Redefining Health Care

Redefining Health Care

Creating Value-Based
Competition on Results

Michael E. Porter
Elizabeth Olmsted Teisberg

HARVARD BUSINESS SCHOOL PRESS
BOSTON, MASSACHUSETTS

978-1-59139-778-6 (ISBN13)

Library of Congress Cataloging-in-Publication Data

Porter, Michael E., 1947–
    Redefining health care: creating value-based competition on results / Michael E. Porter, Elizabeth Olmsted Teisberg.
        p.   cm.
    Includes bibliographical references.
    ISBN 1-59139-778-2
    1. Medical care—Quality control. 2. Medical care—Cost control. 3. Medical care—Cost effectiveness. 4. Value analysis (Cost control). 5. Competition.
I. Teisberg, Elizabeth Olmsted. II. Title.
    [DNLM: 1. Delivery of Health Care—economics—United States. 2. Economic Competition—United States. 3. Quality of Health Care—economics—United States. 4. Health Care Costs—United States.
    W 74 AA1 P847r 2005]
    RA399.A1P67 2005
    362.1'068—dc22

                                                                    2005018631

The paper used in this publication meets the requirements of the American National Standard for Permanence of Paper for Publications and Documents in Libraries and Archives Z39.48–1992.

To Lana, Sonia,
Tyler, and Thomas

Contents

List of Figures

List of Boxes

Preface

THIS BOOK GREW out of a puzzle: why is competition failing in health care? Throughout the economy, competition among private-sector rivals is the most powerful force yet discovered for driving improvements in the quality and cost of products and services. This is illustrated every day in countless industries around the globe.

How could the U.S. health care system, which is largely a private system and characterized by arguably more competition than any other health care system in the world, be performing so poorly? Why are U.S. costs among the highest in the world even though many citizens do not have health coverage? How could costs, already so high, still be rising so rapidly? Why is quality so uneven? Why is there growing evidence of alarming quality problems in the system?

We set out to address these questions in a field that erects daunting challenges for outsiders. The field is huge, multifaceted, and self-contained. Health care scholars tend to work just in health care, for reasons that are understandable. There is an immense body of medical and policy literature. The sheer complexity of the health care system is mind-boggling. The practice of medicine is complicated and arcane, and medical practitioners are notoriously skeptical of non-physicians' ability to contribute. "Health care is different" or "you just don't understand" are phrases one hears over and over again in the field.

We bring a point of view to our research that has not necessarily been a particularly welcomed one. There is quite a low status attached to "management" in the medical field, and *business* is almost a dirty word. The literature on strategy for health care organizations is virtually nonexistent. Finally, in health care, many practitioners consider the whole idea of competition to be suspect. Physicians are taught that competition is wasteful, that it promotes self-interested behavior, and that it undermines patient care. Many equate competition with price cutting. Significant numbers of people are convinced that a monopolistic, state-controlled system is the only way for the United States to extricate itself from its mounting health care problem.

Our interest in health care dates back to the early 1990s. As is the case for so many Americans, we encountered the health care system in a personal way, in the course of addressing medical issues facing parents, relatives, and children. When Elizabeth's newborn son underwent complex—and remarkably successful—heart surgery to address a medical condition that would have been fatal or debilitating just a few years earlier, we experienced firsthand the very best of the U.S. system with all its innovation, medical skill, and human compassion. Yet even as the system was performing a miracle, getting the right doctors required circumventing the normal system. Even more troubling was the protracted struggle, which truly became a nightmare, to obtain reimbursement from supposedly the best health plan available. Other encounters each of us had with the health care system contained elements that were troubling.

We were drawn to try to understand what was underlying the dysfunctional competition in the health care system. Given our backgrounds in the area of industry competition and company strategy, the puzzle of health care competition was immediately apparent. We concluded, in an article with Dr. Gregory Brown published in 1994, that the forces of competition were strong in health care, but that skewed incentives were driving predictable, but undesirable, results in terms of rising costs. The article contained predictions that industry structure would rapidly consolidate, and it put forward some prescriptions for how to modify the skewed incentives in the system. We then turned our attention back to other research.

Yet the puzzle of health care competition would not go away. Managed care took hold, and industry consolidation indeed increased markedly over the rest of the 1990s as we had predicted. Despite the adoption of managed care, which many health care experts thought would control costs, matters only got worse. Reform proposals continued unabated, including efforts to manage and realign incentives, but none seemed to address the deeper issues in the system.

Meanwhile, new research began to document the pervasive quality problems in the system. We were greatly informed and influenced by the research of Jack Wennberg, Elliot Fisher, and others in the Evaluative Clinical Sciences group at Dartmouth Medical School, who found huge quality variations in medical care across providers and regions with no scientific basis; by the work of the Institute of Medicine on the high rates of medical errors and the gap between the care that should be delivered and what is actually delivered; by the work of Don Berwick and Maureen Bisognano at the Institute for Healthcare Improvement illustrating the huge opportunities to enhance processes of care and improve quality; by the work of Brent James and Intermountain Health Care on clinical process improvement and knowledge management; by the work of Bill Knaus on developing risk-adjusted outcome measures for care provided in intensive care units to enable quality to be assessed and compared; and by others who shed light on the many dimensions of health care quality.

This new research revealed that the puzzle was even greater than we had originally thought. Quality was just as big an issue as cost. There was not just too much care, but also too little care, and the wrong care. There were not just skewed regulatory and private-sector incentives, but also a fundamental misalignment between the nature of competition and value for the patient.

It became increasingly clear that the nature of health care delivery needed to be transformed. We also began to believe that to reform health care, one had to reform competition itself. And to reform competition, one had to transform the strategies, organizational structures, pricing approaches, and measurement practices of the various actors in the system. We came to see that the problem was less a technology problem or a regulatory problem than a management and organizational problem. The overall result was that the many talented and well-intended individuals working in the system were often working at cross purposes to patient value and were increasingly aware of, and disheartened by, this conflict.

A new stream of research began in 2000, and we began circulating a new working paper in 2003. Our point of view was greeted with encouragement but also sharp criticism. Many health care experts hold strong beliefs and assumptions about the system—for example, that patients will always want more medical care, that improving quality means higher costs, that technology is driving cost increases, that quality cannot be measured in a meaningful way, that universal health coverage is the only answer, or that empowering consumers is the only solution. We were forced over and over again to confront these perspectives and deepen our thinking.

Our article published in the June 2004 *Harvard Business Review* set forth an overall framework for understanding why competition in health care had failed. Given the experience with our working paper, we were braced for a strong dose of criticism, but instead started receiving voluminous correspondence from individuals representing literally every corner of the health care field, including many in other countries. While there were critics, the vast majority of those who wrote or commented at presentations did not want to challenge our basic thesis but were interested in how to operationalize it. Even more interesting was that many organizations were taking tentative steps in the right directions without the benefit of a broader strategic and organizational framework. We began to realize that major improvements could occur from within the system without the need for government-led reform.

We were inspired, as a result, to undertake this book. It begins with the basic ideas set forth in our article, but two more years of intensive research have allowed us to go much further. We develop here the strategic and organizational implications of our ideas for each of the major actors in the system, and illustrate them with numerous examples. In the process of conducting this research, we have encountered an extraordinarily dedicated and talented group of health care professionals. It has been heartening that so many participants in the system care so passionately about delivering value to patients, in spite of the obstacles and the system's debilitating incentives. The inspired efforts of many of these individuals have given us confidence that redefining health care is not only possible but is already beginning.

Given the scope and complexity of the health care field and the breadth of our agenda, this book would truly not have been possible without the help of many individuals. Our team at Harvard and Virginia, consisting of Natalya Vinokurova, Daniel Rueda Posada, and Kjell Carlsson, has made a major contribution to this research. David Chen, Andrew Funderburk, Steve Godfrey, K. C. Hasson, Diem Nguyen, and Cathy Turco provided invaluable research assistance. Colleen Kaftan, our editor, has brought much greater clarity to our writing, as has our production editor, Sarah Weaver. Lyn Pohl has overseen the preparation of the manuscript, with the able assistance of Kathy Kane, Alfredo Montes, Michelle Walker, and Kathleen Custodio. Lana Porter and Tyler Teisberg offered helpful editorial comments.

Within the field, we have been inspired and informed by many individuals, who are too numerous to mention. We recognize here just a fraction of the individuals whose work, comments, and questions have been essential.

We owe a huge debt of gratitude to a few individuals who have played seminal roles in motivating and supporting this project and reviewing large portions of the manuscript. Our heartfelt thanks go to Charlie Baker, Donald Berwick, Maureen Bisognano, Toby Cosgrove, Ray Gilmartin, Jeff Kang, Bill Knaus, Joan Magretta, Tom Stewart, and Henri Termeer. The flaws in our thinking are entirely our own, but the insights and encouragement of these individuals have been essential.

Among scholars and researchers, our special thanks go to Tenley Albright, David Blumenthal, Bob Bruner, Cindy Collier, David Cutler, Lauren Dewey-Platt, Lynn Etheredge, Elliott Fisher, Steven Hyman, Kenneth

Kaplan, John McArthur, Stacey Ober, Gary Pisano, Carl Sloane, Tom Teisberg, Eoin Trevelyan, Myrl Weinberg, Chuck Weller, and Patricia Werhane.

Among providers and physicians, special thanks go to Elissa Altin, Robert Banco, Robert Bode, Kline Bolton, Mark Chassin, Joseph Dionisio, Andrew Fishleder, Robert Flaherty, Bruce Ferguson, Arthur (Tim) Garson, Jim Green, Marjorie Godfrey, Michael Goldstein, Gil Gonzalez, Gary Gottlieb, Frederick Grover, Martin Harris, Alan Henry, Jeff Hunter, Robert Kolodner, Wayne Lerner, Paul Levy, Bruce Marshall, John Mendelsohn, John E. Mayer, Leonard Miller, Kalani Olmsted, Jeffrey Reynolds, Lidia Schapira, Gail Sebet, Jo Shapiro, Michael Singer, Joanne Smith, John Toussaint, John Triano, Scott Tromanhauser, Kelly Victory, Kanh Vu, Beverly Walters, and Jim Weinstein.

Among health plan leaders, special thanks go to Stephen Barlow, Dave Burton, David Crowder, Mike Ferris, Brent James, Cleve Killingsworth, Karen Sanders, Sharon Smith, and Bill Van Faasen.

Among suppliers, special thanks go to Ashoke Bhattacharjya, Kay Deguchi, Jonathan Hartmann, Elliott Hillback, Hank McKinnell, Lisa Raines, and Brad Sheares.

Among service providers, special thanks go to Paul Eckbo, Kenneth Falchuk, Luciano Grubissich, Mike Hogan, Brian Hughes, Jim Hummer, Harold Jacks, Cynthia Lambert, Richard Marks, Richard Migliori, Lynette Nilan, Robert Reznik, David Seligman, Jeff Wagener, and Rob Webb.

Among government leaders, thanks go to Melanie Bella, Göran Henriks, Peter Koutoujian, Mark McClellan, Ron Preston, Mitt Romney, and Gaudenz Silberschmidt.

We are also grateful to the Harvard Business School, Darden Business School, and Batten Institute for funding and research support.

And special thanks for inspiration go to Dr. John Mayer, Dr. Jane Newburger, and Dr. Gil Wernovsky, whose expertise and warmth set this whole project in motion almost fifteen years ago.

Introduction

THE U.S. HEALTH CARE SYSTEM is notorious for its high costs, which Americans traditionally assumed was the price of excellence. Some American health care is truly superb, but we now know that serious quality problems also plague the system. There is compelling evidence that much care falls well short of excellence, that both too little and too much care is provided, and that alarming rates of medical error persist.

At a personal level, almost everyone has a story about health care. Many of these stories have a happy ending and reveal the extraordinary skill and compassion of doctors and other caregivers. Too often, however, even the happy endings were due to personal determination, connections, or the ongoing intervention of family members. Some good outcomes seem to have occurred almost in spite of the system, rather than because of it.

In the past two decades, health care has gone from being a source of national pride to one of America's preeminent concerns. The nation spends almost $2 trillion annually on health care, and costs continue to escalate to levels approaching a national crisis. As costs rise, more and more Americans have lost access to health insurance. As these individuals face insufficient or nonexistent primary and preventive care, quality suffers and costs rise even further. Unless there is dramatic change, the aging of the baby boomers will drive more cost escalation, followed by intense pressures for cost shifting, price controls, rationing, and reduced services for ever more Americans.

The combination of high costs, unsatisfactory quality, and limited access to health care has created anxiety and frustration for all participants. No one is happy with the current system—not patients, who worry about the cost of insurance and the quality of care; not employers, who face escalating premiums and unhappy employees; not physicians and other providers, whose incomes have been squeezed, professional judgments overridden, and workdays overwhelmed with bureaucracy and paper-work; not health plans, which are routinely vilified; not suppliers of drugs and medical devices, which have introduced many life-saving or life-enhancing therapies but get blamed for driving up costs; and not govern-ments, whose budgets are spinning out of control.

Decades of "reform" have failed to improve the situation; if anything, matters have gotten worse. Costs continue to rise despite determined efforts at cost control. More and more quality problems have surfaced. The endless debates over what to do about health care have taken on increasing urgency, but an overarching solution has remained elusive.

Reformers have tended to focus on a single issue or problem that must be addressed, such as the price of drugs and new technology, the rising numbers of uninsured, the unnecessary administrative costs imposed by health plans, the provider incentives to overtreat, the lack of consumer responsibility for cost, or the slow penetration of information technology. Many different villains have been singled out for criticism—in fact, almost every system participant appears as the villain in the eyes of some reformers.

Solutions tend to target one or two aspects of the system believed to be the core problem. Many activists, for example, aim to control drug costs through negotiating lower prices, encouraging the use of generic drugs, and purchasing from Canada. A sizable constituency argues for a single-payer system in which government provides universal insurance and has the power to control cost, doing away with private health insurance alto-gether. Some advocate a move to large, integrated health systems com-bining a health plan with a captive provider network as the only way to improve quality and rein in the amount of care delivered. Others see the solution as empowering consumers and giving them a big personal stake in the cost of their care. Still others promote advances in information technology (IT) as a sort of panacea.

However, none of these solutions has worked, or can work. Each of them is incomplete, and brings with it new problems. As we will discuss, there are good reasons why other advanced countries are moving away from a single-payer system. Large, integrated health systems eliminate com-petition where it is most needed. Consumers alone, no matter how much they have to pay, will never be medical experts and able to navigate the current system. It may be desirable to encourage health savings accounts, help seniors pay for drugs, and require the use of IT, but none of these steps treats the underlying problem.

The nation needs a new way of thinking about the health care system. There is no one villain here. Neither the problem nor the solution will be found in any single aspect of the system or in any single actor. Indeed, the whole approach of attempting to redress competing interests is doomed from the start. The only real solution is to unite all participants in the system in a common purpose.

The Failure of Competition

There are myriad dimensions of the health care system, and it is easy to get overwhelmed by its sheer complexity. From a strategic perspective, however, the issues in health care can be divided into three broad areas. The first is the cost of and access to health insurance. The second is standards for coverage, or the types of care that should be covered by insurance versus being the responsibility of the individual. The third is the structure of health care delivery itself. All three areas are important, and we will address each in this book.

While the vast majority of attention has been focused on insurance, we believe that the structure of health care delivery is the most fundamental issue. The structure of health care delivery drives the cost and quality of the entire system, and ultimately the cost of insurance and the amount of coverage that is feasible.

The fundamental problem in the U.S. health care system is that the structure of health care delivery is broken. This is what all the data about rising costs and alarming quality are telling us. And the structure of health care delivery is broken because competition is broken. All of the well-intended reform movements have failed because they did not address the underlying nature of competition.

In a normal market, competition drives relentless improvements in quality and cost. Rapid innovation leads to rapid diffusion of new technologies and better ways of doing things. Excellent competitors prosper and grow, while weaker rivals are restructured or go out of business. Quality-adjusted prices fall, value improves, and the market expands to meet the needs of more consumers. This is the trajectory of all well-functioning industries—computers, mobile communications, consumer banking, and many others.

Health care competition could not be more different. Costs are high and rising despite the fierce struggle to control them. Quality problems persist. The failure of competition is evident in the large and inexplicable differences in cost and quality for the same type of care across providers and across geographic areas. Competition does not reward the best providers, nor do weaker providers go out of business. Technological innovation diffuses slowly and does not drive value improvement the way it should; instead, it is seen by some as part of the problem. Taken together, these outcomes are inconceivable in a well-functioning market. They are intolerable in health care, with life and quality of life at stake. They are unsustainable in a sector that consumes a large and growing portion of the national budget.

Why is competition failing in health care? Why is value for patients not higher and improving faster? The reason is not a lack of competition, but the wrong kind of competition. Competition has taken place at the wrong levels, and on the wrong things. It has gravitated to a zero-sum competition, in which the gains of one system participant come at the expense of others. Participants compete to shift costs to one another, accumulate bargaining power, and limit services. This kind of competition does not create value for patients, but erodes quality, fosters inefficiency, creates excess capacity, and drives up administrative costs, among other nefarious effects.

Zero-sum competition is not inherent in the nature of competition, or in the nature of health care. The dysfunctional competition in health care results from misaligned incentives and a series of understandable but unfortunate strategic, organizational, and regulatory choices by each participant in the system that feed on and exacerbate each other. All the actors in the system share responsibility for the problem.

In the current system, actors insulated from competition have sometimes achieved impressive progress. For example, some large integrated health systems, such as the Veterans Administration hospitals, Intermountain Health Care, and Kaiser, have avoided zero-sum competition between providers and health plans, which has allowed improvements in quality and efficiency.

However, limiting competition, as we will discuss, is not the solution. *The only way to truly reform health care is to reform the nature of competition itself.* How to do so is the central focus of this book.

Competing on Value

The way to transform health care is to realign competition with *value for patients*. Value in health care is the health outcome per dollar of cost expended. If all system participants have to compete on value, value will improve dramatically. As simple and obvious as this seems to be, however, improving value has not been the central goal of the participants in the system. The focus instead has been on minimizing short-term costs and battling over who pays what. The result is that many of the strategies, organizational structures, and practices of the various actors in the system are badly misaligned with value for the patient.

This book focuses on the value delivered by the health care system, and how it can be enhanced. This proves to be a highly revealing lens with which to reexamine the current practices of each participant in the system. The simple test is: how does each practice contribute to value for patients? Applying this test, we find that the answers are sobering for all participants.

At the most basic level, competition in health care must take place where value is actually created. Herein lies a big part of the problem. Value in health care is determined in addressing the patient's particular medical condition over the full cycle of care, from monitoring and prevention to treatment to ongoing disease management. (We use the term *medical condition* rather than *disease, organ system, illness,* or *injury* because it will prove to be more closely tied to patient value.) The problem is that competition does not take place at the medical condition level, nor over the full care cycle.

Competition in the current system is at the same time too broad, too narrow, and too local. Participants in the system have misdefined the relevant business from a value perspective. Competition takes place on broad service lines, not individual services. Providers offer every possible service, and gear up to handle any patient who walks in the door. Health plans contract with providers across the board. Yet breadth of services per se has little impact on patient value—it is the ability to deliver value in each medical condition that matters. Health plans and providers have merged and consolidated, but the pursuit of breadth and the duplication of services have only increased. As system participants compete on breadth, competition at the medical condition level has been suppressed or eliminated by health plan networks, captive referrals within provider groups, and the almost total absence of relevant information.

Competition in the current system is also too narrow, a seemingly paradoxical result. The reason is that competition takes place on discrete interventions rather than the full cycle of care where value is determined. Value can only be measured over the care cycle, not for an individual procedure, service, office visit, or test. Yet care is structured around medical specialties and discrete services, not the integrated care of medical conditions. Physicians act as free agents, performing their specialty and billing separately. Navigating the care cycle is challenging. Nobody takes an overall care-cycle perspective, including steps to avoid the need for interventions (prevention) and ongoing management of medical conditions to forestall recurrence (disease management). The current structure maintains ways of organizing medicine that have long been obsolete. The adverse consequences for patient value are enormous.

Finally, competition in the current system is too local, because it is centered on relatively small, self-contained local institutions catering to local needs. Services are both delivered locally and managed locally. The local bias in health care is a throwback to an earlier era when medical care was less complicated, and travel more difficult. It has been institutionalized by prevailing ownership and governance structures for provider institutions, regulatory and reimbursement practices, and a lack of local provider accountability for performance. The local bias in health care means that many providers offer services in which they lack the volume and experience to be truly excellent, and that excess capacity and the tendency for supply to create demand are almost guaranteed.

How to redefine competition around value, and shift competition to the level at which value is determined, will be a central focus in the chapters that follow. This will include restructuring care delivery to provide truly integrated care over the full care cycle. Significant changes will be required not just from providers but from every system participant. As we will see, integrated health systems that combine a health plan with a captive provider network do not ensure integrated care. Such systems are not the only way, or even the best way, to create value-based competition over the care cycle at the medical condition level.

Competing on Results

Competition on value must revolve around results. The results that matter are patient outcomes per unit of cost at the medical condition level. Competition on results means that those providers, health plans, and suppliers that achieve excellence are rewarded with more business, while those that fail to demonstrate good results decline or cease to provide that service. Competition to shift cost and limit services is a zero-sum competition—one actor's gain is a loss for others. Competing on patient results is a positive-sum competition from which all system participants can benefit. When providers succeed in delivering superior value, patients win, employers win, and health plans also win through better outcomes achieved at lower costs. When health plans succeed in better informing patients, better coordinating care, and rewarding good care, excellent providers benefit, as do patients.

Competing on results requires that results be measured and made widely available. Only by measuring and holding every system participant accountable for results will the performance of the health care system ever be significantly improved. The ability to measure results and to control fairly for initial patient circumstances (risk adjustment) has been conclusively demonstrated, as we will discuss. So have the striking improvements in patient value that occur when results are measured and compared. Yet results measurement has been resisted by providers, which are fearful of biases and comparisons, and all but ignored by government, health plans, employers, and even suppliers of technology. *Mandatory measurement and reporting of results is perhaps the single most important step in reforming the health care system.*

Instead of measuring and competing on results, efforts to improve health care delivery have made the fundamental error of attempting to control supply and micromanage provider practices. Health plans attempt to second-guess provider decisions. Review boards attempt to judge whether new capacity or capital investments are necessary. Rather than measuring results and rewarding excellent providers with more patients, the focus has been on lifting all boats by attempting to raise all providers of a service to an acceptable level. The principal tools have been practice guidelines and standards of care that every provider is expected to meet. Evidence-based medicine is another term for practicing based on accepted standards of care.

Recent quality and pay-for-performance initiatives address process compliance rather than the quality of results achieved. These initiatives presume that good quality is more expensive, and seek to reward good performance with small price differentials, which ensure the upward march of provider reimbursement. Process guidelines are comfortable to providers, because competent providers can readily meet them. Value-based competition on results and pay-for-performance, then, are very different models.

However, the whole process-oriented approach is misguided. Standardized process guidelines belie the complexity of individual patient circumstances, and freeze care delivery processes rather than foster innovation. What is needed is competition on results, not standardized care. What is needed is competition on results, not just evidence-based medicine. There should be no presumption that good quality is more costly. In health care, more so than any other industry we have encountered, better providers are usually more efficient. Good quality is less costly because of more accurate diagnoses, fewer treatment errors, lower complication rates, faster recovery, less invasive treatment, and the minimization of the need for treatment. More broadly, better health is less expensive than illness. Better providers can often earn higher margins at the same or lower prices, as we will discuss, so quality improvement does not require ever-escalating costs.

What is needed is to migrate patients to the truly excellent providers, which feeds a virtuous circle of provider value improvement through greater scale, better efficiency, deeper experience, faster learning, and more dedicated teams and facilities at the medical condition level. In contrast, the lift-all-boats model perpetuates the vicious circle where many subscale providers lack the capabilities to achieve true excellence.

Value-based competition on results is the only antidote to the inefficiency and quality problems that plague the health care system. Providers with substandard results will be highly motivated to improve them. Those that remain inefficient or fail to deliver appropriate care will rapidly lose patients. Errors will fall dramatically. When providers have to compete on results, the problem of supply-driven demand, in which available capacity leads to care with questionable benefits, will largely disappear.

The absence of value-based competition at the level of medical conditions will doom reform prescriptions across the political spectrum. Pay-for-performance will only raise costs if providers get higher pay for process compliance but do not have to compete on results. Some observers assert that a benevolent monopoly, such as a single payer or a single integrated health plan serving a geographic region, will avoid the duplication and inefficiencies of the current system. But history tells us that monopolies that are truly benevolent and effective are rare. Competition on results is a far more reliable route to efficiency, quality, and rapid improvements in value. Success in the current system has rested heavily on personal leadership and extraordinary vision to counterbalance zero-sum competition. With competition on results, delivering value will no longer be discretionary.

Value-based competition on results goes far beyond consumer-driven health care. Consumers will only be able to play a bigger role in their care, and make better choices, if providers and health plans realign competition around patient results and disseminate the relevant information and advice. Reform does not require consumers to become medical experts or to manage their own care; it requires providers and health plans to compete on value, which will allow and enable consumers to make better choices and be more responsible. When physicians are driven to compete on results—thus improving both quality and efficiency—even uninformed and uninvolved consumers will benefit. *How to create competition on results throughout the system, and the kinds of information that need to be measured, analyzed, and disseminated, appear as recurring themes throughout this book.*

When competition on results is working at the right level, it will reverberate throughout the system in ways that we can only begin to imagine. There will be no need to predetermine the best way to structure the system, specify the processes of care that should be used, dictate how IT systems should be designed, or decide which new medical technologies should be adopted. If every actor in the system has to measure and report results, professional pride will motivate improvement. If every actor has to compete for every subscriber and patient, improvement and innovation will occur even faster.

Value-based competition on results will unleash major value improvements for all citizens, including those with low incomes. Quality will improve across the board, including at providers that care for the poor. As patient value improves, society will have more resources to provide more services. We chart a path to universal insurance coverage in this book, which value-based competition will make more affordable. Primary and preventive care can be extended to all Americans, which will also produce major savings. Finally, mandatory results measurement will mean that substandard care to any group, including minorities or those with low incomes, will be glaringly obvious. Every provider will face strong pressures to provide excellent care for all patients. Results measurement, more than any other policy, is the best way to eliminate substandard care in the system.

Moving to value-based competition on results will require significant changes by all system participants, as we have noted. However, the system can, and will, change from within. Each system participant can significantly improve value, and reap the benefits, even if nothing else in the system changes.

The Structure of This Book

This book begins by describing the unsatisfactory performance of the U.S. health care system, its underlying causes, and the reasons that past reforms have failed to alter the system's trajectory. It then sets forth the principles of value-based competition on results that are necessary to truly reform the system, and the steps each system participant must take to embrace the new model.

Separate chapters treat the implications for providers, health plans, other system participants (suppliers, consumers, and employers), and government. Since we expect some readers to concentrate on the chapter corresponding to their role in the system, we include a brief review of some of the basic principles of value-based competition to allow each chapter to be read on its own. However, since the value delivered by each participant in the system can be affected by the choices of other participants, we urge our readers to read the entire book.

Chapter 1 details the staggering performance challenges facing the U.S. health care system in both cost and quality. It draws on evidence from a wide array of sources and studies, which, taken together, underscore the depth and breadth of the problem.

Chapter 2 addresses the underlying causes of the problem. It describes the zero-sum competition on cost that has plagued the system, and why it has arisen. Fundamentally, competition has taken place at the wrong level and on the wrong things, the result of a series of skewed incentives, faulty assumptions, unfortunate strategy choices, and counterproductive regulations that are understandable but inconsistent with how value is actually created in delivering health care.

Chapter 3 examines the reasons why decades of efforts to reform the health care system have failed. From the early days of insurance covering "usual, customary and reasonable charges" for medical care to the emergence of the Medicare Prospective Payment System, the advent of HMOs, and the aborted Clinton plan, competition has not been based on results, nor has it been aligned with value. More recent reform efforts, including the consumer-driven health care movement, pay-for-performance, and other efforts to improve quality, show promise of moving the system in the right direction. None of the proposed reforms will, however, address the nature of competition throughout the system. They, too, are doomed to fail.

Chapter 4 defines the basic principles of value-based competition that must guide any high-performing health care system. These principles, drawn from experience in numerous other industries and validated by a huge body of health care literature, describe the way competition in health care should be structured. It is often asserted that health care is different, and that market principles do not apply. It is true that the current zero-sum competition in health care is destructive, but the biggest difference in health care is that the power of market principles is greater, not less, than in most other industries. Better health is inherently less costly. Because of the opportunities for value-based competition to drive care that is both of better quality and less expensive, the market has even more potential in health care if the nature of competition is realigned.

Chapters 5 through 8 discuss the roles of each major system participant in moving to value-based competition. Chapter 5 examines hospitals, clinics, physician groups, and individual physicians, which are the core of the system and the locus where most value is actually delivered. Providers must shift their strategies, structures, and management processes and learn to measure and improve their results. The chapter elucidates the strategic and organizational imperatives for providers in moving to value-based competition. It describes the enabling roles of the care delivery value chain, information technology, and systematic processes for knowledge development in improving value. Chapter 5 also contains numerous examples drawn from the many providers that have already begun to compete on value.

Providers will need to overcome significant barriers in moving to value-based strategies, especially the traditional modes of physician practice and historical ways of organizing medicine. Leading providers are already well down the path of value-based strategies, however, and there is no need to wait for reform by other system participants.

Chapter 6 addresses the role of health plans in value-based competition. (We use the term *health plan,* rather than *payer,* because plans behaving only as payers have contributed to the system's problems.) Health plans have been perhaps the most criticized actors in health care. Some policy makers advocate eliminating them altogether, while others advocate integrating health plans with captive provider networks.

Health plans have deserved criticism by operating in ways that have been badly misaligned with value. In the past, the strategies and practices of health plans increased bureaucracy and administrative costs, restricted the choices of physicians, limited the services available to patients, attempted to micromanage medical practice, and generally gummed up the works through adversarial relationships with both providers and members. We believe, however, that competing health plans are uniquely positioned to play important value-adding roles in enabling health care competition. To do so, health plans will need to reorient their whole approach, and embrace new roles and strategies. While many health plans have moved away from the worst aspects of the old "culture of denial," the overwhelming opinion of patients and physicians we encountered is that the transformation of health plans is only just beginning.

Some of the new roles for health plans—such as actively supporting patient choices, helping patients navigate the care cycle, and assisting them in managing their medical records—may appear to be among the most radical of our recommendations. As with providers, however, a growing number of health plans are already moving in these new directions. To some readers, for example, it will seem utopian to suggest that health plans gauge their success by health results rather than costs, but some plans are already beginning to do so. As with providers, those health plans that move early to embrace value principles will enjoy the greatest benefits.

Chapter 7 maps out the key supporting roles of suppliers, consumers, and employers in value-based competition. Each of these actors can contribute to value, and encourage providers and health plans to do so.

Suppliers of medical products, technology, and services play vital roles in health care delivery and innovation in health care practice. They are often blamed for being a primary driver of cost increases. While that conclusion is simplistic, many suppliers have perpetuated and reinforced zero-sum competition. Suppliers can add far more value to health care delivery than they have yet realized.

Consumers, as health plan subscribers and patients, should be the ultimate beneficiaries of the value delivered by the system. Too often, however, consumers have been uninformed and passive rather than active participants in their health and their health care. The potential of consumers as catalysts for change in the system has been well recognized, with whole books written about consumer-driven health care. But despite the fact that consumers have become more informed and have more choices, the system has not been transformed. Consumers do have the power to influence the health care system. However, their influence will not come from attempting to be medical experts and micromanaging their own care, but from acting responsibly and setting high expectations for results so that the other actors in the system do their jobs well.

Employers cast themselves as victims of health care cost increases. Yet they have the motivation and the clout as the major purchasers of health plans to influence the other actors in the system, including their own employees. About half of employer-provided health plans in the United States are self-insured plans, giving employers even more latitude in designing and administering such plans. Despite this, employers have unwittingly contributed to the problem of zero-sum competition, and missed the opportunity to drive value improvement in the health care system. Employers have also turned increasingly to shifting costs to employees, rather than improving the value of their care. Employers will need to radically transform their whole approach to health care benefits, and focus on value rather than on limiting services and bargaining for discounts.

Finally, chapter 8 turns to government's role in creating the conditions for value-based competition. Government has lacked an overall framework for health care policy, and focused until very recently almost exclusively on cost control and access to insurance. Health care reform will not be complete without universal, mandatory health insurance and consistent standards for health plan coverage. However, policy efforts have missed the critical insight that the government's most important role is to enable competition based on value so that the nation will be able to afford quality health care for everyone. Government has a series of important roles in transforming competition, such as mandating the collection and reporting of results information, eliminating barriers to competition, modifying rules for pricing, and facilitating the penetration of information technology. The operation of Medicare and Medicaid must also be refocused around value and competition on results.

This book concentrates on the U.S. health care system, but the principles are universal. Chapter 8 concludes with a discussion of some of the implications of our ideas for the health care systems in other countries, along with examples of countries that are moving to introduce competition and results measurement into their systems. Many countries have state-dominated or state-run systems with little competition. Their historically lower costs and favorable mortality statistics have led some to advocate that the United States move to emulate them. Yet other advanced countries are now facing accelerated rates of cost increase similar to those in the United States, while new evidence is revealing alarming quality problems that appear to be as bad as or worse than the U.S. experience. Leaders in many other countries are now questioning the future structure of their health care systems.

We believe that the principles of value-based competition can be applied to any health care system, whatever its starting point in terms of structure. There is a growing recognition in other countries of the need to refocus on value, to introduce competition into state-dominated systems, rethink how providers are organized, and collect and disseminate results. In fact, starting from a structure with widespread access to primary care may ease the challenges of transition to a value-driven system, which gives other countries an opportunity to progress quickly.

How Will Redefining Health Care Occur?

The fundamental challenge in health care is how to jump-start a new kind of competition—competition on results in improving health and serving patients. Competing on value is a positive-sum competition from which all system participants can benefit. The goal of improving value for patients will unite the interests of system participants who now too often work at cross purposes. When all parties compete to achieve the best medical outcomes for patients, they are pursuing the goals that led many individuals into the profession in the first place.

Some, even many, of the ideas we discuss here have been advanced at one time or another in the debate over health care—for example, the importance of prevention; the benefits of information technology; the value of a greater role for consumers; the need for better coordinated, team-based care; and the need to create a health care marketplace. What has been missing is an overall strategic framework in which these and other ideas can actually be realized. Competition on results to improve patient value is an irresistible force for transforming the health care system without the need for top-down government intervention. Value-based competition provides a new conception of the health care system, while integrating many threads in the reform discussion. More important, it leads to concrete and actionable strategic, organizational, operational, and policy implications for all system participants, including government.

What gives us confidence that value-based competition on results is possible, and not just a theoretical concept? The answer is that it has already started. A growing number of providers, health plans, employers, suppliers, and other system participants are moving to compete on value, some of whom we describe in this book. None of the strategies, operating practices, and policies we recommend is theoretical. Each of them is already being implemented, though no one organization is yet pursuing all of them.

When we first advanced the value-based competition perspective in our *Harvard Business Review* article of June 2004, we expected both skepticism and attempts to justify current practices. What we failed to anticipate was the pent-up demand for a more rational system that did not resort to government control or rely on impractical leadership by consumers. Our focus on value for patients, and the need to shift competition to new dimensions, fit with many readers' experiences and intuition. In subsequent contacts with countless participants in the health care system, we discovered unmistakable signs of a revolution in the making. Hundreds of organizations are embracing some or many of the principles we advocate. Even Medicare is experimenting with changes that embody value-based competition as never before.

This outpouring of interest in realigning competition around value reveals a system ripe for change. Most everyone now understands that the current model is not working and grasps the futility of past approaches to controlling costs and micromanaging the system. There is a growing awareness that true progress can only occur for patients by measuring results and by creating competition at the level where value is actually delivered. Competition to improve results for patients over the full cycle of care will naturally achieve what successive reform movements and top-down solutions have been unable to deliver.

Fortunately, there is no need to wait for dramatic policy changes or leadership from government to redefine health care. The system can, and will, change largely from within. Each participant in the system can take voluntary steps today to deliver greater value. Those organizations that do so will benefit even if others resist the revolution. Providers will improve their outcomes and efficiency. Suppliers that work with providers to improve outcomes for patients will strengthen their competitive advantages. Health plans will improve the health of their members, and save money. Employers that enhance the value of their health benefits will improve employee productivity while reducing benefit costs. As each actor embraces more of the imperatives we identify, the benefits increase disproportionately.

The changes we describe are self-reinforcing. Changes by health plans and providers to compete on value will reinforce and magnify each other, and will spur innovations by suppliers. As consumers and employers adopt these principles, providers and health plans will be more moti-vated, and more able, to improve the value they deliver. Those providers, health plans, employers, and suppliers that move early to engage in patient-centered, value-based competition on results will prosper. Those organizations that defend their old structures, practices, and mind-sets will fall behind. As we have stressed, this is not a call for altruistic action: those organizations that are excellent at delivering measurable value for patients will benefit tremendously.

There is an unprecedented opportunity to redefine health care by redefining the nature of health care competition. The talent and energy of the many extraordinary individuals working in the health care system will be unleashed in a positive agenda of dramatic improvement in value for patients. Costs will be brought under control, and quality of life will be advanced significantly. America can lead a transformation of health care, which will create compelling benefits for the health and health care of all citizens.

1

Scoping the Problem

THE U.S. HEALTH CARE SYSTEM is on a dangerous path, with a toxic combination of high costs, uneven quality, frequent errors, and limited access to care. This chapter presents a wide array of indicators that document the range of problems confronting the system. While individual measures can be questioned for their precision or implication, these many disparate kinds of evidence, taken together, lead to the same overwhelming conclusion: the system is broken, and the magnitude of the problem is staggering.

Per capita health care cost in the United States surpasses that of most other developed countries. Despite this, U.S. costs are rising at comparable rates. (See figure 1-1.)[1] Although U.S. costs are high, they have not enabled greater access to medical care in the United States than elsewhere. There were 45.8 million Americans without health care coverage in 2004, up from 39.8 million in 2000.[2] Although hospitals provide free care for those who need it, that approach to enabling access to care is far from ideal. Access to primary care, rather than just emergency treatment, is essential to providing care of good quality.[3] Rationing of primary care is one of the important problems in the U.S. system. High costs lead many Americans, including some with insurance, to forgo getting treatment.[4] (See figure 1-2.)

Higher costs would not be so troubling if Americans believed they were getting their money's worth, but U.S. consumers do not see the payoff. Quite the contrary: U.S. consumers report higher dissatisfaction with their health care system than do consumers in other developed nations.[5] (See figures 1-3 and 1-4.) Low-income patients in the United States, facing problems of access and high cost, rate their care the worst among the same group of nations as well.

Unfortunately, Americans' dissatisfaction is well founded. Although some American medical care is superb, overall results are not what they

FIGURE 1-1

Per capita total expenditures on health and compound annual growth rate (CAGR) in the United States versus other developed nations

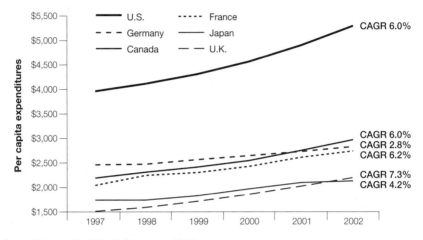

Source: Data from World Health Organization (2005).

FIGURE 1-2

Percentage of citizens by country with health problems who did not get treatment or medication due to cost, 2004

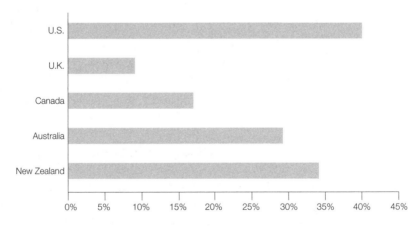

Source: Data from the 2004 Commonwealth Fund International Health Policy Survey, as reported in Schoen et al. (2004).

FIGURE 1-3

Percentage of citizens by country who believe their health care system needs to be rebuilt, 2004

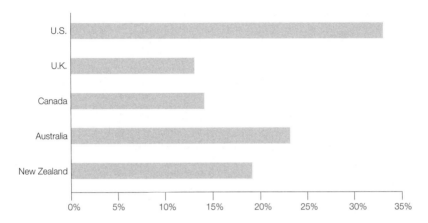

Source: Data from the 2004 Commonwealth Fund International Health Policy Survey, as reported in Schoen et al. (2004).

FIGURE 1-4

Satisfaction of low-income patients in the United States versus in other countries

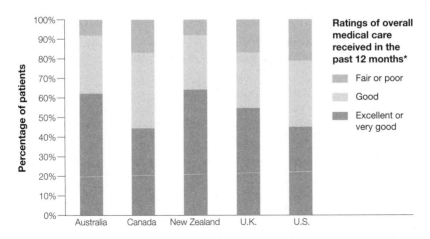

*Ratings based on interviews conducted between April and July 2001.

Source: Data from Commonwealth Fund/Harvard/Harris Interactive (2001).

should be. Higher expenditures on U.S. health care do not result in longer life expectancy for Americans than for citizens of other developed countries, or more years of good health.[6] (See figure 1-5.) Moreover, in a thirteen-country study of health care indicators, the U.S. rank averaged twelfth, with the worst ranking on years of life lost from preventable medical conditions before age 70.[7] As will be discussed in chapter 8, however, health systems outside the United States are facing serious quality (and cost) problems as well.

Yet another sign of a broken system is that the ranking of health conditions on which the United States spends the most money is very different from the ranking of health conditions based on the extent of disability they cause.[8] The Institute of Medicine's (IOM) extensive study of health care quality found that there is not a gap, but a chasm, between the quality of care that Americans should receive and the quality of care that most

FIGURE 1-5

Relationship between health care expenditures and life expectancy in twenty-nine OECD countries in 1996

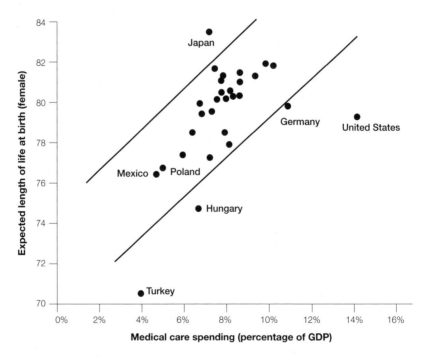

Source: Friedman, Milton, "How to Cure Health Care." Reproduced from *The Public Interest* 142 (Winter 2001), p. 23. Copyright 2001 by National Affairs, Inc.

actually do receive. The IOM found that overtreatment, undertreatment, and medical errors (which the IOM terms *misuse*) are disturbingly common in American medicine.[9] The problem is not that the state of the art in U.S. medical knowledge lags other nations. The best American health care is world-class. But the average quality leaves much to be desired.

Throughout the United States, there is a significant gap between best practice and the actual nature of care delivered. Undertreatment, not just overtreatment, is pervasive. A recent RAND study of thirty types of preventive, acute, and chronic care in twelve metropolitan areas found that Americans receive, on average, only about 55 percent of the care that is suggested by established medical standards.[10] Undertreatment can reflect both quality problems and de facto rationing of care. The problem of disparities in treatments is most extreme for low-income and minority Americans, who experience poor outcomes and excess mortality.[11]

The underprovision of care is roughly equal across broad types of treatment, such as preventive care, acute care, and chronic care. (See figure 1-6.) However, underuse of care is substantially greater for counseling and taking medical history than for interventional procedures and medication. (See figure 1-7.) Undertreatment is less common in conditions such

FIGURE 1-6

Gap between what is known to work and delivered care by broad type of care

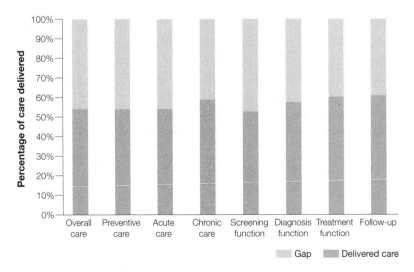

Source: Data from McGlynn et al. (2003).

FIGURE 1-7

Gap between recommended appropriate care and delivered care by nature of the care

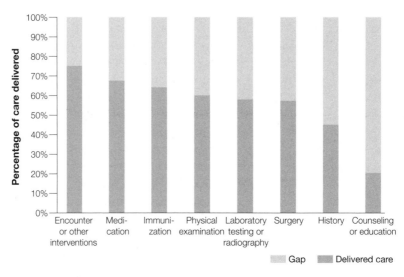

Source: Data from McGlynn et al. (2003).

as cataracts and breast cancer, but in no condition area do Americans, on average, receive even 79 percent of the recommended care. (See figure 1-8.)

Another troubling quality problem in American medical care is the unacceptable rate of errors. Medical errors are a leading cause of death in the United States.[12] (See figures 1-9 and 1-10.) The IOM reported the annual number of deaths in hospitals from medical treatment errors to be between 44,000 and 98,000 in 1999. A 2004 study by HealthGrades estimated that 195,000 people die each year in U.S. hospitals because of preventable treatment errors.[13] Other estimates range as high as 225,000 to 284,000 deaths per year.[14] Even at the lower end of the estimates, such error rates are unacceptably high. Furthermore, while hospital deaths due to errors usually involve people who were already very ill, the studies of errors do not count the estimated one million error-related injuries per year that are not fatal.[15] A number of studies suggest that error rates may be worse in some other countries, as we will discuss, but that does not lessen the urgency of addressing the issue in the United States.[16]

Errors with serious consequences occur not only in treatment but in diagnosis. Studies based on malpractice suits highlight the importance of

FIGURE 1-8

Gap between recommended appropriate care and delivered care by specific condition

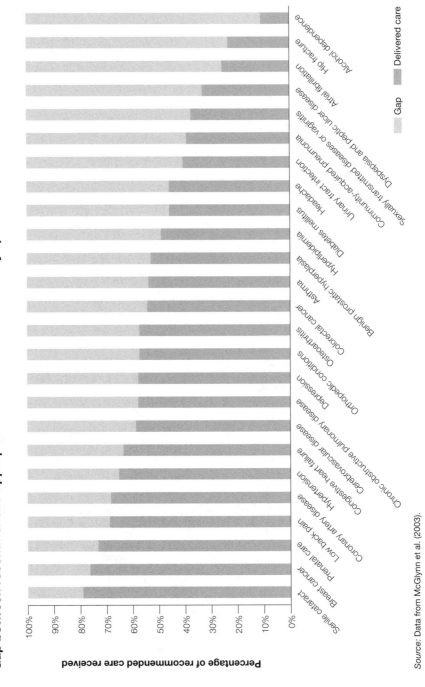

Source: Data from McGlynn et al. (2003).

FIGURE 1-9

In-hospital deaths from medical error versus other major causes of death in the United States, 1998

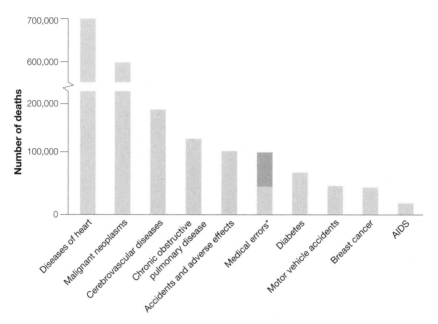

*The Institute of Medicine estimated in 1999 that preventable medical errors kill between 44,000 and 98,000 people per year.

Source: Data from Kohn, Corrigan, and Donaldson (2000), based on 1998 information from the Centers for Disease Control and Prevention, *National Vital Statistics Reports* (1999), and *Hospital Statistics* (1999), published by the American Hospital Association.

diagnostic mistakes. Negligence or errors in diagnosis account for between 30 and 40 percent of U.S. malpractice payments (awards plus out-of-court settlements).[17]

Lower quality does not save money in health care, nor does it in most industries. On the contrary, poor quality leads to complications and the need for additional care, which raises costs substantially.[18] For example, preventable adverse drug events in hospitalized patients increase the costs for the affected patients almost $4,700 per hospitalization. (See figure 1-11.)

The impact and cost of other inpatient errors span a wide range, from little or no additional cost for obstetric trauma to over $57,000 for post-operative infections, over $40,000 for wounds that open after surgery, and about $39,000 for other infections induced by medical care.[19] In the same study, the eighteen types of errors included in the analysis accounted

FIGURE 1-10

In-hospital deaths from medical error versus other major causes of death in the United States, 2002

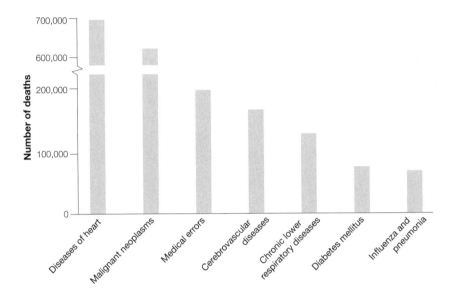

Source: Data from Andersen and Smith (2005) and HealthGrades calculations based on Zhan and Miller (2003).

FIGURE 1-11

Additional per-patient cost and hospital stay from preventable adverse drug events (ADE) in hospitalized patients

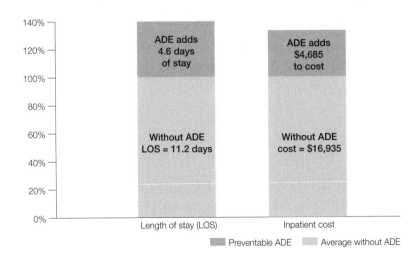

Note: Nearly 2 percent of inpatients had an adverse drug event.

Source: Data from Bates et al. (1997).

for about 32,600 deaths annually and about $9.3 billion in higher costs. Among outpatients, preventable drug-related illness and mortality in the United States are estimated to cost $77 billion due to extra visits to the doctor, additional prescriptions, emergency room visits, hospital admissions, and need for long-term care.[20] The high error rates have led to extensive inspections and reviews by the Joint Commission on Accreditation of Healthcare Organizations (JCAHO), Health Plan Employer Data and Information Set (HEDIS), and public health departments, which add to the cost involved.

The cost of incorrect or missed diagnoses is harder to estimate, but is undoubtedly high as well. Mistakes in diagnosis lead to inappropriate or even harmful treatments, as well as the need for additional care once the actual health condition is diagnosed. Finally, both diagnostic mistakes and inappropriate treatment increase indirect costs because they require additional documentation and extra administration.

There are wide variations in medical practice and costs from one region in the U.S. to another. Dartmouth research on Medicare found not only that there were very different practice standards in different regions, but also that there was no basis in medical theory or medical evidence for these variations.[21] Differences in the patterns of practice, together with variation in the frequency of specialist care and hospitalization, drive regional variations in spending.[22] The highest-cost states spend almost three times as much per patient as the lowest-cost states for inpatient expenses. (See figure 1-12.) Substantial differences in per capita spending among states are present across the board—in Medicare, Medicaid, and private health care spending. (See figure 1-13.)

But higher cost is not correlated with higher quality. Regions with higher spending do not have more access, better outcomes, higher satisfaction, reduced mortality, or improved access to care.[23] There is also evidence of the overuse of care. In regions with a high concentration of specialists, there is more spending on specialists and on end-of-life care. Yet those same locations are less likely to use effective, medically recognized standards of care for all patients.[24] In contrast, locations with more effective care have lower spending and a greater proportion of treatment by general practitioners. (See figure 1-14.)

Quality also varies markedly among providers, even in the same region. In the study on underdelivery of care conducted by McGlynn et al., some providers met 100 percent of the established standards, but the vast majority fell far short. Other careful studies reveal huge variations in risk-adjusted outcomes across providers in areas such as organ transplants, heart surgery, and cystic fibrosis treatment.[25] Moreover, the differences in quality across providers in addressing particular medical conditions do

FIGURE 1-12

Cumulative distribution of expenses per inpatient day throughout the fifty states and Puerto Rico, 2001

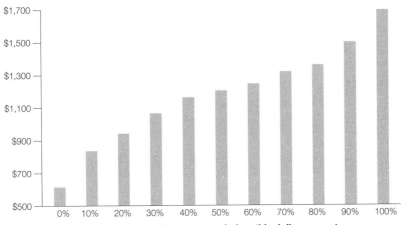

Percentage of states at or below this dollar amount

Source: Data from American Hospital Association (2003).

not conform to common assumptions. For example, community hospitals register equal or better outcomes at lower costs in some types of care than academic medical centers.[26]

Part of the problem is that the diffusion of medical knowledge is slow.[27] It takes, on average, seventeen years for the results of clinical trials to become standard clinical practice.[28] Numerous studies have reached similar conclusions.[29] That huge delay—much longer than in most industries—contributes to low and uneven quality.

Compounding the costs of poor quality are its expense in terms of malpractice premiums and lawsuits. Professional liability premiums are growing at an unprecedented rate, with U.S. doctors spending more than $6 billion per year on malpractice premiums in addition to the billions of dollars spent each year by hospitals and nursing homes.[30] More important than the cost of premiums may well be the threat of malpractice suits, which causes doctors to practice "defensive" medicine in the form of unnecessary tests, overdiagnosis, and redundant or unnecessary treatment to satisfy patients and their families that everything possible was done. This further increases costs while potentially reducing quality, creating a vicious circle.

FIGURE 1-13

Average Medicaid, Medicare, and private spending per beneficiary by state, 2001

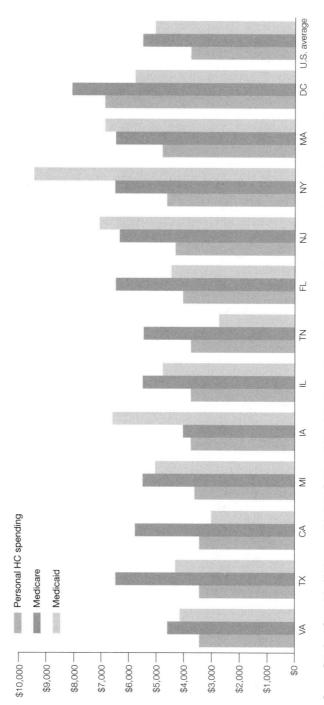

Source: Data from Centers for Medicare and Medicaid Services, Office of the Actuary, National Health Statistics Group, as reported in Martin et al. (2002).

FIGURE 1-14

Medicare spending and quality of care by state, 2001

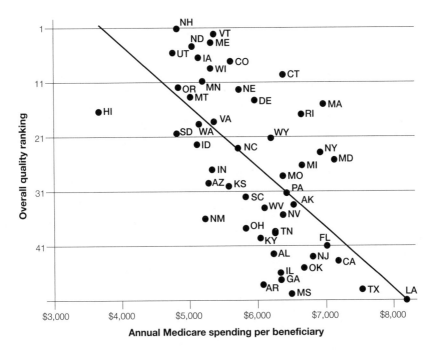

Source: Baicker, K., and A. Chandra, "Medicare Spending, the Physician Workforce, and Beneficiaries' Quality of Care," *Health Affairs* Online. Copyright 2003 by Project Hope. Reproduced with permission of Project Hope via Copyright Clearance Center.

Finally, the current system has resulted in administrative costs that are extraordinarily high and rising. The administrative burden is high across all types of health care delivery, with little apparent benefit in terms of patient care.[31] Surveys find that both doctors and nurses spend between one-third and one-half of their time on paperwork.[32] (See figure 1-15.) Even if these percentages are somewhat overstated, the figure remains strikingly high. Overall, the estimated health care expenditures spent on administration are a staggering 25 percent of hospital spending and are estimated to be over 30 percent of all health care spending.[33] Even as managed care became the norm, the cost of administration, which managed care was supposed to reduce, continued to rise throughout the United States.[34] (See figure 1-16.)

Although the growth rate of insurance premiums slowed in the early 1990s, cost escalation took off again in the mid-1990s. Annual increases in U.S. insurance premiums from 1996 to 2003 have outpaced wage

Administrative burden by type of health care delivery

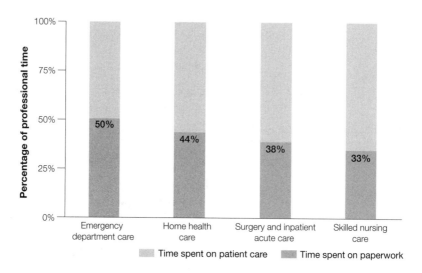

Source: Data from PricewaterhouseCoopers and the American Hospital Association (2001).

Health care administrative costs by state as a percentage of total hospital spending, 1990 and 1994

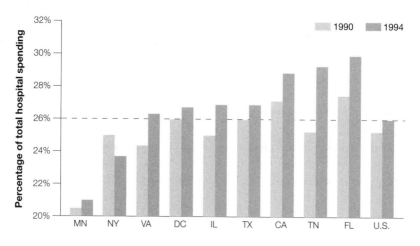

Source: Data from Woolhandler and Himmelstein (1997).

FIGURE 1-17

Annual growth in U.S. health insurance premiums versus inflation and wages

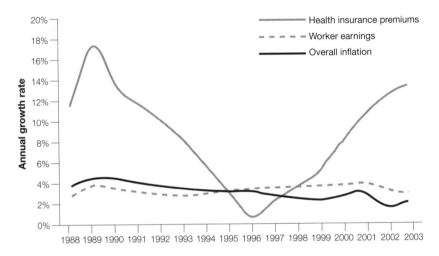

Source: "Employer Health Benefits 2003 Annual Survey" (#3369), The Henry J. Kaiser Family Foundation and Health Research and Educational Trust, September 2003. This information was reprinted with permission of The Henry J. Kaiser Family Foundation. The Kaiser Family Foundation, based in Menlo Park, California, is a nonprofit, independent national health care philanthropy and is not associated with Kaiser Permanente or Kaiser Industries.

growth by a factor of four, and outpaced inflation by a factor of six. (See figure 1-17.)

The costs and the quality problems of American medicine have made health care a critical concern for U.S. businesses. Employers not only purchase health plans from third parties but also self-insure in many cases, so they bear directly the cost of health care and the consequences of quality problems. Average monthly health premiums per employee have risen from about $300 in 1996 to about $600 in 2004. (See figure 1-18.) Indeed, General Motors reports that health premiums add $1,500 to the price of every vehicle it builds in the United States.[35] Ford Motor Company reported a figure of $1,000 in 2003, up from $700 three years previously.[36]

Premium increases understate the problem because less is being covered for employees with insurance. Also, employers have raised the percentage of premiums that must be paid by employees. Although employers have been absorbing substantial cost increases, employee contributions to health premiums rose from an average of 31 to 35 percent for individual

FIGURE 1-18

Average U.S. employer health care premiums, 1996–2004

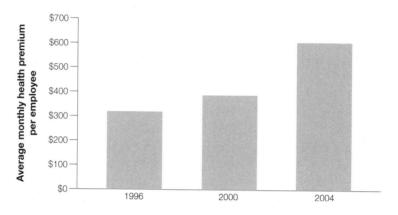

Source: Data from Kaiser Family Foundation and Health Research and Educational Trust (2004).

coverage and from 50 to 57 percent for family coverage in 2003 alone, when pay raises averaged just 3 percent.[37]

A survey of major companies revealed that 96 percent of CEOs and CFOs were critically concerned about health care costs for 2004.[38] A different survey of smaller employers found that 22 percent were considering terminating health benefits for cost reasons, and 74 percent believed that the health care system needed significant government reform.[39]

Taken together, these indicators clearly point to the same conclusion: the U.S. health care system is careening out of control. If the current performance trajectory continues without significant change, the problem will only intensify as baby boomers age. Access problems will compound, rationing will be increasingly likely, and quality promises to be undermined even further.

How could this alarming performance possibly arise? In most industries, competition drives continuous improvement in quality and efficiency, as excellent organizations grow and serve more of the market and ineffective organizations shrink or go out of business. In health care, competition is clearly not working. Explaining this puzzling outcome, and the paradox that higher spending has not led to better care, is a vital first step in any effort to reform the system. Only with an accurate diagnosis can the nation find an effective cure.

2

Identifying the
Root Causes

WHY IS COMPETITION not working in health care? To understand this problem, compare the nature of competition in health care to that which takes place in other industries.

Positive-Sum Competition on Value

Healthy competition is competition to improve value for customers, or the quality of products or services relative to their price. It leads to relentless improvements in efficiency. Product quality and customer service improve. Innovation propels advances in the state of the art. Quality-adjusted prices fall, and the market expands and more customer needs are met. Choice expands as firms work to distinguish their products or services from others. Excellent firms prosper while firms with low quality, poor service, or high costs decline or go out of business unless they make fundamental improvements in the way they operate. This is what value-based competition looks like, but it is a far cry from what we see today in health care.

Value-based competition is positive sum. When value improves, both capable firms and consumers benefit. The firms that find unique ways to deliver superior value are winners, and are rewarded with more business. But customers also win as quality increases and prices fall. The more firms that find ways to provide high value for customers, the more winners there are. The only losers are firms that fail to deliver good value.

Value-based competition is the type of competition we see in virtually every field: retailing, airlines, financial services, aerospace, and computer services. Such competition has transformed previously regulated fields, such as telecommunications and trucking, as well as sclerotic economies, such as those in eastern Europe, with extraordinary benefits.

The beneficial effects of competition are often taken for granted in a country like the United States. When people buy new computers with far more capabilities, speed, and memory for the same or lower prices as their old ones, they are benefiting from productive competition. When automatic tellers and online services make banking possible at all hours, and when cars become safer, more comfortable, and defect free, value-based competition is at work.

But for many individuals—and this is especially true in health care—the word *competition* conjures a different image. Many think of competition as analogous to a sporting event: although someone wins, many others must lose because all the contestants are competing to capture a single prize. Others think of competition as analogous to war. Again, winning depends on defeating the "enemy," which is destructive. Many equate competition with price cutting and inevitable quality reduction. The idea that competition leads to wasteful duplication is also deeply ingrained.

These conceptions of competition overlook the central role of value. Competition that does not improve value, redividing the pie rather than expanding it, is zero sum.[1] In zero-sum competition, no one really wins, even ultimately the customer. Indeed, this kind of competition can actually undermine value because the costs involved in competition sometimes produce no consumer benefit.

Zero-Sum Competition in Health Care

Some have argued that competition does not work in health care because health care is different: it is complex, consumers cannot understand medical practice, services are highly customized, and insurers, employers, or government pay for most of the care.[2] While health care indeed has many of these characteristics, so do other industries where competition works well. For example, the business of providing customized software development and information technology services to large corporations is customized and hugely complex. Yet adjusted for quality, the costs of enterprise computing have fallen dramatically over the past decade.

Others have argued that the problem in health care is *too much* competition. Competition is blamed for duplication, excess investment, and wasteful administrative costs. Competition from specialized hospitals or specialized outpatient facilities is seen as draining revenues from community hospitals. Competition among physicians is seen as driving the overprovision of services.

While these symptoms are real enough, the fundamental flaw in the health care sector is not competition, but the *wrong kind of competition*. Health care competition is not focused on delivering value for patients.

Instead, it has become zero sum: the system participants struggle to divide value when they could be increasing it. Although health care offers tremendous value, the unnecessary costs of zero-sum competition undermine and erode that value. It is the zero-sum competition in health care that has created the unacceptable results detailed in the previous chapter: high costs, low or variable quality, under- and overtreatment, too many preventable errors in diagnosis and treatment, restrictions on choice, rationing of services, limited access, and a raft of costly lawsuits.

Zero-sum competition in health care is manifested in a number of ways, none of which creates value for patients:

- Competition to shift costs
- Competition to increase bargaining power
- Competition to capture patients and restrict choice
- Competition to reduce costs by restricting services

Each of these dysfunctional types of competition has unhappy consequences.

Competition to Shift Costs

Current health care competition takes the form of cost shifting rather than fundamental cost reduction. All system participants seek to lower their own costs by shifting the burden to other parts of the system. Costs are shifted from payer to patient, from health plan to hospital and vice versa, from hospital to physician, from health plan to subscriber, from employer to employee, from employer to government, from insured to uninsured, from government to private insurers, from states to the federal government, and so on. Even patients play the cost-shifting game. They attempt to use political influence and the legal system to obtain expanded coverage from health plans and greater contributions from government.

Passing costs from one player to another like a hot potato creates no net value. Instead, the gains for one system participant come at the expense of others. All this cost shifting does nothing to improve health care at all. It distracts system participants from steps that would improve value, and the added administrative costs and inefficiencies created along the way actually erode value.

Figures 2-1 and 2-2 reveal this pattern. Figure 2-1 shows that reductions in hospital costs for public payers in the late 1980s led to higher payments by private payers in the early 1990s. In the mid-1990s, cost declines for private payers only shifted costs to public ones. Overall, as shown in figure 2-2, costs continued to rise. Total national expenditures more than doubled, from $700 billion in 1990 to $1.9 trillion in 2004.[3]

FIGURE 2-1

Hospital payment-to-cost ratios: Government versus private payers

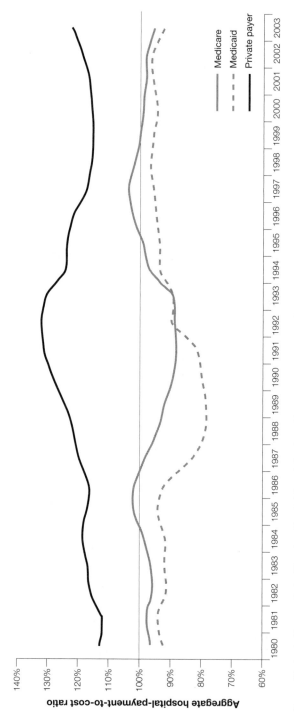

Source: The Lewin Group analysis of American Hospital Association Annual Survey data, 1980–2003, for community hospitals, and the U.S census Bureau. In The Lewin Group and the AHA, *TrendWatch Chartbook 2005*: "Trends Affecting Hospitals and Health Systems." Used with permission.

FIGURE 2-2

U.S. health care expenditures, 1990 and 2003

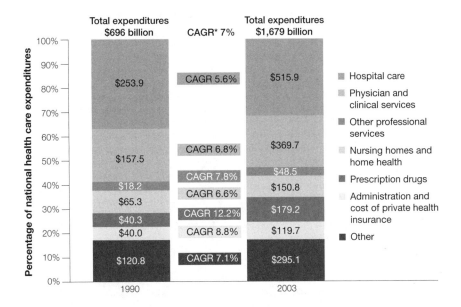

*CAGR: Compound annual growth rate.

Source: Data from Center for Medicare and Medicaid Services, Office of the Actuary, National Health Statistics Group. http://www.cms.hhs.gov/statistics/nhe/historical/t2.asp.

Competition to Increase Bargaining Power

The struggle to shift cost creates strong incentives for system participants to amass greater bargaining power with which to capture more value for themselves instead of focusing on improving health results, raising efficiency, or improving the patient experience. As a result, health plans, hospital groups, physician groups, and suppliers of drugs and devices have all consolidated in recent years. At the same time, intermediaries such as buying groups and pharmacy benefit managers (PBMs) have grown up to aggregate purchases and play the bargaining power game. The primary goal has been to gain more clout in the battle to capture more of the revenues, raise prices, push costs to others, and extract discounts. The quality and efficiency gains from these consolidations are modest; little or no health care value is created.

Health Plan Bargaining Power. In the early 1990s, large employers and large health plans increased their bargaining power by structuring subscriber benefits to include *only* the providers with which the payer had contracted. Health plans then contracted only with those providers that agreed to discounted prices for the group. This triggered competition among hospitals and hospital systems to be included in health plan networks, with the primary method of competition being to offer deep discounts to payers and employers that had large overall patient populations. The rate of increase in health plan costs slowed temporarily, but soon reaccelerated. (See figure 1-17.)

The problem is that there is little or no economic rationale for this kind of volume discount. For the same medical condition, it does not cost less to treat a patient employed by a large company than a patient who is self-employed. Health care delivery does not become more efficient when a hospital treats twice as many patients with a wide distribution of diseases; patients are still treated one at a time and according to their particular circumstances. Any meaningful economies of scale in health care delivery occur at the level of particular medical conditions and their treatment, as we will discuss in chapters 4 and 5.[4] Across-the-board discounts to attract a large group, then, do not boost value but simply squeeze the incomes of hospitals and doctors. This, in turn, creates intense pressure on practitioners to see more patients per day and to pare back care to recoup profits. Health care value is not improved.

Offering large discounts in return for overall patient flow obscures price comparisons, because the prices charged by providers are different for each subscriber group. Discounting also favors large health plans and large employers at the expense of small groups, unaffiliated individuals, patients seeking out-of-network care, and, ironically, the uninsured—with little, if any, compensating value justification.[5] Such cost shifting and perverse cross subsidies ultimately drive up overall costs—even ultimately to large groups—by increasing the number of uninsured patients who lack primary care and must be treated for free or in expensive settings (emergency rooms, for instance). This then increases the amount of free care that must be subsidized.[6] All of this cost shifting and cross subsidizing is zero sum—it creates no value for patients.

Finally, some health plans used their clout to move to capitation, in which providers were paid a fixed amount per member per year to address all the members' health care needs. In so doing, health plans sought to contract only or primarily with full-line providers. As we will see, full-line providers offer limited patient value and can have adverse effects on competition.

Provider Breadth and Consolidation. The squeeze on providers triggered another undesirable competition: a scramble to form the largest, most powerful full-line provider group. While this was a natural response to the increase in health plan bargaining power, it again failed to increase value in health care delivery. Providers sought to control a large share of capacity and form large delivery networks able to offer a complete array of services to gain advantages in contracting. Physicians joined into groups so they would not have to bargain as individual agents. But in both cases, few true efficiencies were gained, apart from modest opportunities to share corporate overhead.

As we have noted, the primary economies of scale in health care delivery are in individual service lines, not for the hospital as a whole. But with few exceptions, hospital mergers have resulted in little or no true consolidation and integration at the service line level.[7,8] Instead, duplicative services were left in place, even when the facilities were close to each other. Savings from consolidating support functions such as laundry, food service, and hotel services are minor, and similar efficiencies are obtainable through outsourcing. Provider groups were not formed to create value, then, but primarily to boost bargaining power vis-à-vis health plans and other system participants.

Between 1996 and 2003, there were more than 850 mergers between hospitals, resulting in significant consolidation in a number of markets.[9] In Cleveland, for example, two hospital systems now control 68 percent of the city's beds. In Grand Rapids, Michigan, one hospital system controls 70 percent; in Richmond, Virginia, three systems control more than 80 percent; in El Paso, Texas, two systems control nearly 80 percent; and on Long Island, New York, two systems control more than 80 percent.[10] In North Carolina, only 18 of 100 counties were served by multiple hospital systems by 2000.[11]

The effect of such consolidation on prices is predictable. With little benefit in terms of value, the primary effect is that prices will rise due to less competition. Throughout Florida, for example, large hospital networks have won price increases far above the rate of inflation after threatening to cut off one of the region's largest health plans. These increases are unconnected to any quality improvements. Recent empirical studies across geographic markets confirm that hospital consolidations, rather than improving efficiency, result in price increases that at least equal, and usually exceed, the median price increases by other hospitals in the same market and that price increases are greater in the most concentrated markets.[12,13] Large provider groups run the risk of severely limiting competition at the level of medical conditions, because their referrals are heavily skewed toward affiliated physician groups and institutions, undermining health care value.

Some hospitals and hospital groups assert that offering a complete array of services in a provider network is necessary for managing co-occurring conditions or addressing unusual illnesses that arise during

treatment. However, there is no need for a single hospital to be able to provide all services for all patients, as we will discuss extensively in chapter 5.
Breadth offers even less of a rationale for multiple hospitals in the same
region to be under common management. Excellent providers in a particular medical condition equip themselves for the common co-occurring
conditions in that practice unit as part of their commitment to providing
superior care for specific patient groups.[14] Unusual cases are readily addressed through consultations and referrals and, in rare cases, patient transport. The M. D. Anderson Cancer Center in Houston, for example, has staff
cardiologists but does not maintain a full-line cardiology practice. When difficult cases arise or heart surgery is required, the physicians at M. D. Anderson consult with outside colleagues or refer their cancer patients to leading
cardiac centers. Patients are best treated by a hospital that is truly excellent in addressing their current condition, not the hospital that treated
them for another condition previously.[15]

Ironically, the current full-service model has contributed to the extreme fragmentation of services. Every hospital offers every service, often
at low volumes. This has little logic in terms of patient value. In today's
system, every hospital aims for its share of patients in every service area,
even if it is not as well equipped to serve some of them as others nearby.
This fragmenting of care is often institutionalized by regulatory practices
and health plan contracts. For example, state rules and health plan contracts require ambulances to take stroke patients to the nearest hospital in
many states, even though most hospitals do not have the experience and
equipment to provide timely, effective care for major stroke. This leads to
deaths and patients with long-term disabilities that could have been prevented in a system oriented to getting patients to the best provider for
addressing their condition.[16]

In today's system, the convenience benefit of each hospital treating all
conditions takes precedence because quality and price information are
not available, and because of network restrictions.[17] If patients and referring
doctors really had information on the disparate results of different providers and physicians, it is hard to believe that they would use the same
hospital for all services and thereby accept an inferior medical outcome.
Today, most referring doctors are not sufficiently aware of even the limited rigorous results information that is available to act on it.[18]

Competition to Capture Patients and Restrict Choice

The struggle to accumulate bargaining power led health plans to merge
and compete fiercely to sign up as many members as possible. But gaining

scale by acquiring members has little impact on health care value. Value is created in helping members to manage their health and obtain excellent care, which has not been the primary focus. Competition to sign up members has taken place primarily through marketing directed at attracting healthy (lower-cost) patients by offering access to many primary care doctors, providing incentives such as health club memberships, and offering a service experience that rates highly in patient satisfaction surveys focused on convenience, amenities, and customer service (not on health outcomes).[19] Such practices have further perpetuated the perception that all health care providers are indistinguishable, when they are anything but that in the most important dimensions of health care value.

The members' annual selection of a health plan is neither the right place nor the right time to focus competition. The vast majority of families choose a health plan when members are healthy, without knowing which illness will need treating or which provider they will desire to use.[20] The information that seems salient at enrollment time covers relatively superficial attributes of routine care. Furthermore, the annual selection of a plan and the churning of subscribers creates an inappropriate time horizon and undermines value for both patient and health plan, as we discuss in chapter 6.

Once members are locked in, health plans have restricted their choices of providers to those offering deep discounts to the group rather than those demonstrating the best results. Such network restrictions would not be so important if all health care providers offered uniformly high quality and efficiency, and if value were improving rapidly. However, as we discussed in chapter 1, there are serious quality problems and tremendous variations in the efficiency and quality of care delivered.[21] Network and approval restrictions undermine health care value by perpetuating these cost and quality problems rather than harnessing competition to uncover and resolve them.

The formation of broad-line providers and provider groups only adds to the problem. Provider groups contribute to the zero-sum competition to capture patients. Strong forces are created to refer patients within the institution or the group, further limiting competition on costs and results at the medical condition level. A common assumption is that provider groups allow continuity of care. In practice, however, service lines in different locations are rarely integrated, communication remains limited, the coordination of care is ad hoc, the multiple physicians treating a patient rarely meet as a team, and the results of the patient's overall care are rarely if ever measured. Fragmentation of service lines is reinforced, then, and patient value suffers.

Competition to Reduce Costs by Restricting Services

Competition has sought to cut costs by restricting access to services, thereby shifting costs to patients or rationing care. Health plans profit by refusing to pay for services and constraining physicians' choices of the amount and type of care. But it is worse than this, because the process of requiring approvals, micromanaging physician judgments, and second-guessing physician and patient choices explodes administrative costs for everyone.[22] None of this benefits patient value. While some health plans have begun to move away from these practices, as we discuss in chapter 6, the legacy of two decades of zero-sum competition remains. Because of this legacy, it is not sufficient just to discontinue the counterproductive practices; additional positive roles by health plans are necessary to create real value in the system.

Not only health plans but also providers have sought to limit services for patients and to restrict access to new treatments. For example, many health plans bargain with hospitals to pay a low, fixed amount per admission for a given ailment. This creates an incentive for hospitals to treat more patients, especially healthier patients for whom the payment clearly exceeds the costs, and to utilize less expensive treatments rather than more effective, innovative ones.[23] If undertreated or inappropriately treated patients must be readmitted at a later time, the hospitals are paid again.[24] Health care value is reduced, not enhanced, by this type of competition.

When the health plan and provider combine together, or vertically integrate, strong incentives are created to deliver less expensive care because the health plan receives a fixed premium per subscriber per year. Hence this structure effectively introduces capitation, with its troubling incentives. Without reliable measures of medical results, patients cannot know whether cost savings are due to efficiency and more appropriate care or to degrading quality or de facto rationing of care. While most Americans have assumed that the care they received was appropriate and up-to-date, this assumption has been shattered by the research discussed in chapter 1. De facto rationing is far more common than virtually anyone had guessed, and it is occurring in the form of partial care.

Dysfunctional Competition Proliferates Lawsuits

These four types of zero-sum competition combine to create many disputes. With all the parties pitted against each other in an adversarial process that adds little or no value for patients, and with no other recourse for the inevitable problems, lawsuits are inevitable. As figure 2-3

FIGURE 2-3

Growth in hospital and professional liability premiums, 2000–2002

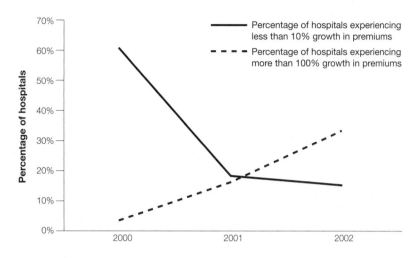

Source: Data from American Hospital Association (2002).

illustrates, malpractice premiums are rising rapidly. In 2002, more than one-third of U.S. hospitals faced malpractice premium increases of greater than 100 percent.

Malpractice lawsuits compound the problems in the health care system. They raise costs directly (through legal fees and administrative expenses) and indirectly (by encouraging the practice of expensive defensive medicine), neither of which creates value for patients.[25] Some lawyers argue that legal recourse creates value because it creates an incentive for physicians to provide good medical care. However, lawsuits have clearly not solved the quality problem in the system. Instead, they drive up cost because most physicians, not just the few who are careless or poorly qualified, are driven to practice defensive medicine to reduce their risks in ways that go well beyond the bounds of careful practice. The result is excessive and duplicative tests and aggressive, redundant, or unnecessary treatment so that "everything possible has been done" in case something goes wrong. Sadly, even the unfortunate patients who experience mistakes scarcely benefit. Less than 30 percent of the billions of dollars that doctors and hospitals pay annually for malpractice insurance reaches injured patients or their families.[26]

The Root Cause: Competition at the Wrong Level

Why is competition in health care not focused on value? The most fundamental, unrecognized problem with the U.S. health care system is that competition operates at the wrong level. Competition is both too broad and too narrow. Competition is too broad because much competition now takes place at the level of health plans, networks, hospital groups, physician groups, and clinics. It should occur in addressing particular medical conditions. Competition is too narrow because it now takes place at the level of discrete interventions or services. It should take place for addressing medical conditions over the full cycle of care, including monitoring and prevention, diagnosis, treatment, and the ongoing management of the condition.

Value in health care is created or destroyed at the medical condition level, not at the level of a hospital or physician practice. A medical condition (e.g., chronic kidney disease, diabetes, pregnancy) is a set of patient health circumstances that benefit from dedicated, coordinated care. The term *medical condition* encompasses diseases, illnesses, injuries, and natural circumstances such as pregnancy. A medical condition can be defined to encompass common co-occurring conditions if care for them involves the need for tight coordination and patient care benefits from common facilities. We will discuss the definition of medical conditions in more detail in chapters 4 and 5.

It is in addressing a particular medical condition that patient value is delivered. Today, multiple entities can be involved in patient care. It is at this level where huge differences in costs and quality persist and where the lack of competition allows providers with worse outcomes and higher charges to remain in business. And it is here where healthy competition would drive improvements in efficiency and effectiveness, reduce errors, and spark innovation.

Yet competition at the level of medical conditions is all but absent. Competition at this level, where it matters most, is stifled by formal and de facto network restrictions, and by lack of information. Patients are referred to doctors and hospitals inside the network, with health plan approval often required at every step of the way. Even if out-of-network care is allowed, it is severely restricted by higher copayments and the requirement to pay list prices.[27] Physicians required or accustomed to referring within the network or within their own provider group are unlikely to know whether an out-of-network specialist has more experience with the patient's particular conditions or could provide more effective or more efficient care.

Information about the most appropriate and effective care for the patient's specific medical needs is virtually nonexistent. Instead, what dominates is what the network provides. The patient backlash against

HMOs with closed networks, administrative preapproval of treatments, and limited choices of pharmaceuticals is now beginning to result in less restrictive plans. However, cost penalties for out-of-network care remain, and provider groups have often taken up where health plan networks left off in insulating service lines from competition based on results.

In addressing a medical condition, health care value is also created not for each discrete intervention but over the entire cycle of monitoring, diagnosing, treating, and managing the condition. The value of surgery cannot be assessed in isolation, but must reflect the other services also required as well as the patient's long-term outcomes. Similarly, value can only be measured over the medium or long run, when the true health outcomes and full costs of care can be understood.

Because of the lack of effective competition at the condition level, the actual organization and structure of care delivery by most providers is not aligned with patient value. Lack of value-based competition on results has allowed care of a patient to be fractured across numerous specialties, hospital departments, and physician practices, each of which focuses on its discrete intervention. Nobody integrates care for the medical condition as a whole and across the full care cycle, including early detection, treatment, rehabilitation, and long-term management.

The need for competition at the level of medical conditions over the cycle of care is only getting more important. Advances in medical practice have blurred distinctions between traditional specialties and treatments. The benefits of prevention and ongoing disease management, not just intervention, are becoming apparent. Medical conditions themselves are becoming more specialized and patient specific. Prostate cancer, for example, is now understood to be six different diseases, each of which responds best to a different cycle of treatment.[28]

Physicians should compete to be the best at addressing a particular set of medical conditions or a particular segment of the patient population, or both. Patients and referring physicians should be free to seek out the provider with the best track record over the full cycle of care. But in the current environment, where patients' choices are determined not by the best provider for their problem but by the network or the provider group they are in, some specialists are all but guaranteed the business.

In the few areas in the current system where competition at the right level is not restricted and physicians must attract patients by competing on price and results, cost and quality have improved markedly. Cosmetic surgery, outside of the mainstream system and not covered by health plans, is an interesting case. As we will discuss in chapter 4, advances in a range of types of cosmetic surgery have simultaneously reduced costs and improved quality during the same period that costs in most of mainstream medicine have doubled.

Why Is Health Care Competition
at the Wrong Level?

It seems obvious that health care value is created in addressing medical conditions for individual patients over the cycle of care, and that health care competition should be centered at this level. So why, despite so much effort by so many well-intentioned people, has competition gravitated to zero-sum competition at the hospital, health plan, and provider group level? Why is care delivery so fractured by procedure and intervention?

The Wrong Conception of Health Care Itself: The Commodity Mind-set

Zero-sum competition has unwittingly treated health care as a commodity when it is anything but a commodity. The system is structured as though health care were one business (service line) rather than many different businesses, and as though all providers were equivalent, all outcomes the same, and all patients shared the same preferences. The net result has been to promote more commoditization and to perpetuate, rather than eliminate, dramatic differences in quality and efficiency.

The commoditization of health care was the first of a series of unfortunate strategic choices made by nearly all the actors in the system. Hospitals thought they should be all things to all people to drive volume. Health plans thought that they should contract with providers based on discounts. Employers, especially, should have been in a position to see the consequences of the commodity mind-set. They should have understood from their own businesses that all service providers are not equal. Unfortunately, however, employers failed to make this connection and went along with forms of competition that were fundamentally unproductive for the system and ultimately more costly for them.

The Wrong Objective over the Wrong Time Horizon

Treating health care as a commodity contributed to the pursuit of the wrong objective: reducing short-term costs. Even worse, the goal often has not been to reduce the actual cost of care but to reduce the costs borne by a particular intermediary—the health plan or employer. Containing costs as a central goal was seductive given the history of incentives to overuse the system. And because health plans were under pressure to hold down premiums, it is not surprising that they focused on reducing their own costs instead of overall costs. But once health plans accepted the mission of driving down *their* costs, almost insurmountable pressures were created to shift costs to providers and patients and to ration care. After all, the surest and easiest ways to reduce health plan costs are to select healthy members (and encourage sick members to disenroll), let patients go untreated or undertreated, or get someone else to pay.

In addition, thinking regarding cost reduction has been short run, relying on quick hits, such as eliminating expensive drugs or diagnostic procedures, rather than on more fundamental cost reduction over the full cycle of care. True costs, and value, can only be measured over the full cycle of care, which begins with prevention and continues through recovery and longer-term management of the condition to limit reoccurrence. The relevant time horizon may be months or even years. What matters for cost is not the cost of any individual intervention or treatment, but the overall cost. An expensive drug, a more experienced surgeon, or more spending on rehabilitation may be a bargain over the longer run.

The right goal is to improve value (the quality of health outcome per dollar expended). Value is created at the level of medical conditions and across the full cycle of care.[29] Competing on costs instead of value makes sense only in commodity businesses, where all sellers are more or less the same. Competing on pieces of costs, not total costs, does not make sense in any business. Yet these perverse assumptions—which neither buyers nor sellers really believe—underlie the behavior of the system participants. The result is that health plans, employers, and even providers pay insufficient attention to the goal that really matters: improving value over time.

The Wrong Geographic Market

Competition should force providers to equal or exceed the value created by the best provider in their region, the nation, or even internationally. For the most part, however, health care competition has been entirely local. This local bias insulates mediocre providers from market pressures and inhibits the spread of best practices and innovations.

Across the United States, there is an almost threefold regional variation in annual costs per Medicare enrollee, with expenditures ranging from less than $3,000 per patient in some areas to more than $8,500 in others. The higher expenditures are not associated with better medical outcomes, nor can they be explained by differences in age, sex, race, rates of illness (which affect the need for care), or cost of living (which affects the costs of delivering care).[30] Such differences are sustained by the absence of geographic competition, either competition for patients across geography or the entry of excellent competitors from other regions.

Numerous studies have also found major differences across regions in quality at the medical condition or specific treatment level, and variations in treatment protocols that are not consistent with established medical standards. Local customs dominate. In the ten procedures that account for 44 percent of Medicare inpatient surgery, for example, the data show very high variation across regions in the incidence of surgery, the quality of clinical decision making, the relationship between clinical practice and the scientific evidence, and the skill with which surgical care is delivered, even after adjusting for variations in illness rates.[31] A number of these procedures would be generally accepted as routine and relatively uncomplicated, and thus seemingly ones where local care would be appropriate. The fact that large variations exist even for these procedures suggests that encouraging patients and referring physicians to consider medical services beyond the closest local options may be important for a wider array of services than one might first assume.

Despite the variation in quality and cost, geographic competition even among nearby providers is severely circumscribed. Most patients are actively discouraged from seeking and securing the best value care, either because their health plan's choices are geographically constrained or because their doctor refers locally. The problem is most acute in rural areas, where there is rarely any local competition at all. But even when multiple providers are readily available, the mind-set of keeping the patient in the provider's own system usually prevails.

Localized competition is also enshrined by health plan policies that require members to pay most of the costs of out-of-network care or that penalize physicians for making out-of-network referrals. This discourages both patients and physicians from seeking providers outside their immediate area. Medicare, for its part, computes payments at the county level, creating little incentive or competitive pressure for hospitals in different counties to match the value of excellent providers elsewhere, even if they are only a few miles apart.

Localized competition is also the result of habit, inertia, and lack of information that would support referrals to a regional center. As a matter of course, physicians refer their patients to nearby doctors with whom they have a relationship—even their Medicare patients, who have no geographic restrictions. Providers routinely compare themselves to other local players rather than the best providers regionally or nationally.

Limiting competition across geographic markets not only perpetuates quality and cost differences, but also stifles innovation that might otherwise occur as physicians are forced to contend with variation in practice patterns and outcomes in different locations. Here again, despite good intentions, health care competition has been "managed" in a way that works against value creation.

Much medical care will be local, but competition should be regional or national. Providers must be held to national standards, not local ones. And more patients should seek care not provided by the closest hospital or physician practice. No provider should be sheltered from competition with providers based elsewhere.

The Wrong Strategies

Value is created in addressing particular medical conditions when providers develop dedicated teams, deep expertise, and tailored facilities in a set of integrated practice units where they can truly excel. (See chapter 5.) Yet most hospitals and provider groups have pursued broad-line strategies to capture referrals and better negotiate with health plans. Hospitals (and other types of providers) made the classic strategic error of becoming more similar to their rivals rather than distinguishing themselves.[32] Broad-line strategies have little positive benefit for value, as we have described.[33] Predictably, however, broad-line strategies have led to extreme fragmentation of service lines—every service is offered by numerous providers, many of whom are subscale. This leads to unproductive duplication of facilities and personnel and more ferocious price discounting. So in their efforts to negotiate better deals, many hospitals and physician groups undermined their ability to compete on dimensions other than price. In a system that rewards volume and bargaining power, many hospitals saw no viable alternative.

The wrong provider strategies have not only made it harder for providers to prosper but also have slowed advances in health care quality and efficiency. As hospitals and physician groups become more alike, they lose the strategic focus necessary to achieve true excellence. The proliferation of providers in every service area only exacerbates the problem that supply in health care can create its own demand. In locations with more specialists, for example, patients get more hospitalizations, more ICU time, more tests, and more minor procedures without higher quality of experience or better outcomes.[34]

The drive to broaden service lines results in some providers offering services for which they lack the scale and experience to attain true excellence. For example, 139 hospitals had adult heart transplant service in 2002. Many handle only a few cases per year, and some have few patients who survive. (See figure 2-4.)

Health plan strategies also went astray. Health plans have focused on discounts and administrative control of members and providers rather than developing a distinctive ability to offer superior health value to patients. (See chapter 6.)

The Wrong Structure of Care Delivery

The wrong provider strategies have reinforced a fractured organization of care delivery that is misaligned with value. Ironically, the drive to offer all

FIGURE 2-4

Heart transplants: One-year survival rate, January–December 2002

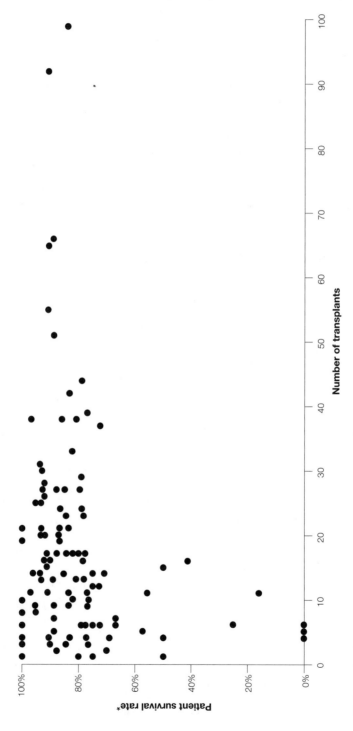

*Patient survival data is not risk adjusted. Patient survival rate is calculated for transplants performed July 1, 2001, through June 30, 2002.

Source: Data from www.optn.org and Dr. Richard Migliori, United Resource Networks.

services has not been accompanied by patient-centered care or integrating care within medical conditions. Rather than building practice units that integrate the talent and facilities required to deliver outstanding care over the care cycle, hospitals and physician groups remain organized along the lines of traditional academic specialties—radiology, anesthesiology, surgery. This not only ensures a disjointed experience for the patient, but makes excellent coordination and communication among the provider team next to impossible. In many situations, the provider team never meets, information is not really shared, and both quality and efficiency suffer. Coordination and communication problems, in turn, raise the incidence of errors and impede the design and implementation of the improvement process. The fractured care structure inhibits conversations about improving results over the full cycle of care, but these conversations and ideas should be a shared source of excitement and professional satisfaction for every medical team.

Each department or physician practice takes a piecemeal view of care. This fractured system obscures information on overall results and the costs and prices of caring for a patient. Few providers measure value over the full cycle of care for a patient.

The Wrong Industry Structure

Zero-sum competition at the wrong level has triggered a revolutionary change in industry structure. Providers have rapidly consolidated, leaving only one or two vertically integrated networks consisting of multiple hospitals and physician groups in many regions. These groups have become quasi-monopolies, with substantial bargaining leverage to restore and then raise prices.[35] The cost "savings" of the early years of managed care were heavily based on cost shifting, and unsustainable. Over time, this industry transformation has been associated with cost escalation.[36] (See figure 2-5.) The recent acceleration of cost increases does not reflect improved value; it is just the latest chapter in the saga of shifting costs, this time back to health plans, employers, and consumers.

Provider consolidation does not inherently destroy value. Value creation or destruction depends on how the provider group is managed. Some groups, such as Intermountain Health Care and the Cleveland Clinic, have rationalized and specialized care across facilities, and sought to make care at the condition level more integrated over the care cycle. Most consolidated groups, however, have failed to produce significant efficiencies. Instead, consolidation into full-line groups has encouraged more redundancy. Ironically, while managed care eliminated the incentives of cost-plus reimbursement that historically led to redundant facilities, its

Annual rate of increase in the Consumer Price Index (CPI) overall and for medical care

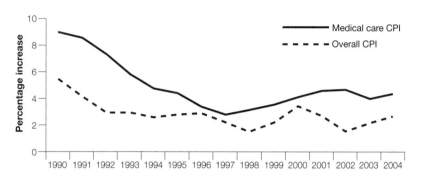

Source: Data from U.S. Department of Labor, Bureau of Labor Statistics.

emphasis on bargaining power introduced new incentives to compete on a full-service basis, which once again encouraged redundant facilities.[37] For example, when Massachusetts General Hospital and Brigham and Women's Hospital (BWH) in Boston became part of the Partners Health-Care System, Mass General chose to expand its obstetrics services rather than direct patients to sister hospital BWH, which had a nationally renowned obstetrics unit treating more than 10,000 patients a year. Provider consolidation, then, does not rationalize service lines but can lead to more duplicative services in a region.

Nor has provider consolidation improved quality. The high rates of errors and inappropriate care suggest that the opposite has occurred, though not intentionally. Instead, the desire to capture volume and patient flow within a full-line provider group creates barriers to *exit* at the service level. Although provider groups do not deliberately maintain substandard services, they are prone to maintaining services that would not survive in genuine service-by-service competition in order to maintain full-service status and minimize out-of-network referrals. Given the lack of relevant information on quality and value and the custom of local referrals, it is easy to unintentionally maintain substandard services.

Yet the worst consequence of consolidated provider groups—that they all but eliminate competition at the medical condition level—was completely unforeseen. Once patients become part of one provider group, it is extremely unlikely that they will ever be served by another group, no matter what medical condition arises or whether the group is truly excellent at addressing it. While provider groups sound like the perfect opportunity for well-coordinated care over the care cycle, most groups have maintained the same old structure of care around discrete intervention and traditional specialties rather than medically integrated practice units.

Consolidation and cross ownership can also inhibit innovation—the only real solution to controlling health care costs in light of demographic trends. While the previous structure—with its many independent providers and cost-plus reimbursement—had its own flaws, there was usually at least one provider in each region in a disease or treatment area willing to experiment with new ideas or treatments. This plurality has been a unique American strength. Consolidation into a few large provider groups, however, has created stronger administrative control that can slow down the adoption of new drugs and devices, at least until patient demand becomes overwhelming. Given the need for reimbursement approvals and lacking rewards for better quality, provider groups have had little incentive to innovate, especially when a new approach raised costs in the short run.[38]

Another consequence of the zero-sum competition on discounting and the shift in industry structure has been the emergence of powerful national buying groups for hospital supplies. Two private buying groups, Novation and Premier, now act as middlemen for about half of U.S. nonprofit hospitals. In a cost-sensitive system, the idea was that buying groups could source the best products at the lowest prices by aggregating the purchasing power of many hospitals. But not surprisingly, the buying groups have become yet another form of gatekeeper that is more likely to slow down innovation than speed it up. Also, buying groups create incentives for hospitals to increase their purchases of given items to obtain better prices. Hospitals find themselves with a limited choice of products and costly excess inventory, rather than purchases tailored to their specific needs. Patient value suffers. Buying groups are discussed further in chapters 7 and 8.

Finally, the shift in health plan and provider strategies, combined with industry consolidation, has led to another counterintuitive result: greater advertising and other marketing by drug companies directly to patients. In the current system, advertising is one of the few ways that drug companies can inform patients about new drugs and overcome resistance in the system to their adoption. Because health plans care about patient satisfaction, they have been more prone to reimburse pharmaceutical treatments demanded by patients. Advertisements, though, should *not* be the patient's sole or primary information source about drugs. It would be far better to disseminate objective data on results and balanced studies of alternative treatments than to target patients with marketing campaigns. While critics point to the cost of advertising as a failure of the current system, limiting advertising is not a real solution. Doing so would address one symptom of flawed competition, but it would not get at the root causes. We return to how to align supplier marketing practices with patient value in chapter 7.

The Wrong Information

Information is fundamental to competition in any well-functioning market. It enables buyers to shop for the best value and allows sellers to compare themselves to rivals. Without relevant information, doctors cannot compare their results to best practice and to other providers. And without appropriate information, patient choice has little meaning.

In health care, though, the information most needed to support value-based competition has been largely absent or suppressed. Physicians generally lack information on results, or their efficiency in achieving results, that is essential for knowing if they are doing their job well or if others are doing their jobs well. Results information was less essential in an earlier era when much of medicine centered on providing comfort and kindness to patients. Today, comfort and kindness remain important, but knowledge, complexity, and specialization of care have grown exponentially. Yet most physicians lack any objective evidence of whether their results are average, above average, or below average. It is human nature for most people to believe that they are above average, which cannot be true.[39] Information that one's results are below average (or not as good as they could be) creates strong incentives to learn from those who are doing better and to improve. For example, in Wisconsin, a study of its hospitals found strong evidence that making performance information public stimulates quality improvement initiatives in areas where the performance was reported to be low.[40] Without results information, referrals for specialty care are based not on measured excellence but on a doctor's personal network.[41] Without objective information, the incentives to improve and learn from others are diminished. Results information, in contrast, allows doctors to work continually to improve their patients' results; this is what value-based competition is all about.

The same type of information on results is crucial for patients. Although most individuals would be quick to say that their health care is critical to them, they have better information available to them about airlines, restaurants, cars, and sellers on eBay than they do about their health care.[42] The information that is available—health plan overviews, subscriber-satisfaction surveys, and doctor and hospital reputation surveys—has modest value. Much more relevant is information about providers' actual experience levels, the treatments they use, the prices they charge, and, most important, the results they achieve.

Even the most basic information—how many patients with a particular diagnosis or medical condition a hospital or a physician has treated—is not yet available. While such information should not be controversial, current information about practitioners' medical experience is largely word of mouth, even among physicians, and usually unsupported by actual evidence. Fee or price information is also nearly nonexistent. Indeed, many providers cannot even quote a price when asked to do so because discount structures and billing practices are so byzantine.

Patient-satisfaction data has become more available, but such data tend to focus on the service experience, not medical results. While a hospital's hotel services and the friendliness of its personnel are important to the overall patient experience, the more critical information is about the speed and accuracy of diagnoses, and the medical outcomes from treatment and ongoing disease management. The little data on patient satisfaction with medical outcomes is not disease or physician specific.

The most widely known efforts to rank providers are not evidence based, and are too general to drive real competition. Medical results are primarily measured through reputation surveys of specialists in the field, not actual results. For example, *U.S. News and World Report* ranks hospitals in seventeen service areas, but to even be considered in twelve specialty areas, hospitals must offer broad service lines and have "extensive" equipment and facilities, as well as be affiliated with a medical school or be a member of the Council of Teaching Hospitals.[43] The rankings also exclude specialty hospitals and community hospitals by assumption rather than based on any evidence. This whole approach reinforces the bias that community hospitals offer lower value care in spite of evidence to the contrary. Studies show that in services that community hospitals perform frequently, they often achieve equal or better outcomes at lower costs than teaching hospitals.[44] Rankings such as this, as well as similar rankings by *Money* and the American Association of Retired Persons (AARP), fall far short of the types of information really needed to support comparisons of value, informed referrals, or practice improvement.

Data on results—the outcome achieved by providers in diagnosing, treating, or managing a particular medical condition—are rarely available to patients or referring doctors. In only a few isolated disease areas—notably cardiac surgery, organ transplants, cystic fibrosis, and kidney dialysis—is broad-based results information available even to physicians.[45] There is essentially no information at all on diagnostic effectiveness or its cost, except in a few forms of cancer screening.

The quality and cost of health care have suffered mightily from the lack of meaningful results information. Lack of the right kind of information and feedback has driven up costs, masked poor results, and allowed poor-quality and high-cost providers to remain in business. A study in Pennsylvania, for example, found that death rates among comparably ill stroke patients ranged from zero to 36.8 percent, depending on the hospital.[46]

Substandard providers continue to receive a steady flow of referrals and patients from their health plan networks. Incredible as it sounds, the lack of meaningful information leads to situations in which patients are sent to providers with both lower quality and higher costs than other local providers, because neither the patient nor the referring physician is aware of the differences. The Pennsylvania Health Care Cost Council, for example, documented that hospitals in one Pennsylvania city had charges for repair or replacement of heart valves that ranged from about $45,000 to $95,000. The study reported an expected number of deaths for each hospital's patient group, adjusting for the case mix in terms of severity of illness. The least expensive hospital had 0.91 expected deaths and one patient who had died. The two most expensive hospitals had 1.3 and 1.22 expected deaths and four and five patients, respectively, who died. Providers often blame poor results or outcomes on a sicker mix of patients. Even after adjusting for this, the most expensive hospitals in the Pennsylvania study had the worst results.[47] Despite this, patients were still referred to the inferior providers because their referring doctors were unaware of the data or did not trust its accuracy and relevance.[48]

With little value-based competition at the right level, even the right kind of information does not guarantee good choices. New York's Cardiac Surgery Reporting System (CSRS) has released data on risk-adjusted death rates following coronary artery bypass graft (CABG) surgery, by hospital and by surgeon, since 1989.[49] Even though a number of peer-reviewed journal articles have documented the scientific validity of this data, referral biases continue to send uninformed patients to hospitals that have consistently mediocre results.

With no information about results and little or no real competition at the disease or treatment level, malpractice suits have filled the vacuum of the lack of a market- and value-based discipline mechanism. Patients constrained in choosing providers, and in no position to make informed choices ahead of time, turn to suits as their only recourse if things go wrong. Unlike normal competitive markets in which poor quality producers lose market share and lawsuits are far less common, the *primary* discipline mechanism in the current health care system is legal recourse that drives up costs while making little impact on the quality problem. There will always be cases in which litigation is justified, but this should not be the first or only market discipline in the system.

Despite its crucial importance, collecting and disseminating the right kind of information has been actively resisted by providers, hampering evidence-based referrals and informed choices. Although the need for better information was explicitly recognized and widely discussed starting over a decade ago, efforts to create such data are still in the early stages.

Providers continue to resist results measurement, even when appropriately risk adjusted to reflect the complexity or severity of the patients' initial circumstances. The collection of outcome information is opposed by some for unfortunate reasons, such as the fear of comparison and accountability. Others fear that flawed risk adjustments will make information misleading. Still others fear that results information will invite lawsuits by revealing mistakes or below-average performance. While fears about litigation are understandable, we believe that widespread collection and dissemination of results information will actually reduce litigation because patients will choose appropriate, experienced physicians and will understand the real risks in advance. Moreover, the reliance on lawsuits will decline with the increase of evidence-based choice by referring physicians and patients because patients will not feel misled.

The few isolated efforts to collect the right kind of information have been promising, as we will discuss extensively in chapter 4. In addition to the Pennsylvania and New York efforts mentioned earlier, Cleveland Health Quality Choice (CHQC) created a large annual database showing multiple performance measures for participating hospitals.[50] The Pennsylvania, New York, and Cleveland initiatives have been small-scale, but they demonstrate both the critical value of having the right information and the feasibility of developing it. They also show the kinds of improvement that can result if results information is put to good use.

When the data from New York's CSRS study were made widely available, for example, cardiac surgery groups began to pursue process and personnel improvements. After four years of publishing this data, New York achieved the lowest risk-adjusted mortality following bypass surgery of any state in the country. Since then, New York has registered not only the lowest U.S. mortality rate but also among the greatest rates of improvement (see figure 2-6), and improvements across the state have continued (see figure 2-7). In Cleveland, death rates at the thirty participating hospitals dropped 11 percent in the first four years of published data.[51] Some system participants continue to try to discredit these attempts to collect relevant information. The Cleveland case, among others, reveals the challenges of mounting and sustaining such efforts in the current system, a subject we will discuss extensively in chapter 4. How to overcome these challenges is a major theme in the second half of the book.

There is a growing recognition of the importance of information, which is a welcome development. A recent spate of quality initiatives involve the gathering of clinical information. Employer initiatives include (among

FIGURE 2-6

Mortality rate and improvement in coronary artery bypass graft (CABG) surgery: New York State versus other states, 1987–1992

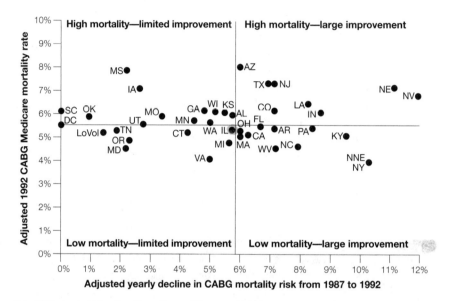

Note: NNE refers to Maine, New Hampshire, and Vermont, which share a provider profiling program. LoVol refers to a composite of ten states performing 500 or fewer bypass surgeries per year (Alaska, Wyoming, Delaware, Idaho, New Mexico, Hawaii, Rhode Island, Montana, and North and South Dakota).

Source: Reprinted from *Journal of the American College of Cardiology* 32(4), E. D. Peterson et al., "The Effects of New York's Bypass Surgery Provider Profiling on Access to Care and Patient Outcomes in the Elderly," 993–999. © 1998 American College of Cardiology Foundation.

others) the Leapfrog Group, the Pacific Business Group on Health, and the Wisconsin Collaborative for Healthcare Quality. The National Committee for Quality Assurance, the National Quality Forum, and the Institute for Healthcare Improvement have done important work. Rankings now exist for nursing services and nursing homes. Finally, Medicare has begun an experiment to introduce quality measurement into Medicare reimbursement. These early efforts focus mainly on process metrics at the hospital level, as well as selected best practices in patient care, such as administration of antibiotics. They are surely a move in the right direction and are slowly beginning to broaden to measures of condition-specific medical results. However, as we will discuss in later chapters, these efforts still stop far short of the information necessary to support value-based competition at the medical condition level.

FIGURE 2-7

Improving coronary artery bypass graft outcomes in New York State

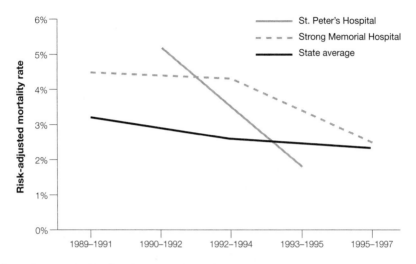

Source: Data from New York State Department of Health (1992, 1993, 1995, 1997, 2000).

Given the information vacuum, a number of companies have sprung up to help patients gather medical information and make decisions on the level of specific medical conditions and treatment choices. United Resource Networks specializes in organ transplants, drawing on the universal, rigorous, and government-mandated data reported by all transplant centers.

Another example, Preferred Global Health, serves members in Europe and the Middle East and helps its subscribers choose among world-class providers and treatments for the fifteen critical diseases it covers.[52] Other companies that have emerged in the United States include Best Doctors, Pinnacle Care International, and Consumer's Medical Resource. While their approaches and scope of services differ, each offers a patient advocate to help assemble relevant and reliable information when someone is sick or injured, and some companies offer help in locating a doctor with appropriate experience and expertise. They lack quantitative, comparative outcome data, however, and must rely mostly on expert panels, surveys, and reputation. In the United Kingdom, Dr Foster Limited is the leading independent provider of information for the National Health Service (NHS).[53] Dr Foster benefits from universal data on all hospital-based care from all NHS hospitals, which is risk adjusted by the company. The United Kingdom, then, is well ahead of U.S. practice.

These organizations, and others like them, make it clear that meaning-ful information, even if imperfect, already exists or can be assembled to support value-based competition in health care. The fact that such ser-vices are not widely known is symptomatic of the absence of value-based competition. The nation can no longer afford to wait for perfect informa-tion to be developed. Nothing will drive improvements in information faster than making existing information widely available.[54] A concerted strategy to develop and disseminate comparative information on results is an urgent priority and a subject we will discuss extensively in later chapters.

The Wrong Patient Attitudes and Motivations

Given the importance of good health and the stakes in obtaining ex-cellent medical care, patients should make every effort to become well informed, to consider their alternatives carefully, and to take personal responsibility for their health and their health care choices. This does not mean that patients should attempt to manage their own health care, or that they will no longer need to rely on their physician and other experts. Consumer-driven health care is an oversimplification. The critical insight is that informed and involved patients, working with their physicians, will help improve outcomes and reduce costs in a competitive system that responds to evidence and rewards excellence.

Recent studies demonstrate that patients who share in decision making often choose more conservative, less expensive treatments and less surgery.[55] More involved patients also experience better outcomes and lower costs,[56] due to better compliance with instructions for medications and self-care,[57] by obtaining care consistent with their values and preferences (including less end-of-life care),[58] and through selecting only care consistent with medical evidence.[59]

Yet in the current system most patients and their families do not behave this way. Instead, they defer important decisions to others. Many patients and their families fail to use the information that is available and are too embarrassed or too afraid to ask doctors about their experience, results, or prices. To be sure, the message often communicated to patients is that asking questions about the logic of a medical recommendation is rude or challenging. Likewise, asking about costs, or inquiring about qual-ifications, is often seen as out of bounds.[60] There are physicians who will drop a patient who seeks care in a regional or national center.

The structure of the system reinforces these attitudes. Why bother to travel for care if you have the impression, or want to believe (but based on no information), that local care is as safe and as effective as anywhere else? Why bother gathering information when restrictions and approval requirements prevent choice anyway? Even if a patient or referring doctor identifies a more effective provider, utilizing that provider may involve greater administrative hassles in gaining approval, much higher out-of-pocket costs for going out of network, and the risk of no insurance coverage if a complication occurs. On top of these problems may be penalties in the form of lower reimbursement for the referring physician and the risk of an adversarial relationship with local specialists who may be important to follow-up care. When patients feel unable to take active responsibility, the threat of lawsuits becomes the only discipline in the system.

Health plans often make the argument that tight control of patient choices is necessary because patients have an endless demand for more care. But that belief confuses better health with more medical care. Most individuals do not want more surgery, more medical procedures, more and longer hospitalizations, or more return visits to address complications. They want *effective* medical care from skilled providers. Uninformed patients do assume that more care leads to better health, as research has revealed.[61] But the same research also suggests that when information is provided and the patient has discussions with his or her physician, the patient's preference for better health, not more treatment, comes to the fore.[62]

There are some situations, such as back pain, where patients are desperate to "do something" even if it is expensive and unproven. In most cases, however, a lack of price sensitivity is simply a logical response to a lack of comparative information on price and quality coupled with existing incentives. Worse still, without relevant outcome information, patients or referring doctors may assume that more expensive providers are better, without realizing that these providers may be higher cost because they provide unnecessary care and make more mistakes.

Health plans introduced copayments, deductibles, and, more recently, medical savings accounts or health savings accounts (HSAs) to give patients an incentive to consider the costs of office visits and treatments. However, because patients have highly restricted choices and little meaningful information on which to base them, copayments, deductibles, and HSAs in the current system mostly encourage patients to self-ration. As we discuss in later chapters, HSAs combined with the right information can encourage more patient involvement in decision making; but the benefit comes from engaging patients in information and choice, not from encouraging patients to skip care, especially cost-effective care.

The Wrong Incentives for Health Plans

Health plans should be rewarded for enabling members to learn about and obtain the best-value care, helping members prevent and manage diseases, simplifying administrative processes, and working effectively with providers to achieve these aims. Instead, health plans currently face several types of skewed incentives that work against value.

First, health plans benefit financially from enrolling healthy people and from raising premiums for sick people. If members turn out to be high cost, health plans can benefit by encouraging them to switch to other plans or by making the process of obtaining coverage for some services so complicated that members pay for it themselves. While health plans cannot legally dump patients, some plans make the process of dealing with claims difficult and time-consuming.

For patients who are not part of a group, these incentives can have dire consequences. Health plans have the incentive to "re-underwrite," or to significantly raise premiums, if a family member suffers an expensive disease or injury. These price hikes occur even if the family has paid premiums for years and filed few claims. After the enactment of a 1996 federal law that prevented insurers from canceling a policyholder for getting sick, the practice of re-underwriting escalated. Unlucky policyholders with expensive medical conditions have ended up paying much more for insurance, which has the same economic effect as cancellation. Re-underwriting is not only unfair, but also defeats the whole purpose of insurance. The unanticipated effect of the 1996 law is a classic example of why piecemeal regulatory solutions fail time and time again.

The incentive to enroll healthy members has also slowed the introduction of disease management programs. There has been evidence for over a decade that disease management is cost effective and improves health and quality of life.[63] But at least one study found that health plans were wary of gaining a reputation as excellent in supporting members with chronic diseases, so as not to attract more of them.[64] While disease management is a clear way to demonstrate improvement in members' health, success for health plans has not depended on improving health outcomes.

Second, many health plans currently have the wrong time horizon. The competition to sign up members on an annual basis is problematic. With no competition on results, the one-year commitment between the subscriber and the health plan motivates both payers and employers to engage in short-term thinking and focus on short-term costs, rather than to invest in services and therapies that have a much higher value when measured over the care cycle. For example, a drug that reduces the chance of subsequent hospitalization will not be encouraged, or may not even be covered, because its immediate cost is certain while the uncertain longer-term cost reduction might accrue to a different health plan.[65] A short-term commitment between health plan and subscriber also creates the incentive for health plans to drag their feet in implementing disease management programs for chronic diseases whose benefits in terms of value occur over the longer run. Annual sign-up also exacerbates incentives for health plans to cherry-pick currently healthy subscribers and raise premiums for individual or small-group subscribers who have had the misfortune to become sick or injured during the year.

Because health plans do not have to compete on results in terms of subscriber health results, they can also benefit from slowing down innovations that do not show immediate, short-term cost savings. They limit referrals, disallow coverage of unproven approaches, and push doctors not to use expensive diagnostics and treatments. Indeed, health plans (and others) have widely assumed that new drugs, new technologies, and new techniques have been driving cost increases. In fact, innovations in health care, including how care is organized and delivered, are the only way, over the long term, to achieve better care for more people at lower cost.

Third, health plans have the incentive in the current system to complicate billing and reimbursement rules. Plans can shift costs by issuing incomprehensible or inaccurate invoices, by delaying or disputing payment, or by making the approval process cumbersome for out-of-network care. Because the insured family or individual remains legally responsible for health care bills, health plans (and even providers) gain time and money by disputing coverage or the payment amount and overwhelming patients or their families with bureaucracy. HMOs attempted to simplify billing with capitated payment plans (a single annual payment to providers to address all of a patient's health needs), but this introduced a powerful set of skewed incentives for providers to undertreat, which again undermines health care value for patients.

As we will discuss further, the billing practices of most hospital and physician groups have become so complicated that their own billing offices often cannot even explain them. There are a myriad of bills issued, including a separate one for each doctor involved. If the bill for buying a car were like today's health care bills, the customer would get a separate invoice for every part in the vehicle. This obscures overall value, as we will discuss. However, it also means that errors such as double billing, erroneous charges, and billing patients instead of the payer are common. Yet they are difficult to discover—especially by inexperienced patients—because of convoluted practices involving multiple bills and poorly labeled charges.

Health plans have extensive experience with medical bills and are in a good position to find errors. Health plans could also work with providers to correct and simplify their bills. Today, however, health plans have little incentive to do so. In fact, they can benefit by not correcting errors that shift bills to patients or by simply allowing providers to bill the patient for the difference between charges and the health plan's negotiated charge.

This leaves the individual patient or the family, who often have the burden of dealing with illness or death, to decipher the bills, figure out whether there are errors or creative interpretations of billing agreements, and deal with the providers' billing departments.[66] Then the patient may have to petition the heath plan to pay the corrected bill. Many patients simply assume that the provider's bills and the health plan's accounting of them are correct, so that payment is shifted to the patient.[67] If the patient cannot pay, the provider bears the burden of unpaid bills. Either way, the health plan has little incentive to insist on simpler, more accurate bills. None of this contributes to value-based competition, but only shifts costs from one party to another, drives up costs in the form of administrative overhead, and wastes patients' time and effort.

Providers too can be overwhelmed by bureaucracy. The process of answering health plan questions and preparing all of the forms and obtaining signatures required for reimbursement is so complicated and time-consuming that providers sometimes give up pursuing reimbursement entirely and record the service as uncompensated. The net effect is more cost shifting.

Fourth, without the discipline of value-based competition on results, health plans have incentives to reduce the time physicians spend with patients, restrict coverage for expensive services, encourage providers to push patients out of the hospital more quickly, and restrict most out-of-network care. The system of network discounts and approvals, decoupled from true costs or value, means that patients are not directed to the most effective provider.

Although some of these practices are now being changed in response to patient pressure, many health plans in the 1990s had elaborate approval processes designed to ensure that most patients needing specialists were directed within the network and to oversee the medical decisions made by the network's physicians. Rules required formal referrals from primary care physicians to in-network specialists, and from in-network specialists to out-of-network specialists. Administrative approval is still often required for the clinical care proposed by specialists, especially when providers are out of network. The approval process is slow, often preventing the patient from being diagnosed and treated in the same visit, thereby creating significant cost, inconvenience, and sometimes risk by delaying treatment. Even when health plans no longer require approvals for each step of clinical care, high copayments on nondiscounted prices have frequently taken their place. Such impediments to out-of-network care limit competition, while the lack of results information obscures their effect on value.

Some approval processes set up a potentially adversarial relationship between patients and their in-network doctors. Instead of accepting a physician's judgment that out-of-network care is appropriate, some plans require referring doctors to state that they are *incapable* of providing the needed care. These rules effectively push in-network specialists to provide care, even if they believe their patients would be better served by going outside the network. Furthermore, a patient seeking out-of-network care faces the risk that even asking for a referral would offend the in-network doctor, since it effectively means asking for a declaration of incompetence. Even when formal approval is not required, the risk of offending the local doctor creates a disincentive for patients to go outside of the usual referral patterns.

Of course, patients can always seek care outside the network without approval and pay the bill themselves. However, in addition to defeating the purpose of health coverage, in this case the patient is charged significantly higher prices.[68] Health plans routinely negotiate 50 percent discounts from list prices, but out-of-network patients without health plan approval are charged the list price.[69] So even when health plans claim to cover 70 percent of a reasonable charge for out-of-network care, they define "reasonable" according to what a large payer could negotiate. In fact, then, the "insured" patient is required to pay 65 percent of the bill.[70] In addition, some plans do not cover the costs of treating complications that arise during out-of-network care, adding to the patient's financial risk. Thus, in the current system, insured patients who need out-of-network care for complex or unusual problems face an unpalatable choice: they can undermine their relationship with their in-network doctor (who often has little results information but believes that in-network care is above average), or they can pay very large medical bills on top of their insurance premiums.

While some health plans have modified their rules and processes, such practices persist in many plans even today. Health plan preapproval for out-of-network coverage remains cumbersome. For example, the patient is required to produce data proving superior quality care by the out-of-network providers relative to the in-network providers. This comparison is made practically impossible because the health plan does not provide data on quality of the in-network provider. So while coverage exists on paper, the reality of payment denial persists. All this serves to further stifle competition where it matters most: in the diagnosis, treatment, and management of specific medical conditions. Moreover, the approvals, controls, and complex battles over who pays have led to an explosion of administrative costs. These costs undermine value too.

Finally, the current system has resulted in pervasive price discrimination, in which different patients pay widely different charges for the same treatment, with no economic justification in terms of cost. Patients covered by the public sector are subsidized by private-sector patients. Within the private sector, patients enrolled in large health plans are perversely subsidized by members of small groups, the uninsured, and out-of-network patients, who pay higher or even list prices. Worse yet, artificially high list prices make more patients unable to pay, driving up uncompensated care expenses, which leads to even higher list prices and pressure for even bigger discounts for large groups. The administrative complexity of dealing with multiple prices adds cost with no value benefit.

The dysfunctional competition that has been created by price discrimination far outweighs any short-term advantages that individual system participants gain from it, even for those participants who currently enjoy the biggest discounts. The lesson is simple: skewed incentives motivate activities that push costs higher. All these incentives and distortions reinforce zero-sum competition and work against value creation.

The Wrong Incentives for Providers

Providers should be rewarded for competing regionally and nationally, or even internationally, to deliver the best value in care for particular medical conditions. Instead, providers' incentives, just like the health plans' incentives, reinforce zero-sum competition. Ironically, however, while health plan incentives reinforce overly broad competition that neglects health outcomes, physician incentives tend to reinforce overly narrow, fragmented care. Physicians are motivated to provide discrete services, rather than compete on value over the full cycle of care.

Fee-for-service medicine was widely believed to create incentives that were a leading culprit in the cost problems in health care during the 1980s. Fee for service was a system that rewarded providers for doing more, regardless of whether it improved outcomes. More procedures, more visits, and more tests meant higher incomes for physicians and hospitals. To curb this overuse, managed care introduced a new set of incentives. But in practice, those too have turned out to be highly problematic.

Some health plans tried capitation, assuming that the fixed fee per covered patient per year would reduce the incentive for doctors and hospitals to order too many tests, perform too many procedures, or make unwarranted referrals to specialists. But in fact, capitation skewed the incentives too far in the opposite direction in the absence of having to compete on results. Because hospitals and doctors received a fixed payment, doctors were pressured to spend less time with patients, do fewer tests, make fewer referrals, and shorten hospital stays. New treatment approaches were avoided if there was uncertainty over the short-term benefits, especially because providers could not count on retaining the contract for a particular patient for multiple years.[71] The bias shifted from "If it might work, try it" to "If we're not sure, don't do it." While some might say this is at least consistent with "first do no harm," the more troubling effect is revealed in the studies, described in chapter 1, that show that Americans now get 55 percent of the care suggested by established medical evidence.[72]

Even where global capitation was not imposed, reimbursement to physicians and hospitals was drastically cut and fees to a doctor were sometimes further reduced when a patient was referred to a specialist or came back for more care. This had an effect similar to that of capitation: intense pressure to see more patients, spend less time per patient, provide less service, order fewer tests, and cut costs even if quality might suffer. When Medicare or health plans pay a set amount per admission without measuring results, hospitals may try to discharge patients as quickly as possible even if there are readmissions. Data indicate a trend since 1995 of more admissions and shorter stays, which is worrisome if the same patients are being readmitted (see figure 2-8).[73]

Many physicians have resisted the pressure to undertreat their patients. But while professional ethics in medicine are strong, the current system essentially asks a lot by expecting doctors to work against their

FIGURE 2-8

Inpatient trends: Total days in the hospital and number of admissions, 1980–2002

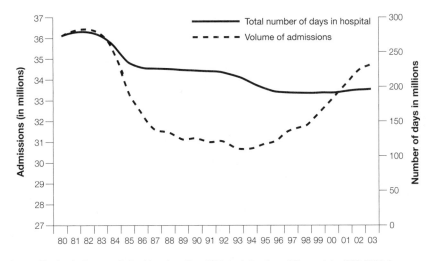

Source: The Lewin Group analysis of American Hospital Association Annual Survey data, 1980–2003, for community hospitals, and the U.S. Census Bureau. In The Lewin Group and the AHA, *TrendWatch Chartbook 2005:* "Trends Affecting Hospitals and Health Systems." Used with permission.

own economic interests to deliver value to patients, especially when information on results that would justify care delivery choices is so limited. This conflict between good medicine and self-interest demoralizes physicians and slows the adoption of best practices.

Ironically, providers' incentives to undertreat due to health plan reimbursement rules and structures coexist with incentives to overtreat, compounding the problems for patient value. Incentives to overtreat have four sources. First and most obviously, physicians and hospitals are paid to treat, not for keeping patients healthy. Second, when reimbursement is squeezed, the incentive becomes stronger to earn more by treating more. Third, the phenomenon known as *supply-driven demand* is a significant problem—providers have a tendency to fill up their capacity.[74] Patients are treated surgically (versus less invasively) when their geographic location has more surgeons. End-of-life care is more specialist intensive when there are more specialists in a region. Hospitals throughout the country fill their beds, and doctors naturally fill their work schedules with care for patients.[75] While this effect may be inadvertent, it is consistent with a system in which payment is for treatment and results are not measured.

Fourth, and more subtle, is that unless doctors know for sure that more care will not improve results for a patient, they may feel obligated to provide it.[76] Pressure for overtreatment stems in part from uninformed patients who pressure doctors to do *something*—such as prescribing antibiotics for a viral infection or operating on a painful back. And all of these pressures are compounded by the threat of malpractice suits, which creates incentives for physicians to overtest, overtreat, and overrefer their patients to reduce their risk.

Unfortunately, the incentives to overtreat do not cancel out the incentives to undertreat, because they affect different aspects and types of care. The net result of the simultaneous incentives to overtreat and undertreat is poor quality and poor value, as we discussed in chapter 1. RAND studies of the medical quality literature from 1993 to 1998 include a ten-page bibliography of peer-reviewed medical articles documenting inappropriate or equivocal treatments.[77] Unnecessary procedures remain extremely common, but quality problems are now compounded by incentives to undertreat. The result is less effective clinical practice, high costs, and mountains of paperwork that drain doctors' time. Rather than trying to patch one set of skewed incentives with more skewed incentives, reform needs to create value-based competition on results.

The lack of competition on results also blunts providers' incentives for improvement. Learning is slowed because providers with a steady stream of in-network referrals have little incentive other than professional ethics to pursue improvements in treatments, and insufficient data to measure how well they are doing. Even the most dedicated medical professionals work under intense time pressures. Without facing competition on results, they are not compelled to devote precious time to looking into possible practice improvements. Ironically, while technology has made knowledge diffusion faster and easier than ever before, the social and economic structures of the health care sector work against the rapid dissemination of learning. The threat of malpractice suits can also deter providers from trying to acknowledge and learn from bad outcomes.

Provider payment approaches can work against improving quality, reducing costs, or innovating. For example, Intermountain Health Care embarked on a project in 1995 to lower the rates of community-acquired pneumonia in Sanpete County, Utah. Treatment process guidelines developed as part of the project focused on the initial triage criteria for hospitalization, the choice of initial antibiotics, the work flow to get antibiotics started quickly, and a conversion protocol to shift inpatients to medications that could be delivered in an outpatient setting. The implementation of the guidelines resulted in a reduction in the rate of complications and a lowering of the patient mortality rate.[78]

While the project lowered the total costs for the episode of care, however, Intermountain's leadership quickly realized that the quality improvements were cutting into the IHC's bottom line. While the IHC's costs of care had dropped by 12.3 percent, the revenues had dropped by 17.5 percent because as the complication rate fell, the Medicare reimbursement rates shifted from complex DRGs with positive margins (e.g., DRG 475), to much simpler DRGs (e.g., DRG 89) with negative margins.[79] IHC continued the efforts but now works to negotiate gain sharing for process innovation with health plans to counter disincentives for improving value.

Providers are also often paid much less for less-invasive procedures that improve results. More generally, there is no reward for innovation when reimbursement for better approaches is lower. (See chapters 5 and 6.) For orthopedic surgery, for example, hospitals whose patients have less than the mean length of stay are paid less by Medicare. Without gain sharing, why would a hospital or doctor invest the effort required to innovate? The only way to stimulate innovation is for providers to compete on results, and be rewarded for delivering superior value.

The Wrong Response from Employers

Employers, who purchase and pay much of the bill for health care in the United States, were in a good position to perceive and work to counter many of those shortcomings. Unfortunately, in seeking to reduce costs, employers have largely reinforced zero-sum competition.[80] They treated health care as a commodity and focused on narrow cost reduction. They concentrated most of their attention on health plan offerings and structures, and allowed patients' care choices to be restricted. Many employers offer only one health plan to their employees, removing competition even at the health plan level. Employers failed to understand that health plans have focused on cost, not value, with consequences for employee productivity and morale. Encouraging competition among health plans is beneficial, but the only real solution lies in promoting value-based competition on results for both health plans and providers.

Most employers were content to go along with these shortcomings, not realizing that the prevalence of substandard care and rate of medical errors were so significant, or that true cost differences across providers were so substantial.

Employers inadvertently encouraged the battle over bargaining power between health plans and providers that, in turn, raised the cost of providing health benefits without any improvement in quality. Now, as an underdog in the bargaining power battle, employers again face a crisis of rising health care costs.

Recently, employers have resorted more and more to cost shifting, by asking employees to pay a bigger share of health premiums, limiting coverage in offered plans, or dropping health benefits entirely. Not only have employees been required to absorb higher costs, but costs of uninsured employees have been shifted onto society.

Health savings accounts (HSAs) have become the most recent vehicle for employer cost shifting. Some employers and health plan administrators believe that the only way to hold down costs is for consumers to have to pay for a significant portion of their care, thereby introducing cost discipline into their choices. However, without relevant value information, the ability to choose providers, and decision support from medical professionals, HSAs devolve to self-rationing. Contrary to the intent of HSAs, the only real choice becomes whether to get care. A real change, and real value, requires enabling relevant choices, not just shifting who pays.

Another round of consolidation and cost shifting will not provide a solution. Zero-sum competition must be replaced with value-based competition on results. As we will discuss in chapter 7, employers must transform their thinking and address health care differently if they are to address this problem. Otherwise, health care costs will erode U.S. companies' competitiveness in global markets.

3

How Reform Went Wrong

THE PROBLEMS with the U.S. health care system are not the result of inattention. Well-intended reformers have long recognized that the system has been on a collision course with demographic and economic reality. However, reform efforts have failed because the diagnosis of the problem was wrong. As we saw in chapter 2, the fundamental problem is that competition in health care operates at the wrong level and focuses on the wrong things. The absence of value-based competition on results has had consequences that have been widely misunderstood by both reformers and system participants. With the wrong diagnosis, the attempts to treat the system have addressed the wrong issues or offered piecemeal, ultimately ineffective solutions aimed at symptoms rather than causes.

In this chapter we briefly review the history of the U.S. health care system and the many attempts to improve it. We examine why the major reform movements have failed despite the concerted efforts of countless dedicated, intelligent, and knowledgeable groups and individuals. These reform movements have overlapped in time, in repeated waves of actions and reactions. Fortunately, a few of the newer initiatives show promise of moving the system in the right direction, but none of the proposed reforms will, by themselves, fix the system. We conclude the chapter by describing the strengths and limitations of these recent approaches, which will be explored in more detail later in the book.

Figure 3-1 offers a perspective on the reform efforts of the past, the present, and the future as we envision it.

The Rise of Group Health Insurance

The first group health plan in the United States became available in Dallas, Texas, in 1929. Baylor University Hospital sought to smooth its revenue stream by offering 1,500 schoolteachers a prepaid ($6/year) plan with up

FIGURE 3-1

The evolution of reform models

Past	Present	Future
Objective: Reduce costs, avoid costs	**Objective: Enable choice, reduce errors**	**Objective: Increase value**
Focus was on costs, bargaining power, and rationing.	Focus is on choice of health plan.	Focus should be on the nature of competition.
Focus was on legal recourse and regulation.	Focus is on provider and hospital practices.	
System characterized by: • cost shifting among patients, providers, physicians, payers, employers, and the government • limits on access to services • bargained-down prices for drugs and services • prices unrelated to the economics of delivering care	System characterized by: • competition among health plans • information on health plans • financial incentives for patients	System characterized by: • competition at the level of specific diseases and conditions • distinctive strategies by payers and providers • incentives to increase value rather than shift costs • information on providers' experiences, outcomes, and prices • consumer choice
System characterized by: • patients' rights • detailed rules for system participants • increased reliance on the legal system	System characterized by: • online order entry • Six Sigma practices • appropriate ICU staffing • volume thresholds for complex referrals • mandatory guidelines • "pay for performance" when standards of care are used	

Source: Porter, M., and E. Teisberg, "Redefining Competition in Health Care," *Harvard Business Review*, June 2004, 64–77. Copyright © 2004 Harvard Business School Publishing Corporation. All rights reserved.

to twenty-one days of hospital care per subscriber. Given the state of medical knowledge at the time, hospital care cost roughly the same for any condition, and twenty-one days would have been a very long hospital stay. Because the plan smoothed uncertain cash flows, this approach was picked up by other hospitals and hospital groups and became the model for Blue Cross, which offered its first plan in 1932 in Sacramento, California.[1] The Blue Cross plan included an array of hospitals that were paid on a cost-plus basis (cost of service plus a percentage to cover the cost of capital). Since the early plans paid only for hospital care, covered patients were treated in the hospital whenever possible.

During World War II, wage and price controls prevented companies from attracting workers by offering higher salaries. Instead, they competed by offering fringe benefits, and employer-paid hospital plans and health insurance spread. To encourage these group health plans, the IRS ruled in 1943 that employer-provided health benefits were income tax exempt for employees and tax deductible for employers, but this tax treatment did not extend to individually purchased employee health plans.[2] By 1950, over one-third of Americans with health insurance were covered by employer-provided plans. After the mid-1950s, most Americans came to expect health insurance coverage from their employers.

To provide a safety net for health care, the Hill-Burton Act, passed in 1946, mandated that any hospital that received federal funds had to offer free hospital care for uninsured people who could not afford to pay.[3] Medicare and Medicaid, introduced in 1965, created public health coverage for the elderly and poor.[4]

Traditionally, insurance companies paid physicians based on "usual, customary and reasonable charges." This made sense in the early days of insurance, when most patients did not have coverage and therefore paid for their own health care. At that time, doctors faced price pressures in setting their customary charges. As health insurance became widespread, however, insurers retained the "usual, customary and reasonable" structure even though insurance all but eliminated most price competition in physician services.

Patients with insurance were no longer attracted by lower prices; in fact, in the absence of other information, they came to view low prices as a signal of low quality. Since any fee could become "usual, customary and reasonable" as long as enough doctors charged it, physicians had the incentive to regularly increase their fees so that future reimbursement calculations would be based on higher charges. Not surprisingly, health care costs rose.

Historically, physician fee structures evolved in ways that favored technical procedures (such as surgery or endoscopy) over cognitive services (such as office visits and physical examinations). As new technology emerged, providers set high prices for novel procedures because they carried higher risk and were offered by relatively few, highly skilled physicians. In a competitive market, the diffusion of technology and an increasing supply of such services would drive down their prices over time. In health care, however, fees were not reduced because patients were not price sensitive, insurance payments were based on customary charges even if costs were declining, and treatment results were not measured or compared.

Limiting Payments to Physicians and to Hospitals

Major reforms in the 1980s attempted to curtail physician fee increases and limit hospital charges. Rather than reducing total system costs, however, the piecemeal fashion in which these reforms were implemented created skewed incentives for system participants.[5] For example, Medicare imposed a fee freeze in 1984 that lasted two years. However, physician groups were able to raise their overall rates by setting high charges for new physicians in the group. Private insurers imposed fixed fee structures, to which some doctors responded by billing the patient for the difference between the list charge and the fixed fee. This practice, known as *balance billing,* not only meant that health care expenditures continued to rise but also that the price sensitivity of health plans was reduced. Patients remained price insensitive because they expected insurance to pay for care and rarely knew in advance the charges for their care. During the 1990s, the practice of balance billing was banned in most states. However, the prohibition usually applied only to networks with negotiated fees, rather than to all insured patients. Some balance billing, and lawsuits disputing its legality, continues to this day.

As fixed physician fees became the norm, incentives were created for doctors to perform more procedures, spend less time with patients, and raise their revenues by having an equity interest in facilities or testing laboratories to which they referred their patients. To counter this last effect, legislation known as the Stark Law was passed in 1989 that prohibited "self-referral" to physician-owned facilities, regardless of whether they were more efficient or produced better results.[6]

Left untouched in the fixed fee for service model was the fact that physicians have the incentive to treat rather than to minimize the need for treatment, prevent disease, or, more generally, improve health care value.

Efforts to control hospital fees created more skewed incentives. Health plans traditionally paid hospitals on a cost-plus basis. The Medicare Inpatient Prospective Payment System, using Diagnosis Related Group (DRG) reimbursement, was implemented in 1983. It granted hospitals a fixed fee based on the admitted patient's diagnosis. The base DRG reimbursement was the same at all hospitals, but there were numerous adjustments that moved the DRG in the direction of cost plus. Other insurers tended to implement reimbursement rules that followed Medicare's lead.

DRG reimbursement was a step in the right direction in that it tied inpatient reimbursement to the medical condition being treated and the complexity of the patient's condition, and bundled discrete charges into a single payment for overall care, which is what is relevant for value. However, DRGs failed to fully capture important differences in the severity of a patient's condition, and this weakness continues today. For example, the DRG payment for a serious stroke is not much higher than the DRG payment for a simpler stroke that requires much less treatment.[7] This weakness created major cross subsidies. Also, the reimbursement was fixed and did not depend on results, thus creating incentives to reduce hospital stays and limit treatment costs even beyond the point where quality was diminished. In the ensuing decade, the average length of stay for an inpatient was reduced by half. DRGs also reimbursed for the episode of inpatient care irrespective of what happened later, including the need for readmission because of poor quality.

In addition, since outpatient treatment continued to be reimbursed by procedure or by service delivered, expensive procedures and drugs were administered whenever possible in the emergency room (considered outpatient) before a patient was admitted. Hospital admission rates dropped 20 percent in the decade following the implementation of DRGs. Outpatient reimbursement for hospital-based care was eventually changed from a cost-based system to a prospective payment system in 2000.

Some, or even much, of the reduction in hospitalization and lengths of stay probably improved health care value, and created a needed counterweight to the cost-plus system's incentives to overtreat and to treat in the hospital. Nevertheless, the DRG system introduced its own set of skewed incentives. With no measurement of results, fixed DRG fees created incentives to undertreat and discharge patients prematurely—reducing the quality of care and ultimately raising costs for remedial treatment. How much hospital stays should be reduced and the extent of care that should be performed in an outpatient setting are questions best answered by attention to results, not just attention to costs and reimbursement structures.

Outpatient reimbursement for physician services remained cost plus until 1992, and in general, the incentive for overtreatment of outpatients remained. In 1992, Medicare took further steps to limit physician fees. It implemented the Resource Based Relative Value Scale (RBRVS) for physician payment, which was designed to tie reimbursement more closely to costs rather than customary prices, and to lower reimbursement for procedures relative to cognitive services. Despite this change, however, reimbursement amounts remain skewed toward higher reimbursement for procedures, and physicians still made money by performing services, not delivering results. Indeed, the lower pay per procedure created incentives for physicians to do more procedures in order to maintain incomes.

Nowhere in this whole approach is the introduction of competition based on results to set prices and determine which providers will serve patients. Instead, there were top-down efforts to set and arbitrarily push down prices, which were set the same for all providers. Predictably, the prices and disease classifications imposed by the government could not realistically always correspond to costs or patient circumstances. Thus cross subsidies were introduced and provider incentives were further disconnected from value. Rather than a price for the cycle of care, separate prices were set for each type of physician, hospital, inpatient service, and outpatient service, none bearing any relationship to results. The response was predictable efforts to manipulate the location and form of services to maximize revenues, all of which worked at cross-purposes to patient value.

Managed Care

The issues of undertreatment and overtreatment led to the view that patients needed someone, preferably a physician, to oversee the appropriateness of their care. The original idea of "managed care" was simple and elegant—a primary care physician close to the patient would ensure that the care delivered was neither too much nor too little, involved appropriate specialists, and reflected the individual patient's needs and values. In its implementation, however, managed care took on a very different character.

By the late 1980s and early 1990s, the high cost of U.S. health care relative to the rest of the world had become widely apparent. Most people assumed that these higher costs reflected a quality of care that was uniformly good or even excellent. As we noted in chapter 2, the implicit assumption was that quality differences among providers were minor. This is the essence of a commodity—a product or service where the offerings of producers are indistinguishable. There was little data to suggest that medical outcomes or rates of errors varied significantly across providers.

Accordingly, the managed care movement devoted its attention primarily toward cutting costs. Reformers believed that competition among health plans would drive down costs as health plans, through primary care physicians, managed the patient's care and bargained with providers.[8] Health plans (health maintenance organizations [HMOs] and preferred provider organizations [PPOs]) were to negotiate aggressively with providers, monitor physicians to control waste, and limit the provision of unnecessary care. The original idea—that care would be managed *for the patient* by a primary care physician intent on appropriate care—evolved over time to management *of physicians* by health plan administrators intent on reducing costs, limiting services, and increasing margins. This notion marked the beginning of the foray into micromanagement of providers and their processes that continues in 2006, albeit in new and revised forms.

For a while in the early 1990s, managed care was viewed as a success. Health plans aggressively accumulated bargaining power and exercised it to shift costs to providers in the form of extracting discounts. Many health plans moved to pay providers using capitation, or contracts that paid the providers a fixed amount per subscriber per period of time to provide all covered services. In this payment system, the provider keeps any of the payment that is not spent, which creates strong incentives to reduce costs. Many observers credit capitation with an even greater effect than the DRG system on reducing hospital admissions and length of stay.

HMOs and PPOs used their bargaining power in the early 1990s by contracting only with providers that would agree to lower rates, allowing them to hold down premium increases.[9] However, providers soon responded to the new clout of health plans by merging and broadening their scope of services to bolster their own bargaining power, as we noted in chapter 2. The direction of the cost shifting reversed, and health plan costs and premiums began to rise more rapidly. Managed care rapidly deteriorated into a zero-sum competition over cost shifting, with patients the ultimate losers as quality suffered.

Patients and doctors began to feel the squeeze of increasing bureaucracy, rushed schedules, less personalized care, and administrative control of decisions previously made by doctors. Health plans moved to mitigate this discontent by offering their subscribers the choice of primary care physician while simultaneously limiting referral networks for secondary and tertiary care. Rather than enabling and supporting competition for referrals based on results, however, health plans attempted to micromanage subscribers' care and who performed that care through approval processes, administrative constraints, and negotiated prices. Health plans also began offering financial incentives for physicians to spend less time with patients, order fewer tests, and make fewer or less expensive referrals. The net result was increasingly rationed and restricted services.

Given this system, hospitals and doctors focused not on improving value but amassing countervailing bargaining power to restore and raise prices. Predictably, the struggle between providers and health plans delivered few true improvements in quality or efficiency. Instead, it dramatically increased administrative costs. As the underlying costs in the system continued to rise, access to care declined as premiums rose and ever more Americans lacked health coverage.

The Medical Arms Race

In parallel with efforts to control costs through managed care, other reformers focused on investment costs and the overbuilding of capacity. The problem of overinvestment became known as the medical arms race.[10] Hospitals competed to enhance their market standing and reputation by acquiring the latest high-tech equipment and building the most up-to-date facilities.[11]

The arms race was predictable under a cost-plus reimbursement system. Until 1992, Medicare's rules dictated that the more a hospital invested in new technologies and facilities, the more it could receive in capital expenditure reimbursements. This system led to communities with multiple CAT scanners or helicopter ambulances even when there was obvious excess capacity.

As regulators became more aware of the strong incentives to overbuild capacity, many states turned to micromanagement. They established review boards to approve investments based on community needs. If a provider wanted to invest in new facilities or capital equipment, it had to obtain a Certificate of Need from the review board. This marked a whole new level of micromanagement, in which regulators attempted to second-guess the investment choices of providers.

In 1992, the Medicare capital reimbursement rules changed, limiting the rate at which major capital reimbursements could be amortized (or recovered in terms of reimbursement levels). However, the effectiveness of this change in slowing down investment was diluted by significant adjustments to the mandated amortization rates based on geographic location, overall case mix, numbers of residents in training, and percentages of uninsured patients. Cumulatively, these adjustments made the system similar to cost-plus reimbursement in its effect.

Ironically, the advent of managed care networks inadvertently fueled a new arms race. At the same time that health plans moved away from the cost-plus reimbursement of providers that had led to overbuilding, providers began to consolidate into large, broad line groups to counter health plans' negotiating power. More redundant services, equipment, and facilities were put in place to ensure that groups were state of the art. As a result of all this history, many observers came to the conclusion that advances in medical technology were the key problem driving up U.S. health care costs.[12]

More recently, efforts by states to prevent overinvestment in medical facilities have come to include restrictions on entry of specialty hospitals. Some states with Certificate of Need legislation have blocked specialty hospitals in the name of avoiding excess capacity, limiting the so-called cherry picking of profitable services from community hospitals, and reducing the fragmentation of patient volume across institutions.[13] While fragmentation of providers within a service line is a major problem, as we will discuss, limiting competition is not the solution. The unintended consequence of a policy of arbitrarily blocking specialty hospitals has been to protect local incumbents from competition that could drive improvements in the diagnosis and treatment of specific medical conditions. Also, given the lack of results information currently available, community review boards may be protecting the patient volume of local providers who are substandard.

All the efforts to contain the arms race have failed. With the dominant incentive being to treat in order to obtain payment (rather than to deliver value), attempting to control provider investments was futile. More and more providers invested in expensive facilities, and everyone got their share of the business. Costs went up and quality suffered. The only real solution to controlling investment is to create value-based competition on results. Only by measuring results and prices, and directing patients only to high-value providers, will the right level of investment needed to deliver value be ensured.

The Clinton Plan

As managed care was penetrating the system, attention also began to focus on the fact that over 15 percent of Americans under 65 were uninsured despite the nation's high overall health care spending.[14] Reformers continued to assume that health care was uniformly good and that reducing costs was the primary objective. In 1993, President Clinton introduced a 1,342-page bill to reform health care. The bill proposed creating a National Health Board to oversee the pricing of insurance premiums, specify the benefits that had to be covered, and enforce overall spending limitations at the state and national levels. It also required every American to obtain health insurance, and created a system of state-based health insurance cooperatives to oversee the availability of health plans and enforce the national insurance regulations. Increases in public and private insurance premiums were to be capped, and the rate of increase was to be ratcheted down each year until it was in line with the increase in the overall consumer price index.

Under the Clinton plan, the entire population would be organized into health insurance purchasing cooperatives (HIPCs). HIPCs would only negotiate with entities that combined a health plan and providers, so-called Accountable Health Partnerships (AHPs), which could provide a full array of health care services, demonstrate quality outcomes, and control costs.

Health plans and providers were convinced that the changes proposed in the Clinton plan were imminent. Many states had already started to create purchasing cooperatives. Employers were increasingly offering exclusive contracts to manage the health care of their employees that only integrated, full-service providers could bid on. This spurred providers to combine with health plans to form larger integrated plan-provider networks, and to broaden services and geographic coverage within their region.[15]

The Clinton health plan failed to become law and was widely criticized. It revealed, however, an increasing fervor for top-down control of providers and the overall amount of health care to be delivered by the system. The Clinton plan contained some attractive elements that we support in chapter 8. However, it made some unfortunate bets in terms of how to structure competition and was doomed by heavy government control of both public and private insurance that made most Americans understandably uncomfortable.

More remarkable to us, however, was the lack of focus of the Clinton plan on the actual structure of health care delivery. As we discussed in the introduction, health care policy, broadly speaking, addresses three sets of issues: insurance (who gets access and who pays), coverage (what services health plans and society should be responsible to pay for), and delivery (what rules, structures, and type of competition should govern the actual delivery of health care services).

The Clinton plan focused heavily on insurance. In addressing the delivery of care, the Clinton plan fundamentally misunderstood the drivers of patient value. It addressed cost, not value. It bet on consolidation and vertical integration between plans and providers that would only have exacerbated zero-sum competition, rather than fostering open competition among multiple providers based on results at the level of specific medical conditions. Instead of enabling competition in the delivery of patient-centered care to improve value, the plan sought governmental control to hold down spending while requiring all citizens to be covered. Without the powerful mechanism of competition to drive value higher, holding down spending, while enforcing wider access, implied increasing the rationing of care. Like many other reformers, the architects of the Clinton plan seemed to view rationing of health care as inevitable. They failed to consider the question of how to make the health system more productive. They bet on top-down control and government oversight, not the power of competition.

Much of the philosophy underlying the Clinton plan remains widely accepted in other countries, with their monolithic state-controlled systems in which providers are often state owned and managed. However, escalating health care spending is now an alarming concern in virtually all of these countries. Although the amount of spending abroad is not as high as in the United States, government-controlled systems do not appear to provide a solution to rising costs. Moreover, there is mounting evidence that government-run systems are not as good at delivering many aspects of quality as the U.S. system. In addition to the well-recognized problems of long waits for specialized care and other forms of rationing, countries such as Canada, Denmark, the Netherlands, Sweden, and New Zealand, among others, are recognizing that their health care systems are prone to medical error.[16] Rates of adverse medical events are estimated to be between 10.6 and 16.6 percent in Australia, between 10 and 11.7 percent in the United Kingdom, and about 9 percent in Denmark, versus in the range of 3.2 and 5.4 percent in the United States.[17] Deaths from preventable medical errors in Organization for Economic Cooperation and Development (OECD) nations are estimated to range from 400 to 700 per million of population,[18] representing the third leading cause of death, compared to a range of 160 to 360 deaths per million in the United States based on the Institute of Medicine estimates, or as many as 675 U.S. deaths per million using HealthGrades estimates.[19] Countries such as Japan and Singapore are launching programs to reduce rates of error, and soul searching about the health care system is going on in virtually all advanced economies. (We will discuss the structure and performance of health care systems outside the United States further in chapter 8.)

It is ironic that despite mounting evidence abroad of cost and serious quality problems in government-controlled systems, the idea of government control and a single payer system is gaining a new legitimacy in the United States. As desperation grows with the runaway costs of our system, and with no good alternatives evident, reformers throw up their hands and accept the need for rationing. The power of the right kind of competition to deliver huge improvements in value goes unrecognized.

Patients' Rights

Responding to patient and provider backlash against managed care, the next wave of reform attempted to create new regulations that limited unpopular HMO practices and gave patients more legal rights to sue health plans for injury or death resulting from decisions to withhold or limit care. Advocates hoped to temper administrative control by health plans with stronger rights for patients to have their medical decisions made by a doctor, see a medical specialist, have a pediatrician serve as the primary care doctor for children, ensure access to the closest emergency room, be entitled to a fair and independent appeals process if care was denied, and hold their health plan accountable for harm done. Less understood by reformers was that there were already thousands of pages of state "patient protection" statutes and rules for HMOs that had proved not to be effective.

As Congress got bogged down in hammering out differences between versions of the Patients' Bill of Rights law passed by the House and the Senate, a number of states passed their own patient protection laws. In the summer of 2004, however, the Supreme Court ruled that only Congress, not the states, could pass laws giving individual patients the right to sue health plans. Congress has yet to pass such a comprehensive patient rights law as of 2006, but the debate has had an impact on how HMOs are perceived and has revealed the dissatisfaction of Americans with the health care system. The threat of legislation has also led to the elimination of some of the most egregious examples of cost-driven rationing.

Among those well-intentioned patients' rights initiatives that were passed, there were once again unintended effects. For example, the protection of the right to privacy of a patient's health information was part of the Health Insurance Portability and Accountability Act of 1996 (HIPAA). The idea of protecting private, personal health information seems obvious and desirable. However, the realities of getting written consent from every patient to use information at the time of care have saddled health care providers with extra administrative costs and delays. From a patient's perspective, signing the HIPAA form is a prerequisite for care, so it is rarely read carefully or understood; thus, the new legislation does not have the intended effect.[20]

The rights of patients are important. However, it is clear from past experience that more patient rights legislation will not fix the U.S. health care system. More regulatory patches on a deeply flawed system do not alter dysfunctional competition. Each new layer of regulation adds more costs unrelated to actual health care value. Inevitably, new loopholes, omissions, and distortions in behavior are created that need to be addressed with yet more regulation.

Similarly, attempting to require participants in the system to behave contrary to their interests is futile. Making the health plan–patient relationship more adversarial only exacerbates the problem. More litigation only leads to escalating legal costs, wasteful defensive medicine, and more burdens on patients. More rules and bureaucratic procedures only stifle innovation and drive more talented people from medicine. Unless the nature of competition in the system is changed and aligned with value, the problems will continue or get worse. What patients need is better health care, not more recourse for care that is denied or poorly delivered.

Consumer-Driven Health Care

Even before the patients' rights debates heated up, concerns with high cost, restricted care, and the poor experiences of patients with health plans and the health care system gave rise to another stream of reform proposals centered on consumer choice. Over the past decade, advocates of so-called consumer-driven health care have raised the important issue of the need for consumer choice and information. The consumer-driven approach renames patients as "consumers" and stresses that consumers are capable of making their own medical decisions.[21] Harking back to the era when patients actually paid for health care directly, the consumer-driven health care movement also stresses that greater responsibility for consumers will reintroduce price sensitivity. The introduction of health savings accounts and other mechanisms that give consumers a stake in paying for their own care are prominent features of the consumer-driven health care movement. Many observers equate consumer-driven health care with the introduction of the "market" into the health care system.

We share some of the perspectives underlying the consumer-driven approach, but it by itself is too simple. Consumers alone cannot realistically drive a transformation of the system, though they can play a supporting role in it. A transformation in competition will be needed, along with shifting roles, incentives, and time horizons for each of the major actors in the system. Indeed, introducing value-based competition among providers and health plans will revolutionize the value delivered to patients even if consumer behavior is slow to shift. Changes in competition at the provider and health plan levels will do more to shift patient choices than increasing consumers' payment responsibilities in the system.

Consumer choice proposals have focused primarily on the choice of health plans as the locus of change, rather than the far more critical choices of providers and treatments.[22] The role of the consumer is taken too far, as if consumers can replace doctors and make medical decisions entirely on their own.

Consumer choice proposals highlight the role of employers in enabling information and choice for employees, but again through the mechanism of health plans. Without confronting the structural problems of closed networks that prevent meaningful choice of providers, however, consumer choice will not affect the decisions that most influence health care value.

Many critics of consumer-driven reform proposals point to the consumer's need for advice and decision support, but the advocates of consumer-driven care clearly recognize this. Relevant, appropriate information is what enables consumer choice. However, less recognized is the need for providers to compete on results and efficiency over the cycle of care at the medical condition level. Without results competition at the condition level, consumer choice is far less meaningful. Unless providers also have to compete over the full cycle of care, consumers will be faced with the need to coordinate their own care over the care cycle, a daunting challenge.

Proponents of consumer-driven health care frame the problem as health plans not paying for value, rather than the absence of value-based competition at the level of specific conditions in the first place. The consumer-driven movement has led to some positive benefits, such as attention to the critical need for more information, but it cannot achieve its potential as long as the dysfunctional competition persists.

Part of the reason for the dysfunction, as we discussed in chapter 2, is failure to recognize that value is created over the full cycle of care for a disease—from prevention and monitoring through diagnosis, preparation, intervention, recovery, and long-term management. Value-based competition on results requires medically integrated care over the full care cycle, not focused factories[23] delivering specific procedures or piecemeal care.

Introducing the market mechanism into health care, then, goes way beyond empowering consumers. It requires transforming the nature of competition throughout the system. The combination of the failed Clinton plan, which was seen as including a market element, together with the limited impact of consumer-driven health care proposals, has led many thoughtful participants in the national debate about health care to conclude that competition simply cannot work in the health sector. An ever-louder chorus of voices, for example, is lamenting that consumer-driven health care will not work.[24] But the important role of provider competition, together with the new roles for health plans, has not been recognized. Consumer choice is a key element of successful health care reform, as we will discuss, but only together with the fundamental changes in competition that we advocate in chapters 4 through 8.

Quality and Pay for Performance

Since 1999, with the publication of the Institute of Medicine's report *To Err Is Human: Building a Safer Health Care System,* reformers' attention has shifted to quality and initiatives to reward quality known as *pay for performance.*[25] The accumulating evidence of quality problems and the magnitude of medical errors finally reached the point of challenging the deeply held assumption that U.S. health care is uniformly outstanding. As we discussed in chapter 1, compelling data published by researchers at respected organizations, such as Dartmouth Medical School and the RAND Corporation, reveal that not only are errors common but most Americans receive less care than medical evidence suggests is appropriate. Many receive unnecessary or ineffective care. There are also significant variations in care delivery processes and medical outcomes in different regions of the country.[26] A seminal shift in mind-set has occurred, and cost reduction is today no longer the dominant focus of reform. Safety, error reduction, and (to a lesser extent) quality of care have finally been brought into the mainstream of health care reform.

The issues of safety and quality are valid and essential. It simply is not acceptable to have preventable medical errors as a leading cause of death. Information on quality and outcomes is essential to any effort toward value improvement, as we have discussed. Moreover, and this is less understood, poor quality almost always raises costs through inefficiency, prolonging the need for care, and requiring remedial treatments or surgeries. The Juran Institute and other researchers estimate that poor process quality accounts for 30 percent of U.S. health care costs.[27] While the researchers acknowledge that their estimate is crude, there is little doubt that poor quality is costly.

Many efforts, both public and private, are now underway to address poor quality. Some solutions seem relatively straightforward, such as reducing the working hours of residents and interns based on the clear evidence that sleep-deprived physicians make significantly more errors.[28] Other initiatives to improve quality are far more complex, including the efforts of not-for-profit organizations such as the National Quality Forum (which is developing consensus-based measures of care delivery standards and outcomes with which quality can be reported and assessed), the Institute for Healthcare Improvement (which supports and enables provider initiatives to improve quality), and the National Committee for Quality Assurance (which develops and publicly reports information comparing health plans).[29]

Employers have also finally recognized the importance of quality, especially the dimension of safety. Employer quality initiatives, such as the Pacific Business Group on Health and the Leapfrog Group, are expanding. The Leapfrog Group, a consortium of employers with a membership of more than 160 public and private companies and endorsement by the Business Roundtable, is probably the most prominent effort. Leapfrog is attempting to improve safety, its primary focus, by requiring hospitals to meet a number of conditions: initially, entering treatment orders into a computerized system, maintaining appropriate staffing in intensive care units, and meeting volume thresholds for referrals in some treatment areas.[30] Over time, Leapfrog aims to broaden its approach.

Leapfrog members have used their combined influence to pressure and encourage hospitals to improve safety and quality. Leapfrog also advocates and encourages financial rewards by health plans to providers that improve the quality, safety, and affordability of health care. Leapfrog has developed seventy-seven programs in the United States that have some version of incentive pay for better performance, including seventeen programs that base incentives on meeting Leapfrog's measures. Such pay-for-performance initiatives are now widely endorsed as a way to reduce errors.[31] There are many other pay-for-performance systems being designed, and we applaud their long-overdue focus on safety and quality.

However, these current efforts are just a start, and they carry some risks. Most current quality initiatives are not actually about quality (results), but processes. Most "pay for performance" is really pay for compliance. Programs have the important but still limited aim of getting providers to comply with accepted medical standards of practice. Providers are expected to conform to specific *processes*, but are not necessarily rewarded for better *results*.[32]

This approach has serious limitations. First, the incentives may not be large enough to shift behavior, and certainly not large enough to compensate for lower reimbursement if quality means that less treatment is needed. It is disconcerting to note that a recent study finds that hospitals participating in pay-for-performance programs may not even have better process compliance than nonparticipating hospitals, much less better results.[33]

Second, given the many variables and judgments required in medical care, it is possible for providers to have wide variation in outcomes even if process compliance is uniform. This has been the case, for example, in the treatment of cystic fibrosis.[34] Pay for compliance, then, will not guarantee excellent quality.

Third, and even more troubling, if extra pay is tied to process conformance rather than to outcomes and results, the wrong incentives are created. This is especially true if rewards to an overall institution are tied to conformance to a small number of hospital processes. For example, many pay-for-performance incentives, including the experimental program introduced by Medicare, involve compliance with specified processes in a few discrete areas of medical care (as we will describe in chapter 8). Other pay-for-performance initiatives address a few hospital processes on which consensus has been achieved and data are available. These are not the most important processes, however, but a lowest-common-denominator starting point. Yet the rewards accrue to the entire hospital, whether or not its other processes conform to good medical practice, much less whether it achieves excellent results. Mediocrity, errors, and out-of-date practices in the majority of the hospital's activities go unmeasured. Thus providers' attention and resources are naturally directed to the few processes being measured, rather than to a fundamental transformation in care delivery needed to drive major improvements in value.

Compliance to too many process standards also runs the risk of inhibiting innovation by the best providers. If all providers are held to currently acceptable practices, this can deter innovation to find better ones. This again points to the dangers of a system that rewards conformance rather than results.

Yet there is a fourth and even larger problem. Focusing on process compliance, instead of results, is problematic because there are simply too many dimensions of process to track and too much heterogeneity among patients. Focusing on just a few visible process steps creates a checklist that providers can address, but oversimplifies the problem. A good example is the administration of tPA (tissue plasminogen activator) to stroke patients. While tPA is very beneficial to some patients, it is usually ineffective in addressing clots in a large vessel, unnecessary for some patients whose obstruction will be addressed naturally, and dangerous to others in whom it may cause a brain hemorrhage. A universal guideline to administer tPA, then, can fall far short of delivering the best results or the best value for many patients.[35] Measuring results and costs, adjusted as well as possible for the mix of patients, is the only way to ensure that providers are delivering care of excellent value.

Fifth, not only can uniform process guidelines lead to inappropriate care for some patients, but the understanding of appropriate processes changes over time. Updating process measures and reflecting the latest learning is challenging. For example, current medical research has identified some patients for whom the accepted process guidelines on angiotensin-converting enzyme (ACE) inhibitors are not appropriate. Yet doctors in some hospitals are reluctant to stray from the guidelines. Technically, the guidelines allow for exceptions, but justifying deviations from the guidelines is difficult and doctors are loath to risk their compliance ratings. As a result, some patients are being treated with an out-of-date process in the name of obtaining higher "quality" rankings!

Sixth, process compliance also ignores the important dimension of how providers work with patients to improve their choices and avoid unnecessary care. Rewarding value, rather than process compliance, would enable physicians to benefit by helping patients to become better informed and choose the most appropriate care, even when that means less care.[36]

Finally, pay for performance, even in its name, remains stuck in the mind-set of increasing costs. In health care, better care often costs less. Better health is inherently less expensive than disease. Better care reduces costs through less invasive treatment, more expert care delivery, better management of chronic care, and improved risk prevention. Thus, higher pay will often not be necessary to reward better results. Excellent providers will often achieve higher margins through greater efficiency. With higher margins, attracting more patients is a far greater reward than a few percentage point increases in prices because excellent providers can expand the advantages they enjoy through increased learning and improved efficiency (see chapter 5). The pursuit of quality should not presume that better care must cost more. There are so many inefficiencies, errors, and unnecessary expenses in the current system that many gains could be made without driving up costs at all. "Rewards for results" is a more appropriate mind-set.

Overall, attempting to micromanage hospitals and doctors by specifying processes is a difficult task that will only become a morass. In the extreme, process specification by health plans and employers is just a new version of the most problematic aspect of managed care. Specified processes and process guidelines easily morph into administratively determined medical decisions, as they did in some HMOs. Administrators, rather than caregivers, specify what care may be and should be provided to patients. Americans have already found that approach to be unacceptable and ineffective.

The only truly effective way to address value in health care is to reward *ends*, or *results*, rather than means, such as process steps. The relevant results can be measured only at the level of medical conditions and over the cycle of care, where health care value is determined for patients, not for a hospital or other provider entity overall. Guidelines are important to coach doctors and spread knowledge about best practices, but rewards for excellence must be tied to results, not compliance. Providers should have to compete for patients based on value and not be rewarded for delivering just acceptable care.

A Single-Payer System

A recurring suggestion in health care reform discussions, both before and after the proposed Clinton reforms, has been to create a single-payer system. A bill proposed in Congress in 2003 terms this "Medicare for All."[37] This proposal is gaining momentum as an increasing number of reformers see no viable alternative, believing that all the alternatives to fix the system have been attempted and failed.[38]

A single-payer system would have some benefits, especially in the area of insurance coverage. Notably, it would end the practice of excluding high-risk subscribers from health plans because there would only be one insurer, obligated to cover everyone. In theory, a single payer could also simplify paperwork, because there would only be one health plan and thus one set of forms and procedures. A single payer could limit price discrimination, which gets in the way of competition on value, because there could be one set of payment schedules, rather than different prices for different patients with different sources of coverage. If the single payer required data to be collected and reported for all patients, information could improve. In theory, a single payer could also have a longer-term perspective on care, because there would be no subscriber churning among plans. All of these shifts would be desirable ones.

However, a single-payer system would create serious, and in our view, fatal, problems for health care value. It would eliminate independent health plans, and thereby eliminate competition among health plans to add value by serving subscribers in their quest for excellent care. Given today's skewed incentives and the past behavior of health plans as patient adversaries rather than advocates, the idea of potential benefits from competing health plans strains the imaginations of many observers. But as we discuss in chapter 6, competing health plans can play crucial roles in value-based competition that are inconceivable from a monolithic government entity.

A single-payer system would create a government monopoly with absolute bargaining power relative to other participants. With the inevitable and irresistible pressures to control its budget, the single payer would undoubtedly engage in major cost shifting to providers, suppliers, and patients. In time, rationing of services and deterrents to the adoption of innovative new approaches to care would seem inevitable, as we have seen in other countries.

Government efforts to oversee practice and to micromanage health care would be launched with the best of intentions. However, as we already know from the experience with managed health systems such as HMOs, top-down administrative control of medical decisions often compromises patient care, retards improvement and innovation, and limits patient rights. The United States needs a system that will drive quality up and costs down over time, rather than top-down limits on the amount and types of care.

While it is theoretically possible for a single payer to make consistently good decisions about services, treatments, processes, and reimbursement rates, this is unlikely, especially in what would be a very large system. And when questionable choices are made, the checks and balances of competing health plans would be absent. Providers and patients would have no recourse except the legal system and political pressure, both of which are slow, expensive, and hardly conducive to value creation and innovation.

It simply strains credulity to imagine that a large government entity would streamline administration, simplify prices, set prices according to true costs, help patients make choices based on excellence and value, establish value-based competition at the provider level, and make politically neutral and tough choices to deny patients and reimbursement to substandard providers. Medicine as currently structured is deeply flawed in all these areas, and a single-payer system would do little to correct the problems. More likely a single payer would be just a payer, not a true health plan.[39]

Even if one assumes that an efficient, nonbureaucratic single payer could be created, this step only scratches the surface of the real problems with health care. At best, it could offer only a partial solution. Eliminating health plans does not address the root causes of dysfunctional competition and lack of a value focus in the system. Unless competition is transformed so that providers must compete on results, a single-payer system will only make things worse by exacerbating the skewed incentives and zero-sum competition present in the current system. Even more consolidation of providers and limited choices would be inevitable.

The United States does need to move to mandatory health insurance for all, as we will discuss in chapter 8. The system must provide quality care for all, including primary care (not just catastrophic care), with subsidies for those who cannot afford to pay the full cost. But achieving this does not require a single payer. Issues of risk pooling and cross subsidies can be addressed in other ways, as we will discuss in chapters 6 through 8. Pricing reform, paperwork reduction, and information collection can be accomplished with much less government intervention. Health plans can become value-adding participants in the system, as the best plans are today, operating as true health plans and not just financial organizations.

The real solution is not to make health insurance a government monopoly or to make all physicians government employees, but to open up value-based competition on results at the right level.

Medical or Health Savings Accounts

The notion of private savings accounts to cover medical expenses, now known as health savings accounts (HSAs), has been part of the health reform discussion for decades. However, the notion has recently taken on greater prominence as part of the effort to rein in costs. HSAs introduce some important elements that can support the shift to value-based competition in health care delivery. However, by themselves, HSAs are far from the solution to the health care problem, because they do little to address the value of health care delivery. If they simply become a tool for shifting costs to patients and rationing care, the cure may be even worse than the disease.

The earliest form of HSA was the flexible spending account (FSA), introduced in 1979.[40] FSAs were potentially available to all employees (provided that their employer offered one), but not to the self-employed. FSAs created a vehicle to pay for unreimbursed medical expenses with tax-exempt funds. Employees specified at the beginning of the year how many pretax dollars they wanted to deduct from their income to place in an FSA. If they failed to spend the entire amount during the calendar year, however, the unspent balance was forfeited. Employees who switched employers also lost any unspent funds. Thus, while FSAs offered employees the opportunity to cover some medical expenses with pretax dollars, they ran the risk of wasting money and thus created strong incentives to use any remaining money—perhaps for an extra pair of glasses, discretionary dental or medical services, or sometimes more questionable services—at year-end or before switching jobs.

The notion of a medical savings account, or "medical IRAs" as they were then called, was proposed in 1984 as a way to reform Medicare.[41] After much discussion, the idea evolved into medical savings accounts (MSAs), which were proposed as an alternative to the Clinton plan. A pilot MSA plan was introduced in 1997.[42] However, MSAs applied only to the self-employed and employees of small businesses who had to simultaneously subscribe to a high-deductible health plan. Either the employer or the employee, but not both, could contribute pretax dollars to the account. Funds in the account could carry over from year to year, and employees could retain their accounts if they switched jobs. Funds could be withdrawn and used for nonmedical purposes, subject to income tax and a penalty fee if the individual was below 65. The number of MSAs was capped at 750,000 in the pilot plan, but in practice it only reached one-tenth of that number due to the many restrictions on the accounts.

In 2002, a new variation, health reimbursement arrangements (HRAs), was allowed by the Internal Revenue Service. These arrangements allowed employers (with no employee contributions) to create tax-exempt accounts for their employees for unreimbursed medical expenses. Funds would carry over from year to year (without interest). The employer determined whether employees could get access to the HRA after leaving the firm.

The current incarnation of the idea, health savings accounts, was signed into law in 2003. HSAs extend medical savings accounts to *all* individuals with high-deductible health plans. HSAs allow individuals to contribute up to $2,600 per individual ($5,150 for families) on a pretax basis to pay for unreimbursed medical costs and for insurance premiums during times of unemployment. The accounts carry over and are portable from one employer to another, and both the employer and the employee can contribute to them. As with MSAs, money can be withdrawn to pay for nonmedical costs and can be inherited, but subject to income tax and penalties.[43]

Coupled with relatively high-deductible health plans, HSAs introduce the consideration of price and value into a portion of medical purchase decisions by giving patients the responsibility to pay the first $1,000 to $3,000 of costs. This is in lieu of money many patients already pay for deductibles. However, HSAs create the possibility of moving to high-deductible plans without shifting costs to the employee.

Some health plans have marketed HSAs, together with high-deductible plans, to encourage better patient medical decisions. The idea is that since patients pay some of the costs, they will be more sensitive to cost and, hopefully, to value. Early evidence with HSAs drawn from case studies and experiences in other countries is promising. Individuals who control their own medical spending consider price as well as the quality of care, including preventive care.[44] Aetna, for example, has found that subscribers with HSAs spend more money on preventive care, seek more information about health care choices, use the emergency room less, use more generic medications, and experience significantly lower rates of increase in health care costs (1.5 percent versus double-digit rates) compared with a similar group of subscribers without health savings accounts.[45] The majority of Aetna subscribers who elected HSAs earned less than $30,000 in annual income and had money to roll over at the end of the year.[46]

It is possible that subscribers who choose HSAs do so because they are healthy. However, the differences in behavior of those with HSAs are still striking enough to suggest that individuals will consider value in making medical decisions if they feel responsible for the choice, not just the payment. The finding that people with HSAs seek more information is promising because early studies of the effect of price incentives on patient behavior essentially assumed all care was equal and that the only choice was between more care or less care.[47] If that is the case and employees cannot choose among treatments and providers, or if employees have insufficient information and decision support, then HSAs simply become a way to encourage self-rationing.

HSAs have helped a growing number of subscribers understand the appeal of high-deductible plans. While only one percent of Aetna's employees elected to have a health savings account in the first year it was offered, by the third year more than 70 percent of employees had chosen an HSA. Similarly, when Whole Foods offered voluntary health reimbursement accounts (essentially an HSA), 95 percent of its employees opted for the HRA with a high-deductible health plan, though only 65 percent had chosen any health plan the year before. Whole Foods' medical claims costs fell 13 percent, and hospital admissions per employee fell 22 percent.[48] Employees rolled $14.2 million into the next year, suggesting that some individuals who were choosing not to buy insurance will buy it if unused HSA funds can be carried forward for future health care needs.

HSAs can also streamline administrative processes and reduce the need for health plans to process small transactions for routine care, thus creating the potential for administrative cost savings. Most families typically spend less per year than the HSA deductible, so they pay for their own care directly unless they experience a serious accident, acute illness, or have chronic conditions. For families with chronic care needs, health savings accounts will not help accumulate savings because these families will usually exceed their deductible. Such families, however, may benefit from the ability to direct how the deductible is spent and from the mind-set of focusing on the value of care and managing diseases to avoid unnecessary hospitalizations and services.

Yet HSAs are not the solution by themselves. HSAs will have the greatest impact where there is real provider choice, good information about results, and competition on value. Within a restricted network or in situations in which there is little or no information to enable choice, in contrast, HSAs run the grave risk of becoming a vehicle for self-rationing because the only real choice is whether to seek or forgo care, especially for families managing chronic conditions. Without the ability and information to choose among providers and among treatments, HSAs may simply become a new kind of cost shifting to patients. Even when choice is theoretically available, many patient choices are constrained in practice by patients' need to maintain good relationships with their doctors and by a lack of support for making informed choices. Until services are available to enable results-based referrals and value-based decisions, HSAs will be primarily a cost-shifting vehicle.

As with consumer-directed health care, HSAs can only have the desired effect if other elements of the system evolve to support value-based competition on results at the level of diagnosis, treatment, management, and prevention of medical conditions. HSAs are a part of the puzzle, but only one piece.

Non-Reforms

A number of other prominent proposed and actual reform efforts are not reforms at all. Migration of consumers from Medicare to private insurance does not solve much from a value perspective if the private system is not working. While proponents of privately administered Medicare believe it creates an immediate benefit through avoiding the inefficiencies of government administration, this does not address the root problem—the lack of value-based competition in the delivery of care to patients. The private insurance system is high cost and fails to focus on value as well.

Changing tax laws so that individuals rather than employers choose their insurance may well be desirable, as we will discuss in chapter 8. The provision of health insurance through employers was a pragmatic step at the time, but the employer's involvement offers limited intrinsic benefit in terms of health care value, especially if health plans play the roles we discuss in chapter 6. Unfortunately, as health care costs have risen, a dynamic has been created in which fewer employers provide health benefits for employees and retirees, and those employers that do offer benefits cover less of the cost. Furthermore, the asymmetry between those employed by large organizations and other individuals has created major complexities and cross subsidies that continue to plague the system, both in terms of tax deductibility (which now creates a disincentive for individuals to buy their own insurance) and bargaining power. But tax equalization alone is not a real solution because it ignores the dysfunctional competition in health care delivery.

Other proposed reforms have attempted to regulate provider structure, but may well make zero-sum competition worse. For example, some employer groups, such as the Buyers Health Care Action Group which represents twenty-seven major employers in the Minneapolis–St. Paul area, advocate "system to system" competition, in which physicians are forced to commit to one closed network or another.[49] Similarly, the Community Health Purchasing Corporation in central Iowa is forcing competition among "care systems" (provider networks).[50] These initiatives accentuate the power of a few full-line systems but undermine effective competition at the level of diseases and treatments. As we have discussed, there is little logic to suggest that such groups will offer medically integrated, better-quality, or more efficient care.

Buying drugs from Canada is just the health care system's latest example of shifting costs, in this case to drug companies or to the citizens of other countries. U.S. citizens pay a disproportionate share of the cost of the world's drug development, which should be shared by other industrialized nations. However, if drugs are purchased by U.S. consumers or intermediaries from a country such as Canada that uses its clout as a government buyer to obtain lower prices, this represents just another form of cost shifting rather than value creation. Pharmaceutical companies, in this case, can withhold exports to re-exporting countries, raise prices abroad, cut back investment in the development of new treatments, or accept lower profits. While it would be desirable to have a more equitable sharing of drug development costs, buying drugs from Canada will at best be a bandage, not a solution.

The system needs strong incentives for innovation in treatments (pharmaceutical or otherwise) that improve value if there is any hope of controlling cost increases. Opening up more competition among pharmaceutical companies, and requiring drugs to demonstrate not just efficacy but meaningful patient value, are the only policies toward pharmaceuticals that will improve value in the system.[51]

Finally, much current "reform" simply throws more money at the system. Adding prescription drug coverage to Medicare does little to address health care value. Neither does pressuring providers to provide more free care or subsidized prices to deserving groups, instead of equitably subsidizing the purchase of heath plans for those people who genuinely cannot afford them. These reforms are just more examples of cost shifting.

Reforming Competition: The Only Answer

All but missing in the discussion about health care reform is an understanding of the structure of health care delivery to patients, and the crucial role of value-based competition in driving improvements in quality, safety, and efficiency. Only competition on results to improve the diagnosis, treatment, management, and prevention of specific medical conditions will lead to true value improvements for patients. Reform must focus on how to get competition right and how to put in place the enabling conditions, such as the right information, the right incentives and time horizons, and the right mind-sets.

4

Principles of Value-Based Competition

THE ZERO-SUM COMPETITION of the 1990s and early 2000s in the United States health care system has clearly failed. It did not produce widespread improvements in the quality and cost of delivering care, nor widen access to care for all Americans. Instead, zero-sum competition perpetuated inefficiency and substandard quality. It also drove up administrative costs, inhibited innovation, and resulted in alarming cost increases for patients, employers, and the government. More and more Americans are without health plans. Participants in the system have been pitted against each other, to no one's benefit.

Health care competition must be transformed to a value-based competition on results. This is the best way, and the only way, to drive sustained improvements in quality and efficiency. The experience in numerous other industries tells us that this transformation is possible. It also tells us that there can be stunning progress when the right kind of competition is unleashed.

Value-based competition on results is a positive-sum competition in which all system participants can benefit: When providers win by delivering superior care more efficiently, patients, employers, and health plans also win. When health plans help patients and referring physicians make better choices, assist in coordination, and reward excellent care, providers benefit. And competing on value goes beyond winning in a narrow sense. When providers and health plans compete to achieve the best medical outcomes for patients, they pursue the aims that led them to the profession in the first place.

What would value-based competition in health care look like? It would be guided by the eight principles shown in figure 4-1. As rational and self-evident as these principles may seem, they do not describe the health care

FIGURE 4-1

Principles of value-based competition

• The focus should be on value for patients, not just lowering costs.

• Competition must be based on results.

• Competition should center on medical conditions over the full cycle of care.

• High-quality care should be less costly.

• Value must be driven by provider experience, scale, and learning at the medical condition level.

• Competition should be regional and national, not just local.

• Results information to support value-based competition must be widely available.

• Innovations that increase value must be strongly rewarded.

system currently in place in the United States. A host of flawed assumptions, misguided strategies, and counterproductive policies have led participants to behave in ways that have driven health care further away from what makes medical and economic sense.

This chapter describes the principles of value-based competition and their underlying rationale, together with supporting evidence. One need not rely on experience from other industries to make the case that these principles hold; there is compelling evidence in health care itself. Fully achieving the right kind of competition in health care will require embracing all eight principles. The process of moving to value-based competition, however, does not require achieving prior consensus. Chapters 5 through 8 describe how providers, health plans, suppliers, consumers, employers, and governments can act on these principles in their strategic, organizational, and policy choices. Indeed, as many examples illustrate, many participants are beginning to move in these directions.

Focus on Value, Not Just Costs

The right objective for health care is to increase value for patients, which is the quality of patient outcomes relative to the dollars expended. Minimizing costs is simply the wrong goal, and will lead to counterproductive results. Eliminating waste and unnecessary services is beneficial, but cost savings must arise from true efficiencies, not from cost shifting, restricting care (rationing), or reducing quality. Every policy and practice in health care must be tested against the objective of patient value. The current system fails this test again and again.

When measuring value, patient outcomes are multidimensional, and far more complex than whether the patient survives. Recovery time, quality of life (e.g., independence, pain, range of movement), and emotional well-being during the process of care all matter. The relative importance of different outcomes will vary for different individuals. In a system of value-based competition on results, each provider and health plan may excel in different ways and serve different groups of patients. This is one of the benefits of a competition-based system relative to a top-down or centrally managed system, which assumes one size fits all.

Value must be measured for the *patient,* not the health plan, hospital, doctor, or employer. This is an important distinction in practice. For example, much health care delivery is organized around the traditions and preferences of physicians rather than around patient value, as we discuss in chapter 5. Similarly, health plans and employers often focus on the costs they bear, rather than on the overall cost of delivering care. This encourages them to attempt to ration services or shift costs to providers or patients rather than to improve value.

Value in health care can only be understood by focusing on the level at which it is actually created, which is in addressing *particular medical conditions*, such as diabetes, knee injuries, or congestive heart failure. (We will discuss the definition of medical conditions later in this chapter.) Only at the level of medical conditions can outcomes and costs be compared directly to determine value. It is much less revealing to attempt to measure the nation's or even a provider's results overall (see the box "Does the United States Spend Too Much on Health Care?").

Value improvement is occurring at the medical condition level in some areas, though not as often and as much as it could. To understand value, the results per dollar expended at the medical condition level must be measured over time. Consider some examples. In coronary heart disease, the death rate has fallen so much since 1965 that this trend alone accounts for more than 70 percent of the increase in Americans' life expectancy. While spending on cardiac medicine has risen rapidly, the cost per procedure is rising at less than the rate of inflation. When adjusted for improved mortality rates, expenditures have actually fallen by about 1 percent per year.[1] In gallbladder surgery, aggregate spending has also risen, but that is due to increased demand for the lower-risk, highly successful laparoscopic surgery that has improved the quality of life for many patients. The procedure has virtually eliminated inpatient hospital costs and reduced the cost of physicians' services in addressing gallstones by 50 percent.[2] These examples illustrate the potential to achieve major improvements in value. The challenge is to create the right kind of competition in the system to ensure that this takes place, and at all providers.

When measuring value, both outcome and costs must be measured over the full cycle of care, not for discrete interventions or procedures.

Does the United States Spend Too Much on Health Care?

The value perspective makes it clear that the share of U.S. GDP that goes into health care is not the right measure of the success of a health care system. Success can only be measured by the value delivered per dollar spent. Spending more is not necessarily a problem; the question is whether Americans are getting their money's worth. Americans collectively spend more on computers than they did ten years ago, for instance, because today's computers offer much greater value.

Health care is more expensive today than it was in the 1930s, but the average life expectancy has increased from about sixty years to seventy-seven years, and the quality of life for older Americans is substantially better. Hence, it is clear that there have been important advances.[3] It is also clear that the efficiency of the system is far less than it could be, and that quality falls well short of the ideal. However, looking at health care in aggregate terms is not the best way to understand how to increase value significantly, and attempting to fix the system with top-down solutions will continue to fail. Instead, meaningful change will need to focus on value at the medical condition level, and redefine competition around value.

Short-term cost savings that lead to long-term cost increases do not improve value. A low-cost diagnosis that is mistaken and leads to unnecessary treatment is not a good value. Conversely, high-cost stroke intervention that avoids decades of nursing home care is a bargain.

The cycle of care involves not just treatment but rehabilitation and long-term management of a medical condition to minimize recurrences. The care cycle also encompasses assessment of the risk of disease and steps to prevent its occurrence or progression. Value must be understood as the outcomes and costs over the whole cycle, not just for the individual components. (We define the care cycle more precisely in chapter 5.)

There are opportunities for major improvements in health care value through new medical technologies. Even more important, however, will be new ways of organizing, measuring, and managing health care delivery over the full cycle of care. There are tremendous gains to be achieved from simply using today's medical science more effectively. We have come to believe strongly that technology is important, but that the major problem the system is facing today is not technology but management.

A focus on value over the care cycle, rather than just short-term cost and benefits, would transform much thinking about health care delivery. For example, the current focus on controlling prescription drug spending trades short-term drug savings for higher spending down the road,[4] pushes some patients into noncompliance,[5] and stifles innovation.[6] Focusing on value over the care cycle would shift this debate from one about controlling spending to one about the most effective use of drugs and other treatments to improve quality and efficiency in treating and managing specific diseases. In today's competition, the most cost-effective drug is not always chosen. For example, in the treatment of hypertension, a landmark, long-term study revealed that the shift away from lower-cost thiazide-type diuretic drugs to newer drugs (from 56 percent of the total prescription volume in 1982 to 27 percent in 1992) increased costs $3.1 billion without improving, and frequently worsening, patient outcomes.[7] A better approach to controlling drug costs is to create more competition among providers and drug companies based on results.[8] The current system is not structured to compete on value across the full cycle of care, much less measure and sort out the value differences among alternative diagnostic approaches and treatments.

Redefining health care competition around value will require changes in the structure, organization, measurement, and time horizon of patient care, as we describe in chapters 5 through 7. The activities of all those involved in the cycle of care must be integrated and coordinated, something that is rare today.

With coordination of care will come joint accountability for outcomes and cost over the full care cycle by all those involved. In today's fractured system there is little accountability even for individual results, and joint accountability sounds radical. In other fields, however, individuals and organizations bear responsibility for working together to get the total job done. In health care, where results are critical to the quality of patients' lives, everyone involved in the patient's care should bear responsibility for the patient's overall outcome.

Competition Is Based on Results

The only way for value to increase rapidly and broadly in health care is through competition based on results. Unless providers have to compete to be excellent, there is simply no feasible way to create the same incentives for rapid and widespread improvement. It is not realistic or effective to attempt to second-guess provider practices, review their choices, and specify from the outside the way care should be delivered. It is also not realistic to rely on specialized training or board certification to keep physicians up to date. Nor is it feasible to think that providers who do not know how they compare, and who do not have to compete, will always sift through the voluminous literature on clinical trials in search of ways to improve their outcomes.

Health care delivery is simply too complex, too subtle, too individualized, and too rapidly evolving to be manageable by top-down micromanagement, as we discussed in chapter 3. While following treatment protocols can contribute to value, for example, the results achieved in following the same protocol vary substantially from case to case.[9] Efforts to specify provider processes or choices in advance, then, will inevitably disappoint or fail. It is also an approach that is very costly and demoralizing.

The real proof of success is better patient results (quality versus cost), not compliance with processes specified by outside experts or administrators. Providers need to be compared on results, and excellent providers rewarded with more patients.[10] Information about results, which is appropriately risk adjusted, must become the critical driver of behavior in the system—by referring physicians, by health plans, by patients, and by providers themselves. Results (outcomes versus cost) also must be the ultimate basis on which drugs, medical devices, other technologies, and services are selected.

Results, it must be stressed, mean actual health value for patients. A hospital's ranking in *U.S. News and World Report* is not a result, nor is the fact that the hospital is a teaching hospital, or has a good reputation, or administers aspirin to patients arriving at the hospital with heart attack symptoms.[11] Neither are results meaningful at the level of the hospital or network. Competition on results must take place at the level at which value is determined—in addressing specific medical conditions over the full care cycle.

Unrestricted competition based on results is the best and the only real cure for the problems of medical errors, undertreatment, and overtreatment. Practice guidelines have failed repeatedly to drive widespread process improvement. Outside review of treatments or investments has failed to control excess capacity and unnecessary care. Some observers are now arguing for government limits on the supply of physicians to limit excessive care.[12] However, simply limiting the number of physicians will not ensure that the services that physicians deliver will be higher value; unless there is information and competition on results, fewer physicians could mean that higher-value services are curtailed. Competition on results, not trying to control supply, is the only effective way to create accountability, motivate and inform process improvement, and drive up patient value.

If, and only if, providers have to demonstrate excellent results in addressing specific medical conditions will errors decline, unnecessary tests not be performed, unnecessary treatments stop, the use of ineffective treatments cease, and the withholding of effective services come to an end.[13] Supply-induced demand for unneeded care will decline when results are measured and compared. Physicians who cannot demonstrate patient value will go out of business. (Note that other changes that we discuss in later chapters, such as organizing diagnosis as distinct from treatment and modifying billing structures, will also help reduce the incentives to overtreat that are endemic in the current system.)

Some observers worry that because competition on results can create incentives to reduce costs, providers will ignore best practices or use obsolete processes—but the reality is quite the opposite. The lack of measured results in the current system invites unwise short-term cost cutting. It also makes attention to best practices optional rather than required. Today, excellence depends too much on enlightened leadership and unusual commitment. In competition on results, staying abreast of best practices is mandatory, not discretionary. Competition on results will clearly reveal obsolete or substandard approaches to care to physicians as well as to patients. Better mechanisms will surely be needed to help physicians improve their methods and keep up with innovations, which we will describe in later chapters.

Competition on results will also do much to eliminate a bias in feedback that now occurs for physicians. Satisfied patients return, but patients who have experienced poor results will often seek care elsewhere. Physicians sometimes never know why a patient lost contact, and it is human nature to assume that the care they delivered was effective. Results tracking and reporting will give physicians the honest feedback they need.[14]

Providers should earn their right to practice. Competition on results must be unrestricted by network, geography, provider group, or ownership. Value-based competition requires physicians and teams to compare themselves to the best in the region, the nation, and the world, not only locally or within their own health care system. It also requires that providers have to compete, in the best sense of the word, by improving patient results. No provider can be guaranteed patients because of its past reputation, health plan contract, system affiliation, or location.

Some observers have raised concerns that providers competing to achieve the best results will withhold their learning and process improvements from other providers, in contrast to today's more collegial system. We suspect that the opposite will occur. As is the case in other industries, the introduction of competition will trigger more willingness to exchange ideas as part of the process of staying excellent.

Today, systematic process improvement is voluntary, and largely uninformed with comparative data. Proponents of "evidence-based medicine" have made valiant efforts to enable the spread of documented effective practices. Still, as we discussed in chapter 1, best practices are notoriously slow to diffuse in health care. With measurement and competitive pressure to improve results, the effort devoted to improving care delivery structures and methods will increase dramatically. In practice, each particular provider does not compete head to head with most providers in other regions, even if there are no network restrictions. Thus, formal and informal collaboration among providers to exchange ideas and share expertise is likely to proliferate. Medical schools, medical societies, quality improvement organizations, outcome measurement organizations, and others will also be conduits for learning among providers who are more motivated to learn. Finally, as we have observed in other industries, sharing process insights even with competing providers will take place, and will not eliminate the advantages of leaders. In cystic fibrosis care, for example, the collection of results information triggered widespread diffusion of best practice protocols, raising the average level of results across all providers. However, the best providers have continued to outperform the average. Their care delivery activities and organization cultures are hard to replicate, and they do not stand still but continue to innovate. (We discuss the case of cystic fibrosis further later in this chapter.)

We are mindful of the possibility that some providers will respond to results competition by trying to game the system to manipulate their numbers. However, competition will also create a strong motivation to expose manipulation, while advancing results measures and risk adjustment methodologies that make manipulation difficult. Results competition is sure to trigger an intense and sorely needed discussion about how to measure and compare results fairly. If some providers game the system by referring the sickest patients to leading centers, patient value will still improve. And even if some manipulation of results occurs in the short run, the value improvement from competing on results will still be much better for patients than a status quo in which physicians do not even know where they stand. Today, providers who deliver below-average care have no accountability short of malpractice lawsuits.

Some critics downplay competition on results, asserting that outcome variations will quickly diminish. If this actually occurs, patient value will have improved tremendously! History suggests, however, that outcome variations will be persistent. Even for medical conditions in which good outcome measures have been available, variations persist even though the average outcome improves. Moreover, even if the gap is closed on one outcome measure (such as mortality) and performance becomes truly excellent across the board, competition will shift to improving the next outcome dimension. Results outcomes are always multidimensional. As outcomes improve, competition will shift more toward efficiency. Competition on results is dynamic and never-ending.

Finally, value-based competition on results must extend to referring physicians and health plans. Referring physicians whose patients are habitually treated by substandard providers should have to examine and justify their practices. This will not only benefit their patients, but also reinforce value-based competition at the provider level. Health plans need to be held accountable primarily for the health value they achieve for their subscribers, as we discuss in chapter 6.

Competition Is Centered on Medical Conditions over the Full Cycle of Care

In health care, as in all fields, identifying what constitutes the relevant business or market is critical to making good choices and ensuring that markets work. It is common to talk about health care as if it were one service. Instead, it is a myriad of distinct services. But each discrete service is not the relevant business either. The relevant businesses in health care delivery are specific medical conditions seen over the cycle of care. A medical condition (e.g., chronic kidney disease, diabetes, pregnancy) is a set of patient health circumstances that benefit from dedicated, coordinated care. The term *medical conditions* encompasses diseases, illnesses, injuries, and natural circumstances such as pregnancy. A medical condition can be defined to encompass common co-occurring conditions if care for them involves the need for tight coordination and patient care benefits from common facilities.

As we have discussed, value and results can only be measured in a meaningful way at the medical condition level. Providers can offer services for a range of medical conditions, but the value they create is overwhelmingly determined by how well they deliver care for each one. Competition on results, then, must be centered on the medical condition level.

How to define the medical conditions around which to organize care delivery involves important judgments. A medical condition should be defined from the patient's perspective. It should encompass the set of illnesses or injuries that are best addressed with a dedicated and integrated care delivery process. Knee injuries and spine injuries, for instance, may be best treated as separate medical conditions because addressing each of them involves different monitoring, different diagnostic expertise, different interventions, and different forms of rehabilitation.

Setting the start and the end of the care cycle for each medical condition is also an important judgment. As we discuss in chapter 5, for example, chronic kidney disease is probably best seen as a separate medical condition with a care cycle, and kidney dialysis as a separate medical condition with a different care cycle, rather than combining them into one. While there are clearly links between earlier renal stage care and dialysis care, and these links should be managed, the nature of the care delivery processes is very different. Hence there are two medical conditions that will benefit from dedicated focus and a dedicated care delivery structure.

Providers should organize themselves around medical conditions, not skills or discrete specialties or services necessary to address a medical condition. Integrated practice units, as we term them, should include all the services necessary to address a medical condition, usually in dedicated facilities. Providers will define integrated practice units somewhat differently, based on their patient populations and their approaches to structuring and coordinating care. We will discuss integrated practice units and the definition of medical conditions in chapter 5.[15]

Competition in addressing medical conditions must take place over the full cycle of care, not on discrete interventions, treatments, or services. As we have noted, value can only be accurately measured over the cycle, not just a particular intervention.[16] A low-cost surgery is no bargain if it results in avoidable complications or long-term reoccurrence of the condition. Conversely, an expensive drug may be a bargain if it replaces an even more expensive (and painful) surgery or the need for chronic rehabilitation. A pervasive problem in care delivery and clinical investigations is a time horizon that is too short. Interventions and treatments must compete on results with disease management and prevention.

There is room for value improvement in each aspect of care delivery, but the potential for value improvement is far greater by managing the full cycle of care. In today's fractured and procedure-centric system, however, tapping into this potential is still in its infancy. In the diagnosis and treatment of a medical condition, numerous specialties, departments, and even different organizations are typically involved. There are major opportunities to improve patient value through better information sharing and handoffs among the players. There are also important linkages or interdependencies across care delivery activities that must be optimized. Better preparation before treatment, for example, can make treatment more effective. More attention to rehabilitation and posthospitalization follow-up can raise the success rate of a surgery, not to mention reducing time in the hospital. We explore these and other opportunities in chapter 5.

Health care delivery today is centered on acute treatment. However, care-cycle thinking also exposes the crucial role of disease management, which involves closely managing a patient's illness over an extended period of time to improve compliance with medication and desirable life practices, detect impending problems early, and initiate timely remedies involving less costly interventions. Disease management is often most effective when it starts early, highlighting the value of early detection. The evidence for long-term quality and cost improvements through disease management is becoming so compelling that a journal has been created to chronicle advances in the field.[17] (For further discussion see chapter 6.)

A good example of both the importance of early intervention and disease management is chronic kidney disease. A timely diagnosis and treatment for early stages of the disease prevents or delays the evolution of the disease to end stage renal disease, which must be treated with dialysis or transplantation.[18] Early intervention improves the benefits of coaching patients in healthy living habits and the management of related health issues such as anemia, bone disease, hypertension, dyslipidemia, and malnutrition.[19,20] Disease management also enables appropriate preparation for successful dialysis if the disease progresses.[21] Yet today, early intervention and systematic management of chronic kidney disease is far from the norm; only 43 percent of the individuals on dialysis had seen a nephrologist even once in the year prior to dialysis.[22] Competition on value over the care cycle will lead to more attention to the prevention, detection, and long-term management of illness relative to treatments and acute interventions.

At its most fundamental level, care-cycle thinking points to the importance of understanding those factors (lifestyle, environment, genetic, or otherwise) that increase the risks of contracting a medical condition, and of working with high-risk individuals to forestall or limit disease (with lifestyle modification or other steps) and detect it early, when it is the most treatable.[23] Using genomics to predict and help treat disease is currently a hot topic, but there are huge gains to be reaped even by measuring and addressing well-known risk factors. Such opportunities, which offer large potential value improvements, have been rare because they are not encouraged by the prevailing strategies, organizational structures, reimbursement practices, and types of competition in the system (see chapter 6).

Competing on results in addressing medical conditions over the cycle of care will require a move to joint accountability, as we have noted. Specialists will no longer be responsible just for what they do, but for the overall results. A surgical team will no longer be responsible just for the surgery, but for patient value over the long term. Creating and enabling this joint responsibility is one of the central agendas in health care.

Tools for understanding and structuring health care delivery from a medical condition and care-cycle perspective, and the role of health plans in reinforcing this perspective, are discussed in chapters 5 and 6.

High-Quality Care Should Be Less Costly

The right kind of competition on results, at the level of medical conditions over the care cycle, will lead to major improvements in efficiency. It will also drive huge improvements in quality. But what is crucial to understand is that quality and cost will often improve simultaneously. The extent of this opportunity in health care is one of the most important and encouraging findings of our work. It carries profound implications for the behavior of the actors in the system. In health care, it is essential not to think or act as if there were an inevitable cost versus quality trade-off.

The widespread opportunity to achieve simultaneous improvements in cost and quality in health care arises for several reasons. First, much U.S. health care delivery lags the state of the art, as discussed in chapter 1. This leaves ample room for simultaneous improvement in quality and cost, even in the short run. Just by implementing known best practices, virtually all providers can improve both quality and margins without raising prices. One can imagine a productivity frontier, which relates the quality of the health outcomes achieved in addressing a particular medical condition to the full cost of providing care for that condition (see figure 4-2).[24] The productivity frontier incorporates all available best practices in terms of process protocols, technologies, drugs, and other aspects of care. If a provider is not at the frontier (and it is clear that much of health care delivery is far from the frontier), catching up and moving to the frontier will allow delivering current outcomes at lower costs, improving out-

FIGURE 4-2

Productivity frontier: Operational effectiveness versus strategic positioning

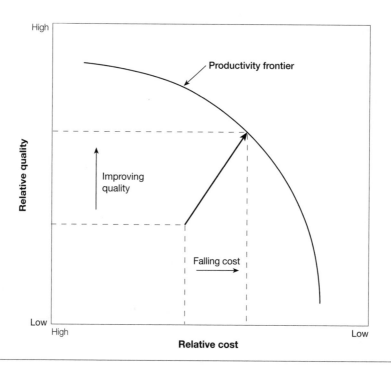

comes at the same cost, or, in many cases, attaining better outcomes at lower cost.[25] For example, timely administration of drugs will produce better results with no cost increase, or a new arthroscopic procedure may improve quality in terms of complications and recovery time while lowering cost through shorter operative time and time in the hospital. When providers fail to use best practices, conversely, more spending will often not improve outcomes.[26]

Second, improving quality and cost simultaneously is also made possible by eliminating mistakes and getting it right the first time. In every industry, eliminating defects lowers cost because it reduces wasted effort and lowers remedial costs. In health care, the benefits of error reduction are especially great since the costs of preventable errors and complications are very high due to slower recovery and the need for repeated or extra treatments. Indeed, in some types of care, the failure to use the right approach the first time can never be fully corrected, no matter how much remedial care is provided. The cost of a poor diagnosis is also potentially huge, in the form of wasted or inappropriate treatment, repeat visits, and the delay of appropriate care.

The incidence of mistakes and errors in health care is far higher than in many industries, partly because measurement is so recent. The Institute of Medicine estimates that preventable medical errors involve between $36.7 and $50 billion each year in unnecessary costs, with over half of that estimate representing direct costs of remedial health care.[27] We believe that these estimates are highly conservative and look narrowly at cost rather than consider the full care cycle. The Juran Institute, for example, estimates that 30 percent of direct health care outlays are due to poor process quality.[28] An ongoing Dartmouth Medical School study of Medicare across the United States concluded, "It is hard to find evidence that more resources are required to improve the quality of care in fee-for-service Medicare. There is, instead, evidence of large-scale waste and inefficiency in the delivery system."[29] The potential to improve quality and cost through reducing or eliminating mistakes is enormous.

Third, the inherent nature of health care itself proliferates fundamental opportunities to improve quality while reducing costs over the long term. For example, better diagnosis means that the right condition is treated, improving outcomes and avoiding ineffective treatments. Less invasive procedures have shorter recovery times and fewer complications, and are often less costly to perform and can be delivered in less expensive settings. Migrating diagnosis and treatment toward addressing causes, rather than mitigating symptoms, will often make care more effective and less costly, especially over the long run. (See the examples discussed in the section on health care innovation later in this chapter.) Better coordination and

integration over the care cycle avoids wasted effort while improving patient results. Better management of chronic conditions, including the simple act of informing patients about steps they can take, lessens the severity
of these conditions while reducing cost through eliminating or reducing
illness and the need for expensive treatment. Risk assessment and the prevention of disease or injury, the ultimate improvement in quality, avoids
treatment and its cost altogether. At the most fundamental level, better
quality lowers cost in health care because better health is inherently less
expensive. Maintaining health is the ultimate cost saving.

Advances in care delivery that simultaneously enable better outcomes
at lower costs are often not dramatic breakthroughs. For example, a leading hospital noticed large variations among its physicians in the number
of days of hospital stay required to restore a normal heartbeat in patients
experiencing atrial fibrillation after bypass surgery for coronary artery
blockages. All of the relevant practitioners—cardiologists, cardiac surgeons,
and intensive care nurses—were called together to determine the causes of
the variation and identify what could be done better. Note that this approach
of improving care through the integrated effort of all the specialists and
skilled practitioners involved is extremely powerful but far from the
norm. (We discuss the organization of care delivery further in chapter 5.)

After reviewing the health status of each patient and how he or she was
managed, the team identified three effective treatments (two drug therapies and shocking the heart). The analysis revealed that the timing with
which the three treatments were performed varied considerably. Some
doctors performed all three in rapid succession, while others waited for a
response after each treatment. The conservative approach of waiting
between treatments proved not to improve results but led to significantly
longer hospital stays. With this new understanding, a relatively simple
change in patient management significantly improved health outcomes,
shortened hospital stays, and reduced total costs.

Major improvements in cost and quality in health care are possible
even without heroic efforts or breakthrough technology. A good example
is the Veterans Administration (VA) hospital system, which has achieved
major improvements in cost and quality as a result of measurement and
better patient information. Between 1994 and 1998 under Dr. Ken Kizer's
leadership, the previously disjointed thousand sites of care were reorganized into twenty-two integrated service networks that competed with each
other based on cost and quality.[30] Information systems connect all sites,
providing the medical staff with access to a patient's complete medical
record going back to the mid-1980s.[31] As the number of enrollees rose by
70 percent between 1999 and 2003 and process quality metrics improved,
the VA's funding (not adjusted for inflation) went up only 41 percent.[32]

Such opportunities are legion, as is made evident by the work of organizations such as the Institute for Healthcare Improvement. Imagine the value improvement that would occur if such efforts were not an unusual event, but a normal, expected activity of every provider. Today, a growing number of providers, such as Intermountain Health Care in Utah, M. D. Anderson Cancer Center in Houston, and the Cleveland Clinic in Ohio, have such processes.[33] Imagine if the right kind of competition—competition to improve results in addressing medical conditions over the cycle of care—demanded such efforts by every provider in every medical condition and practice unit. The potential in terms of value improvement for patients is staggering.

Despite the unmistakable opportunity to improve quality and lower costs simultaneously, a surprising number of system participants still assume, and act, as if advancing the state of the art in health care required more services and more expensive technology. This can sometimes be true, especially early in the life of a new technology, but the far greater opportunity today is to use better the technologies known already. Value-based competition will be instrumental in shifting old mind-sets.

Value Is Driven by Provider Experience, Scale, and Learning in Medical Conditions

Value in health care delivery is created by doing a few things well, not by trying to do everything. Yet health care delivery is currently not organized this way—indeed, the current system encourages just the opposite.

As in every field, health care providers that concentrate their effort and learn from experience in addressing a medical condition usually deliver the most value and innovate the most rapidly. Organizations with experience in a field will tend to have more skilled teams, develop more dedicated facilities, and achieve faster rates of learning. Experience allows individuals and teams to hone more effective techniques and routines and to get better at spotting and dealing with problems. Experience and specialization also tend to attract the most demanding patients. Serving them drives even more rapid learning.

Scale in a medical condition is also important. For example, scale allows a provider to develop dedicated teams rather than relying on part-time practitioners, and to afford dedicated, tailored facilities for the medical condition rather than shared facilities. Scale results in multiple colleagues doing similar things who can consult with and get feedback from one another. Surgeons at New England Baptist Hospital, for example, cite the benefits of having numerous colleagues performing similar orthopedic procedures.

Scale allows greater integration in a practice area, such as in-house testing, which can greatly improve information and coordination compared to the current fractured system. By allowing multiple physicians, operating rooms, or other facilities, scale allows flexibility and efficiencies in scheduling. Scale leads to clout in purchasing devices, information technology, and other inputs. With a meaningful volume of cases in a medical condition, the fixed investments in results measurement and process improvement can also be amortized across higher revenues, reducing the cost per patient. (Note that a provider that lacks the scale to support its own study of value improvement can partially offset this by affiliating or contracting with an excellent larger provider, something that will become increasingly common in value-based competition.)

Note that while experience and scale are important in particular aspects of care, they can have an even greater impact across the cycle of care. This relationship has not been well studied because of the focus on health care delivery as discrete interventions. The ability to control the care cycle, manage handoffs across the cycle, share information, and optimize across various aspects of care (e.g., rehab versus inpatient care) are all enhanced by patient volume and experience at the medical condition level. What is needed in health care delivery, then, is not narrow specialization, but critical mass and experience in a medical condition over the care cycle.

A good example of the role of provider scale, experience, and learning in driving excellence is St. Luke's Episcopal Hospital, the home of the Texas Heart Institute (THI). St. Luke's prides itself on having surgical costs that are one-third to one-half lower than those at other academic medical centers, despite taking on the most difficult cases and using the newest technologies. Because of its excellence, St. Luke's attracts the most complex and demanding patients, whose needs drive even more rapid learning opportunities.[34]

St. Luke's has performed more than 100,000 coronary bypasses. To learn from this experience, the hospital has conscientiously examined and improved its practices and facilities. It has the scale to invest in dedicated facilities. Computers track every second of each operation for quality control. Sterile corridors connect different procedure rooms to allow greater efficiency. Improvements in treatment are made standard: for example, the surgical and nursing staffs developed protocols for early removal of ventilator tubing in some patients to yield fewer lung complications and faster recoveries. Although the number of cardiac patients it sees is rising, St. Luke's is now reducing the number of bypasses through the use of less traumatic interventions such as stents when surgery is unnecessary to achieve good outcomes. As we noted earlier, today's reimbursement practices actually work against the pursuit of such value improvements, an issue we will return to in subsequent chapters.

FIGURE 4-3

The virtuous circle in health care delivery

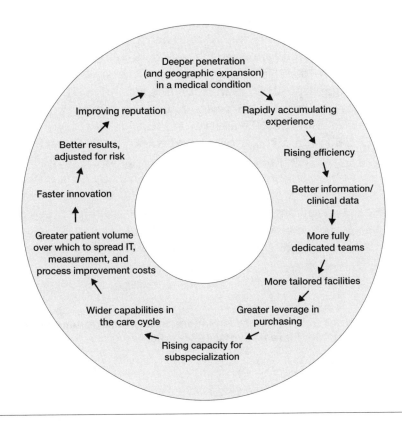

The combined effects of experience, scale, and learning create a virtuous circle, in which the value delivered by a provider can improve rapidly (see figure 4-3). (We discuss this dynamic for health care providers further in chapter 5.) Deeper penetration in a medical condition leads to accumulating experience, rising efficiency, better information, more fully dedicated teams, increasingly tailored facilities, the ability to control more of the care cycle, greater leverage in purchasing (many key purchases are practice-unit specific), rising capacity for subspecialization within the practice unit, efficiencies in investing in practice development and marketing, faster innovation, and better results. Better results lead to an improving reputation, which attracts more patients and feeds the circle further. Competition on results at the medical condition level drives this virtuous circle. Today, however, the reality is instead a vicious circle of fragmentation, subscale services, dependence on less dedicated resources, shared facilities, quality problems, and inefficiency.

In this regard, medicine is not different from other types of human endeavor: focused attention, experience, learning, and scale in addressing particular medical conditions lead to better results and faster improvement. These principles are especially important in a field where services are so fragmented. As in all fields, however, the virtuous circle is not automatic, and depends on healthy results competition. The ideal is not a single large provider in each medical condition but an array of providers competing to distinguish themselves.

The relationship among volume, experience, and outcomes makes intuitive sense. It is validated statistically in hundreds of studies that show that physicians or teams that learn from treating a high volume of patients who have a particular disease or condition register better outcomes, and sometimes also lower costs.[35] Studies of surgical procedures often find lower mortality rates in high-volume hospitals versus low-volume ones (see figure 4-4). There is debate among the scholars who

FIGURE 4-4

Mortality rates in low-volume providers versus high-volume providers by treatment, Medicare patients, 1994–1999

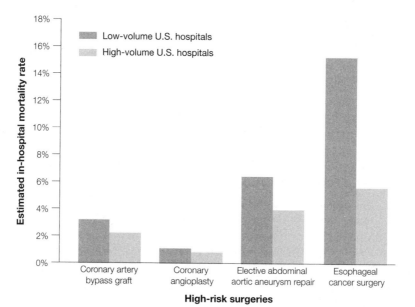

Source: Data from Birkmeyer et al. (2000).

study the empirical relationship between patient volume and outcomes, and the literature on this topic includes over 500 papers.[36] The evidence is overwhelming, however, that at least a threshold level of experience in a particular condition is critical for good quality.[37] The effect of scale on costs and outcomes in a medical condition has not been extensively studied. However, there are countless indications that a threshold level of volume in a practice unit is desirable for effectiveness and efficiency.

Scale and experience are also important in making accurate diagnoses, not just in care delivery. For example, even with common tests such as mammograms, many early-stage cancers are missed. Studies over the past twenty years have shown that women receive more accurate diagnoses when the reader of the mammogram is highly experienced and when the original film is reread every time a mistake is discovered in order to facilitate learning. Studies suggest that women should have their mammograms read by a radiologist who reads at least 1,000 films per year,[38] and perhaps over 2,500 per year.[39] Today, digital images can be transferred almost instantly, so high-volume, experienced centers for reading tests can be utilized without inconvenience to the patient or physicians.[40]

Success in diagnosis can also benefit from the ability to effectively integrate a range of specialties that contribute to understanding a patient's condition. The ability to support a team of dedicated experts in a medical condition is another reason a minimum volume of patients is necessary. The Mayo Clinic, headquartered in Rochester, Minnesota, combines the ability to integrate across medical specialists with extensive scale and experience to achieve extraordinary renown in diagnosis.

Clearly, the relationship among experience, scale, and results is not automatic, especially when providers do not have to compete on results. An important factor is learning. It is possible to repeat the same mistakes or poor practices over and over, but conscious learning is a powerful driver of improvement. Studies suggest that outcomes of specific procedures improve more in high-volume hospitals with active clinical trials, implying active learning, than in high-volume hospitals not involved in trials.[41] Yet, many providers today use inconsistent clinical processes that disguise the sources of problems and deter improvement. Many providers are also not structured and organized to systemize and capture learning. (See chapter 5.) Studies suggest that, in general, the number of years since medical school does not correlate with better patient results.[42] This implies that many experienced doctors are not keeping up with improved practice approaches.

Learning requires an active process of review and improvement. Physicians and teams need to keep up to date with clinical evidence, study and compare their results, highlight differences and problems, and then analyze what to do about them. When this happens, more experience drives faster learning. In cystic fibrosis, an example we discuss further later in this chapter, excellent providers improved more than the average providers even when best practices were shared among all providers. As attention focuses more and more on value, and providers have to compete on results, the rate of learning will become even greater.

Note that today, the relationship among experience, scale, and results is discretionary. Since providers do not have to compete and results are not measured, experienced providers are not required to learn, nor are higher-volume providers under pressure to reap every scale benefit. Indeed, the way much care delivery is structured neutralizes or minimizes these advantages. Studies drawn from existing practice, then, are only suggestive of the potential. Imagine if providers were truly focused on leveraging their scale and experience to drive results.

Given the importance of scale and experience at the medical condition level, health care delivery today is far too fragmented. Many providers offer too many services without enough patients, as we discuss in more detail in chapter 5. Providers are poorly structured to leverage the scale and experience they have. The current nature of competition accentuates fragmentation. Health plans and government programs aim to lift all boats and support all providers in achieving a minimum standard of practice, instead of rewarding excellent providers with more volume. The net effect is a huge number of providers for most services, even in complex conditions such as neonatal cardiac surgery and organ transplants. With little or no accountability for results, providers enter every service perceived as profitable.

Reimbursement practices also work against building volume and experience in diagnosis. M. D. Anderson Cancer Center, known for its remarkable cancer expertise, had an overwhelming number of breast cancer patients seeking second and third opinions because of the complexity of the disease and differences in outcomes resulting from different combinations and sequences of treatment. This high demand for consultations caused long waiting times for appointments of patients being treated by the hospital, so M. D. Anderson decided in 2004 to suspend the practice of providing second opinions to breast cancer patients not considering receiving their care at the hospital.[43] This was a natural and logical choice given the incentives in the current system, which bias compensation toward treatment. From a value perspective, however, diagnostic and second-opinion services should be dramatically expanded at the best centers.

Some observers, given the considerations we have discussed, have suggested that certain types of care should be restricted to high-volume centers. We are sympathetic to the idea that subscale and inexperienced providers should not be practicing on uninformed patients, and that physicians should gain experience only under the supervision of high-volume teams with excellent outcomes. However, volume per se is not the goal, but value measured by results. Volume is only a proxy for results. Assembling information on results, combined with opening up competition based on value, is far superior to setting arbitrary volume thresholds. Introducing volume restrictions without considering results could protect established providers from competition, which would actually reduce patient value.

Value-based competition on results will lead naturally to a significant reduction in the number of providers serving particular medical conditions. It will also lead to stronger and deeper affiliations between the truly excellent centers and other providers in that field. The effect on patient value will be enormous.

Competition on results, coupled with the virtuous circle of value improvement, will produce far greater value improvement than attempting to improve all providers across the board ("lifting all boats"). As patients move from being treated by below-average providers to excellent ones, patient value will rise substantially. As excellent providers grow, the virtuous circle of value improvement is reinforced. Since innovations that improve the state of the art tend to be driven by top performers, expanding their volume can accelerate the rate of value improvement further.

In this kind of competition, capacity in a medical condition will be reallocated from less effective providers to more effective providers. Some physicians at the less effective providers will shift their practice to other services where they can be excellent. Other physicians, or their institutions, will affiliate with excellent centers and benefit from their training, process expertise, and more effective management structures to significantly improve their performance. Overall, every physician will have an opportunity to become truly excellent. Patients will no longer have to accept substandard providers.

Competition Is Regional or National

The relevant geographic scope for competition in health care delivery is regional, national, or even international, not just local. Geographic scope begins with provider mind-set. Physicians and teams must compare their risk-adjusted results to those of the best providers anywhere, not just providers nearby. Also, providers should pursue relationships with national and regional centers to obtain consultations and other services to ensure that they can meet the highest standards of value even if they are the only hospital or clinic in their region.

The Importance of Regional Competition: Stroke Care

Stroke care highlights the importance of regional competition on results.[44] Strokes are quite heterogeneous, varying by location within the brain, the size of the clot, and the type of vessel affected. Caring for stroke patients requires personnel with a wide set of skills, including emergency physicians, neurologists, neurological intensive care specialists, radiologists, interventional radiologists, and specialized nurses. While many strokes are relatively mild and can resolve by themselves or with modest intervention, a portion (about 20 percent) of strokes occur in large vessels and are life threatening or may lead to major long-term disability unless treated immediately.

A clot in a large vessel, if it is identified early and the appropriate facilities and expertise are available, can be treated successfully. However, relatively few hospitals have the combination of twenty-four-hour CT machines, MRI machines, on-call radiologists, and brain angioplasty expertise needed to pinpoint the nature and location of the stroke and intervene mechanically if necessary to open the clot. (Clots in large vessels will often not respond to drug therapies.) We discuss the care delivery value chain for major strokes in more detail in appendix B.

In the greater Boston metropolitan area, the Massachusetts General Hospital (MGH) is one of just two or three hospitals with the necessary expertise and facilities to care for the most difficult stroke cases. MGH treats about 1,000 strokes per year, or about 10 percent of the total number in the region.

In obtaining care, patients, referring physicians, and health plans should seek out excellent care that best meets patient needs wherever it is located. Even for emergency and primary care, which will normally be delivered nearby, a regional perspective is important.

As discussed in chapter 1, there are significant differences in outcomes and costs across geography, even for conditions that occur frequently. For unusual or complex conditions, variation in outcomes is even greater. This should not be surprising given the benefits of expertise and scale at the medical condition level.

The notion that seeking out the best regional facilities will improve the quality of care is not a new one. Trauma centers, for example, replaced the 1970s practice in which every local emergency room treated patients involved in car accidents or having other serious injuries. The advent of trauma centers has saved countless lives and reduced disability. Today, taking this approach one step further, the treatment of major strokes in

Of these, about 200 involve major arteries, and between 50 and 100 are suitable for mechanical intervention.

MGH has the capacity to treat fully half of all the major strokes in the entire region. However, ambulances are required to take every suspected stroke patient to the nearest hospital, even if the patient or family specifies otherwise. Since most strokes are relatively mild and reimbursement rates are attractive, all hospitals want their share of stroke patients. For most patients, those who have minor strokes, this approach results in acceptable outcomes. For major stroke patients, however, the "send everyone their fair share" model may mean death or total incapacitation. Subsequent transfer to a second hospital will not work in these cases because the window of time to treat a stroke patient successfully is roughly three hours. Today, given the absence of value-based competition on results at the medical condition level, patient value is too often not well served.

The costs of failing to get patients to the right provider are significant in terms of life, quality of life, and dollars. Strokes are the leading cause of long-term disability and the third leading cause of death. Both long-term disability and death rates could be dramatically reduced if patients showing signs of a major stroke, something which can be ascertained by emergency medical technicians, were taken only to the centers with the best capabilities and results for these cases. Health plans should require ambulance companies to follow this practice. Laws in some states requiring transport to the nearest hospital should, at minimum, have an exception for major stroke. (Laws already allow trauma patients to be taken to the nearest trauma center rather than the nearest emergency room.)

appropriate centers would save lives and reduce disability (see the box "The Importance of Regional Competition: Stroke Care"). However, state laws and health plan contracts often require ambulances to take stroke patients to the nearest hospital rather than the most appropriate hospital that can be reached in time.

While traveling to a preeminent regional facility may sound expensive and inconvenient, cost savings and better short- and long-term medical outcomes can make travel clearly worthwhile for both patients and health plans.[45] The costs and inconvenience of travel are easily justified by avoiding other, higher costs that arise with inferior outcomes (longer recovery times, less complete recovery, chronic pain, complications, and mistakes). We do not suggest that *all* (or even most) patients should or will travel, but that it should be an option.

It is frequently asserted that patients will always choose convenient local care rather than seek out or utilize more distant providers. Yet current patient behavior is the result of an almost total absence of relevant outcome information, as we discussed in chapter 2. Patients, referring doctors, and health plans simply do not know just how uncompetitive many providers actually are, in both cost and quality. When they do, established patterns of behavior will rapidly change. The fact that patients tend to utilize local providers is also the result of numerous restrictions on patient choice and economic disincentives to seek out-of-network providers. (We discuss new roles for health plans and employers in encouraging competition across geography in chapters 6 and 7.)

Finally, the local bias in health care, as several physicians have pointed out to us, grows out of a time when medicine was more about comfort than cure. Local referrals made sense when outcome differences were probably smaller and matching patients to doctors was largely a matter of interpersonal chemistry. Today, the sophistication and complexity of care is far greater, which can lead to a substantial variation in results between excellent and undistinguished providers.

When relevant information, choice, and support for nonlocal care are expanded, patients and referring doctors can choose when to seek regional or national care based on the patient's condition and preferences. The pressure to meet or exceed the value offered by regional and national competitors will accelerate value improvement locally. And as more and more physicians have to compete and hold themselves to national expectations in terms of results, the need to travel should decline, though the opportunity must remain.

In a health care market without geographic restrictions, many patients would still choose to obtain care locally or within their region. However, the opening up of competition, and the encouragement of results comparisons across providers and geography, will jump-start condition-by-condition geographic competition even if just a fraction of patients actually elect to take advantage of it.[46] Doctors have explained to us that when they realize some patients are choosing to go elsewhere for care, they are more introspective and inclined to explore new approaches.

In today's system, a patient's desire to explore an excellent regional provider is too often taken as a sign of disloyalty and may undermine the working relationship with the local physician. In value-based competition, physicians will build relationships with excellent providers and facilitate the process of getting the patient to the right center for various parts of the care cycle. This will be one of the ways in which physicians distinguish themselves.

Regional and national competition only amplify the need for strategic focus by providers, and expand the opportunity to develop expertise and scale. Excellent providers in a medical condition will expand geographically by managing services in multiple locations, thereby leveraging scale, expertise, care delivery methods, staff training, measurement systems, and reputation. Patients will benefit tremendously from the acceleration of re-sults improvement.

Some argue that every city or town must have all services and specialties. But this argument is often made by hospitals that are located very close to several others. No one institution needs to provide every service. There is also no reason, in terms of health care value, for a patient to be cared for by the same hospital, physician group, or network for different conditions that occur at different times. Value for the patient is determined by how effective a provider is in addressing that patient's specific medical condi-tion, not by how good a job was done previously for some other condition.

The goal should be to encourage excellent providers to grow in their areas of expertise, rather than to lift all boats. Raising every provider to an acceptable standard in every medical condition will perpetuate fragmen-tation of service lines. Drawing from a wider geographic area, providers treating less common conditions could serve enough patients to benefit from scale, experience, and learning.

Increased scale and more regional and national competition would also enable excellent providers, wherever they are located, to train more interns and residents. Already, interns work at different hospitals through-out a region during their education. However, the location of training is often not based on evidence of excellent results. Training interns at cen-ters with excellent results would help disseminate best practices as young doctors begin their careers (see the box "Implications for Medical Educa-tion" in chapter 5).

As geographic competition increases, pressure will grow for providers to become more strategic about what services to offer. Excellent providers will offer services regionally and even nationally or internationally. Even for primary and emergency care, where much care is localized, local providers will build relationships and obtain consultations from excellent regional centers to increase the value delivered. As such relationships pro-liferate, local providers will be able to tap into economies of scale and experience in particular medical conditions and to speed the diffusion of care delivery innovations.

For rural hospitals there is no need to offer all services, except for emergency care, routine and preventive care, disease management, and follow-up care, unless the hospital has enough experience, scale, and expertise and meets a standard of true excellence. Rural hospitals should no longer operate as isolated, stand-alone organizations, but as organiza-tions connected through well-established medical relationships with other providers. An ideal health care system would encourage close working relationships between rural and community hospitals and regional and national centers. These relationships would be dedicated to integrated care in particular medical conditions over the full care cycle.

The potential benefits of such a collaborative model are revealed in traumatic brain injury (TBI). For TBI patients, better outcomes take the form of improved functionality or reduced disability, as is the case in many other medical conditions. Better outcomes dramatically reduce cost, because many of the 235,000 Americans per year that are hospitalized for TBI need expensive long-term care.[47] Standards of care that have been approved by the American Association of Neurological Surgeons are fully implemented in only 16 percent of the hospitals treating TBI.[48] A firm called CarePath is delivering Web-based information to local hospitals on TBI, backed up by telephone coaching by leading experts if local emergency physicians have questions.[49] The same sort of relationship could be developed between local hospitals and a leading national brain trauma center.

Such relationships—which today are rare and sometimes resisted— would markedly increase quality and value throughout the system. This example reveals the roles that service companies can play in a new type of health care competition. A growing number of specialized service companies are assisting providers and health plans in improving value at the medical condition level, a subject that we discuss in chapters 5 and 6.

As competition moves to the level of medical conditions rather than overall entities, community and rural hospitals would become known for their excellence and expertise in particular areas of care. Referrals from tertiary care centers back to such hospitals would be common and would increase value by locating care in an appropriate, lower-cost setting.

Some observers worry that rural hospitals might not survive financially if they refer profitable patients to other centers. We believe that more focused strategies by rural hospitals would significantly improve efficiency and margins. However, value delivered by rural hospitals could be enhanced if reimbursement practices were changed that currently undervalue the types of services that rural hospitals (and other rural providers) are best equipped to perform. Today's reimbursement works contrary to sound strategy and patient value. We discuss strategy for rural hospitals and community hospitals further in chapter 5 and propose some new approaches to reimbursement in chapters 6 and 8.[50]

Results Information Is Widely Available

Competition can produce rapid improvement when decisions by providers, patients, their families, referring physicians, and health plans are based on objective knowledge of results—medical outcomes and the cost of care over the full care cycle. Without such information, providers are deprived of the most powerful source of motivation and insight for improving their practice. Without appropriate information, referring physicians and patients are in the dark, and patient choice has marginal benefit.[51]

The Information Hierarchy

There is a hierarchy of information needed to support value-based competition (see figure 4-5). At the top of the hierarchy is information on *results* at the medical condition level. Results consist of patient outcomes, adjusted for risk, and the cost of care, both measured over the care cycle.

Next in the information hierarchy is data on the *experience* each provider has in addressing a medical condition, measured by the number of patients. Experience is a rough proxy for skill and efficiency, and affects the results achieved, as discussed earlier in this chapter. Experience is also a tool for matching providers and patients.

The third level in the hierarchy is information on *methods*. Methods are the processes of care itself, which are important to understanding how the results are achieved. Methods information is important to guiding process improvement.

FIGURE 4-5

Information hierarchy

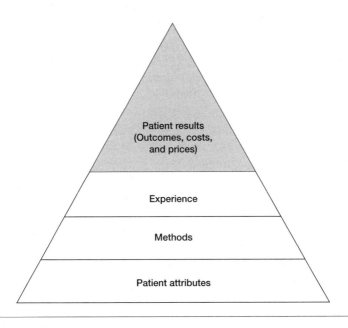

At the base of the information hierarchy is data on *patient attributes*. These include factors such as age, gender, co-occurring conditions, and, ultimately, genetic makeup. Patient attributes affect the process of care and are important to control for initial conditions or risk. (The information hierarchy is discussed further in chapter 5.)

The current focus of information gathering is on methods. A variety of organizations, as we have indicated, are collecting process information. Much of it concerns generic processes such as the use of computerized order entry (to reduce errors) and procedures for infection control. Less developed is the collection of process information at the medical condition level. Information about whether providers meet (or fail to meet) established standards of care for treatment of specific conditions gives referring physicians, patients, and health plans an important indication of quality. It also encourages providers to offer care consistent with established medical knowledge. Process compliance information is being collected in some medical conditions, as we have discussed in chapter 3.

Process compliance, however, is not an end in itself. What really matters is results. Process guidelines are related to results, but different providers utilizing the same protocols achieve very different results (as in the example of cystic fibrosis, mentioned earlier). Health care delivery is complex, and protocols do not capture the entire care delivery process. Good medical practice involves adjustments to address each patient's particular circumstances. Providers differ in skill, facilities, and organizational structure. Also, the best process is constantly changing. It is difficult, if not impossible, to keep process guidelines up to date. A narrow focus on process compliance, then, can actually slow innovation.[52]

There is a fine line between diffusing best practices and standardizing medicine. The current rates of medical errors and inappropriate standards of care are unacceptable, so diffusion of guidelines to encourage appropriate practice is essential. Yet standardizing medicine is not the goal. Standardization focuses on processes, not results. Process information, then, is just a tool to enhance the true goal—improving risk-adjusted results.

Results information is by far the most important type of information needed for value-based competition. Ultimately, medical outcome and price information should cover the full care cycle. When accurate risk-adjusted outcome and price information is available, large-scale external reporting of process comparisons will eventually be unnecessary. In the interim, however, external reporting of process data can be important to ensure that providers who lag behind prevailing medical practices are motivated to update their standards of care and reduce their rates of error.

Note that all providers should and will collect process information internally at increasing levels of granularity and sophistication. Internal analyses of the relationship between processes and the outcomes will be essential to organizational learning and improvement, as we discuss further in chapter 5. Providers will share process information, and researchers will mine such information for clinical studies. Providers will conduct their own studies of care delivery methods, rather than wait for clinical trials. However, the requirement to report detailed process data to external parties is burdensome, and ultimately unnecessary.

In measuring results, data on medical outcomes is essential, but price information is just as important. Together, outcome and price data enable judgments to be made about value. As we discuss in later chapters, current pricing practices are opaque and they obscure price reporting and price comparisons. It is difficult, if not impossible, to learn the price in advance of services, and many providers are actually unable to quote a price.

Current piecemeal prices for discrete interventions and services are not the prices that patients really want, or that matter for patient value. Prices should cover service bundles involved in episodes or full cycles of care. The relevant price is the overall price for care, not the price of a visit, treatment, or service by an individual physician. Health plans are beginning to post negotiated prices for specific medical services on their Web sites. Aetna, for example, posts the negotiated prices for a wide variety of services and interventions in the Cincinnati area.[53] However, the posted prices cover specific services and interventions and are nearly impossible to aggregate and make sense of. We discuss pricing and billing practices more fully in chapters 5, 6, and 8.

Measuring provider experience is more straightforward than collecting information on results and methods. Yet systematic data on provider experience with particular medical conditions would be a huge step forward. Just knowing how many patients each provider has diagnosed or treated in a medical condition would improve choice significantly. Experience is not a perfect predictor of results, but is a helpful and less threatening start. Reporting of experience data should be an immediate goal, either voluntarily or, if necessary, as a mandatory requirement to practice medicine.

Experience data is more valuable if it includes not just the overall number of patients cared for during a time period, but also finer breakdowns related to parts of the care cycle, methods, and patient attributes. For example, experience in diagnosis, experience by treatment approach, experience by disease subtypes, and experience for particular patient populations (e.g., age, risk factors) are all valuable to patients, health plans, and other physicians. Simply having systematic data to help physicians locate experts to consult on particular cases would pay immediate dividends in medical practice.

The final type of information that is important to value-based competition, data on patient attributes, is essential in understanding the causal chain leading to results. Patient attributes such as age, co-occurring conditions, state of illness, and so forth can affect the appropriate methods, define the relevant experience, and influence results. Patient initial conditions are crucial for risk adjustment, so that the results of providers can be fairly compared. As the causal relationships between patient attributes and effective treatment become understood, however, the risks of patients with those attributes should fall as excellent providers incorporate them into care delivery. Hence, risk adjustments should not be fixed, but modified as learning occurs.

The set of patient attributes collected should err on the side of too many rather than too few. The list will grow as providers accumulate knowledge of care delivery. For attribute data, collecting possible measures even before the need is fully validated is beneficial because it enables learning. The reporting of some patient attribute data will be mandated for risk adjustment purposes. Providers should collect more patient attributes internally and use it in analyzing and improving care delivery processes. Genetic data offers the potential for a quantum leap in this area.

The State of Results Measurement

Outcome measurement is complex. Some health care experts assert that meaningful outcome measurement is not feasible and that appropriate risk adjustments cannot be made. However, meaningful and reliable risk-adjusted outcome data is already available.[54] High-quality, comparative outcome data exists in a number of medical conditions, including pediatric oncology, cystic fibrosis, end stage renal disease, intensive care, cardiac surgery, and organ transplants. (See the box "How Good Outcome Information Arose" for a description and brief history of these information initiatives.) Each case carries its own lessons for how outcome measurement should be spread to every medical condition.

As a group, these cases demonstrate, beyond a doubt, that it is possible to develop robust outcome measures, collect comparative information, and adjust it for risk. These cases also demonstrate that doing so leads to substantial improvements in terms of patient value. The existing outcome measurement efforts, even though imperfect, have reduced mortality and improved other outcomes, benefited clinical decision making, and motivated major process improvements. The improvement in patient value has been enormous, and reveals the potential for results measurement systemwide.

The cases described in the following box begin to define the parameters of an effective outcome reporting system. Outcome measures need to be defined in a rigorous process, and improved and expanded over time with expert input. Reporting needs to be universal, mandatory, and unblinded. Outcome information should be risk adjusted, and risk adjustment methods

How Good Outcome Information Arose

Pediatric Oncology

In the 1960s, childhood cancer was nearly always fatal within five years. Today, the five-year survival rate is over 75 percent and has improved by 20 percent in boys and 13 percent in girls over the past twenty years.[55] The improvement is remarkable in its own right, but also relative to adult cancer, where results have improved but not nearly as much.

In pediatric oncology, the tragedy of young children suffering and dying created a sense of urgency and a sense of community to improve treatments. Physicians in this relatively small field developed a strong commitment to refer patients only to academically based cancer centers that were actively researching the relationship between the treatment process and outcomes. As a result, the vast majority of pediatric oncology patients are treated under research protocols tracked by clinical trials, unlike adult cancer patients.

Outcome data in pediatric oncology is compared by protocol, not by center or provider. The unstated assumption in this approach is that use of the most successful known treatment protocol is the best way to produce excellent care. Pediatric oncology reveals the substantial potential of disseminating best practices to improve outcomes. This approach to practice improvement in pediatric oncology has benefited from a relatively small community of physicians with good communication and a culture of mutual support.

Complying with process guidelines, however, is not the same as competing on results. The implementation of a specific protocol is never exactly the same from physician to physician, even if it is a successful one. In pediatric oncology, differences among providers have not been a focus of analysis. Nor is provider outcome data readily available to the parents of patients or referring physicians; rather, blinded data is collected and used solely for comparing treatment protocols in clinical trials.

Patient value could improve even further in pediatric oncology if comprehensive outcome information was collected and disseminated. Such data, at the physician and center level, would allow even faster process improvement for physicians and allow referring doctors and parents to make even better decisions. This case also highlights the need for systematic patient registries rather than relying on patient data assembled in a series of clinical trials, each focusing solely on a small number of variables. Comprehensive data collection would enable faster innovation by improving statistical power and allowing researchers to examine more aspects of care.

(continued)

Cystic Fibrosis

The impetus for outcome data collection on cystic fibrosis came from the Cystic Fibrosis Foundation, founded in 1955.[56] In the early 1960s, Dr. Leroy Matthews at Rainbow Babies and Children's Hospital in Cleveland reported the amazing statistic that he and his colleagues were witnessing mortality rates of less than 2 percent per year, compared to a U.S. average of more than 25 percent per year. In 1964, in part to test Dr. Matthews's claims, the Cystic Fibrosis Foundation awarded Dr. Warren Warwick a $10,000 budget to collect information on all the patients treated at the thirty-one cystic fibrosis centers in the United States. The data backed Dr. Matthews's claims, and his pioneering preventive approach became the gold standard for cystic fibrosis treatment.

Cystic fibrosis outcome data, unlike the case in pediatric oncology, is collected and assembled center by center. The unstated assumption here is that the best way to improve value is not just to focus on protocols but to learn from the methods of the best centers. However, as in pediatric oncology, the data is blinded for individual centers. Physicians know their own results and how their patients fared relative to the national distribution, but cannot compare themselves to specific other centers.

The cystic fibrosis data has supported rapid improvements in the expected lifespan of cystic fibrosis patients, from ten years in 1966 to eighteen years in 1972 and thirty-three years in 2003.[57] Yet patients treated at the best-performing centers continue to live significantly longer than even the rising national average. In 2003, the expected lifespan of a cystic fibrosis patient at the best clinics was forty-seven years versus the average center's thirty-three years.[58]

Outcome reporting in cystic fibrosis centers has been, and continues to be, voluntary.[59] The Foundation encourages reporting by making research grants to each clinic proportional to the number of its patients in the registry. The grants range from $25,000 to $200,000, averaging approximately $75,000. All participating cystic fibrosis centers are required to follow Institutional Review Board processes at their institutions and obtain explicit patient consent to submit patient data to the registry. The Cystic Fibrosis Foundation estimates that the patient registry contains data on 93 percent of patients.[60]

As beneficial as the data has been, competition on results in cystic fibrosis is not yet fully enabled. Neither cystic fibrosis care centers nor their patients and referring physicians have access to unblinded center-by-center outcomes. Doctors would learn faster, and patient choice would benefit, if unblinded data allowed identification and learning from the best-performing centers.

Kidney Dialysis

In the1970s, kidney dialysis technology had been developed, but the procedure was so costly that it was inaccessible to all but a few patients. The American Association of Kidney Patients brought national attention to the fact that patients with end stage renal disease (ESRD) could lead near-normal lives with dialysis, but would die without it. In response to public concern, Congress passed the End Stage Renal Disease Act in 1972, making all ESRD patients eligible for Medicare coverage before age sixty-five.

In 1978, Medicare organized the oversight of ESRD care into eighteen regional administrative networks.[61] The networks are financed by a fee of 50 cents per dialysis treatment, deducted from the reimbursement. The U.S. Renal Data System (USRDS) was established in 1988 to collect, analyze, and disseminate data about ESRD outcomes to foster research and to monitor quality.[62,63]

Initially, few dialysis providers regularly measured even the filtration rate, which is the most direct outcome of dialysis. Since 1994, when the first comprehensive clinical ESRD database was in place, virtually all facilities began to measure and report outcomes because it became a requirement for Medicare reimbursement. Unlike the cases of pediatric oncology and cystic fibrosis, comparative data on dialysis facilities is unblinded and public. Patients and referring doctors can look at anemia, hemoglobin, and mortality results for all providers in the United States except the Veterans Administration hospitals (which are not reimbursed via Medicare).[64] Medical review boards of each regional ESRD network examine results[65] and intervene with coaching when the outcomes of a dialysis facility fall below accepted guidelines or when providers request help.[66]

While outcome data reporting is mandatory, the current data reported by the ESRD networks is restricted to a sample of 5 percent of all patients measured for the period from October to December of each year. The absence of electronic reporting has, until recently, made the reporting of data on all patients impractical.

As in the other medical conditions where outcome data has been collected, the results data have made a significant impact on the quality of dialysis care. Between the first collection efforts in 1989 and 1997, a 17 percent decline in mortality for dialysis patients was recorded.[67] The results data have also revealed that attention to quality is crucial for cost reduction; when providers fail to follow accepted processes of care, increased spending often does not improve outcomes.[68]

The dialysis data still reveal large differences in outcomes across providers. Improved risk adjustment as well as reporting for all patients will help drive further improvements. The data has also supported clinical research with potential major implications. For example, dialysis outcomes are clearly affected by care in earlier-stage renal disease. Kidney disease is a striking case of the importance of disease management and care-cycle thinking.

(continued)

Intensive Care

The genesis of a system to monitor and evaluate the risk-adjusted outcomes of intensive care grew out of the belief of William Knaus, an intensive care unit (ICU) physician at George Washington University Hospital, that the quality of clinical decisions and confidence in their outcomes would never be better than the quality of the information supporting decisions. In 1978, Dr. Knaus and his colleagues began work on an information system to support quality improvement by analyzing the relationships among outcomes, patient physiology, and processes of care. The Acute Physiology and Chronic Health Evaluation (APACHE) system analyzes patient data to rate the severity of acute illnesses and probabilistically predict outcomes.[69] An ICU team can compare its actual outcomes to the risk-adjusted predicted outcomes to see whether its outcomes are better or worse than a large body of actual data on clinical practice would suggest.

APACHE became a widely used methodology for driving process improvement in ICUs. One of the early studies applied APACHE predictions to 5,030 patients at thirteen hospitals and found that patient outcomes, controlling for risk, were related to differences in the coordination of care, including the degree of communication and the effort devoted to quality control in the medical, surgical, and nursing staffs.[70] Despite APACHE's ability to support process improvement, however, funding for outcome modeling was scarce, and the team was unable to raise enough funds from grants and philanthropic sources to sustain continued development. In 1988 a company was formed to raise venture capital to support additional research and development. (APACHE Medical Systems Inc. was ultimately acquired by Cerner Corporation in 2001.)

APACHE has been continuously improved, releasing versions III and IV. Case studies have documented significant results improvements and process enhancements at hospitals using the system, such as Sarasota Memorial Hospital in Florida and St. Mary's Medical Center in West Virginia.[71] Rather than embracing the learning generated by APACHE, however, some members of the medical community have resisted modifying methods until expensive and time-consuming clinical trials were conducted to document each specific aspect of process improvement revealed by outcome analysis.[72] Discomfort with the use of risk-adjusted outcome data has been due in part to aversion by physicians to being assessed, and in part because the education of physicians has not included outcome evaluation.

The Mayo Clinic, which has used APACHE for over a decade, has demonstrated how a clinically robust measure of outcomes can reveal variations in results that are associated with specific clinical and administrative processes. With data from 50,000 of its ICU patients, Mayo investigators found that its

ICU discharge policies were resulting in higher than predicted hospital mortality rates. Mayo is working to improve them.[73]

APACHE is now used in hundreds of ICUs for internal process improvement and is the basis of over 5,000 medical research articles.[74] Hospitals that use the system can compare their outcomes for ICU patients to the expected outcomes for patients with similar severity of illness.

APACHE uses outcome measures in modeling, but is not a system for outcome reporting. In spite of the existence of well-vetted risk-adjusted outcome measures, public reporting of ICU results is not required. Thus, no center-by-center comparisons of ICU outcomes are yet available. APACHE outcome measures have been endorsed by the Joint Commission on Accreditation of Healthcare Organizations (JCAHO). Disappointingly, however, JCAHO uses only process measures for ICU accreditation.[75]

If ICU outcome reporting were mandated by Congress, by states, or by Medicare, process innovation and patient value in ICU care would almost certainly improve markedly.[76] In this case, providers' fear of accountability for results has continued to trump the greater good of driving dramatic and widespread value improvement.

Cardiac Surgery

Cardiac surgeons pioneered the development and use of outcome measures more than three decades ago. In 1972, the Veterans Administration, facing concerns over quality, established the first multihospital database for monitoring outcomes for cardiac surgery, beginning with volume of procedures and unadjusted operative mortality.[77] By 1986, with growing public attention to the safety of cardiac surgery, the Health Care Financing Administration (HCFA, the predecessor to the Centers for Medicare and Medicaid Services) began publishing mortality data for cardiac surgery based on administrative data. The Society of Thoracic Surgeons (STS), uncomfortable with the HCFA methodology, began developing its own risk-adjusted outcome measures using clinical data sources. By 1989, STS had developed measures and began collecting voluntary adult cardiac surgery data and compiled a national risk-adjusted database.[78] As we have discussed, there is no better way to motivate improvement in results measures than to start publishing what is currently available.

Facing the same public concerns, the New York Department of Health in 1989 required that the hospitals performing coronary artery bypass graft (CABG) procedures report outcome measures and risk information from patient records.[79] Measures and risk adjustments were designed by a group of cardiothoracic surgical experts, but independently of STS. The program, which continues today, reports risk-adjusted mortality rates of CABG procedures by

(continued)

hospital and by surgeon to the general public. In the first four years of New York's reporting program, deaths from cardiac surgery fell by 41 percent.[80] The New York experience was replicated in a number of other states, such as New Jersey, Pennsylvania, and California,[81] which now collect and publish risk-adjusted cardiac surgery data.[82]

STS has expanded its program to include as many as 200 data points per patient.[83] The sophistication of risk adjustment methods has improved and is widely accepted as the most advanced outcome measurement in health care. STS is also tracking an increasing array of other surgeries. Individual surgeon and hospital STS data is blinded to other surgeons, and only national averages are available to patients and referring doctors. Some providers, such as the Cleveland Clinic, publish their outcomes with comparisons to the national outcomes (see appendix A).

All these experiences in cardiac surgery provide compelling support for the principle that feedback and comparison of risk-adjusted results heighten awareness, self-assessment, analysis of processes, and improvement of outcomes for patients.[84] STS data, as with the other outcome measurement efforts, documents significant improvements in surgical outcomes in cardiac surgery despite the worsening risk profile of surgery patients.[85] In addition to the use of the data in numerous peer-reviewed studies,[86] practice innovations are showcased at professional conferences with demonstrations to enable learning for practicing surgeons.[87] Studies document that the evidence-based nationwide communication about ways to improve clinical processes in heart surgery has lowered national mortality levels.[88] These experiences also point to the power of public reporting to drive improvement measurement beyond that which public reporting requires.

Medical societies can play a fundamental role in results measurement and reporting, a role that most societies have abdicated. (See the box "Implications for Medical Societies" in chapter 8.) The STS has not only improved its own measures but worked to improve public reporting. For example, STS members worked with the National Quality Forum (NQF) to create a consensus set of cardiac surgery process and outcome measures, announced in December 2004.[89] While the NQF measures are available to be used by JCAHO, Medicare, and other accrediting or reporting bodies, there is as yet no national collection and reporting.

The next step envisioned by STS is to include cost as well as outcome data to enable the measurement of value. Efforts are currently under way to link the STS National Database data with Medicare Part A payment data. The preliminary results of this effort provide further confirmation that the highest-quality providers frequently incur the lowest costs.[90]

Participation in the STS database remains voluntary. However, starting in the 1990s a number of health plans, including several Blue Cross Blue Shield affiliates, made participation in the database a criterion for being included in their preferred provider list.[91]

Organ Transplants

Government intervention in organ transplants was motivated by public outcry over the fairness of organ allocation and concerns about organs donated in the United States that were going to foreign patients. In 1984, Congress passed the National Organ Transplant Act establishing the Organ Procurement and Transplantation Network. The Network is operated under federal contract by the United Network of Organ Sharing (UNOS), a nonprofit organization. Providers of any type of transplant wanting to receive an organ must report data, so reporting is effectively mandatory.

The data is national and complete, and goes beyond the sum of individual institutions' reports. The database reveals if a patient has a re-transplant at another institution, even if the original center is not aware of the repeat surgery. UNOS also uses the Social Security death database to track long-term mortality, even if providers lack this information.[92] The registry of transplant data now contains information on over 317,000 transplant recipients. UNOS is not only responsible for data collection but also makes recommendations to the Department of Health and Human Services about policies for how organs should be allocated to patients on the waiting list. Thus, statistical data on transplant outcomes affects allocation rules.

The transplant outcome data is publicly available on the Web.[93] It is sorted by organ type, and whether the patient is adult or pediatric. Results are reported for each transplant center by name. In addition to reporting the raw data on the survival of the patient (at one month, one year, and three years) and the survival of the graft (organ), the results are risk adjusted based on a model that is regularly updated using statistical analysis of the national data. For each transplant center, expected survival rates are calculated given the risk factors of the patients treated. That expected rate is compared to the actual rate, and calculations are performed to determine if the difference is statistically significant. The data are presented in clear and well-annotated charts.

Nonetheless, patients need help with interpreting the results in this complex condition. Also, not all referring doctors utilize the data yet. Transplant surgery teams, however, are very aware of their own results and their comparison with other centers. Performance in transplants has continued to improve, while better results have led to successful transplants in sicker patients.

(continued)

This consistent, national, unblinded data is a crucial tool not only for providers and patients, but also for health plans, researchers, and health information services. For example, as we discuss in Chapter 6, services are now available to support patients and referring doctors in making results-based choices about transplant providers. More patients are being treated by excellent providers, who often are willing to negotiate lower prices.

improved over time through expert input. Data needs to be made public in a form that is accessible. Cost data must be integrated eventually. Such an ideal results management system is a tall order, but transplant outcome data is already approaching this ideal. To reach a high standard of outcome measurement quickly in many medical conditions may well require independent, not-for-profit organizations (such as UNOS in transplants) to develop and implement reporting and analysis. Oversight of all of these organizations could be assigned to the Department of Health and Human Services (which oversees UNOS) or to a respected, quasi-public organization such as the Institute of Medicine. We explore these options further in chapter 8.

To date, the development and use of outcome measures has progressed far too slowly. For example, the APACHE system of risk-adjusted outcome measures for intensive care (discussed in the preceding box, "How Good Outcome Information Arose") was developed twenty-five years ago, continually improved, and validated by numerous reviews and use by prestigious providers such as the Mayo Clinic. Yet there is still resistance and foot dragging to reporting APACHE measures broadly. The Joint Commission on Accreditation of Healthcare Organizations (JCAHO) undertook a pilot project to include ICU outcome measures in accreditation. In July 2005, however, JCAHO backtracked and replaced the outcome measures with process measures.[94] JCAHO has been slow to utilize outcome measures for accreditation not because the methodology is problematic, but because providers have resisted it. An accreditation organization strongly influenced by those being measured may not be the best vehicle for driving results measurement versus much less threatening process compliance.

Similarly, despite the good intentions of the National Quality Forum (NQF) to move beyond process to outcome measures, vested interests have delayed the development of specific measures and risk adjustments. Vested interests have also slowed the widespread implementation of existing outcome measures.[95] NQF's consensus model may not be up to the task of overcoming resistance to outcome measurement and accountability.

Providers seem to fear, to put the best face on this resistance, that the collection and dissemination of outcome data will be simplistic and unfair. Providers, including individual physicians, are understandably wary about making results measures public, pointing to problems with the accuracy of measures and the appropriateness of risk adjustment methodologies. Poorly adjusted data can create incentives for doctors to turn away the sickest patients. But the medical community is far too sophisticated to be thwarted by such obstacles. Clinging to such reasoning to avoid collecting and publishing any results information is no longer acceptable, especially in the face of the successes already achieved.

A system of checks and balances is necessary in outcome measurement and reporting, and has characterized all the efforts described in the preceding box ("How Good Outcome Information Arose"), which reveal important principles for future efforts. There needs to be an array of measures to capture the multidimensionality of outcomes. Providers and medical societies need to participate in defining measures. Providers must be able to check and correct the accuracy of data before (and after) it is published. When reports appear accurate but counterintuitive, expert judgment must be applied to determine if the problem rests in measurement biases. The sophistication of measurements will inevitably improve with time, and measures will be refined. Nothing will speed the development of new outcome measures and improvements in existing measures more than the widespread dissemination of the data already available.

To be fair, health plans, not just providers, must bear some of the responsibility for the slow pace of development in outcome and price measurement. Health plans have expressed fears that the collection and utilization of outcome data will give excellent providers too much bargaining power to raise prices. Health plans also fear that members will use outcome data to demand more care and more expensive care. These fears are a manifestation of the zero-sum mentality that has consumed health plans. As health plans shift their focus to value, they will learn that excellent providers will often be less costly because quality and efficiency often improve simultaneously, as we have discussed. Health plans will also need to trust their members and inform them. Empirical evidence shows that *informed* patients tend to choose less invasive, less expensive care and achieve better outcomes, as we discussed in chapter 2.[96] Results measurement, then, is not something to be resisted but a core role for health plans, as we discuss in chapter 6.

Comprehensive results measurement can and must become available in every medical condition. Huge value improvement will occur as all system participants come to expect and use such information. The universal development and reporting of results information at the medical condition level may well be the single highest priority to improve the performance of the health care system. The nation can no longer afford to wait for "perfect" outcome or price data. Even imperfect data are better than no data, because they will spur learning and improvement. We return to a strategy for developing results information in chapter 8.

Collecting and Disseminating Results Information in Practice

Experience makes it clear that just collecting outcome data is not enough. Information must also be broadly disseminated and, ultimately, acted upon. One of the early efforts at results measurement, a pioneering initiative by Cleveland Health Quality Choice (CHQC), verifies the power of information but reveals the practical challenge of collecting and disseminating it.[97] CHQC, created by Cleveland's leading corporations, asked hospitals for substantial amounts of outcome information twice a year and then published reports showing death rates (adjusted for patient risk factors such as age and degree of illness) for a range of illnesses, together with patient-satisfaction ratings. The information was made public with a delay, and was covered in the local newspapers.[98] With so many employers in the program, Cleveland hospitals had little choice but to cooperate by providing data. After seeing the comparisons, hospitals revised their diagnostic and treatment practices to improve their results. In 1997, in-hospital death rates at thirty Cleveland hospitals were down 11 percent from the time that CHQC's efforts began in 1993.[99] This alone represents a substantial value improvement.

However, both employers and their health plan administrators, who now had highly relevant information, failed to act on it. The flow of patients was not altered, and provider contracts were not modified in any way to reward excellent providers and penalize lagging ones. As we discuss in chapter 6, neither health plans nor employers saw the selection of excellent providers as a way to add value, nor did they have the mind-set of rewarding excellent providers with more patients. Patients, without assistance and advice, remained largely unaware of the information.

As a result, neither the hospitals with better-than-expected results nor the hospitals with worse-than-predicted results felt any significant impact in terms of employer or patient decisions.[100] In addition, some leading hospitals questioned measures that cast them in an unfavorable light or failed to show them to be as superior to other hospitals as public perception had assumed. Since information reporting was not mandatory, and since there was no mechanism to improve the measures over time, the effort was vulnerable. By 2000, the leading hospitals, perceiving little benefit to cooperating, refused to provide the information, and the data collection ended. This promising but truncated experiment makes it clear that other system participants must be aware of and be motivated to act on results information if it is to achieve its full benefit.

Another pioneering and instructive effort to disseminate results information is the program by New York State to collect and publish statewide information about outcomes of coronary artery bypass graft (CABG) surgery. (This effort is described in the box "How Good Outcome Information Arose.") In this experiment, as in the Cleveland case, hospitals were acutely aware of the data, and overall outcomes improved dramatically throughout the state.[101] After the first four years of published data, New York had the lowest mortality rate following CABG surgery in the nation and one of the fastest rates of improvement.[102] Critics argued that much of the improvement came from discontinuing the privileges of certain surgeons who had low volume and high mortality rates, and from referring difficult patients out of state to nearby specialty providers such as the Cleveland Clinic. But these steps are exactly what patients (and society) should want to happen! Researchers have refuted the claim by some skeptics that hospitals refused to treat difficult patients.[103] But even if they had, patient outcomes will improve if complex patients are referred to more specialized providers.

In the New York case, dissemination and use of the information outside of providers was again limited. Tragically, patients and referring doctors again continued to use hospitals with the worst risk-adjusted outcomes. Some critics have seized upon this phenomenon to argue that the data did not have the desired impact. But the improvements by providers were clearly significant. Also, the data were not widely known to patients. At the same time there were health plan and other restrictions on choice of providers, and health plans and physicians failed to utilize the information to counsel patient choices. In short, competition in the system was not based on results.

Just developing measures is not enough. Even participating in clinical trials is not enough. Open dissemination of outcomes is also necessary to accelerate improvement in patient value. The case of cystic fibrosis (see the box "How Good Outcome Information Arose") illustrates the benefits of openness. Cystic fibrosis outcome data were collected on a blinded basis, with individual providers disguised. The data revealed enormous variations in outcomes, and pride and professional responsibility motivated providers to improve. Because of anonymity, however, it took a special agreement to allow the identities of the top performers to be revealed to allow best practices to be studied.

However, even dissemination just to physicians is not enough. In cystic fibrosis and pediatric oncology, the results of specific providers remain mostly unavailable to patients and their families. This dampens the sense of urgency to demonstrate good results and to improve them. The case of cystic fibrosis reveals that patients will not abandon providers who share even mediocre data while demonstrating a clear commitment to improve. The Institute for Healthcare Improvement made grants available to cystic fibrosis providers to fund process improvement, but on the condition that they would share their results data openly with the parents of patients. Cincinnati Children's Hospital decided to reveal its average and below-average results to parents while pledging to get better. in spite of the fears of Cincinnati's physicians, not a single family left the practice. Parents, who believed in the unit's integrity and commitment to learning, explained that they would go elsewhere only if results did not improve.[104]

Experience shows that patients are responsive to data presented in an accessible form and interpreted by a trusted adviser.[105] Patients tend to trust their own physicians, who may themselves be unaware of outcome evidence. In organ transplants, for example, referring physicians are sometimes still in the dark about the comprehensive results data available, sending patients to a substandard local provider unless an intermediary calls and explains that the patient has coverage at a medical center with more experience and better risk-adjusted outcomes. Independent health advisers who work with both patients and physicians are beginning to play the role of advising patients; they are employed by health plans and specialized information services. Over time, as more results information becomes available, health plans will treat advising patients and their physicians about results information as a core role, as we discuss in chapter 6. Physicians who fail to embrace and utilize results information will eventually begin to lose patients.

The benefits of better information and advice, coupled with the right kind of competition, will be striking. Even given the current state of information, value improvement opportunities are substantial. Companies such as Honeywell, for example, have added services to assist their employees in obtaining specific medical information when they need it. Honeywell estimates that it has cut more than $2 of health care expenditures for every $1 it spent on a program that enabled employees to call a medical information company, Consumer's Medical Resource, for up-to-date, practical information on forty specific diseases. The information helps employees learn which treatments and drugs are most effective. Even though no provider results information was included, the benefits were substantial. Of the Honeywell employees who used the service, one in thirty discovered they were misdiagnosed; one in ten discontinued a treatment considered unnecessary, ineffective, or unproven; and one in five changed doctors.[106]

Independent information services companies have been emerging to meet the pressing need for information and advice to improve results in the current system. For example, Best Doctors (U.S.) offers a service for subscribers that enables those with an unclear diagnosis or complex situation to have their records reviewed by a carefully chosen group of expert physicians from around the country. In situations that are complicated and have proven mysterious to the local physicians, reaching an accurate diagnosis can dramatically improve the effectiveness and efficiency of care. Another independent patient organization operating in Europe and the Middle East, Preferred Global Health (PGH), also helps its members diagnosed with critical illnesses achieve significant improvements in outcomes by providing medical information and directing patients to the best centers of medical excellence in the United States, while offering financial protection. PGH has been able to identify world-class providers even with the rudimentary information that is currently available, beginning with a hospital's focus on particular conditions or diseases and its cumulative volume of patients and experience with the most advanced treatment. The patient benefits have been substantial.

Over time, as comprehensive results information becomes available, such services will become commonplace, and provided by every health plan. Someday, using results information to support choices will become routine. For most patients, there will always be roles for their doctor, health plan, and potentially an independent medical adviser in helping them understand and weigh their choices.

As all the parties become aware of the power of making medical decisions based on results, providers will improve value much more rapidly. Providers will forge relationships with leading centers to improve the accuracy of their diagnoses and the outcomes of treatment. Where significant differences in risk-adjusted results persist, patients will migrate to the better providers. Over time, those providers with excellent results will see their demand rise significantly. Those with poor outcomes will be highly motivated to improve their relative standing.

The current model for addressing the information problem in U.S. health care is to mount many public and private experiments in the hopes that a solution will emerge. A variety of efforts are under way, as we have discussed. For example, the National Quality Forum was established in 1999 with the explicit goal of improving American health care by enabling public reporting of medical performance data. With a distinguished board, the NQF has become an important body endorsing information standards and process measures, which Medicare is beginning to utilize. NQF is also beginning to move beyond methods and include some mortality outcome measures in its set of consensus measures. However, NQF's consensus-based approach has its disadvantages in terms of pace and avoidance of the tendency to move to the lowest common denominator. Also, there is no mechanism to ensure that NQF's consensus measures are actually used.

Given the stakes, the United States needs to move beyond an incremental approach. The focus needs to be on results, not process compliance. Mandatory reporting of outcome information by medical condition on a state and national scale will be necessary to truly transform the value delivered in health care. The process needs to start with existing measures of risk-adjusted outcomes, and broaden over time. We discuss a strategy for defining and disseminating results information at the medical condition level on a national basis in chapter 8.

Innovations That Increase Value Are Strongly Rewarded

Value-based competition on results will not only lead to more patients being cared for by excellent providers, but also inspire and drive innovation in medical care. Innovation, broadly defined as new methods, new facilities, new organizational structures, new processes, and new forms of collaboration across providers, is fundamental to value improvement in health care. Innovation is the only way the U.S. health care system can address the needs of an aging population without rationing services or experiencing huge cost increases.[107] Innovation will reduce the costs of medical care far faster than the current efforts to control medical practice.

The importance of innovation in health care is no different from its role in other industries. In other industries, firms prosper if they innovate, and fail if they stick to old approaches. In health care, however, innovation has often been discretionary and hit or miss because superior value is not measured and rewarded. What is worse, innovation is sometimes viewed with suspicion and even resisted by providers, health plans, employers, and the government, partly grounded in the problem of oversupply of care. When expensive new technologies are adopted and used with the hope of benefiting patients but without compelling evidence of value creation, technology gets blamed as a problem for health care, not a solution.[108]

The skepticism about innovation is not supported by the data in many areas of medicine. For example, estimates suggest that investments in health care innovation over the past twenty years in four areas of care (heart attack, type 2 diabetes, stroke, and breast cancer) have returned from $2.40 to $3.00 for every dollar invested.[109] This is illustrated by a succession of new treatments for acute myocardial infarction (heart attacks), which have improved results and reduced mortality rates. At the same time, lengths of stay in intensive care and in the hospital have been reduced, thereby reducing costs (see figure 4-6).

Advances in medical technologies are often viewed as driving up costs because medical advances increase capabilities.[110] Even curing diseases is

FIGURE 4-6

Effects of innovation in treatment of acute myocardial infarction (AMI)

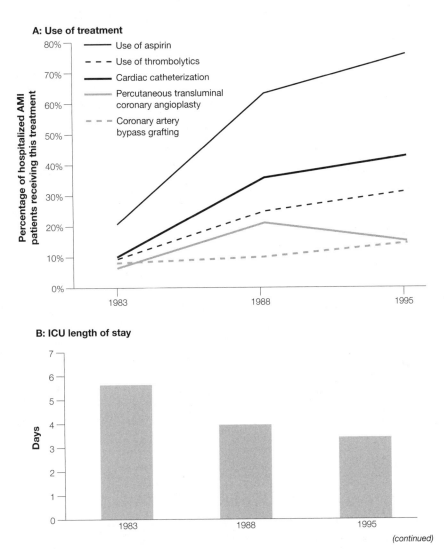

A: Use of treatment

B: ICU length of stay

(continued)

sometimes assumed to raise costs because some researchers have asserted that individuals will only become sick with something more expensive later in life. In the extreme, such an argument boils down to saying that the cheapest patient is a dead patient.

It is nonsensical to argue that disease-curing innovations do not lower costs and increase value. That stance confuses value creation in the treatment of a medical condition with the costs of treating other conditions in

FIGURE 4-6 *(continued)*

Effects of innovation in treatment of acute myocardial infarction (AMI)

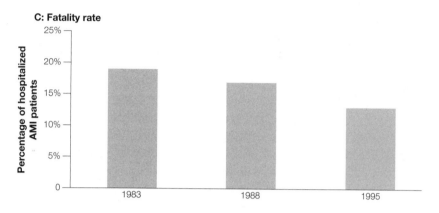

C: Fatality rate

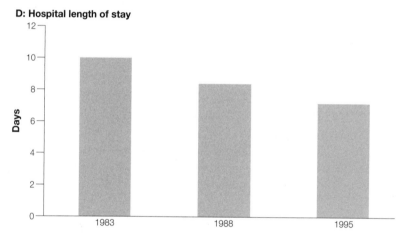

D: Hospital length of stay

Source: Data from Heindenreich and McClellan (2001).

the future. It ignores the productive contributions of more healthy individuals, including the revenues they contribute through premiums to the health insurance system, and the value (including less need for care) of a better quality of life for patients. Also, a substantial portion of health care costs occur earlier in life, so a patient may have decades of good health before succumbing to a different disease.

Contrary to conventional wisdom that assumes that end-of-life health care spending increases with age, research reveals that that Medicare costs in the last two years of life are *lower* for persons dying at later ages.[111] This is true in part because individuals who live longer lives tend to have experienced fewer chronic diseases that add cost and complexity.[112] It is also due to the preferences of many older individuals for noninvasive end-of-life care.[113]

An estimated 70 to 75 percent of the nation's health care spending goes to treating chronic conditions (diseases that are not cured), such as heart disease, arthritis, cancer, diabetes, ulcers, AIDS, birth defects, schizophrenia, and depression, that occur at many ages.[114] Clearly, medical innovations that prevent, cure, or minimize the effects of chronic conditions will make dramatic improvements in quality of life while significantly reducing the lifetime health care costs of the affected patients. Similarly, advances in disease management for chronic conditions promise to improve quality of life and decrease costs. In short, the assumption that innovation in medicine *must* drive up costs is wrong and needs to be abandoned.

Innovation is not the problem; rather, it is the lack of competition on results. The issue is not whether new tests or technologies should be developed, but that doctors need results data to know whether and how to use them to improve value. Also, the trajectory of innovation has been skewed by the incentives in the current system for drugs and devices. Huge opportunities to improve the organization, methods, facilities, and coordination in care delivery have just begun.

Innovation and the Nature of Competition

The right kind of competition, enabled by results information, will unleash rapid innovation and lead to dramatic improvements in value. Value-based competition will dramatically speed up the rate of adoption of new methods and technologies, making innovations even more valuable. Even when an innovation leads to increased total spending, value-based competition will ensure that society will get its money's worth.[115]

Innovations in health care take many forms, including advances in technology and equipment. However, as we have noted, we believe that some of the greatest opportunities lie in new types of strategies, organizational structures, facilities, processes, and partnerships. Some innovations are easier to adopt because they yield better quality and lower cost right from the start. For example, new antibiotics that reduce dosing requirements from every three or four hours to once in twenty-four hours lower nursing costs and allow some patients to be discharged from the hospital and receive outpatient care. New, minimally invasive surgery, such as laparoscopic surgery, reduces both costs and recovery time.

Other innovations involve extra costs, but increase value by reducing the need for expensive services elsewhere in the care cycle. For example, administering thrombolytic drugs after a heart attack increases drug costs but lowers the rate of re-hospitalization for follow-on heart attacks, yielding clear net savings. Some drugs actually save more (in averted hospital care, for example) than they cost to administer, such as long-term anti-coagulant therapy for lung cancer patients with acute deep venous thrombosis. Many other drugs, while not immediately saving money, are cost-effective in providing care-cycle benefits far exceeding their costs.[116]

However, some medical innovations, especially new drugs or devices, begin as more expensive approaches that allow patients to live with a disease rather than die or be debilitated by it.[117] For example, cataracts once left people blind. When cataract surgery was first developed, it was dangerous, improved vision only marginally, and required up to a week's hospital stay. However, a technology is refined over time. Today, cataract surgery is a painless outpatient procedure that restores near-normal sight, and patients simultaneously get nearsightedness or farsightedness corrected. The current surgery achieves better quality at lower costs, but this was possible only after a period of learning (see figure 4-7).

FIGURE 4-7

Improvements in cataract surgery costs and outcomes, 1947–1998

Year	Procedure	Inpatient nights	Surgeon*
1947	Extracapsular extraction	7	N/A
1952	Intracapsular extraction by freezing and/or suction	7	N/A
1969	Intracapsular extraction; routine use of operating microscope	3	1
1972	Controlled extracapsular extraction with phacoemulsification	1	1
1979	Intracapsular and extracapsular extraction; inserting intraocular lens in increasing use	1 or outpatient	1
1985	Extracapsular extraction with intraocular lens	Outpatient	0.8
1994	Extracapsular extraction with intraocular lens developed for small incisions	Outpatient	0.7
1998	Extracapsular extraction and inserting intraocular lens Quicker operations allow reduced anesthesia Multifocal intraocular lens becoming more common	Outpatient	0.5

*Units normalized with the surgeon fee in dollar terms equal to the cost of spending one night in the hospital
N/A: not available.

Source: Shapiro, I., M. Shapiro, and D. Wilcox, "Measuring the Value of Cataract Surgery." In *Medical Care Output and Productivity*, edited by D. Cutler and E. R. Berndt, Universit of Chicago Press, 2001. Data used with permission from University of Chicago Press.

Another pattern in health care innovation is the evolution of care upstream in the causal chain, which we spoke of earlier. Ulcers, for example, once required surgery. Later, the acid production that triggered the ulcer was treated. Today the bacterial cause of ulcers can be cured with antibiotics.

Whatever the trajectory of innovation, innovation in health care often experiences another cycle that has confused some observers. As improvements in care occur, demand for care can grow as more patients can benefit. Costs can actually go up even if the value of care for each patient improves dramatically, especially if costs are measured in the short run versus taking a life-cycle perspective. Eventually, though, further improvements will lower costs and overall spending.

Shifting the nature of competition, as we have outlined in this chapter, will dramatically speed the trajectory of innovation in health care. As we noted in chapter 2, innovation is discouraged in the current system by a wide variety of factors, including lack of accountability, reimbursement practices that penalize better methods, buying group structures focused on short-term costs savings, and rationing mind-sets. There may be a role for a government or philanthropic fund to encourage the adoption and deployment of initially higher-cost new procedures and treatments, at least during a transitional period, as we discuss in chapter 8.

A New Innovation Model

While innovation has produced major improvements in health care delivery, the current model is too narrow. The current approach is focused heavily on drugs and medical devices, and centered around carefully designed clinical trials that often cost $10,000 or more per trial patient. The United States spends by far the most on this kind of research of any nation in the world, funded by the National Institutes of Health, other research sponsors, and drug and device companies. Trials are complex, time-consuming, and appropriately dedicated to using methodologies that prevent biases. Trials involve relatively small patient populations that are laboriously enrolled and willing to be randomly assigned to a treatment or control group. Patients are screened to minimize statistical variations. A limited number of results measures are normally explored, with the focus on a single endpoint, even though results are inevitably multidimensional. Rarely if ever are trials concerned with cost. The aim is to isolate the effects of a particular treatment or therapy rather than to assess the value of the overall care delivery process. Often years of time and effort go into challenging and validating seemingly straightforward findings.[118]

Clinical trials must continue, and this model of innovation needs to be improved upon. In particular, much greater attention needs to be directed at isolating which particular patients benefit from drugs or therapies, as we discuss in chapter 7. One of the major causes of waste in the system is therapies that benefit only a fraction of patients, but for which the particular patients that will benefit are known only after the fact. Multiple therapies are attempted and fail until one works.

Another high priority for clinical investigation is longer-term studies covering the full care cycle to get at longer-term outcomes, including total costs of care. These sorts of investigations will be essential in measuring the true value of alternative therapies. We discuss this issue further in chapter 7.

Trials would also be greatly improved by better understanding of biomarkers of the progression of disease, which has been slow to develop.[119] In addition, risk-adjusted outcome data could be used to simulate human testing of a new molecule before designing the actual trial, to target the trial more effectively and reduce its costs.[120]

While the clinical trial model is important, a second innovation model is also necessary and of potentially equal, if not greater, significance in value terms. Studies using risk-adjusted results data and focused on detailed examination of the organization and processes of care delivery can make a huge contribution to patient value. Many improvements with a major impact on patient results are relatively simple changes in procedures or approaches, not tied to a particular drug or device per se. In ICU care, for example, mortality is reduced significantly with the use of lower volumes of mechanical ventilation for patients with severe respiratory failure.[121] Also, tighter control of blood glucose, positioning of the head of the bed correctly to reduce the incidence of aspiration pneumonia, and the routine use of prophylaxis for deep venous thrombosis deliver major value benefits.[122]

Results-based studies can retrospectively investigate large populations of patients over extended periods of time and uncover practical ways to improve outcomes and efficiency. The best clinicians have always learned by looking for what is associated with good results, but there is the opportunity to make the process much more systematic and rigorous.

Risk-adjusted outcome measures enable researchers and clinicians to understand the effects of variations across institutions and treatments. Effectively, hundreds of thousands of natural experiments occur daily in U.S. hospitals and physician practices as medical teams deliver care, doing the best they can. The variations in patients' conditions, treatments, and outcomes can be analyzed for patterns that reveal the relative effectiveness of processes and therapies that are currently in use. And the outcomes can be considered granularly as multiple dimensions of results are considered. Unlike a prospective clinical trial, data can be reused to explore and test new insights. Indeed, evidence-based medicine, at its foundation, involves widespread gathering and reporting of risk-adjusted outcome data. With a standardized set of outcome measures in each area of practice, analysis can be done both within an institution and across institutions to rapidly advance the understanding of effective care.

Today, there is little funding for studies of this type, and their findings are resisted or belittled as data mining. Ironically, there is much greater acceptance of animal models, which often do not translate well to humans. The best providers use analysis of outcomes and processes to drive improvements in-house. But in professional publications, research on care delivery structure, organization, process, and measurement is vastly underrepresented despite its huge importance to value for patients.

As the widespread and mandatory reporting of results information expands, these kinds of studies should proliferate. Use of results data to improve patient care provides a path to avoiding the huge amounts of wasted effort, inappropriate treatment, and physician judgments inconsistent with systematic evidence that occur in today's system. Every provider should have a formal knowledge improvement program, as we discuss in chapter 5. Today, as we discuss in chapter 8, research on processes, quality, costs, outcomes, and patient safety comes under the Agency for Healthcare Research and Quality, which has a far smaller budget than the NIH. A significant proportion of overall federal health research funding, as well as funding from health plans, should be allocated to such research. The United States will earn a much higher return on its huge investment in medical research if care delivery structures and processes are greatly improved. It is care delivery methods at the medical condition level that translate new medical knowledge and technology into patient value, while also contributing to new knowledge.

The Opportunity of Value-Based Competition

The potential of value-based competition on results is evident in the numerous examples we have described and in the medical conditions where outcome information has been available. The promise of value-based competition is also evident in those parts of health care delivery that fall outside the normal structure. In areas such as cosmetic surgery, competition works much more like it does in other industries: it is focused on the level of particular medical conditions over the care cycle. Patients take responsibility for choice and pay the bills themselves. Doctors have to compete for patients by convincing them of the value of services offered, and are fully accountable for the patient's results. In this field, rapid advances have improved quality while significantly reducing costs (see figure 4-8). This example clearly illustrates that better medical

FIGURE 4-8

Price differential of traditional versus innovative cosmetic surgery, 2002

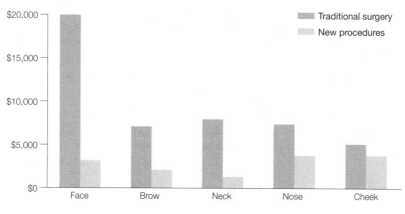

Source: Data from Parker-Pope (2002).

care is not necessarily more expensive than existing treatments. The case of cosmetic surgery, though it is neither mainstream nor without controversy in terms of patient benefit, is suggestive of the rate of progress that could be unleashed if the nature of health care competition changed.

If competition on results drove the pursuit of health care value for patients, the gains would be enormous. Huge gains are possible by reducing the variations in the value of care across geography and providers, reinforcing and rewarding excellent providers, and encouraging physician and consumer choices based on information and results. It is within the nation's capability to increase health care quality and lower cost dramatically, even using today's technologies and methods. The enormous savings that could be achieved would help pay for improved care for every American, especially those who lack access in the current system.

To reap these benefits, however, the nature of competition must change. Each constituent in the system must shift its roles, strategies, and policies. We turn to the steps required to do so in chapters 5 through 8.

5

Strategic Implications for Health Care Providers

PROVIDERS, INCLUDING HOSPITALS, clinics, physician groups, and individual physicians, are the central actors in the health care system and the place where most value is actually delivered. Other system participants—whether they are health plans, employers, suppliers, government, or patients themselves—can reinforce or detract from this value through their roles and choices. Ultimately, however, it is how medicine is practiced, and the way patients are cared for, that will determine the success or failure of the health care system.

Today, the strategies, organizational structures, and operating practices of many health care providers are misaligned with value, as revealed in the staggering array of evidence on poor performance and practice variations we presented in chapter 1. We believe that the problem is due less to shortcomings in technology than to weaknesses in how care delivery is structured and managed, although continued technological innovation is surely necessary.

Moving to positive-sum competition on results offers the only real way to address the long-standing weaknesses in health care delivery while also enhancing the entire system's ability to innovate. This chapter describes how providers can compete on value—a subject vast enough to fill an entire book by itself. We begin by framing the strategic challenges for providers in clarifying their goals and rethinking the service lines they will offer. We then describe eight strategic and organizational imperatives to compete on value, and show how an array of providers are addressing them. The consequences of these eight imperatives will be a different and far more productive industry structure than exists today. Providers that anticipate this new structure will be best positioned to take advantage of it.

Three important enablers will help providers to address these strategic and organizational imperatives. The first is a systematic approach to process identification and analysis. We introduce the care delivery value chain as a framework for value improvement. The second enabler is information technology (IT). Information technology is sometimes seen as the answer to the system's problems. However, simply automating current modes of practice will yield limited benefits. The real opportunity is to transform the delivery of care in ways that IT can help support. The third enabler is the use of systematic processes for knowledge development. Ongoing and formal knowledge development at the medical condition level is necessary to support continuous improvements in care delivery.

Finally, moving to value-based strategies will require overcoming a series of barriers ranging from entrenched mind-sets to the ways physicians have been organized, prevailing reimbursement models, and obsolete regulations. We identify some of the most important barriers, and some ways that providers are addressing them. Despite the barriers, we are confident that new strategies and structures are possible, because leading providers are already embracing them.

Moving to new strategies and structures need not wait for regulatory changes or leadership by other system participants. Every provider can begin immediately to take voluntary steps toward competing on value. Leading providers are already doing so, and reaping the benefits in the form of better patient care, greater expertise, better clinical data, improved margins, and strengthened reputations, even in today's flawed system.

Too many providers are still content with the status quo, waiting for perfect solutions or for uncertainties surrounding future government regulation to be resolved. Too many providers have blamed problems in the system on other participants, rather than taking responsibility for what they can control. Too many providers, slow to measure their results even internally, have found reasons to resist accountability to the outside world. Such foot-dragging will leave providers behind in the coming realignment of the way health care is delivered. Those providers that want to earn a place in a value-driven health care system and remain in control of their own destiny need to act.

The Strategy Vacuum in Health Care Delivery

Delivering health care, whether it involves a hospital, physician group, or individual physician practice, is a complex undertaking involving a myriad of activities and challenges. Providers grapple with contracting with health plans, negotiating reimbursement, complying with regulatory requirements, assimilating new medical technologies, improving customer service, and recruiting and retaining staff. A growing body of literature reveals numerous opportunities for process improvement in all aspects of care delivery that can reduce errors and complications, improve treatment outcomes, and boost efficiency. Assimilating all these best practices, and improving operational effectiveness, can be all-consuming.

A dedication to improving operational effectiveness is important for any organization, but it is not sufficient. Every organization needs a guiding strategy, which defines its goals and purpose, the business or businesses it will operate in, the services it will offer, and the ways it will seek to distinguish itself from peers. Without a strategy, an organization lacks the clarity of direction to attain true excellence. Without direction and focus, it is difficult even to be truly efficient in operations.

Health care delivery cries out for strategy, given the stakes, the scale, and the sheer complexity of the task. Hospitals and physician practices need clear goals, given the myriad forces pulling on them. They also need to define what array of services they will offer. Providers need to chart a path to true excellence in their service areas, given that their patients' well-being is at stake. Clear goals and strategy should determine organizational structures, measurement systems, and the use of facilities.

For many health care providers, however, these strategic and organizational questions have been answered by default. Goals are undefined or framed in terms of financial sustainability or community service rather than patient value. Service lines are broad and mirror those of comparable organizations—other academic medical centers, other community hospitals, other nearby practices. Actual health care delivery is governed by established practices and traditions. Organizational structures are supply driven rather than customer driven, consisting of traditional specialty groups and shared functions. Few providers measure or hold themselves accountable for results at the patient level. Management considerations tend to be well down the priority list.

The absence of clear strategies among health care providers is perhaps understandable, given the community service orientation in the field and the strong influence of physicians who tend to want to do a little of everything.[1] But that legacy is counterproductive in modern health care, where the number and complexity of services has risen dramatically.

Health care providers tend to suffer from three characteristic types of strategy problems. First, their range of services is often *too broad* in terms of service lines, especially in the case of hospitals but also in some physician groups. Second, within each service line, the service delivery approach is *too narrow*, and the services offered are unintegrated. Third, the geographic focus of most health care providers is *too localized*, both in terms of market scope and the organization of care itself. These three problems often compound within the same organization to substantially detract from patient value.

Too Broad

At the level of the range of services they provide, many health care providers have non-strategies—they offer almost every service possible, with overly wide service lines serving an overly narrow geographic market. Hospitals, especially, are prone to try to be one-stop shops and maintain a full line even if the number of patients in a service line is small compared with experienced providers. A similar tendency occurs in physician practices. An orthopedic practice will be prone to treat every type of orthopedic problem that comes in the door, or an anesthesiology group will cover a multitude of types of surgical procedures.

Yet overall provider size and breadth have little impact on patient value. It is experience, scale, and expertise in each service that matters, not overall breadth of services. There is little justification for going back to the same provider for another medical condition unless the provider is excellent in addressing that new condition. Providers sometimes assume that unless they can diagnose, and subsequently treat, every patient that appears, they will lose referrals. Yet patients only benefit if the provider is excellent in diagnosing and addressing their specific condition. A typical argument for breadth is the presence of co-occurring conditions. However, excellent providers in a medical condition equip themselves to deal with important co-occurrences, as we will discuss. In contrast, many broad-line providers treat co-occurring conditions but fail to coordinate care.

The broad-line model has serious consequences for patient value, given the principles we described in chapter 4. In some service lines, many providers lack the scale to be either experienced or efficient. They maintain facilities and equipment that have excess capacity. This creates pressures to utilize the capacity, leading sometimes to further broadening of services. The result is that providers offer services in which they are competent but not truly excellent.

Some providers do focus on addressing specific medical conditions, such as M. D. Anderson Cancer Center or New England Baptist Hospital (orthopedics), but these remain exceptions. Insulated by a lack of competition and with no accountability for results, the more common mind-set is to maintain every service in-house and strive to be good enough at everything instead of concentrating resources on areas of distinction. The lack of focus makes improvement all the more challenging. Providers try to improve, but fail in many services to deliver superior value.

The problem of too much breadth afflicts all types of hospitals. Academic medical centers offer many routine or standard services in inherently high-cost facilities. Community hospitals maintain expensive high-tech facilities to treat patients with uncommon or complex conditions. Rural hospitals set out to meet all the needs of their local community even though patient volume is limited.

In part because of the issue of breadth, there is a notable absence of the types of strategic partnerships between organizations that one observes in other fields. Organizations tend to go it alone, and deal with others at arm's length. (This is partly due to the misguided Stark laws, which we discuss in chapter 8.)

Prevailing governance structures accentuate the tendency for health care providers to try to be all things to all people. Most hospitals and clinics are nonprofit organizations overseen by well-meaning volunteer boards, mindful of their mission in the community and their legal obligation to serve. Community service, though, is interpreted as offering everything. Taken too literally, then, such noble aims can actually work against patient value as providers attempt to cater to the needs of all constituencies. To maintain financial viability while supporting a broad array of services, providers also seek charitable donations to support uneconomic, subscale services.

The governance of physicians is also problematic for strategy, not to mention for the organization of care delivery. The free agent model is pervasive in health care. Many physicians work for themselves, even if they practice in a hospital's facilities. This raises challenges for executing a concerted strategy and coordinating and integrating care across doctors. Physician groups tend to be loose confederations of independent practitioners, each of whom wants to do his or her own thing. Many doctors have resisted the idea that they should restrict themselves to those services where they are the most effective. They are stimulated instead by taking on a range of cases, confident that they will be good enough at handling them.

To be fair, the strategic and organizational choices of providers are also affected by a variety of external factors that we have described in earlier chapters. The need to assemble bargaining power has led some hospitals and physician groups to broaden their service lines, for example. Similarly, generous reimbursement levels in areas such as orthopedics have led to substantial duplication of services.

Too Narrow

While many providers are too broad in terms of service lines, strategic thinking within service lines is often far too narrow. As we have discussed in earlier chapters, most providers are structured narrowly to deliver discrete services, not to provide truly integrated care. Hospitals, for example, are organized by traditional specialties such as internal medicine, surgery, radiology, and so on, not around the needs of the patient. Physician groups are also structured by specialty. Instead of operating as an integrated team, shifting groups of independent specialists come together around individual cases. All of this detracts from patient value.

The narrow focus of providers also extends to the delivery of care across time. Providers tend to define their services in terms of a series of discrete interventions, not an overall cycle of care. Even within a given hospital or clinic, the various units or departments tend to focus narrowly on their own procedure or function. Each unit devotes limited attention to what has come before for the patient, or what will come later.

The various units involved in the care cycle, which frequently include separate organizational entities, rarely work jointly and accept responsibility to improve the overall value of care. Instead, relationships across the care cycle tend to be arm's length, even within a hospital or provider group. This fractured delivery of patient care across the cycle seriously undermines patient value, as we have described in earlier chapters.

The fragmentation of actual care delivery has its roots in medical traditions. The medical field has inherited structures from an era when medical practice was less complex and more individualistic. Yet today, it makes little sense for patient value that, for example, cardiologists, cardiac surgeons, and interventional radiologists are often independent actors in treating heart patients through separate offices and facilities. Nevertheless, medical training, medical societies, and other traditions enshrine the current structure. Similarly, there is little rationale in terms of patient value for physicians to accumulate costs and bill individually for services, or, for that matter, to bill separately from the hospital. However, these legacies, and many others, have needlessly complicated the process of integrating and improving health care delivery.

It is challenging, to say the least, to get groups of physicians aligned and working strategically to deliver medically integrated care via shared processes. It is even harder to get free agents, who in effect work for themselves, to accept joint responsibility for their results and work together to systematically improve patient value. To be strategic, providers will need everyone involved in care delivery to have a common goal centered on the patient, and a shared commitment to overall results, not individual agendas.

The curious combination of excessive breadth and excessive fragmentation in health care delivery has also complicated process improvement. Many providers are devoting attention to improving processes, but the focus has tended to be on generic, institution-wide processes that fit the current structure, such as infection control, telephone triage, and prescribing, rather than the integrated care of specific medical conditions.

Too Local

Many of the realities that we have described also lead providers to think and behave in ways that are predominantly local. Anchored in a particular community or region, most providers see their options in local terms. Boards, which are also overwhelmingly local, usually define service to the community as the organization's principal mission. There is little inclination to expand or compete geographically even in areas of medical excellence.

The local focus of providers accentuates the problem of breadth. Viewing their market as the local community, providers are prone to want to provide all the services that the community needs, rather than leave some services to other providers. With a local orientation, growth opportunities are constrained. Widening the service line, rather than expanding geographically, appears to be the natural path. State-level licensing and other regulatory complexities also reinforce a local orientation in health care delivery, as we will discuss in chapter 8.

A local orientation extends not only to the home region but all the way down to individual campuses or facilities. Providers have a tendency to treat facilities as self-contained. Sites offer all the services demanded in the immediate area, rather than the set of services for which a particular location is cost-effective. Downtown teaching hospitals, for example, often include primary care practices and extensive outpatient services in a location that is inherently expensive and inconvenient for many patients. More providers are establishing satellite facilities, but the matching of services to facilities and true integration across facilities remain hit or miss.

Defining the Right Goal: Superior Patient Value

How can health care providers create more effective strategies and improve their performance? The starting point for strategy is to define the right goal. For every health care provider, the primary goal must be excellence in patient value. Value is the health outcomes achieved per dollar of cost compared to peers. A provider's size, range of services, reputation, and whether it earns a comfortable operating surplus are secondary. Unless a provider is delivering value to the patients it serves, it is failing at its fundamental mission even if it is financially successful. A provider that delivers superior patient results will be in a position to prosper even in the current system.

As we have discussed, patient value can only be measured at the level of medical conditions, and assessed relative to peers. Competence alone is not enough. A provider must be able to achieve results that compare favorably to others that provide similar services.

The overall value delivered by an organization is built up medical condition by medical condition.[2] Excellent value in some services does not offset mediocrity in others. Patients, not to mention the entire health care system, are not well served if providers maintain even one service line in which they do not achieve results equal to or better than peers. The truth is, not all providers will be equally effective at everything, nor should they try to be. In value-based competition, excellence, not breadth or convenience, should shape the choice of services by providers and the overall configuration of the health care system. ThedaCare, a Wisconsin health care delivery system, has articulated this aspiration in a forceful way. ThedaCare seeks to operate only in those service areas where it can achieve world-class clinical performance at the 95th percentile level.

While the goal of patient value may seem self-evident, goal definition in health care delivery has been clouded by a variety of factors. Many health care delivery organizations are nonprofits. Nonprofit organizations, as a group, face special challenges in agreeing on goals because each constituency sees its values and desires as worthy. Governance structures, as we described earlier, introduce community considerations and a local focus that can inadvertently trump patient value as the central goal. Finally, and this is by no means an exhaustive list, professional standards and ethics in medicine offer considerable scope for differences in opinion in setting institutional priorities. The result is that providers can end up trying to care for every patient that comes in the door.

Financial viability often appears as an important goal. But financial results are an outcome, not the goal in and of itself. A comfortable operating surplus cannot offset mediocrity in serving patients. In a value-based system, as we will discuss, excellent results will lead to more patients, greater efficiency, and higher margins.

Patient value, then, is the compass that must guide the strategic and operational choices of every provider group, hospital, clinic, and physician practice. Every provider must do its best to measure patient value, service line by service line, and compare its performance to others. If value for patients truly governed every provider choice, the health outcomes per dollar expended in the U.S. health care system would improve dramatically.

Providers clearly do not operate in a vacuum. The benefits of value-based provider strategies will be greater if other system participants (notably health plans, employers, and government) embrace the goal of patient value. This is a subject we will discuss extensively in the following chapters. However, even if providers act alone, the potential to improve value for patients is enormous. By taking the lead, providers can also act as a catalyst for change throughout the system.

Moving to Value-Based Competition:
Imperatives for Providers

How can providers compete on value? To do so, they must embrace a series of strategic and organizational imperatives, shown in figure 5-1. We describe the imperatives in the context of hospitals and physician groups. However, they apply even to the practice of an individual physician. A growing number of providers have begun to address several of the imperatives, but few, if any, providers are currently addressing all of them. The shift to a value-based model is self-reinforcing. As more of these imperatives are addressed, the benefits grow disproportionately.

Redefine the Business Around Medical Conditions

The starting point for developing strategy in any field is to define the relevant business or businesses in which an organization competes. Health care delivery is no different. Health care providers do not think of themselves as businesses, but they are in the business of providing services to patients. (Those who are uncomfortable with the notion of businesses in health care can substitute the term *service lines*.)

The question "What business are we in?" is an important one because it guides an organization's thinking about who its customer is, what needs it is trying to meet, and how it should organize. Implicit in every business definition is a view of how value is created. Aligning an organization's view of value with actual value is a precondition for excellent performance.

In some fields, defining the relevant business is straightforward. In health care this is not the case, in part because of the way medicine has traditionally been structured and organized. Many hospitals, for example,

FIGURE 5-1

Moving to value-based competition: Imperatives for providers

- Redefine the business around medical conditions
- Choose the range and types of services provided
- Organize around medically integrated practice units
- Create a distinctive strategy in each practice unit
- Measure results, experience, methods, and patient attributes by practice unit
- Move to single bills and new approaches to pricing
- Market services based on excellence, uniqueness, and results
- Grow locally and geographically in areas of strength

see themselves in the "hospital" business or the "health care delivery" business, competing with other hospitals based on their overall service offering. An even broader definition of the business, "health care," is common among experts in health policy. This leads them to favor large health systems, believing that health care is best organized by combining insurance and health care delivery into one vertically integrated, full-line system.

Other providers, including most physician practices, define their business around specific functions or specialties. An anesthesiology group defines itself as in the anesthesia business; a nephrology group sees itself as in the nephrology business. Hospitals, to the extent that they think in terms of service lines, normally define them in terms of specialties such as internal medicine, radiology, urology, surgery, and so on.

Both of these prevailing modes of business definition in health care providers represent obstacles to value creation. They are doctor centric, procedure centric, or institution centric, not patient centric. They are also misaligned with how patient value is actually created.

Patient value in health care delivery, as we have discussed, can only be understood at the level of medical conditions. Overwhelmingly, value is determined by how well a provider delivers care in each medical condition, not its overall breadth of services. The value delivered in a medical condition arises from the full set of activities and specialties involved. It is not the individual roles, skills, or functions that matter, but the overall result. Moreover, for each aspect of care, value is determined by how well the needed set of skills and functions come together. In surgery, for example, value depends on not only the surgeon but also the anesthesiologist, the nurses, the radiologist, the skilled technicians, and others, all performing well. Yet no matter how skilled the surgical team, the overall care cycle is crucial. Unless the patient's problem is accurately diagnosed, the patient is properly prepared, and recovery and rehabilitation are managed well, patient results will suffer. Indeed, the impact of the cycle of care is even broader. Value may be enhanced by not performing the surgery at all, and treating the case in a different way. Value may be still greater if preventive care and advice is provided over time so that little or no treatment is needed at all.

The relevant business in health care delivery, then, is a medical condition seen over the full cycle of care. The business is congestive heart failure, for example, not heart surgery, cardiology, angiography, or anesthesiology. Traditional specialties are often too broad. The business is not nephrology, but chronic kidney disease, end stage renal disease (dialysis), kidney transplantation, and hypertension. The medical condition is not orthopedic care, but several conditions, including spine disorders, hip disorders, and so forth. Cancer care also involves many distinct medical conditions.

Note that in academic medical centers, laboratory research and teaching should also be treated as separate businesses from patient care in most cases, rather than co-mingled as they are today. Clinical outcome research, however, needs to be expanded and better integrated with patient care.

Business definition always involves a geographic component. A health care provider must understand the geographic market or service area over which it must compete. Otherwise, the provider will misunderstand the true benchmarks for performance it must meet and the strategic options it has available. As we have discussed, even if some services must be provided locally, the relevant market for most medical conditions should be regional or even national. Providers that fail to think in these terms will become more and more vulnerable to competition. They will also miss opportunities to grow and form partnerships across geography.

Medical conditions represent the basic unit of analysis for thinking about value in health care. Medical conditions are patient centric, not provider centric. We use the term *medical conditions,* rather than *diseases, injuries,* or other patient circumstances, such as pregnancy, because the term is more general. The term *organ systems,* used by some providers, is provider centric and not a medical condition at all.

How to define the appropriate set of medical conditions around which to organize care sometimes involves judgments, as does where to begin and end the care cycle. Different providers can, and should, define medical conditions differently based on their strategies, the complexity of the cases they undertake, and the patient groups they serve. The ultimate arbiter of the appropriate definition is patient value. We will return to these issues later in this chapter and in appendix B.

Every provider, then, must clearly and explicitly define *the set of medical conditions in which it participates*. For each of these medical conditions, the provider must define *where it currently fits in the care cycle*. Addressing these questions is the first step in devising a strategy, organizing care delivery, and measuring results.

Choose the Range and Types of Services Provided

Perhaps the most basic strategic decision for every provider is the set of services to be delivered. In other words, what businesses does the provider *want* to be in? Providers must choose the set of medical conditions in which they can achieve true excellence in terms of patient value, given their particular patient mix, skills, and other circumstances. In each medical condition, providers must decide what roles they will play in the care cycle, and what services to offer to ensure good overall patient results. The choices will be different for each provider. Academic centers will make different choices than community or rural hospitals. A provider may make different choices from peers nearby.

Part of the strategic choice of service lines is to match the complexity and acuity of the conditions diagnosed and treated with the skill, technology, facilities, and cost base of the institution. Routine or simple services should not be offered by institutions that cannot deliver them at competitive cost. Conversely, complex or unusual services should not be offered by institutions that lack the experience, scale, and capabilities to provide excellent results.

In value-based competition, most hospitals and physician groups will retain an array of service lines but will stop trying to offer everything. Most institutions should narrow the range of medical conditions served, or at least the types of cases they seek to address. Some practices may be phased out completely, while others are significantly reorganized. In most businesses, it is common sense to concentrate on products and services that create unique value. For many hospitals and other health care providers, however, doing so will require a significant change in mind-set in a field used to handling any patient who walks in the door. And deciding what *not* to do is an even more radical idea. In health care, the need for strategic choice of services has been avoided because of the lack of information and the lack of accountability for results.

An array of specialized hospitals, which are or are among the leaders in their fields, is testament to the ability to deliver superior value without serving all needs. Many of these hospitals, such as the Bascom Palmer Eye Institute (Miami), the Hospital for Specialty Surgery (orthopedics, New York), M. D. Anderson Cancer Center (Houston), and Memorial Sloan-Kettering Cancer Center (New York), are among the top-rated institutions in the United States in their fields. While specialization is not a prerequisite for excellence, as wider-line providers such as Massachusetts General Hospital and the Mayo Clinic attest, it is not a disadvantage.

Strategic focus is not about narrow specialization, but the pursuit of excellence and deepening penetration in the chosen fields. At Fairview–University Children's Hospital (Minnesota), for example, a long-term commitment to excellence in the area of cystic fibrosis has resulted in the top treatment facility for cystic fibrosis in the country, with a median patient survival age of forty-six years compared with the U.S. average of thirty-two.[3,4] The Minnesota Cystic Fibrosis Center has developed age-specific programs serving the needs of particular patient groups: pediatric (through age twelve), adolescent (ages thirteen to twenty-two), and adult (over the age of twenty-two). Its expertise with adult patients has led to the development of a specialized reproductive practice for cystic fibrosis patients, with excellent results.[5] The center also has specialized diabetes and gastro-

FIGURE 5-2

The virtuous circle in health care delivery

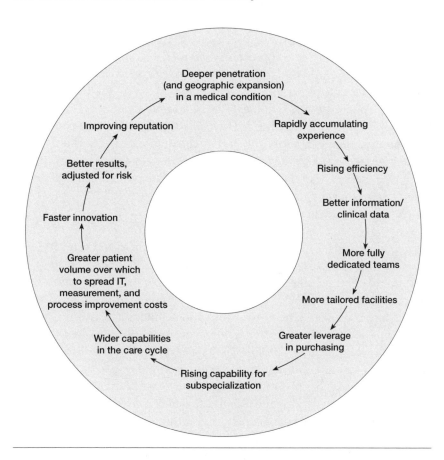

intestinal clinics to help its patients deal with conditions that frequently co-occur with cystic fibrosis, as well as a lung transplantation program for cystic fibrosis patients that has achieved a 76 percent one-year survival rate and a 66 percent five-year survival rate, well above the national averages.[6]

When a provider makes a strategic choice of medical conditions and service lines, it feeds the virtuous circle of value in care delivery in its favor (see figure 5-2). Deeper penetration in areas of excellence triggers a cascade of benefits, as we discussed in chapter 4. (We explore organizational and other changes needed to achieve these benefits throughout this chapter.)

A strategic choice of medical conditions and services does not require shrinking the overall organization, but growing some areas and limiting or exiting others. The net result can be a larger institution in terms of size, but a far more effective and efficient one. The impact on health care value would be enormous if organizations only provided services where they were excellent relative to peers. The huge variations in performance across providers reveal the magnitude of the opportunity.

The need for a strategic approach to service lines does not rule out large provider groups, but will require major changes in the way they operate. Most provider groups, as they are currently structured, are holding companies. Their constituent hospitals, clinics, and physician practices operate largely as stand-alone entities. In a value-based health care system, provider groups will retain a role only if they can demonstrate excellent results in each service line and medically integrate services across the entities in the group. Rather than duplicating care and relying on bargaining power, care delivery must be radically restructured or groups will lose share once they have to compete on value.

Why have health care providers resisted service line choices? In health care delivery, bigger has been seen as better, and providers tend to overstate the importance of breadth. Focused providers are criticized as cherry pickers and often provide specific procedures rather than a full cycle of care for a condition. Incremental thinking has led to the illusion that each new service line is contributing to overhead and profitability, without considering whether redeploying the facilities and space to grow areas of true excellence would be more profitable. (As we will discuss later in this chapter, provider cost accounting remains primitive.) Today, paring back service lines tends to occur only in cases of severe financial distress. Few providers realize that pursuing breadth in unrelated or loosely related services has a large opportunity cost, namely, dissipating the focus and investment needed to become truly excellent and grow in particular medical conditions.[7]

The bias toward breadth is revealed in the response of broad-line hospitals to new, specialty institutions in cardiac care and orthopedics. Motivated by generous reimbursement rates for these services and enjoying the benefits of focus, such hospitals have taken business from full-service institutions. Broad-line providers have actively opposed specialty hospitals and even sought regulation to outlaw them altogether (see chapters 3 and 8).[8] Yet, specialized providers can offer compelling benefits in terms of value in some fields, provided that they can demonstrate high standards and are required to compete on results. Efforts to outlaw such competitors to perpetuate today's full-line model are misguided. Instead, full-line providers need to rethink their own strategies. Nothing prevents existing institutions from competing through focused attention to the service lines targeted by specialty providers, including establishing "hospitals within hospitals" on their campuses.

Implementing Service Line Choices. The particular services to offer will be different for academic medical centers, community hospitals, and rural providers. Community hospitals in urban areas should compete in a different array of service lines than academic medical centers, because their strengths differ. Studies reveal that community hospitals offer equal or superior quality, and lower cost, in types of care for which they have adequate volume.[9] Community hospitals also demonstrate faster learning on new techniques they perform frequently, while tertiary hospitals learn faster in new techniques for more complex cases.[10] If their experience and patient volume are low in a medical condition, community hospitals may be better off referring these patients elsewhere for parts of the care cycle. However, community hospitals should have medically integrated relationships and even formal partnerships with the excellent providers to whom they refer patients. This will improve value in diagnosis, follow-up care, and ongoing patient management.

Rural providers also play an essential role in a variety of service areas, including emergency care, diagnosis, treatment of relatively common conditions, follow-up care, and disease management for chronic conditions. However, most rural providers lack the volume, expertise, and facilities to support excellence across all services. They are drawn to offer many services because of the absence of other local providers in a system that has been biased toward local care. This makes little sense from a value perspective except in areas where a rural hospital can demonstrate true excellence.

In lower-volume service lines, rural providers can and should establish medical relationships (such as formal referral or partnership relationships) with centers that have the experience and facilities to achieve excellent results. Such relationships cannot be at arm's length, but require actively integrated care delivery. In some cases, urban and rural providers will establish joint care cycles involving an integrated approach to diagnosis, treatment, follow-up, and monitoring. In such models, each institution undertakes the roles where it can deliver the greatest value. In other services, a rural provider can deliver care but team up with a high-volume center to obtain support in terms of training, measurement, information technology, and consultations on cases. Rather than try to capture the local patient volume for every service, then, rural providers should select the services they will perform while in other services distinguishing themselves through the quality of their relationships with excellent providers, modifying facilities and staff accordingly. In so doing, rural hospitals will dramatically improve their efficiency and reduce the need to maintain underutilized capacity while improving patient outcomes.

Beth Israel Deaconess Medical Center (BIDMC) in Boston, an academic medical center, provides an example of an institution beginning to make choices in its service lines. BIDMC discovered that the average acuity index for its services was quite similar to that of a community hospital, despite the fact that its urban campus had technologically sophisticated facilities, highly skilled personnel, and a hard-to-get-to location for many patients. BIDMC began a conscious process of migrating services not requiring its skill and cost base to other providers, such as to referring physicians and community hospitals. Its approach to attracting referrals shifted more toward specialists rather than primary care physicians, because it sought only the more complex cases that matched its capabilities.

Ironically, many hospitals are severely short of space and lack the resources to expand capacity. They overlook the most obvious solution that BIDMC understood—utilize space only for those services where the hospital offers unique value. This means redeploying and redesigning facilities to expand excellent services while phasing out others or moving them to other locations.

As compelling as it is for patient value, migrating the right services to the right providers is not an easy task in health care even though today's division of work is far from ideal. Doctor preferences often bias service line choices, in some cases for their personal convenience. Institutions lack a sophisticated understanding of cost, leading them to believe that incremental services are profitable even though they could be provided much more cost-effectively by other providers. There is wariness about sharing referrals or directing patients to other providers, for fear that this will be a one-way street.

Patients, too, can work against the efficient allocation of work across locations when they patronize inherently costly tertiary medical centers for less complex or routine services. Patients and referring physicians, lacking results information, are drawn to the strong reputation of an academic medical center and presume that its results will be better across the board. Often, the cost to patients in terms of copayments and deductibles will be the same as if care were obtained at a community hospital. In this and many other ways, information, pricing, and reimbursement practices work against health care value, as we will discuss further.

The challenges of choosing and allocating services efficiently are substantial even in affiliated institutions within a wholly owned network. Here each institution is prone to want to maintain its autonomy and preserve a full line, even if services are duplicated or inefficiently divided. Sites asked to give up complex services have bruised egos. The centers-of-excellence approach, adopted by some multiunit providers, often encounters this kind of resistance. To make centers of excellence work, structural changes in practice organization, management, and care delivery processes are also necessary, as we will discuss further.

The problem of inefficient division of labor is even greater across independent provider organizations. The case of Beth Israel Deaconess reveals the challenges and the opportunities. When BIDMC sought to migrate some services to community hospitals while gaining referrals for more complex cases, some physicians were wary of giving up control over patient care to another institution and leaving important decisions to other doctors. At the same time, independent community hospitals were suspicious that BIDMC would attempt to capture referred patients. In cardiac care, BIDMC established a formal relationship with Milton Hospital, a community hospital five miles south of BIDMC's campus in central Boston, to overcome such obstacles. The two hospitals began marketing cardiac care jointly, encouraging patients in communities south of Boston to present themselves at Milton. BIDMC and Milton agreed on a common protocol for evaluating patients with heart symptoms. Milton physicians make the preliminary diagnosis. Patients with serious conditions are transported to Boston using a dedicated ambulance, while other patients are treated more cost-effectively at Milton. In order for this effort to succeed, BIDMC physicians had to develop the confidence that Milton would meet their high-quality standards, while Milton physicians had to believe that BIDMC physicians were responsive, would involve them in continuing care, and were not out to steal their patients. This case illustrates how good coordination of the care cycle can take place across separate organizations, a topic we will discuss further.

The Cleveland Clinic has sought to address some of these same issues without formal affiliations with other provider organizations. The Clinic has a policy of trying to return patients to the referring doctor, and keeping the referring doctor well informed. The referring doctor gets a telephone call, fax, and letter with operative findings immediately after surgery, and the same three notifications of the hospital summary upon discharge. The Clinic also contacts patients to remind and encourage them to schedule an appointment with the referring doctor after discharge. Recently, the Clinic has begun to utilize information technology to deepen coordination and integration across the care cycle. It provides referring physicians with real-time access to the patient's complete medical record so that the referring doctor has access to all test results and orders and can track the care delivered.[11]

Separating Providers and Health Plans. Health care providers face an important issue of strategic scope in deciding whether to combine with a health plan into one vertically integrated organization. In the early

1990s, numerous providers also operated HMOs, though the number has fallen as some providers became disillusioned with the combination. Kaiser Permanente has long been a commonly cited role model, operating an entirely closed system involving an HMO, owned hospitals, and salaried doctors. Other vertically integrated groups, including Sentara Healthcare (Virginia) and Intermountain Health Care (Utah and Idaho), are widely regarded as outstanding providers. A number of respected health care policy experts believe that such vertically integrated, broad-line systems are the best way to organize health care.[12]

There are benefits from combining health plan and provider, especially where zero-sum competition is the rule. Vertical integration mitigates the adversarial relationship between health plan and provider and allows incentives to be better aligned. For example, integrated organizations can incorporate gain sharing into the compensation system to motivate process improvement at the provider level. Vertical integration can also facilitate the health plan's ability to exchange information and coordinate across provider entities. Vertical integration can simplify billing transactions to achieve administrative savings. Finally, the vertically integrated model allows strict budget control of the provider network, so that the amount of services provided and the costs can be managed. Such budget control can potentially mitigate supply-driven demand.

While these benefits are real in the current flawed system, we are wary of the integrated system model as the sole model, or the dominant model, for health care delivery. A structure that mitigates some dysfunctional aspects of the current zero-sum system is not necessarily the best structure for a new, value-based system. There are two core problems with the vertically integrated model. First, combining the health plan and provider network eliminates or suppresses competition at the provider level where it matters most—in addressing particular medical conditions. An inherent conflict of interest arises when patients are treated only (or primarily) by providers in the integrated group, which are thereby insulated from competition. It is unlikely that a vertically integrated system will contain the highest-value providers in every single service area, or improve the fastest. Moreover, without outside competition, measuring and communicating results at the level of medical conditions remains discretionary. If the integrated model becomes predominant, the system will consolidate to a small number of integrated systems so that competition on results at the health plan level is suppressed. Competition at the provider level for specific conditions will be eliminated.

The second problem with the vertically integrated model is incentives. Combining insurance and the provision of services essentially recreates a system of global capitation. The global capitation model creates strong incentives to reduce costs and limit services because the health care system receives a fixed amount per subscriber. Since the health plan controls the provider organization, however, the checks and balances that come with separate health plans and providers are lost. Hence patients must trust the health plan to put them first, at the expense of near-term revenues and margins.

Separating health plans and providers, in contrast, harnesses the power of competition to drive patient value. Independent health plans will be motivated to compare providers and assist patients in obtaining excellent care. Providers, with no guaranteed patients and referrals, will be motivated to demonstrate and improve excellent value.

As competition shifts to value, the incentives and administrative benefits enjoyed today by integrated systems will fade. Independent health plans and providers will learn to simplify administration, share information, and contract based on gain sharing. Indeed, competition will drive even faster progress than large, monolithic systems with dominant regional positions are likely to achieve.

Finally, managing a provider is a fundamentally different business from running a health plan. Both have important and unique roles that are best played when they are independent. Both health plans and providers will benefit from total dedication to their roles, unencumbered by any conflicting interests.

Integrated systems, then, look attractive given the flaws in the current system, but are a second-best solution. They appeal to those who believe that top-down control and oversight of providers is the only hope, including some leading advocates of managed care. They appeal to those who see today's zero-sum competition as inevitable, rather than those who envision a world of value-based competition on results.

Vertically integrated systems can have a place in a value-driven system, but they must earn it. Integrated systems should have to compete on results at the medical condition level with nonintegrated providers. Also, the provider organizations in vertical systems must be subject to results measurement and reporting at the medical condition level. Without transparency on results, subscribers in a closed system will have no assurance that their care is excellent. The share of the market served by vertically integrated systems should be determined by the results achieved, not top-down policy decisions.

Organize Around Medically Integrated Practice Units

The typical organizational structure of health care providers is what is known in management terminology as a functional structure. Hospital staff, for example, are organized into departments reflecting traditional medical specialties (e.g., radiology, surgery, internal medicine, cardiology, anesthesiology) and shared functions (e.g., operating rooms, imaging, laboratory services, intensive care, hospital wards). Individual practitioners, drawn from these functional departments, come together in temporary groups to treat individual cases, using shared facilities. Doctors sometimes participate in such temporary groups in multiple hospitals. In one Boston group, for example, some anesthesiologists handle cases at five or more hospitals involving numerous different types of surgery.

The functional structure is supply driven; it organizes around the types of skills and facilities. This is the way businesses in the rest of the economy were organized many decades ago. Outside of health care, functional structures have long since been replaced with a far more effective organization around products or service lines, commonly known as business unit structures.

Business unit or service line structures organize around the customer—the demand side. Under a general manager with overall responsibility, they marshal all the skills and facilities to meet the overall needs of the customer, and enable the integration of service delivery. In business unit structures, individual practitioners sometimes maintain an affiliation with similarly trained colleagues through informal or dual reporting structures. In a less formal model, individuals with a particular skill (e.g., marketing) report to a business unit but are also part of a marketing council that creates a forum to share marketing knowledge. In a dual reporting structure, sometimes known as a matrix structure, individuals have reporting relationships to both the business unit head and a senior functional head (e.g., a corporate vice president for marketing). In a true business unit structure, however, the primary reporting relationship is to the business unit.

In health care, the traditional functional structure must radically shift to a structure that medically integrates the care of patients with particular medical conditions. We term such a structure the *integrated practice unit* structure.[13] Integrated practice units are defined around medical conditions, *not* particular services, treatments, or tests. An integrated practice unit includes the full range of medical expertise, technical skills, and specialized facilities needed to address a medical condition or set of related medical conditions over the cycle of care. Ideally, the individuals and facilities involved in a practice unit are *dedicated*—that is, they are focused solely on that practice unit. The fundamental organizational unit in health care delivery should be the integrated practice unit (IPU). It is the overall care of a medical condition that creates value for the patient—not the radiology department, the anesthesiology group, or the cardiology group.

Most providers will operate multiple IPUs. We do not advocate special-ization per se, as we have already discussed, but a new approach to orga-nizing and managing those areas in which a provider operates. However, if a provider cannot support a medically integrated practice unit in a ser-vice line, then there are serious questions about whether it should be practicing medicine in that line.

Some experts have argued that practice unit thinking will tend to frag-ment health care delivery around narrow specialties. We strongly dis-agree. Health care delivery is highly fragmented today, but *not* in a way that creates value for patients. Many providers and individual physicians are generalists and free agents, treating a little bit of everything in their field. Much of the actual delivery of care is not medically integrated, in the sense of groups of skilled individuals working together consistently over time in a focused way to attain true excellence. Too many providers offer services in which they lack the volume and experience to achieve efficiency and superior medical results.[14]

Health care delivery today is also highly fragmented across the care cycle. Individuals and entities involved in different aspects of care are organized separately and work almost independently. There is little conti-nuity and integration over time in care of both acute and chronic condi-tions. The concept of practice units is far more medically integrated, then, than most existing health care delivery.

A growing number of providers are moving to the IPU model via insti-tutes, clinics, centers, and other more integrated structures. The Cleveland Clinic, M. D. Anderson Cancer Center, and New England Baptist Hospital are examples we will discuss further. However, even the leading centers have yet to implement the IPU model completely.

Principles of the Practice Unit Structure. The practice unit model rests on a number of basic principles. We discuss the principles in this section, and give examples of how particular hospitals and physician practices are actually deploying IPU thinking in the next section.

IPUs are patient centric and results driven. Individuals in a practice unit work together, as a group and on a sustained basis, to achieve excel-lence in care delivery through continuous learning, improvement, and innovation. Physicians and physician groups, even if they are indepen-dent, understand their role as part of and are integrated closely with the hospital-based IPU, rather than seeing their particular specialty as a sepa-rate business.

The IPU model embodies the growing recognition of the importance of multidisciplinary approaches to diagnosis, treatment, and disease man-agement.[15] However, IPUs focus not on disciplines per se but on the best way to deliver care. There appears to be a trend toward the blurring of traditional specialties as medical practice advances. For example, cardiologists, vascular surgeons, and radiologists are all now repairing arteries from the inside with catheters and devices such as stents. In a practice unit, the best approaches from all fields are brought together to achieve the best results for the patient.

IPUs in a medical condition should include (or have access to) the capabilities to address the prevalent co-occurrences. Some providers may choose to define their practice units around just those patient groups with co-occurrences. IPUs can also encompass closely related medical conditions that involve similar skills, facilities, and care delivery approaches.

IPUs should encompass the full cycle of care for the patient. Figure 5-3, for example, illustrates the broad range of stages involved in care for organ transplantation, an example that we discuss further in chapter 6. (We present a framework for delineating the care cycle in more detail later in this chapter.)

In the IPU model, a patient may have a lead physician, but care is provided by a team. In the current system, patients tend to "belong" to a single physician for each aspect of care. In the practice unit model, the patient belongs to the IPU, which manages information, integrates decisions, and ensures continuity during handoffs. Practice units, then, are patient centric, not procedure centric or doctor centric. IPUs also need to accept responsibility for, and be held accountable for, the entire care cycle *even if other entities are involved.* For example, referring physicians, rehabilitation specialists, and independent disease management providers are integrated into the care delivery process.

Sentara, a Norfolk, Virginia, group that includes hospitals, salaried physicians, and affiliated physicians, illustrates the benefits of moving to a care cycle perspective even without formal practice units. In delivering care for congestive heart failure, Sentara found that patients improved in the hospital, but many floundered once they were discharged and had to be

FIGURE 5-3

Organ transplant care cycle

Evaluation	Waiting for a donor	Transplant surgery	Immediate convalescence	Long-term convalescence
			Addressing organ rejection	Adjustment and monitoring
			Fine-tuning the drug regimen	

readmitted. Sentara devised a program involving home visits and telehealth visits using easy-to-use monitoring technology to maintain an ongoing interaction with discharged patients. Nurses were able to identify exacerbation of symptoms in time to alert the primary care physician and avoid trips to the emergency room. In cases where the patients' symptoms could not be controlled using the existing treatment plan, the nurses recommend readmission. Overall, the program decreased hospital readmissions by 82 percent and emergency room visits by 77 percent. In addition to better patient outcomes and huge cost savings, participants reported an improvement in their ability to eat and sleep and felt less of a burden on their families.[16] With a shift to IPUs and new reimbursement models involving single bills for episodes of care (discussed later in this chapter), such examples will proliferate.

In the IPU model, many if not most staff are dedicated—they work exclusively in a medical condition. Staff, including nurses and specialized technicians, are co-located in dedicated facilities: dedicated clinics, dedicated imaging facilities, dedicated operating and recovery facilities, dedicated wards, dedicated floors, and even entire dedicated buildings. This allows and encourages better medical integration, deepening of expertise, and the tailoring of facilities to the medical condition. At Sentara, for example, stroke patients once residing in multiple locations were concentrated in a single ward. Care by dedicated staff with specialized expertise has virtually eliminated pneumonia, a common stroke complication, and significantly shortened the length of stay. This ability to support dedicated and tailored facilities is another benefit of aggregating a threshold level of volume through a strategic focus on a service area both within and across locations.

Ultimately, the IPU model lends itself to the notion of hospitals within hospitals and practices within practices, rather than monolithic, functionally structured entities. Practice units are designed around the integration of care, rather than a collection of discrete specialties.

Within the practice unit structure, there are significant benefits from organizing diagnosis as a distinct function, rather than co-mingled with treatment.[17] Diagnosis involves its own set of discrete activities, including medical history, testing, evaluation, and treatment plan definition. Mobilizing a range of disciplines and specialties to jointly examine the case can improve the quality and efficiency of diagnosis and the recommended treatment compared to sending the patient to a sequence of specialists who will have a natural tendency to diagnose what they know. Also, the best diagnosticians and the most skilled interveners may well be different. Finally, highlighting diagnosis as a distinct role can better align incentives. It is human nature for diagnosticians who are paid primarily for treatment to recommend treatment, and to recommend the treatment the diagnostician is equipped to provide.

Diagnosis itself can be costly, and the quality of the diagnosis has a huge impact on quality and cost in subsequent care. A correct and timely diagnosis often enables a better chance at full recovery, while an incorrect or indeterminate diagnosis will require further diagnostic costs and may lead to ineffective or contraindicated care. Diagnostic accuracy and cost need to be measured and compared, not just treatment.

Organizing diagnosis as a distinct subunit within an integrated practice unit, then, can improve value through enabling consultation and knowledge sharing, focusing attention on improving methods, and encouraging measurement of results. For some providers, diagnosis (including second opinions) is a business in its own right and a tool for attracting patients. The Mayo Clinic, for example, has dedicated attention to diagnosis as distinct from treatment. Incoming patients are assigned a physician to coordinate the diagnosis, from the initial interview about the symptoms to custom formulating a battery of tests and assembling a multispecialty team of medical experts. The team provides a thorough explanation of the diagnosis and possible therapies, and advises the patient in choosing the course of treatment. Of course, diagnosis can be iterative, so close links are necessary between diagnosticians and those involved in treatment and other care.

The Cleveland Clinic has taken focus on diagnosis a step further. It offers a national service of second opinions for three hundred life-threatening or life-altering diagnoses at a fixed fee, enabled by its comprehensive information technology infrastructure. Each practice unit, then, has a vehicle for providing its diagnostic services nationally. The Clinic has been forced to overcome some challenges in introducing this product, such as state-level licensing of physicians. However, the patient results in terms of number of improved diagnoses and enhanced treatment plans are encouraging.

Just as diagnosis can benefit from focused attention, so can the longer-term functions such as prevention, risk management, and disease management. Units managing acute treatment may not be equipped to manage and implement such functions. The Sentara example illustrates the benefits of having an explicit program and staff dedicated to these longer-term roles rather than expecting acute care and hospital-based personnel to pick up these roles along with their other responsibilities. However, units focused on diagnosis or long-term patient management must be housed and integrated within a practice unit with full care-cycle responsibility and accountability.

Finally, the integrated practice unit model can be applied to primary care. Primary care can be thought of as a set of practice units, whose range depends on the patient population served. One IPU is what might be termed general health maintenance. This encompasses patient monitoring, general preventive care, and the diagnosis and care of routine diseases or injuries. Other practice units involve more complex conditions such as asthma care, cardiac care, and chronic kidney disease. Here, the primary care provider is part of larger care cycles. In these more complex conditions, primary care physicians and their staff act as the front end (e.g., initial monitoring, preliminary diagnosis, preventive care) of the care cycle or the back end (disease management) of the cycle, or both.

In primary care practices, recognizing and distinguishing these practice units, and organizing around them, will pay dividends in terms of patient value. For general health maintenance, the primary care practice manages the entire care cycle. For more complex care, the primary care practice should establish strong relationships and efficient coordination with other providers for each medical condition. Primary care practices, like all providers, must also measure and be accountable for results. Results for general health maintenance and results for the management of each complex medical condition should be measured separately.

Some primary care practices may choose to concentrate on some complex conditions, and refer patients with other conditions to practices with deep expertise in those areas. There are primary care practices, for example, that concentrate on older patients or postmenopausal women, among other patient populations.

Moving to Integrated Practice Units. Many providers have begun to move in the direction of dedicated practice units, although the process is just beginning. An essential early step in the practice unit concept is to get physicians and other skilled personnel working together in a medically integrated team rather than as separate practitioners. Intermountain Health Care (IHC), based in Utah, began to form precursors to true IPUs in the 1990s. After identifying ten disease areas (including conditions that accounted for 90 percent of its costs), IHC's initial focus was on cost-reduction efforts in each area. When this met with limited success, IHC moved in 1995 to shift its model explicitly from managing cost to managing care delivery.[18] In so doing, it identified and reinforced the natural groupings of physicians involved in treating each disease or condition. IHC has made great strides in quality and cost ever since. Between 1999 and 2002, for example, the cardiovascular surgery mortality rates at IHC have been 19.5 percent lower than the intensity of the case mix would predict.[19] This case illustrates the benefits of simply getting physicians involved in a medical condition together.

The Boston Spine Group at New England Baptist Hospital, a hospital with a large majority of its practice in orthopedics, illustrates how physicians in the same medical condition can begin working together and begin the evolution toward a true IPU. At New England Baptist, as in many hospitals, all physicians are independent, free agents in private practice. In 1997, four spine surgeons decided to come together in a focused physician group dedicated to providing the best spine care based on outcome measurement. Measurement is especially significant in the spine field, where there has been skepticism about the benefits of some types of back surgery.[20] By 2004, the group was performing about two thousand spine-related surgeries annually.

The Boston Spine Group was formed as a corporation, with each surgeon contributing capital to establish a common administrative support structure. While this is common in physician groups, what makes this group more interesting is that the surgeons are invested in collecting and pooling detailed information, using a common structure, on each patient's initial condition, the care delivered, and the medical outcomes achieved (such as functionality and range of movement before and after treatment). The group invests time and extensive internal meetings to understand patient outcome trends, explore problems, and improve treatment methods and technologies. A variety of published studies and specialized medical devices have emerged from the group. This case illustrates a central aspect of the integrated practice unit model: a dedication to working as a group to achieve systematic improvement in care delivery and patient value.

Like many hospital-based practices, the Boston Spine Group is an independent physician group that is not formally part of the hospital. The Boston Spine Group contracts with the hospital for most infrastructure and many services. However, the group has worked closely with the hospital and other physician groups to build a de facto dedicated team of nurses, anesthesiologists, radiologists, and technicians who concentrate on spine care. Spine patients are all housed on the same floor, with nurses who have specialized expertise in this medical condition. The group is moving to secure even more tailored, co-located, and dedicated facilities within the hospital.

The Boston Spine Group markets itself to health plans like a practice unit, using its growing body of clinical evidence. It has achieved significant improvements in clinical results, and its market share of patients in its region increased from 8.6 percent in fiscal 1998 to 11.1 percent in fiscal 2002 and has continued to rise. The Boston Spine Group, then, is well on the way to operating as a practice unit. It illustrates the case of an individual practice unit arising spontaneously based on the vision of its physician partners and the support of the hospital. As the group and the hospital continue to evolve their structures and ways of operating, the potential to strengthen the practice unit, improve the medical integration of care, accelerate process improvement, and improve facilities will grow.

The Texas Back Institute, founded in 1978 with the vision of becoming the spine equivalent of the Texas Heart Institute, illustrates a more established and more medically integrated practice unit in the same field as the Boston Spine Group. The staff of the institute is integrated across medical specialties and includes occupational and physical therapists and fitness trainers. Texas Back Institute operates out of a dedicated facility at the Plano Presbyterian hospital, together with nine freestanding feeder clinics with a strong focus on the care cycle rather than interventions. Only about 10 percent of Texas Back Institute patients end up having surgery. Patients who do have surgery enjoy rapid recovery times.[21]

The Cleveland Clinic illustrates a more fully developed integrated practice unit in cardiac care. The Clinic's Heart Center is contained in a multi-floored building on the hospital's main campus. All the specialists (cardiologists, cardiac surgeons, and anesthesiologists, among others) are co-located, with offices in the Heart Center. All nurses and other staff are dedicated to cardiac care. Operating rooms and other procedure rooms are designed for, and dedicated to, cardiac care. The intensive care units serve only cardiac patients, as do the regular hospital beds. Patients in the intensive care units are grouped by their particular cardiac condition. While physicians still report to their traditional specialty group, the co-location of dedicated physicians is an important step toward true practice integration. The Heart Center will soon become the Cardiovascular Institute, incorporating specialists in vascular care into the practice unit and operating in a larger dedicated facility currently under construction. In addition to an integrated practice unit in cardiovascular care, the Cleveland Clinic has a similar unit in eye care (the Cole Eye Institute). The Clinic is moving to the integrated practice unit model (through what it terms *institutes*) in all major fields.

The M. D. Anderson Cancer Center is another example of an advanced, integrated practice unit model. Over the last decade, M. D. Anderson has established more than a dozen clinics that integrate care for particular types of cancer. Each clinic brings together dedicated medical oncologists, surgeons, radiologists, pathologists, radiation therapists, and other specialists in common clinical space, where patients can see multiple specialists in the same visit. Clinics include co-located imaging facilities, and include facilities for chemotherapy on a nearby floor. In-patient facilities are also specialized by type of cancer, as are many in-patient staff.

The specialists caring for a patient act as a team, with one physician designated as the team captain. The team captain and an advanced practice nurse follow the patient through diagnosis, treatment, and recovery, as well as follow up to check on progress. The team captain may change as care progresses, with both the physician and the patient holding veto power over the relationship.

Each clinic is managed by a physician head and a center administrative director (usually a senior nurse). When practicing in the clinic, all physicians are under the supervision of the clinic head. The clinic head leads regular practice improvement meetings, utilizing multiple results measures and process metrics. However, as is the case at the Cleveland Clinic, physicians retain their affiliation with their traditional specialty departments. Department chairs take responsibility for recruiting and mentoring.

In these more advanced integrated practice unit examples, the important medical specialists and skilled personnel (including nurses and technicians) are fully dedicated to the practice unit. One of the major benefits of volume and experience in a practice unit is just this ability to support a dedicated team.

Reporting structures in which physicians remain in traditional specialty groups or in which there is dual reporting both to a practice unit head and the specialty group remain the norm. Over time, however, we believe that the primary reporting relationship for operational purposes should be the IPU, not the medical specialty.

As we will discuss further, the traditional model of contracting with physicians, in which physicians are independent free agents, complicates the process of moving to integrated practice unit structures. Even at the Cleveland Clinic, where all physicians are salaried staff, cardiologists and cardiac surgeons continue their affiliation with their departments. Over time, however, providers with staff physicians should be able to move more quickly to truly integrated management.[22]

IPUs need to accept responsibility for the full cycle of care, even if they do not directly control all of it. We have discussed how the Cleveland Clinic and M. D. Anderson are proactive in managing the continuity of care with the hospital and reaching out to referring physicians. At the New England Baptist Hospital, care managers specialized in each medical condition guide patients through the cycle of care after diagnosis. Specialized patient education classes are held prior to admission for surgery. The care manager shepherds the patient while he or she is in the hospital, and oversees the development of a detailed, written discharge plan. This plan, which is approved by all the physicians involved, documents the subsequent steps required by the patient and others, and what to do in the case of difficulty. Providers are just scratching the surface in learning how to better integrate care over the cycle and manage the patient relationship both inside and outside the confines of the hospital or physician practice.

Organization into practice units, co-location of staff in common facilities, and the use of care managers, however, are a means to an end, not ends in themselves. The central goal is to deliver care in a different way that is centered on patient value. Unless the staff involved embrace the goal of patient value, grouping them into a practice unit will have little impact. Similarly, unless the principle of medically integrated care is accepted, dedicated facilities will yield little benefit.

ThedaCare, mindful of these issues, chose to begin its process of moving to practice units with week-long, team-based process improvement workshops. These aim to encourage the staff in service lines to rethink and restructure care delivery from a patient value perspective. Over time, ThedaCare management expect that this new focus will create the conditions for successful medically integrated practice units. ThedaCare has resisted physician groups seeking a dedicated facility unless they are clearly committed to patient-centric practices, have a results orientation, and are dedicated to process improvement.

In addition to the examples we have discussed, there are a growing number of providers moving toward the IPU model. For example, other cancer centers, such as Dana Farber, have made strides toward IPUs focusing on types of cancer. Dartmouth-Hitchcock Medical Center has developed an integrated Spine Center. Brigham and Women's Hospital has recently announced a new Cardiovascular Center, which will have a dedicated building. Whether such groupings are called institutes, clinics, centers, or other designations, the essential principles are the same. But calling a group a center or an institute does not make it an integrated practice unit. The acid test is whether care is patient centered for a medical condition, dedicated and integrated over the cycle of care.

Create a Distinctive Strategy in Each Practice Unit

Organizing around medically integrated practice units will enable a major improvement in patient value. Patient value will benefit even further if providers find ways *within* each practice unit to establish distinctive areas of excellence. There are numerous ways in which a provider can distinguish itself in a practice unit—through concentrating on complex diagnoses, serving particular patient groups such as women or older patients with co-occurring conditions, offering extraordinary timeliness or efficiency, demonstrating excellence in long-term disease management, and others. These are all means to an end, which is even better outcomes per dollar expended.

In health care, there is a tendency to think that there is a single gold standard for how to practice in each field. Providers search for the "best" protocol or standard of care. This tends to be emulated by all providers that offer services in a field. There are certainly important gains to be achieved from practice guidelines, as we have emphasized. However, a generic, "me too" approach to practice that emulates leaders might raise a provider to average performance but is not the path to true excellence. Standardization of care in a medical condition, though advocated by many, belies the complexity of care delivery and the variety of patient circumstances.[23]

Instead of standardized care, the better long-term model is competition on results. As providers compete to improve on current practices and distinguish themselves through expertise in addressing patient differences, results will improve more rapidly than through adherence to standard guidelines.

Another instinct among providers is to gear up to handle any case that might present itself and attempt to deal with every conceivable patient circumstance. Yet this approach impedes the development of deep expertise while making it more difficult to match facilities and needs. If a provider gears up for every possible circumstance, excess capacity is virtually guaranteed.

In each IPU, a provider should seek a distinctive focus that differentiates it from other local and regional competitors. This does not mean that everything about a practice unit should be different. It does mean, however, that a practice unit should aim to deliver superior value (in quality, cost, or both) in some aspects of the care cycle or for some meaningful group of patients. The pursuit of a distinctive approach will drive the development of deeper expertise and stimulate innovation in facilities and methods.

The strategy for an IPU, then, needs to define the types of services where the provider will build special expertise and the particular patient groups it will be expert in serving. These choices will affect how care delivery is configured and the nature of the facilities needed. They should also become a central focus of provider marketing. As providers differentiate themselves, patient value will grow rapidly.

There are myriad opportunities for providers to distinguish themselves in a medical condition, though no one provider should pursue them all. The following choices are by no means exhaustive.

Types of Services Provided
- The overall severity or complexity of cases
- The degree of specialization in particular subconditions
- The emphasis on diagnosis and second opinions versus treatment
- The range of procedures or services performed
- The comprehensiveness of in-house services over the care cycle

- The relative emphasis on risk management, prevention, rehabilitation, and disease management versus acute treatment
- The quality and depth of partnerships or relationships with leading centers in the medical condition
- The convenience of locations
- The timeliness of services (e.g., waiting time)

Types of Patients Served
- The age, gender, or ethnicity of patients
- The degree of emphasis on patients with multiple conditions
- The particular types of patients served in terms of disease or genetic variations (e.g., as in cancers)
- The extent of foreign or non-English-speaking patients

Providers will choose different ways to distinguish themselves based on their locations and expertise. An urban provider will typically make different choices than a rural provider because of the presence of numerous nearby competitors. Urban providers, because they draw on larger populations, will have more scope to differentiate themselves in terms of particular medical conditions, patient groups, and types of treatments provided. Rural providers will tend to differentiate themselves more by their role in the cycle of care. For example, rural providers can distinguish themselves in selected medical conditions, the quality of their referral relationships, and their medical integration with centers for complex conditions.

Within an IPU, individual physicians can be encouraged to develop unique expertise and subspecializations that deepen the overall competence of the group. At the Heart Center at the Cleveland Clinic, for example, individual surgeons are not all generalists treating the full range of heart-related conditions but tend to concentrate in order to develop deeper expertise in particular areas. Most surgeons perform coronary bypasses, for example, but some concentrate on mitral valve surgery, while others focus on surgery of the aorta. Yet the entire group collects a common set of clinical information and works together to improve the care delivery process. A similar process of subspecialization is under way at the Boston Spine Group.

Measure Results, Experience, Methods, and Patient Attributes by Practice Unit

Among the most important provider steps in moving to value-based competition is the measurement of results and the factors that influence them. It is difficult to improve value without measuring results. No physician or provider organization will be truly effective in attaining and sustaining excellence without knowing where it stands. A move by providers to measure results, make results transparent, and use results information to improve value would be the single most important step in transforming the health care system

Most providers have been woefully slow to collect results information even for internal purposes, much less for comparing themselves with others. Provider reticence about measurement has brought on, to a considerable extent, the attempts at micromanagement by outside parties that providers detest. Fortunately, the tide is turning, and results measurement will eventually be unavoidable. Unless providers take the lead in collecting, analyzing, and disseminating results information, they will open themselves to increasingly intrusive second-guessing and reporting imposed by outside parties. More and more providers are concluding that there is no longer a choice. For example, Tenet Healthcare, with its history of problems, has embraced participation in all legitimate quality measurement initiatives, including a commitment to public reporting.

As we have discussed, a range of information initiatives are under way. Most are focused on process information (methods) rather than results, and on institution-wide measures such as the incidence of computerized prescribing or overall infection rates. As we have argued, the most relevant unit for measurement is medical conditions, not broad functions, physician practices, or hospitals as a whole. Information also needs to encompass the full cycle of care for a patient.[24]

Measuring the Information Hierarchy. What information should providers collect for each integrated practice unit to guide value improvement? We introduced the information hierarchy in chapter 4 (see figure 4-5). Providers should collect information by medical condition at each level of the hierarchy: results (outcomes, costs, and prices), experience (a tool for matching patients and providers and a rough proxy for the skill and efficiency), methods (the processes used in care delivery), and patient attributes (to control for initial conditions and identify causal factors affecting methods and expected results).

Each IPU must be required to develop and implement a measurement plan. There is no simple formula that determines the specific measures that a provider should track, because each medical condition differs. Ultimately, each IPU must be charged with proposing and developing its own metrics in each part of the hierarchy and improving them over time, drawing on external best practices. Providers should develop, collect, and analyze far more measures for internal management purposes than are required to be disclosed externally.

Patient Medical Outcomes

- *Outcome measures.* There are multiple dimensions of medical outcomes in a medical condition. In spine care, for example, there are a number of validated measures covering pain reduction, improvement in the range of movement, and functional ability. Another important outcome is time between the beginning of care and the return to work or restoration of normal activity.

  At minimum, and to the extent possible, providers should collect all the outcome measures that have been validated in clinical studies. In spine care, as in other fields, some validated metrics have been developed for use in clinical testing of medical devices or drugs. The Food and Drug Administration and the Centers for Disease Control and Prevention have also defined some useful outcome measures for particular diseases. Use of such validated measures improves rigor and facilitates external comparisons.

  There is a pressing need, however, to expand the number and sophistication of outcome measures in virtually every medical condition. Practice units should be encouraged to develop and experiment with new measures. For internal purposes, providers should err on the side of more outcome measures rather than less. The development of measurement standards should be a major agenda item for medical boards and societies, as we will discuss.

  Outcome measures should cover the full cycle of care, not just individual interventions. The time period over which outcomes are measured must be matched with meaningful patient results. Short-term outcome measures, such as thirty-day survival rates, are misleading and can encourage counterproductive care to game the measures.

- *Complications, errors, and failed treatments.* Measures should be collected for each type of complication (and its severity) that can arise in treating a medical condition across the care cycle, along with the consequences in terms of additional care. Errors that might occur in treatment or patient management (e.g., medication errors, procedural errors) also should be identified and measured, along with their consequences. Finally, providers must measure treatments that fail or need to be repeated, which have major consequences for patient value.

- *Diagnostic accuracy.* As we have discussed, diagnosis should be treated as a distinct set of activities with major consequences for patient results. Measures of diagnostic quality (e.g., accuracy, completeness, timeliness, and cost) should be devised and collected. Treatment plans should also be compared with actual care and its effectiveness.

- *Patient registries.* Registries should be established to track treated patients over long periods of time. Periodic contact with patients over time is invaluable in judging the true value of care. Registries can also reveal insights about how to modify care to improve long-term outcomes. Providers should take the lead in long-term tracking to improve their care delivery. Suppliers of drugs, devices, and services can be partners in such efforts, and bear some of the costs.

- *Patient feedback.* Patient surveys should be conducted during the cycle of care to gain supplemental information on medical outcomes as well as the fit between the care delivered and the patient's values and preferences. Surveying patients on their service experience (e.g., waiting time, amenities) is beneficial, but ultimately less important than determining their perceptions of the medical outcomes of their care.

Cost by Activity over the Care Cycle. Cost information is necessary to measure the value of care and, ultimately, to set prices. Costs need to be measured by activity over the care delivery value chain (see the discussion later in this chapter). Currently, cost measurement and accumulation by providers is crude. Costs are accumulated and billed separately for office visits, tests, supplies, procedures, hospital rooms, and so on. Physician costs and hospital costs are treated separately. The full costs for a patient over the care cycle are rarely, if ever, aggregated and analyzed. The costs of individual services tend to be an average derived from arbitrary allocations of the costs of shared facilities, equipment, and staff, rather than the true costs borne in treating a particular patient for a particular condition. Other costs crucial to the overall cost of care go unmeasured, such as the cost of drugs and other expenditures borne by the patient or by other providers that bill separately.

It is striking that in a field so preoccupied with cost, the understanding of cost is often so primitive. The focus has been less on understanding and reducing costs than on learning to bill creatively to maximize revenue. Charges have simply been passed on. The attention that has been paid to cost has tended in many cases to be focused on throughput, physician productivity (e.g., patients per day), and bargaining down the prices of big-ticket inputs (e.g., implants, drugs, and supplies). Minimizing these costs, however, may not be the best approach to improving value.

Providers need to design cost systems around IPUs, not functions, transactions, or procedures. Costs should be aggregated by activity (e.g., in-house rehabilitation) for individual patients. The total costs of episodes of care (such as diagnosis) should be measured, including tests, consultations, and evaluations by specialists. Shared costs should be allocated based on the time, capacity, or resources involved in addressing a particular patient (e.g., time to perform an imaging scan, operative time), not overall averages. Cost should be accumulated and compared for each patient over the cycle of care. To support this kind of cost measurement, careful process definition is essential. The discrete activities involved in care delivery must be defined and documented to allow costs to be assigned to meaningful categories using activity-based costing systems. (See the discussion of the care delivery value chain, a tool for delineating and analyzing the process of care delivery, later in this chapter.)

Ultimately, costs must be matched with clinical outcomes to determine value for patients. To enhance and systematize such a process, Intermountain Health Care entered into a ten-year, $100 million joint venture with GE Healthcare in 2005 to develop an activity-based costing system that would also enable the storage and analysis of a longitudinal electronic medical record of each patient.[25] IHC found that current IT systems failed to embody the ability to characterize detailed clinical processes needed to integrate financial and clinical data.[26]

With appropriate cost information, providers can move beyond ad hoc analysis to understand the true cost of providing care to each patient, and the factors (such as complications and recovery time) that affect these costs. Providers can begin to understand how costs in one part of the care cycle affect costs elsewhere. Costs must be combined with medical outcomes to understand value. Value and costs can then be analyzed in terms of experience, methods, and patient attributes. In the long run, this will enable setting prices based on value.

Experience. Providers need to measure their annual volume and experience (cumulative volume) in terms of patients served for each medical condition. Volume and experience should also be tracked for each activity in the care cycle (e.g., tests of each type, surgical procedures, rehab cycles, diagnoses). Such information should be collected for individual doctors, teams, and sites, not just for the hospital system or physician group as a whole.

Volume and experience data should ultimately be supplemented by data on *each individual patient*. This way, experience can be further broken down by patient attributes such as age, gender, initial severity of illness, and co-occurring conditions.

Methods. Methods are the actual processes used in delivering care. Measures should be devised and collected on the relevant aspects of each care delivery activity and on the quality of coordination across activities (e.g., sequence of actions; length of time involved; types of personnel involved; and use of inputs such as tests, devices, supplies, information sharing, and consultations across activities). In parts of the care cycle, such as risk management and disease management, process measures should cover extended periods of time.

The process characteristics that can affect patient value (outcomes and costs) are very numerous, and the number of relevant measures will tend to expand as providers learn. Providers should err on the side of capturing more measures in order to facilitate such learning, and prune measures with no predictive value over time. As medical records are automated, outcome, cost, and methods metrics will be able to be compiled at far lower cost than is the case today.

Patient Attributes. Patient attributes are important to control outcomes and costs for initial conditions, characterize experience more precisely, and better understand the causes of the relationship between methods and results. Over time, as knowledge grows, care delivery will be tailored more to the particular patient's circumstances. Providers need to begin laying the groundwork for such approaches. Such standard patient attributes as age, gender, race, weight, and the presence of other diagnoses will be relevant to collect for most medical conditions. Other patient attributes that are important will be specific to particular medical conditions. Over time, as technology progresses and costs of information storage and testing decline, genetic information, digital images and diagnosis, and complex test results can be captured as initial conditions. As with methods, providers should err on the side of capturing more patient characteristics even if their link to results has yet to be definitively established. As a provider learns and its sophistication grows, the array of patient attributes tracked will continually evolve. Retrospective collection of patient attribute data is very costly, except for invariant patient attributes such as genetic makeup. Some providers are considering the step of seeking blood samples from consenting former patients to obtain genetic traits as the ability to personalize care becomes closer to reality.

Many providers are beginning to collect more results and process information, as we have discussed in earlier chapters, though few if any providers are measuring the full hierarchy. An example of a provider that is moving down the path of collecting outcomes and methods information is the Boston Spine Group, as shown in figure 5-4. In addition, New England Baptist Hospital is undertaking a registry of all its orthopedic patients, including spine patients.

Collecting and Acting on Clinical Information. Why has clinical information not been collected by many providers until recently? We

FIGURE 5-4

Clinical and outcome information collected and analyzed by the Boston Spine Group

Outcomes

Patient outcomes
(before and after treatment, multiple times)

Visual Analog Scale (pain)

Oswestry Disability Index, 10 questions (functional ability)

SF-36 questionnaire, 36 questions (burden of disease)

Length of hospital stay

Time to return to work or normal activity

Service satisfaction *(periodic)*

Office visit satisfaction metrics (10 questions)

Overall medical satisfaction

"Would you have surgery again for the same problem?"

Medical complications

Cardiac
   Myocardial infarction
   Arrhythmias
   Congestive heart failure

Vascular deep venous thrombosis

Urinary infections

Pneumonia

Postoperative delirium

Drug interactions

Surgery complications

Patient returns to the operating room

Infection

Nerve injury

Sentinel events (wrong-site surgeries)

Hardware failure

Methods

Surgery process metrics

Operative time

Blood loss

Devices or products used

Source: The Boston Spine Group.

have discussed some of the reasons in earlier chapters. Collecting and analyzing data is costly and has not been rewarded. Providers fear misuse of data and question the accuracy of risk adjustment. Providers with limited numbers of patients are concerned that data will be unfair or unreliable.

Though these concerns are important in explaining why data has not been reported publicly, few providers have collected comprehensive information even for internal purposes. Organizational structures centered on functions rather than practice units complicate measurement. Physicians and other skilled personnel involved in care maintain separate practices. Care and measurement is structured around discrete procedures or interventions, not care cycles. Care delivery methods are often idiosyncratic and not codified, so that collecting consistent measures is difficult. Different provider units often collect different information, which is not integrated. At New England Baptist Hospital, for example, the Boston Spine Group collects all the pre- and post-treatment patient information, such as the extent of pain and ability to function, while the hospital collects information about the surgery and hospital stay (e.g., operating time, blood loss, infections, days in the hospital). In many hospitals, even when such highly relevant information is collected, it is rarely assembled across the care cycle. Some providers have appointed senior corporate executives with responsibility for quality, but current quality initiatives are too narrowly focused on process compliance.

Few providers have established and assigned responsibility for clinical and cost information, or institutionalized process improvement. With no one assigned clear responsibility for improving patient results, the process of measurement has been left to the vision and conviction of individual physicians. It is no coincidence that Fairview's Minnesota Cystic Fibrosis Center, discussed earlier, became a leader in collecting results information. The center is led by Warren Warwick, the same physician who accepted the mandate from the Cystic Fibrosis Foundation in 1964 to collect the first systematic outcome data from the thirty-one cystic fibrosis practices operating at the time.[27] His personal commitment to measurement and benchmarking was later institutionalized and has driven rapid value improvement at Fairview for decades.

In a practice unit structure, information becomes the central management tool. It is how leaders evaluate IPU performance, measure the performance of individual contributors, and set priorities for enhancing care delivery. There needs to be a physician with clear responsibility for practice information, and an administrator to coordinate the process of assembling information and preparing reports and analyses. While there can be a central support group, the fundamental responsibility for information must rest with each practice unit.

For many providers, the initial task will be to pull together existing information that resides in multiple places in the organization, and to code information contained on paper charts. Providers that have moved to electronic records will gain major advantages in assembling a basic core of results, experience, and methods measures. Recapturing historical patient data can be cumbersome, but providers can begin the process of assembling such histories to build a critical mass of data.

Information needs to be compiled for specific teams and individuals so they know how they compare. ThedaCare, for example, provides performance data for each physician group and site, as well as for each physician. Also, referring physicians need information on how their referred patients fare. More providers are moving to collect results and cost information at the physician level. Sentara now provides doctors with individual reports showing how their clinical results and costs compare to the average and best results in the system. The decision whether to keep individual physicians' data confidential or to make it public should rest on the level of confidence in the data and whether physicians have had an opportunity to act on the data to improve their performance. At ThedaCare, unblinded physician feedback on some measures has been provided for several years.

The amount of information to be collected can seem daunting, but the important thing is to get started. Starting early is important because the value of the information rises as it accumulates over time. More data points begin to reveal patterns and unusual variations in results and processes. More data allows greater statistical validity, and makes results more convincing to outside parties.

Information initiatives need to start with simple steps rather than grand solutions. Even relatively straightforward information can yield an astonishing impact on patient value, as some of the examples we have discussed in this and other chapters make clear. The range of measures collected can expand over time once the process of measurement has begun. The impact on health care value will be enormous, as the experience in those areas where comparative information is available demonstrates (see chapter 4).

Assembling Comparative Information. Comparative information is not necessary to improve value, because a provider can benchmark against itself: across time, across sites, across patients, across teams. However, the value of information rises even further when a provider is able to *compare* itself to others. The process of assembling comparative national information on medical conditions has been halting and has occurred in relatively few fields, as we discussed in chapter 4 (see especially the box "How

Good Outcome Information Arose"). Outside of these fields, the only comparative information across many providers and practice units is the all-payer claims data. This data can be used to create imperfect but indicative measures of experience, complications, and mortality by provider, though it has rarely been utilized this way. Though validated risk adjustment models exist in just a few fields, these fields are highly complex and involve very sick patients, suggesting that risk adjustment should be feasible in many IPUs.[28] There is no better way to improve the understanding of the effect of patient attributes on results than for providers to analyze their own data.

Since comparison of results with other providers remains challenging, the place for most providers to begin is *internally*. Each integrated practice unit should be charged with seeking out, measuring, and analyzing all available national benchmarks that can be drawn from the literature and medical societies. For example, the Boston Spine Group utilizes a number of validated functional metrics (shown in figure 5-4), while the Cleveland Clinic utilizes national benchmarks developed by the Society of Thoracic Surgeons. Providers need not, and should not, wait for generally accepted risk adjustment algorithms, but must start developing their own insights into the effect of patient initial conditions. Providers that engage this task early are likely to benefit more in terms of learning and process improvement.

One way to jump-start the effort of developing comparative information is to pursue a collaborative approach with other providers. Health plans and employers can also be included. A pioneering example is the Wisconsin Collaborative for Healthcare Quality (WCHQ), a voluntary consortium involving numerous hospitals, clinics, and health plans in the southern part of Wisconsin.[29] Beginning in 2003, WCHQ has published comparative results on forty-two measures, drawing on a variety of sources. While most of the measures published remain process measures, some are disease-specific outcome measures. The aim is to broaden this important initiative over time.

Making Information Transparent. Once a provider begins to develop a body of information, there are strong benefits to communicating it externally. This reveals a true commitment to patient value and catalyzes internal efforts at improvement. As Donald Berwick, founder of the Institute for Healthcare Improvement (IHI), has stressed, making information available to patients is an enabling condition for true commitment to excellence. In addition, transparency and dissemination speed the rate of improvement and begin to establish the reputation of the provider. At ThedaCare, where data began to be made public beginning in October 2003, there was a stepped-up focus on improvement by its affiliated physicians.

The Cleveland Clinic, long associated with excellence in patient care, has been publishing an annual report on its experience and clinical outcomes in cardiac and thoracic surgery since 1999. By 2005, outcome reporting had expanded to numerous other practice units. The Clinic is moving to require *every* clinical department to develop and publish outcome measures over the coming years. (An overview of the Cleveland Clinic outcome reports and excerpts from a recent edition are contained in appendix A.)

Other hospitals are beginning to follow suit, a very encouraging development. The Clinic's reports have been part of the motivation for similar reports by the University of Pennsylvania Hospital, Brigham and Women's Hospital (Boston), and Dartmouth-Hitchcock Medical Center. The Dartmouth-Hitchcock case is particularly interesting because the hospital does not rank at the top on all the measures reported.[30]

The mentality of secrecy in health care is deeply ingrained, and physicians and hospital administrators fear that less than stellar results will cause them to lose patients and increase the risk of lawsuits. A large majority of hospital administrators surveyed in 2005 were against public reporting of medical errors.[31] The Dartmouth case and the Cincinnati Children's Hospital's positive experience in sharing below-average results data with parents, described in chapter 4, belie this sort of thinking. Patients will admire a provider that is willing to measure and hold itself accountable even if it currently does not rank at the top. Transparency sends a strong message about commitment to patients and commitment to improvement. Also, a move to making results transparent may actually reduce the risk of litigation. If results information is transparent and true risks are known, patients will be better informed and claims of malpractice harder to sustain except for truly substandard providers. Interestingly, the hospital administrators surveyed in states where there was already mandatory public reporting were more supportive of disclosing hospital names than administrators who had never faced required reporting. Again, the tide may be turning.

Ultimately, we believe that collection and reporting of results information will be a condition of practicing medicine, and no longer discretionary. If a provider cannot offer sufficient evidence to document its results in a medical condition because of limited patient experience, there are real questions about whether the provider should be offering that service.[32] If a provider cannot demonstrate good results over time, there are real questions about whether it should continue to practice.

Move to Single Bills and New Approaches to Pricing

The shift to value-based competition will require a transformation of cost accumulation, billing, and pricing. Today, providers issue a myriad of bills for discrete charges. Hospitals issue multiple bills for each visit, and even for the same treatment. Each doctor issues a separate bill. This approach is hugely expensive for everyone in the system, with no compensating patient value benefit. Indeed, the current model undermines value by obscuring costs (and value delivered) for all parties. Finally, the current system results in many different prices for the same service, depending on the patient's health'coverage. This raises administrative expenses and makes it nearly impossible for prices to be truly transparent to anyone— even physicians and billing departments often do not know the price in advance. Providers will need to improve the efficiency of billing methods even in the short run. Otherwise they will be overwhelmed by the trend toward higher deductibles (as with health savings accounts) and thus the increased need for direct billing of patients rather than health plans for small charges.

Over time, the whole approach to cost accumulation, billing, and pricing will need to change. Providers will need to issue a single bill for each episode of care and eventually the full care cycle. It is the entire episode, not a discrete service, that is the meaningful cost for assessing the value delivered. Providers must understand these full costs, and take responsibility for managing them. Aggregating these total costs will also lead to exactly the kind of scrutiny by providers themselves that will improve value. The charges for each specialty service or function will be compared to its contribution to overall value. Individual entities whose costs are out of line with value will see their share of reimbursement fall or will be replaced. These decisions will be made by knowledgeable providers rather than outside parties. Customary charges will fade in importance.

The conventions and obstacles that prevent single billing can and must be overcome, as they have in other businesses. The biggest obstacles are inertia, the fragmentation of independent practitioners, primitive cost accounting systems, and the reluctance to diverge from the billing practices of Medicare. None of these are insurmountable obstacles today. All will ease as obstacles in the future.

Building the capability for combined billing can start with discrete care episodes such as diagnostic office visits (combining physician fees, all tests, and other associated charges) and hospitalizations. Over time, the capability to bill for multivisit treatment cycles will follow. Eventually, providers must learn to accumulate costs and bill for the full cycle of care. All these steps will also help providers better understand their costs and facilitate price comparisons with peers.

Single billing will require independent practitioners to become team players. It will also require providers to sort out the issue of who the aggregator is—that is, which entity will assemble the bill and direct the resulting payments to the various parties. The hospital is the most obvious aggregator for hospital-based care. Some physicians do not view hospitals as partners and may not trust the hospital's motives or its ability to efficiently manage such transactions. However, similar issues have long since been addressed in other industries. There is simply no valid justification for the current billing system. We are convinced that health plans and employers will begin to exert increasing pressure for single, unified bills.

Providers that start now to create the capability for single billing will gain an advantage in preparing for this eventuality. Moreover, preparing for single billing will have huge benefits for providers even if they never issue one, because it will equip them to understand their costs. The movement toward billing for cycles of care will spread much more rapidly if Medicare joins this trend, as we will discuss in chapter 8.

A logical and, we believe, inevitable next step beyond single bills is a single fixed, agreed-upon price for episodes or care cycles (or periods of time for a chronic condition). Instead of simply aggregating all the actual charges, the price would be set up front. This model further aligns pricing with value, and creates even stronger incentives to coordinate and integrate care. Care-cycle pricing is already in use in transplant services, as we discuss in chapter 6, and was used successfully in a Medicare demonstration, as we discuss in chapter 8. To avoid an unnecessary risk premium in the price, the care cycle will need to be clearly specified. Also, providers should be compensated for unexpected complications at an agreed-upon rate (see chapter 6).

Why has single, bundled pricing not already occurred? An extreme version of single pricing was attempted in the 1980s in the form of capitation, or a fixed fee per person per year for all the services provided by a hospital. Capitation was another unfortunate example of thinking at the wrong level—the level of the hospital or provider group as a whole. Capitation covering all treatment for any condition put providers into the risk management business and created almost irresistible incentives to withhold services. Providers found this system untenable. Today, capitation is rare except in the case of integrated health plan and provider systems such as Intermountain and Kaiser Permanente. These organizations are successful because they have been attentive to measuring quality and care processes to ensure that patients get appropriate care. A single price stated (by the provider) for addressing a known medical condition is an entirely different matter from capitation. Risk is much lower, and can be further mitigated through provisions for unexpected complications.

Historically, the absence of results information and competition for patients has given providers little incentive to move to single prices, which could turn into another mechanism for cost shifting by health plans.

However, health plans will begin to accumulate charges across the care cycle even if providers do not, and use such information to their advantage. As results data expands, the question for health plans will shift from "How big a discount can we obtain for this procedure?" to "What is the overall price for obtaining a good outcome?" Superior providers will benefit from higher prices or from higher margins due to greater efficiency at equal or lower prices.[33]

We believe it is only a matter of time before health plans will move to expect single prices, with provisions for unexpected complications billed at or near cost (with no margin). Hence, providers will have no incentive to withhold care (especially if results are publicly reported), nor will they be rewarded for providing more care than is expected or needed. Providers that habitually experience complications will ultimately lose patients, unless the data justifying their substandard results are compelling.

Those providers that can begin to offer such pricing models to health plans and patients, together with robust data on results to support them, will be in a position to gain market share. In this and in so many other of the areas we have discussed, providers can either find reasons to resist change or become leaders. Those providers that move proactively to align their practice with value will not only better serve patients, but also will increasingly prosper as competition on value grows.[34]

Eventually, prices will start to vary based on the location of service. For example, patients desiring to receive care in a higher-cost setting where there is no meaningful difference in terms of quality (e.g., a teaching hospital campus for routine care) should bear a higher price and a higher deductible. This will help migrate the care delivered by providers to more cost-effective locations.

Also, as we will discuss further in chapter 6, pricing needs to incorporate gain sharing so that providers are not penalized for improvements in care delivery methods that result in revenues falling faster than costs. Today, reducing the need for hospitalization or expensive procedures or tests can result in a loss.[35] Care-cycle pricing, instead of service-based pricing, will help to eliminate this problem. In the interim, however, providers need to propose contracts with gain-sharing provisions.

Ultimately, as costing and pricing practices evolve, providers can begin to differentiate their prices from other providers in medical conditions. Those providers that can demonstrate superior results in a practice unit may choose to seek higher prices that capture some of that value, or to match or reduce prices to attract a greater volume of patients, thus feeding the virtuous circle of value improvement we discussed earlier.[36]

We believe that the current model of setting many prices for the same service based on the insurance group is unwise and works against health care value. Cost and value have nothing to do with the group or government program to which a particular patient belongs. The current model also creates complexity for both providers and health plans that drives up total costs while obscuring price comparisons.

We believe that each provider should begin to move toward more consistent pricing across its patients, and seek to persuade health plans and other system participants of the benefits of a new system. Consistent prices will greatly improve price transparency, because posted prices will be far more meaningful than current list prices, which are far higher than the actual price paid by most patients. Providers with true posted prices will be able to communicate their value to patients and attract patients covered by health plans with which they do not have a contract. Health plans will also benefit in the long run by eliminating the huge expense and limitations of contracted networks.

Moving to reduce or eliminate price discrimination based on group affiliation is controversial, and system participants currently benefiting from cross subsidies may resist it. Regulatory changes may be required to limit the gap between the highest and lowest price, as we discuss in chapter 8.

Market Services Based on Excellence, Uniqueness, and Results

The current marketing of health care services is based largely on reputation, breadth of services, convenience, the building of referral relationships, and word of mouth. Some providers are utilizing patient and physician amenities and services as marketing tools. Hackensack University Hospital (New Jersey), for example, attracts patients with in-room flat screen TVs and designer gowns, and attracts physicians with new operating rooms. Amenities and nonmedical services can attract patients and generate incremental revenue if patients are willing to pay extra for them.

The focus of marketing in health care delivery must shift to patient value. Value is determined at the medical condition level, not the hospital or practice overall. More providers are publicizing rankings such as those in *U.S. News and World Report*, but these rankings are largely based on reputation. More providers are beginning to market their capabilities in individual service lines, a very encouraging trend. Yet, these efforts are still based largely on reputation surveys or assertions that the provider is experienced and has good-quality physicians. Concrete evidence on experience and results is mostly lacking.

Marketing must shift from breadth and reputation to practice unit excellence. This means that providers must begin to communicate their areas of unique excellence at the IPU level, such as their dedicated teams and facilities, their strengths in diagnosis, their expertise in addressing particular types of cases, and their ability to coordinate care over the cycle. Instead of making general claims, providers should begin to disseminate the information that patients, employers, and health plans really want—their experience, expertise, methods, and results. The outcome reports of the Cleveland Clinic, described earlier and excerpted in appendix A, are a good example of marketing that is tied to patient value.

The role of brands also needs to change. Brands should migrate from broad institutional brands to brands (or sub-brands) associated with practice units. Also, the current model of maintaining brands for each acquired or partner institution should migrate to fewer and more integrated brands across sites and geography. We will discuss these issues further when we examine geographic expansion.

In reorienting their marketing, providers can wait for health plans or the government to require disclosure of results and experience, or they can move proactively. Those providers that begin voluntarily to disseminate results and experience information will send a powerful message both externally and internally. They will define their reputations in new and ultimately more beneficial ways for patients. And by making results public, providers will hasten the shift in internal culture to patient value.

Providers must also reorient their marketing to health plans. While this will take time, marketing must shift from price and breadth to patient value in particular medical conditions. Contracts must focus on value over the care cycle, not piecemeal costs. Instead of struggling over the micromanagement of care, providers and health plans must agree to do business based on results. Pricing must embody the principle of gain sharing: value improvements should benefit both sides. We discuss these and other aspects of a new relationship between providers and health plans in more detail in chapter 6.

Grow Locally and Geographically in Areas of Strength

Most providers have grown by expanding overall patient volume in their local area, often expanding the range of services offered. Local acquisitions (e.g., community hospitals, physician practices) have figured prominently in growth strategies. As we have discussed, however, overall size and breadth have little to do with patient value. The effort to build groups of full-line institutions across geography has achieved only modest success, because the benefits of this model are largely one-time purchasing, contracting, and overhead benefits with a modest impact on value.

Growth strategies should be centered on practice units, not broad-line institutions as a whole. Providers should grow by deeper penetration in their areas of excellence (see figure 5-2). This feeds the self-reinforcing, virtuous circle of value in care delivery that we have described.

Most providers will have opportunities to increase penetration in their most distinctive IPUs, even in their local region. In so doing, they will reallocate precious beds, space, resources, and management attention to the most productive uses. Deepening local penetration may require new facilities and often a restructuring and medical integration of existing personnel and facilities in the practice unit. Care will be coordinated over the full care cycle, with services performed in locations that are cost-effective for patients. Single large broad-line facilities, which have been the norm, should decline in importance.

Geographic expansion in particular medical conditions offers a huge, untapped growth opportunity for health care providers. Excellent providers in a practice unit can grow regionally, nationally, and even internationally. In the process, they will leverage scale, expertise, care delivery methods, staff training, measurement systems, and reputation to serve more patients. A rising number of patients in the practice unit feeds economies of scale, the subspecialization of teams, and more efficient division of labor across locations. Ultimately, the best providers in a practice unit can operate nationally through extensive networks of dedicated facilities. While this possibility seems radical today, the main barriers are attitudinal and artificial (e.g., state licensing requirements and archaic corporate practice of medicine laws).

The current structure, in which many local providers operate at modest scale in their home region, is an artifact of history and has little logic in terms of patient value. Even if most services are provided locally, services in each practice unit can be managed or supported by premier integrated national organizations. Part of the value benefits of cross-geographic competition arises from patients traveling to higher-value locations. However, an equal or greater benefit will result from the integrated management of services in a medical condition across locations, leveraging the expertise and efficiencies of a multiunit organization. Such a cross-geographic structure is what we observe in other complex professional services, such as information technology and accounting.

Geographic expansion can take a variety of forms. In some practice units, expansion may involve feeder locations providing diagnostic services and follow-up care, with complex interventions taking place at a central campus. In other cases, new facilities covering the full care cycle can be established in new locations, with only specialized cases treated at a national or regional center. Geographic expansion can involve co-location or facilities agreements with existing provider institutions, other types of partnerships, or the establishment of new, wholly owned facilities in new locations.

Whatever the ownership structure and configuration of the geographic network, however, each IPU must be medically integrated across geography. That is, all the sites need to be part of a truly integrated and coordinated practice unit under common management that spans the care cycle. In this structure, unified processes, common information infrastructure, common performance measurement systems, shared training of physicians and other staff, and efficient division of labor by location take place under an integrated management structure.

In principle, geographic care delivery networks in practice units can be international, or can compete for patients internationally by utilizing diagnostic centers and referral relationships in other countries. Interventions in the care cycle can take place in the most cost-effective location, which may be another country. Today, most international linkages involve referrals, knowledge sharing, and training of physicians, rather than integrated practice units across countries. However, international competition in health care services is sure to increase.

The potential of regional and national integration and expansion in IPUs is just beginning to be realized. Initiatives take a variety of forms. The Beth Israel Deaconess Medical Center example involving Milton Hospital, discussed earlier in this chapter, is a regional model based on a formal partnership and extensive integration. Here, a regional medical center has formed a partnership with a community hospital, Milton Hospital. Both institutions remain independent, but the partnership coordinates and medically integrates the cardiac practice. Facilities have also remained separate, but the service is co-branded. Dartmouth-Hitchcock Medical Center, in New Hampshire, has pursued a broader hub-and-spoke model involving independent physician practices and other providers in its region.

Cleveland Clinic's operations in the greater Cleveland area constitute a different model, involving a combination of wholly owned facilities and independent referrals. Like many other hospitals, the Clinic merged with a number of hospitals in its region as well as a number of family health centers and physician practices in order to offer a single source for negotiations with health plans.

Simply merging stand-alone broad-line institutions, however, makes little sense in terms of patient value. The Cleveland Clinic is beginning to truly integrate care across facilities at the medical condition level from a regional standpoint, beginning with cardiac care. In cardiac care, all hospitals and physician practices are coming under a common management structure. All cardiac surgeons in the region are part of the same integrated practice unit, collect the same information, and follow the same practice standards. The aim is for care to be delivered at the location within the region that is the most cost-effective, but at a consistently high level of quality. In other practice units, the Clinic has also moved to focus service lines among its various Cleveland-area hospitals. For example, obstetrics has been moved off the main campus and relocated to community hospitals. Psychiatric care is being combined at Lutheran Hospital to achieve the benefit of focus and scale.[37]

Geographic expansion of integrated practice units outside the home region is still rare, but will grow in the future. A few hospitals, such as the Mayo Clinic and the Cleveland Clinic, have broad-line facilities in multiple locations. The Mayo Clinic, for example, has campuses in Rochester, Minnesota; Jacksonville, Florida; and Scottsdale, Arizona. In addition, for-profit hospital chains have pursued the model of aggregating numerous broad-line hospitals across multiple markets. However, these approaches are still characterized by only modest levels of medical integration across regions.

Geographic expansion via broad-line institutions is not well aligned with value in health care delivery. There are limited synergies across geographically separate broad-line institutions. The potential benefits, in cost of capital, shared procurement, and centralization of overhead, are incremental. The real leverage is in integration across geography in practice units. As a result, chains of stand-alone, broad-line hospitals will offer limited benefits for patient value. For-profit hospital chains will need to embrace the principles we describe in this chapter or they will gain few real advantages over community hospitals and regional medical centers.

Geographic expansion should be focused on medical conditions in which a provider can offer truly excellent care in an integrated structure. One approach to doing so is managing a practice unit within another institution's facilities. The Cleveland Clinic, for example, operates the cardiac surgery practice at the Rochester General Hospital under a management contract. All the cardiac surgeons at Rochester General Hospital are employed by the Cleveland Clinic, practice under the same standards, report the same information, and are evaluated by the same top management. The Rochester physicians benefit from, and contribute to, the deep expertise and innovation of the overall practice. Rochester also enjoys the purchasing power of the overall IPU for medical devices and other costly inputs, a major area for savings.

In this example, the Rochester General Hospital owns the facilities and provides supporting services, contracting out the management of a particular practice unit to the Clinic. However, an institution with a premier practice unit could actually own the practice unit at one or more hospitals in other regions, contracting with these hospitals for facilities and shared services. Or, a premier provider could own or contract to operate a "hospital within a hospital" that is located on another institution's medical campus. Finally, IPUs could construct entirely new, dedicated facilities in other regions. Given the excess capacity already in place throughout the United States, managing, partnering, or taking over and enhancing existing facilities and existing hospitals may be more practical and more economic than greenfield investment in many cases. Through these various approaches, one can imagine a new model of a medical center in which a series of world-class providers manage the important practice units in dedicated but co-located facilities.

Whatever the ownership structure, however, the most essential aspect of geographic expansion is a focus on practice units and true medical integration across geography. Here is where the leverage lies for patient value.

Rural hospitals, with natural limits on patient volume in many services, should also be aggressively pursuing geographic integration models, both with regional centers and across contiguous rural regions. There is no reason that rural institutions, through medical integration and careful choice of partnerships in complex practice units, cannot offer truly world-class care at high levels of efficiency to their communities.

Remote medicine approaches can and should reinforce such geographic structures. Across Mayo's three campuses, for example, consultation on specialized cases occurs regularly using a state-of-the-art communication and videoconferencing network. More generally, telemedicine technology enables consultation on diagnoses, consultation on difficult cases (even for inherently local emergency care), better preparation before treatment, and better follow-up care for treatment performed at another location.

Sentara illustrates the value benefit of distance medicine approaches within a practice unit. In 2000, Sentara started utilizing distance medicine to integrate the operation of intensive care units (ICUs) across its various hospital locations. The ninety ICU beds in four hospitals are monitored from one central location. ICU patient information is continuously transmitted to a central monitoring center. A camera in the patient's room also provides visual observation. One remote intensivist (a critical care physician) monitors all patients, together with local nurses in each ICU who actually deliver care.

The remote ICU, which supplements regular hospital rounds and in-person care, enables better anticipation of the needs of patients and quicker reaction times. Lab test results that arrive in the middle of the night, for example, are integrated into patient treatment immediately. In the first nine months with the remote ICU model, Sentara's per-patient ICU cost declined by $2,150, with a total savings of $4.9 million on an initial investment of $1.9 million, or a 155 percent return on investment. Mortality fell by 20 percent and length of hospital stay by 17 percent.[38]

Distance medicine was especially beneficial in the smaller hospitals. It also reduced turnover of critical care nurses, and improved the quality of life of the intensivist physicians by providing them with a more predictable schedule. Before the remote ICU, an on-call intensivist's beeper went off every thirty to forty-five minutes, day and night. The new system allows late-night calls to be referred to the remote intensivist after 9:30 p.m., so the on-call local doctor gets far fewer calls.

Gaining the most important benefits of distance medicine, however, requires medical integration of a practice unit across geography. Without common information, shared practice structures, common training, common management oversight, and personal relationships among the members of the team, the ingredients to make distance medicine truly effective are missing. Unleashing the potentially major benefits of distance medicine for patient value will require the same kinds of restructuring of care delivery into practice units and across geography that we have described in this chapter. It will also benefit by moving beyond the "we can do everything" mentality that is still prevalent in medicine.

Some of the benefits of practice unit expansion across geography can be reaped via a consulting or shared services network model. For example, the Texas Back Institute's former head of development founded a company, Prizm Development, that works with physician groups in many states to improve clinical results in spine care. In some cases, dedicated spine care centers are established. Prizm provides treatment process improvements as well as IT systems to track outcomes and patient satisfaction. Prizm has affiliates in New Mexico, Colorado, South Carolina, and Kansas, and its model of physiatrists working closely with spine surgeons is now widely emulated.[39] The value benefits of this approach can be substantial, but they could be even greater in a truly integrated practice unit structure.

Geographic expansion in all of its forms has implications for branding. Hospitals have had a tendency to position their brands as broad institutional brands spanning all their services. Instead, brands need to become associated with excellence in particular practice units. There has also been a tendency to maintain historical hospital names even after acquisitions. This is understandable in a system where the local area has been the focus. In a value-based model, where care is truly integrated within practice units across geography, however, the entire network in a practice unit should operate under the brand of the premier institution in that practice unit (or, at minimum, the co-brand). This sends the right message both to patients and to staff about the standard of excellence that will be met, and reinforces the fact that a given facility is not a stand-alone institution.

Imagine the impact that the geographic care delivery models we have described could have on the quality and cost of medical care. Patients in most communities, if not every community, could be served directly or via partnerships with excellent providers. Local physicians could deliver care in state-of-the-art facilities and enjoy the benefits of expertise, training, and management by the best in the world in their field. Consultation on any aspect of care would be easy and instantaneous. Referrals of complicated or specialized cases to an appropriate center would become the norm. Interventions would take place in locations where they would be the most efficient and effective. Continuity of care after treatment elsewhere would be automatic. Physicians, nurses, skilled technicians, and managers would be trained, measured, and coached by true experts and have a career path in their practice unit across locations based on their skill level, experience, and performance.

The eight strategic imperatives we have just described are important not just for health care organizations but for individual physicians. Some implications for individual physicians appear in the box "Implications for Individual Physicians."

How Would Industry Structure in Health Care Delivery Change?

The eight strategic imperatives imply a transformation of health care delivery that is already in the offing. Leading providers have been moving in these directions, and it is only a matter of time until the movement gains momentum. As this redefining of health care delivery plays out, what will industry structure look like?

Competition will shift to integrated practice units, based on results. Health care delivery will be fundamentally reorganized and integrated across the care cycle. Results measurement and other comparative information will expand dramatically. Information technology will permeate every aspect of health care delivery.

In each medical condition, care delivery will migrate to excellent providers with adequate volume, extensive experience, better processes, and dedicated facilities. Substandard providers unable to demonstrate results will phase out service lines. Errors, complications, overuse, and underuse of care will fall markedly as results become the arbiter of what works and who should provide care.

The supply of less valuable or unnecessary services will decline as results data reveal them, a far more powerful solution than attempting to restrict supply. Variation in outcomes across providers will diminish. The quality of health care for all Americans, including historically underserved groups, will rise markedly because the results achieved for every patient will count toward determining the results for which providers are held accountable.

Implications for Individual Physicians

*   Medical practice must be designed around *value for patients,* not convenience for physicians.
*   The business of physicians is addressing *medical conditions,* not performing a specialty. Physicians must understand what different businesses they are in.
*   Patient value comes from expertise, experience, and volume in *particular medical conditions.* Physicians must choose those medical conditions in which they will participate and achieve true excellence, rather than try to do a little of everything.
*   Health care value is maximized by an *integrated team,* not individuals acting and thinking as free agents. Physicians must know what team or teams they are part of, and ensure that these are functioning as teams.
*   Physicians rarely have full control over the value delivered to patients, but are *part of care cycles.* They need to know what care cycles they are involved in, and how to integrate care with both upstream and downstream entities to ensure good patient results.
*   Every physician must be *accountable for results.* Intuition and personal experience are no longer enough.
*   Physicians have no right to provide care without *demonstrating good results.* Results should be made available to patients, other providers, and health plans as soon as measurement is reliable.
*   Physician *referrals* should be based on excellent patient results, together with the ability of referred providers to share information and integrate care across the entities involved in the care cycle.
*   *Electronic records* and the ability to exchange and share information are indispensable to excellent medical practice. Physicians will limit effectiveness unless they wholeheartedly embrace IT.
*   Every physician should be responsible for *improving his or her own process of care delivery,* using systematic methods based on measurement of results, experience, methods, and patient attributes.
*   Physicians must seek out *partnerships and relationships with excellent providers* in their areas of practice in order to access knowledge and improve the integration of patient care.

Providers will expand significantly in the service lines in which they excel and choose to concentrate, while phasing out or relocating others. Space at hospital campuses will be realigned. Space and resources freed up by shrinking less distinctive services and moving less advanced services offsite will be reallocated to areas of true excellence.

Patients will no longer think it natural to seek all their health care from the same institution. However, the coordination of their care across providers, across the cycle of care, and across time will be significantly greater.

Fewer providers will offer care for each medical condition, and the care they deliver will have far higher value. The fragmentation of local care will decline, and today's duplicative and excess capacity will be significantly reduced. The problems of supply-driven demand will decline substantially.

Competition will span geography, with most patients able to access outstanding care outside the local area. Competition to improve results relative to national benchmarks will reduce variation in outcomes. Over time, then, there will be less need to travel to access excellent care.

There will be a growing number of regional and national providers operating in multiple geographic areas, linked to local institutions through various types of partnerships. These partnerships will enable learning through knowledge management across a broader base of practitioners and patients and will speed diffusion of best practices.

Community hospitals and rural hospitals will become more focused, but tightly connected into relationships and partnerships with regional centers. Telemedicine and remote consultations will become a normal occurrence in ways that are inconceivable today. Financial viability will be achieved by community and rural hospitals as a natural outgrowth of demonstrated value in the services they provide.

Primary care physicians will remain central actors in the system. Indeed, armed with much better information and more alternatives to which to refer patients, primary care physicians will add more value than ever before. Primary care practices will increasingly become the front end and back end of integrated care cycles. Over time, disease management will become an integrated part of the care cycle of most providers, closing the gaping hole now addressed by stand-alone disease management companies. As a net result of all these shifts, health care value will increase dramatically.

Enabling the Transformation

Moving to value-based competition presents a formidable agenda for providers. Three important enablers will help to address these strategic and organizational imperatives. The first is the care delivery value chain, a systematic approach to process identification and analysis. The second enabler is information technology. Introducing IT into current modes of practice will yield limited benefits. The real opportunity is to utilize information to transform the process of care delivery. The third enabler is the use of systematic processes for knowledge development to support continuous improvements in care delivery. Most process improvement efforts today are informal, and focus primarily on ensuring compliance with practice guidelines. Systematic knowledge development at the medical condition level will unleash a far greater rate of improvement in the methods of care delivery encompassing the entire care cycle.

Analyzing the Care Delivery Value Chain

Value-based competition requires a transformation of health care delivery. The practice unit model implies a very different conception of care delivery from the prevailing approach. Care is organized around medical conditions, and medically integrated across specialties, treatments, and services, and over time. Dedicated teams utilize facilities designed for maximum value in care delivery for the medical condition being addressed. Care over the full care cycle is tightly coordinated, and patient information is extensively and seamlessly shared. Results (outcomes and costs) are measured, analyzed, and reported. All the entities involved in the IPU accept joint responsibility and accountability for performance.

In order to implement this new model of care delivery, providers need to systematically delineate and analyze their process of care delivery at the medical condition level. The value chain, a tool developed for analyzing competition in business and other organizations, offers such a framework.[40] The value chain is based on the observation that delivering any product or service consists of performing numerous discrete activities. The choices made about how these activities are configured and integrated drive value, and should guide organizational structure.

Based on our research and discussions with an array of physicians in a variety of medical fields, we adapted value chain thinking to the delivery of health care. The care delivery value chain (CDVC), shown in figure 5-5, is the premier tool for designing an IPU. It portrays the types of activities involved in caring for patients with a particular medical condition over the entire cycle of care. This generic starting point can be specialized to a particular medical condition or combination of co-occurring conditions. (We discuss the framework in more detail, including examples applying the framework to chronic kidney disease, breast cancer, and stoke care, in appendix B.)

Every provider already has care delivery value chains for each medical condition, though these may not have been delineated explicitly. The CDVC framework first describes the current activities in each medical condition and then, more important, analyzes ways to increase the value of services to patients. The configuration of activities should then determine how the IPU should best be structured organizationally.

FIGURE 5-5

The care delivery value chain for an integrated practice unit

	Diagnosing	Preparing	Intervening	Recovering/ rehabilitating	Monitoring/ managing
Knowledge development	(Results measurement and tracking, staff/physician training, technology development, process improvement)				
Informing	(Patient education, patient counseling, pre-intervention educational programs, patient compliance counseling)				
Measuring	(Tests, imaging, patient records management)				
Accessing	(Office visits, lab visits, hospital sites of care, patient transport, visiting nurses, remote consultation)				
Monitoring/ preventing	**Diagnosing**	**Preparing**	**Intervening**	**Recovering/ rehabilitating**	**Monitoring/ managing**
• Medical history	• Medical history	• Choosing the team	• Ordering and administering drug therapy	• Inpatient recovery	• Monitoring and managing the patient's condition
• Screening	• Specifying and organizing tests	• Pre-intervention preparations	• Performing procedures	• Inpatient and outpatient rehab	• Monitoring compliance with therapy
• Identifying risk factors	• Interpreting data	◦ pretesting	• Performing counseling therapy	• Therapy fine-tuning	• Monitoring lifestyle modifications
• Prevention programs	• Consultation with experts	◦ pretreatment		• Developing a discharge plan	
	• Determining the treatment plan				

Provider margin

Patient value (health results per unit of cost)

Feedback loops

Providers should delineate and analyze the CDVC in a medical condition for the entire care cycle rather than for particular interventions or services. The activities in the CDVC can be divided into two broad categories. Those activities involved in patient care itself are the focus of our analysis here. Providers also engage in support activities, such as contracting, billing, procurement, and facilities management,[41] that often consume a great deal of management attention. We have not included these activities in figure 5-5, but they should be configured to reinforce, and not detract from, patient value. We do include one type of support activity, knowledge development, which refers to the set of activities involved in learning how to improve care processes and outcomes. Formal knowledge development by health care providers remains rare, but must become standard. Knowledge development is a crucial enabler of value-based competition, as we discuss later in this chapter.

Every care delivery value chain begins with *monitoring* and *prevention*. Monitoring and prevention include tracking a patient's circumstances, assessing risk, and taking steps to prevent or reduce the seriousness of illness or injury. The CDVC progresses through *diagnosing, preparing, intervening*, and *rehabilitating*, and ends with *monitoring* and *managing*. The latter are the activities involved in managing a medical condition over time to sustain good results and minimize reoccurrences.

Cutting across the stages of the care cycle are three additional types of care delivery activities: accessing, measuring, and informing. *Accessing* refers to the steps involved in gaining access to the patient, including patient visits, movement within the hospital or other care setting, and other means of access, such as remote monitoring and Internet consultations. *Measuring* refers to the measurement of a patient's medical circumstances. *Informing* encompasses the activities involved in notifying, educating, and coaching the patient.

These three cross-cutting activities, discussed further in appendix B, pervade each stage of the care cycle—that is, there is measurement involved in monitoring, diagnosis, intervening, and so on. Since they cut across the care cycle, these activities are the glue that binds the care cycle together. Managing them well from an integrated and cyclewide perspective is important to patient value, and absolutely essential to prevention and disease management.

The CDVC provides a framework with which to describe the current care delivery process, analyze how the care delivery process can be enhanced, examine facilities and the location of services, design geographic expansion, measure results, and accumulate costs. (We describe in more detail how to map and delineate the value chain for a cycle of care, and provide some examples, in appendix B.) The CDVC is also a tool for thinking about where to begin and end the care cycle and draw the appropriate boundaries for practice units. We will further discuss these issues later in this chapter, and in appendix B.

Current efforts at process improvement (e.g., infection control) tend to cut across the CDVCs for all conditions a provider targets. Rethinking the care delivery process for each specific medical condition will offer the greatest potential for value improvement.

The Care Delivery Value Chain in Practice. The CDVC will differ for each medical condition, and can vary somewhat in the same medical condition for different groups of patients due to their individual circumstances. Partly for this reason, the CDVC for addressing a particular medical condition can differ significantly across providers. Providers can have differing patient populations and may also have made different historical choices about how to organize care. The analysis of provider differences in the CDVC for a medical condition, and their consequences for patients, is often illuminating for value improvement.

Figure 5-5 emphasizes that the extent of the full care cycle goes well beyond the perspective and field of vision of most of today's provider organizations. In care-cycle terms, for example, release from the hospital is not the end of the cycle, nor is admission to the hospital the beginning.

Many parts of the CDVC, such as informing or preparing, are often not treated as distinct activities in overall care delivery, nor are they measured and analyzed from a value perspective. Part of the problem is the lack of information systems. Existing information systems tend to be structured around discrete functions or "silos" in the care delivery process and are difficult to integrate.

The stages in the cycle of care often unfold iteratively. An initial diagnosis and intervention, for example, can lead to a feedback loop that clarifies the diagnosis and results in further intervention, and so on. Or, deterioration of a patient's condition during recovery may trigger a feedback loop leading to new intervention. Monitoring that identifies the progression of the condition (e.g., for a patient with chronic kidney disease) leads to a feedback loop to diagnosis and perhaps a revised treatment plan. Or, if a patient does not tolerate a particular treatment or drug well, there is a loop back to the treatment to find one that works better. These iterations create cost and reduce patient quality of life until good results are achieved.

The iterative character of care delivery is inherent in medicine to some degree, but can be reduced by careful design of methods and reduction of errors. Iteration or recurring effort is a danger sign in any process or business. Much of today's iteration is caused by mistakes, poor processes, and inattention to the full care cycle. An incorrect diagnosis, for example, can send a patient down an entire care cycle that is ineffective or even harmful, making iteration inevitable. Excellent providers will tend to minimize iteration. Analyzing the incidence, nature, and causes of iterations in care is an important aspect of improving patient value.

The care delivery value chain will usually involve activities that are performed by numerous different individuals, teams, departments, and even completely different organizations. In stroke care, for example, some crucial activities are performed by emergency medical technicians (EMTs), who transport the patient to the hospital. Coordination and the management of linkages across activities, units, and entities are crucial to patient value. Thus, the ability of EMTs to make a sound preliminary assessment of stroke patients and communicate this information to the hospital during transit can be important to the timeliness and appropriateness of subsequent diagnosis and intervention.

Within a provider, operating units must see beyond their individual activity and recognize that they are part of a broader process. Imaging is not a separate service, for example, but an activity in a larger care cycle. Today, the many entities or departments involved in care tend to focus on their own roles, with little integration with upstream and downstream units. To use our earlier terminology, they see their business far too narrowly. Thus, individual entities do not accept or even perceive responsibility across the care cycle. Physicians who do try to assist their patients over the cycle, then, must often spend large amounts of time ensuring that the correct care is delivered.

Excellent providers not only integrate across the value chain within their own organizations, but also with independent entities involved in the care cycle (e.g., primary care physicians, rehabilitation clinics). M. D. Anderson Cancer Center is an interesting example, because only about one-third of its patients live in the vicinity of the hospital. M. D. Anderson offers a personalized Web portal designed to expedite patient referrals and improve communications between M. D. Anderson and referring physicians. Referring physicians have access to a patient's appointment schedule, transcribed documents, secure messaging with M. D. Anderson staff, information regarding M. D. Anderson clinical trials, and a link to M. D. Anderson's research medical library. Out-of-town patients are returned to the care of a local oncologist when they return home, but an M. D. Anderson physician teamed with an advanced practice nurse also follows each patient's progress. The nurse makes follow-up calls to check on ongoing local care, and the referring physician can continue communicating with the treating physician via the personalized Web portal.[42] Such integration with independent entities can be complicated unnecessarily by the Stark laws, which need to be modified, as we discuss in chapter 8.

Providers can deepen their understanding of the CDVC by delineating the parallel activities that patients need to perform, both inside and outside the hospital or office setting. Identifying a patient activity chain that corresponds with the care delivery chain will reveal insights for how to improve care, inform the coordination of care as a patient moves between entities in the care cycle, and suggest ways to help patients comply better with recommended actions and contribute more to the value of their care.

Delineating the CDVC also highlights an observation we made earlier—there is a significant mismatch between today's reimbursement structures and value for patients. Pay is linked to what is done in a particular unit or by a particular specialist, not to overall value. For example, a provider organization that imposes or shifts costs downstream or upstream in the care cycle does not have to bear those costs, just the costs incurred within the organization itself. This is one of the reasons why single bills for episodes and cycles of care will be important to value-based competition in the long run. Also, some of the most important activities in the CDVC are not reimbursed at all but must be subsidized by charges for other functions. A good example of this is informing patients and helping them navigate the care cycle. However, there are major opportunities to improve patient value even within the existing reimbursement system.

The CDVC is not only a framework for providers but also a way for other actors in the system to examine the roles and activities. Suppliers, for example, must understand where their products or services fit into the care delivery chain, and how they can both measure and improve the value they deliver (see chapter 7). Similarly, health plans can use the CDVC to better understand where they can add value either in supporting providers, counseling patients, or coordinating across activities and entities (see chapter 6).

While developing a good description of current activities is important, the real payout is normative—finding ways to improve care. A series of fundamental questions should guide the analysis of the CDVC for a medical condition (see the box "Transforming the Care Delivery Value Chain"). The answers to these questions will often reveal insights into how care delivery can be improved.

Harnessing the Power of Information Technology

Information technology is a powerful tool to enable many of the strategic, organizational, and care delivery changes we have described. Virtually every aspect of health care delivery is information intensive. Every activity in the care delivery value chain can be enhanced and made more efficient with IT. For example, prescribing can become more efficient,

Transforming the Care Delivery Value Chain

1. Is the *set and sequence* of activities in the CDVC aligned with value?

The simple act of delineating the activities involved in patient care will yield important insights. It will reveal gaps, duplication of tasks, redundant testing, and inconsistencies due to the idiosyncratic practices of individuals.

Careful study of the CDVC, for example, reveals that much effort is often not value-adding for patients. Studies show, for example, that the percentage of time nurses and doctors actually spend with patients is a small portion of their overall time.[43] This occurs, in no small part, because care delivery processes have not been systematically analyzed.

Simply documenting the CDVC and individual activities will reveal opportunities for improvement. Each activity should be compared to known best practices. Examining the CDVCs of other providers will be revealing as well.

Delineating the CDVC will often suggest a more efficient division of labor across entities, and ways to increase patient value from combining, reordering, or relocating steps. The act of laying out activities can also highlight important types of activities that are omitted or not systematically managed (e.g., informing). For example, employing a dedicated patient educator and advocate, even if he or she is not reimbursed by health plans, can improve outcomes while freeing many hours of physician time.

2. Is the appropriate *mix of skills* brought to bear on each activity and across activities, and do individuals work as a team?

Multiple skills and specialties are needed for all stages in the care cycle for a medical condition. In care of chronic kidney disease, for example, primary care physicians, nephrologists, cardiologists, endocrinologists, and urologists can be involved, among others. The question is, what is the best set of skills from a value perspective? Is care structured so that the necessary skilled individuals come together as a team?

Today, the individuals involved and the division of labor often vary for the same medical condition. In breast cancer care, for example, both breast surgeons and general surgeons perform surgical interventions, with breast surgeons more likely to undertake other roles in the care cycle as well (see appendix B). Which individuals, with which skills, should take the lead in the care cycle? Would shifting the mix of skills, or better integration of skills, improve patient value?

3. Is there *appropriate coordination* across the discrete activities in the care cycle, and are handoffs seamless?

Identifying the activities in the CDVC will reveal the numerous areas for coordination in care delivery, both between particular activities and across

(continued)

the care cycle. Specialists need to consult and coordinate with one another, for example, while a sequence of treatments and services for the patient must be scheduled with minimum delays. Identifying the types of coordination necessary and how well they are taking place will reveal opportunities to improve value. One indicator of ineffective coordination is delays, which introduce inefficiencies into care delivery and worsen outcomes. Other danger signs are the need to recreate information, check or verify schedules and decisions, and conduct numerous bilateral communications involving different parties.

Coordination is improved through better processes and information systems. It is also enhanced through co-location of staff and better design of facilities. Within a hospital or clinic, for example, co-location of clinical facilities for specialists and the use of shared support staff can greatly improve coordination, as well as enable both formal and informal learning by multifunctional teams.

4. Is care structured to *harness linkages* across different parts of the care cycle?

Examining the care delivery value chain in a medical condition will usually reveal significant opportunities to harness linkages across the care cycle. A linkage occurs when the way one activity is performed affects the outcomes or costs of others. For example, more effort or different effort in one activity will reduce effort required in others. Linkages create opportunities to improve value by examining the care delivery chain as a whole, not just improving each activity separately.

Linkages are pervasive in health care. Better patient monitoring can reduce the cost of treatment or improve its results. More complete diagnosis can improve the value of treatment. Management of recovery can improve the results of surgeries. For example, New England Baptist Hospital has learned that devoting extra resources to immediate in-hospital physical therapy pays dividends in shorter rehabilitation time and better overall patient outcomes. Also, since patients often talk more frequently and freely to a physical therapist than to the physician, immediate in-house therapy creates an opportunity to identify and manage problems more rapidly.

Given the fragmented nature of care delivery today, such linkages in care delivery are often overlooked and unaddressed. One pervasive opportunity to improve value will be devoting more attention to informing patients and involving them in care.

5. Is the *right information* collected, integrated, and utilized across the care cycle?

As we have stressed, information is fundamental to delivering value in health care delivery. Information is needed to make good medical decisions, deliver care efficiently, and track costs and results over the care cycle. The CDVC is a basic tool for defining, organizing, auditing, and improving the information utilized in both medical decisions and in managing the care delivery process. The integrated practice unit is the basic unit around which information systems must integrate.

In addition to defining and capturing the right information, providers must ensure that it gets to the right individuals. Part of the assessment of a CDVC, then, is whether information is shared effectively and supports the coordination needed in the care cycle.

6. Are the activities in the CDVC performed in *appropriate facilities and locations*?

Identifying the CDVC provides a systematic framework for examining the appropriateness of the facilities utilized in care delivery. The opportunities for value improvement through better provider facilities are numerous. Many hospitals and other treatment centers have grown up organically through incremental expansions or renovations rather than systematic design around the care delivery process. Activities often take place in facilities that are more costly than necessary, and in locations that are far from ideal. Space is organized around specialties and shared services (e.g., imaging suites, operating rooms, specialty clinics) rather than the care cycles for medical conditions. Shared facilities, which are not tailored to particular medical conditions, often introduce inefficiencies into the care process. Moving patients and physicians is costly and leads to substantial waiting and downtime. Facility designs frequently impede coordination across staff and services, complicate the integration of care across the full care cycle, and work against learning and innovation by staff. Overall, expansion and improvement of facilities in health care delivery tends to be incremental and heavily tradition bound.

The CDVC allows a reexamination of facilities throughout the care cycle from a patient value standpoint. For each activity, what kind of space will maximize value delivered? What specialists and staff should be co-located? What parts of the care delivery chain should be housed in facilities dedicated and tailored to the practice unit? Diagnostic and examination space? Operating and procedure rooms? Imaging and other testing? Recovery and rehabilitation units? Hospital wards? Facilities that are patient centric and designed for the specific needs of a practice unit will usually be more productive than facilities shared across multiple practice units, but some highly specialized and low-volume facilities may be shared.[44]

How should services in the care delivery value chain be located? In a single dedicated building? In a network of dispersed locations? How can the cost and overhead structures of facilities be matched to the needs of the activities

(continued)

involved? The answers to these and other facilities questions will be unique to each provider and practice unit. The Cleveland Clinic and M. D. Anderson Cancer Center, discussed earlier, offer striking examples of facilities designed around medical conditions and care cycles. A major rethinking and reconfiguration of facilities in health care delivery is urgently needed, not just in hospitals but across all types of care.

7. What provider departments, units, and groups are involved in the care cycle? Is the provider's *organizational structure* aligned with value?

Organizational structure and management reporting relationships should reflect and reinforce the process of care delivery. As we have discussed, the fundamental organizational unit should be the integrated practice unit dedicated to a medical condition. The CDVC defines the appropriate boundaries for a practice unit. A practice unit should encompass all the important activities in the care cycle in which a provider is involved. There should be an individual with overall responsibility for the practice unit, and for results over the entire care cycle. Subunits for particular services must be clearly identified with the practice unit even if there is not formal reporting. Explicit responsibility and accountability for coordination and handoffs in the care cycle must be clearly assigned. Each organizational unit and physician group should be measured and held jointly accountable for overall results.

8. What are the independent entities involved in the care cycle, and what are the relationships among them? Should a provider's *scope of services* in the care cycle be expanded or contracted?

The involvement of independent entities in the CDVC for a medical condition can complicate the coordination of care and the ability to harness linkages across separate parts of the care cycle. Where independent entities are involved in the care, there must be a formal structure for coordination, joint measurement and accountability for results, and a structured mechanism for process improvement in which the separate organizations work collaboratively to evaluate results and enhance methods. A move toward more formal partnerships and alliances among entities in care cycles for particular medical conditions is likely to be a growing trend. The partnership between Beth Israel Deaconess and Milton Hospital, discussed in this chapter, is a good example.

Each provider must also examine its scope of services in the care cycle. At the same time as it works to improve coordination with all independent entities involved in care, a provider must ensure that its scope of services allows excellence in value delivery. In some cases, the delivery of care by fully integrated units can enable better results. Memorial Sloan-Kettering Cancer Center, for example, has reported that it achieves better results when chemotherapy is delivered by its own units rather than independent service providers. Providers need to make conscious choices about the appropriate scope of services in each IPU, mindful of the fact that in-house control is a means to deeper integration of care, not an end in itself.

An example of the types of needed choices in terms of service lines and locations is Sentara's move to establish cost-effective, convenient, freestanding outpatient rehabilitation facilities rather than attempt to protect its hospital-based business. By operating its own freestanding facilities, Sentara has the opportunity to better integrate rehabilitation into the care delivery cycle compared to hospitals that must coordinate at arm's length with independent rehabilitation providers. Freestanding facilities have allowed Sentara to compete successfully with independent rehabilitation providers. However, its ability to take full advantage of this opportunity will require a true practice unit model with seamless coordination and with an integrated view of the full care cycle.

convenient, and less subject to error. Medical records can be generated and compiled more easily and completely, and shared with those who need them. Remote medicine is enabled.

More broadly, IT provides the backbone for collecting, compiling, and utilizing information on patients, activities, methods, costs, and results for each patient across the cycle of care and across time. As care delivery moves from discrete interventions to care cycles, and from silos to integrated teams, IT only becomes more important.

Information technology has been recognized as a powerful tool in health care for more than a decade. Until recently, however, its promise was far greater than the reality. Introducing IT was resisted by physicians, who viewed it as costly but with uncertain benefits. The capital costs of developing and implementing IT systems deterred many financially strapped provider organizations, especially since many of the early initiatives were far too expensive for the value they delivered. The net result has been a striking underinvestment in information technology in the health care field. IT investment per worker in the health care sector averages about $3,000, versus a private industry average of $7,000, and of $15,000 per worker in a similarly information-intensive field such as banking.[45]

Today, however, the question is no longer whether IT investments are needed, but how to implement them. Calls for moving ahead on IT come from every important constituency, including the federal government. IT applications tailored to health care are increasingly available, and numerous case studies demonstrate the benefits.[46] Physicians are now embracing some types of IT with much less hesitation. There are myriad IT-related products, initiatives, programs, and committees under way. Keeping up with all the developments can be daunting.

While IT is crucial, it is not a panacea. Automating current modes of practice will yield limited benefits. IT is not the end in itself, but an enabler for value-based competition. Gaining the full benefits of IT will require the fundamental restructuring of care delivery that we describe in this chapter. It will not work well until IPUs are defined, the care delivery value chain is delineated, and information standards have been established. The real opportunity is not just automating currently paper-based transactions such as orders, records, and schedules, but using IT as a platform for integrated, results-based management.

A number of principles apply in introducing IT in health care delivery. First, the patient must be the fundamental unit around which information is collected and stored, not physicians, functions, departments, or cost categories. Patient value is the ultimate goal of health care delivery. All information must be able to be tied to each individual patient longitudinally.

Second, electronic medical records (EMR) for each patient, including images, are the backbone. Electronic patient records have many benefits in their own right. They improve legibility (a big source of errors), documentation, and the information available to clinicians, while reducing the duplication of tests and information gathering. Electronic records allow better integration across physicians and locations and make it far less costly than current methods to extract results, experiences, methods, and patient attribute information. Recording what is done, the core of an electronic record, is the front end to sophisticated costing systems. Moving to electronic records for new patients, and gradually coding records for past patients, is a strategic priority for every provider. (See also our discussion of patient medical records in chapter 6.)

Third, clinical, administrative, and financial information must be brought together. Automating financial and administrative information without the ability to link it to clinical information, or vice versa, misses the point that value is the ultimate goal of care delivery. Intermountain, for example, failed twice at process improvement based on cost data alone, each time devoting millions of dollars to an effort that had to be abandoned. Intermountain succeeded in using information to drive improvement only when it brought clinical results, service measures, and costs together.

Fourth, all data in the system must be sharable and all applications interoperable to support care-cycle integration, not create information silos. Systems for admitting, scheduling, prescribing, and other functions need to integrate seamlessly with each other. In addition, it is essential to select platform technologies, data standards, and security standards that enable and facilitate exchange, integration, and comparison of records across providers and with other outside entities.

Fifth, the units for aggregating information should be the integrated practice units and medical conditions, not the entire hospital, physician group, or function. The medical condition is the basic unit where value is driven and where tracking patients is most meaningful. Templates and screens across the care delivery value chain must be tailored to each practice unit to allow ease of data entry and usage. A common mistake is to attempt to introduce IT without first getting agreement on practice unit and process definitions. At ThedaCare, for example, IT implementation in one key practice unit was put on hold until process definitions had been agreed upon, a lesson ThedaCare learned the hard way in other service areas.

Finally, the most successful IT implementation proceeds in manageable increments based on a long-term plan. The system is rolled out in steps designed to build confidence and secure usage.[47] For example, moving to decision support systems for physicians captured much attention in 2005. However, decision support will fail unless basics for prescribing and records management have been accepted by doctors.

The Cleveland Clinic offers an example of a provider that has moved well down the path we have outlined in the development of information technology. The Clinic's IT infrastructure, known as e-Cleveland Clinic, utilizes a single common database organized longitudinally by patient. All applications are views of this common database, in contrast to the more common structure involving different databases for financial data, scheduling, clinical records, and so on. The system employs the most accepted and robust information standards for each type of record: for example, standard identifiers of visits and services (Clinical Procedural Terminology, CPT4; and Evaluation and Management Codes, E&M), National Drug Code (NDC) tables, and standard disease categorizations (International Classification of Diseases, ICD9). In order to allow data exchange, the Health Level 7 standard is utilized. The database captures a rich array of digital data, including images, test values, and doctor reports. When possible, lab computers and medical devices transmit data to the database directly. Where digital data is unavailable (e.g., echocardiograms), digital values are extracted and entered.

Drawing on the common database, the Clinic has implemented a series of applications. For patients, MyChart provides real-time online access to all a patient's information, with the exception of some sensitive information that is filtered so the physician communicates it first to the patient.

MyChart can generate a health screening profile with implications, and keeps track of all prescriptions. A recently added feature, automatic prescription renewal, is driving major increases in site usage.

MyPractice is the site for Clinic physicians and other staff. It brings together data for patient care and all the clinical and administrative functions.

Dr.Connect is a site for referring physicians. Referring physicians can access online all the information related to their patients in real time. This site yields significant benefits in terms of fewer phone calls, time savings, and the avoidance of duplicative tests. The Clinic had to overcome obstacles posed by the Stark laws in providing this software to outside physicians, a barrier that should be removed, as we discuss in chapter 8.

Finally, MyConsult offers access to second opinions for patients (and their doctors) in about three hundred life-threatening or life-altering diagnoses. This service, which we described earlier, extends the same processes utilized to make in-house diagnoses nationally to outside patients.

The Clinic is continually improving, extending, and deepening its electronic infrastructure. The structure is designed to allow as much flexibility as possible in applications, views, and ways of aggregating the data. For example, an eResearch site is being introduced to support laboratory research and clinical trials. As more data accumulates, historical data is added, and data from other providers is integrated, the benefits of the technology in improving patient value will only grow.

Every provider needs a comprehensive, long-term IT plan that reflects and reinforces its strategy and service lines. Since the value of information grows as more is accumulated, those institutions that start early will get major benefits. Still, providers must remember that IT will not transform the organization. It will enable and speed change when practice units are defined, the care delivery chain is delineated, and information standards have been established.

Systematizing Knowledge Development

In every practice unit, there needs to be a formal process of knowledge development. This is the only way that an organization can truly learn and enable continuous improvements in care delivery. Knowledge development needs a systematic process, rather than being left to chance.

Systematic knowledge development by providers remains uncommon. There are many process improvement efforts under way, but they are often not part of ongoing management. Also, much process improvement is focused on common or hospital-wide processes (e.g., nurse triage, patient admitting, limiting infections). There is much low-hanging fruit to pluck in these areas, but the even larger payoff will take place at the medical condition level.

The most common process improvement model in clinical care at the medical condition level currently centers on practice guidelines. Guidelines can serve as a floor or jumping-off point for care delivery improvement, but they are just a start. The goal is not standardized or generic medicine, but excellent results. Providers can learn from guidelines, the practices of excellent centers, and their own experience how to transform and improve their structures, methods, and facilities to deliver better results.

Systematic knowledge development consists of at least three components: measuring and analyzing results, identifying process improvements, and training staff. The effort needs ongoing management by physicians and skilled staff working together as a team under active leadership.[48] It requires a structured, data-driven approach. Measuring and synthesizing all four levels of data in the information hierarchy for a practice unit provide the essential raw material. Integrated practice units need to set aside time for regular meetings to review results, examine the causes of problem areas, explore possible solutions, and learn from anomalies and variations in results across patients. Substandard outcomes must be discussed and analyzed so the entire group learns and improves. (This approach has been more common in surgery, but it must spread to other disciplines and medical conditions.) New ideas must be actively sought from outside, and from top-performing units elsewhere, as well as inside the unit. Finally, physicians and other skilled staff must be integrated into the process, and compensated and held accountable for progress.

In larger organizations, consultants and corporate resources can supplement practice unit teams. At Intermountain, for example, physicians have access to a decision support database. At M. D. Anderson Cancer Center, informatics teams assist clinic heads in compiling data and analyzing results.

Relatively simple process enhancements can make a big difference in patient value. For example, an award-winning quality initiative in New Hampshire involved a structure in which the various doctors treating the same patients did rounds at the same time so that they discussed the patients together. This relatively simple change improved critical communications and markedly reduced errors, lowering the mortality rate to 2.1 percent from an expected 4.8 percent.[49] This change required only that physicians be open to thinking about patient care differently and looking for ways to do it better. (Chapter 4 described other examples of good process improvement.)

The Institute for Healthcare Improvement's path-breaking program to save 100,000 lives in hospitals is also based on disseminating knowledge about relatively modest changes in processes performed at virtually all hospitals. The six process changes—assembling response teams based on specified symptoms, applying an evidence-based process to treat heart attacks, preventing adverse drug events, preventing surgical site infections, preventing central line infections, and preventing ventilator-associated pneumonia—all require little or no new investment or advanced technology for most providers. Yet if widely adopted, these principles could reduce error-induced mortality dramatically.[50]

The value gains available from knowledge development can be enormous, even in today's system. Intermountain Health Care, for example, has become well known for its systematic efforts at process improvement. Its efforts to get it right the first time have led to system costs for Medicare patients that are 34 percent below the national average and 14 percent below non-Intermountain hospitals in Utah.[51] Notably, the process improvements efforts at Intermountain are heavily weighted toward improving clinical care for specific medical conditions. Intermountain's approach is based on a philosophy that improvement comes from measuring clinical and financial results, learning what works, and making it easy for practitioners to practice what works. As Intermountain's Brent James explains it, "managed care means [clinicians] managing processes of care [for patients], not [administrators] managing physicians and nurses."[52]

A number of organizations provide knowledge and resources for process benchmarking and improvement. A leader is the Institute for Healthcare Improvement, a not-for-profit organization that aims to improve health care by assisting providers to improve safety and quality. It provides training, tools, literature, and discussion forums to support provider efforts to improve both general hospital practices and processes in a number of specific practice units.

One of the most important responsibilities for a provider CEO is establishing and overseeing formal knowledge development activities in each practice unit. Knowledge development needs to be an accepted and celebrated part of the culture of every provider organization.

Overcoming Barriers to Value-Based Competition

How can organizations overcome the barriers to transformation that almost inevitably exist? To compete on value, providers must overcome an array of external and internal barriers. Given their history and structures, some providers will have an easier time doing so than others.

Health Plan Practices. Health plan practices have historically worked against value-based competition. Plans have focused on the size of discounts rather than patient value. They have sought contracts with broadline providers and fostered unproductive duplication of services. They have attempted to micromanage providers rather than rewarding excellent results with more patients. Integrated health plan and provider networks have mitigated many of these dysfunctional practices, which has allowed such organizations to make strides in enhancing value over the past decade. As we discussed earlier, however, value-based competition will work better if health plans are separate from providers.

Chapter 6 will discuss how health plans must transform their roles and practices.

Medicare Reimbursement. Medicare reimbursement, which exerts a strong influence on reimbursement throughout the system, has worked against value-based competition, as we have described. For example, Medicare reimbursement levels are not tied to cost or value, leading to cross subsidies and excess capacity. Reimbursement has been biased toward treatment procedures, rather than improving value over the care cycle. The reimbursement structure is also unintentionally biased against cost-reducing innovations in treatment methods. Chapter 8 will elaborate on how Medicare can modify its practices to encourage value-based competition on results.

Regulation. Numerous regulatory and legal impediments work against value-enhancing strategies and structures. Certificate of Need regulation has tended to protect established institutions rather than encourage new, high-value competitors. The Stark law and corporate practice of medicine laws inadvertently work against care-cycle integration. State-level licensing works against cross-geographic integration of care delivery. We will discuss the areas where regulatory reform is needed in chapter 8.

Governance. Legal requirements and provider governance structures inadvertently work against value-based strategies, as we have discussed. A local orientation and a full-service bias are reinforced by local boards of directors and community service obligations. There is resistance to closing any service, and closing an entire hospital is almost unthinkable even if there are other nearby institutions of better quality. The mind-set that "closer is better" is deeply ingrained among boards, community leaders, and politicians. Some hospital boards have begun to pursue value-based strategies, but they have been in the distinct minority.

Boards must embrace patient value as the central goal. A hospital or clinic will create more value for more patients if it provides only services where its results are excellent. Local patients will also benefit from care that is integrated regionally, and which draws on partnerships with other excellent institutions.

Attitudes and Mind-sets. Old assumptions, attitudes, and mind-sets are pervasive in health care. The bias toward breadth of services is deeply ingrained. Some physicians bristle at the idea of being held accountable for results. Another pervasive mind-set in medicine is that it is wrong to compete, because medicine is collaborative and competition will only result in price cutting. These attitudes and mind-sets will begin to change as the system realigns its focus around patient value, providers implement the steps we outline in this chapter, and other actors in the system shift their strategies and approaches (see chapters 6 through 8).

Management Capabilities. Management expertise within health care providers is limited, especially among individuals with medical training. These limited managerial resources will be sorely tested by the kinds of organizational structures and delivery methods and processes we have described, which are far more management intensive than traditional care delivery structures. Improving managerial capability will be a challenge for nearly every provider, especially since the culture of medicine has not viewed "management" as important or prestigious.

Providers will need to mount a conscious strategy to equip medical staff with appropriate training as their managerial responsibilities expand, while recruiting new talent with managerial backgrounds. Management schools are expanding curricula tailored to health care professionals. Medical education will also need to expand its managerial component (see the following section).

Medical Education. Medical education does not equip young physicians for their role in a value-driven health care system, nor does it serve the needs of experienced physicians. Medical education fails to address such crucial agendas as the role of teams, integrated care, care cycles, results measurement, knowledge development processes, information technology, and practice unit management. A broader rethinking of medical education is needed (see the box "Implications for Medical Education").

The Structure of Physician Practice. Improving care delivery is difficult to accomplish when free agent physicians see process improvement as a chore, which is the current norm. What we are describing is also a far cry from typical rounds in which senior doctors grill residents as part of medical education. Process enhancement, then, is one of many ways in which physicians' traditional attitudes and habits will need to change.

Perhaps the most complex barrier to value-based strategies arises from the traditional structure and organization of medical practice. As we have noted, traditional ways of grouping and organizing physicians are not

Implications for Medical Education

Both the content and the culture of medical education need to be realigned around achieving excellence in patient value. Medical education needs to break out of the specialty straightjacket, and embrace integrated care delivery and its improvement.

Modifying medical curricula will be challenging at schools organized around traditional specialties that have often focused on preparing students for exams and boards instead of clinical practice. The shift in mind-set will be substantial, from academic credentials and laboratory research as the source of prestige to excellence in clinical care. Based on our own experience in curriculum redesign at academic institutions, entirely new medical schools may need to take the lead in making some of the structural changes that are necessary.

Where Clinical Training Should Occur

Providers entrusted with the clinical training of future doctors should have to demonstrate excellent results. Today, students are trained in clinical care by practice groups that have academic credentials but may lag behind the state of the art in actual care delivery. Worse, these groups may not know where they stand because they do not measure and analyze their own outcomes. No hospital or physician practice without outcome measurements and the willingness to report them should be allowed to educate students.

In each field, students should be trained at a local or regional center that has demonstrated excellence in results in that field. The university hospital or other nearby hospitals may not be the best location for clinical training in every practice unit. Already, at some medical schools, students with an interest in a field not practiced at their school's affiliated hospital can apply for that rotation in another location. Restricting training to centers with demonstrated excellence in each practice unit would have the added benefit of making medical students and other physicians aware of where excellent results are being achieved.

Working in Integrated Practice Unit Teams

Today, training is organized around specialist roles and driven by specialist departments, reflecting the typical functional organization of hospitals. Medical education needs to prepare future doctors to work in integrated, multi-specialty teams that address specific medical conditions. Also, many doctors learn clinical care as practiced by ad hoc groups of staff on a series of largely unrelated cases. They are not taught how to deliver care in stable teams that

(continued)

work together over time to improve results for patients through systematic process improvement.

Medical curricula are moving toward a better appreciation of the role of interspecialty collaboration and of the contribution of nonphysician medical staff, but curricula are changing only slowly. As providers reorganize around practice units, there will be major opportunities for improved models of medical training in which groups of medical students and residents work as part of new, integrated organizational units.

Managing the Full Cycle of Care

Medical training reflects and reinforces the fractured system of care built around discrete procedures and interventions. Yet patient value depends on coordination and integration of care across the full care cycle. Ideally, students should develop expertise in the entire care cycle, including training in screening, prevention, and long-term disease management. They should understand what needs to happen before their specialty becomes involved in care, and what should happen afterward.

Today's training is focused on high-acuity hospital settings. The medical education system also needs to provide doctors with expertise in lower-acuity outpatient settings, and insight into the more chronic stages of managing diseases or injuries. Training could be structured, for example, so that a resident involved in the treatment of an acute congestive heart failure episode would maintain involvement with the patient's care after discharge.[53]

Demonstrating Competence in Clinical Practice

The medical school curriculum is based on two years of course work followed by a series of fixed rotations. The balance between basic and applied (clinical) science needs to be reexamined. Topics such as basic anatomy, for example, are covered extensively because of tradition and the content of exams. Some schools offer molecular pharmacology but omit clinical pharmacology, and students are expected to learn about drug interaction during residency.

A number of schools are moving to competency-based curricula that emphasize what students must actually learn and be able to do, a welcome development. However, the definition of competency is still biased toward exams rather than the realities of clinical practice.

At the graduate level, medical education has been organized around the "see one, do one, teach one" approach, a model in which a resident is expected to learn a procedure by watching and practicing it on patients until he or she gets it right.[54] This not only raises a dilemma in terms of balancing the patient's well-being with the training of doctors, but it is hardly a system conducive to achieving clinical excellence. Some teaching hospitals are beginning to require training in common procedures before students and residents are permitted to work with patients. For example, the Partners hospitals in Boston now require central line insertion training for all incoming residents.[55]

Some academic centers also have established or are developing bioskills labs, in which individual doctors and teams can train on models and cadavers before working with actual patients. The use of simulators is also growing. Where it is feasible, both new and experienced doctors should have to practice and demonstrate competence on simulators, just as airline pilots are required to do every two years.

Training in Results Measurement

Designing outcome measures, collecting clinical information, and systematically investigating the relationships between clinical methods and outcomes are all topics not currently part of the medical curriculum. Yet tomorrow's doctors need to know the best available measures of clinical results and what they mean, how to appropriately adjust for patients' initial conditions, and how to find and use the results information that is already collected. Every clinical rotation should include attention to outcome and process measurement. Doctors need to know how to identify the national and regional centers where the best results are being achieved. They need to know how to find those physicians with the deepest experience in specialized areas, and how to utilize outcome data to make evidence-based referrals.

Doctors must also be taught that measuring themselves compared to peers is a normal part of professional development, not to mention an obligation to their patients. If measurement becomes normal and expected, this will go a long way toward reducing the fear of assessment and create strong incentives for every doctor to improve continuously.[56]

Improving Clinical Processes

Every aspiring physician should receive training in systematic approaches to improving care delivery. This includes tools for explicit process definition, analysis of practice variations and anomalies, methods of benchmarking care delivery methods versus other providers, and best practices in how to organize and manage team problem-solving processes. Participating in formal care delivery improvement should become an expected part of a doctor's job, not an unusual event.

New Models of Continuing Education

There are long-established requirements for continuing medical education, but current practices are a far cry from what is actually needed. What physicians need is structured training on the latest clinical practices, and coaching in

(continued)

mastering state-of-the-art care delivery methods. Training needs to be structured in a way that is sensitive to the realities of the time pressures and information overload that physicians face.

Doctors initially learn clinical practice in inpatient tertiary hospital settings, surrounded by many colleagues. Yet many doctors actually practice through treating patients by themselves in primary or secondary outpatient care environments. Once their formal training is completed, physicians rarely get a chance to observe colleagues or obtain feedback on their own performance. Doctors often have precious few opportunities to master new care delivery techniques in a supportive environment free of supplier involvement.[57]

The current design of most medical meetings misses the mark. Meetings consist of loosely structured presentations and research papers, with doctors left to sort it all out. While cardiac and orthopedic surgeons see demonstrations of new surgical techniques at professional meetings, this kind of practical curriculum oriented toward care delivery is uncommon.

Continuing education should be organized around medical conditions. Medical schools, medical societies, and provider groups need to design and offer practitioner-oriented courses focused on care delivery. Such courses need to synthesize and integrate research findings together with learning from clinical practice into structured courses on the latest methods of clinical care and how to measure it.

Intermountain Health Care has moved in this direction. Each of IHC's clinical programs (e.g., cardiovascular, preventive care, women, and newborns) has an experienced team of physicians dedicated to analyzing and learning from both the medical literature and IHC's own data on results and clinical practices. These teams train line clinicians about new findings as well as assist them in implementing, improving, and updating best-practice treatment protocols. The idea is to make the act of keeping current with the state of the art easy, expected, and normal.

Decision support systems for physicians are being introduced as part of electronic medical records initiatives. Such systems will be most useful if they are designed to improve the information on which physicians make judgments rather than handcuff them with process guidelines. The use of decision support systems needs to be taught in medical school.

Finally, simulators and other tools for learning by doing without involving actual patients also have a role in continuing clinical education. Even without such high-cost technology as full-body simulators, bioskills labs can enable clinicians to learn new surgical techniques in a hands-on environment. For example, the Orthopaedic Learning Center in Rosemont, Illinois, has a bioskills laboratory with twenty-five surgical stations that allow doctors to practice on cadavers or models.[58] The New England Baptist's Bioskills Learning

Center has two operating rooms with multimedia and teleconferencing capabilities in which physicians can practice techniques and originate demonstrations. Two-way communication technology allows trainees not only to watch best-in-class surgeons perform the latest procedure but also to ask questions and receive immediate feedback on their performance.[59]

Developing Practice Unit Management Skills

As early as their residency years, doctors are asked to take on tasks such as triage and scheduling without the benefit of any management training. Later in their careers, division chiefs and hospital leaders are expected to master care delivery process design, multidisciplinary team management, strategic planning, budgeting, human resource management, and mentoring roles, again without any training.[60] Some hospitals and professional organizations, such as the Society of Thoracic Surgeons and the American Academy of Family Physicians,[61] are beginning to provide opportunities for future leaders to attend management education programs. However, the need for better management training is urgent, which includes the concepts of practice units and managing full care cycles as well as basic training in process improvement, managing innovation, systems analysis, and managing information technology.

well aligned with patient value. Physician organization is enshrined in medical boards and societies involved in certification, and in medical training. Medical societies, as currently constituted, are sometimes constraining the shift to new care delivery structures and results measurement rather than enabling it (see the box "Implications for Medical Societies" in chapter 8).

Another formidable barrier to strategy is the free agent model so common in medicine. Many physicians are largely independent practitioners with only loose affiliations to hospitals and physician groups. Each free agent is in effect a separate business, often issuing a separate bill and bearing separate administrative costs. The result is multiple bills, redundant staff, and poor coordination.[62] The free agent model also enshrines fragmentation. It is difficult to get free agents to be on the same team, and moving in the same direction. Free agents want to handle an array of cases and do things their own way, rather than to agree on standard processes.

More broadly, the free agent model means that health care delivery is physician centric, rather than patient and value centric. Without measurement and competition on results, processes and structures are organized around what physicians want. Many physicians still view the desire of patients to be better informed or seek referrals to other excellent providers as a sign of disloyalty, not as something they should encourage.

These problems are particularly acute in academic medical centers, where physicians often practice, teach, and conduct research simultaneously. Patient care can represent only a modest portion of a physician's time, limiting the focus on the process of care delivery. The chief of a group or department is chief of everything rather than specifically charged with improving patient care. The challenges of getting physicians together into integrated practice units, organizing care around care cycles, and engaging in disciplined information collection and process improvement are compounded in the academic medical setting, where the focus on traditional specialties is even greater because of the research and teaching missions.

Academic medical centers are also notoriously broad line, providing services even in areas requiring few specialized skills or technology. Academic medical centers justify broad service lines as necessary to fulfill their teaching mission, but are not required to demonstrate excellent results to qualify to train future doctors. Traditional structures and processes of care delivery are further entrenched.

Some providers, including academic centers such as the Cleveland Clinic and the Mayo Clinic, have a model in which physicians are salaried staff members with clear reporting relationships. This model offers significant advantages for moving to value-based strategies. The salaried model tends to make it easier to reorganize into practice units, collect the right information, and institute systematic process improvement. Also, the appropriate design of compensation structures in a salaried model can mitigate incentives to overtreat or take on an excessive number of cases.

However, while a staff model offers advantages in moving toward value-based approaches, it is far from a panacea. A staff model alone will not work unless organization structure, care delivery structures, and measurement practices are modified. Moving to a staff model is complicated by potential incentive problems, such as adverse selection of physicians who are less capable and productivity issues that can arise when physicians do not own their practice.[63] These incentive problems are overcome by prestigious institutions such as the Cleveland Clinic and the Mayo Clinic, but can be a challenge for the average provider.

The move to integrated practice unit structures will require new contracting and incentive structures. Some hospitals and group practices are paying stipends for administrative time devoted to practice unit management and process improvement. For example, Beth Israel Deaconess pays for a portion of referring doctors' time to support their involvement in such efforts.

Intermountain Health Care addresses this issue by selecting from its independent physicians a number who are distinguished in their field and willing to take leadership roles in assisting their practice unit to achieve its clinical goals. These physicians are compensated for one-quarter of their time, using a scale recognizing income differences among specialties. They are responsible for studying the literature, meeting with the other practitioners, and attending Intermountain committee and board meetings as appropriate.

A number of providers are also moving to modify the traditional relationship between the hospital and affiliated physicians. Traditionally, contracts with doctors have been largely financial agreements. However, contracts are beginning to include goals and results measurement. At ThedaCare, orthopedic surgeons are now required to measure SF-36 performance for hip and knee surgery.[64] At Tenet Healthcare, doctors seeking to perform bariatric (obesity) surgery have to agree on practice standards to be met or exceeded before being permitted to use hospital facilities. These sorts of conditions, and others that need to be developed, will focus attention on value, information, and practice improvement. Over time, the conditions should be reciprocal, with hospitals as well as physicians committing to meeting high standards.

Academic medical centers need to take the lead in moving to value-based competition, given their actual and symbolic roles in medicine. Many academic medical centers will need to compete more strategically, paring back service lines and partnering with other providers to deliver greater patient value. Here, models such as Beth Israel Deaconess's partnership with Milton Hospital, and the Cleveland Clinic's management agreement with Rochester General Hospital's cardiac surgery practice, are instructive.

Academic medical centers must recognize that research, teaching, and patient care are different businesses, and must be managed as such. In patient care, academic centers must be held accountable for results. Training and laboratory research cannot compromise patient care. Physician training should occur only in practice units with demonstrated excellence in results. Significant changes in medical education will also be necessary to align training with the imperatives of excellent care delivery.

The Benefits of Moving Early

How should the process begin? Who will take the lead? The reality is that the transformation of health care providers is already under way. Despite the barriers and challenges, some providers are moving rapidly to develop value-based strategies; realign their structures around practice units; integrate across the care cycle; collect, analyze, and disseminate results; and provide integrated care across geography. The more of these steps that are taken, the more rapidly value will rise because the steps are mutually reinforcing.

Competing on value will benefit providers and patients, even if nothing else in the system changes. Value-based competition is positive sum. When providers win, patients, employers, and health plans also win because quality and cost will improve markedly. None of the steps we advocate are radical or risky; leading providers are already taking them.

Providers that move early will gain major benefits as they feed the virtuous circle of health care delivery. Early movers will get a lead in establishing greater strategic focus and creating areas of excellence. They will build reputations in a less crowded field. Early movers will begin sooner to learn about appropriate organization structures and practice standards and to accumulate clinical information. Early movers will get first crack at establishing strategic partnerships and new types of relationships with other providers and will have the inside track in serving health plans that are moving, and will increasingly move, to more value-driven models.

Moving early is particularly important in the area of clinical information. More information will not only improve practice, but will also allow more convincing demonstrations of excellence, and better insight into costs. Providers that are early and aggressive in collecting and analyzing results information will also be in a position to influence the measures used and to set the standards that others will have to live with.

There is no need to wait for perfection. Virtually every provider can make major improvements in the value of health care it delivers that will become self-reinforcing.

6

Strategic Implications for Health Plans

HEALTH PLANS HAVE a unique and essential role in value-based competition in health care, as some forward-looking plans are beginning to demonstrate. Most health plans, however, are not living up to this potential. Instead, many have acted in ways that reinforced zero-sum competition and failed to deliver the most value to their customers. Significant changes will be needed in health plan mind-sets, attitudes, and ways of operating.

In the past, the strategies and practices of health plans detracted from value through bureaucracy, administrative costs, restricting physicians' and patients' choices, limiting services, attempting to micromanage medical practice, and generally gumming up the works through adversarial relationships with both providers and members. Such practices not only failed to add value from a health perspective, but also failed to achieve their intended result of controlling rapidly rising costs. Instead, health plans came to be widely vilified and became perhaps the least trusted and admired participants in the health care system. The perception of health plans is so negative among subscribers, providers, and policy makers that many question whether plans can ever add value.

We believe they can, but health plans must rethink and reorient their whole approach around value-based competition. Health plans must become health organizations, not just insurance organizations. They must be participants in health, not just payers, a term we believe has become counterproductive. As they become focused on health value for patients, health plans can win back the respect of patients, physicians, and other system participants.

In this chapter, we first describe how the roles of health plans need to shift. We then outline the strategic, organizational, and operating practices that will allow health plans to truly add value for patients. This needed shift, from accentuating zero-sum competition to enabling value-based competition, will not only dramatically benefit patients but also open up many more opportunities for health plans to distinguish themselves and create meaningful competitive advantages. As providers also transform themselves, as we describe in chapter 5, the transformation of health plans and providers will be mutually reinforcing. Patient value will improve exponentially.

Many health plans will have to overcome formidable barriers to adopting these new value-adding roles. It will be difficult for some plans to move beyond the discount mind-set, the attitude that providers and members need top-down micromanagement, and the culture of denial. We are encouraged, however, by the growing number of plans that are beginning to address these challenges, with promising results. As with providers, those health plans that move early to embrace value-based competition will reap enduring benefits.

In this chapter, we treat fully insured and self-insured plans together. As we outlined in this book's introduction, health plans fall into these two broad categories. About half of employer-based health coverage is self-insured, meaning that the employer bears the financial risk, though self-insured plans are still normally administered by a health plan company. Self-insured plans have much greater flexibility in defining coverage, terms, and conditions because they are not regulated as insurance.

The two types of plans are treated together here because the principles and the roles we outline apply to both. The past practices of health plans reflect a combination of choices not only by health plans and plan administrators, but by employers (e.g., benefit caps, lack of disease management). Shifting the role of health plans, then, will also require that employers adopt new approaches. Employers will need to move beyond short-term thinking about costs and instead structure plans to embody value principles (see the discussion of implications for employers in chapter 7).

Past and Future Roles of Health Plans

In the past, and to a large extent still today, the roles of health plans have been defined by the zero-sum mentality of cost shifting and by the misguided assumption that health care services could be treated as a commodity whose cost should be minimized. As we have described, cost shifting is a dead end that has failed, and health care is anything but a commodity. In fact, the more health care is treated as a commodity, the more efforts to shift costs and micromanage providers will drive costs up even further.

FIGURE 6-1

Transforming the roles of health plans

Old role: culture of denial		New role: enable value-based competition on results
Restrict patient choice of providers and treatment	➡	Enable informed patient and physician choice and patient management of health
Micromanage provider processes and choices	➡	Measure and reward providers based on results
Minimize the cost of each service or treatment	➡	Maximize the value of care over the full care cycle
Engage in complex paperwork and administrative transactions with providers and subscribers to control costs and settle bills	➡	Minimize the need for administrative transactions and simplify billing
Compete on minimizing premium increases	➡	Compete on subscriber health results

It is common for system participants—and especially the advocates of a single-payer system—to blame nearly all of the problems in health care on health plans and their practices. We disagree. Health plans offer unique potential to add value in important ways. But in order to do so, they have to shift their roles in five broad areas, shown in figure 6-1. Many health plans have moved away from the old roles. However, few (if any) health plans have fully embraced the new roles. Instead, most plans today are operating in ways that fall short of value-based competition.

Enable Choice and the Management of Health

In the 1990s, health plans attempted to control costs by limiting the choices of patients and referring physicians to networks of approved providers. Networks were determined based on favorable contracts rather than evidence of quality or value. Health plans also required approval for referrals to specialists even if they were in the network, and approval of treatment options. Plans got in the business of defining "medical necessity," which often placed them in an adversarial relationship with their members and their doctors. Patient and physician discontent with this approach bordered on outrage.

In value-based competition, in contrast, the fundamental roles of health plans are to help members improve their health and to enable the choice of excellent providers by referring doctors and patients. Health value will only improve in the long run if the patients together with their doctors and medical advisers take responsibility for choice, not the health plan.[1] This will involve major changes in health plans' mind-sets. Health plans must become organizations dedicated to patient and physician information, support, and service, not organizations for administrative, auditing, and financial services. Everything plans do must first and foremost be centered on patients and their health.

Health plans must move from being adversaries to true partners in value creation for patients, not just paternalistic intermediaries. In response to backlash, health plans have created much broader provider networks and eliminated many of the cumbersome approval requirements. But most plans have remained focused on contracting discounts and maintain the network mind-set.

Health plans must also shed the attitude that constraining patient choice and overseeing physician practices are needed to ensure good health care. More than once, we have heard health plan executives quip that consumers and physicians want the right to make their own bad choices, so the plan needs to protect them. Instead, health plans should see their essential role as *enabling* patients and their doctors to obtain excellent care, without trying to constrain their choices.[2] To play this role, plans will need to alter deeply held assumptions and build a level of trust that is today often lacking.

Health plans are in an inherently better position than any single provider organization to support and enable the choice of providers and treatments. Providers have an almost unavoidable tendency and incentive to refer within their provider group and to recommend treatments they are in a position to deliver. Health plans, especially those independent of any provider, should care only about what provider and what treatment will create the most value, because that is in their customers' and their own interest. Also, health plans, in a different way than any single provider, should be concerned with a patient's total health needs and have the perspective of the full cycle of care all the way from monitoring and prevention to ongoing disease management—especially if plans can adopt a longer-term perspective.

As health plans move to measure results, enable informed choice, and recognize provider excellence in addressing medical conditions, they will also encourage and motivate the right type of competition among providers. As providers redefine their strategies around results as described in chapter 5, health plans will be better able to help members and their physicians make good choices.

Measure and Reward Providers Based on Results

Health plans fell into the trap of assembling large networks of providers, and then using their clout to bargain down price while attempting to micromanage health care delivery by reviewing or specifying provider activities. This second-guessing of providers has failed, and the accompanying build-up of administrative cost has revealed the deep flaw in the way managed care was implemented.

Top-down micromanaging is not only costly and requires considerable effort, but it also alienates providers, stifles innovation, and may actually not serve patients, as we have discussed in earlier chapters. The efforts of some plans to control expensive diagnostic tests through approvals and process specifications illustrate some of the pitfalls of micromanagement. Aetna, for example, hired radiologists to review requests for expensive MRIs and other scans, second-guessing the physicians ordering the scans rather than measuring and comparing the quality and overall cost of the diagnoses of the physicians utilizing the scans to see if they achieved good results, and whether use of the scans in diagnosis added value versus alternative approaches.[3]

Highmark, a Blue Cross Blue Shield affiliate, went a step further, specifying how imaging clinics should be operated. Highmark refused to cover diagnostic imaging at any clinic that did not offer a broad line of services (including five different kinds of imaging tests), that was not open at least forty hours a week as well as on some Saturdays, and that did not have at least one full-time accredited radiologist on staff.[4] The rationale was to steer tests to high-volume facilities in order to avoid costly duplication of equipment. Instead, these rules created the incentive for every imaging provider to perform every kind of scan, hence leading to more duplication of investment. Also, the notion that a high overall volume across a broad line creates value, versus volume in a particular test, is questionable. For instance, physicians have pointed out that for musculoskeletal injuries it can be more effective to have an orthopedist rather than a radiologist read the scans. In such cases, a smaller, specialized imaging center within an orthopedic practice could provide more cost-effective results, but the health plan policy encouraged the opposite. Even if Highmark's motives were good, this example illustrates the difficulty of and futility of regulating processes instead of tackling head on the task of measuring and rewarding results. What matters should be the cost, accuracy, and usefulness of scans, not how imaging providers choose to organize.

In addition to the philosophy of process micromanagement, many health plans remain oriented toward attempting to raise the standard of providers across the board instead of rewarding excellent providers with more business. There are surely opportunities at most providers to incorporate best practices, but the goal is not to bring all care to the average or to lift all boats. Leveling the playing field will further fragment the delivery of services and retard value improvement.[5] Instead, the goal is for more care to be delivered by truly excellent providers. This is what will dramatically raise the average value delivered in the system.

A basic tenet of economic and management theory is that it makes more sense to set goals and measure results than to specify methods and try to enforce them. Patients should be assisted in accessing the truly excellent providers in a given service, not spread among the excellent and the mediocre. Still focused on bargaining power to control costs, however, health plans remain concerned that they need large networks to gain leverage over providers. Health plans worry that seeking the best providers for their members will drive up costs. But the best providers are often the lowest cost, as we discussed in chapters 4 and 5. Those health plans that are moving to build quality-based networks (see the discussion later in this chapter) are finding that the excellent providers often will offer more favorable fee structures because of their inherent efficiencies.

Getting patients to the best and most efficient providers drives down cost and feeds the virtuous circle of value improvement pictured in figure 5-2. Rewarding good results with patients is the most powerful way to motivate every provider to improve. It is also the best way to limit excess supply, because providers that cannot demonstrate value in a practice unit will no longer be viable.

In value-based competition, providers and health plans will need to develop a whole new type of relationship. Providers will compete, in the best sense of the word, to demonstrate value and innovate in care delivery to improve patient outcomes and efficiency. Health plans will assist referring physicians by providing information and educating patients, and by working collaboratively with providers to understand what works. But forging such a constructive relationship, which seems radical today, will require major cultural changes for both parties. Most physicians still see health plans as obstacles to care. However, the move of some health plans to embrace disease management services is beginning to shift physician attitudes.

Currently, many health plans are embarking on quality initiatives under the banner of pay for performance. As we have discussed in earlier chapters, however, most of these efforts focus not on quality per se but on process compliance.[6] While it is a useful transitional step, then, pay for performance runs the risk of becoming just the latest version of micro-management, trying to specify all of the practices that providers must follow. Pay for performance also presupposes that the reward for quality must be higher prices. If, instead, good outcomes are rewarded with more patients, then excellent providers will earn higher margins due to increased learning and efficiency. This rewards quality without requiring ever-increasing prices.

Maximize the Value of Care over the Full Care Cycle

In the current system, subscriber churn rates mean that up to one-quarter of subscribers may change health plans within five years. As a result, many health plans have consciously or unconsciously taken a short-term perspective, focused on controlling and minimizing the cost of each office visit, service, drug, or treatment. Focus on discrete interventions accepts and even exacerbates the fragmented and transactional nature of health care delivery that erodes value. Today's churning of subscribers is accepted as inevitable and even encouraged. As we have discussed, it is not in the patient's, the employer's, or even the health plan's true interest.

Health care value is determined over the full cycle of care. The appropriate care can only be understood over the full cycle, as we have discussed in earlier chapters. There are also powerful linkages across the cycle—for example, risk prevention can minimize the need for intervention.

A care-cycle perspective shifts the very nature of the role of a health plan. As some health plan managers have described it, the mandate must shift from reducing the payment for a day in the hospital to figuring out how to help keep the patient healthy enough not to need hospitalization.

Health plans must become the driving force for organizing, evaluating, and facilitating medical care across the full care cycle. Plans must also accept the role of assisting patients in navigating the full cycle, supporting coordination, facilitating the exchange of information, and ensuring continuity. Plans must take a leading role in compiling and analyzing member health results over the full cycle. This shift in focus will pay huge dividends in terms of patient outcomes, cost management, and administrative simplicity. Patients, providers, and health plans will all be winners. Plans are in some ways better equipped than any one provider to play this role, contrary to conventional wisdom.

Health plans are just beginning to move to care-cycle thinking. While many plans offer some disease management, there has sometimes been a reluctance to fully embrace this approach so as not to attract "expensive" patients. Few plans have yet assembled the information to track patients over the care cycle. Also, plan administrators for employer-insured plans have sometimes not forcefully communicated the value of a care-cycle approach to plan sponsors, perhaps out of a misplaced concern that employers will inevitably embrace plan structures that minimize costs in the short run.

Minimize the Need for Administrative
Transactions and Simplify Billing

In the old system and often still today, health plans engage in extensive paperwork to approve referrals and treatments, pay bills, control spending, limit services, and communicate with patients. Contracts with providers remain complex. Even for an individual medical condition, health plans routinely deal with a multitude of entities, negotiate a myriad of separate contracts, and run a plethora of checks to ensure that contract conditions are met. Numerous bills are processed even for a single episode of care. Billing and collection procedures are intricate and contentious. Administrative processes are not transparent to subscribers, who are not provided with the overall cost of their care and cannot understand what goes into their bills. Administrative costs borne by health plans themselves represent about 10 percent of the premiums at health plans. Requirements set by health plans impose even greater costs elsewhere in the system.[7] In any other field, companies that operated in this manner would soon go out of business.

Administrative complexity remains a significant tool used by health plans to control costs. For example, even though many plans have eased network restrictions, some plans require the *member* to establish that an out-of-network provider is superior to the contracted (in-network) providers in order to secure reimbursement. Yet the plan provides no information on in-network quality or experience. The inescapable conclusion is that the exercise is not aimed at securing the most appropriate care for members, but simply at avoiding reimbursement for out-of-network care. It is inexplicable why so much effort and expense is devoted by some to justifying the denial of payment, rather than simply asking out-of-network providers to match the in-network contract price. The whole approach to controlling cost is misguided.

This whole mind-set of health plans needs to be turned on its head. Many if not most of the administrative transactions in the current system do not add value. The focus should be on how to minimize or eliminate them. How can health plans make payments simpler? How can health plans move from discrete interventions and multiple bills to a single bill for episodes of care? How can health plans aggregate and manage patient medical information to eliminate redundant paperwork, duplication of tests, and repeated medical histories?

Many of the current health plan administrative functions should and will become anachronistic as plans restructure their roles. As they provide information and advice to patients and physicians rather than creating restricted networks, shift to measuring results rather than attempting to micromanage care delivery, and reorient around the full cycle of care rather than discrete interventions, administrative complexity should decline.

Most health plans recognize the goal of reducing administrative costs, but lack the mind-set to truly succeed at it. Almost every plan has reduced its requirements for administrative approvals, and the more forward-looking plans are allowing electronic transactions. But these incremental approaches focus on performing the old tasks more efficiently, rather than restructuring the system to improve value.

Compete on Member Health Results

Health plans have competed primarily by attempting to lower their costs and limit the growth of premiums. The means to this end has been zero-sum competition. In the future, health plans need to compete based on the health results of their members adjusted for initial conditions. They must provide evidence that their members' health outcomes per unit of spending are excellent. This is the ultimate manifestation that a plan has created value.

Health plans should be measured and motivated by the overall health of their members. This will create a strong focus on member health. Helping members reduce the risk of illness and manage their medical conditions to stay healthy will become central to a health plan's (and its members') self interest. Helping the patient find the provider and treatment that delivers the best value will become a necessity. Health plans will also be motivated (and well situated) to enable the accumulation of members' health information from all providers and maintain a comprehensive medical record, as we will discuss. Competing on member health results will also yield a further bonus—it will open up much greater opportunities for health plans to distinguish themselves from their peers.

Health plans complain that employers only seek the lowest premiums and are preoccupied with short-term cost minimization. But what should plans expect, given that they have not measured health results and educated employers about how a model centered on provider excellence, care-cycle management, and risk prevention is the way to improve value?

Some health plans are beginning to measure their success differently. For example, CIGNA published data about improvements in outcomes and costs for diabetes patients in its disease management programs in a peer-reviewed journal in 2004.[8] Blue Cross Blue Shield of Minnesota has published evidence of improvements in results and costs from a combination of disease management and risk management.[9] In these cases, evidence of member health results was not marketed directly to subscribers or plan sponsors. However, leading plans are moving in this direction. In 2005, some health plans were beginning to market their ratings not just on member satisfaction but on process and quality measurements compiled by the National Committee for Quality Assurance (NCQA).[10] For example, Harvard Pilgrim Health Care, in New England, can market itself as the nation's top health plan among 260 plans ranked by NCQA in 2004.[11] Over time, the measures utilized in assessing results must shift from process measures to true health outcomes per dollar of premiums. Some leading health plans are already analyzing measures of health for their members relative to the overall population. So far, this member health data has been kept private. Ultimately, however, the most forward-looking health plans will begin publishing the data on their own members' outcomes. One leading health plan will begin publishing a composite member health index, including measures of outcomes, safety, and prevention, in 2006.

A health care system in which health plans compete to deliver superior health results for their members will drive far more value improvement and innovation than a single-payer system.[12] Unlike a single payer without competition or accountability, competing health plans will strive to provide the most useful information, facilitate the best care, and make transactions simple for patients and providers. This model will drive far more rapid improvement in patient value, while maintaining the checks and balances of competition.

Today, some health plans and providers are vertically integrated into a single organization. As we have described, a single integrated organization can mitigate some of the dysfunctional aspects of the current system by improving the working relationship between plan and providers, lessening the incentive to shift costs, and simplifying contracts and paperwork. Integrated organizations such as Intermountain Health Care and Kaiser Permanente have reaped considerable benefits and so far have been able to move more quickly in improving care delivery methods.

However, integration of the payer and provider creates an inherent conflict of interest in the choice of providers within a closed network. This runs the risk of stifling competition at the level of medical conditions, as discussed in chapters 2 and 5. System-to-system competition will ultimately be less effective. Integrated organizations must also deal with the inescapable incentive to limit provider services and ration care because the organization as a whole receives a fixed payment per member, covering all health care needs—known as capitation. An independent plan, with no provider infrastructure or capacity in place, will have more degrees of freedom to improve value by migrating services to excellent providers and to new, more effective treatments than an integrated network with a defined provider base and cost structure. With value-based competition, this flexibility of independent plans should enable them to achieve greater value improvements in care for specific medical conditions than an integrated payer-provider that must depend on process improvements or cost controls by a fixed set of providers.

Integrated organizations should have a place in the future health care system that their results should ultimately determine. However, we believe that patient value is best served by a system in which most health plans are independent of providers, where payment for services is for cycles of care at the medical condition level (rather than systemwide capitation), and where competing health plans harness competition among providers to improve value.

Open competition and unrestricted choice will be increasingly important as published information on risk-adjusted outcomes becomes the norm, so that good results in a specific medical condition can be rewarded by an increased flow of patients. As the perverse incentives, restricted competition, and high administrative costs of the current system are corrected, the advantages of vertical integration will recede in importance, while the value of open and unbiased referrals will grow.

Moving to Value-Based Competition: Imperatives for Health Plans

To support these new value-adding roles, health plans must change their strategies, organizational structures, operating practices, and ways of dealing with providers and members. These steps will require substantial change, but we know that they are possible because they are already occurring. As was the case for providers, each of our recommendations for health plans is being implemented or is under development at some plan or service provider, though no one plan has yet embraced all of them. Figure 6-2 summarizes the steps that health plans can take in these broad areas.

FIGURE 6-2

Imperatives for health plans

Provide health information and support to patients and physicians

- Organize around medical conditions, not geography or administrative functions
- Develop measures and assemble results information on providers and treatments
- Actively support provider and treatment choice with information and unbiased counseling
- Organize information and patient support around the full cycle of care
- Provide comprehensive disease management and prevention services to all members, even healthy ones

Restructure the health plan–provider relationship

- Shift the nature of information sharing with providers
- Reward provider excellence and value-enhancing innovation for patients
- Move to single bills for episodes and cycles of care, and single prices
- Simplify, standardize, and eliminate paperwork and transactions

Redefine the health plan–subscriber relationship

- Move to multiyear subscriber contracts and shift the nature of plan contracting
- End cost shifting practices, such as reunderwriting, that erode trust in health plans and breed cynicism
- Assist in managing members' medical records

Provide Health Information and Support
to Patients and Physicians

The central strategic transformation for health plans is to redefine their business from administering health benefits and controlling costs to providing health information, counseling, and ongoing support to members. The primary customer must become the member/patient, not the plan sponsor. The physician must be treated as the health plan's ally in enhancing member health, not its adversary. We are certain that if health plans create value for subscribers, the support and loyalty of plan sponsors will follow.

Organize Around Medical Conditions, Not Geography or Administrative Functions. Health plans, like providers, need to align their organizational structures around the central drivers of value creation. As we have discussed, health care value is created in addressing particular medical conditions over the full cycle of care. In health plans, the principal organizational units should be defined around clusters of health conditions, together with a unit dedicated to primary care. For ease of exposition, we will term these organizational units *health condition management units* (HCMUs). These units are analogous to the provider integrated practice units we described in chapter 5. Just the act of aligning the organizational structures of both health plans and providers around medical conditions will itself proliferate opportunities for value creation. A whole new dialogue and working relationship can be created.

HCMUs should take responsibility for assembling the best medical knowledge on prevention, diagnosis, treatment, and long-term management of the health conditions they address. They should measure and contract with providers, compile and interpret member information across the care cycle, interact with referring physicians, support subscribers/patients in their choice of both providers and treatments, and assist members in navigating the care cycle.[13] Analysis of the care delivery value chain for each medical condition (discussed in chapter 5 and appendix B) provides a tool for health plans to understand and play these roles effectively as well as facilitate the better integration of care. In some cases, HCMUs will develop subunits with special expertise in aspects of the cycle of care, such as risk assessment and prevention, diagnosis, treatment, and long-term disease management. HCMUs should be measured based on member health results in the medical conditions they oversee relative to the cost of care, and on their health results compared to those achieved by other plans.

Some health plans, such as CIGNA, are beginning to move in this direction. Such plans have units responsible for case management of acute care in a number of medical conditions, and other units responsible for disease management for some chronic conditions. Such a structure is a good start, but can be extended across all the important medical conditions. Ultimately, the structure needs to embrace the care-cycle model rather than artificially separate acute and chronic care.

HCMUs should cut across geography when a health plan operates in multiple regions. This will lead to depth of expertise as well as efficiencies in information gathering, patient advising, and cross-regional provider measurement and relationship management. Organizing by region, in contrast, only perpetuates a local mind-set in care delivery, and shelters local providers from meeting the standards of the best competitors. A regional model can also gravitate to contracting with the few large entities present, rather than a practice unit–by–practice unit approach driven by true excellence.

In addition to the HCMUs, health plans need a common unit dedicated to assembling, validating, and analyzing comprehensive member health information, working closely with each HCMU to compile the right information and utilize this information to enhance member health and the effectiveness of their care. This unit, which might be termed the member information management unit (MIMU), should be charged with finding innovative ways of working with members and their physicians to ensure that all the necessary member health information is available to members and physicians, that duplicative testing is avoided, that heath risks are understood, and that information from all involved physicians and providers is assembled and exchanged. Eventually, this unit should also oversee the process of assembling and verifying complete patient medical records for members (discussed later in this chapter). This unit should be measured based on the quality of the information provided.

Other health plan administrative functions, such as information technology (IT), transaction processing, marketing, member services, accounting, and maintaining relationships with employers and plan sponsors, are supporting functions. These units should be organized as service organizations whose job it is to enable the core HCMUs and the MIMU to meet their health value goals and to communicate with the various constituencies. They should be rewarded for providing excellent service and meeting specific functional goals.

Develop Measures and Assemble Results Information on Providers and Treatments. One of the most important ways that health plans can add value arises from their ability to assemble and marshal objective health information for the benefit of patients and referring physicians. Unlike any one provider, health plans have experience and data across many members, many providers, many individual physicians, multiple treatments, virtually all medical conditions, and over the full care cycle. Health plans, through HCMUs, should be able to measure and compare providers at the level of medical conditions. They should also be able to assemble external evidence and develop their own data on the effectiveness of various treatments. Ultimately, health plans should become essential drivers of competition among providers based on results. Health plans will not need to second-guess the appropriate treatments, because provider results will reveal them.

As described in previous chapters, four types of provider information are particularly relevant: results, experience, methods, and patient attributes. Medical results, consisting of outcomes, costs, and prices, are the most important. Outcomes are multidimensional, as we have discussed, and include measures of patient functionality, length of life, quality of life, recovery time, pain, complications, and errors. Outcomes that bear on the personal values of patients can also be important in areas such as side effects, the aggressiveness of treatment, and the need to be treated in an institutional setting.[14] Outcomes relative to prices determine value.

While patient service (such as amenities and friendliness) is significant and should be surveyed, medical results are ultimately more important. Therefore, patient surveys need to address the patient's perspective on medical outcomes, not just the types of customer service metrics that have been the focus of most subscriber feedback processes.

Given the current limitations on outcome data in many areas of care, too many health plans fall back on looking just at short-term costs and discounts. This reinforces the old model of focusing on discrete services and steering patients to providers willing to offer low prices, rather than informing and enabling patients' choices based on value over the care cycle.

Patients and plans need information not just on treatments but on other parts of the cycle of care: diagnosis, disease management, and disease prevention. Some plans are making progress in measurement in these areas, but current practice is just scratching the surface. Measuring the diagnostic effectiveness of providers (e.g., accuracy and full cost, including tests and the need for repeat visits) is crucial to value, not only in terms of achieving good patient outcomes but also of avoiding unnecessary and even harmful treatments that can hugely increase costs. Health plans must see this part of care as separate from treatment and know who the excellent diagnosticians are.

Health plans also need expertise on disease management approaches and measures of the effectiveness of various disease management providers or the health plan's own efforts. Finally, health plans must become experts in helping members understand the factors that affect a member's risk of developing various medical conditions, the best approaches to disease prevention, and the success rates of disease prevention services providers (including, potentially, the health plan itself).

To measure value, health plans will need to take the lead in aggregating patient information over multiple interventions and ultimately full cycles of care. This involves both longer-term outcome information as well as information on total charges, including repeat or recurring treatment. Health plans will need to assemble and integrate information on discrete interventions that is now usually collected, analyzed, and acted upon separately. Over time, as providers shift their care delivery structures (see chapter 5), providers themselves should be expected to present their results and cost information this way.

Health plans can begin the process of results measurement by drawing on numerous sources for information, none of which is yet complete or fully satisfactory. First, health plans have access to information about their present and past members, as well as the providers who have treated members and the approach to treatment. This information has rarely if ever been analyzed systematically at the level of medical conditions and over full care cycles. Yet it has significant potential to inform improvements in value. CIGNA, for example, has recently been combining lab test results and pharmacy data with its medical claims data for members enrolled in disease management programs. It has found that it can improve the detection of errors, gaps, or omissions in patient care and measure the effectiveness and return on investment of alternate disease management vendors and approaches.

Second, Medicare claims data is an important source of insight and comparison, as is all-payer data (which includes non-Medicare patients) where it is available. These data enable comparison of costs of discrete interventions or treatments for specific conditions across providers and across geography. The data also reveal differences in treatment patterns and in one dimension of results: mortality. While the data do not yet easily support broader outcome measurement or comparison of patients through entire care cycles, sophisticated analysis can utilize codes to infer complications and adjust for patients' initial conditions.[15] Some health plan executives believe that the sophisticated analysis of existing all-payer data can provide a good starting point for comparative data on results of treating specific conditions across many providers. They point out, however, that data remains sparse on individual physicians and on care provided outside of hospitals.

Third, objective and systematic outcome data is already collected on certain disease areas, including some complex medical conditions, as we discussed in chapter 4 (see the box "How Good Outcome Information Arose" in chapter 4). For example, data on end stage renal disease has been collected by the federal government, and measures of the effectiveness of care are available for every hemodialysis center for patients over age nineteen in the United States. Although dialysis patients often have numerous other health problems, much has been learned from the analysis of this data. They reveal, for example, huge variation in years of survival after kidney failure, with much of the variation linked to the care received. About 20 percent of patients die within a year, about 50 percent die within three years, and about 30 percent live for more than five years. There is also large variation in the filtration rate (a measure of the effectiveness of dialysis). Even this data, however, is not yet used to nearly its full potential. While providers with poor results are reviewed and coached on process improvement, the information is not used by Medicare to get patients to the excellent providers. This would not only lead to better health results but would spur improvement by providers with below-average results.

Another example of existing outcome information is nationally collected data from the Scientific Registry of Transplant Results, which similarly reveals huge variation in transplant outcomes. Few referring doctors appear to be aware of the power of the data, relying instead on their personal experience and relationships in making referrals. However, in the case of transplants, some health plans and their subcontracted service providers are beginning to use the available data to enable patients and referring physicians to make better provider choices, as we discuss later in this chapter. Even if physicians are slow to seek out and utilize results data, health plans can play a facilitating role.

Fourth, a number of independent organizations already collect quality-related information on hospitals and some physicians, much of it still through reputation surveys or data on process metrics. Reputation surveys are a start, but unfortunately they often reinforce impressions that are not based on objective outcomes.

Finally, every health plan can simply ask providers to present their results and prices at the medical condition level in the most meaningful way possible. There is no need to wait for standardized measures or national coverage. If health plans challenge providers to measure results at the condition and care-cycle level, and reward those who do excellent jobs, it will accelerate improvement in the state of the art.

The amount and range of outcome data are certain to grow dramatically. There is no more important role for health plans acting as catalysts in improving the availability of results information, individually as well as in collaboration with other health plans, employers, and providers. Indeed, the health plan industry should be investing collectively in research on results measurement and the study of the relationship between results and clinical practice. There is no area more important to the long-term value delivered by the industry.

To achieve reported results across all medical conditions, as we discuss in chapter 8, government or quasi-public organizations such as the Institute of Medicine may need a public mandate to ratify measures and risk adjustment models, oversee information collection, and disseminate results. However, health plans must move aggressively toward utilizing what is already available today, as some leading plans and service companies are doing.

Much of the information gathering and analysis function of a health plan should be performed in-house because medical information is absolutely central to a health plan's mission and its competitive advantage. However, outsourcing certain information collection and analysis functions, such as responsibility for certain specialized medical conditions, can improve efficiency and tap into a greater depth of expertise.

Over time, health plans will evolve many configurations for in-sourcing and outsourcing of information gathering and patient counseling functions. The economies of scale of specialists in performing certain information functions will be compelling in some fields, especially for more unusual medical conditions where a particular health plan lacks a meaningful number of cases. Health plans can also choose strategically to specialize in building up deep internal capability in some medical conditions, becoming a service provider to other health plans. This is just one way in which moving to value-based competition will allow health plans to better distinguish themselves. Those health plans that begin early to assemble and understand results information by provider at the medical condition level will gain a crucial competitive advantage.

Actively Support Provider and Treatment Choice with Information and Unbiased Counseling. A fundamental role of health plans is to help the patient and referring doctors obtain the right care from a provider that is excellent in addressing the patient's particular medical condition. Health plans have too often assumed that patients will not or cannot make good decisions about their own health care. Worse yet, many health plans have assumed that patients will always opt for more care. Yet this is not supported by careful studies, as we discussed in chapters 2 and 4. Informed patients often choose less care and less expensive care because they are equipped to make good choices about their own health care and motivated to avoid risky, painful, and time-consuming medical procedures.

When better results information is available and accessible, many health plan members and their doctors will make better choices. But it is not sufficient for health plans simply to post information on the Web and hope their members (and referring physicians) will find it. Proactive counseling and support in decision making are needed. Health plans that raise options early and assist patients in securing excellent care will add enormous value, especially in complex or chronic medical conditions.

The old model has been to attempt to control patient choices via network restrictions or approvals. Instead, the patient and referring doctor must be allowed, and indeed encouraged, to find an excellent provider. Health plans must build the capabilities to actively support this process, and be skilled enough to understand each provider's areas of unique specialization and distinctiveness (see chapter 5) versus a patient's particular needs. Doing so will not only improve health outcomes but also contain costs. Providers that are experienced and expert enough to utilize the most effective and least invasive methods will get it right the first time, avoid costly complications and errors, and achieve faster and fuller recoveries. If the patient receives care from an excellent provider, there is a higher probability not only that outcomes will be better but also that both short- and long-term costs will be lower. Results and value become the dominant considerations, not whether the provider is local or whether the plan has contracted the lowest price with that provider for a particular service.

Patients will and should continue to rely on physicians for advice. The idea that patients can or should become medical experts and direct their own care is misguided and unrealistic. Physicians will inevitably be part of the process, and supporting referring physicians with information will be an important health plan role. However, health plans should themselves play a role in informing and advising, because they are independent and their affiliation is with the patient, not any provider or treatment. The health plan, when it is not wedded to any provider network, should be able to be more objective than any provider, and better placed to recommend a regional center over a local provider if this is justified. By imparting results information and support to patients and physicians, health plans will become the crucial market makers and enablers of value-based competition.

To play these roles, health plans will need to build trust and credibility, both with patients and referring physicians. When choices are constrained and networks are defined based on cost without regard for value, trust is destroyed. Based on years of experience, members are suspicious that the sole motivation of health plans is to restrict treatment and steer them to the provider with whom the plan has the biggest discount. As long as they retain network restrictions and artificially high out-of-network costs for patients, the objectivity and credibility of health plans will be compromised.

Many health plans are beginning to try to shift their relationship with members and physicians to one of becoming a health adviser or health advocate. The growing number of health plans moving in this direction, among them Harvard Pilgrim and UnitedHealth Group, shows that a transformation of the health plan–subscriber relationship is possible. However, it will take sustained effort to win the trust of subscribers, not to mention that of physicians.

The efforts of United Resource Networks (U.R.N.), a unit of United-Health Group, illustrate the opportunity for successfully enabling patient choice. U.R.N. is not a health plan itself, but provides services to health plans, including its parent company. Leveraging the availability of national data, U.R.N. has specialized in serving organ transplant patients so well that other health plans in addition to UnitedHealth have contracted with U.R.N. to serve their transplant patients. Overall, U.R.N. manages over 7,000 cases per year. Its organ transplant program helps patients find excellent providers, achieve good outcomes, and reduce costs through improved care. Sometimes this means enabling a transplant, while in other cases it means getting the patient to a provider with the expertise to treat the patient successfully without the need for a transplant.

To identify centers of excellence, U.R.N. uses the national organ transplant data on outcomes and experience as well as its own credentialing process, which is based on in-depth interactions with numerous excellent providers. Centers of excellence in transplanting each organ are identified separately; for example, the best centers for a bone marrow transplant may not be the best for liver transplants because each requires a different care delivery value chain. U.R.N. negotiates contracts only with centers that are among the most experienced and that have demonstrated superb outcomes.

U.R.N. does not dictate patient choice of provider; its patient clients are not confined by their health plan to a network. Instead, U.R.N. provides information to referring doctors and patients about each provider's outcomes, patient ratings of the provider's service experiences, and the out-of-pocket costs the patients will bear in being cared for by the provider given the patient's particular health insurance coverage. Each patient is guided through the process by a skilled nurse who not only supports the initial choice of provider but also becomes the adviser over the course of treatment. The ultimate decision remains squarely with the patient. U.R.N. has found that the excellent outcome data available in the transplant area, while freely available on a Web site, is simply impossible in its current form for most patients to understand. Also, as we mentioned earlier, referring doctors do not consistently use this data.[16] Thus, the role of a trusted adviser is essential to explain the data and the available choices to the patient as well as the primary care doctor or referring physician.

U.R.N. has delivered excellent results. Its patients have achieved better outcomes at lower costs. For example, John Deere contracted with U.R.N. in 1993. By 1999, 129 covered patients had undergone transplants. In each case, with no constraints on choice, the patient chose a very high-quality provider. John Deere saved an average of 35 percent of standard transplant charges per transplant episode.[17] U.R.N. has found that about one-quarter of the cost savings came from fewer complications. The balance came from lower rates that excellent providers were willing to offer for greater patient volume. This is consistent with the greater efficiency of excellent providers, a result of the virtuous circle of care delivery we described in chapter 5. And with the availability of outcome data, no network restrictions were needed to achieve the flow of patients to the better transplant centers. Patients did not simply choose the most convenient, nearby provider.

Building on this success, U.R.N. is expanding its services to other areas of care where credible evidence of quality exists or can be constructed. For example, less than 3 percent of adult cancers are treated under research protocols, and cure rates for adults lag far behind those for children.[18] U.R.N. is working to improve the results for adult cancer patients by collecting outcome data on those types of cancer for which peer-reviewed research has already demonstrated that better clinical results are achieved by providers with experience and high volume. When U.R.N.'s data reveals better clinical outcomes at an experienced center, U.R.N. seeks a relationship with that center and seeks to negotiate a contract to serve its patients. Again, U.R.N does not restrict the patients' or referring physicians' choices, but enables better choices by providing results information and advice.

In some cases, the preferred treatment and provider for a medical condition will be outside the local area. Here, a health plan can assist in facilitating appointments and travel. U.R.N. has found that when comparative data is available, the prospect of traveling to obtain truly expert care proves to be far less daunting to patients than many assume it will be. As U.R.N. has extended its services to neonatal congenital heart disease, for instance, it seeks to ensure that couples expecting a child with a heart anomaly travel to the right place so that a child can obtain expertly performed surgery when he or she is born. As in heart transplants (see figure 2-4), surgery on congenital heart defects is performed at many hospitals throughout the United States, but with widely varying success rates. Excellent providers reduce the risk of both physical and cognitive impairment, literally making a lifelong difference for the patient. U.R.N. has found that expectant parents are highly receptive to travel when they are well informed.

To facilitate patient choices of excellent providers, health plans should pay for travel when significant value differences are present (as with all our health plan recommendations, this applies to employer self-insured plans as well). As U.R.N. has found, covering travel for the patient and a companion will encourage the choice of the best provider and, in many cases, save money because the best provider is actually less costly over the cycle of care. Many employers, stuck in a cost minimization mind-set, have been hesitant to include travel reimbursement in their health plans. Some health plans have also hesitated to reimburse for travel out of fear that doing so would harm competition among local providers. Instead, the effect will be the opposite. Having patients compare local providers with the best providers across the nation will dramatically enhance competition locally by motivating local providers to meet a higher standard.

While U.R.N offers one example of how to assist patients in finding the best providers, there are a variety of other models being introduced as well. Some health plans, following the basic principles we have described, are beginning to define new types of networks that do not involve restricted choice. Tiers of providers are created based on quality and value, rather than location. By encouraging patients to consider high-quality providers without constraining choice, health plans further harness competition to improve provider quality.

CIGNA, for example, has developed "quality networks" for several diseases for which data is available. The guiding principle is that these networks should not constrain patient choice, but motivate patients to make better choices by providing information, access to health advisers, and economic incentives. These incentives come in the form of lower cost sharing for patients obtaining care at excellent providers. Similar to the U.R.N. approach, excellent providers should be rewarded with higher patient volume as the health plan communicates their good results. CIGNA negotiates better rates from these centers and shares that savings with subscribers.

CIGNA has also found that quality and efficiency are correlated. For example, cardiologists who are 10 percent better or more on outcome measures (depending on the measure) are, on average, approximately 10 percent more efficient. Overall CIGNA has found that top-tier physicians are 8 to 10 percent less costly, including all medical and pharmaceutical costs for inpatient and outpatient care. CIGNA's data indicates that over 80 percent of physicians recognized by the National Committee for Quality Assurance (NCQA) are also more efficient than nonrecognized physicians.[19] Unfortunately, NCQA recognition is only available for heart, stroke, and diabetes care because these are the medical conditions for which objective, good-quality national results information is currently available.

CIGNA has taken its approach further by identifying hospital centers of excellence for nineteen specific admissions (corresponding to medical conditions) based on a number of other information sources: risk-adjusted results from all-payer data (in the states where it is collected), Medpar data (Medicare data for states without all-payer data), Leapfrog data, and internal CIGNA data on the total cost per episode of hospital care. Overall, care in these centers of excellence is not only of better quality (measured by better survival rates or fewer complications, or both) but also less costly.[20]

It is essential that approaches such as quality networks or centers of excellence be truly results driven, not based on discounts. They also must be truly optional, rather than simply repackaged network restrictions. The integrity of so-called quality networks will become suspect if the sole criterion for network qualification is lower cost. Subscribers and referring physicians need to be clearly informed as to how a given provider qualified for the network when both quality and cost measures are used to delineate the network. Also, the quality network model will be diminished if health plans revert to coercion by making out-of-network care prohibitively expensive. The use of restrictive networks is an unneeded crutch. Without networks but with information, the incentives of both health plans and providers to improve value will be compelling.

Some observers have questioned whether patients will actually use information to alter their choices, citing the experiments in Cleveland and Pennsylvania in which published information had little impact on patient behavior.[21] We believe that patients and referring physicians will be very receptive, but health plans must play an enabling role that remains rare today. In the earlier experiments, there was no one acting as an informed, trusted adviser, which was a role that health plans had abdicated.

Health plans need to gather, package, and communicate information in a form that patients can understand. As the U.R.N. example illustrates, skilled and specialized staff such as nurses or even physicians will be needed to oversee information collection at health plans and play the adviser/counselor role. Health plans will learn how to configure and deliver such services cost-effectively, including the management of chronic care. The recent evidence of health plans or their subcontractors playing advisory roles in diagnosis, treatment, and disease management is encouraging.

Health plans may also choose to offer additional counseling as a premium service for those subscribers (or plan sponsors) who desire it. CIGNA, for example, is offering a nurse health adviser program that provides telephone, e-mail, and mail communication between the nurse and patient. The nurse adviser provides outreach education to patients before and after hospitalization, guidance on health risk assessment, and health coaching and referral assistance in response to patient-initiated requests for help, among other services. The health adviser program has to date been selected by employers with a total of one million plan members.

Health plans will need to develop the internal capability to provide information and counseling services for many medical conditions, because this is essential to their value proposition and their ability to distinguish themselves from their competitors. For highly specialized conditions, however, those functions can be outsourced to specialists, such as U.R.N., that aggregate patients across many health plans. Such specialists will be able to afford to invest in deep expertise and specialized medical personnel and to track results nationally. They will also have the volume of patients needed to form meaningful relationships and be influential with the best providers. Specialists may also be especially cost-effective in those conditions where rarity means that providers across multiple regions need to be measured and assessed.

U.R.N. is an example of such a specialist service provider in organ transplants, end stage renal disease, infertility treatment, and neonatal cardiac surgery. Another example is Preferred Global Health, a patient service organization that offers decision support and enables access to world-class care for patients in Europe and the Middle East who face any of fifteen serious diseases.[22] When one of these diseases is suspected, the member is provided with expert help in confirming the diagnosis and understanding treatment options and their implications. As with U.R.N., a nurse specializing in the particular disease works with the patient to be sure that the information available is understood. Preferred Global Health also provides support in identifying and accessing a world-class provider of the treatment approach chosen by the patient.

Some health plans may choose particular medical conditions for which they will develop the capability to serve not only their own subscribers but also those of other health plans. Such services may be tailored to the needs of particular patient populations. For example, expertise related to the elderly would involve providing counseling and tracking on diseases, injuries, and co-occurring conditions that often occur later in life. Such a service also might help members understand Medicare coverage, provide information on the quality of care at nursing homes or retirement communities, and assist in tracking multiple conditions and medications. Such services could be marketed regionally or nationally. Providing such services to other plans is another means for health plans to distinguish themselves in value-based competition.

Organize Information and Patient Support Around the Full Cycle of Care. The information, advice, counseling, and patient support roles of health plans must encompass the full cycle of care, not just discrete visits, tests, procedures, or treatments. We have discussed the rationale for a care-cycle focus extensively in this and previous chapters. The current mind-set of trying to reduce piecemeal costs (for drugs, tests, visits, or discrete procedures) encourages cost shifting rather than true value creation. It fails to harness the powerful linkage across the parts of the care cycle that can lower overall cost. It also ignores the fundamental importance of disease prevention and long-term disease management.

Organization around care cycles is challenging because neither health plans nor providers are currently managed this way. Comprehensive patient information is rarely collected and aggregated across time because most medical care occurs in response to the appearance of a symptom or condition and most reimbursement and payment is organized by service visit, procedure, or treatment type. Health plans obtain most information about member health only when they are in the process of paying, and insurance records are based on discrete coded interventions. Traditionally, patients have not wanted information that bears on their risk of future medical issues to come to light for fear of losing health coverage or facing increased insurance premiums in a zero-sum system. Providers have been organized around discrete interventions, not the care cycle, as we discussed in chapter 5. Numerous separate units and entities are involved in care. Coordination of care and handoffs across the care cycle leave much to be desired.

The health plan is arguably the entity in the best position to aggregate information on the patient's entire cycle of care, including follow-up care, since a combination of physicians, pharmacists, therapists, and other health care professionals in different entities may well be involved. Health plans can use the care delivery value chain (discussed in chapter 5 and appendix B) to map the cycle of care; identify and facilitate the linkages among different providers, labs, and service organizations involved in care; and anticipate potential gaps in coordination.

The health plan is also in the best position to help the patient navigate the care cycle. This involves making sure that handoffs are smooth, that information needed for care is transferred, that breaks in care do not occur, and that follow-up takes place. It may not be practical or feasible for any one provider to play this role, though providers need to dramatically step up their responsibilities. Organizing health plans around medical conditions, encompassing the full care cycle, will greatly facilitate the ability to play these roles.

U.R.N.'s organ transplant services provide a good example of the role of health plans across the care cycle. As described in chapter 5, organ transplants involve a protracted and multifaceted process of care stretching over years. U.R.N. studies and supports the entire cycle, from confirming the diagnosis to selecting the provider and waiting for an organ, all the way through surgery and long-term follow-up. Value depends on the combined excellence of all stages, not just a successful surgery. So does the ultimate cost of care.

In managing the full care cycle, it is important to distinguish diagnosis as a discrete set of activities, separate from treatment. As we have discussed, getting the diagnosis right has huge cost and value benefits. Managing the process of obtaining an accurate and complete diagnosis is a fundamental health plan responsibility. Health plans may find that some providers are especially effective at diagnosis, even if treatment is conducted elsewhere. Independent diagnosis is also important to eliminating treatment bias, as discussed in chapter 5.

Providers' efforts to integrate care over the care cycle are just beginning, as we discussed in chapter 5. Health plans can encourage this integration by aggregating and sharing their own care-cycle information, and working with providers to identify opportunities for better coordination. Strong care-cycle integration should become one of the hallmarks of excellent providers that a health plan recommends. Some inducements or incentives can also encourage providers to move more quickly, as we will discuss further.

Aggregating member health information, organized around cycles of care for medical conditions, should be a central role of the member information management units of health plans described earlier. Health plans will need new types of information systems to support care-cycle management. Today, most health plans have records only of service visits and covered treatments, not of the results. Increasingly, plans are compiling information about prescriptions that can be used to help with case management. In some circumstances, health plans also have access to lab results. However, large gaps in information limit the ability of health plans to see across the care cycle, much less measure overall results and costs. Patient data can be aggregated over time and around medical conditions even with the technology that is available today. Health plans should not wait for fully electronic medical records to begin this effort.

Provide Comprehensive Disease Management and Prevention Services to All Members, Even Healthy Ones. A fundamental implication of care-cycle thinking is that health plans must widen their scope and accept responsibility for the full cycle. As we discussed in earlier chapters, this means measuring and minimizing the risk of disease (so-called prevention or risk management) and managing medical conditions over the long term to improve results and prevent or minimize recurrences (so-called disease management).

Recognition of the value of disease management is perhaps more advanced. There is voluminous and rapidly growing evidence that disease management, not just the initial diagnosis and treatment of a medical condition, contributes substantially to health care value. The Institute of Medicine reviewed the literature and concluded that there is "substantial evidence that programs providing counseling, education, information feedback, and other supports to patients with common chronic conditions are associated with improved outcomes."[23] More and more examples of the return on investment in disease management are becoming available.[24] Blue Cross Blue Shield (BCBS) of Massachusetts, for example, has registered improved outcomes while also reducing costs through disease management programs in congestive heart failure, diabetes, coronary artery disease, and rare diseases such as multiple sclerosis and Tay-Sachs disease. CIGNA has documented outcome and efficiency improvements for diabetes, congestive heart failure, chronic obstructive pulmonary disease, asthma, and lower back pain.[25] Wellpoint data documents the improved clinical outcomes and lower costs of members participating in disease management programs for asthma, diabetes, and heart disease, including a 27 percent reduction in emergency room visits and a 15 percent decrease in average blood sugar levels for diabetic patients in the program for three years.[26]

Blue Cross Blue Shield of Minnesota (BCBSMN), which has been a leader in this area, has expanded its disease management program to seventeen diseases that affect 12 to15 percent of its member population.[27] To create a program of this scale, several million medical records were assembled, 120 nurses were hired, a call center was established, and a ten-year agreement was signed with American Healthways, which specializes in disease management services. BCBSMN identified eligible members using claims data, prescription data, and referrals. It enrolled every member who was eligible unless the individual chose not to participate. The result was a 97 percent participation rate among eligible members. Because BCBSMN did not apply the program to employer-funded plans (which would have had to pay for the program and were skeptical of its value), BCBSMN automatically had a control group with which it could compare results. Relative to the control group, outcomes were better and costs were lower by $500 per member in the first year.[28] In its first year, BCBSMN reported a 14 percent decrease in the rate of hospital admissions, an 18 percent drop in emergency room visits, and a return of $2.90 for every dollar invested (for a total savings of over $36 million) relative to a similar cohort that was not enrolled in the program.[29] Based on this success, BCBSMN is expanding the program to include nine cancers, chronic kidney disease, and depression.[30] Since some experts suggest that the benefits of disease management kick in about nine months after programs begin, and the program benefits should persist over the long range, these results are very encouraging.

Disease management is especially important for chronic conditions, which represent as much as 75 percent of total health care expenditures and are projected to affect more patients in the coming decades.[31] Currently, the 45 percent of the population that has one or more chronic conditions accounts for 69 percent of hospital admissions, 80 percent of hospital days, and 55 percent of emergency room visits.[32] While individuals over the age of sixty-five often have a chronic condition, 75 percent of people with chronic conditions are under age sixty-five. The impact of improving the value of health care delivery for chronic conditions would be enormous for Medicare and Medicaid, which pay for 40 percent of medical care for chronic conditions (excluding nursing home expenses), versus 20 percent of acute care expenditures. While chronic conditions are not curable, quality of life can be greatly enhanced and the need for medical services can be significantly reduced with the right kind of care.

Risk assessment, together with care that reduces the risks of or prevents disease or injury, is also fundamental to value-based competition. Risk assessment, coupled with information and counseling, creates a personalized understanding of the need for behavior modification and compliance with preventive therapies. This is another critical change of mind-set: from paying for treating an acute stage of disease to minimizing or preventing the disease with earlier intervention. Learning about such preventive approaches is accumulating rapidly, and will only become more important with advances in genetic and personalized medicine. For example, predictive models are being developed that anticipate which individuals are at the greatest risk of developing particular medical problems. BCBSMN, whose disease management programs we described earlier, also offers a program for high-risk members who have not yet had an acute event.

An example of a health plan embracing risk management and prevention is BCBS of Massachusetts, which is piloting a program with its own employees in which individuals voluntarily provide information that can be used to predict the risk of future disease, particularly coronary artery disease. While employer plan sponsors have not yet been convinced to embrace this approach, the health plan's own employees have been very forthcoming in providing information to assist in reducing their medical risk. The voluntary program is garnering far more participation than expected, and the initial results are positive in terms of patient satisfaction.

Patients for whom elevated risk is identified are offered a Blue Health Coach who calls weekly in the initial months (and less frequently later) to advise and answer questions on issues such as medication compliance, weight, exercise, how to talk to the doctor, and what test results really mean. Preliminary results, based on a small sample of pre–coronary artery disease patients, indicate both improved health outcomes and reduced costs.

CIGNA's health adviser service, mentioned earlier, also includes the opportunity for members to participate voluntarily in risk assessment and subsequent coaching on risk reduction. This service is being offered through self-insured employer plans and has attracted greater participation than initially anticipated.

Another example of the benefits of risk management is Aetna's program focused on high-risk pregnancies. Consultations with perinatologists and home visits by nurses educate high-risk expectant mothers about the signs of preterm labor. While Aetna once had a blanket policy of seeking to enroll all pregnant women in a general wellness program, it now focuses exclusively on the high-risk population. Aetna reports a 20 percent reduction in time spent in the neonatal intensive care unit for children whose mothers entered the program in the first trimester. This reduction equates to better health for the baby and a savings of $4,000 a day for care.[33]

The value benefits of risk assessment and management are also revealed by U.R.N.'s healthy pregnancy program to improve the early recognition of babies who will be born with complex conditions. This program complements the congenital heart disease services mentioned earlier in this chapter.[34] U.R.N. has found that appropriate and timely care can improve the health outcomes of at-risk babies while achieving cost reductions of a remarkable 50 percent. Medical results for the covered newborns are far better when they are born at a provider with appropriate facilities and capabilities to treat them. Risk assessment is important in this case because it is often far easier and less expensive to find and secure treatment by such a provider before the child is born, rather than on an emergency basis.

In each of these examples of risk management, the health plan does not attempt to manage how the provider cares for patients, nor second-guess the care that was delivered after the fact. Instead, risk management is designed to provide understandable, trustworthy information to patients (and referring physicians) at the time it is needed, and even before symptoms have presented. This enables choices that minimize disease and that enable well-planned care in what would otherwise be an emergency situation.

Applying such predictive thinking in many medical or disease areas, and across a health plan's full subscriber base, offers large potential gains in value. Risk management not only benefits patients but further reinforces competition among providers to achieve excellent medical results—the kind of competition that is consistent with physicians' professional and ethical obligations.

Every health plan needs comprehensive programs for risk assessment and prevention and disease management in which many if not most subscribers participate. Most plans currently offer few areas of disease management (typically one to four), although interest in them is now increasing. As plans increasingly compete on health results and their time horizons lengthen, prevention and disease management programs will be core elements of health plan strategies. With their capacity to embrace the full care cycle and to aggregate member information, health plans have a unique capacity to add value in this way.

One reason many plans cite for not offering more disease management (and prevention) programs is that such efforts will only benefit competitors if subscribers move to another plan. However, prevention and disease management programs are very likely to increase subscriber loyalty and reduce plan churning. Health plans have also sometimes seen chronically ill (and thus relatively expensive) or high-risk members as something to be avoided, slowing the spread of prevention and disease management programs over the past decade. However, such programs are value creating, and every subscriber and plan sponsor will benefit from them. Health plans without such programs will lose market position in the new competition.

Employers (and some health plans) focused on short-term costs have sometimes dragged their feet on prevention and disease management. The excuse has been that the gains from such programs are hard to measure and that the benefits of such programs are hard to isolate from other causal variables. This thinking is obsolete, as evidenced by the numerous studies discussed earlier in this section. CIGNA is confident enough to provide all five of its disease management programs in all health plans in which it bears the financial risk. In contrast, only about 65 percent of employers who contract with CIGNA for plan administration choose to include *any* disease management programs in their self-insured health plans. There are indications, however, that more and more employers are beginning to embrace disease management and pay for it. This trend will accelerate as companies measure the value and health outcomes, not just the short-term costs, of their health benefits programs. We discuss this further in chapter 7.

The success of risk assessment and prevention depends on relationships with subscribers and physicians that are no longer adversarial and zero sum, but trust based and value creating. Without trust, patients simply will not participate. Also, the dark side of risk management and predictive medicine is the fear that health plans will use them to justify re-underwriting and discrimination, both forms of zero-sum competition. Patients must be convinced that this is neither the motivation nor the planned outcome of these programs. In a system of trust and partnership, members would voluntarily provide information to assist in managing their health.

All health plans will need to develop some in-house capabilities in prevention and disease management, because these are core functions for improving health and health care value. Most prevention and disease management programs involve skilled personnel who interact with members, with titles such as a health coach (BCBS of Massachusetts), life coach, or patient adviser. Over time, an increasing percentage of health plan employees will require these skills.

Health plans can outsource some elements of the prevention and disease management roles to specialists. There were approximately 160 disease management vendors in 2005. Over time, providers will also begin to incorporate prevention and disease management services into their service lines, as part of seamless care-cycle delivery models.

Restructure the Health Plan–Provider Relationship

Competing on value and playing new supporting roles with patients will require that health plans develop very different relationships with physicians and provider organizations. Some physicians would describe their interactions with health plans today as "war."[35] This adversarial mind-set needs to disappear, and some health plans are already taking steps to eradicate it. In its place should arise a spirit of collaboration regarding value creation for patients. When health plans and providers work together around value and health results, efficiency will improve exponentially and administrative costs will fall.

Physician support is critical to health plan success because most patients will (and should) make medical decisions and behavioral choices with the advice of their doctor. If the health plan and the doctor offer information and advice that conflict, patients will usually trust the doctor. Conversely, if the health plan and the doctor are in sync, the ability to make good decisions and secure appropriate patient behavior is amplified.

Restructuring the relationship between health plans and providers involves two areas: changing the nature and type of information sharing, and shifting the incentives built into patient flows and reimbursement.

Shift the Nature of Information Sharing with Providers. Health plan executives often express frustration that what they know is not listened to and utilized by physicians. Given the history, this is no surprise. There has not been a collaborative relationship centered on patient value.

Health plans need to recognize that doctors are and will always be important, if not the most important, contributors to patient choices.

The health plan can assist patients and their doctors to gather information, understand their treatment options, seek the best provider to address their circumstances, ensure that the providers involved in care have up-to-date patient information, and assist in navigating handoffs in the care cycle. For example, U.R.N. has found that before it becomes involved, many patients have already been given a referral to a transplant surgeon. The information U.R.N. brings to bear can suggest that the referral is a questionable one given the outcome evidence. U.R.N. will contact the referring physician and explain that while U.R.N. cannot know everything, its data points to a different choice. It asks the referring physician to help U.R.N. learn about the suggested specialist, and ensures that the referring physician is aware of the patient's range of covered choices. In most cases, the referring physician is surprised to learn that the patient has access to the best care, and would prefer to have the patient treated at one of U.R.N.'s identified centers of excellence. The physician can then talk with the patient about the wider set of choices.

Health plans can also support doctors with many other kinds of information that is difficult or impractical for physicians or even any one provider organization to assemble. Prescription claims, for example, can offer opportunities to uncover and share information about compliance. One health plan manager described a case in which a member with diabetes was experiencing ongoing problems keeping sugar levels under control. The health plan's system for checking prescription compliance uncovered that the member's prescription for medication twice a day was being refilled exactly half as often as it should have been. The health plan shared this observation with the physician. It turned out that although the physician had previously asked if the patient was taking medication regularly, and was assured that this was the case, the patient had misunderstood the frequency. This member's sugar levels are now under control, reducing health risks. Through a collaborative relationship based on sharing information, the doctor is delivering better care, the patient is enjoying better health, and costs will be lower. These kinds of examples can become commonplace.

Health plans can also assist physicians in gathering outcome data before making referrals. In today's system, referral patterns tend to be routine, rather than based on actual evidence. Only reliable, relevant information shared with physicians can change these patterns and enable referring physicians to improve results for their patients.

Health plans should also share with physicians ongoing feedback about the results achieved by their referrals, in terms of patient outcomes. If doctors could compare how their referred patients fared relative to patients at other providers, the right kind of investigation and scrutiny about referrals would take place.

Health plans can also provide resources to support physicians in terms of diagnosis and treatment. For example, about fifty health plans and reinsurance companies use the services of Best Doctors to assist in obtaining the correct diagnosis and the best treatment plan for complex patients. Best Doctors has a team of internists who review difficult cases and identify the types of specialists who need to be involved. It is also able to contact and retain leading experts to assist the treating doctor by reviewing the diagnosis and treatment plan. Sometimes a leading expert is recruited to participate in treatment. Best Doctors' reviews have led to modification of the diagnosis in 22 percent of cases and alteration of the treatment plan in over 60 percent of cases. A retrospective analysis of these services by the reinsurance company American Re revealed more accurate diagnoses, a 27 percent reduction in permanent disability, avoidance of one or more invasive surgical procedures by 63 percent of patients, and a $44,000 per case savings on rehabilitation expenses.[36] Such information sharing, which only in extreme cases involves changing doctors, can not only improve care but also help doctors improve the value they deliver.

In complex trauma cases, when a patient is brought to the hospital, Best Doctors is contacted by the insurer and sends one of its nurses to the patient's location to serve as the case manager and to coordinate communication. Best Doctors quickly assembles a team to provide expertise and telephone consultation to the physicians who are caring for the patient. This approach has significantly reduced unnecessary complications, which American Re has estimated as saving $250,000 per trauma case.

As value-based competition grows, more patients will be referred to excellent providers, and providers themselves will build networks of relationships with experts who will consult on difficult cases. However, health plans will have an enduring and important role in bringing information and expertise to bear that draws on their independence and relationships with numerous providers. As long as this process is collaborative and focused on patient results rather than limiting services, it will contribute to value.

Finally, health plans have a role in overcoming provider wariness of measurement. Given subscribers' loyalty to their providers, health plans have sometimes been wary of comparing providers for fear of backlash. This has reinforced the tendency to treat all providers as equal. Closer scrutiny of provider results requires a disciplined process that is perceived as objective and fair. It also requires measures that are relevant and meaningful indicators of medical results. The excellent providers will welcome such measurement, especially if the value they deliver is rewarded with more patients and higher margins. The move to measurement will also trigger much new data collection if providers come to see that health plans will use the best information available. Once providers understand that outcome measurement is inevitable, they will contribute to refining it.

Progress in developing outcome measures can be more rapid if health plans engage with providers in creating meaningful clinical measures specific to each medical condition. Some health plans, such as Anthem (Virginia, now owned by Wellpoint), are asking physician groups in specific areas of care to develop the measures on which their performance will be assessed. This helps ensure that the metrics are meaningful and encourages buy-in. Physicians also need to be involved in reviewing and improving the metrics.

Health plans should communicate results data to providers and allow time for them to make corrections. This will improve the accuracy of the data and increase physicians' confidence in the fairness of the process. The inclination of physicians to make evidence-based referrals will be strengthened by the knowledge that they and their colleagues have checked the data.

Reward Provider Excellence and Value-Enhancing Innovation for Patients. Current health plan contracting and payment practices are not tied to value. Either all providers of a given service are reimbursed equally, or contracted rates depend on bargaining power. Rate structures tend to closely follow Medicare, whose flawed reimbursement structure is not aligned with costs, outcomes, or value. Health plan reimbursement is tied to transactions and discrete services rather than episodes or full care cycles. There are separate charges for each physician, for the use of facilities, and for pharmaceuticals.

Providers are not rewarded for excellence. What is worse, they get paid for treatment, not for devising better or less expensive methods. In fact, providers can be penalized for better performance or innovations utilizing a less invasive treatment. Reducing treatment and office visits, or avoiding serious complications, leads to lower revenue for the provider. Revenue can drop more than costs, thus creating a *penalty* for value improvement! In the current system, providers also get little reward other than professional satisfaction for counseling patients in managing or preventing disease. There are still not well-developed mechanisms for compensating providers for services in these areas.

Overall, there is a lack of gain sharing in the system, either for providers achieving better results or for providers who improve results over time. None of this makes any sense in terms of patient value. Health plans must find new ways to reimburse providers that reward, rather than work against, value and value improvement. Health plans can no longer simply take the easy solution and follow Medicare, but must help lead reimbursement toward value-based competition in all the ways they can influence.

Rewarding Provider Excellence. First and foremost, health plans need to reward provider excellence. Some health plans are taking steps in this direction through pay-for-performance programs, as we have discussed in previous chapters. Harvard Pilgrim's pay-for-performance contract with Partners HealthCare System in 2001, for example, was the first cooperative performance incentive contract between a plan and a large delivery system in the United States. Harvard Pilgrim has expanded its pay-for-performance system substantially, and publicly recognizes outstanding providers in its Honor Roll.

BCBS of Massachusetts has established quality-related pricing models for primary care physicians, specialty group practices, and hospitals. Available results measures are still rudimentary, however, so that BCBS and similar initiatives base their bonuses primarily on process measures. For primary care physicians, BCBS uses improvement in the National Committee for Quality Improvement's HEDIS[37] measures, such as mammography rates and diabetes treatment protocols.[38] In addition, there are rewards for prescribing generic versions of antibiotics and using a medical decision support tool (of their own choosing, not a particular tool specified by BCBS). All of these are process measures. BCBS's ultimate goal is to base rewards on publicly reported outcome measures.

For hospitals, BCBS bases bonuses on mutually established performance improvement goals that are specific to each hospital, rather than utilizing the same goals for all providers. In the chosen areas of improvement, broad outcome measures developed by the Agency for Healthcare Research and Quality (AHRQ) are utilized, such as infection rates and acute myocardial infarction rates after surgery. Hospitals that exceed their specific improvement goals can receive a 2 percent increase in reimbursement, which can involve millions of dollars for a medium-sized hospital. Again, the longer-term goal is to base rewards on outcomes rather than processes.

From Processes to Results. As we have discussed, current pay-for-performance approaches, with their emphasis on process compliance, are only a start. Pay for performance does not actually reward excellence. While the BCBS of Massachusetts program rewards areas of improvement, for example, it is less likely to set an improvement goal in an area where the provider is already very good. The incentive to develop true excellence would be far stronger if BCBS went a step further and created a reward for hospitals that further distinguish their best services.

Ultimately, providers should be encouraged not just to improve clearly substandard processes but to achieve clearly superior results. From a value perspective, results are best measured and rewarded at the level of medical conditions, not overall outcomes such as mortality or generic complications. Pay-for-performance bonuses should be specific to medical conditions, not across the board. Rewards for improvement need to be the same for all providers. Health plans should encourage providers to strengthen the areas in which they are already very good.

The process focus of current pay-for-performance initiatives reflects a desire to promote safety. However, if safety *results* are measured, such as numbers of patients with postsurgical infections or ventilator-associated pneumonia, the attention to safe *practices* will markedly increase. Health plans do not have to be in the business of monitoring everything a hospital does, but should ensure that physicians and patients are appropriately focused on results.

Competition for Patients. While bonuses to reward excellence are beneficial, perhaps the most powerful reward for excellence and value is more patients. Providers that are excellent and efficient will earn higher margins, even at the same prices as other providers. It is the margin (revenue net of costs), not the price, that really matters for providers. Increasing a provider's volume of patients in a medical condition should drive major improvements in value and margins, as we have discussed (see figure 5-2).

Health plans should resist the temptation to try to level the playing field by seeking to raise all providers to an acceptable level. Instead, the best providers in a medical condition should be rewarded with patients. Leveling the playing field works against the powerful role of volume and expertise in driving value, as we have discussed. Also, the motivation of weaker providers to win back lost patients by improving results will be far stronger than incremental pay-for-performance incentives.

Gain Sharing. Reimbursement structures must evolve to reward providers for value-enhancing improvements that reduce the need for services. Today, health plans penalize them. Since current payments are tied to providing services, and the price for a given service reflects its complexity, moving to a less invasive treatment or minimizing the need for admissions or office visits can reduce revenue faster than cost, as we described in chapter 4. In its contracts with commercial health plans, for example, Intermountain Healthcare discovered that its care improvements for community-acquired pneumonia reduced its costs by 12.5 percent, but that revenues fell by 17 percent. Intermountain is beginning to point out these anomalies and define models to share savings.[39] One model, for example, might be one in which a health plan guaranteed equal provider margins *for the care cycle* for innovative new care delivery methods, together with a formula to share net savings. Ideally, health plans would also reward process innovations with more patients.

Another way to encourage value improvements is to allow providers to capture gains of efficiency improvements by leaving prices stable for periods of time (while measuring outcomes). Providers will be motivated to improve efficiency (without sacrificing measured quality) because they will retain the benefits of efficiency improvements during that time.

Value-Based Pricing. In true value-based competition, prices should be based on health value rather than effort, the complexity of the service, or overall cost. In value-based pricing, for example, diagnosis would be recognized, measured, and rewarded as a discrete service. The price would reflect the overall efficiency and effectiveness of the diagnosis, and the fact that an accurate diagnosis can have a huge influence on subsequent costs and results.

One of the greatest flaws in the current pricing system is that consultation is undervalued relative to performing procedures. Value-based pricing would change this. Consultation-based services that have a clear health impact, and that reduce the need for expensive treatments, should be rewarded with attractive reimbursements. This will also help avoid the bias toward treatment.

An encouraging example of value-based thinking is the move to reward doctor-patient communication via telephone or e-mail. Such consultation has typically not been reimbursed at all. A bias is created for office visits or for not addressing issues early, which drives up costs. Some health plans are beginning to pay for doctor-patient communication by e-mail, including Blue Cross and Blue Shield plans in California, New York, Florida, Massachusetts, New Hampshire, Colorado, and Tennessee, as well as Anthem Blue Cross (now owned by Wellpoint), CIGNA, Harvard Pilgrim, and Kaiser Permanente. The physician is typically reimbursed $24 to $30, and patients typically make copayments of $5 to $10 to discourage unnecessary communication. Medicare has also been conducting experiments with online patient-physician communication, and House legislation has been proposed to let Medicare make "bonus payments" to physicians for e-mail consultations. These moves are a step forward in recognizing the importance of consultation, but they create yet another example of extremely fragmented payment. More comprehensive pricing models for services such as preventive care and disease management will be needed.

Value-based pricing models will also be necessary for risk assessment, prevention, and disease management services. Prices should reflect the value delivered in terms of patient health outcomes and cost savings. The onus should be on providers to demonstrate value, which will improve the availability of outcome information and comprehensive cost data. In each of these service areas, the best providers should also be rewarded with patients.

Ideally, providers would some day set their own prices based on value, rather than be presented with the amount of reimbursement. Different providers may well seek different prices depending on the cases they address and the results they deliver. As we mentioned earlier, however, providers with better results will often be more efficient and thus will earn higher margins even while charging the same price as rivals. The principles of value-based competition make it clear that the most powerful reward of all is patients. If health plans encourage and support competition to attract patients based on results in addressing medical conditions, this will not only enable excellent providers to improve value further (through the virtuous circle) but will also drive substandard providers to either improve or lose business.

Move to Single Bills for Episodes and Cycles of Care, and Single Prices. Aligning reimbursement and patient value will ultimately require that the current model of separate reimbursement for each doctor, hospital, charge, and service be replaced with a system involving single prices for service bundles, episodes of care, and ultimately full care cycles. The current system introduces unnecessary transactions and complexity that have no health benefit for patients. The current system also obscures value. The most important reasons for single, unified prices are to make prices transparent and to match price with value.

Value and cost can only be measured over episodes of care and complete care cycles, as we have discussed in earlier chapters. It is the results of all the interventions taken together that matter, not individual services. Only by adding up all the costs can the true cost be measured, including the cost of follow-up care, repeat treatments, and the cost of addressing any errors and complications. Moving to a single price for the entire care cycle will encourage appropriate care delivery structures and appropriate trade-offs among types of treatment (such as pharmaceutical treatment versus surgery; newer, less invasive surgeries versus older methods; more preparation versus treatment; and greater attention to follow-up care).

Moving to single prices will also be a huge step in making it possible for prices to be transparent. Without a single bundled price, transparency of the many prices for discrete services is much less useful to patients, health plans, and other system participants. It is the total charges that we should care about, not the prices of hundreds of line items. Billing and the explanation of benefits are hugely simplified with a single-price method.

The shift toward care-cycle pricing is already occurring. In transplants, for example, U.R.N. negotiates a single price with each provider covering the full cycle of treating the patient. The full cycle of care is carefully defined and includes an early post-transplantation phase of 90 days and an extended follow-up phase ending after 365 days. As noted earlier, U.R.N. contracts only with high-quality providers. In return for favorable prices, U.R.N.'s clients (the health plans) agree to reduce the provider's financial risk in unusually complex cases. If a patient's treatment cost goes above a pre-agreed ceiling, the additional expense is reimbursed at cost. Because the provider does not bear the risk of cost overruns, the contracted price for most patients is held down.

One of the valid arguments against single prices for cycles of care is that patients differ so much that the price must be raised to cover the risk of unanticipated care. As illustrated by the U.R.N. example, however, reimbursing providers for complications at an agreed-upon rate can mitigate the need to raise prices for all patients. Of course, providers with habitual complications will ultimately suffer in quality and value comparisons, and in the flow of patients.

Note that the single prices we are describing are very different from capitation, in which a provider organization receives a fixed payment for *any* needed medical services. Capitation addresses the wrong level of competition—the hospital or provider organization as a whole. It creates strong incentives to cut costs without regard for quality, rather than to improve the value of care for a defined medical condition.

Diagnosis could also be subject to a single price, encompassing all consultations, tests, and analysis. Diagnosis prices could also be structured to include recommendations regarding the best course of treatment. This will highlight diagnosis effectiveness and efficiency, while separating diagnosis from treatment to minimize the risk of bias. While diagnosis can be iterative with treatment, the diagnostician group could remain responsible for diagnostic services under the single price until the diagnosis is complete. This highlights the full cost of diagnosis and will draw attention to improving the processes involved.

Moving to single prices for cycles of care will lead to other significant changes both for health plans and providers. Health plans will contract more efficiently, with less need for detailed specifications of the care itself and what specific care is paid for. Instead, providers will be measured on results. Single pricing will also trigger beneficial changes by providers. Providers will be motivated to measure overall costs, rather than piecemeal costs. Ultimately, providers will have strong incentives to integrate care medically across facilities and specialists. The patient health benefits and economic benefits will be striking.

In moving to single prices, an intermediate step is to ask providers for a single bill for an episode of care, which lists all component charges and provides a total. A designated entity (e.g., a lead provider) could assemble the bill, as discussed in chapter 5. Alternatively, the health plan could initially assemble the single bill from discrete charges if providers were reluctant to do so. For each episode, the health plan would make one payment, and the designated provider or other entity would then be responsible for settlement with each physician or other party involved. As data from single bills is accumulated, the move to single prices will be less intimidating for both plans and providers.

Health plans can offer incentives to providers for a single bill in view of the cost savings in reduced paperwork. However, transaction simplification is far from the most important benefit. Both health plan and provider will benefit from bill simplification in terms of facilitating better health results. Beginning a dialogue about the bill as a whole, and how it can be brought down, will in itself be beneficial.

Simplify, Standardize, and Eliminate Paperwork and Transactions. The current system encourages administrative complexity because it is based on discrete services and multiple separate entities involved in care. Administrative complexity is also inherent in restricting services, shifting costs, and contesting bills. Value-based competition, in contrast, seeks to minimize any cost that does not contribute directly to patient value. Health plans will need to drastically simplify and streamline their administrative processes. Yet entrenched bureaucracy and mind-sets will stand in the way, both at health plans and at providers that have evolved their own defensive bureaucracy.

Reducing administrative complexity will require a step-change reduction in the number of transactions. Avoiding the need for many transactions altogether, by moving to single bills, to single prices, and contracts based on cycles of care, will make a major dent. Substituting measurement of results for process documentation requirements and treatment reviews will also dramatically reduce administrative costs. Interactions with providers can be further simplified by standardizing information requests and establishing information standards across health plans, thus avoiding parallel information gathering and reporting systems.

The introduction of online transactions by leading health plans is relatively recent. Electronic transactions have major benefits in cost, accuracy, and reduction of claims disputes. The introduction of electronic medical records will eliminate even more paperwork, further simplify transactions, and greatly reduce the need for redundant information. Proactive use of information technology will also enable patients to more easily request sharing of their records with providers and disease management services vendors. (We further examine the issue of electronic records and the role of IT later in this chapter.)

Standardization, interoperability, and open systems are vitally important for reducing administrative costs throughout the system. Health plans as an industry need to attach a high degree of urgency to achieving agreement on standardization of definitions, forms, and interfaces. As a legacy of the cost-shifting mind-set, health plans still use a myriad of different claims and reimbursement forms. Standardization offers important opportunities for value improvement. The Health Insurance Portability and Accountability Act (HIPAA) has been a step in the right direction in terms of standardization, but the specifics are still to be put in place.

Further progress on standardizing data definitions and formats will not only increase value but also enable health plans to outsource processing to outside vendors. As has been demonstrated in many other industries, the outsourcing of specific information services to specialists can reap scale economies and benefit from their greater management focus and expertise. Selective outsourcing can also allow health plans to redirect more attention to functions that add value from a patient health standpoint.

High-deductible plans with health savings accounts (HSAs) provide yet another important opportunity to reduce administrative paperwork for the majority of plan members who tend to have relatively low medical expenses. Many patients do not spend more than the HSA threshold of $1,000 to $5,000 per year on health care. Hence, much of the paperwork and overhead involved in the processing of provider bills could be reduced for these subscribers, leading to direct cost savings. Employers wary of HSAs argue that processing savings may be consumed in the costs of transitioning to the HSA model. But transition costs are not a good reason for avoiding a change with potentially large benefits in terms of administrative efficiency as well as benefits in encouraging informed, value-seeking consumer behavior.

Through steps such as these we have described, the administrative savings of a single payer can be achieved without the need to eliminate health plan competition or introduce a heavy role for government, as discussed in chapter 3.

Redefine the Health Plan–Subscriber Relationship

Competing on value will also require a new relationship with subscribers. Traditional forms of health plan contracting must change in order to lengthen time horizons and better align the health plan's and subscribers' interests. Cost-shifting practices involving subscribers must give way to a relationship based on value added and mutual responsibility for health. Finally, health plans must truly assume responsibility for members' total health over the long term. Assisting members in assembling and managing a complete medical record is an important health plan role and a service that health plans should offer.

Move to Multiyear Subscriber Contracts and Shift the Nature of Plan Contracting. The annual health plan contract with subscribers is an artifact of zero-sum competition and is misaligned with health care value. Choices about effective treatment from a patient standpoint, not to mention prevention and disease management, require a multiyear time horizon. As we have discussed, value can only be understood over care cycles. Also, many medical conditions are slow to develop and take time to fully address. Early diagnosis is often beneficial, so approaching diagnosis with a longer-term perspective adds value.

Moving to voluntary, multiyear contracts will better align the incentives of health plans, patients, and employers. Health plans will be more motivated and better able to consider long-term patient health value rather than short-term costs. Patients will be more motivated to establish supportive relationships with their plans and physicians, as well as to participate in caring for their health. Multiyear contracts will also allow significant transactional savings through avoiding marketing costs, contracting costs, and related information technology costs, none of which has health value for patients.

Historically, subscribers have wanted the flexibility to opt out of a plan that is not performing or whose premiums escalate. This is understandable in a system built on adversarial relationships and cost shifting. However, a multiyear period is necessary for both members and health plans to achieve good results.

Health plans should be cultivating loyal, long-term members. Subscribers and employers should be building long-term relationships with excellent health plans (see chapter 7). The current rate of subscriber churning says more about the current system's flaws than about the value of a long-term relationship. Health plans have sometimes encouraged churn to weed out expensive members, rather than focusing on health value. As health plans shift their roles with members along the lines we have described, churn rates should decline markedly. However, multiyear contracting will add to the benefits.

Multiyear commitments should be voluntary, but health plans can offer some inducements to persuade subscribers and plan sponsors to adopt them. The transaction cost savings alone from multiyear contracts could fund meaningful plan improvements (a gain for members) or potentially lower premiums (a gain for both members and plan sponsors). A cap on premium escalation over defined time periods could also encourage multiyear commitments.

Health plans also need to design products that facilitate portability so that subscribers can be retained. Subscribers who lose employer coverage could be allowed and encouraged to roll over to a comparable, fully insured plan on similar plan terms.[40]

Even with annual contracts, health plans can play a much more constructive role by offering more cost-effective plan structures and assisting subscribers to select the right plan structure for their family. Offering health plan structures involving HSAs can encourage better patient choices while creating a structure for saving to meet future medical needs. Studies suggest a noticeable shift in behavior when patients perceive more responsibility for health care choices, as we discussed in chapter 3. However, a financial stake in care decisions is not a panacea. Without the other health plan roles we have described, copayments and deductibles will add little value and result only in self-rationing and cost shifting (see chapter 7).

Health plan product offerings are changing, and the number of plans and plan alternatives in terms of deductibles, copayments, flexible spending accounts, and HSAs is growing. Many subscribers lack the information or the expertise to select the plan structure that is most cost-effective for them and to understand what their plan will actually cover and how to take advantage of its services. Health plans can play an important role in these areas. Harvard Pilgrim, for example, has introduced a new approach to subscriber contracting, tested initially with its own employees, in which it provides information on a subscriber's past medical spending (both the employer and employee payments) together with simple financial tools to assist the subscriber in picking a plan. Harvard Pilgrim has found that many subscribers conclude that they have been buying more insurance than they really needed. Premium growth has slowed markedly as subscribers shifted to less expensive plans involving higher deductibles.

End Cost-Shifting Practices Such as Re-underwriting That Erode Trust and Breed Cynicism. Zero-sum competition leads not only to inefficient plan churning but also to adversarial interactions with members and practices such as re-underwriting, in which members with expensive conditions are winnowed from plans by sharply increasing their premiums. Many plans use such practices to attempt to boost profits. These cost-shifting practices persist even at health plans that are otherwise value oriented.[41]

Such practices not only lead to financial hardship for patients but also break the continuity of care that is often essential to health results. Such practices also contribute to the anger and cynicism that many subscribers feel toward health plans. Even if a subscriber has not experienced these practices, he or she often knows of a friend or neighbor who has been affected.

Outright patient dumping is legally prohibited. Re-underwriting should also be legally prohibited (and already is in some states), as we will recommend in chapter 8. Both practices are unfair and inconsistent with the rationale for insurance in the first place. Health plans should move away from re-underwriting voluntarily, even if it is legal. Churning subscribers who are not protected by membership in large groups, rather than providing the value the subscribers paid for when they bought insurance, undermines trust with subscribers and physicians.

Re-underwriting and other adversarial practices also reinforce the wrong internal mind-set. A plan that truly embraces the approaches we have described cannot treat any member in ways that violate these core principles. Doing so will only erode its effectiveness in serving all its customers. Instead, plans should be pursuing low subscriber turnover and multiyear contracts to better align interests and reinforce their focus on risk reduction, prevention, and disease management. These approaches are far better ways to deal with members who are high risk or who become ill.

Our research concludes that the United States must move to require everyone to have a health plan, as we discuss in chapter 8. Together with mandatory insurance should come risk pooling, in which every plan must bear its fair share of the cost of expensive members. One of the many benefits of such a policy is that the incentive to push out high-risk patients will be dramatically reduced because another expensive patient will replace the one eliminated. Health plans will have to focus instead on their proper role: adding value.

Assist in Managing Complete Member Medical Records. There are compelling health value reasons for complete, integrated, and verified patient medical records that are easily, and rapidly, accessible to any provider or adviser for whom the patient has authorized access.[42] It improves the information available to physicians, improving decisions and reducing error from unknown allergies or unanticipated drug interactions. A complete record reduces the costs of information gathering and duplicate testing, and reduces delays in diagnosis and treatment while records are being awaited. Today, many diagnoses and other medical decisions are made without access to full (or even any) medical records.

Without a complete record, it is easy for patients to overlook important facts that are relevant to their current condition. Even when patients conscientiously bring their own records, the records are not organized, and the next physician has no verification of the accuracy of past test results or the quality of past care. Without verification, past records can be disregarded—and sometimes appropriately so.

A full medical record not only improves each aspect of care but facilitates the medical integration of care across the full care cycle. A complete record is indispensable to risk management, prevention, and disease management. Finally, a full record enables positive-sum competition among providers by lowering the switching costs of shifting providers and utilizing multiple providers.

The importance of a complete medical record is well understood, but the United States has been stumbling on how to implement the idea. Given the understandable concern of Americans about privacy, a central government repository of individual medical records would not be an option even if it was practical. HIPAA legislation has given patients the right to obtain and add to their own medical records, which reside with each provider entity that has been involved with their care. This has made the accumulation of one's individual records theoretically possible. In practice, however, assembling and maintaining a complete record remains difficult at best.

Today, medical records are scattered. There are separate records at individual physician offices and at various treatment facilities. Specialists usually send summaries to the patient's primary care provider or family physician, not the full record of their care. Records are not kept in a form that is easy to integrate.

Current proposals for records management aim to facilitate requests for records, when needed, from the various providers (the so-called pointer system). However, this approach is cumbersome, technologically questionable, and inherently costly. Patients need to have ownership of their own medical records. They need a secure, complete personal medical record that is all in one trusted place (though there is no need for everyone's records to be in the same place). Electronic availability (with appropriate permission) will enable records access on a timely basis and in emergency settings.

A trusted third party will be needed to play the role of maintaining, accumulating, and verifying the patient's records and making them available when, and only when, the patient has given approval. Although the primary care physician is a trusted party and has the perspective of the whole patient, primary care physicians are not in the business of assembling and maintaining comprehensive medical records for their patients and providing complete records whenever requested. For primary care providers to take on this role is simply impractical.

Health plans are in a unique position to add value in this area. Health plans are the other entity in the system that should be focused on the whole patient, across all of his or her medical needs and across all providers. Today, health plans already maintain some records of services performed and paid for, but these are not full medical records.

This is a radical idea, and is unthinkable given historical attitudes toward health plans and the traditional roles health plans have played. If health plans can establish trust and partnership with patients, they will be in a good position to serve as the repository and integrator of a patient's medical records, in a way that no provider (including the primary care physician) can feasibly replicate.

As health plans shift their roles, they will need to accumulate more and more member health information, as we have described. Moving to maintain a complete record is a logical next step. A consolidated, accessible, verified medical record yields health value benefits that are very much in the health plan's interest, and which support its other roles as well. Medical integration over the full care cycle, improved disease management, and more effective disease prevention are all core health plan functions. Indeed, maintaining a complete record at the health plan would create major synergies because the plan will need much of the information anyway to play the value-adding roles we have described. And because health plans will also be measuring provider results, there are synergies in validating the quality of the record. The member, however, must own the individual record so that the right to privacy is clear, and so that the integrated record will be transferred on a timely basis under transparent rules and guidelines if a subscriber shifts to another health plan.

A number of plan affiliates or independent service providers are beginning to offer individual patient health records, either through the health plan, through providers, or directly to the individual.[43] Aetna Health Information Management, for example, is working toward assembling a personal health record for Aetna members based on information on diagnoses, lab results, and prescriptions for which reimbursement has been sought. Others, such as the service company eHealth Trust, are marketing individually controlled medical records through providers, who are compensated to enter the records on the eHealth system. Patients can utilize the records and can input their medical history on a Web-based form before going to the doctor. An alternative approach to creating individually controlled records that are verified is being developed by Patient Command, Inc. Health plans or employers could sponsor the service for members. Subscribers would authorize electronic transmission of the complete record to providers, who would have assurance of the data's accuracy. The need to rerun tests would be reduced, and providers would be able to reduce errors by detecting allergies, other prescriptions, and existing medical conditions before treating the patient. These are just some of the numerous models that will be explored to meet the need for an integrated patient medical record.

Trust in managing medical records is critical. Members must be assured of confidentiality, and that their health plan will not use the information in the medical record to set rates or plan requirements. If re-underwriting and selective terms and conditions are outlawed, as we recommend in chapter 8, this risk declines.

For a health plan, providing the service of medical records aggregation would not only facilitate the value-adding roles we have described, but also boost loyalty to the plan. It would strengthen the common interest in the patient's well-being, and encourage long-term subscriber relationships.

Ideally, full medical records management (provided by the plan or an independent subcontractor) could become a standard health plan service, with the cost included in the plan premium. The direct savings may well pay for part or all of the cost. The records management function could also be offered as a value-added service of some plans. In the interim, health plans may want to experiment by subscribing to or designing a medical records management model that is implemented, with member permission, for patients with multiple chronic diseases, complex acute conditions, potentially dangerous allergies, or other complicated medical needs. Here, improved records access could produce immediate cost and value benefits. Health plans may also want to offer medical records services first to their own employees, where trust can be more easily established, learning can accumulate, and credibility can be built.

Winning patient trust to allow health plans to perform medical records management will be challenging. Health plans will need to radically transform their relationships with members and physicians if they want to play this value-adding role in the system. However, the health value benefits are so great that it is worth a very significant effort to overcome the trust hurdle. At least in the interim, plans may need to contract with an independent medical record service company on behalf of their subscribers.

Clear privacy standards and access safeguards must be built into the process, no matter who performs the records management role. Also, information standards, as well as accepted procedures for the verification of records, will clearly be important, no matter how medical record storage and access is organized. Finally, the ability to easily shift records to another health plan or independent contractor with certainty is essential, so health plans must structure services so that the member owns the record.

Overcoming Barriers to Health Plan Transformation

Shifting the roles of health plans is not without challenges. To make this transformation, health plans will confront an array of barriers, similar in many respects to those confronting providers that we discussed in chapter 5.

Establishing Trust

Many subscribers view health plans with trepidation, if not outright distrust. Many patients and doctors see health plans as a prime villain in health care. These attitudes have built up over years and will die slowly. Building trust will be critical for any health plan if it is to fully succeed in transforming its roles. Visible changes will be needed to convince subscribers and doctors.

Total honesty must characterize these relationships. Patients need to trust health plans not to use "quality" as a smokescreen for the same old behavior—limiting services and steering patients to favored providers with which they have negotiated the best deal. Health plans must work hard to ensure the accuracy and reliability of their clinical outcomes data, and take care to distinguish where valid information exists and where it is not yet well enough developed.

Improving Information

As we have noted, relevant information about results remains inadequate, which limits health plans from playing some value-adding roles. Every avenue needs to be taken to improve this state of affairs, including collaborative efforts. As we discuss in chapter 8, there is a role for government in ensuring that appropriate and consistent outcome and cost information is collected and disseminated.

Building Health Plan Capabilities

To successfully play these value-adding roles, health plans will need to improve their internal capabilities. Two areas stand out: human resources and information technology. Performing the new roles of health plans will require new skills and new types of people. Health plans will shift from administrative and processing organizations to true health organizations. Greater medical expertise will be necessary. More doctors, nurses, and other medical professionals will be employed by health plans, not to second-guess providers but to play the range of value-adding roles we have described. More substantive subscriber and physician interactions will require far more knowledge.

Without the right expertise and people at health plans, conversely, value-based competition is set back. We encountered providers attempting to move to results competition who lamented that health plan managers sometimes lacked the expertise to evaluate their experience and outcome data. Instead, interactions turned into bargaining discussions focused almost exclusively on discounts. Shifting the employee mix will be an urgent priority, even as health plans begin to outsource some administrative functions.

Information technology is also a major enabler of many of the value improvements we have described. Information technology will automate and reduce the cost of administrative transactions, but this is just the start. The new roles of health plans are very information intensive and involve gathering and aggregating information for members while also tracking outcomes and costs across numerous medical conditions. The information systems to support this activity will need to be far more advanced than the systems in place today.

While a detailed treatment of IT issues for providers and health plans is beyond the scope of this book, it is clear that an electronic medical record (EMR) is central and indispensable from a health value standpoint. A well-designed EMR has a series of compelling health value benefits for providers, health plans, and, ultimately, patients:

- Reducing the cost of transactions and eliminating paperwork.
- Lowering the cost of maintaining complete records of all actions taken on behalf of the patient and of all facilities utilized. This not only supports medical decisions but also enables detailed understanding of cost at the activity level.
- Making patient information easily and instantly available to physicians.
- Allowing the sharing of information in real time across doctors and institutions to improve decision making and eliminate redundant tests and effort.
- Facilitating the aggregation of patient information across episodes of care and across time.
- Integrating decision support tools into care delivery, as physicians place orders and specify treatments, to reduce errors and bring learning about diagnosis and treatment best practices to providers.
- Creating an information platform from which provider results, process, and experience metrics can be extracted at very low cost compared to manual entry of data from charts.

Health plans have an urgent need to play a leadership role in making EMR a reality and in harnessing the benefits. They also have a strong economic incentive to do so, which is as great as or greater than that of providers. Health plans should support efforts to move to universal EMRs by providers, in collaboration with other health plans, and the entire health community in a plan's geographic territories. BCBS of Massachusetts, for example, has taken a leadership role in the eHealth Collaborative initiative in its home state, helping to bring together a consortium of thirty-three organizations to develop a plan to roll out EMR statewide. BCBS of Massachusetts sees EMR as a foundation technology for its business, and has committed $50 million to support the pilot.

Health plans should be prepared to provide financial incentives for providers who are early movers to EMR. These can be structured in various ways. One approach would be to add a small premium on all reimbursements of EMR-covered services. Another is to advance a portion of the capital costs of installing EMR systems, which are recouped through small deductions from reimbursement. Medicare's offer to provide free EMR software to physician offices is a step in the right direction. Whatever approach is taken, health plans should insist on open systems and data standards that allow consistency of information as well as easy exchange across the systems of different vendors. Otherwise, the most important benefits of EMR will be needlessly squandered.

Overcoming Provider Skepticism

Some providers will resist greater health plan involvement in results measurement, advising patients, and coordinating care over time, seeing these as provider roles. Other providers will be threatened by the collection of results data, and complain that reporting data is too costly. Some providers, caught up in historical contracting practices and resistant to coordinating with other providers on charges and bills, will balk at single bills, not to mention single prices, for episodes of care. There will be providers who have the bargaining power, at least initially, to opt out of having to compete on value.

Health plans will need to work sensitively but firmly with providers in making the transition to value-based competition. Physicians must be treated as respected partners in improving patient health. The provider relationship must shift to one in which results matter, and the focus is on the cycle of care, instead of discrete interventions. Gain sharing must become a reality so that providers benefit financially from improving outcomes and efficiency. Providers need to have a say in what data is required and what measures are used. Common measures need to be defined so that providers do not have the burden of different requirements for every plan. Once information is analyzed and compiled, providers should have an opportunity to check and respond to the data before it is used. This will improve the accuracy of data and increase the incentive of providers to improve results that are lagging.

However, health plans need to leave no doubt that the status quo is unacceptable. It will be necessary for health plans, individually and collectively, to forcefully make the case that the system must change. Large health plans with more clout should pursue the advantage of moving early. Health plans must act on the idea that quality and results really matter and will be rewarded (or their lack penalized). Once it is clear that the issue is which measures to use, rather than whether information must be provided at all, the pace of change will accelerate. Once it is clear that a single bill is required to obtain payment, providers will rapidly learn how to assemble one.

As in making any change, health plans should first seek out the most enlightened providers. Over time, providers that are unwilling to change will have to learn to live with the consequences in terms of reputation and flow of patients. Efforts can initially concentrate on a few medical conditions. Over time, success and patient enthusiasm will propel the movement to widen.

Moving Ahead of Medicare

Medicare creates practical constraints on what the private sector can do in terms of reimbursement and other policies. Even large health plans can be small compared to Medicare. (In Massachusetts, for example, the top two plans account for just 30 to 35 percent of the typical provider's revenues versus 50 percent for Medicare and Medicaid.) Providers have to maintain the administrative infrastructure to support the Medicare and Medicaid business, which is growing.

However, Medicare practices do not prevent progress. Leading health plans are demonstrating every day that all of the recommendations in this chapter can be implemented irrespective of Medicare and Medicaid. Every health plan should move ahead in each of these areas.

There are major benefits if Medicare practices move in the directions we advocate. Other health plans would follow, as has occurred repeatedly in the past twenty-five years. We discuss directions for Medicare and Medicaid, including some promising experiments currently under way, in chapter 8. Health plans, individually and collectively, must nudge Medicare in the right direction.

Cultivating New Mind-sets

Perhaps the biggest barrier facing health plans in adopting these new roles is deeply ingrained internal mind-sets. One is that consumers are not sophisticated enough to deal with health care decisions. As we discussed in chapter 2 and will amplify in chapter 7, consumers are already proving this assumption invalid. Instead of finding excuses to maintain the status quo, health plans need to find ways to embrace and encourage a more constructive consumer role.

There is a telling parallel in the experience of financial services. When employee pensions were managed by others, employees were relatively uninformed and passive. Now that many individuals must manage their own Keoghs, 401(k) accounts, and IRAs, they have sought advice and become far more knowledgeable about financial management. Individuals rarely manage all their funds themselves but get help in doing so. Prior to this shift, it was widely believed that financial markets were too complicated for individuals to be able to gather information, seek advice, and make sound decisions. In retrospect, it is clear that this thinking underestimated the ability of individuals to take an active role in choices important to their well-being.[44]

The early experience with HSAs is also encouraging. As we discussed in chapter 3, evidence reveals that HSAs shift buying patterns and reduce costs,[45] as well as encourage patients to seek more information about their medical care and spend more money on preventive care.[46] The benefits of HSAs will only rise as competition shifts toward value. Patients will have more information and more support services to make value-based choices, together with their doctors, about where to obtain care.[47]

A second health plan mind-set that will retard change is the assumption that patients will always choose more care, or more expensive care. In the current system, with so little results information, patients have a hard time knowing what treatments and providers are effective, and what their alternatives are. In the absence of other information, higher price is often viewed by patients as a signal of higher quality. Academic medical centers are assumed to be universally better in delivering care.

Results data at the medical condition level will have a major influence on behavior, as we discuss in chapter 7. The belief that consumers have an endless demand for health care confuses better health with more health care. Most consumers want more effective care, not more surgery, longer hospital stays, or more complications. The evidence suggests that informed and involved patients choose less invasive care, comply with medical instructions better, and show higher satisfaction with their care.[48]

Another dangerous mind-set affecting health plans is that patients will not travel. Yet there is little information to justify travel in the current system, little counseling about the provider alternatives outside the local area, and numerous impediments to seeking nonlocal care. For example, referring physicians tend to have local relationships and knowledge and may actively resist nonlocal referrals as a sign of patient disloyalty. In managing transplant patients, U.R.N. frequently encounters patients who have been referred by their doctor to a nearby center with substandard results. Once the patient understands the relevant outcome data, reluctance to travel for excellent care is overcome. Health plans can have a major influence on securing excellent care outside the local area, as we discussed earlier.

Finally, health plans are hobbled by the pervasive mind-set among both health plans and employers that discounts and restricting care are the way to save money. Health plans must discard the crutch of networks, and focus instead on supporting results-based choice and involvement in care by physicians and patients.

No health plan CEO should underestimate the task of rooting out these old ways of thinking. No matter how committed the CEO and top management are to change, the organization will need to be brought along. Some significant turnover of the management of health plans will probably be necessary.

Redefining Culture and Values

The new roles for health plans involve a radical transformation not only in their relationships with subscribers and providers but also in the internal culture that is needed. The legacy at many health plans is the culture of denial: denial of claims, denial of services, denial of choice, denial of physician autonomy, and denial of responsibility for members' health results. While health plans are trying to move away from this culture, most retain the paternalistic view that they need to oversee provider processes with pay for performance, and to continue to constrain members' choice of providers via networks.

Health plans must replace the culture of denial with a culture of patient health. Communicating these values will involve not only what a health plan says but also what it does. Responsiveness, fairness, consistency, reliability, integrity, and the ability to listen will be needed in every interaction with every party to dismantle the distrust that has accumulated.

Those health plans that succeed in moving in the directions we have outlined will have employees who are far more motivated and dedicated. The satisfaction of creating value for patients and working with providers centered on results, instead of restricting and second-guessing decisions, will be palpable for all concerned.

The Benefits of Moving Early

As with providers, those health plans that move early to change in these ways will gain compelling benefits. They will get a head start in assembling data, learning how to aggregate information, developing relationships with the best providers, recruiting the best staff, implementing the right information systems, and sourcing from the best specialists and outsourcing partners. The reputational benefit with patients and plan sponsors will be striking. Health plans do not have to move in all these new directions simultaneously. However, the more of these steps that are undertaken, the greater the benefits, because the benefits are complementary. Each step makes other steps easier and more effective.

Instead of behaving as a commoditized industry—as many health plans have done in the old model—the early movers will open up a wealth of opportunities to differentiate themselves from their peers. Along the way, they will discover many different strategic positions that will appeal to different groups of customers. Health plans will be able to build exciting and sustainable competitive advantages.

Imagine if a health plan were seen as an expert on health and the member's greatest advocate. Imagine if a health plan informed and advised members and reduced the anxiety of illness. Imagine if members knew that their health plan was dedicated to their getting the best provider for their condition, and receiving the most effective and up-to-date treatment. Imagine if health plans took responsibility for helping a patient navigate the system. Imagine if members and health plans worked jointly to keep the member healthy. Imagine if the interests of health plans, patients, providers, and plan sponsors were all fundamentally aligned. If health plans were truly dedicated to health, the consequences in terms of creativity, innovation, and health care value would be enormous.

7

Implications for Suppliers, Consumers, and Employers

PROVIDERS AND HEALTH PLANS are the central actors in health care delivery, and we have described how their strategies and operating practices need to change in order to unleash value-based competition. Suppliers, consumers, and employers also have important roles in catalyzing and supporting such competition. By moving to value-based thinking, suppliers, consumers, and employers will benefit while speeding systemic transformation. There is no need to wait for regulatory reform or for other system participants to act.

Suppliers of products, technology, and services to the health care sector include a wide range of companies producing a vast array of products, such as pharmaceuticals, diagnostic tests, medical devices, imaging equipment, medical supplies, pharmacy benefits management, and medical information technology. Each type of supplier has its own distinct characteristics. A detailed discussion of the strategic issues for each type of supplier is beyond the scope of this book, but the principles of value-based competition apply to all of them. Here we take a high-level look at how suppliers as a group can better enable and support such competition.

Consumers, as health plan subscribers and patients, should be the ultimate beneficiaries of the value delivered by the system. Too often, however, consumers have been uninformed and passive rather than active participants in their health and their health care. The potential of consumers as catalysts for change in the system has been well recognized, with whole books written about consumer-driven health care.[1] But despite the fact that consumers have become more informed and have more choices, the system has not been transformed.

The notion of consumer-driven health care oversimplifies the problem. Consumers will never be medical experts, nor should they be expected to be. Consumers should not be forced to play roles abdicated by health plans. Consumers should not have to manage and coordinate their own care across a fractured care cycle. Also, no matter how informed and value sensitive consumers try to be, they will be unable to meaningfully affect their care unless results information is available and providers have to compete at the medical condition level. In this chapter we describe the roles that consumers should play in a value-based system, and the expectations they should set for health plans and providers.

Employers, the third actor we consider here, have the motivation and the clout to influence the other actors in the system, including their own employees. Employers are the major purchasers of independent health plans. In addition, about half of employer-provided health plans in the United States are self-insured plans, giving employers even more latitude in how such plans are designed and administered. Employers can exert a strong influence on providers, especially through collaborative efforts with other employers. Finally, employers can influence the way employees think about their health and health care. We discuss here why employers have missed the opportunity to drive value improvement in the health care system, and how they can reinforce the shift to value-based competition.

Implications for Suppliers

Suppliers of medical products, technology, and services play vital roles in the value of health care delivery and innovation in health care practice. Despite this, many suppliers have perpetuated and reinforced zero-sum competition. Suppliers can add far more value to health care delivery than they have yet realized.

Missed Opportunities

Suppliers have manifested zero-sum competition in a number of ways. First, facing increasingly powerful customers and price pressures, suppliers have been prone to merge and broaden product lines to enhance their bargaining power. This sometimes means producing competing entries in many product segments, even if products are similar to competitor products or offer only marginal additional patient benefit. The focus seems to be on giving sales forces more products to sell, and gaining more negotiating clout with distributors, buying groups, and customers, rather than increasing value for patients. In pharmaceuticals, for example, "me-too" drugs with minimal therapeutic differences are common. Such products can potentially improve value if offered at significantly lower prices.

However, in practice this has not usually been the case. Even if me-too drugs are introduced at lower prices, incumbents have rarely responded by bringing their prices down. After a respectable introductory period, me-too producers are prone to raise their price to approximate that of the incumbent.[2] This practice increases supplier margins but means that competing products yield little patient value.

Second, supplier sales and marketing efforts often seem more focused on volume than on patient value. Suppliers of drugs, devices, supplies, and equipment seek preferred positions on formularies or approved lists through discounts, rebates, and volume incentives. They make payments to buying groups to secure placements, behaving as if their products were interchangeable commodities instead of justifying their value to defined groups of patients. Suppliers are drawn into competing by offering incentives for physicians to use their products, rather than by demonstrating superior results or offering meaningfully lower prices. For example, suppliers have sometimes entered into questionable consulting agreements with doctors to secure product usage.

In sales, many suppliers have pursued the reach and frequency model. In this model, large sales forces are deployed to call on as many physicians as possible, and to see those physicians as often as possible. The idea is to engender maximum awareness and physician loyalty to secure the maximum usage of a drug, device, or test. Suppliers have sought to expand usage to as many patients as possible rather than focusing on reaching those patients for whom their products offer the best value. This has contributed to the unfortunate situation in which many therapies produce disappointing results for too many patients. In cancer care, for example, drugs such as Erbitux, Herceptin, Tarceva, and Iressa are each effective in only about 10 percent of patients. Thus, a succession of drugs is often tried, which boosts overall supplier revenue; however, repeated failures mean that treatment cost is wasted and patients are exposed to side effects. Value is dramatically eroded.

In pharmaceuticals, some companies open themselves to criticism and controversy through implicit support of off-label usage for patients who get only marginal benefit. Similarly, equipment suppliers encourage providers to match each other's investments in expensive technology, even when there is low utilization. These approaches raise revenues for suppliers, but erode patient value in the system.

The same mind-set afflicts supplier advertising. Suppliers invest in costly direct-to-consumer mass advertising campaigns to raise many patients' expectations, rather than competing through more targeted communication of meaningful outcome and price information to those patients who will benefit the most from their products.

Third, suppliers, like providers and health plans, have tended to concentrate too narrowly on the drug, device, or diagnostic test they produce, rather than the entire cycle of care for the patient's medical condition. This is akin to the mind-set of providers, who have been procedure driven and organized around discrete interventions rather than overall care delivery. Suppliers are also prone to highlight selective indicators of patient benefit, rather than overall measures of long-term value.

Suppliers have sometimes not been sufficiently attentive to the care delivery processes in which their products are actually used. This results in lost opportunities for value improvement. For example, General Electric, Siemens, and other manufacturers of imaging equipment have overlooked opportunities to improve value through improving the utilization of their machines in the care cycle. A CT scan, for example, takes only two to three minutes using current technology. Yet it can take fifteen minutes or more to get a patient onto and off the machine's table, especially if the patient is attached to intravenous lines or is being monitored. An MRI machine typically involves an even longer period before and after scanning. These delays not only waste precious time in the treatment cycle but also require extra staff to move and lift patients. They tie up costly technicians and dramatically reduce throughput. In any given day or hour, expensive imaging machines experience mostly downtime.

Imaging equipment vendors have devoted little attention to improvements that would most increase the value of their products. For example, there is little attention to designing tables that facilitate simpler and rapid patient access and egress. Also missed have been opportunities to design and manufacture modular tables that would be compatible with both CT and MRI machines, speeding up imaging of seriously ill patients. Nor have imaging companies taken leadership in designing multipurpose or modular tables that could be utilized for patient transport, treatment, and imaging, also offering huge value advantages.

These kinds of missed opportunities to add value in care delivery are common. They occur because supplier interests are not always aligned with overall patient value (e.g., increasing machine utilization means fewer machines are needed). They also occur because siloed product organizations (e.g., CT and MRI business units) fail to talk to each other. Finally, suppliers have overlooked opportunities for value improvement by organizing around discrete products rather than the full care cycle.

It is no wonder, given the supplier practices we have described, that drug companies and suppliers of technology have often been portrayed as a major cause of the cost problem in health care. Researchers have reinforced this simplistic view by reporting correlations between the availability of new technology and higher spending, rather than investigating

the overall implications of new technology for long-term costs and patient value.[3] For example, implantable defibrillators can reduce the amount
and cost of drug therapy while reducing physician visits, emergency room
visits, and hospital stays. Focusing on the cost of the device alone misses
the point, but such a narrow viewpoint is common.

Suppliers, however, deserve some of the blame. It is up to suppliers to
provide compelling evidence of overall value improvements. However,
the studies that are most relevant to providers and patients have simply
not been done.

Why have suppliers been drawn into these types of competition? In
fairness, supplier competition on value has been deterred by the sluggish
pace of adopting evidence-based medical practice, for all the reasons we
have already discussed. When the ability of a drug, device, or test to improve value for patients is not clearly the driver of its adoption, suppliers
turn to other ways to compete. The structure of health care providers also
plays a role. Fractured providers, each worried only about its small part
of the care delivery cycle, make choices that boost their margins but fail
to consider overall patient value. Hospital or clinic department heads,
worried about their own budgets and not sufficiently aware of the consequences for the organization as a whole, make unwise decisions in adopting therapies.

In addition, supplier practices are a logical consequence of the zero-
sum competition endemic in the system. As health plans and providers
focused on cost shifting, accumulating bargaining power, and restricting
services, it should be no surprise that suppliers were drawn to strategies
that reflected this reality. For example, when health plans buy drugs or
devices based on discounts rather than measuring their value (results per
dollar cost) in terms of patient health[4] and the total long-term costs of
care, suppliers naturally try to secure the clout and the relationships necessary to play the cost-shifting game. They expend huge resources navigating their way through a maze of negotiations and approvals and run
the gauntlet to secure listings on hundreds of formularies rather than
invest in things that add value for patients.

Finally, faulty provider reimbursement structures undermine supplier
competition on value. A defibrillator with a longer battery life will have
to be replaced less often, a major benefit in terms of cost and patient discomfort. However, if a provider gets paid the same fee for implanting any
defibrillator and chooses a cheaper one that has a shorter life, it increases
its margin and increases revenue by doing more implanting procedures.

The irony is that the kind of supplier practices we have described have
not only failed to address patient value, but also are ultimately bad strategy for the suppliers themselves. Zero-sum competition has reinforced

price competition and tactics that aim to maximize volume, undermining the ability of suppliers to distinguish themselves.

Moving to Value-Based Competition: New Opportunities for Suppliers

How can suppliers support value-based competition? Some of the most important steps are summarized in figure 7-1.

Compete on Delivering Unique Value over the Full Care Cycle. The most fundamental implication for suppliers is to base strategies on creating unique value for patients, measured over the full cycle of care. Products must deliver truly better results, or meaningfully lower cost for equivalent results. Me-too products either need to be improved, repriced, or phased out.

Value can only be measured accurately by examining the overall cycle of care and by measuring costs and patient results over the longer term. The care delivery value chain (CDVC), described in chapter 5, is a powerful tool for examining the role of a product in the overall care cycle. Sup-

FIGURE 7-1

New opportunities for suppliers

Compete on delivering unique value over the full cycle of care

- Base strategies on creating unique value for patients
- Focus on cycles of care rather than narrow product usage
- Sell not just products, but provider and patient support

Demonstrate value based on careful study of long-term results and costs versus alternative therapies

- Use evidence of long-term clinical outcomes and cost to demonstrate value compared to alternative therapies
- Conduct new types of long-term comparative studies in collaboration with providers and patients

Ensure that products are used by the right patients

- Increase the success rate instead of maximizing usage
- Target marketing and sales to minimize unnecessary or ineffective therapies

Ensure that products are embedded in the right care delivery processes

- Help providers to utilize products better and minimize errors

Build marketing campaigns based on value, information, and customer support

- Concentrate marketing efforts on value, not volume and discounts

Offer support services that add value rather than reinforce cost shifting

- Support provider efforts to measure and improve results at the medical condition level

pliers can use the CDVC to understand how their products affect and are affected by other activities outside the activity in which they are used. A good example, discussed earlier, is the effect of an imaging machine on the overall value of the care delivery process, including downtime and the full cost of patient transport and movement. Analyzing how a machine affects the CDVC will reveal opportunities to improve its contribution to overall value. In addition, the CDVC enables suppliers to find other points of contact with providers and patients that present further opportunities to add value. For example, suppliers can offer services such as process consulting to help providers better realize their products' value.

In order to compete on overall value, the product development thinking of many suppliers needs to shift markedly. Suppliers must understand, and address, what happens before and after their product or service is used in the care delivery value chain. They must understand the linkages across the care cycle that affect total cost and the long-term health consequences for patients. This way of thinking not only allows product performance to be improved, but also opens up new possibilities for differentiation and ancillary services.

Suppliers can also add value by engaging directly with patients, assisting in the "informing" part of the CDVC. Suppliers can produce patient brochures, design Web sites, and operate call centers, among other points of contact. Novo Nordisk, for example, hosts an online patient community and provides glucose diaries, cookbooks, and articles on diabetes to patients. All of these offerings contribute to value in the care delivery process and contribute to better long-term patient results, helping to distinguish Novo Nordisk from its competitors. Suppliers can also work collaboratively with patient organizations that provide information and support for those with particular diseases, especially complex and unusual ones. Genzyme, for example, has worked closely with the Gaucher's Foundation to improve care and assist patients with this rare disease. Collaborative Web sites with patient organizations and physicians can also further patient and physician education.

These examples all involve chronic conditions, where the need to think about the long-term care cycle is perhaps the most apparent. However, virtually every drug, device, or diagnostic test is embedded in a broader care cycle. Understanding the broader set of factors that affect the true value of a product is important for every supplier.

Demonstrate Value Based on Careful Study of Long-Term Results and Costs Versus Alternative Therapies. Value can only be convincingly demonstrated through sophisticated clinical and cost evidence. Suppliers historically concentrated on demonstrating the efficacy of their products in a narrow sense, being content to meet the minimum requirements for

FDA approval. This has begun to change over the past fifteen years. For example, pharmaceutical companies have greatly increased the amount of "pharmaeconomic" analysis of the medical benefits of drugs relative to costs. However, these analyses have traditionally focused more on the regulatory approval process than on supporting decisions about health care delivery. Moreover, suppliers have offered little long-term outcome information for patients; for example, if a new device helps diabetes patients manage their blood-sugar levels but requires more primary care visits, credible long-term evidence of cost reductions due to fewer long-term complications is essential.

Suppliers must accept responsibility for demonstrating value by assembling information on results and costs over the whole cycle of care.[5] A new kind of postapproval clinical study is necessary. Patients, their care, and their results need to be tracked for far longer periods of time. We are confident that patients will participate in such efforts if there is confidentiality and suppliers widely disseminate findings, because such studies will be contributing to product improvement and to helping other patients. Given the time required and the cost of longer-term studies, suppliers will need to rethink the design of preapproval trials to facilitate ongoing tracking of enrolled patients, rather than having to start all over with new studies.

The most useful studies will investigate long-term value relative to alternative therapies. Comparative information is what actually matters for health care value, not the absolute improvements in study endpoints. Value needs to be examined not just in stand-alone therapies but also in combination or sequence with other therapies. Moreover, the relevant information is not just the average rate of effectiveness of a product but how effectiveness varies for different identifiable groups of patients. Suppliers should devote much more attention to delineating the patients who will benefit most from a given therapy (or have the fewest side effects), to increase the overall impact on patient value.

Some suppliers are moving in the direction of collecting such evidence through postapproval testing; this should be the norm. To be credible, such investigations may need to be undertaken by independent researchers or third-party organizations such as patient-sponsored groups. The National Institutes of Health (NIH) has funded some studies of long-term outcomes for patients, such as studies of the long-term developmental outcomes beyond the immediate results of the surgery for pediatric cardiac surgery patients.[6] However, these assessments are relatively uncommon for NIH, much less for suppliers. Finally, the Centers for Medicare and Medicaid Services (CMS) is also playing a growing and welcomed role in catalyzing the collection of long-term results and cost information.

Suppliers need to get ahead of this trend, rather than wait until such studies are mandated. To encourage and enable longer-term studies, however, the industry and regulators will need to set reasonable scientific and legal standards which govern the use of such studies and their findings. Otherwise, suppliers will not be motivated to expose themselves to the added risks.

By studying the role of their products over the full care cycle, suppliers gain the opportunity to better understand how their products create value and how other aspects of care matter. Suppliers can also learn which patients will benefit the most from their products, which is fundamental to good marketing (discussed later in this chapter). Suppliers should also relish opportunities to work with providers to improve the processes of care in which their products are embedded because this provides a powerful opportunity for supplier differentiation. Conversely, suppliers who fail to perform robust studies on the full cycle of care will lose precious insights that could help them better differentiate their offerings.

Suppliers also need to gather information on value by directly tracking the experience of consenting patients who use their products. A number of suppliers have moved in this direction, such as Medtronic and Genzyme. Genzyme, for example, has maintained a patient registry since 1991 that tracks the therapy used and the results achieved for Gaucher's disease patients using its Cerezyme product as well as other treatments.

Ongoing contact with consenting patients is valuable for gathering evidence of usage patterns and outcomes over a large cross section of patients and over an extended time period beyond the immediate treatment or hospitalization. Especially in the case of a rare disease with a small patient population, interaction with many patients, not just those enrolled in a trial, can enable much faster learning about value. Direct patient contact is also a vehicle with which to learn about compliance with treatment and ways to improve compliance. As all these examples suggest, some of the most important research should be done after product approval, contrary to conventional wisdom.

Moving in the direction of measuring value will not only require new kinds of data and analyses, but also require suppliers to establish new types of relationships with providers, health plans, and patients. Suppliers will benefit from working jointly with groups of providers to collect and analyze care cycle information, because such information is difficult for suppliers to obtain otherwise. The costs of gathering information can be shared, and participating providers will benefit from gaining earlier and more in-depth access to clinically relevant information. Suppliers will also benefit from joint projects with health plans, leveraging their patient data and their ability to interact with referring physicians.

Suppliers should take an active role in working with providers and medical bodies not just on the research itself, but also on developing metrics for outcomes and cost for particular practice units. We have discussed in previous chapters the pressing need to develop objective, quantifiable results measures in every medical condition for use in long-term studies. Providers such as Intermountain Healthcare, Children's Hospital Boston, the Cleveland Clinic, and Dartmouth-Hitchcock Medical Center, among others, have serious results measurement efforts already under way. Their work creates prime opportunities for suppliers to contribute as partners.

Ensure That Products Are Used by the Right Patients. The value delivered by a product is highest when the right patients use it. Product development programs and sales efforts should aim at identifying and reaching the patients for whom a product is most beneficial. They should also identify patient groups who gain limited benefits or who experience debilitating side effects. The goal should be for treatments to succeed in the highest possible percentage of cases. This approach creates far more value, and justifies higher prices, than therapies that deliver poor results for many patients and impose wasted cost and effort on the system.

As noted earlier, new kinds of clinical investigations are needed. Trials need to focus less on justifying the largest possible overall market and more on delineating the attributes of patients who will respond best to a particular treatment or will have the fewest side effects, or both. Suppliers who can assist patients, providers, and health plans in avoiding unnecessary or ineffective therapies will gain a formidable competitive advantage.

Getting products to the right patients, and supporting patient successes, will require a new role for supplier sales forces. Rather than the traditional reach and frequency approach, the new model should involve fewer, more substantive physician relationships for each sales representative, whose job would be to add more value to each physician's practice. Sales representatives would see their role as helping identify the particular patients who will benefit most from their products. Sales programs with health plans, hospital formularies, and other purchasers would no longer push greater product use across the board; rather, they would offer targeted, multistage programs to create value for specific segments of patients. In this approach, low-cost generic products could be the first line of treatment, with newer and more costly therapies prescribed only if less costly products yielded poor results for particular patients. Major cost savings for suppliers will accrue from such targeted marketing, not to mention far greater patient value.

Ensure That Products Are Embedded in the Right Care Delivery Processes. The value of a product depends critically on its correct and effective use. Moreover, even a correctly used product can be ineffective if other aspects of the care cycle undermine results. Suppliers add value if they assist providers and patients in addressing these issues. Genzyme, for example, works with physicians treating patients with Gaucher's disease to determine the right dosage of Cerezyme for the patient. Because the disease is very rare, most physicians have limited experience, and Genzyme's expertise and extensive experience is invaluable in helping providers achieve better results.

Suppliers that track the usage and value of their drugs, devices, and other equipment over the long term, as we have suggested, will gain insights about the comparative effectiveness of the care delivery processes of different providers. Through serving many providers, suppliers are in an excellent position to contribute to provider process improvement. Suppliers have an important role to play in diffusing knowledge about the care delivery value chains that are most effective.

Taking responsibility for the care delivery process also means that suppliers need to understand how their products are misused, and assist in minimizing errors. As we will describe in chapter 8, the American Society of Anesthesiology had to take the lead in investigating the sources of errors in administering anesthesia and in identifying changes that could minimize them. The resulting new measurement capabilities, disconnect alarms, dial designs, hose size standards, and drug container changes should have been already addressed by suppliers as part of their ongoing efforts to ensure that products were utilized effectively in actual practice.

Taking responsibility for effective product use in the care delivery process also has major implications for the role of suppliers' sales forces. Sales forces should become more knowledgeable about fewer products, and understand far better the nature of the practices of the physicians they call on. Sales forces can add value by transferring the latest knowledge to physicians, their staffs, and their patients about methods for diagnosis, treatment, and effective compliance.

Merck embarked on such a new sales force model in December 2004, realigning the responsibilities and territories of about 7,000 sales representatives. The number of products promoted per representative was reduced significantly, and the number of physicians called on per representative went down by 20 to 25 percent. For a given physician, the number of Merck representatives seen was drastically reduced. Sales representatives shifted their emphasis to helping identify candidate patients for therapies, transmitting disease and treatment information, helping physicians keep track of which formularies and plans had approved the product, and helping to educate patients. An Internet site that provided convenient access to in-depth specialized information about therapies and risk assessment was made available to physicians and other interested parties.

Merck also set out to collaborate with health plans to assist them in playing some of the value-adding roles we describe in chapter 6. The goal was to support health plans in reinforcing appropriate treatment guidelines with physicians, and monitoring adherence to therapy by patients. An example of such an initiative is Merck's asthma program with Blue Cross Blue Shield of California. Here Merck and Blue Cross identify high-risk members, bring them to the attention of physicians, and provide the physicians with risk assessment tools, treatment information, and patient materials.

Build Marketing Campaigns Based on Value, Information, and Customer Support. Marketing that adds value is marketing that communicates clinical and cost evidence to help providers make better choices and improve their care delivery processes and methods. Value-added marketing also helps patients select and use products more effectively. Suppliers need to reallocate marketing budgets toward these types of activities.

Given the current fractured organization of care delivery in many hospitals and physician practices, suppliers will sometimes need to educate and build bridges between separate units or departments within provider organizations in order to help them understand the overall value impact of a product for the institution. Suppliers may also need to educate and provide convincing evidence that brings the various stakeholders together around a treatment: providers, the health plan, the family, and the patient. As competition shifts toward value, the need for suppliers to play these roles should diminish.

Offer Support Services That Add Value Rather Than Reinforce Cost Shifting. For service providers, the most basic question is whether the services they offer contribute to patient value or whether they reinforce the zero-sum competition that has plagued the system. Many traditional service providers fail this test. There are still too many service providers in the business of supporting old-style cost shifting. Service companies that focus on controlling usage, rather than improving patient results, are not adding value. Service providers whose sole function is securing discounts are reinforcing a cost, not a value, mind-set. For example, many pharmacy benefit managers are still preoccupied with bargaining power, rebates, and discounts. They have been slow to use their rich data on prescriptions and drug usage to add value.

Service companies that assist providers to maximize reimbursement by billing creatively are helping system participants game the system rather than adding value. Software companies that market stand-alone packages for discrete functions (such as scheduling) or for single departments perpetuate information silos and reinforce the fragmentation of care, rather than add real value. Survey research firms that survey patients on the service experience, while ignoring medical outcomes, are reinforcing old mind-sets.

As we discussed in chapters 5 and 6, a new breed of health service company is emerging. A growing array of information companies, software companies, decision-support companies, and disease management companies, among others, has emerged to enable and support value-based competition at the medical condition level over the care cycle. These new service suppliers are working with providers and health plans, as well as with employers and consumers, to measure results and support value-based choices. Companies such as U.R.N., Preferred Global Health, and Best Doctors, for example, seek out and disseminate the best available results information to assist providers, health plans, employers, and consumers.

There will be an explosion of opportunities for service companies in value-based competition. Established service companies, just like providers and health plans, will need to transform their thinking and redefine their roles and product offerings.

Getting Started

Over time, suppliers could dramatically speed the process of value improvement in health care by moving in these directions. Leading suppliers are already beginning to adapt: focusing on value, not just discounts; measuring long-term results; practicing targeted marketing; and collaborating with providers. As competition in the system changes and as other system participants adopt new roles and strategies, these shifts in supplier strategies and operating practices will no longer be a matter of choice. Those suppliers that move early in the directions we have described will be rewarded in terms of depth of knowledge, clinical expertise, better reputation, and the ability to develop more differentiated offerings.

Implications for Consumers
as Subscribers and Patients

In value-based competition, patients and their families, freed from health plan restrictions and empowered with better information, would accept more responsibility for their health care choices and their own health. The importance of consumers moving from being passive to active health care customers has been well recognized. Indeed, some have advocated consumer-driven health care as the solution to the problems of the health care system.[7] Yet, more informed consumers and greater choice of health plans have not led to the transformation of the system that advocates anticipated.

Limits of the Consumer-Driven Model

The unfulfilled promise of consumer-driven health care stems from two problems. First, the conception of the consumer's role has been oversimplified. Second, even if consumers change their behavior, there are major obstacles to reaping the benefits without significant changes by providers and health plans in the nature of competition.

Most of the literature and attention in consumer-driven health care has focused on the choice of health plans. Although having a choice of health plans can be beneficial, the choice of providers and treatments is far more significant. Today, even well-informed, committed consumers face impediments to improving the value of their care because of the lack of competition on results at the medical condition level.

Consumer-driven health care is also unrealistic in assuming that individuals can fully take charge of their own care. Very few consumers will be expert enough, or should be expert enough, to oversee their care on their own. They will need to rely heavily on their doctors, their health plan, and other advisers.

Consumer choice is not the goal in and of itself, as consumer-driven health care advocates sometimes seem to imply. Rather, the goal is to increase dramatically the value of care delivered. Significantly increasing value in health care will require more than just consumer choice. It will also require a shift to value-based competition on results involving providers and health plans.

The problem is not just that consumers have been slow to adopt the new mind-set of the consumer-driven care movement, but that the needed changes in the structure of health care delivery are not yet in place. Today, the choice of providers and treatments is restricted, yet the results of providers vary markedly. Care is so fractured by procedure, specialty, and service that coordinating care requires great effort from both the patient and a guiding physician. Even basic coordination, such as the exchange of medical records, is not taking place. There is often no physician to help navigate the system and ensure follow through.

Consumers also lack the right information to improve the value of their care even if they want to. Evidence shows that uninformed consumers tend to assume that more health care leads to better health. While the need for advice and decision support is widely recognized, the consumer-directed health care literature is silent on what information should be assembled and reported, and how.

Patient advocacy groups are playing an important role in the current flawed system, particularly those focused on medical conditions. These groups are filling the information void and helping to guide patients to excellent providers. Some groups, such as the Alpha-1 Foundation, are directly catalyzing the development of centers of excellence by particular providers. Patient groups, however, are not a substitute for value-based competition in the system. They can address weaknesses, but their impact will be constrained until competition is working in the same direction.

The transforming power of competition on results among providers and health plans will unleash the benefits of informed consumer involvement. As providers and health plans compete to improve value for patients, it will get easier and easier for consumers to make good decisions. Thus, value-based competition will accelerate the adoption of a new consumer mind-set. However, even if most consumers are slow to adopt the new way of thinking, value-based competition will ensure that patient value will still improve markedly. The nation cannot depend on major attitudinal changes by consumers alone to transform the system.

Moving to Value-Based Competition: New Responsibilities for Consumers

Consumers can enable value-based competition in a number of ways, as summarized in figure 7-2.

Participate Actively in Managing Personal Health. Consumers must accept personal responsibility for their health.[8] This means directly influencing the risk, frequency, and severity of health problems by adopting a healthy lifestyle, participating in testing for early detection, complying with treatments, and taking steps to reduce the severity and complications of disease. It also means that consumers must participate actively in disease management and disease prevention programs. As prevention, risk management, and disease management become more central to competition, and as more health plans integrate these as core functions, the scope of responsibility for consumer involvement will only increase. As value-based competition becomes more widespread, consumer involvement will reap larger and larger benefits.

Skeptics of any consumer role in health care, who remain numerous despite the consumer-driven health care movement, argue that patients do not want to assume responsibility for choices, preferring that their doctor make decisions. Skeptics also assert that patients will always choose the most convenient provider, and will always opt for more care. However, current patient behavior reflects the lack of focus in the system

FIGURE 7-2

New responsibilities for consumers

Participate actively in managing personal health

- Take responsibility for health and health care
- Manage health through lifestyle choices, obtaining routine care and testing, complying with treatments, and active participation in disease management and prevention

Expect relevant information and seek advice

- Gather information on provider results and experience in medical conditions
- Seek help and advice in interpreting information from physicians and the health plan
- Utilize independent medical information companies when needed

Make treatment and provider choices based on excellent results and personal values, not convenience or amenities

- Choose excellent providers, not the closest provider or the past provider of unrelated care

Choose a health plan based on value added

- Expect the health plan to be the overall health adviser
- Choose cost-effective health plan structures involving deductibles together with HSAs to save for future health care needs

Build a long-term relationship with an excellent health plan

- Seek a long-term relationship instead of plan churning

Act responsibly

- Accept responsibility for health and health care
- Communicate personal intentions regarding organ donorship and end-of-life care
- Designate a health care proxy and prepare a living will

---

on maintaining health, the prevalence of restricted choices and zero-sum competition, the difficulty of navigating through poorly coordinated care cycles, and the lack of relevant information on results. As these things change, the pendulum will swing in consumers' favor.

Even in the current system, informed and involved patients tend to choose less invasive care and follow through on self-care more effectively.[9] Patients who adopt self-management of chronic diseases have better outcomes and sometimes also lower costs.[10] When appropriate information on outcomes and prices is transparent and available, the choice of more expensive care with worse expected outcomes will decline markedly. As health plans play the new roles discussed in chapter 6, greater involvement and responsibility by patients will be inevitable.

Though some health care experts are skeptical that consumers will ever accept responsibility for their health, many consumers are already doing so in spite of the challenges thrown up by the current system. We are confident that many more will do so over time as competition in the system changes. However, as we have noted, value-based competition will drive huge improvements in value even if consumers are slow to change their attitudes and behaviors.

Expect Relevant Information and Seek Advice. As consumers begin to accept more responsibility for their health, the first task is to become informed. Already, the third most common use of the Internet is seeking medical information.[11] In addition, a growing number of patient organizations are disseminating information about the most effective and experienced providers of care for various illnesses. The role of patient advocacy groups partly reflects the absence of such services at health plans.

Health plans have estimated that about 25 percent of patients already seek information, and that another 50 percent would do so if they had more assistance in learning how to find relevant information and advice in understanding it. These percentages are striking in view of the limited information available in the current system and the restrictions on the choice of providers. As health plans shift their roles, the proportions of informed consumers will only increase, and their knowledge and involvement in their health and health care will only grow.

Most consumers today simply do not know that provider quality and cost differences are so large. They would be horrified if they did, in our opinion, and act accordingly. Many consumers also do not understand that referrals can be biased and, even where there is the best of motives, uninformed by evidence. As discussed in chapter 6, referring doctors also lack results information. They often do not know how dramatic the differences in outcomes among providers are, or are loath to raise anxiety by referring a patient to an excellent provider that cannot be accessed given the patient's insurance coverage. A recent survey of consumers and primary care physicians, while far from definitive, found that an overwhelming percentage of patients and doctors desire more cost and quality information, and a huge majority of consumers would be likely to ask their doctor to change hospitals in favor of one that offered better quality at lower cost.[12]

The trend toward patients researching their own medical problems makes some doctors uncomfortable. Patients are arriving with unprecedented amounts of information and questions. However, an informed patient is more likely to make good choices and to comply with lifestyle and treatment recommendations. Doctors need to be able to spend the time to answer questions, help patients understand the alternatives, support good patient decision making, and advise patients on their ongoing care. Doctors and other health personnel should be compensated for this time. Unfortunately, as discussed in earlier chapters, the current provider incentives encourage just the opposite. The recent move to compensate doctors for e-mail communication with patients is an encouraging start.[13]

A growing number of patients are not just gathering information but actively seeking alternatives in terms of treatments and providers. One thing that motivates physicians to adopt new processes and techniques is when they hear their patients, or potential patients, considering alternatives.[14] Experience in other industries reveals that it is not necessary for all consumers to use information aggressively to reap the benefits in competitive terms; even if just 15 to 25 percent actively base choices on comparative information, this is sufficient to refocus competition on value.

There will always be some patients who do not seek out information, who want others to make their choices, or who just make bad choices, but such patients will become more the exception and less the rule. As value-based competition develops, far more support, advice, and integration of care will be available. Consumer-driven health care rests on a social movement and new belief systems. With the right kind of competition, however, patient value will increase dramatically even if consumers are slow to change or reluctant to get involved in their care.

We do not advocate a system in which patients are expected to direct their own health care. This conception of consumer-driven care is too simplistic. So is the idea that making consumers personally responsible for some of the costs of their care will solve all problems. The goal is not consumer-driven care per se but patient-centric care driven by value-based competition.

Consumers will need assistance in interpreting and drawing insight from medical information. As health care competition evolves, doctors should continue to play a major role in informing and advising patients about treatment and disease management choices. Patients will continue to rely on their doctors' help in interpreting data on provider experience, outcomes, and cost; understanding what is known medically; and deciding where to get the best care for their condition. In a value-based system, providers will be organized and rewarded for playing this role well.

Health plans, which are independent of any particular provider, will also have a growing role in advising and assisting patients, as we discussed in the previous chapter. Health plans can add far more value by supporting consumers in obtaining excellent care than by simply shifting payment responsibility so that consumers will be more price sensitive. Finally, patients and their families can seek out independent advisers, especially during the transition to a value-based system. Firms such as Best Doctors have the knowledge and access to experts that allow patients to obtain an accurate diagnosis more quickly and find an excellent provider that can address their condition.

Make Treatment and Provider Choices Based on Excellent Results and Personal Values, Not Convenience or Amenities. Consumers can reinforce value-based competition through the way they choose treatments and providers. Consumers should expect their providers to disseminate results at the medical condition and treatment level and to make their charges known in advance. Consumers should choose providers that can demonstrate excellent value in addressing the care they need. The closest provider is not necessarily the best provider. And just because a consumer has been treated by a physician group or hospital for one medical condition does not mean that this is the right or the best provider for every other medical condition. The hospital that provided maternity services, for example, may not be a good choice for treatment of breast cancer or heart disease.

Indeed, just because the consumer has been diagnosed by a physician does not mean that treatment should be provided by the same physician, physician group, or hospital network. The focus should be on demonstrated excellence, not familiarity. Part of excellence is coordination of care. Consumers should evaluate their provider in terms of the ability to integrate care over the full care cycle, including ongoing disease management.[15]

Some argue that insured consumers will never make good provider and treatment choices because they are spending someone else's money. We advocate some cost sharing by consumers for a number of reasons, as we will discuss. However, ascribing all the problems in the system to a lack of cost sharing is simplistic. It ignores the fact that health care has many nonmonetary costs, such as risk, pain, time, inconvenience, and diminished quality of life. Patients want better health, not more health care. Patients also want care that is consistent with their preferences in terms of the invasiveness of treatment, side effects, changes in lifestyle, and quality of life. Patients surely have enough at stake to care about their health care choices if they come to understand that better choices result in better outcomes. In the current system, seemingly poor choices are often due to absence of information and lack of value-based competition by providers and health plans.

Choose a Health Plan Based on Value Added. As consumers' responsibilities and involvement grow, health plans and results information take on more, not less, importance. Consumers will never be medical experts, nor should they have to be. Together with their doctor, health plans should play a central role as the consumer's overall health adviser. Health plans should also be the consumer's advocate with providers.

The choice of health plan is crucial to value, yet consumers have tended to select health plans for the wrong reasons. Over time, consumers need to understand that access to information, advice, support, and freedom to choose among providers and treatments should be the most important criteria they use to select a health plan. Does the plan provide information comparing treatments and provider results by medical condition, not just locally but regionally and nationally? Does the health plan eschew networks and help access excellent providers based on results? Does the health plan offer comprehensive disease management services? Does the health plan work with subscribers to assess their medical risks and mitigate them? Does the health plan work constructively with doctors to ensure good care that is coordinated over the care cycle? Does the health plan assist in assembling an overall medical record? These and other value-adding roles of health plans should determine the plan chosen, not attractive amenities, health club memberships, the number of physicians in the network, the lowest price, or satisfaction surveys focused on the service experience rather than health outcomes.

Consumers should select health plan structures that include appropriate coverage and deductibles. First-dollar coverage is not cost-effective for many, if not most, individuals. Instead, consumers should be willing to bear some of the financial costs of their care because this will reduce premiums. Copayments and deductibles in good health plans should be designed to encourage the choice of excellent treatments and providers as well as healthy living practices.

Consumers must also begin to save for their own health care, because they are likely to share in its future costs. Health savings accounts (HSAs) combined with high-deductible plans, as we have described in earlier chapters, provide a vehicle to save for health care while encouraging active patient involvement in making health care choices based on value. Even in the current system, with its limited information and restrictions on choice, there is growing evidence that HSAs can improve buying patterns and reduce costs.[16] Aetna has found that HSA subscribers spend more on preventive care and make greater use of available information about health care choices.[17] Since more informed patients tend to comply better with physicians' advice, which improves outcomes, building patient responsibility and knowledge helps to create a virtuous circle of improving outcomes without increasing costs.

But HSAs will not have the desired effect unless they are combined with a health plan that provides the information and advice that consumers need, and gives them the right to choose providers. Without information, advice, and choice, the idea that giving consumers a financial stake in their decisions will improve value is simply unrealistic. Without provider choice, HSAs become a vehicle for self-rationing because the only real choice is whether to seek or forgo care—more zero-sum competition.[18]

Some experts seem to think that giving consumers "skin in the game" in terms of financial consequences for each health care decision will solve the problems of the health care system. This is yet another example of simplistic, piecemeal thinking. HSAs (or copayments) alone are not the answer. However, they can be a real step forward in a system in which there is value-based competition on results at the medical condition level involving all parties.

As we mentioned in chapter 6, HSAs can also reduce administrative costs if they are implemented in a way that eliminates the need to process small claims. Imagine the cost savings from getting health plans out of the business of processing the numerous small transactions that typically make up the first several thousand dollars of health care expenditures per family. While there will be costs for making the transition to HSAs, the net administrative savings could be substantial.

Build a Long-Term Relationship with an Excellent Health Plan. Consumers need a health plan that accepts responsibility for their total health and takes a long-term perspective in terms of provider and treatment choices. Consumers need a health plan that shares their interest in disease prevention and disease management. A long-term relationship between plan and member fosters such an alignment of interests. Instead, some consumers are prone to shop around and switch plans in search of lower premiums or enticing coverage options. Employers encourage such plan churning when they add and drop health plan choices from year to year.

Plan churning is inconsistent with the proper time horizon in health care decisions. It also works against developing personal relationships with advisers and limits the plan's ability to assemble a comprehensive picture of the member's health needs. It is also inconsistent with the time horizon required by both members and plans in modifying behavior and improving health via prevention and disease management programs. A long-term relationship aligns the interests of consumers and health plans, and facilitates value-based choices. Consumers should find an excellent plan and seek a long-term relationship unless their plan fails to deliver good value. If health plans move to multiyear contracting with subscribers, as we recommend in chapter 6, consumers should be receptive.

Act Responsibly. Patients and their families are doing themselves a disservice if they fail to accept responsibility for their health and their health care decisions, and look to others to bear the cost. This behavior not only leads to worse health outcomes, but also inflicts unnecessary costs on society—yet another form of cost shifting.

Too many consumers see the costs of their health care as someone else's responsibility. Individuals who can afford insurance opt out of the system when they are young and healthy. A bevy of lawyers helps older citizens transfer assets to their heirs so that the government will pay for their nursing home care. These types of cost-shifting tactics by consumers are unfair and unsustainable. Public assistance should serve only those who are truly needy, as we discuss in chapter 8.

Too many consumers are passive until something goes wrong, but then quick to sue their hospital or doctor. Yet malpractice suits do not restore health, nor have they fixed the health care system because quality problems remain common. Instead, lawsuits impose large direct costs on the system and even larger indirect costs in the form of defensive medicine.

Patients who play the role of victims and who abdicate personal responsibility for health but then turn to lawsuits are one of the tragedies of American health care. Consumers can strongly affect their health and the quality of the care they receive if they accept responsibility, become informed, and modify their behavior. Even in the current system, well-informed consumers and their families can do much to ensure that they are receiving the right treatments from the right providers. When value-based competition kicks in, careless, negligent, and out-of date providers will go out of business. Lawsuits will be needed far less frequently.

Finally, consumers can avoid much unnecessary confusion and cost by clearly articulating their wishes about end-of-life care. Every individual should designate a health care proxy and prepare a living will, including instructions about whether to be an organ donor and which types of care to attempt in extreme circumstances.

Consumers do have the power to influence the health care system. However, their influence will not come from attempting to be medical experts and micromanaging their own care. Instead, their major leverage will come from acting responsibly and setting high expectations so that the other actors in the system do their jobs well. When health plans and providers have to compete to add value, consumers who become informed and participate in their health and health care will reap larger and larger dividends.

Like other actors in the system, however, consumers need not wait for the system to change. Even in the current system, consumers can significantly improve their own health results and speed up the transformation of providers and health plans.

Implications for Employers

Employers have a great deal at stake in the performance of the U.S. health care system. Businesses' health care costs have outpaced inflation in fourteen of the past eighteen years. Over the past ten years, the average spending on health care per employee increased 140 percent, to more than $8,400 per employee in 2006.[19] In 2005, General Motors reported that health care expenses added $1,500 to the cost of every car it manufactured.[20] Estimates of the cost per employee of lost work time due to poor health are even higher than the direct cost of health care benefits.

Employers are no longer willing or able to absorb the full cost of these increases. As a result, cost shifting is taking place in a variety of forms. Employers are shifting a rising proportion of health care costs to employees through higher premiums, reduced services, or higher deductibles. About half of large employers shifted costs by reducing benefits or raising copayments and deductibles in 2003, according to Mercer Human Resources Consulting.[21] Mercer found that over 20 percent of employers planned to increase deductibles and copayments in 2005.[22] (Figure 7-3 provides data on employer health benefit changes.)

Unfortunately, HSAs are being utilized by many employers primarily as a cost-shifting tool, rather than as a way to improve health care choices. Some companies have shifted costs by forcing working spouses to enroll in their employer's health plan or pay higher premiums to join the company's plan. Some employers have shifted costs by dropping health coverage altogether for workers or retirees. They are also outsourcing jobs to suppliers without health coverage, or outsourcing jobs to offshore locations. Finally, some employers have shifted cost to employees and society by denying any benefits to part-time workers instead of making a contribution to benefits proportional to working hours.

Ultimately, many of these costs land on society. While each incremental employer decision seems to benefit the company involved, the per employee unit cost of health care rises for everyone as less revenue flows into the system. Hence the decisions by employers consciously or inadvertently drive everyone's costs up. Shifting costs, then, does not really solve employers' health care cost problem. It may mitigate the problem, but only temporarily.

Employers are also attempting to reduce costs through approaches to managing health coverage that are self-defeating. When employers use their clout to insist on discounts (rather than working to increase the value of coverage) they set in motion a vicious circle that raises costs, as we discussed in chapter 2. Large discounts to employers shift costs to small groups, the self-employed, and the uninsured, who are charged list price. More bad debts, more people who drop insurance, and more uncompensated care drive up costs to employers that offset the discounts. (Even if each year's discounts remain large, then, employers face major premium increases.)

The entire approach of employers to purchasing health benefits has failed miserably. By buying health care services (and structuring self-insured plans)

FIGURE 7-3

Changes in employer health benefits, 2003 to 2004

A: Premium increases

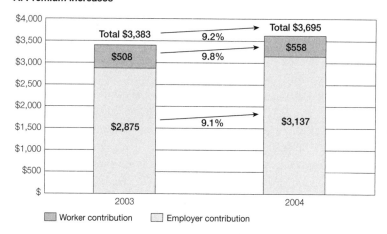

Worker contribution   Employer contribution

B: Percentage of workers covered by their employer health benefits

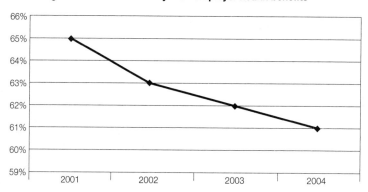

C: Level of benefits for covered workers compared to previous year

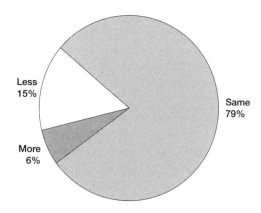

Source: Data from Kaiser Family Foundation and Health Research and Education Trust (2004), based on 1,925 randomly selected firms with three or more employees.

in a way that focuses on short-term cost savings, employers are reducing the health value that both they and their employees get for their money.

Many employers now understand that the status quo is unacceptable. A Hewitt Associates study of 650 major U.S. companies found that 96 percent of CEOs and CFOs were significantly or critically concerned about health care costs for 2004, and 91 percent voiced serious concerns about the impact of health care costs on their employees.[23] But more cost shifting is hardly the answer. Asking employees to pay a bigger share of premiums without changing the nature of competition in the system only reduces the income and morale of employees with no compensating health value benefit. And by not providing health benefits at all, some employers saddle their employees with worry and financial exposure that will hardly engender employee loyalty.

As we discussed in chapter 3, some experts have suggested that employers should get out of the loop and no longer be the funders of health insurance. Instead, some advocate that the tax incentives that now apply to employer-sponsored health benefits should be provided directly to individuals. Such a step would allow individuals to purchase directly a health plan that meets their needs rather than one preselected or designed by their employer. It would also solve the problem of portability of health coverage, important because plan churning erodes value. And, most importantly to some, providing the tax benefit directly to individuals would get employers out of the health care business.

While such a model is certainly a reasonable way to design a health care system from scratch and a direction in which the system should move in the long run, it will not happen overnight. Moreover, it should not happen until risk pools, mandatory coverage, and subsidies for low-income Americans are in place. Moving the purchase of health insurance solely to individuals is not only impractical in the near term, but also fails to address many of the value problems that beset the system. Realistically speaking, then, employer-based health benefits are likely to be the predominant model for the time being. Rather than wait for a new model, employers must move now to improve the employer-based system while also helping to lay the groundwork for direct individual purchase of insurance in the future.

Missed Opportunities

Employers, working individually and collectively, have the clout as major purchasers of health care services to influence the roles and practices of health plans and the nature of competition in the system. Employers can also enable, and provide incentives for, better health and health care choices by their employees. Unfortunately, however, many employers have failed to grasp these opportunities. Instead, they have contributed to the zero-sum competition in the system by letting themselves be drawn into the game of cost shifting.

In purchasing health care services, employers have forgotten or over-looked basic lessons about competition and procurement that are second nature in other goods and services they buy. Instead of placing responsibility for health care benefits at senior levels in the organization, many employers have outsourced the management of their health benefits to health plan administrators. Worse, they have done so without setting the proper mandate: improving health value and employee well-being.

Rather than managing health, employers have attempted to manage costs. Instead of understanding the quality and value differences in health care offerings, employers have bought health plans based on price—an easy mistake if health care is seen as a commodity. Rather than working strategically with health plans to find ways to improve value and reduce the long-term costs of health care for the company and employees, many employers have pushed for discounts and the lowest annual premium increases, thereby biasing health plans even more toward short-term cost reduction and cost shifting. As employers shuffled health plan offerings almost every year in search of cost reductions, they triggered more plan churning instead of encouraging longer time horizons that would align health plan, provider, and employer interests. As big companies pushed for larger and larger discounts, they widened the cross subsidies in their favor that inflicted higher costs elsewhere in the system and, ultimately, drove up their own costs.

Employers should have known better. Smart companies realize that all suppliers are not equal. Few products or services are actually commodities, especially complex services like health care. Companies know that the relevant standard for choice is value, not just cost. They understand that greater experience and expertise of service providers can improve quality, reduce errors, and lower costs all at the same time. Companies know that innovation is crucial to progress, not something to be minimized. They know that relevant information is essential to good decision making, and that well-informed buyers get better value. They also understand that intermediaries, such as health plans, must add value. Finally, companies know that the right kind of competition among their vendors is crucial. Yet despite the fact that it had become one of their largest cost items, amnesia set in when employers bought health care.

Employers failed to apply the same rigorous practices to buying health care that they bring to other decisions. Just as troubling is that the vast majority of attention has been focused on the *direct* cost of employee health care, while the *indirect* costs (absenteeism, lost work time, low productivity) were largely ignored. What is worse, in an effort to negotiate lower-cost plans, employers frequently failed to invest in services that significantly improve employee health, such as preventive health services, screening programs, and disease management. Many companies, then, all but abdicated responsibility for improving value in the health care system and behaved in ways that made the problem worse.

While CEOs complain endlessly about health care costs, they too have failed to take responsibility. The management of health benefits has usually been assigned to employee benefit departments several levels down from senior management that often lack a broader perspective and the proper mandate. Also, CEOs have failed to measure and hold staffs accountable for the health results achieved from all the spending. The poor results, then, are hardly surprising.

Promising Initiatives

Employers have begun to move beyond their myopic, short-term cost reduction mind-set and have come to understand the quality problems that plague the system. Some employers have started to purchase health care services differently. Employer consortia, such as the Leapfrog Group, the Pacific Business Group on Health, and others, have been formed to influence health care delivery. Especially in the area of safety, these employer groups have begun to communicate new expectations to providers about acceptable practices and set forth criteria that employers will use in choosing providers.[24]

The best-known employer consortium is the Leapfrog Group, a coalition of 150 public and private organizations providing employee health care benefits. Leapfrog has been working primarily to reduce the high incidence of medical errors. In July 2001, Leapfrog launched its first stage—a market-oriented initiative in which members agreed to purchase health care only from hospitals that adopted three quality standards: electronic prescribing systems to reduce errors in prescription orders; staffing of intensive care units by physicians trained in critical care; and provider volume thresholds governing patient referrals in five high-risk adult surgeries, to ensure that the hospitals treating their employees have sufficient experience to achieve acceptable outcomes.[25]

In 2003, the referral requirements were extended beyond minimum provider volume to include documented adherence to certain clinical processes known to improve outcomes. In 2004, Leapfrog added a quality index to its standards for choosing providers, based on the National Quality Forum's list of thirty safe practices, ranging from having a "culture of safety" to using standardized processes for labeling x-ray and other images, and to prophylactic use of beta blockers before elective surgery for patients with high risk of an acute ischemic cardiac event during surgery.[26] Leapfrog lists hospitals on its Web site that are adhering to its standards, as well as those that fail to do so. The organization estimates that its "quality leaps" have the potential to save more than 65,000 lives and $9.7 billion annually.[27]

Such employer consortia are an important step in the right direction, and Leapfrog has done much to combat the commodity mind-set in employers' health care purchases while highlighting the importance of safety. However, medical errors and safety are only a part of the overall quality and value equation. Leapfrog is still too focused on process compliance, rather than results, and is falling into the trap of trying to specify how hospitals should run their operations. It is also attempting to certify hospitals as a whole, rather than at the medical condition level. Leapfrog's efforts to expand the amount and types of information are welcome initiatives. But they are still just tentative, early steps toward true value-based competition.

Employer consortia need to move to a broader focus on value and measurement of results. As we discussed in earlier chapters, results are multidimensional. The goal is not to identify a single metric, but a set of results measures on which providers compete. Employers need to worry less about controlling provider practices and use their clout to create the right kind of competition in the system—competition on results at the level of specific medical conditions. Getting competition right will unleash a force far more powerful than any amount of provider oversight. Employers also need to motivate the adoption of value-adding roles by health plans, and hold them accountable, rather than to insert themselves as another layer into an already complicated system.

Another recent employer initiative, which has spread to some health plans, is "pay for performance." In this approach, higher reimbursement rates are set for providers that comply with specified standards for care delivery. The aim is to eliminate low-quality care by encouraging the widespread use of proven practice standards. These standards mostly involve hospital-wide practices or basic treatment standards for a few medical conditions, but they are beginning to include some genuine measures of outcome.

Pay for performance can be a useful transitional step until results information is more widely available.[28] It can also be a mechanism to support the accumulation of comparative data on provider processes. However, pay for performance is not a long-term solution, as we noted in chapter 3, especially if it rewards providers for following mandated practices in performing discrete interventions rather than for achieving excellent results over the full cycle of care in particular medical conditions. Pay for performance also remains too closely aligned with the fee-for-service model, which creates incentives for intervention, not health outcomes. When performance is defined as compliance rather than results, providers and health plans cannot raise their performance metrics with prevention, but only through acute treatment.

Current pay-for-performance thinking also assumes that the way to reward quality is with higher prices. This puts the system on a path of inevitable cost increases as more providers are able to meet process compliance thresholds. Instead, as we discuss in chapter 4, higher quality should be associated with lower costs because better health care is often inherently less expensive. This means that excellent providers often enjoy higher margins at equal prices. The far greater reward for good performance is more patients, which will reinforce the virtuous circle of value improvement discussed in chapters 4 and 5.

This observation is startling to many providers. Why, they ask, do we pay more for a better car but may not need to pay more for better medical care? We discussed the answer extensively in chapter 4. Much health care today is far from the frontier of best practice. This creates low-hanging fruit, in the form of practices improving quality without raising costs. All that is necessary is better management. Also, health care is a field where the advancing quality has a particularly strong potential to lower costs through faster recovery, fewer errors and complications, more accurate diagnoses, less invasive methods, reduced disability, and, most important, better health through prevention of illness and disease management.

Already, pay for performance is devolving into the micromanagement of providers, and threatening to move down the same blind alley as managed care. Employers are not well equipped to second-guess provider practices and decisions. They would be better advised to ensure that the right kind of provider competition is put in place, enabled by the right kind of information and the value-adding roles of health plans (see chapter 6). Then, excellent providers in a medical condition will be rewarded with more patients, which will help them become even more efficient. In the process, average quality will rise markedly, and value will rise even faster.

Moving to Value-Based Competition: New Roles for Employers

At the broadest level, employers must use their influence to create the right type of competition in the system together with the information, incentives, and participant roles to support it. They can do this in seven broad ways (see figure 7-4).

Employers will exert the greatest influence by selecting the right health plans to offer, defining the right value-adding roles that health plans must play, and directly supporting their employees with appropriate services. Employers can surely influence provider competition, but they will

FIGURE 7-4

New roles for employers

Set the goal of increasing health value, not minimizing health benefit costs

Set new expectations for health plans, including self-insured plans
- Choose plans that demonstrate excellence in playing the roles shown in figure 6-2
- Select plans and plan administrators based on health results, not administrative convenience

Provide for health plan continuity for employees, rather than plan churning
- Align interests by encouraging long-term relationships between the plan and subscribers

Enhance provider competition on results
- Expect demonstrated excellence from all providers involved in employee care
- Collaborate with other employers in advancing value-based competition

Support and motivate employees in making good health choices and in managing their own health
- Offer encouragement, incentives, and support to employees in managing their health
- Provide independent information and advising services to employees to supplement other sources
- Offer health plan structures that provide good value and encourage saving for long-term health needs

Find ways to expand insurance coverage and advocate reform of the insurance system
- Create collaborative vehicles with other employers to offer group insurance coverage to employees or affiliated individuals not currently part of the employer's health plan
- Support insurance reform that levels the playing field among employers

Measure and hold employee benefit staff accountable for the company's health value
- Health benefits must ultimately be a senior management responsibility, with staff responsible for results

---

never possess the deep medical expertise necessary to direct health care providers. Nor will it usually make sense for employers to attempt to assume the health plan roles described in chapter 6. Current employer initiatives have attempted to address providers directly because employers do not trust health plans. Instead, a better approach would be to rapidly change the expectations for the health plans, which are, or should be, the medical experts, which already have extensive subscriber health information, and which deal directly with providers every day.

Set the Goal of Increasing Health Value, Not Minimizing Health Benefit Costs. Success in addressing the health care problem starts with defining the right goal. The aim must be to drive up employee health and the value of health care delivered, not minimize the costs of health benefits. Cost minimization is a one-way street to cost shifting, discounting, and rationing, a combination that has failed.

Employers must measure not just the direct costs of health care but also the indirect costs of poor health and reduced productivity (such as lost work days). Employee health and the value of care can only be measured over a several-year period, like all other aspects of company operations. Employers must adopt the proper time horizon, rather than focus on minimizing cost in the short run. As we have discussed, a short time horizon will cause health plans and providers to make choices that are not in the interests of employees or ultimately the company.

Set New Expectations for Health Plans, Including Self-Insured Plans. While employers can positively influence the nature of provider competition, as we will discuss, it is rarely advisable for employers to attempt to become true health care experts. Instead, employers should expect their health plans and plan administrators to do their jobs well, with clear accountability for health results. To reinforce these expectations, employers must purchase health care services differently.

About half of employer-funded health plans are self-insured, though most self-insured plans hire a health plan or third-party administrator to manage their health benefits. Employers with self-insured plans have the most flexibility to shape coverage and the roles of health plans, because self-insured plans are not regulated as insurance and thus have wider latitude to define benefits.

More employers are talking about value in health care, a welcome development. However, too many are still acting as if short-term discounts were the dominant consideration in purchasing health benefits.

In chapter 6, we described the ways that health plans can add value. These roles for health plans (see figures 6-1 and 6-2) should define the expectations that employers set for their health plans, plan structures, and plan administrators, and the criteria used in selecting them. Employers must then be willing to invest in the steps and plan structures that will foster improved care and healthy behaviors rather than only seek the lowest short-term cost per employee and the deepest discounts.

A good plan will assist the patient in securing the correct diagnosis. It will provide meaningful results information and advice so that patients can select and obtain care from an excellent provider using an effective treatment, even if such a provider is not available locally. Good plans will facilitate access to excellent out-of-network providers at reasonable cost. If travel is beneficial from a value perspective, a good plan will cover travel for the patient and a companion. It will also provide a medical coach for patients during complex treatments. A good plan will offer integration of care and coordination across the care cycle, both rarities in a system where different entities provide each aspect of clinical care: physical therapy, mental health services, disability management, and pharmacy benefits. A good plan will also enable and support information sharing across providers.

A good health plan will also enable health, and build in incentives for employees and their families to participate in managing and improving their health. Comprehensive and well-structured disease management programs should be part of every plan. Many employer-insured plans still do not cover disease management at all, or cover it only for a few chronic conditions. In 2004, only about 50 percent of the large employers surveyed by Mercer Human Resource Consulting offered disease management programs for diabetes and heart disease/hypertension, up from about 40 percent in 2002. Among very large employers (20,000 employees or more), 70 percent offer one or more disease management programs. Of those companies that have attempted to measure a return on their investment in disease management programs, the great majority have found the returns to be positive in spite of measuring only the direct reduction of health care costs while ignoring indirect costs savings such as lower absenteeism.[29,30] The evidence is compelling that the long-term benefit of disease management is substantial in both value and cost terms (see chapter 6).[31]

A good health plan should also include screening, risk assessment, and preventive services. Employers should expect their health plans to work with primary care physicians and others to identify member risk factors and provide systematic programs for disease prevention for high-risk members. Finally, a good plan should reward behavior that improves health and mitigates the risk of disease, and vice versa. Scotts Miracle-Gro, for example, requires employees to pay an additional $40 per month in health care premiums if they do not fill out a health assessment questionnaire that enables the company to involve them in health management and disease management programs.[32]

The selection of plans should be based on the health results achieved for members per dollar of spending. Health results can only be measured over the two- to three-year period that it takes for some programs, such as prevention and disease management, to achieve the full benefits. Results need to be adjusted for the nature of the employee population. Employers can also begin to negotiate contracts in which health plan or plan administrator compensation is tied to improvements in the health status of their covered population.

In order to offer excellent health plans, the best solution may not be to select a single plan that covers all the geographies in which the sponsoring company operates. The administrative savings from dealing with a single plan or plan administrator will be overwhelmed by the health value benefits that excellent plans can deliver. Employers should select plans that can deliver the most value in each geographic area in which they operate. They should also aim to offer a choice of plans to allow employees to select a plan with distinctive ability in managing their particular health issues.

Provide for Health Plan Continuity for Employees, Rather Than Plan Churning. In order for a health plan to best deliver health value, there needs to be a long-term relationship between plan and subscriber. A long-term relationship creates incentives to seek out excellent care as well as to invest in prevention and disease management. Continuity of care and stability of relationships with providers and health plan advisers will improve the value of care. With a long-term relationship between the plan and subscriber, everyone's interests are aligned.

Employers, then, must structure their health benefits to allow and reinforce plan continuity, rather than consciously or unconsciously increase plan churning. In chapter 6 we discussed the concept of multiyear contracting, which not only fosters goal alignment but should also produce administrative efficiencies for employers as well as for health plans. Employers can also offer incentives for repeat contracting.

Employers should be conservative in removing well-performing plans from the list of options available to employees, because this forces plan churning. Employers should be conservative in changing plan administrators and other health service management companies except in cases of meaningful value differences. It is usually better to adjust cost-sharing ratios with employees rather than to eliminate a well-performing plan altogether, in order to allow plan continuity. In return, employers should expect their plans and plan administrators to demonstrate excellent results, and adopt a long-term perspective regarding their roles, their services, and their member relationships.

Enhance Provider Competition on Results. Employers, individually and collectively, will have the greatest impact on providers if they can shape the nature of competition at the provider level. Through their health plans, employers should expect the providers who serve their employees to make data on results and experience available at the medical condition level over the full cycle of care. Employees should be cared for only by providers that have demonstrated excellence. Employers should also expect providers to put a process in place that will lead to a single, transparent fee for episodes of care, not a myriad of discrete charges. Over time, provider contracts should be revised to reward value improvements.

Finally, employers should outlaw billing of employees by providers for covered services, except for copayments and deductibles. Once true provider competition begins, it will spread. As one provider has to compete, it will put more pressure on others with which it has referral and other relationships.

Employers should redirect their focus from provider discounts to demonstrated results. Despite all the focus on bargaining for discounts, health costs have continued to rise rapidly. Obtaining a discount on substandard or inefficient care is no bargain. Indeed, discounted care with above-average rates of complications may be significantly more expensive. Well-designed disease and injury prevention programs will often be more cost-effective than even the best negotiated discounts on the treatment of the same diseases and injuries once they occur.

Expecting a company's employees to be cared for by providers at lower prices than other patients will only contribute to a vicious circle of cost shifting and cross subsidy that leads to cost increases for everyone. Instead, the focus should be on making sure that the providers serving their employees are delivering superior value at the medical condition level.

Support and Motivate Employees in Making Good Health Choices and in Managing Their Own Health. We have described how patients and their families, working with their physicians and advisers, need to accept more responsibility both as consumers of health care services and in managing their own health. Employers can encourage and support such a shift in mind-set and behavior. The best way to lower health care costs is to help employees and their families remain healthy, or as healthy as possible given their medical circumstances. Employers can educate and encourage employees to take responsibility for their health. More and more employers are offering educational sessions, fitness programs, financial incentives, and other efforts to further these objectives. Also, especially until health plans play these roles well, employers can support employees in gathering health information, choosing providers, and managing chronic conditions.

Pitney-Bowes, for example, allows employees to earn reductions in health plan deductibles by attending classes about lifestyle and disease prevention, and becoming more savvy consumers of health care. Scotts Miracle-Gro includes disease management programs in its health coverage. Scotts also offers reimbursements to employees for participation in Weight Watchers and smoking cessation programs. It offers free membership in an on-site fitness center to employees who use it an average of at least ten times per month. It also has announced that, in states where it is legal, it will employ only nonsmokers beginning in fiscal 2006.[33] Employee incentives such as discounts on healthy choices in the employee cafeteria and vending machines, subsidies for health club memberships, and reimbursement for preventive health services are becoming mainstream. Over time, asking employees to bear some of the cost of unhealthy choices will also spread. Such steps are not cost shifting, but improve health value.

More employers are embracing programs that encourage workers to undergo basic health screening and help them correct problems with weight, blood pressure, and other issues. Some companies give cash incentives to employees who complete health risk assessment questionnaires. Blinded data from such questionnaires are used *in the aggregate* to structure prevention and wellness programs at employee work sites.[34] Furthermore, about a third of large employers are focusing on obesity reduction among workers, up from 14 percent in 2003.[35]

Employers are also increasingly providing health information services for employees. Many employers are offering access to medical Web-based services that contain information on medical conditions, diagnoses, and treatment choices, as well as prevention and healthy lifestyles, as part of their health benefits. Some employers are offering third-party information and advisory services to assist their employees. As we discussed in chapter 4, for example, Honeywell achieved good results when it retained Consumer's Medical Resource, a decision-support service company, to provide independent information on diagnoses and treatments to employees. Best Doctors is another company that offers services that enable patients with complex conditions to secure the correct diagnosis and determine where they can get experienced and expert care.

Finally, more employers are offering on-site primary care clinics for employees and, in some cases, their families. The on-site delivery model allows convenient access to primary care services, which reduces lost work time. Furthermore, easy face-to-face access to preventive care, health coaching, and disease management improves compliance with treatment regimens. Coupled with evidence-based referrals for secondary and tertiary care, this approach also improves the ability to track value.

Whole Health Management, for example, is an operator of on-site primary care and wellness clinics for major corporations. It provides primary care and preventive services as well as handling worker's compensation cases. Whole Health contracts directly with large self-insured employers in open-book, cost-plus-fee arrangements covering a five- to ten-year period. The contracting structure rewards Whole Health for long-term improvement in health value, including the indirect costs of poor health such as absences and turnover. Studies of value improvement achieved by the approach at an array of large employers, such as Freddie Mac, Discovery Communications, and Nissan North America, are encouraging.[36]

Ultimately, health plans, not employers, should take the lead in providing patient advice; educating subscribers about treatment and provider choices; and enabling disease management, disease prevention, and healthy living. Health plans will enjoy advantages of scale and expertise that employers need not recreate. However, employers need to assist and motivate their employees to actively participate, while challenging health plan administrators to move quickly in these directions.

Employers can also help employees be better purchasers of health plans and save for their future health needs. Employees need help in choosing the kind of health plan structure (e.g., coverage, deductibles) that offers the best value given their needs. Harvard Pilgrim, which we discussed in chapter 6, provides a good example of the role of an employer in helping its employees save money by purchasing only the insurance that they really need. Employers can also build incentives into plans that will help employees and their families save money, such as Sprint Nextel's steep reductions of copayments when members use generic drugs.

An increasing number of employers are offering high-deductible health plans (which hold down premiums) together with a health savings account.[37] HSAs provide for out-of-pocket costs to meet deductibles and encourage savings for future health needs. We believe that all employers should offer HSAs. However, it is important that HSAs not be used as a new tool for cost shifting. Instead, HSAs need to be accompanied by health plans that provide relevant information, provider choice, advice to subscribers, and programs in disease management and risk prevention.

Find Ways to Expand Insurance Coverage and Advocate Reform of the Insurance System. The current insurance system has left numerous individuals without any health insurance, including many who are working. Some employers have opted out of providing health benefits, which shifts costs to employees, to other employers who provide coverage, and often to society when employees need free care or public assistance. Some individuals not covered by their employers, but who could afford insurance, opt out of the system because they are healthy or willing to take the chance that their health care expenditures will remain affordable. If their wager proves wrong, they fall back on public assistance to cover care they cannot afford.

As a first step in improving the insurance system, employers must end the cycle of cost shifting by devising affordable ways to organize and provide coverage for employees who are not now part of the system. The Affordable Health Care Solutions Coalition, a group of sixty employers, has recently taken a first step toward enabling coverage for part-time workers, temporary workers, contractors, and early retirees. They have

banded together to assemble a pool of participants large enough to qualify for lower insurance rates than individuals, and offered these plans to
the affected employees.[38] The companies involved do not subsidize the
plan, but they are willing to enable it because they understand that they
ultimately pay for the uninsured population as hospitals pass on their
costs for nonpaying patients. Every employer that does not offer health
insurance to all employees should be participating in such an effort at the
very least. Such an initiative can significantly improve the coverage of the
insurance system and bring down health plan premiums.

To expand coverage to currently excluded groups, there are other
avenues as well. Employers can devise plans with more limited coverage
or higher deductibles, which can substantially reduce premiums (ways to
design plans that are more affordable are discussed further in chapter 8).
Alternatively, employers can offer to part-time workers a partial contribution toward health coverage in their existing plans (for example, proportional to hours worked), which will bring more workers into the system.

Employers should also have a strong interest in more fundamental
reform of the insurance system. While we will discuss insurance reform in
chapter 8, the bottom line is that there is no efficient and fair solution
except mandatory health insurance for all, with subsidies for those who
are truly needy. Employers must be in the forefront of advocating this
change at the state and national level. If everyone becomes a contributor
of revenue to the system, the cost per person is likely to go down, including the cost borne by employers.

In addition, some mechanism is needed to level the playing field
among employers and limit free riding. Employers that are not providing
health insurance benefits to all employees, and therefore not contributing their fair share to the system, must not gain an artificial advantage
over other companies. We suggest some avenues of reform to resolve this
issue in chapter 8. It is in the interest of the business community to support reasonable rules that level the playing field among employers, which
will also serve to bring down insurance costs for everyone. Without such
changes, less attractive regulatory solutions may ultimately be imposed
that will prove to be far more onerous.

**Measure and Hold Employee Benefit Staff Accountable for the Com-
pany's Health Value Results.** Many employers have delegated the management of health benefits to administrative staff units, normally in the
human resource department. Health care is lumped with other employee
benefit purchases, and decisions are frequently delegated to brokers or
consultants. Companies have traditionally separated the management of
employee health benefits from management of worker's compensation

(typically housed within the safety department in manufacturing companies), even though they are both part of overall health care services. Internal medical departments, where they are present, are often not required to demonstrate their value versus independent providers. In the vast majority of companies, no one in the organization measures or is responsible for health results.

Company personnel managing health benefits often have limited seniority and are far from health care experts. They are rarely oriented toward thinking about the role of health plans in fostering better health and healthy behaviors by employees and dependents, nor are they given this mandate. Despite the huge costs involved, we have found that few corporate CEOs interact directly with the staff responsible for health benefits.

Steeped in the flawed system of today, health benefits staff can unwittingly become part of the problem. Since staffs often work more closely with the health plan than with employees, they can become communicators of health plan constraints rather than advocates for health care quality and value for employees.

The kinds of steps we have outlined for employers will not occur unless the right management team is in place and held accountable for performance. Health value must be the ultimate responsibility of a senior executive in the company. Employers need to develop measures to track health value, using blinded data drawn from their own human resource records together with information from health plans and plan administrators. The confidentiality of individuals can be protected in measuring aggregate results across the employee population.

Improving health care value is different from minimizing short-term benefit costs. Health value can only be measured over rolling multiyear periods. Health outcomes and costs are improved by organizational choices and program investments that will take time to yield results.

Some possible measures of health value are shown in figure 7-5. The question is, how much value is the company receiving in terms of overall health outcomes per dollar expended on health benefits and other health-related expenditures? At the broadest level, employers need to track the aggregate health circumstances of their employees and their families, using measures such as the number of treatments or hospitalizations, lost days, and the extent of disability, controlling for the attributes (e.g., age, health history, severity of chronic conditions) of the employee population. Employee satisfaction with health services should also be surveyed. Health plans and plan administrators should be expected to assist in compiling such information, while strictly preserving the confidentiality of individual records.

FIGURE 7-5

Illustrative measures of health value received

Employee health

- Employee health outcomes, such as extent of illness, number of health care interventions (e.g., office visits, treatments), sick days and lost time, absences, extent of disability, and progression of chronic conditions
- Employee health results per dollar of spending, controlling for employee demographics, health status, and location
- Measures of health results for family members

Health plan performance

- For each health plan, overall employee and family health results per dollar expended
- For each health plan, employee and family health results by medical condition
- For each health plan, results measures compared to external benchmarks

Provider performance by condition

- Comparative results of providers serving employees and their families, by medical condition

At the second level, employers need to track the value delivered by each health plan with which they contract, with a focus on health results. Employers should expect plan administrators to provide health results by medical condition, including success in the management of chronic conditions. Weaknesses in plan performance for a particular medical condition or group of subscribers should be identified and addressed. High-value plans should be rewarded with more attractive cost sharing by the company and more subscribers. New plans should be solicited with expertise in poorly performing geographic regions or in medical conditions where employee health results are disappointing.

The third level of measurement is the performance at the medical condition level of providers that care for employees and their families. Plans should be asked to compile this data. Employers need to know how well the providers that serve their employees stack up relative to peers, including primary care physicians. Employers, in dialogue with their health plans and plan administrators, should expect that excellent providers will be rewarded with more patients.

By making health care a senior management responsibility, and by creating management accountability for health value, employers can transform their approach to health care. In the process, they can speed the transition to value-based competition.

8

Health Care Policy and Value-Based Competition

Implications for Government

GOVERNMENT HAS A MAJOR INFLUENCE on the health care system in the United States, as it does in virtually every country. State and federal policy makers set numerous rules and regulations that affect the nature of competition in health care, as well as incentives and constraints for system participants. Government also participates directly in the system through the operation of Medicare, Medicaid, health plans for government employees, and health care delivery systems for the active armed forces and veterans. Because of the size of government insurance programs, the way they are structured has ripple effects throughout the system. Finally, government has a prominent role in the development of medical technology, notably through the National Institutes of Health and other public R&D programs.

Health care policy has been both a reflection of and a contributor to the zero-sum competition that plagues the system. Government policies have contributed to the cost shifting and flawed incentives that we have described. At the same time, government has attempted to step in and deal with perceived abuses in the system such as restrictive HMO practices, the cancellation of insurance by health plans, and self-dealing by doctors. These well-intended efforts, however, have mostly amounted to treating symptoms rather than deeper, but unaddressed, problems. In most cases, regulatory solutions have created new problems.

The fundamental flaw in U.S. health care policy is its lack of focus on patient value. There has been no overall framework guiding reforms. Instead, policies are piecemeal, reactive, and incremental. And they are rife with unintended consequences. If there is any overarching perspective that has guided public policy, it is government's version of zero-sum competition: drive down the cost of government programs by policing costs, forcing down prices, and shifting costs to the private sector. Medicare, for example, requires lower charges for Medicare patients than private patients in providing the identical services. This cross subsidy in Medicare's favor keeps prices high for non-Medicare patients and deters price reductions that would require corresponding reductions in Medicare charges.[1] The zero-sum mind-set and neglect of patient value as the guidepost of policy also have the unacceptable result of a system with almost 46 million uninsured people, who often receive substandard care (see the box "Health Care for Low-Income Americans").

Health care policy is highly controversial, with strong advocates for widely differing models: a government-controlled national health care system, a single-payer system, a consolidation into integrated health systems combining a health plan with a captive full-line provider network, or a consumer-driven system in which consumers bear personal responsibility for cost. As we have discussed, none of these models is a real solution. A government-run system can allow universal coverage and tight cost control, but will eliminate competition altogether and worsen the problems with the value of care that plague the current system. Government-run health systems in other parts of the world are encountering increasing problems with quality, costs, and rationing.

A single-payer system appeals to those who believe that health plans are the culprits and that controlling the supply of care is the way to rein in costs. However, as we discuss in chapter 6, we believe a single-payer system offers limited real efficiencies and will only increase the payer's bargaining power to shift costs. This is why a number of other advanced countries have moved away from the single-payer approach. For the United States, moving to a single-payer system would not be a solution, but an admission of failure.

Integrated health plan/provider systems are appealing in the current flawed system because they can mitigate zero-sum competition between providers and health plans and control the supply of care at the regional level. As we discuss in chapter 5, however, the price is high: eliminating competition at the provider level, while limiting it among health plans.

Finally, consumer-driven health care is an oversimplification. No matter how much costs and decision making are shifted to consumers, they cannot succeed unless providers and health plans have to compete on results and the right information and advice is available. As we have discussed in chapters 6 and 7, shifting costs to patients will just lead to self-rationing unless the nature of competition changes—and consumers cannot cause competition to change on their own.

Health Care for Low-Income Americans

In today's system, many low-income Americans receive substandard care. How would a move to value-based competition affect the poor? Is a system in which there is competition on results, and where everyone has access to excellent providers, too expensive for low-income citizens?

A shift to value-based competition will unleash major value improvements for everyone, including those with low incomes and those who receive free or subsidized care. Quality will improve across the board, including at providers who care for the poor. Americans should not have to pay more for better quality. Even in the current system, the best providers are often the most efficient. Public programs can and should guide patients to excellent providers, as we discuss in this chapter.

We outline a path to universal, mandatory health coverage for all Americans, including low-income citizens. Universal insurance must be part of any true solution to the problems of substandard care for the poor. However, achieving the goal of universal coverage will be far less expensive in a value-driven system, where competition will free up resources to allow society to provide more services. As insurance coverage widens, primary care and preventive care will also be extended to everyone, yielding major long-term cost savings.

Universal coverage provides a payment mechanism that covers everyone but does not guarantee good-quality care. Changing the structure of health care delivery is fundamental to improving care for the poor. Value-based competition on results will be necessary to ensure that excellent care is received by all patients.

A system of two-class care as a way to contain the cost of wider insurance coverage is not a good solution. When some individuals are deliberately provided a lower standard of care, there will be inescapable incentives to shave costs by paring back services even further. Also, employers and governments will be prone to push more individuals into the low-service group. Thus the problem of zero-sum competition will be exacerbated, and patient value will suffer. The only way to contain the cost of universal coverage is to establish an appropriate minimum standard of care that applies to everyone, and introduce competition on results to transform the value delivered.

Mandatory results measurement is especially important, because it will mean that substandard care for any group, including minorities and those with low incomes, will be glaringly obvious. Poor results in serving any patient will bring down a provider's reported results, creating strong pressures to improve results or lose patients. Results measurement, more than any other policy, is the best way to eliminate substandard care for any group.

In all of these disparate views, however, there is agreement on one thing: the current system is not working. A fresh approach is clearly needed to address a health care system that is consuming a larger and larger share of public, corporate, and individual resources with questionable results.

This chapter outlines an overall framework for health care reform that is centered on value for patients. Unless the value of health care delivered can be increased substantially, Americans will face ever-increasing cost escalation and pressure to ration care as the baby boom generation ages. Unless value can be increased substantially, de facto price controls will become more and more likely, with far-reaching consequences for providers and other system participants. Everyone has a stake in getting reform right.

We believe that the central policy goal of health care reform must be to unleash and enable value-based competition on results.[2] Only through harnessing the power of competition can major improvements in value occur. If competition on results starts working at the right level, it will reverberate throughout the system. There will be no need to predetermine the best way to structure providers or health plans, specify the processes of care that should be used, dictate how IT systems should be designed, or decide which new medical technologies should be adopted. If every actor in the system has to measure and report results and compete for every subscriber or patient, value will rise and innovation will flourish.

Fortunately, government is not the key to health care reform. We believe that health care reform can come, and will come, largely from within. As numerous examples in this book reveal, each participant in the health care system can take steps that will significantly increase patient value without the need for new regulations or new legislation. Yet progress toward value-based competition can be accelerated by changes in public policy. Medicare and Medicaid policy are particularly salient, since together these programs account for about 46 percent of U.S. health care expenditures, and that share will rise as the baby boom generation ages.[3] Medicare, which is engaged in a range of promising experiments embodying value-based competition principles, can be a catalyst for positive change since other system participants often follow its lead.[4] If Medicare falters, state governments are poised to be the innovators.

Public policy affects health care in numerous ways, and the details can be arcane. We offer here not an exhaustive treatment, but a strategic perspective that identifies the range of steps that will foster the right kind of competition in the system. Some of our recommendations fall outside of the current policy dialogue, and others may appear radical. If attention can migrate from cost shifting to patient value, however, these bold steps will seem straightforward.

While our focus is on the United States, the principles of value-based competition can be applied in any country. We conclude this chapter with some implications for health care policy in other nations, and discuss some of the promising developments that are under way internationally.

Broad Issues in Health Care Policy

There are myriad discrete policy areas in health care, ranging from the licensing of physicians and facilities to the Stark laws, and from the way Medicare sets prices to the portability of health insurance. It is easy to get overwhelmed by the sheer complexity of the policy agenda. From a strategic perspective, however, there are three broad areas of health care policy, shown in figure 8-1. (We briefly described these in the book's introduction and in chapter 3.)

First is the set of policies addressing health insurance and access to insurance: who has health insurance, how health plans operate, and how insurance is paid for. Many countries have addressed this issue with a government-run system that provides insurance for all. We believe that everyone must have a health plan, but that there are better ways to achieve universal coverage than a single-payer system, as we shall discuss.

Health insurance draws the majority of policy attention in the United States. As health insurance has become more and more expensive, individuals are being asked to pay more toward their coverage. As the number of uninsured grows, the debate about access and the structure of insurance is taking on ever more urgency. Recently, much attention has been focused on enabling health savings accounts. These are the front-line issues in health policy.

A second broad issue in health care policy is coverage: what services insurers, and society, should be responsible for covering and what services

FIGURE 8-1

Issues in health care reform

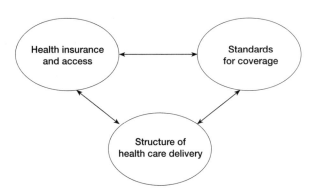

individuals should pay for themselves. This includes difficult issues surrounding the extent of treatment that is justified in terms of its health value (for example, treatment near the end of life), the types of care that should be discretionary (for example, fertility treatment), and the responsibilities of patients in participating in their health and their health care (for example, should subscribers who refuse to participate in health risk screening pay more for their health care?).

What is covered by insurance is a major determinant of the costs of public and private plans. Historically, states have weighed in on this issue through mandating the services that must be covered in private health plans, while Congress plays a big role in what is covered by Medicare. The tendency toward too many mandates has significantly increased the cost of insurance and expanded the number of uninsured.

However, many issues of coverage have been all but undiscussable. Instead of explicit policy attention, this area has tended to be left to politics, individual negotiations between subscribers and health plans, and the courts.[5] Determined patients and their families can appeal and seek coverage for treatments on a case-by-case basis. Coverage differs by state, with more generous reimbursement in some states than others.[6] Some experts assert that the only way to reduce the rate of growth in health care costs is to make tough rationing choices about what is covered. Recently, employers who self-insure (and hence avoid state mandates) have been in the forefront in paring back coverage and expanding subscribers' responsibilities in terms of cost contribution and personal behavior.

The third broad issue in health care policy is the structure of health care delivery itself. It is the delivery of health care that actually creates value for patients, but this area has received less attention until recently because U.S. health care was assumed to be uniformly good. The result was more and more public and private money poured into health care with little attention to the value delivered.

The policy attention directed at health care delivery has been dominated by how to reduce cost—for example, requiring Certificates of Need for new facilities, preventing self-referral to doctor-owned facilities, ensuring the lowest prices for Medicare, buying drugs from Canada. More recently, attention has been focused on the importance of information technology and pay-for-performance initiatives to reduce errors and improve quality. These are welcome steps, but their focus is still largely on attempting to control the supply of care and bargain down prices, rather than on enabling competition in terms of value.

All three policy areas are clearly interdependent. Access to insurance and the extent of coverage clearly affect the effectiveness and cost of health care delivery. For example, access to primary care significantly affects costs and outcomes.[7]

All three areas—insurance and access, coverage, and the structure of health care delivery—are important. However, we believe that the structure of health care delivery is the most fundamental. Delivering value for patients (in terms of health outcomes per dollar expended) is the central purpose of the health care system in the first place. The value delivered will determine the cost of insurance, and what can be covered. Improving the value delivered, not just shifting costs, must be the central focus of health policy instead of an afterthought.

In the pages that follow, we outline an overall policy agenda that addresses each of the three areas and would radically transform the nature of competition in the system. It is simply not feasible here to discuss every aspect of health care policy in detail. However, the central principle that should guide decisions in every policy area is clear: unleash, enable, and reinforce competition on results to improve the value of the health care delivered to patients.

Moving to Value-Based Competition: Improving Health Insurance and Access

There is simply no way to truly reform health care without moving to a system in which everyone is covered by health insurance. Universal coverage, together with value-based competition, will also produce dramatic improvements in efficiency and effectiveness of health care delivery. Achieving universal coverage will require a series of steps, including some changes in insurance rules and regulations.

As we have discussed, we believe that a system of competing health plans is far more likely than a single-payer system to improve the value delivered to subscribers. However, the rules governing the operation of health plans need to be modified. Employer self-insured plans, which represent a large share of subscribers, are not currently subject to state regulation. Some of the regulatory modifications we advocate should apply to both types of plans because they will contribute to value-based competition while deterring employers from unfairly imposing health care costs on others.

Finally, improving health insurance will require shifts in the roles of Medicare and Medicaid as insurance providers. Figure 8-2 summarizes the important steps in improving health insurance and access.

Enact Mandatory Health Coverage

Both fairness and value require that health coverage be mandatory for all individuals. (As we will discuss in later sections, subsidies will be needed for lower-income individuals and families.) In health care, where an individual can impose costs on society, the need for mandatory insurance is

FIGURE 8-2

Imperatives for policy makers: Improving health insurance and access

Enact mandatory health coverage

Provide subsidies or vouchers for low-income individuals and families

Create risk pools for high-risk individuals

Enable affordable insurance plans

Minimize distortions from uneven employer contributions

Eliminate unproductive insurance rules and billing practices
- Ban re-underwriting
- Clarify legal responsibility for medical bills
- Eliminate balance billing

---

common sense. Everyone who wants to drive an automobile, for example, is required to have insurance so that they will not inflict costs on other citizens if they have an accident. Making insurance mandatory also means that all individuals pay their share of the costs of the insurance system every year, not just the year that they think they might have an accident. If everyone pays their share every year, this lowers the average annual cost of insurance for everyone.

Health insurance involves the same principles; if anything, the rationale for mandatory health coverage is stronger. While individuals can choose not to drive, they cannot choose not to need health care. The cost of treating an illness or injury can be huge, and can continue for years or even decades. Hence the cost that an uninsured person can impose on others is substantial.

People think of the uninsured as low-income individuals. Yet mandatory health coverage will bring many individuals into the system who today choose not to buy coverage. In Massachusetts, for example, an estimated 168,000 people without health insurance (37 percent of the state's uninsured) have annual incomes over $56,000.[8] These individuals who can afford insurance (or who can afford to pay at least part of its cost) opt out and take the chance that they will not need care. When they are injured or become ill, they seek care and are charged list prices (which are often twice those charged to patients with health plan coverage). In many cases, the resulting bills are beyond their means to pay. Inability to pay medical bills is a leading cause of bankruptcy in the United States. When uninsured patients cannot afford to pay, the cost of their treatment is borne by those who are insured, either in the form of higher health plan premiums, free care pools paid for by the private sector, or public subsidies financed by taxes.

Insurance depends on everyone paying premiums every year to hold down the cost per person. Even if uninsured individuals remain healthy, then, they deprive the insurance system of revenues. If those who opt out join the system later on, they will not have contributed their fair share of the costs that they are likely to impose on the system. Mandatory coverage would end this cost shifting and free riding by people who can afford (or afford to contribute to) insurance but prefer to take the risk and go without it because they are young, currently healthy, or have other financial priorities.

There is another important reason why mandatory health coverage makes sense: it leads to a far more efficient and effective system. In a way, America already has a form of universal care because hospitals and doctors are obligated to treat all patients when they present themselves for urgent or emergency care.[9] However, this form of universal care is arguably the worst kind of universal care imaginable.

In the United States, the uninsured tend to obtain urgent care in very expensive emergency settings. They present themselves for treatment of serious diseases at later stages that are more difficult and more expensive to treat. They lack continuity of care, and experience a truncated care cycle, with no access to cost-effective preventive care or long-term disease management. Empirical research indicates that universal access to primary care is a major driver of health value, and the lack of it is an important explanation for America's lagging infant mortality statistics and other poor aggregate health outcomes versus other countries.[10] Racial disparities in care, related to lack of insurance coverage, also have a big effect on America's lagging overall health outcomes.[11] For all these reasons, the current form of safety net care in the United States is expensive, inefficient, and often ineffective.

Everyone should be required to have some form of health coverage for life. This not only makes economic sense, but also makes sense for reasons of compassion and fairness. The only fair way to provide access for all is to make health coverage mandatory for everyone, with subsidies for those who need them so that everyone becomes a paying customer and contributes what they can to the costs of the system. It is important to enact mandatory coverage at the same time as providing more subsidies. Otherwise, the subsidies will only encourage more individuals to drop private coverage.

The preferred policy would be to institute mandatory coverage nationally. This would minimize incentives to relocate or shift jobs because of state-to-state differences. However, states may well have to take the lead in moving to mandatory coverage, and there are promising state-level initiatives already under way.

Provide Subsidies or Vouchers for Low-Income Individuals and Families

Moving to mandatory health coverage will require subsidies for those who cannot afford it. Subsidies should be based on a sliding scale where individuals pay what they can, rather than an all-or-nothing model. Ideally, everyone would pay something toward his or her health care.

There are a variety of ways to provide subsidies. The most elegant solution would be vouchers based on income that enable individuals to buy into a plan. This turns everyone into a paying customer, with the same access. It will also minimize some of the unfair cross subsidies in the current system, such as the charging of list prices to the uninsured. More affordable health plans will need to be established to make this approach feasible, as we will discuss.

An alternative proposed by some experts is to enroll automatically everyone without another health plan in a state Medicaid program or Children's Health Insurance Program, with premiums adjusted for income.[12] This approach has the advantage of making everyone eligible for Medicaid, which would enhance continuity of care and potentially reduce administrative costs. Subsidies would be provided to reduce or eliminate the premiums for low-income families.

Moving to mandatory coverage will certainly involve new costs to cover subsidies, but there will be some major offsetting revenues and savings. People who are currently uninsured but can afford insurance would contribute new revenue to the system. Employer cost shifting and termination of coverage altogether may well decline significantly, generating more revenue and extending coverage to more individuals. More revenue will work to moderate premiums on a per person basis, reducing the size of needed subsidies. Cost sharing by those with modest incomes would offset some of the subsidy.

In addition, the expense of treating those now without health coverage is already largely borne by the system through pro bono services and uncompensated care that providers recoup by raising average prices. With required health coverage, everyone becomes a paying customer, so the huge cost of free care would be eliminated, and providers would no longer have to raise their prices to cover it.[13] With lower premiums, the cost of subsidies goes down.

Providing full access to primary care will reduce some of the cost of free care already borne. Preventive care, risk screening, earlier diagnosis, disease management, and continuity of care should produce major savings compared to the free care model.[14] The Agency for Healthcare Research and Quality, for example, estimates that provision of primary care would save $26.5 billion per year in preventable hospitalizations.[15]

Subsidies would also be reduced by eliminating costly practices such as cost shifting and patient dumping, which mandatory, universal coverage would eliminate. Finally, subsidies could also be reduced by allowing higher health plan premiums for individuals who do not accept responsibility for their health. For example, premiums could be higher for smokers, now permissible in only some states. Higher premiums could be allowed for those who fail to participate in health screening and prevention programs, or who fail to participate in disease management programs after a confirmed diagnosis of a chronic disease. Such rules, if implemented broadly, will bring in new revenue in the short run and bring down the cost of health care in the long run.

The move to mandatory coverage should also be accompanied by tightened rules that prevent individuals from transferring assets or income to heirs or relatives to avoid paying for their own health care. This practice has been particularly common in avoiding the responsibility to pay for nursing home care, and shifting the costs to the government and taxpayers. Every individual should have the responsibility to save to pay for his or her own health care. Public assistance should be provided only to the truly needy. This glaring loophole needs to be closed, ideally on a national basis.

Mandatory health coverage would greatly expand the commercial market for both providers and health plans. Therefore, moving to mandatory coverage should be accompanied by a significant across-the-board reduction in health plan premiums. The shift to mandatory coverage can also be made contingent on enactment of other policy changes we describe in this chapter affecting health plans and providers. (Note that even if mandatory coverage is not instituted immediately, other steps we describe, such as risk pools and changes in coverage mandates, should still be implemented because they will ease the move to mandatory coverage.)

Create Risk Pools for High-Risk Individuals

An important step in the move to mandatory coverage is the creation of mechanisms to make it possible for high-risk or ill individuals who are not already covered to buy insurance at reasonable cost. This is especially important for those not working for large employers. A system of assigned risk pools, probably aggregated at the state level, would address this need. High-risk individuals (or their costs) need to be spread proportionally among all health plans to remove the incentive to avoid or disenroll them. Although some states now have a subsidized insurance plan of last resort for all high-risk individuals who are refused insurance, this is not a sufficient solution.[16]

The inherent nature of health insurance is that a modest percentage of patients accounts for a large percentage of costs during any given time period. Every health plan (including self-insured plans) should have to serve its fair share of patients with expensive diseases or conditions, or pay into a fund to cover their costs. Otherwise, there will be strong incentives for health plans to find ways to avoid, disenroll, or deny coverage to unlucky subscribers who become ill. With a pool requirement, health plans will have no such incentive because pushing out one high-risk subscriber will just lead to the acquisition of another expensive subscriber from the pool. The advent of pools would end re-underwriting (discussed later in this chapter), because the same rates would apply to all pool members. Risk pools are not a new invention, and are already used in auto insurance.[17]

Enable Affordable Insurance Plans

The cost of mandatory health coverage can be moderated if health plans are required to cover only essential services. The coverage required in health plans varies by state. In many states, the setting of mandates has become problematic. Mandates add incremental requirements in response to the desires of particular interest groups, each of which seems reasonable. As layers are added on, however, the required coverage becomes greater than is reasonable or necessary in a basic plan. This raises the cost of insurance for everyone, and makes it far more costly to provide coverage for everyone. Self-insured employers can offer leaner benefits packages, so that mandates fall disproportionately on individuals, smaller businesses, and state government programs.

Health plans also become more affordable when they move from first dollar coverage to coverage for major and catastrophic care. This shift can be accomplished through plans with deductibles up to a cap. Deductibles are more efficient than copayments, which involve higher administrative costs.

Plan structures involving relatively high deductibles coupled with a health savings account (HSA) allow lower premiums while encouraging individuals to save for their own health care. Such structures have the added benefit of encouraging subscribers to consider value in their health care decisions. Congress made HSAs widely available in 2004. (Chapter 3 discusses the benefits and risks of HSAs.)

As we have discussed, however, moving to high deductibles and HSAs without also introducing information, choice, and competition at the provider and treatment level becomes just another form of cost shifting. Patient choices to obtain less care due to cost sharing are often not value-based decisions.[18] Also, to the extent that high deductibles and HSAs discourage primary care, risk prevention, and disease management, they will also erode value for patients.

Finally, health plans can be made more affordable if individuals and small businesses without access to a large group plan can buy into a group to gain the benefits of lower premiums. One alternative would be to allow individuals to purchase policies through the Federal Employees Health Benefits Program (or a similar federal group option) at the federal group rates.[19] Or, states could allow individuals to join the plan for state employees. Another approach would be for states to create a statewide group that any individual could join. Health plans would compete to offer plans to this group, and subscribers could select from among the available plans. The state group would not be the repository for high-risk patients, because every health plan and every self-insured plan would be required to cover its share of the most expensive and most risky subscribers through a risk pool system, as we discussed earlier.

Over time, as risk pools and other nonexclusive groups are expanded, the need for employer-sponsored group plans could, in principle, be phased out altogether. Employers could choose to provide a cash amount for health benefits indexed to inflation, allowing individuals to buy their own plan. Also, the current problem of differential prices based on the size of the group would be mitigated if everyone had access to a large group.

Minimize Distortions from Uneven Employer Contributions

The costs of mandatory coverage will be reduced by minimizing the distortions created by the uneven contribution of employers to employee health benefits, particularly for part-time employees and employees of small businesses. As we discussed in chapter 7, some employers free ride by not offering health benefits at all or not offering them to part-time workers. Individuals not covered by their employer may then require free care or public assistance, another form of cost shifting. Employers that avoid health insurance gain an artificial advantage unconnected to their true quality or efficiency, distorting competition.

We recommended in chapter 7 that employers that do not provide health benefits should, at minimum, be subject to a number of requirements. First, they should be required to disclose the cost of forgone health benefits so that their compensation levels can be readily compared with those of other employers. Second, employers who do not provide insurance should pay higher state and federal Medicare and Medicaid tax rates on their wages to cover the public expense of treating uninsured employees.

Third, the United States needs to move in the long run to a system where there is tax neutrality between employer-purchased and individual-

Implementing Universal Coverage: The Case of Massachusetts

The Massachusetts governor has proposed a plan to dramatically expand coverage and ultimately make health coverage universal and mandatory. While there are a number of variations being debated in the state legislature, the governor's plan illustrates the types of steps required in moving from the current system. The first step in the governor's plan is to enroll everyone who is eligible in Medicaid at the time they present themselves for care. The state has approximately 100,000 individuals (22 percent of uninsured) who are eligible for Medicaid but are not enrolled.[20] Other states have found that enrolling individuals as they seek care brings more people into the Medicaid system.[21]

A second component of the Massachusetts plan is to establish a basic health plan with coverage that is less extensive, and therefore less expensive, than the minimum insurance plan currently available. This basic plan will provide an insurance option that is more affordable to more families.

Insurers estimate that paring back mandated coverage will allow health plans for individuals at a price of $140 per month instead of the current minimum of $500 per month. Modifying the minimum coverage list for all citizens of the state would be desirable, but a basic plan designed for those who are not now covered is seen as more practical in the near term. The design of the new minimum coverage list will be important both for reasons of value and equity. It is important that the basic plan covers primary care and risk

purchased plans. If an employer does not use the tax deduction by providing health benefits to an employee, the employee should get the deduction.

A number of states are moving in the direction of universal and mandatory coverage. The example of Massachusetts is described in the box "Implementing Universal Coverage: The Case of Massachusetts."

Eliminate Unproductive Insurance Rules and Billing Practices

To encourage competition on value rather than cost shifting, a number of unproductive insurance rules and billing practices should be eliminated. Doing so will benefit the system as a whole and aid in moving to coverage that is mandatory and universal.

Ban Re-underwriting. Health plans are already prohibited from simply dropping coverage of patients who develop expensive medical conditions. However, the practice of re-underwriting, or raising the premiums management, not just acute care. The design of the coverage list is also crucial because subscribers will remain uninsured for any condition not covered.

Third, together with instituting a basic plan, Massachusetts seeks to make health insurance mandatory, with serious penalties to ensure compliance. Massachusetts currently has 100,000 people in households with incomes over $75,000 who do not buy health coverage, and an additional 68,000 people with family incomes over $56,000.[22]

A fourth element of the Massachusetts approach is a safety-net care network for low-income residents who do not qualify for Medicaid, which includes screening for diseases that can be prevented or mitigated with early detection and appropriate response, and preventive care. In the current administration's proposal, provider choices would be tightly restricted for those whose insurance is being paid for by the state. We are highly skeptical of such network restrictions, as we have discussed. While it is theoretically possible to manage networks around value for patients, the overwhelming temptation for the administrators is to focus on short-term costs and withholding of services. As appealing as it is to reformers, administrative oversight of care delivery has failed again and again. A far better model is to measure results and assist subscribers in accessing excellent care.

Finally, Massachusetts is debating various ways to ensure that employers that do not provide health coverage contribute to the cost of dealing with the uninsured, such as through higher Medicaid payments. This will help to minimize the distortions from uneven employer contributions.

of individuals who become ill, should also be banned. Re-underwriting is already illegal in some states, such as Massachusetts. It is particularly harmful to individuals who purchase their own insurance or are members of small groups.[23] It is a pernicious practice that is unfair and inconsistent with the very purpose of insurance. It also distracts health plans from their real job—delivering value and assisting patients in obtaining excellent care. New regulations should require that any increase in health plan premiums must apply to all subscribers or to a large class of subscribers, not to isolated individuals.

Clarify Legal Responsibility for Medical Bills. Today, the ultimate responsibility for medical bills rests with subscribers, even if they have health insurance in good standing. Instead, health plans should assume full legal responsibility for the medical bills of paid-up subscribers, except in cases of fraud, designated breaches of important plan conditions, or deductibles and copayments. Closing this loophole would deter plans from trying to shift costs to patients. It would motivate plans to simplify bills and administrative processes that now sometimes result in de facto cost shifting. Finally, giving plans legal responsibility would also deter attempts to shift costs by denying payment to providers for legitimate care and thereby forcing providers to seek payment from patients. Much of the gaming and delays over billing in the current system could be eliminated.

Eliminate Balance Billing. Balance billing, in which providers charge patients the difference between what the health plan chooses to reimburse and what the provider chooses to charge, should also be eliminated. Balance billing distracts from value by allowing some health plans to pass on costs to patients rather than help patients secure good value. For providers, balance billing is a vehicle for raising charges through stealth rather than transparent pricing. Balance billing also creates much patient confusion and unnecessary administrative costs.

All billing of patients for covered services should be eliminated, except for agreed-upon deductibles and copayments. Balance-billing restrictions should apply both to fully insured and self-insured plans. Assigning the legal responsibility for bills to health plans will also contribute to reducing balance billing.

Although balance billing is illegal for HMOs, it still occurs. Health plans have policies against balance billing, but these policies are not always enforced. Providers may hope that some patients will just pay the bill rather than question it. If the only enforcement mechanism is to discontinue a provider's contract, the health plan may overlook the practice. Finally, though officially prohibiting the practice, some health plans may ignore it because it may lead to bigger discounts.

Health plans should take more aggressive steps to enforce rules against balance billing. Some states, such as Ohio, have established hotlines to make it easier for Medicare patients to report its occurrence.

Moving to Value-Based Competition: Setting Standards for Coverage

Most Americans would probably agree that health insurance should pay only for health care that is necessary, not discretionary, and that meaningfully improves quality of life and life expectancy.[24] However, what is necessary versus what is discretionary is debatable. Also, many Americans still believe that everything possible should be tried even when prolonging life offers no prospect of recovery or quality of life. Health care that affects matters of choice rather than personal health, such as fertility treatment, is also a gray area. Even the responsibility for health care that affects only recreation (one's tennis game, for instance) can engender debate. Unfortunately, then, the specifics of what should be covered, and the extent of personal responsibility for health care, quickly become complicated.

The United States (and each state) needs a better process for deciding these questions that ideally establishes a common minimum standard applicable to everyone. Today, the question of what is covered is determined by state mandates, plan-by-plan coverages, and countless individual negotiations and lawsuits. The process is mostly legal, political, and adversarial rather than based on dispassionate medical judgments. The current process also encourages gaming of coverage by system participants, diverting attention from improving patient value. In some of the most important areas of coverage, such as end-of-life care, the issue is virtually undiscussable as a policy matter. Money spent fighting over what is covered drives up costs, with little or no health value benefit. The discussion takes place largely case by case and state by state, creating inequities and incentives for employers to move jobs to states with fewer mandates. A better process of defining minimum coverage is clearly needed. Ideally, a binding national standard for minimum required coverage should be established (figure 8-3). If the federal government is slow to move, a consortium of states can take the lead.

A minimum standard for coverage should include primary care and preventive care in addition to essential acute coverage. Discretionary services and nice-to-have mandates must be avoided to allow a basic affordable plan to be available in every state. The minimum required coverage needs to be reviewed periodically to ensure that new types of high-value care are added and ineffective or obsolete care is no longer covered.

Standards for coverage need to be based on demonstrated results and evidence on patient preferences, rather than on the assumption that

---

FIGURE 8-3

Imperatives for policy makers: Setting standards for coverage

Establish a national standard for minimum required coverage

- Include primary care, preventive care, and essential coverage
- Review minimum coverage standards periodically to update for evolving types of care
- Use Federal Employee Health Benefits as an initial standard

Consider medical outcomes and patient preferences in covering end-of-life care

- Require a medical power of attorney and living will as a condition of health coverage

Introduce individual accountability for participation in health care

everything possible should be done. Studies demonstrate that much of the expensive care that takes place at the end of life does not improve outcomes, nor does it meet the needs of patients and families.[25] Indeed, many patients and families do not desire heroic care. Physicians may be unaware of this evidence or ignore it because they believe they are providing the best-possible care. Or, physicians may provide care that is unnecessarily invasive to prevent lawsuits, or because treating may be easier than helping patients and their families make well-informed decisions consistent with their own values and medical evidence.

To establish standards for minimum coverage, a respected expert body must act on behalf of all Americans. The Institute of Medicine (IOM), an independent advisory group that is part of the National Academy of Sciences, has undertaken a study on this issue. The IOM cannot set a binding standard, however, so government action will be needed to implement the IOM's recommendations. Until such a national standard is agreed upon, the coverage included in the Federal Employees Health Benefit Plan, which applies to members of Congress, could serve as the interim national minimum list. We are confident that an open process by a respected body would gain the support of most Americans, who will have the good sense to understand that some care is appropriate for coverage while some care should be their own responsibility.

Once a minimum standard is established, health plans could choose to exceed the minimum coverages, but only voluntarily. Plans could offer coverage beyond the minimum levels at higher prices, with much higher deductibles, or both. Alternatively, noncovered, discretionary services could be covered by supplementary insurance. Individuals would be responsible for saving to pay for noncovered services, with strict rules to limit improper subsidies and other public assistance due to inappropriate asset transfers to relatives or other means.

There are two main arguments against minimum required coverage. First, if the standard is too high, health insurance is too expensive. This issue must be addressed head-on through thoughtful standards together with encouragement for higher deductible policies. Second, a national standard for minimum coverage could make it more expensive, or even impossible, for some people to obtain insurance because of their medical history or risk in a newly covered area. This is one of the reasons why mandatory health coverage is needed, and why assigned risk pools are necessary to ensure that all health plans cover their fair share of the most expensive patients.[26]

As part of the move to a standard for minimum coverage, government should also enact a requirement that each health plan member provide a medical power of attorney or living will to record individual preferences for desired treatment. Such a statement should become a condition of insurance.

This will avoid care that is inconsistent with the patient's own preferences, which will lower the system's cost while improving value for the patient.

A final issue in the area of standards for coverage is the extent of personal responsibility to participate in healthy living practices and comply with treatment. Currently, the implicit standard is that there is little or no personal responsibility. Unhealthy practices such as smoking, poor diet, and others do not affect most health insurance. It is illegal to reflect these conditions in insurance premiums in many states. Compliance with treatment or disease management programs is discretionary. Risk screening and health monitoring are voluntary. Coverage and the cost of coverage, then, is unaffected by whether individuals participate in practices that will greatly improve their health and substantially improve the value of their health care.

This approach is no longer acceptable, or sensible. America cannot afford to take on the obligation of coverage for all unless all Americans take on some obligations concerning their health. New regulations are needed that clarify a reasonable set of obligations for subscribers regarding their health care, and allow consequences in terms of plan premiums or benefits. It will be important to be sensitive to the addictive or physiological nature of some unhealthy practices, and the difficulty of modifying behavior. However, America can no longer afford a laissez faire approach, especially when so much evidence now highlights the importance of prevention and disease management in an individual's health. The benefits to health care value of making individuals more accountable will be enormous.

Among employer self-insured health plans, a movement is beginning in which employees and sometimes their families are being asked to meet higher expectations. Individuals are being offered more screening, preventive, and disease management services. Members who fail to participate in screening for unhealthy practices or programs to mitigate their medical condition are bearing some consequences, usually in the form of higher health plan premiums. This greater individual accountability should spread to all health plans, including public plans.

Moving to Value-Based Competition:
Improving the Structure of Health Care Delivery

While expanding insurance and clarifying coverage are essential steps, we believe that the greatest leverage in health care reform lies in transforming the structure of health care delivery. The goal of public policy should be to enable value-based competition on results at the medical condition level. Government's role lies in several areas (figure 8-4). Its single most important role lies in the area of ensuring that results information is universally available.

FIGURE 8-4

Imperatives for policy makers: Improving the structure of health care delivery

Enable universal results information

- Establish a process for defining outcome measures
- Enact mandatory results reporting
- Establish information collection and dissemination infrastructure

Improve pricing practices

- Establish episode and care-cycle pricing
- Set limits on price discrimination

Open up competition at the right level

- Reduce artificial barriers to practice area integration
- Require a value justification for captive referrals or treatment involving an economic interest
- Eliminate artificial restrictions to new entry
- Institute results-based license renewal
- Strictly enforce antitrust policies
- Curtail anticompetitive buying-group practices
- Eliminate barriers to competition across geography

Establish standards and rules that enable information technology and information sharing

- Develop standards for interoperability of hardware and software
- Develop standards for medical data
- Enhance identification and security procedures
- Provide incentives for adoption of information technology

Reform the malpractice system

Redesign Medicare policies and practices

- Make Medicare a health plan, not a payer or a regulator
- Modify counterproductive pricing practices
- Improve Medicare pay for performance
- Lead the move to bundled pricing models
- Require results-based referrals
- Allow providers to set prices

Align Medicaid with Medicare

Invest in medical and clinical research

Government also has key roles in opening up competition, improving pricing practices, encouraging the penetration of information technology, improving the structure of publicly managed health plans (especially Medicare and Medicaid), and continuing to support medical research, with a greater emphasis on research in the area of clinical outcomes.

What follows is a strategic road map for government policy, not an exhaustive treatment of each policy topic. For every aspect of health care policy, including areas not discussed here, the same core principles apply. Government's role is to create an environment that requires and enables competition based on patient value.

Enable Universal Results Information

Perhaps the most fundamental role of government in enabling value-based competition is to ensure that universal, high-quality information on provider outcomes and prices for every medical condition is collected and disseminated. This single step will have far-reaching and pervasive effects throughout the system, as we have described. A role for government does not mean that government itself should develop the measures, or take on collection and dissemination. Instead, the role of government is to ensure that these activities take place at a high level of quality and integrity, as it has in areas such as transplants and dialysis (see the box "How Good Outcome Information Arose" in chapter 4). Also, a role for government in information does not mean that the government should set prices based on this information, or try to mandate pay for performance. In fact, the clearer it is that this is not the intent, the easier it will be to start collecting and disseminating the critical information. The current approach to information collection and reporting—which relies on numerous, overlapping, and largely voluntary efforts—is too slow and will not deliver the quality and universality of information necessary.[27] The foot-dragging by providers and medical bodies that has characterized past measurement efforts is no longer tolerable. Results information is so vital to patient value in health care that it must be mandated. We advocate a systemwide government information strategy, not just one focused on Medicare.

The information hierarchy, which we introduced in chapter 4, sets forth the types of information needed to support value-based competition: results (outcomes, costs, and prices), experience, methods, and patient attributes (see figure 4-5). As we discussed in chapter 4, stopping at measuring process compliance is not sufficient. By far the most important information for value-based competition is information on outcomes, adjusted for patient attributes and prices. Experience information, ideally by types of patients served, is also extremely valuable in connecting patients with providers. Since experience information is less controversial, its collection can move faster than full-blown outcome measurement. Information on methods is also surely valuable, but such information collection should be left primarily to internal provider, health plan, and other efforts in the private sector. Government should not get into the game of trying to measure or specify process improvement.

For results information, the relevant level is medical conditions, not hospitals or overall physician practices. Ideally, information should be measured at each care location. Data for individual physicians or other skilled personnel (e.g., rehabilitation therapists) at a given location is essential for internal management. Professionals in a shared practice or shared care cycle should know each other's results for accountability and improvement, but public reporting may be unnecessarily controversial and less valuable. When outcome information is available by condition and by care location, teams will have strong incentives to work together to improve the results of individuals. The complexities and volatility inherent in public reporting of individual data are avoided (except in solo practices).

Public reporting should not aim to cover every conceivable outcome measure or patient control attribute. Instead, the aim should be a set of measures and risk adjustments that capture the most important dimensions. Most providers should collect and analyze far more detailed results (and methods) information for their own internal purposes than will be publicly reported, because this is part of the process of learning and practice improvement. The same is true for health plans. Also, every patient will ultimately need an accurate, secure, comprehensive personal medical record that government will never see.

The numerous information initiatives already under way have laid important groundwork, but a more forceful role for government is necessary. Measures that are standard across providers and geographies are required. Every provider must be required to disclose results in an accurate and timely manner. Value-based competition will benefit the most if information collection and dissemination is standardized nationally. However, states or consortia of states can take the lead if the federal government is slow to move.

It is telling that federal or state legislation has played a decisive role in many of the instances where comprehensive outcome information is currently available (see the box "How Good Outcome Information Arose" in chapter 4). These initiatives grew out of scandals, alarm over deaths, or high costs. The United States needs to build a system in which the collection and reporting of results information for all providers is not exceptional, but assumed.

Past experiences in comprehensive outcome reporting are also revealing in terms of approach and methods. In organ transplants, an independent, not-for-profit organization was tasked with collection and reporting. Here, progress has been faster than in dialysis, where responsibility remained within government agencies. In cardiac surgery, state governments initiated their own public reporting, but their initiative spurred the Society of Thoracic Surgeons (STS) to push the state of the art much further. (STS outcome data, however, is not shared publicly.) This illustrates the important role that medical societies can play in the outcome measurement process. Finally, in each of these cases where government initiative led to outcome information, results for patients have improved significantly.

Government is already involved in a variety of broader measurement initiatives, but the effort must expand to an entirely new level. Within the Department of Health and Human Services, the Agency for Healthcare Research and Quality (AHRQ) has undertaken a number of useful projects in developing quality measures and clinical information.[28] To date, however, the scope and the dissemination of these efforts remain far too limited.[29]

The Centers for Medicare and Medicaid Services (CMS) also already collects a significant amount of outcome information. In addition to transplant and dialysis information, CMS collects and publishes information on nursing homes and home health agencies. It also requires hospitals to file cost reports in order to obtain Medicare reimbursement.[30] Sophisticated users can analyze these reports to glean comparative information not only on costs but also on complications and some risk-adjusted outcomes by hospital department. However, the data do not allow analysis of the full cycle of care, which includes activities before and after hospital episodes, nor can the data isolate the performance of individual locations.

Medicare has some other measurement initiatives under way. For example, it launched Hospital Compare, a Web-based database that compares hospitals on seventeen process compliance measures for treatment of conditions such as heart attack, heart failure, and pneumonia. However, none of these other initiatives are focused on results. Nor is their scope nearly comprehensive enough. Medicare should actively participate in a systemwide process of results measurement, not one focused solely on Medicare patients.

In 1998, the Presidential Commission on Consumer Protection and Quality in the Health Care Industry suggested that organizations be set up to develop and widely disseminate quality measures, a sign of growing awareness of the issue.[31,32] Yet, only one organization to develop measures was actually established: the National Quality Foundation (NQF), which was formalized in 1999. NQF is an independent, not-for-profit public-private membership organization, and it has undertaken some valuable programs, largely in the area of process measures. However, the structure of NQF and its requirement of consensus have limited its effectiveness in developing outcome measures.

At the state level, twenty-two states have adopted all-payer reporting, in which hospitals (and in some cases ambulatory surgery facilities and emergency departments) are required to file cost reports for all patients, not just Medicare patients. These state-level initiatives are a good beginning, but the data collected is still far from true results reporting. It is also not compiled and presented in a transparent way to system participants. A number of insurers, such as Harvard Pilgrim and CIGNA, analyze the all-payer data and make the analysis available to their members. The data, however, fall well short of what is needed.

An immediate priority for each state public health or insurance department is to compile and disseminate the state-level data that are already available. Data need to be presented in a useful and accessible way for assessing results, and made more available to health plans, providers, and the public.[33] Also, state-level reporting requirements should be expanded to include outpatient care.

Another practical interim step to improve the availability of results information would be a federal policy requiring all-payer reporting in all states. This would enable national comparisons and lay a foundation for further improvement in outcome measurement.

Ultimately, however, national standards for results measurement and mandatory reporting are needed across all medical conditions. Outcomes for every provider by medical condition, combined with improved cost reports, are needed to maximize the rate of value improvement.

A government role in overseeing the development of results reporting should not, and will not, supplant private-sector initiative. As value-based competition on results takes hold, private organizations will go well beyond the minimum reporting standards. Providers will develop and use additional outcome methods and patient attribute data for internal management purposes. As with SEC filings, providers, health plans, employers, and independent information companies will analyze the mandated information in whatever ways they find useful and collect additional information. The goal of public policy is not to limit the information collected or slow down innovation in measurement, but to ensure that a minimum set of accurate, timely, consistent, and useful results information is collected and made available.

Establish a Process for Defining Outcome Measures. Government should establish and oversee a process of defining and ratifying a minimum set of outcome measures for each medical condition. Consensus on outcome measures is harder to achieve than on process measures, and this is why voluntary, consensus-based organizations such as NQF have moved so slowly. Yet, there is no need to wait. As we discussed in chapter 4, validated outcome measures and risk adjustment models have existed in complex medical conditions for over two decades. The slow acceptance of outcome measurement has been due more to provider discomfort and apathy about the importance of results measurement than to substantive issues.[34]

There is no more time to waste. The federal government, or a consortium of states if progress is slow at the federal level, should charge a series of medical societies and/or independent organizations (following the model of U.N.O.S. for organ transplants) to lead a process of defining a minimum set of outcome measures to be reported in each medical condition. Where multiple medical societies are relevant to a medical condition, they should be expected to collaborate or provide input to an independent organization. (See the following box, "Implications for Medical Societies," for a discussion of the broader implications of value-based competition for medical societies.) If there is no appropriate society, an expert panel can be convened. The organization charged with developing measures needs to maintain the perspective of improving patient value rather than representing the interests of providers or individual physicians. While expert input is critical, the goal is not consensus per se, but a set of measures with scientific integrity.

The development of outcome measures should have a fixed deadline. If the deadline for a medical condition is not met, government should contract with different independent experts or organizations to define the measures to be reported.

The initial focus should be on a core set of outcome measures for each significant medical condition. Outcomes are multidimensional, so every condition will have and should have multiple measures. Measures also will be needed for diagnosis and, eventually, for preventive care and long-term disease management. The process of developing measures will be less controversial if it is clear that results measures are multidimensional, and that they are designed to support competition and innovation rather than to set pay-for-performance prices.

Whenever possible, reported measures should include risk adjustment. However, the inability to perfect risk adjustment algorithms should not delay the beginning of public results reporting. As the cardiac surgery field has demonstrated, public reporting speeds the development of improved measures as well as improved risk adjustment models.

The process of defining the outcome measures and risk adjustment algorithms should be open and subject to public and professional comment. (Note that providers that have moved early to measure themselves will be in a position to influence the direction that public reporting takes.) The initial tranche of measures will inevitably be improved and expanded upon. The process should provide explicitly for improvement and extension of measurement on a regular basis. There is no better way to spur improvement in information than to get started in disseminating it.

A public or quasi-public entity, along the lines of the Bureau of Labor Statistics (BLS), may be needed to oversee the process. Existing organiza-

Implications for Medical Societies

Medical societies have important roles to play in enabling value-based competition in health care delivery, but few societies have yet taken up leadership. Societies are well equipped to drive results measurement, benchmarking, and process improvement. However, most societies will need to modify their traditional roles and boundaries in order to play these roles effectively. In particular, societies must shift from reinforcing silos around traditional specialties to supporting the focus on patient value in medical conditions and over the care cycle.

Developing Results Measures and Risk Adjustment Methods

Perhaps the most important and the most pressing role for medical societies is in the area of results measurement. Medical societies should be instrumental in developing outcome measures at the medical condition level. These measures should be developed through systematic, collaborative processes involving doctors with deep expertise in each field, which societies are well placed to organize and lead. Societies should also be instrumental in developing and validating risk adjustment methodologies.

Some medical societies are rising to this challenge. The Society of Thoracic Surgeons (STS), for example, is a leader in results measurement and comprehensive risk adjustment. Societies such as the Society of Breast Surgeons are in earlier stages of developing results measures and championing results reporting. Other medical societies, however, continue to resist result measurement. The American College of Surgeons, for example, was reported to be instrumental in the decision of the Joint Commission on Accreditation of Healthcare Organization to utilize process measures in ICU accreditation rather than risk-adjusted outcome measures.

Medical societies face real challenges in persuading members to move beyond process compliance and embrace results measurement. The tendency to cater to the lowest common denominator can lead societies to avoid controversial agendas—after all, not every society member will have results that are above average. Medical societies are not doing their jobs, however, unless they lead the process of improving patient value, which only results measurement can truly enable.

Information Collection and Benchmarking

Medical societies can serve as catalysts and focal points for universal information collection and reporting, whether unblinded or blinded. Societies are also well placed to establish national benchmarks on specific outcome measures. Here, the Society of Thoracic Surgeons is again a leader. The STS database, built over a long period of time, is perhaps the most comprehensive of any medical field. STS also uses its data to establish national benchmarks by type of surgery on metrics such as mortality. As we described in chapter 4, the STS national database has enabled its members to drastically reduce surgical morbidity and mortality. However, STS does not yet make its results data publicly available, a serious shortcoming.

While the American College of Surgeons has been reticent about external results comparisons, it has developed a prospective, peer-controlled, validated database to measure thirty-day risk-adjusted surgical outcomes. This allows physicians and hospitals to compare their outcomes to the database of blinded results. The database is part of the society's National Surgical Quality Improvement Program, which also enables sharing of best practices and site visits.

Results databases should become the norm for treatment of every medical condition. This data will raise the bar in terms of patient value and help physicians learn when their results are substandard. Results measurement also focuses competition on achieving improvements in quality and efficiency, rather than on demonstrating compliance with process specifications.

Medical societies can also be vehicles for tracking *experience*, or how many patients each provider has treated in a medical condition. Experience information is especially important in dealing with rare or complex conditions, where societies can assist health plans, referring physicians, and patients seeking to locate experienced providers. Much inappropriate and ineffective treatment can be avoided by helping patients and referring physicians find providers with appropriate experience.

Care Delivery Process Improvement

Medical societies should have a primary goal of enabling their members to deliver excellent, state-of-the-art care. The speed of change and the reality of information overload make it difficult for even committed physicians to keep abreast of the most effective therapies and new care delivery approaches. Doing so is especially challenging for primary care providers that treat an array of medical conditions.

Because keeping up with the latest learning in care delivery is costly, many physicians and providers cannot afford to develop in-house capabilities and need outside sources of training and coaching. Some large provider organizations, such as Intermountain Health Care and the Cleveland Clinic, provide these services to their physicians. However, most smaller providers lack this capability, and societies can be an invaluable resource.

The American Association of Family Physicians (AAFP), for example, develops and disseminates a series of evidence-based protocols in the medical conditions its members treat most often. AAFP also reviews and selectively endorses clinical

(continued)

protocols from other organizations, such as the American Academy of Pediatrics and the Centers for Disease Control and Prevention.[35]

Societies should be offering publications, Web sites, courses, and consulting services that enable physicians to stay on top of excellence in patient care delivery. Services should be structured around practice units, medical conditions, and care cycles, not discrete services, techniques, or treatments.

Smaller specialist groups, such as pediatric oncologists and breast surgeons, have been able to develop and disseminate care delivery improvements more easily based on personal connections in relatively small fields. Larger groups will need to devise more formal mechanisms.

Safety Improvement and Error Reduction

Professional societies must take a leadership role in the area of safety. A good example is the work of the American Society of Anesthesiology (ASA). The ASA launched a study in 1985 of closed malpractice claims to determine sources of patient injury and ways to avoid them, motivated in part by reducing malpractice insurance costs. The study revealed that one-third of the claims were due to respiratory injuries, which usually resulted in death or permanent brain damage.[36] Further analysis concluded that better monitoring would have prevented adverse outcomes in 72 percent of these cases. The ASA then developed guidelines and training materials that encouraged its members to switch to the use of oximetry and capnography—automated means of monitoring the oxygenation of a patient's blood and the level of carbon dioxide exhaled. Most hospitals viewed the $10,000 cost of two more machines as an expense to be avoided. When the ASA guidelines became official, however, out-of-compliance hospitals were exposed to malpractice liability. All hospitals acquired the new equipment, and major safety improvements had been achieved by 1990.[37]

The ASA has also taken a number of other steps to address safety and medical errors, such as hosting biennial international symposia for sharing advances in patient safety. The Anesthesia Patient Safety Foundation was established in 1985 to further research on safety.[38] In addition, the ASA has worked closely with equipment suppliers to improve safety. For example, the ASA took steps to standardize the direction of hand wheels controlling the release of oxygen and anesthesia gases to avoid error, develop different standard hose diameters for various gases so that hoses would not be accidentally interchanged, and to specify differently shaped bottles for each medication used in anesthesia to reduce medication errors.[39] These changes, taken as a whole, have resulted in a reduction of deaths associated with surgical anesthesia from one patient in 500 in the mid-1980s to one patient in 200,000 to 300,000 in 2005.

Aligning Medical Society Structures and Patient Value

Many medical societies have long histories, with roots in traditional definitions of medical specialties and ways of practicing. As a result, their scope and
boundaries may not be aligned with integrated care delivery teams or the full
cycle of care. Many societies are structured around specialties or procedures,
not medical conditions or practice units.

Broader societies, such as the American College of Surgeons, may need to
evolve programs around distinct medical conditions. This is already happen-
ing in the areas of trauma and bariatric surgery. Narrow societies may need to
merge. Societies more aligned with medical conditions will be in a better
position to push the state of the art in terms of outcomes measurement, risk
adjustment, and practice improvement.

Ideally, restructured medical societies will emerge that group physicians
not by their specialty, but by the condition they treat. Major improvements
will follow in terms of the value of care delivered to patients.

tions that could potentially play this role include AHRQ (part of HHS),
the Institute of Medicine (a quasi-public organization), and NQF. AHRQ
could potentially take the lead if its mandate is modeled after HHS's role
in overseeing the work of U.N.O.S. in organ transplants (see chapter 4). As
is the case for transplant data, AHRQ would not itself develop the measures or collect the data, but would contract with independent not-for-
profit entities. Even that role, however, would require a significant
increase in AHRQ's budget relative to today.

The Institute of Medicine is more centered in the scientific community, and more independent. We believe that charging IOM with the
responsibility for information standards could greatly speed the process
of development while maintaining scientific integrity. IOM could solicit
an array of medical societies, the NQF and other organizations that have
been working on measurement, or newly created entities to submit recommendations in each medical condition. IOM would ratify measures
and risk adjustment approaches, and oversee an ongoing process of improving them. The NQF's structure and history would make it more difficult
for it to adopt the coordinating role.

As a transitional step while outcome measures are being defined, a set
of experience measures by medical condition should also be developed by
an expert body, ideally supervised by the same organization charged with
outcome measure oversight. All providers should be required to report
experience data on an annual basis by medical condition as soon as possible, and eventually for subgroups of patients and individual treatment

options. This is a low-cost and less controversial place to begin public reporting. It will also assist in compiling a universal set of definitions for medical conditions. Experience is not a clinical outcome and is not necessarily an indicator of results, but it is useful information in its own right in connecting providers and patients.[40] It will be useful for health plans, referring physicians, treating physicians, and patients alike.[41]

In addition to outcomes, a process will be needed for mandatory reporting of prices. Both outcomes and prices are needed to ascertain value. Initial efforts could build on the all-payer reporting system, expanded to all states and to outpatient care. Definitions will need to be aligned between the outcome-measurement and price-reporting efforts. Also, pricing practices will need to shift to allow bundled prices that are more transparent and useful, as we will discuss further.

Enact Mandatory Results Reporting. Once a minimum set of outcome measures and risk adjustments is established, government should mandate that every provider in a particular medical condition report the designated outcome measures and certify the accuracy of the information as a condition of practice. After a phase-in period, this data would be publicly reported. Once again, if the federal government is slow to act, a consortium of states should take the lead.

Mandatory reporting is already the case in organ transplants, dialysis, and, in some states, cardiac surgery. These cases illustrate both the feasibility and the benefits. Over time, no provider should have a right to practice medicine without measuring and providing evidence of outcomes, and ultimately value, as charges are combined with outcomes.

Mandatory reporting is justified by the pressing public need for such information in health care delivery. Just as the SEC has strict, detailed reporting requirements for public companies designed to protect investors, the same is needed for health care providers. The social benefits of results information will be even greater in health care than in the financial markets, because the physical well-being of Americans is at stake.

Establish Information Collection and Dissemination Infrastructure. Government also needs to ensure the formation or designation of a trusted entity or a set of entities to collect and disseminate results information to all interested parties, ideally via the Internet. Again, government need not operate the system but should ensure its creation and its operation at high standards of accuracy and integrity.

There are a variety of ways to structure an information collection and reporting system. U.N.O.S., the nonprofit corporation that operates the transplant information registry under contract, is an example of one way of accomplishing these objectives. The same quasi-public or independent entity charged with establishing outcome measures could also oversee the collection and dissemination structure. If the federal government is slow to take up collection and dissemination, once again, a coalition of states could initiate the structure.

Improve Pricing Practices

Current pricing practices in health care delivery work against value-based competition, as we have discussed.[42] Health care pricing is complex and opaque, which is a symptom of two underlying problems. The first is a pricing system that is centered around discrete services and interventions rather than service bundles or care cycles. Thus there can be numerous prices and bills for the same service or episode, covering each physician, room charge, test charge, and so on that is involved. Such a pricing system obscures value, because what is relevant for value is the overall price for a diagnosis or for care of a medical condition, not the components. This system also makes price disclosure far more complex and much less useful.

Second, pricing transparency and complexity are further compounded by the fact that, even for the same discrete services, prices vary widely for different patients based on their group affiliation, health plan, or government program. In the current system, neither patients nor, often, doctors know the governing price. Even provider billing offices are often unable to quote prices. The distortions created by negotiated prices based on group bargaining power rather than differences in cost or quality undermine value for patients, or shift value but create no real savings.

As we have discussed in chapters 5 and 6, value-based competition will be greatly enhanced by a pricing and billing model in which prices cover the full bundle of services and products delivered together, and in which prices are based on a patient's medical condition, not his or her group affiliation. Prices should be clearly disclosed in advance, which will become far easier than in the current system. Such a pricing approach will greatly reduce administrative costs, curtail cost shifting, and remove incentives for restrictive networks. It will also facilitate provider choices based on value, and create strong competitive pressure for providers to improve value and efficiency. Limiting discounts for large groups (or limiting price discrimination) is highly controversial because large groups mistakenly believe cost shifting benefits them. As we discussed in chapter 4, however, this thinking is myopic and misguided. Limiting price discrimination would be one of the most effective ways to refocus competition on value and bring down prices or price increases. But, given the resistance to the idea, we want to emphasize that bundled or episode pricing rules should proceed even if limiting price discrimination takes longer to accomplish.

Establish Episode and Care-Cycle Pricing. After a phase-in period, providers should be required to tender bills, and post prices, for episodes of care. These should include all physician charges, facilities charges, tests, and supplies involved in the episode. Separate bundled prices should be established for diagnosis, risk assessment, prevention, and disease management services. The latter two will probably be based on time periods. For each medical condition, complexity groups need to be established so that prices reflect initial conditions that significantly affect care. In stroke care, for example, care for a stroke in a major blood vessel and a stroke in a small blood vessel should have different prices. Ultimately, single bundled prices should be posted for full cycles of care, including procedures, office visits, drugs, supplies, and the services of all the involved entities.

Prices for episodes, service bundles, and ultimately full cycles of care should be required to be reported and be readily accessible, ideally via the Internet, in a single place for all providers to facilitate comparisons. Reporting of hospital-based bundled prices should be the responsibility of hospitals, which will aggregate all charges, including outpatient visits. Prices for service bundles delivered solely from physicians' offices should be the responsibility of physicians.

Required price disclosures can begin with a set of commonly occurring medical conditions, and expand over time. Over time, providers could also be required to provide cost estimates in advance for episodes of care.

Set Limits on Price Discrimination. Competing on results is encouraged when prices are based on value rather than on the bargaining power of health plans or employer groups. Price discrimination across patients based on group affiliation is not justified in terms of patient value or by the economics of health care delivery. The cost of caring for a medical condition has little or nothing to do with the patient's employer or insurance company. While price discrimination in other industries usually reflects economies of scale or other efficiencies, this is not the case in health care. Price discrimination is not only unfair, but also involves an inevitable cross subsidy across patients. Health care is an essential service, and the individuals who must pay the highest prices in the current system are often those least able to pay—the uninsured, members of small groups, individually insured patients, or patients with insurance who are seeking out-of-network care.

Limiting pricing differentials for favored groups is especially important for low-income patients who can ill afford paying higher prices than the more affluent. Medicare, in an effort to prevent overcharging of its patients, requires that providers charge Medicare patients a lower price than all other patients (no matter how poor).[43] The result, however, is that low-income patients who are not enrolled in Medicare or Medicaid are charged full list prices unless their care is provided for free. Medicare rules also required providers to make real efforts to collect bills from non-Medicare patients, so as to prevent de facto discounts when providers collect only part of the bill.[44] The Department of Health and Human Services has since backed off, but the overall approach remains flawed.[45]

Limiting price differentials will also correct the incentive to direct patients to in-network care without evidence of quality. The current practice of tiered (higher) deductibles or copayments for out-of-network care works against value. Even though this structure offers the appearance of choice, tiered copayments strongly discourage the choice of out-of-network providers even if they are superior because out-of-network care is billed at list price, which is typically about double the in-network rate, while the health plan's contribution is calculated based on the in-network rate. Hence, the patient ends up responsible for more than half of list price.[46] Moreover, if a complication occurs in the course of out-of-network care, insurance often will not cover any of the costs related to the complication. As a result, the cost and risk of out-of-network care are prohibitive for many patients, even if the out-of-network provider is far superior. Ending in-network contracting altogether by limiting price discrimination is a far better approach than tiered deductibles.

We advocate the move to a system where providers charge the same price (or a price within a reasonable band) to any patient for addressing a given medical condition, regardless of the patient's health insurance or group affiliation. More complex conditions would involve higher prices than simpler cases, but price differences should be tied to medical complexity, not to the bargaining power of the health plan.

A practical way to shrink price differentials for favored groups is to limit (or band) the spread between the most discounted price and the highest price charged by a given provider for a particular service, adjusted for complexity. The allowed band could be narrowed over time.

Doctors and hospitals would be free to set different prices from those of their competitors. However, charges by a given provider for the same service would not vary more than the allowed band simply because one patient was insured by Aetna and another was covered by Blue Cross. Ideally, the same band would apply to Medicare pricing.

The idea of provider freedom to set prices evokes a concern that providers specializing in complex and rare fields, especially those involving serious conditions, might charge excessively high prices because there could be little price sensitivity.[47] However, the experience of United Resource Networks (U.R.N.) in obtaining discounts for organ transplant patients suggests just the opposite. The most successful providers of highly specialized, life-saving transplant surgery offer larger than average discounts to

U.R.N. Their ability to offer such discounts results in part from the expertise, efficiencies, and learning that come from serving more patients. In a value-based system, there is the additional deterrent that charging high prices not justified by results would lead to declining patient volume.

There is also a concern that the excellent providers would have too much pricing power because of limits on capacity. Yet, the very existence of 139 heart transplant centers in the United States, many of them demonstrating acceptable results, suggests that the ability to charge attractive prices will draw enough additional high-quality providers into the market to moderate prices, even in highly complex fields.[48] The market for complex conditions can also be expanded to be regional or national, limiting the pricing power of local players. (Note that impediments to competition, such as arbitrary Certificate of Need regulations or state-level licensing, need to be reduced.) In any medical conditions for which there is not effective competition, price caps could be established during the transition period to value-based competition.

In the system we propose, health plans, employers, and government programs would be free to negotiate on price, but a lower price would shift the band and benefit all patients, not just their own. In the short run, limiting price discrimination will reduce the cross subsidy in favor of the biggest cost shifters in the current system, such as the largest health plans and Medicare. In the long run, all system participants, including the largest health plans, will benefit from a fairer system in which prices are based on value delivered. More efficient providers would bring prices down, improving patient value. The new approach will also reduce administrative costs, reduce billing complexity, improve price transparency, and support competition, which will drive down value-adjusted prices over time.

Without the substantial price discrimination that exists today, network restrictions that limit patient choice of providers would tend to disappear. Subscribers seeking care from a provider would be assured of a reasonable price, not an inflated list price. Combined with results information, such a pricing system would thus refocus health plans away from networks and on working to improve value for their members.

Some efforts to limit price discrimination are already under way. The state of Maryland requires that a provider charge the same price to every health plan, Medicare, and the uninsured. The Maryland system allows prices to vary among providers, but not among the groups of patients each provider serves. Maryland illustrates a system in which the uninsured are not subsidizing the insured, since everyone faces the same prices. Also, a given provider will have the same price whether patients are in or out of network, so there are fewer barriers to choices of providers. But in Maryland, prices are set by the government, not by the providers, as would be preferable.

The need to limit price discrimination is partly due to the zero-sum competition in the current system. If there were free and open competition at the level of medical conditions supported by transparent information on outcomes and prices, price discrimination would naturally decline and price differences would come to reflect differences in value. Thus, in the long run, regulatory limits on price discrimination may be unnecessary. However, new pricing rules would greatly speed the transition to value-based competition.

Open Up Competition at the Right Level

Government has a crucial role in eliminating artificial barriers to competition throughout the health care system. There are a wide variety of such barriers, many of them unintentional. Some laws that impede competition, for example, were enacted in an effort to address abuses that occur when information on quality and cost is unavailable. Other impediments to competition arose from the local focus of care delivery.

Government should not only eliminate barriers but safeguard competition by preventing anticompetitive practices and combinations. While value-based competition will lead broad-line provider groups to be dismembered naturally, for example, the federal government and state attorneys general need to be on the lookout for excessive consolidation and excessive bargaining power without a demonstrable value or productivity benefit.

Reduce Artificial Barriers to Practice Area Integration. Piecemeal regulation to correct skewed incentives often yields unintended consequences. Two such examples are the Stark laws and corporate practice of medicine laws, both of which constrain providers' ability to organize by practice units and integrate care delivery across the care cycle.

Modify the Stark Laws. Physicians are prohibited by law from self-referral of patients to medical practices in which they have a financial interest. The Stark laws (I and II) are examples of the need for complex regulatory approaches to control undesirable behavior in the absence of value-based competition on results. Self-referral is a problem when referrals are made based on financial interest and without regard for value. Uninformed patients may be referred to physicians, testing centers, rehab providers, or other service providers with higher prices, worse outcomes, or both. The Stark laws aim to prevent such abuses, but have the unintended consequence of fracturing the care cycle. They also impede clinicians from working together, sharing information,[49] and providing coordinated care. The Stark laws also make it more difficult for physicians to organize integrated practice units addressing the care cycle.

In value-based competition on results, the Stark laws are unnecessary. Inappropriate referrals will harm a provider's results and drive up bundled prices. Self-policing will weed out inefficient or ineffective members of a care-cycle team. Rather than prohibit practice coordination and integration, a results justification should be added to the Stark law exceptions. As results information becomes available, Stark law restrictions on coordination can be eliminated.

Phase Out Corporate Practice of Medicine Laws. Corporate practice of medicine laws also deter value-creating integration in health care practices. Laws are on the books in many states that bar physicians from being employed by a corporation (either nonprofit or for profit) for the purpose of practicing medicine. These archaic laws have outlasted any conceivable purpose. They deter the salaried employment of physicians by hospitals and other entities, which works against integrated practice delivery across the care cycle. While providers can often circumvent these laws through complex structures, the laws are inconsistent with value and should be repealed.

Require a Value Justification for Captive Referrals or Treatment Involving an Economic Interest. While self-referral by physicians has been regulated, self-referral by health plans to affiliated providers, or by providers to affiliated providers, has been ignored. Yet these self-referrals can create at least as much distortion of competition as physician ownership—if not more. Health plans and providers should be required to disclose to patients all affiliations with providers to which patients are referred, and to offer an alternative referral if requested. Until results information is widely available, referrals to affiliated, partially owned, or captive providers (including testing services) should require a value justification based on objective data on quality and cost. Referral of all or a great majority of patients to the same provider or provider group, even if there is no formal affiliation, should constitute de facto indication of possible bias and require a value justification. As results information becomes widespread, these rules can also be eliminated.

There are also cases in which physicians or providers have an economic stake in a medical device, drug, or service utilized in a particular treatment. While some experts seek to eliminate all financial ties to treatment approaches, this model is misguided and will work against innovation and patient value. Instead, providers should be required to disclose any financial interest in the particular treatment recommended and provide a value justification, including evidence of good results. As with all such policies, however, the widespread availability of results information and the introduction of true competition will eliminate the need for special rules. Results competition is by far the best mechanism to police ineffective care delivery.

Eliminate Artificial Restrictions to New Entry. Government should eliminate bans and restrictions on specialty hospitals or other new providers, and base approvals solely on qualifications and medical results. Efforts to restrict the entry of specialty hospitals have been especially common in recent years. The 2003 Medicare drug law included a moratorium on new specialty hospitals through June 8, 2005; Florida's July 1, 2004, legislation also banned specialty hospitals. These laws were the result of aggressive lobbying by the American Hospital Association and community hospitals.

Outright bans of specialty hospitals, and similar efforts such as zoning restrictions, are nothing more than efforts to protect incumbent providers and limit competition where it is often much needed. The attacks on specialized hospitals reflect the failed hospital strategies of trying to be all things to all people and of offering all services through shared facilities (see chapter 5).[50]

The criticism that specialty hospitals treat less sick patients reflects the same obsolete mind-sets.[51] In an efficient division of labor, patients not needing an expensive setting are exactly the patients who should be treated in a more cost-effective location. Specialty hospitals that track and report their outcomes, demonstrate good results, and use evidence-based practice standards will drive significant value improvements in health care delivery.

There is preliminary evidence of actual benefits to community hospitals that come from competing with specialty hospitals. A recent study found that community hospitals responded to competition from specialty heart hospitals with cost reductions, expansions in other surgeries, rehabilitation, pain management, neurosurgery, aggressive price negotiations with private payers, and, in some cases, recruiting new surgeons into the community.[52] This description is a vivid example of value-based competition at work. The same study found that the profits of community hospitals were not affected by the entry of specialty hospitals.

Some existing academic medical centers and community hospitals may choose to team up with specialty hospitals through joint ventures. MedCath, for example, is pursuing this strategy in cardiac catheterization labs.[53] These types of new relationships follow the principles we discussed in chapter 5. However, relationships between specialty hospitals and incumbent hospitals should be voluntary, not forced by anticompetitive restrictions to entry by specialty hospitals motivated by incumbents.

Innovation in the structure and organization of health care delivery is badly needed, and new models should be encouraged. Both new and incumbent providers, however, should have to compete on results.

Another common restriction on new competition is Certificates of Need (CONs). In some states, CONs are required for new facilities or large capital investments. Instead, the system should move to Certificates of Good Results. Ironically, CON regulation is sometimes supported by advocates of outcome data collection, because the threat of withholding approval ensures compliance with outcome data reporting. However, this is yet another example of using complex regulation to address a problem that would be better addressed directly. Data reporting should be mandatory, rather than using flawed CON rules as a lever to make data reporting appear voluntary.

Institute Results-Based License Renewal. Renewals of provider and individual physician licenses to practice should be based on patient results. Renewal should require objective evidence of results that meet or exceed national benchmarks at the medical condition level.[54] As value-based competition spreads, substandard providers will either improve or go out of business naturally. In the interim, license renewal based on the best available results measures can raise the bar.

Strictly Enforce Antitrust Policies. Over the past fifteen years, provider groups that shield substandard individual provider entities from competition have been deemed acceptable. However, the consolidation of providers into a few large groups runs the risk of thwarting competition in a region with little or no health value benefit. As we discussed in chapter 2, studies of hospital consolidation show that higher concentration often is associated with price increases for both not-for-profit and for-profit hospitals. Studies also document the absence of efficiency gains from acquisitions, because actual operations are not combined.[55]

Antitrust policy has a crucial role in the health care system that has not been widely recognized. Antitrust authorities must scrutinize the behavior of all system participants to ensure that no provider, hospital group, health plan, or integrated system can concentrate excessively, unfairly dominate, or unfairly compete in an important market. Given extraordinary cost increases, the need to do so is as great or greater than elsewhere in the economy.

While health care has not been a primary focus of antitrust attention in the past, the Federal Trade Commission (FTC) and Antitrust Division of the Department of Justice (DOJ) issued a welcome report on the role of antitrust enforcement in the sector.[56] Between 1994 and 2004, the FTC and DOJ challenged seven hospital mergers and lost each case. The courts, perhaps not appreciating the consequences of a lack of effective competition in the health care sector, disagreed with the federal agencies on market definition, prospects for new entry, and the magnitude of possible efficiency gains, among other things. New guidelines or new legislation may well be necessary to clarify the tests for effective competition in the sector and set new standards for courts to apply.

Instead of a move to more vigilance on health care competition, there is a steady stream of proposals from health care experts and system participants to eliminate or relax competition. These steps are usually justified through hoped-for efficiencies from avoiding duplication and encouraging collaboration. Such flawed arguments are typical in other industries seeking to avoid competition. At best, these proposals are naïve. There is no evidence that such efficiencies of consolidation or collusion will be achieved—in truth, the evidence shows the opposite. Consolidation leads in practice to higher prices.

The only way to lower cost and increase value in health care is to insist that providers compete on results. Competition will define the best configuration of the system for patient value. Competition is the only way to eliminate uneconomic duplication of investment and excess capacity, as we discussed in chapter 4.

Curtail Anticompetitive Buying-Group Practices. Group purchasing organizations (GPOs) aggregate hospital purchases of supplies and medical devices in order to bargain down prices. GPOs are the subject of heated and ongoing debate about whether they improve efficiency or are anticompetitive. On one hand, most hospitals choose to utilize at least one and often two GPOs for purchases, which provides evidence of some benefit. Yet there are serious concerns that some GPO practices erode value and slow the rate of innovation. Hospitals, for example, explain that GPOs achieve volume discount targets by overbuying inventory that hospitals must then hold and manage. Inventory carrying costs can be hidden because separate hospital departments are often involved in procurement and care delivery. Also, hospitals that buy a product that is not on the GPO's list not only lose the discount but must also repay savings from previous purchases of the GPO-approved item.[57] This creates a strong bias toward the products the GPO has selected, which may have been determined more by the discount offered by the supplier than by the health care value of the product. In addition, critics of GPOs allege anticompetitive practices such as tying, bundling, and exclusive dealing, all of which would work against value-based competition.[58]

Most troubling is that some GPOs are funded by suppliers rather than solely by hospitals. The fees that suppliers pay, which would normally be considered illegal kickbacks, are allowed by the 1986 amendment to the Social Security Act.[59] Thus, buying groups may serve the interests of the suppliers that provide their funding, not providers, thereby undermining value-based competition.[60] While the extent of this bias is contested, the potential for conflict of interest is indisputable.

To enable value-based competition, every buying-group practice should be consistent with open and fair competition. There is no valid reason for buying groups to accept financing or any payments from suppliers: if a buying group adds value, the customers (hospitals) should voluntarily pay for it.

Eliminate Barriers to Competition Across Geography. A variety of regulations and practices artificially limit competition in health care across states and geographic regions. We discuss just a few examples here, but all such impediments to provider or health plan competition need to be eliminated.

Establish Reciprocity in State-Level Licensing. Reciprocity across states in the licensing of physicians, provider organizations, and other skilled personnel would encourage integrated care delivery systems across geography, including the use of telemedicine. Licensing of providers from other states that meet reasonable standards in terms of training, experience, and results should be automatic. Otherwise, licensing becomes a barrier to competition that can only reduce health care value. Eventually, state-level licensing should be de facto eliminated in favor of national licensing, which could be administered by states.

Modify Tax Treatment of Medical Travel. Currently, IRS rules for the deductibility of medically related travel hamper value-based competition. The rules allow 14 cents per mile for travel and $50 per day for room and board. These amounts are unreasonably low and deter competition among providers across geography. A better policy would be to harmonize the rules with the reimbursement rules for business travel.[61]

Establish Standards and Rules That Enable Information Technology and Information Sharing

Information technology (IT) promises to enable major value improvements in health care delivery, as we have discussed in earlier chapters. Substantial benefits are possible through improved medical records, better coordinated care, more integration across providers, improved results measurement, and better patient information, among other things. Deploying IT in health care is the job of the private sector, but government has important roles to play in enabling the sharing of medical information and speeding IT adoption.

Develop Standards for Interoperability of Hardware and Software. Standards need to be developed that ensure interoperability of IT software and hardware. Today, providers and other system participants operate a myriad of legacy systems, many of them built around particular applications such as scheduling or financial management. Vendors often support their own proprietary systems, especially in the area of software.

In order to reap the full benefits for patient value, however, information systems within and across health care organizations need to be able to talk to each other. Interface standards are essential, which all vendors providing systems for medical applications should be required to meet. A federal commission on systemic interoperability was established by Congress in 2003 to advance these aims. The commission's report, released in 2005, contains a set of useful recommendations. Implementing these recommendations after vetting takes on high importance.

Develop Standards for Medical Data. Standards for medical data are necessary so that records from different providers, health plans, and other parties can be exchanged, compared, and aggregated. Any type of information that appears in a medical record must be specified using a standard that is recognizable and compatible with the way other parties record the same type of data. This means that standard or compatible disease categories, diagnosis codes, pathology results, definitions, and so on must be utilized. Such standards for medical data are important not only for patient care, but also to allow the efficient compiling of results and process information.

Enhance Identification and Security Procedures. Rules and regulations are necessary to protect the security and privacy of medical information while allowing its efficient exchange. Rules are needed to make electronic signatures legal and verifiable. This would enable electronic prescribing, among other applications. Patients also need a unique identifying number to allow the reliable matching of records and individuals. Finally, procedures are necessary for requesting and releasing medical records that are verified and that protect privacy while ensuring timely access. HIPAA regulations already give patients the right to obtain their own medical records, which previously belonged to providers and health plans. While a step forward, however, this model is far from ideal. We believe that records must eventually become the property of individuals, not just providers, in order to allow a practical and efficient medical records system. Verifiable electronic signatures will ease the transition to a consumer-owned record that physicians can use in care delivery.

The notion of transferring medical information electronically makes many individuals uncomfortable. This concern has a parallel in the history of electronic financial transactions, where security concerns regarding online banking and commonplace commerce were initially great but were largely overcome. As information standards and security measures are established, the exchange of sensitive medical information will also become expected and normal. The benefits for patient value will be enormous.

Provide Incentives for Adoption of Information Technology. Government has a role in encouraging the adoption of electronic medical information and information technology because the benefits are systemwide. Broader adoption leads to a disproportionate increase in benefits because information can be exchanged among more and more parties, much like the case of electronic mail. Also, results data can be far more easily assembled and reported.

Medicare is taking a welcome initiative in speeding IT adoption by making free software available to some doctors. Medicare could accelerate IT deployment by requiring electronic transactions and electronic data reporting by a fixed date. Other models can also be explored, such as IT requirements for accreditation. Financing mechanisms to address the capital costs of introducing IT systems may also be necessary, especially for smaller providers.

Reform the Malpractice System

The current malpractice system has been an ineffective means of eliminating poor quality in medicine, as we discuss in chapters 2 and 7. Although some lawyers point to the threat of malpractice as creating strong incentives for appropriate and careful medical practice, the fact is that numerous errors, incorrect diagnoses, and inappropriate treatments persist. Perhaps the greatest cost of malpractice lawsuits is indirect, through their pervasive effect on care delivery. Malpractice risk leads to unnecessary and duplicative tests, overdiagnosis, the use of the most invasive and aggressive treatments, and other self-protective behaviors that contribute to overuse and overtreatment.[62]

There are far better and less expensive ways to motivate excellence in health care than malpractice litigation, as we have described. Value-based competition is a far more powerful tool for addressing medical mistakes and poor quality than the legal system alone, and one without the huge direct and indirect costs of the malpractice system. Value-based competition on results will promote careful practice while driving process improvement, better outcomes, and greater efficiency. With information on results, physicians and patients will be able to measure the appropriateness and effectiveness of care. Together they will choose treatments and providers based on a rigorous understanding of true results and risks. Malpractice litigation will occur less often as poor providers decline and physicians discontinue use of substandard processes.

In today's system, with little systematic results information to rely upon, the malpractice system becomes the pass/fail grading system for providers. One bad outcome can brand a physician as a failure, so defensive medicine makes sense. With better results information and no artificial restrictions on the choice of providers, the whole approach will be different. Patients, their families, and referring physicians will be able to learn in advance and act on knowledge about which providers have high success rates and low rates of complications and errors, rather than discovering this information only after a problem occurs. The system will move away from disciplining poor practice in court and toward comparing treatments and providers in advance. Also, patients will know the real risks based on actual results, rather than engage in wishful thinking and ignore the real risks until after the fact. When a bad outcome occurs, it can be considered in the context of overall outcomes. And the dynamic can shift from defensive medicine to the more positive pursuit of a track record of superb risk-adjusted results.[63]

As outcome and value improve markedly with competition on results, the frequency of malpractice litigation should decline. Better results information should reduce the grounds to sue, because the true risks will be better known. Given the complexity and uncertainty in medical treatment, however, there will always be some bad outcomes and some liability questions.

Technically, the current system limits lawsuits to cases of truly bad medical practice such as negligence in using obsolete treatments or carelessness. But there is so much inherent variability in care delivery practices and results, and so little actual data available today, that substandard care is difficult to define. Increased transparency of the results of all providers will reduce this problem to some extent. Of course, there will always be room for debate about medical judgment and the appropriateness of treatment in specific circumstances.

We believe that the American public will accept reasonable limits on litigation, such as tougher sanctions for bringing cases that lack merit, caps on damage awards, and caps on lawyer fees for contingency cases, but only if patients and their families first gain better information and more choice.[64] Calls for malpractice reform without steps to address the underlying value problems have a hollow ring. This is one of many reasons that competition on results at the level of medical conditions is so necessary. Value-based competition will create far more discipline for providers than litigation while avoiding its destructive and costly effects.

Redesign Medicare Policies and Practices

Medicare policies and operating practices have a strong influence on the behavior of other actors in the health care system because Medicare is the health plan for 42 million Americans (14 percent)[65] and accounts for about 17 percent of total health care spending. Providers are reluctant to meet one set of requirements for Medicare and another for other health plans. While this does not prevent health plans from operating in new ways, as we discussed in chapter 6, the fact remains that Medicare will inevitably have an influence on the system.

Make Medicare a Health Plan, Not a Payer or a Regulator. Perhaps the most fundamental challenge is for Medicare to shift its mind-set from a payer to a health plan. Medicare can jump-start value-based competition by embracing the roles for health plans we discussed in chapter 6. Medicare is beginning to move in these directions, and an impressive range of promising experiments is under way. Medicare's efforts to publish data comparing hospitals, offer disease management for some medical conditions, pay for prevention in the form of counseling to stop smoking, provide free medical records software to physicians, and, more tentatively, recognize and reward results and not just processes are all on target. The challenge is to move from experiments to systemic change. Also, an array of core Medicare policies still work at cross purposes to patient value, notably in reimbursement practices. These must be modified.

Making Medicare a health plan would be easier to achieve if its regulatory roles were assigned elsewhere. Government should require outcome data reporting from all providers, freeing Medicare from the need to tie reimbursement to the reporting of data. Medicare should focus solely on improving health results for subscribers. Ideally, Medicare would operate less and less as an entity unto itself and more and more under rules that govern the entire system.

We cannot hope to lay out a complete strategy for Medicare here, nor would doing so be appropriate given the complexity of the subject. However, we can offer some implications for Medicare arising from the principles of value-based competition. Some of these may seem radical, but we are convinced that all of our recommendations are feasible and can substantially improve the value the nation receives from this vital program.

Modify Counterproductive Pricing Practices. Medicare took a big step in the direction of paying for episodes of care when it moved to the prospective payment system (DRGs) for hospital reimbursement. The rationale was sound albeit limited: create incentives for efficiency by paying according to the diagnosed condition rather than on a cost-plus basis. If prices were set to reflect costs and held stable for a period of time, providers would be motivated to improve their efficiency in order to improve margins. Prices could be reduced periodically and the process restarted, bringing costs down further.

However, the hoped-for benefits were not fully realized. Two big reasons stand out. First, the strong incentives for cost reduction were not accompanied by outcome reporting, so the incentives were simply to cut costs, not to improve value. Second, the DRG reimbursement rates were not accurately related to costs over time. This created a system of cross subsidies in which the reimbursement for some services was well above cost. Areas such as cardiac surgery, orthopedic surgery, organ transplants, and imaging were widely seen by providers as "profitable," while many other services were seen as marginal or money losers. Providers then used profitable services to offset low or negative margins from other services. This also created a strong bias to enter "profitable" fields. Numerous providers crowded into such fields as orthopedics and heart surgery, leading to excess capacity and many patients being treated by low-volume providers without demonstrated excellence. Excess capacity also can lead to practice patterns that overuse some treatments without evidence of improved outcomes ("supply-driven demand").[66] Health care value suffers. Also, the DRG system led providers to devote significant efforts to coding records to achieve the maximum allowed reimbursement.

Physician reimbursement under Medicare, using the Resource Based Relative Value Scale (RBRVS), still pays fees for services, rewarding inputs instead of outcomes. It offers higher reimbursement when more discrete steps are performed, rather than when care is performed efficiently or effectively.[67] Moreover, physicians are paid more for procedures than consultation, despite the fact that skilled consultation can add equal if not greater value. So despite its name, reimbursement in the RBRVS system is based on a highly imperfect notion of cost, rather than patient value.

This current Medicare model motivates physicians to recommend and perform procedures, which are well reimbursed, rather than provide alternative treatments, which may involve consultation and ongoing disease management. Because payment is for treatment rather than results, physicians are discouraged from improving in ways that reduce the need for reimbursed treatment or involve treatments that are reimbursed less generously. In breast cancer treatment, for example, the Medicare physician reimbursement in Roanoke, Virginia, for a modified radical mastectomy is $943.48. For early-stage breast cancer, a lumpectomy (partial mastectomy with axillary dissection) is equally effective for some patients but substantially less disfiguring. While it is equally time-consuming for the surgeon, it has a reimbursement of only $776.09. This creates a disincentive for surgeons to learn and use the higher-value technique. Reimbursement is also lower for sentinel node biopsy, a new and improved procedure, than for a complete axillary lymphadenectomy, which removes all of the lymph nodes under the arm. In this case, the older procedure involves significantly *worse* outcomes.[68] Again, the financial incentive is against practicing with a technique that can improve value for patients.

Further incentives misaligned with patient value are introduced by the "sustainable growth rate policy" intended to control aggregate Medicare spending. Essentially, if the volume of services goes up, the fee schedule is ratcheted down. Doctors are prone to attempt to recoup their incomes by ratcheting up the volume of services, with the risk that supply creates more demand.

Medicare is experimenting with some new reimbursement practices, such as reimbursing physicians for answering e-mails and paying for counseling to help patients stop smoking, that recognize the value of consultation and avoid office visits. The fact remains, however, that the current reimbursement model is often working at cross purposes to patient value and value improvement.

Improve Medicare Pay for Performance. Medicare is beginning to experiment with factoring quality into pricing, recognizing (and in some ways leading) the trend toward pay for performance that we discuss in earlier chapters. The idea of rewarding results is a major step forward. However, the way this idea is being implemented may not achieve the desired effect. Instead, it may turn into another futile attempt to micromanage care delivery processes.

Medicare's initial pay-for-performance program, begun in 2004, had many of the same pitfalls as other pay-for-performance programs. In its initial efforts directed at hospitals, Medicare made the mistake of focusing on the hospital as a whole instead of medical conditions. A hospital's entire product line was deemed high quality based on twenty process checks in four areas of care.[69] The measures used were broad process metrics (e.g., in heart failure, the percentage of patients given an ACE inhibitor, the percentage given smoking cessation advice, the percentage assessed for left ventricular function, and the percentage given discharge instructions). The hospital did not have to demonstrate good medical *results* even in the measured areas. By rewarding the entire hospital based on a few areas, the program masked or even unintentionally subsidized substandard services in unmeasured areas of care.

Medicare's pay-for-performance initiative is evolving rapidly, to Medicare's credit. By 2005, Medicare had ten pay-for-performance initiatives or demonstration projects. It is beyond the scope of this book to critique each of them, but we can offer some general comments. One of Medicare's initiatives is to collect information on thirty-four process measures in five medical conditions. Hospitals in the top 10 percent in a condition are rewarded with a 2 percent bonus for Medicare patients with that condition, and hospitals in the next 10 percent are rewarded with a 1 percent bonus. In the third year of the program, hospitals below a predetermined threshold will have payments reduced for Medicare patients with that condition.

The direct association of rewards with the specific medical conditions being measured is a major step forward. Also, the approach encourages the best to become better. This is essential because, as we have discussed, the top performers tend to be the providers that advance the state of the art, not average players.[70] Encouraging further improvement by already excellent providers will speed the rate of improvement for others.

However, the new initiative still rewards processes, not results, which is a serious weakness. The nation needs to move to true results measurement as soon as possible, and we have discussed a systemwide approach earlier in this chapter. Because Medicare's fixed price system creates incentives to minimize costs, it is especially important that Medicare become a leader in encouraging and utilizing results measures. Otherwise, there are incentives to skimp on care once a patient is admitted, and to provide too much care to too many patients if capacity is available.[71]

Medicare has also assumed that the best way to reward quality is to pay a little more. As we have discussed in earlier chapters, however, rewarding excellence with more patients will improve margins and raise the standard of care much faster (see chapter 4). For example, Medicare could require referring physicians to inform patients if a provider is below the 20 percent threshold and assist them to identify the nearest providers in the top 20 or top 30 percent. Patients and their physicians would then be encouraged to seek out better providers and accelerate the virtuous circle of health care delivery we have described.

Some commentators have raised concerns that directing patients to excellent providers would lead to insufficient capacity and long waits. This would certainly be a risk in a single-payer system in which the payer's bargaining power could push down provider margins and remove the incentive for capacity expansion. However, we are confident that with value-based competition, the capacity of excellent providers will respond quite rapidly (see chapters 4 and 5). Excellent providers would expand facilities and reallocate capacity away from other, less distinctive, services.[72] They would also recruit physicians from less successful providers who would benefit from the training, coaching, process learning, and practice experience that come from working in a high-performing organization. Waiting time can also become one of the reported measures, so that patients will choose providers with good results and reasonable waits.[73]

Lead the Move to Bundled Pricing Models. Medicare can lead the process of moving to single prices for episodes and ultimately cycles of care, combining hospital and all physician charges. Medicare has already shown that bundled price models are feasible, even for complex services. In the 1992 Medicare bypass demonstration project, for example, seven hospitals agreed to charge a fixed combined physician and hospital price for bypass surgery. The Texas Heart Institute, renowned for its expertise and efficiency, set its charge at $27,040, compared with the national average of $43,370.[74] Unfortunately, legislation to implement this initiative nationwide died in conference between the House and the Senate.

Medicare's pilot program to improve chronic care is also a step in the right direction. Providers of disease management services will be paid a monthly fee per patient in two medical conditions—congestive heart failure and complex diabetes. Providers must guarantee Medicare a cost savings of at least 5 percent (including the disease management fee) relative to a similar population of Medicare beneficiaries who are not in a disease management program in order to participate.[75] Payment of disease management fees is also contingent on meeting specified measures of quality, patient satisfaction, and provider satisfaction. Since this project is being carried out by nine service providers in nine different regions, it should not only pay for itself but also establish valuable data on disease management for the two medical conditions as well as raise incentives to develop disease management services. Although studies of disease management (discussed in chapter 6) show cost savings and improved results, many employers do not yet include disease management in their health plans. This pilot is an exciting example of how Medicare can help advance the state of the art.

Require Results-Based Referrals. Medicare should be a major driving force in a national results measurement program, because it will benefit the most. As results measures are developed, Medicare can begin to communicate outcome thresholds for providers, just as other health plans will inform members and referring physicians about results of competing providers. Results thresholds can be rolled out condition by condition. Since clinical outcomes are multidimensional, thresholds will involve a number of measures, just as *Consumer Reports* gives multiple types of ratings for readers to consider. Patients and referring physicians could select the combination of considerations that meets the needs of the patient.

The next step is to require referrals to providers with good results adjusted for risk. This step will improve value since Medicare prices are the same or similar for all providers. Results-based referrals will significantly improve the results experienced by the average Medicare patient, and create almost irresistible pressures for results improvement. It will also begin to limit excessive entry of providers into "profitable" services, because all providers, including new entrants, will have to demonstrate good results to obtain patients.

Results-based referrals do not imply that every patient must be referred to the top provider based on a single metric. Given differences in patients' preferences and desire for convenience, the best-value provider for one patient will not be the same as the best-value provider for another. In transplants, for example, where outcome data and appropriate patient counseling about provider choice are available, counseled patients choose different providers (see chapters 4 and 6). Today patients and referring doctors are simply unaware of all the alternatives, much less able to evaluate them.

Results-based referrals will challenge assumptions and alter some long-standing care patterns. For example, community hospitals will prove to offer results comparable to those at tertiary care medical centers in some services, not to mention greater patient convenience. Indeed, one of the benefits of results measurement will be to better guide patients to the setting in which the best-value care can be obtained.

Allow Providers to Set Prices. Once there is information on results at the medical condition level, Medicare will be able to ask providers for prices, rather than setting them. It is extremely difficult for the CMS to keep up with all of the advances in medical practice. In a new model, providers would set their own prices for service bundles (including physicians' fees and all other charges). Prices would be posted on the Web.

The top-down prices in the current system are not well calibrated with value, as we have described. Some are too high (so every hospital wants to provide those services), and others are too low to be attractive to providers. In the current system, there is also no incentive for an excellent provider to offer the well-reimbursed services at lower rates. The methodology for top-down price setting can be improved, but never perfected.[76] Administered prices will never really work. Hence, preserving the current Medicare pricing structure will only perpetuate the system's problems. The suggestion that providers and physicians set their own prices may be too radical for many observers to even imagine, but with the creation of value-based competition on results, its time can come.

A major advantage of letting providers eventually set their own prices, in a system with results-based referrals, is that excellence will automatically be rewarded, but not necessarily by higher prices. Efficient providers can choose to attract more patients with equal or even lower prices, while still earning attractive margins due to efficiency, fewer complications, and few mistakes.

Some fear that allowing providers to set their own fees would result in sky-high price increases, but competition and results measurement will limit gouging. Price caps could help to alleviate that concern, as we have discussed.

Align Medicaid with Medicare. Medicaid was established in 1965 to pay for medical coverage for low-income citizens. While it is primarily a state-run program, each Medicaid program must comply with national rules to obtain federal matching funding. Medicaid covers over 40 million people, but states differ in interpreting and implementing the program. In addition, Medicaid is often perceived more as a social welfare program than as a health care program, which leads to a lack of focus on the value delivered.

In practice, there is a separate Medicaid program in each of the fifty states. Examining each of them is beyond the scope of this book. However, there are some important general principles of value-based competition that apply to Medicaid programs in every state. See also the sections on insurance and coverage for implications for Medicaid and state health care policies.

Just as we suggested for Medicare, the Medicaid program must move toward becoming a value-based health plan as discussed in chapter 6. Doing so has a series of implications for Medicaid policy. First, a central focus of Medicaid should be primary and preventive care, both of which represent gaping holes in health care for low-income Americans and a major cause of high costs and poor health outcomes. Enabling such services will ultimately lower costs, not increase them. In the interest of ensuring universal access to care in emergency situations, federal rules for Medicaid now prohibit copayments for emergency room care. When expensive emergency room visits are free to the patient and a visit to the doctor is not, there is a strong incentive to overuse emergency care. Health coverage for all will reduce this overuse.

In the current Medicaid system, providing for primary and preventive care is complicated by the fact that the eligibility of individuals tends to change frequently. People move in and out of the Medicaid system over time. When they do not qualify for Medicaid, individuals often become uninsured. At minimum, individuals should be able to remain in Medicaid but pay premiums.

Medicaid programs also need to incorporate disease management. Thirty-nine percent of Medicaid beneficiaries have one or more chronic diseases. States are just beginning to create disease management programs to improve results while lowering costs.[77] For example, North Carolina's Community Care Plan for asthma resulted in 34 percent lower hospitalization rates and 8 percent lower emergency services for participants under age twenty-one. Including higher drug costs, the average total cost per enrolled beneficiary was reduced by 24 percent, while health was improved.[78] Disease management programs may also have benefits beyond the health care sector because they raise the probability of holding a job in good standing.

Like all other health programs, Medicaid programs must also embody results information. Here, North Carolina's Community Care Plan is also taking steps to encourage clinical best practices, tracking information to learn which practices improve quality and reduce costs. Its nurses help train local providers in care and case management strategies.[79] However, these steps are just a start toward true results measurement and value-based referrals.

Invest in Medical and Clinical Research

Innovation is fundamental to improving value. Innovation, broadly defined as new processes, technologies, and organizational structures, is the only way to solve the health care problem in the United States and around the world. Unless diagnosis, treatment, prevention, and disease management improve markedly, demographics will ensure that health care cost rises sharply in the advanced economies over the coming decades.

Moving to value-based competition will unleash a surge of innovation in health care delivery and create powerful incentives and pressures for sustained innovation. Many of the needed changes in care delivery will take place in the form of better organizational structures, enhanced processes, better information, and improved results measurement. However, government will continue to have a vital role in ensuring that the appropriate technological infrastructure for medical advances is in place, as well as providing incentives to spur the diffusion of knowledge.

Support for basic scientific and medical research is an essential foundation for innovation in health care.[80] The United States has a long history of such investment, and the National Institutes of Health and other entities have had a profound influence on life science technologies. This not only benefits patients, but also U.S. competitiveness in health care–related technologies and services. This is an area where U.S. leadership is strong and can be extended. Ironically, however, the current nature of competition in health care delivery has worked against, or slowed down, the effective application and commercialization of all this new life science technology. The changes outlined in this chapter, and elsewhere in the book, will contribute to a higher payoff for America's life sciences research spending.

As we discussed in chapter 4, however, support needs to increase significantly for research on clinical outcomes and processes. The insights from such work are just as important as those from laboratory research, if not more so.

A transitional step to accelerate the transformation of health care delivery, with major symbolic importance, would be a mechanism to encourage the diffusion of promising new approaches to care delivery that are initially more expensive than traditional approaches. As learning accumulates, the value and cost of new therapies and delivery models often improve dramatically, as we have stressed in other chapters.

One proposal would be for Medicare to create an adoption-of-innovation fund to support the spread of promising clinical approaches. These could involve drugs, medical devices, and services, as well as entirely new categories of innovation. Providers, working with health plans and suppliers, would compete to win matching funds to deploy new care delivery models and new, better facilities based on the potential to increase patient value. Projects would follow established institutional review processes and informed patient consent guidelines, plus be subject to extensive longitudinal measurement. In time, such an innovation fund may not be needed as value-based competition kicks in. As a transitional device, however, it could speed new care delivery methods toward lower costs and wider adoption.

Implications for Health Care Policy in Other Nations

Our focus in this book has been on the U.S. health care system, but the principles we describe are universal. Moving to value-based competition on results at the level of medical conditions, supported by the right information, pricing structures, and health plan roles, will produce huge dividends in terms of patient value in any system no matter what the starting point.

Most health care systems in other countries involve far less competition than is present in the United States. Thus, other nations have fortuitously avoided the zero-sum competition that has driven up U.S. costs. In addition, health care systems in other advanced countries benefit from providing wide access to primary care, which is inherently efficient because it fosters prevention, early detection, and delivery of routine treatment in a low-cost setting. The combination of less zero-sum competition and more primary care is a major contributor to the lower costs of other systems. However, a portion of the lower costs of foreign systems comes from limiting or rationing services.

Aggregate statistics such as life span and infant mortality are superior in many other industrialized countries than in the United States.[81] This is due in part to lower poverty rates and better access to primary care in countries with universal coverage.[82] At the same time, however, it is acknowledged that leading U.S. centers have highly advanced medical technology and excellent care for complex cases compared to other countries. This is evidenced by the widespread travel of patients and doctors to the United States for care and training.[83] Because of lower costs, better access, and good performance on some quality metrics, however, many observers have concluded that other countries have a superior health care model. Therefore, these experts believe that a greater government role in the U.S. system is needed. Evidence is growing, however, that government-run systems are experiencing serious problems, and other countries are questioning their models. We believe that the introduction of value-based competition is the only way to drive more rapid improvement in both the U.S. and government-run systems.

Serious quality problems are not limited to the United States. Instead, every country that investigates the issue of health care quality concludes that quality problems have reached unacceptable levels. In the United States, the Institute of Medicine reported between 44,000 and 98,000 deaths per year from preventable medical errors, or between 160 and 360 deaths per million of population, and HealthGrades estimated about 675 deaths per million.[84] International studies are mixed on this measure, but some studies indicate that other countries perform worse.[85] A recent Commonwealth Fund study interviewed patients in five countries and found that Americans reported more mistakes in medications and tests and more fragmented care (as we have discussed).[86] As we noted in chapter 3, deaths from preventable medical errors in other industrialized nations range from 400 to 700 per million of population, which makes them the third most common cause of death.[87] Also, while the rates of adverse medical events (not necessarily causing death) are estimated to be between 3.2 and 5.4 percent in the United States, they are estimated at about 9 percent in Denmark, between 10.6 and 16.6 percent in Australia, between 10 and 11.7 percent in the United Kingdom, and even worse in developing countries.[88] In addition to the much-discussed problems of long waits and other forms of rationing, countries such as Canada, Denmark, the Netherlands, Sweden, New Zealand, and France have concluded that their health care systems are suffering from serious quality problems.[89]

At the same time as concerns about quality rise, the much-cited lower health care costs in other countries are under severe pressure. In most other countries, health care costs are now rising rapidly. Thus, there is now widespread concern and even alarm about health care policy in these countries, as there has been in the United States. The demographic pressures facing the United States are even worse in some other industrialized nations. Finally, it is now being better recognized that the United States subsidizes the cost of drugs and drug development for other countries, because drugs developed and patented in the United States are normally sold outside the United States at prices much lower than in the U.S. market.[90] Few if any countries today are complacent about their health care systems, and there is a new receptivity to different approaches. All countries perceive an urgent need to improve value in health care delivery.

How can state-run or state-dominated systems deliver more value for citizens? The answer is to move in the direction of value-based competition on results, at least among providers.

Interestingly, a number of countries are embracing value-based competition principles in various ways, and some of the results are encouraging. One way to introduce competition into state-operated systems is to require public hospitals and physicians to compete for business. In Singapore, a small island nation, the government health care delivery system has been divided into two provider groups: the National Healthcare Group and Singapore Health Services. Each group is organized as an autonomous independent entity that competes fiercely for patients. Each group, in turn, is encouraged to minimize unnecessary within-group duplication of services in its constituent hospitals. This encourages strategic focus at the individual hospital level instead of attempting to be all things to all people.[91] The initial results in Singapore are promising.[92]

Sweden has introduced some results competition among providers by publishing and comparing risk-adjusted outcome data, process metrics, waiting times, and total health expenditures for each of its twenty-one *lans* (counties or states). Sweden also publishes results data for specific medical conditions for each of the country's sixty-seven hospitals. For primary and secondary care, patients must use a hospital within their *lan*. Here pressure for improvement is created primarily by the availability of information, which motivates physicians because of professional pride. The process and outcome data of providers relative to others (both locally and nationally) are widely known. Physicians and administrators are not content to be below average even if their patients have a limited choice of providers within their *lan*. The fact that information exists at the level of medical conditions is crucial in making it motivating and actionable for physicians.

This example reveals that moving in the direction of value-based competition on results does not require consumer choice as the driving force, which is the premise of the consumer-driven health care movement. Public information about results at the medical condition level creates direct motivation for improvement among providers themselves.

In tertiary care, Sweden has national competition. Doctors may refer patients to any of the eight university hospitals in the country, which compete on quality and price. Swedish hospitals vigorously pursue quality improvement, with ongoing benchmarking against the world's best hospitals. The results of this competition on value are striking. In one of the most progressive *lans*, Jönköping, for example, the rates of infection and mortality from errors are about one-fifth of those in leading American hospitals for patients with the same condition.[93] Sweden has not moved all the way to value-based competition, but it is several steps along the way.

When a state-run system introduces competition by publishing results information and allowing patients to choose, it is important that excellent providers be rewarded and provided with the resources to increase capacity. Otherwise, the best providers will be penalized by forcing them to work harder.

National systems will also benefit from relaxing the constraint that every local provider or hospital must offer full services. Allowing for strategic focus by hospitals and physician practices, as we described in chapter 5, offers significant benefits for value. However, it is important that there are enough providers to produce meaningful competition in every medical condition.

Another way to introduce value-based competition into state-run systems is to allow private providers to compete with public delivery systems. Most countries have a private system that is parallel to the public system, but these have typically been kept quite separate. Some countries are moving to allow the two to truly compete. In the French health care system, for example, patients have the choice of private care. Private clinics account for over 40 percent of health care delivery by volume but only 22 percent of the costs, highlighting the efficiency advantage of the private sector.[94] The share of private clinics in France is growing. In Singapore, the competing public systems must also compete with private providers. Public-private competition works best if it takes place at the medical condition level and if high-quality results information at this level is collected and widely disseminated.

Competition between public and private health care services becomes truly significant if public health insurance or funds from health savings vehicles can be used in either system. In Singapore, for example, every citizen has a tax-exempt, interest-earning Medisave account that can be used to buy services from either of the two public provider groups or from private providers.[95] Prices in the public delivery systems are regulated by the government, but they compete with private hospitals and clinics that can set their own prices at the individual service level.

Introducing competition into the insurance or health plan market can also encourage value improvement. In South Africa, for example, deregulation of the health insurance market in 1994 allowed a wide range of insurance plans. By 2004, medical savings accounts (MSAs) represented about two-thirds of private insurance. Typically, these health plans have no deductible for hospital care but an annual deductible of about $1,000 for outpatient care. Most drugs involve high deductibles, except for those that the insurer wants to encourage to lower overall costs. Results in South Africa indicate that MSA holders spend about half as much on outpatient services as non-account holders, and there is no evidence that these subscribers self-ration primary care in ways that lead to higher inpatient costs. Although lower costs could be partly due to self-selection of MSAs by healthy subscribers, the incidence of catastrophic claims does not suggest healthier enrollees.[96]

Finally, competition within national systems can be introduced via opening them to international competition.[97] International competition is an emerging force for improving value in health care delivery. Differences in the value delivered by health care providers in different countries are giving rise to growing medical tourism. While the United States has long served foreign patients, the practice is spreading. India attracted about 150,000 medical tourists in 2003, and Thailand attracted at least 1 million, just to cite a few examples.[98] Clinics in Cuba are destinations for patients from Central and South America. Jordan attracts patients from across the Middle East. Malaysia and Singapore provide care for numerous patients from neighboring countries.

Providers are also beginning to move to international strategies. Apollo Hospital in Chennai, India, for example, is pursuing a strategy to attract patients from abroad in joint replacements, heart bypass surgery, cataract surgery, and even elective treatments such as in vitro fertilization and cosmetic surgery. To support its strategy, Apollo is establishing telemedicine links with Britain, where family doctors can consult with specialists in India and, eventually, refer patients to them. Governments can reduce barriers to international travel for health care in order to encourage such value-enhancing competition, including allowing reimbursement for foreign services by insurance or health savings vehicles.

Any model of introducing provider competition into state-run systems, if it is to be truly effective, must center competition on results at the level of medical conditions, not only at the level of hospitals or networks. Competition must take place across care cycles rather than in discrete interventions. Competition must include prevention and disease management.

To support value-based competition, other nations will need to develop and disseminate the same kinds of results information we have described, and hold providers accountable. Indeed, even without provider competition, the collection and dissemination of results information can go a long way in driving improvements in value. Other countries will need to confront the same challenges that exist in the United States in developing outcome measures that encompass the entire care cycle.

There are positive information initiatives under way in a range of countries, from which the United States can learn. In Singapore, for example, information on experience (the number of procedures performed by disease area), average length of stay, cost for the fiftieth percentile of patients, and cost for the ninetieth percentile of patients for all public and most private hospitals is available for seventy procedures and accessible online from the Ministry of Health. In Sweden, a national database tracks sixty-eight measures of quality. Clinical data and treatment cost data are beginning to be integrated to achieve a true measure of value.

Substandard providers will feel strong pressures to improve value as results information is disseminated. National systems, however, will face extra challenges in addressing weaknesses because health care professionals are often government employees. If governments cannot reward and discipline government-employed managers, doctors, and other skilled professionals based on the value they deliver, achieving real improvements in health care will be difficult.

State-run providers will need to address the same strategic and organizational principles we describe in chapter 5. More focused services, integrated practice units, dedicated teams and facilities, and so on, are just as applicable for government-owned providers, if not more so.

Finally, in addition to introducing provider competition and accountability, the ideas in this book suggest the need for a fundamental reorientation of the roles of national health insurance agencies. National health authorities are often preoccupied with bargaining down prices and controlling services, not increasing patient value. Heavy administrative oversight and micromanagement of health care delivery networks is endemic.

National health authorities need especially to adopt a whole new philosophy and mind-set based on value, as we have described here. National health agencies must also play the value-adding roles of health plans described in chapter 6. Separating health insurance authorities and delivery systems from an organizational standpoint will make it easier for both entities to effectively play their roles.

Single government payers especially need to be held accountable. It may be desirable for single payers to be divided into multiple payer (health plan) service organizations that, at a minimum, have to publish their results. Ideally, citizens would be free to choose among them. Each organization would then have to compete to add value and improve its services.

Every nation faces different circumstances, and there is no one best plan of action to reform a nation's health care system. However, the principles of value-based competition on results offer a road map for improvement.

Other countries, by starting from a structure of widespread access to primary care, can face fewer challenges in some respects than the United States. Dramatic improvements in value delivered are possible in every country. As the United States and other countries move toward value-based competition on results, learning and patient value will accelerate.

Conclusion

HEALTH CARE IS ON A collision course with patient needs and economic reality. Without significant changes, the scale of the problem will
only get worse. Rising costs, mounting evidence of quality problems, and
increasing numbers of Americans without insurance are unacceptable and
unsustainable. The escalating problems with the U.S. health care system
seem imponderable and even insurmountable to many observers. Many have
come to believe that, like it or not, government management of the health
care system is inevitable. We too suspect that, absent a new approach, the
system will evolve toward more arbitrary budget cuts, price controls,
rationing, and a single payer. Sadly, none of this will be a solution, but an
admission of failure. Fortunately, a better outcome is within reach.

The future of health care is not predetermined. It is a mistake to extrap-
olate and attempt to respond to trends within the current structure.
Instead, the most pressing task for leaders in health care is to create a new
and better structure. Effective leaders have the insight to revisit the fundamental purpose of an organization and imagine a different and more
effective way to attain it. Government control in health care is not
inevitable. Indeed, countries with government-dominated systems are
moving away from that model. America can move now to a system that
serves patients far better than either a government-run model or the current U.S. system.

This book sets forth a new and different vision of the health care system, in which everything in the system is realigned around its fundamental purpose—patient health. Ironically, the solution to the crisis lies
in refocusing the health care system on health. Imagine a world in which
America's best talent—its most accomplished care delivery organizations,
its most skilled doctors and nurses, its best managers of health benefits,
and its most creative developers of new technology—were all focused on
improving value for patients, and rewarded for it. Given the personal

aspirations and values that prevail, we are confident that the many talented individuals in the health care system will embrace this different structure once they have gotten a glimpse of it.

In this book, we describe a health care system that harnesses the power of competition on results to drive stunning improvements in value for patients. Zero-sum competition to shift cost is a road to nowhere. Competing on value is a positive-sum competition in which all participants in the system can win. When providers succeed in delivering superb care more efficiently, patients, health plans, and employers also succeed. When health plans help patients and referring physicians make better informed choices, seek out superior care, and assist in the coordination of care, excellent providers also benefit. Competing on value also goes beyond economic success. When physicians and other health professionals compete to achieve the best medical outcomes for patients, they pursue the aims that led them to the profession in the first place. No longer are economic realities and personal values in conflict.

The right kind of competition drives stunning value improvement in other parts of the economy, and it will do so in health care. Health care, by its very nature, is ripe for a value revolution. Better quality in health care is often less costly due to more accurate diagnoses, fewer complications and errors, less invasive treatments, faster recoveries, and reduced risk or severity of disease. In health care, prevention is less expensive than treatment, and managing a disease is less expensive than reacting with acute care. At the most fundamental level, better health is less expensive than poor health. Competition on results can and will trigger improvements in quality and efficiency that are unimaginable in the current system.

To unleash this power of competition in health care, a transformation in the very nature of competition in the system is necessary. This will require strategic and organizational changes by all participants. In pursuing new strategies and structures based on value and results, all the key actors in the system will establish a dynamic for improvement far more powerful than consumer activism alone. And the new strategies will arise from each player's self-interest rather than from government-imposed regulations that are never a real solution.

Value for patients will align the interests of all system participants, who now often work at cross purposes. Like a compass pointing the way, the goal of value will guide everyone's choices. In the context of today's system, what we propose may sound radical to some and utopian to others. However, competing on value will call into question many assumptions and choices that have been taken as given.

What will the health care system look like when all participants focus on patient value? Providers will offer services where they can be truly excellent, rather than attempting to offer all services to every patient. Care will be organized around medical conditions and coordinated across the cycle of care. The current organization of hospitals and physician practices around traditional specialty departments will evolve to integrated practice units. Prices will cover the full care cycle, doing away with a myriad of bills for individual services. Every provider will measure and disseminate its results.

Fewer providers will offer care for each medical condition, but the care they offer will be far more integrated. Few hospitals will close, but providers will phase out less distinctive service lines and reallocate their efforts to areas where they can achieve true excellence. Today's duplicative and excess capacity will be significantly reduced. A growing number of excellent regional and national providers will operate across multiple geographic areas, linked to local institutions through various types of medical partnerships and relationships. Community hospitals and rural hospitals will not try to be self-contained, but will be tightly connected to regional centers. Over time, the variations of results across providers and geography will narrow, so that patients will not need to travel to obtain excellent care, as they do today.

Primary care physicians will remain central actors in the system, with far better support in caring for patients. Armed with much better information, more choices about where to refer patients, and better prevention and disease management programs, primary care physicians will add more value than ever before. Primary care practices will increasingly become the front end and back end of integrated care cycles for medical conditions. Over time, stand-alone disease management companies may become less needed as this gaping hole in the current system is closed.

Suppliers of drugs, devices, and services will stop trying to maximize usage and start focusing on maximizing value for the patients they serve. They will convincingly demonstrate the value of their products (in terms of outcomes and costs) compared to alternative therapies through long-term clinical studies. Suppliers will focus on getting their products to the patients who will benefit from them the most, and take responsibility for ensuring that the care delivery processes in which their products are utilized are at the state of the art.

Health plans will move from a culture of denial to a culture of health. They will align their strategies with patient value, and measure themselves based on member health results per dollar of premiums. Health plans will become true health partners with their members. They will improve dramatically the advice and assistance they provide to members and their physicians. Dictating to members and micromanaging providers will become a thing of the past.

Employers will stop complaining about health care costs and start improving health and health care value for employees and their families. Health benefits will be redesigned around prevention, disease management, and employee involvement. Employers will insist that their employees and their families are cared for by excellent providers. Health benefits will be evaluated not in terms of short-run costs but in terms of employee health, greater employee productivity, and reductions in time lost from work.

Consumers will experience a health care system that is far simpler and more effective than today. They will work closely with their health plan and their doctors to understand their health risks and actively manage their health. They will bear more responsibility for unhealthy behavior. Access to excellent care will not depend on personal connections or the ability to pay for out-of-network care. Every patient will have the information and the help to obtain superb care. Supported by their health plans, all patients will expect their care to be seamlessly coordinated. Confusing bills, and debates with the health plan over what is covered, will come to an end. Doctors, freed of much wasted effort, will have more time to assist their patients.

While redefining health care will require fundamental change, governmental reform is not the most important driver. Each system participant, acting in its self-interest, can begin now to take steps that will significantly increase the value delivered. Each step will make participants better off while moving the system in the right direction.

As individual actors modify their strategies and operating practices, the benefits will become self-reinforcing. For example, as health plans seek out the best providers, the virtuous circle of value for providers will be reinforced. Advances by one participant in the system will encourage, and better reward, advances by others.

Government's fundamental role in this revolution is to put in place the infrastructure and rules that enable value-based competition. Government must ensure that the right kind of competition takes place. This will require overseeing the development of risk-adjusted outcome measures for every medical condition, requiring mandatory reporting of results, opening up provider and health plan competition, defining new rules for pricing, and speeding the introduction of information technology, among other steps. At the same time, government must ensure that health insurance is available to all citizens, with consistent standards for minimum coverage. With a new kind of competition, universal insurance will become a practical reality, rather than a hope that the nation cannot afford.

Universal and mandatory health coverage will bring everyone into the system, including low-income citizens. Everyone will become a paying customer, with access to primary and preventive care dramatically improving the efficiency of the health care system. Substandard care for any group, including the poor or minorities, will become glaringly obvious in a results-based system. Providers and health plans that fail to deliver value will be forced to improve or go out of business.

How will redefining health care start? It is already under way! There are numerous examples of organizations and individual physicians moving in the directions we have outlined. As this book was being written, new examples presented themselves almost daily through our many communications with system participants. The case studies we discuss in this book are just the tip of the iceberg. The readiness to embrace change is widespread and palpable. There is a transformation in the making.

The recommendations we offer are not theoretical. Each recommendation is included based on proof by example—some organization with unusual insight and leadership is already implementing it. Yet even today's forward-thinking organizations can go further, and reap disproportionate benefits. Combining better strategies with better organizational structures, better care delivery processes, better information, and better incentives will have a snowball effect in terms of value improvement. Measuring results, and making results information widely available, is probably the single most important catalyst to triggering cascading changes in the system.

Once competition on results starts working, improvements in value will no longer be discretionary. Every participant in the system will be compelled to refocus on value. Improving care delivery will no longer be optional. Competition will continually raise the bar. Progress will not depend on extraordinary leadership, unusual commitment, or special vision. No provider, health plan, supplier, or employer will be able to resist these changes and remain viable. Consumers will be drawn to and supported in new roles. The right kind of competition will bring to health care its immense power to make things better, as it has in so many other fields.

Value-based competition on results is a positive-sum competition in which all participants can win, so long as they are dedicated and capable. However, those participants that will enjoy the greatest rewards will be those that move early. For anyone in the health care system, the time to act is now.

The coming transformation will unleash the talent and energy of the many extraordinary individuals working in the health care system on a positive agenda of dramatic value improvements. Costs will be brought under control, and the health of citizens will advance significantly. As this happens, the benefits will accrue to every U.S. health care consumer and will spread to other countries as well. And all of this could happen sooner than now seems imaginable.

Appendix A

Making Results Public

The Cleveland Clinic

The Cleveland Clinic, long associated with excellence in patient care, has been publishing annual reports on clinical outcomes since 1998. The Cleveland Clinic is well known for taking on the most difficult cases, which has not deterred it from publishing these data. The first outcome report covered thoracic and cardiovascular surgery. Two years later, in 2000, a specific outcome report for thoracic surgery was introduced. In 2002 and 2003, new reports were introduced for heart failure, digestive diseases, and aortic surgery.

In 2004, the Clinic set out to expand its outcome reporting to every major clinical area. New outcome books were published for vascular surgery, neurology, neurological surgery, infectious disease, head and neck surgery, general internal medicine, nephrology and hypertension, dentistry, orthopedic surgery, rheumatic and immunologic diseases, obstetrics and gynecology, emergency medicine, psychiatry and psychology, endocrinology, diabetes and metabolism, general surgery, cardiovascular medicine, urology, spine care, brain tumors, respiratory diseases, and radiation oncology. The following chart shows all the outcome books that have been published covering years through 2004, with others expected over coming years. It is planned that outcome books will be published either annually or biennially.

In addition to outcome reports, the Cleveland Clinic has established a quality Web site (www.clevelandclinic.org/quality). This site contains downloadable copies of all outcome reports as well as detailed experience data by procedure and a range of other comparative information utilizing All Payer DRG data.

The original outcome report on thoracic and cardiovascular surgery, as well as some of the other reports, contain comparisons to national benchmarks. Such benchmarks are not yet available in many medical fields, and the benchmarks that exist in cardiovascular surgery were in part stimulated by the Clinic's leadership in outcome measurement. The Clinic is committed to seeking out and publishing benchmarks wherever they are available, and challenging medical societies to develop benchmarks in every field of medicine.

This appendix contains excerpts from the first edition of *Surgical Outcomes for Heart Failure*. While the comparative charts presented in this excerpt are not adjusted for patient risk, risk-adjusted results would likely improve the Clinic's results relative to national benchmarks because it treats some of the most difficult cases.

Outcome Reports by Medical Area and Year, The Cleveland Clinic

Surgical Outcomes Guide	1998	1999	2000	2001	2002	2003	2004
Thoracic & Cardiovascular Surgery	▓	▓	▓	▓	▓	▓	▓
Thoracic Surgery			▓	▓	▓	▓	▓
Heart Failure						▓	
Aortic Surgery Center						▓	
Digestive Diseases					▓		
Vascular Surgery							▓
Neurology							▓
Neurological Surgery							▓
Infectious Disease							▓
Head and Neck Surgery							▓
General Internal Medicine							▓
Nephrology and Hypertension							▓
Dentistry							▓
Orthopedic Surgery							▓
Rheumatic & Immunologic Diseases							▓
Obstetrics and Gynecology							▓
Emergency Medicine							▓
Psychiatry and Psychology							▓
Endocrinology, Diabetes, Metabolism							▓
General Surgery							▓
Cardiovascular Surgery							▓
Urology							▓
Spine Care							▓
Brain Tumors							▓
Respiratory Diseases							▓
Radiation Oncology							▓

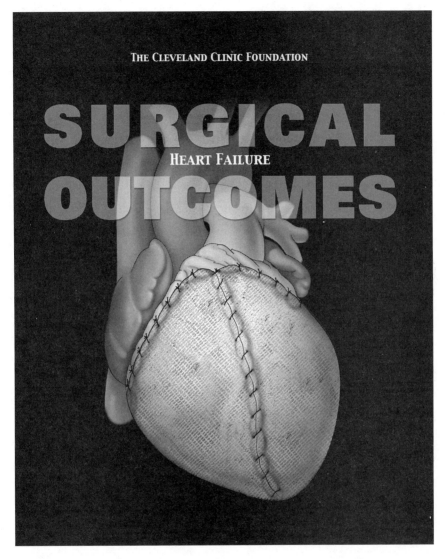

THE CLEVELAND CLINIC FOUNDATION

SURGICAL

HEART FAILURE

OUTCOMES

The Department of Thoracic and Cardiovascular Surgery at the Cleveland Clinic and the George M. and Linda H. Kaufman Center for Heart Failure are pleased to publish the first edition of *Surgical Outcomes for Heart Failure.* In the past decade, deaths from coronary artery disease and stroke have declined, yet there is a significant increase in the prevalence, morbidity, and mortality from heart failure. This disease and its tragic consequences are major health problems in the United States, accounting for over 23 billion health care dollars each year. Surgeons at the Cleveland Clinic are continuing to aggressively pursue surgical, medical, and device-based therapies, both conventional and novel, for patients with heart failure. These therapies have given many heart failure patients their best opportunity for a meaningful life. We are indebted to many for our successes of the past, and with great optimism, we welcome the challenges of the future.

Contents of the Full Report

Note: Page numbers are from the original report.

Overview

It is now estimated that more than 5 million people have been diagnosed with heart failure, with an additional 550,000 new cases diagnosed annually.

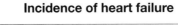

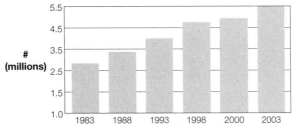

Incidence of heart failure

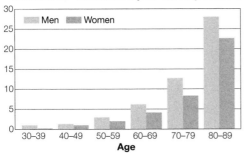

Annual HF incidence per 1,000 persons

With an aging population, the incidence of heart failure will escalate.

Heart failure results in more deaths than cancer, accidents, and strokes combined, costing more than $23 billion annually.

Heart failure in the U.S. (2002)	
Prevalence	>5 million patients
Incidence	550,000 patients per year
Mortality	>287,000 deaths per year
Cost	>23 billion dollars per year (7% of all healthcare costs)

Cardiac Transplantation

The Heart Transplantation Program at the Cleveland Clinic is the third largest program in the United States with 73 procedures performed in 2003.

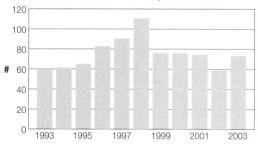

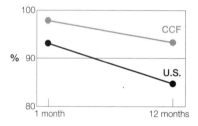

Survival after heart transplants at the Cleveland Clinic surpasses the U.S. benchmark.

On January 14, 2003, the Cleveland Clinic team performed the 1,000th transplant, an achievement accomplished by only five other transplant programs in the United States. Importantly, we continue to achieve excellent outcomes following transplant, with survival of 90%, 79%, and 59% at 1, 5, and 10 years, respectively.

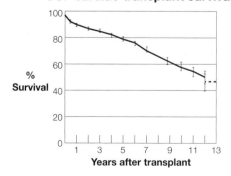

Non-Transplant Therapies

While extremely effective, cardiac transplantation will benefit only a small number of patients with heart failure because of the limited number of donor organs.

Cleveland Clinic physicians have pioneered medical and surgical alternatives to transplantation. Of 1,147 patients with advanced heart failure referred for transplantation evaluation, approximately two thirds were successfully managed with non-transplant therapies.

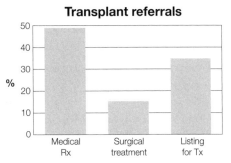

Transplant referrals

Referrals and transplant listings

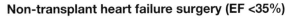

The success of this strategy is evidenced by a decreased number of patients listed for transplant, while transplant referrals remain stable.

Over the past decade there has been a doubling of the number of patients undergoing heart surgery with ejection fraction <35% with a simultaneous 50% reduction in mortality.*

Non-transplant heart failure surgery (EF <35%)

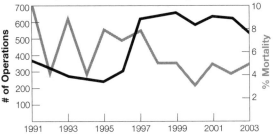

*Author's note: In general, a lower ejection fraction indicates a malfunctioning of the heart. In a healthy person, the fraction of blood ejected from the pumping heart into the body should be over 50%.

Valve Surgery

Aortic valve replacement (AVR) is the most common valve replacement operation at the Cleveland Clinic. In the past, patients with severe aortic stenosis or aortic insufficiency with poor ventricular function were thought to be poor surgical candidates. For patients with aortic stenosis with severe LV dysfunction and a low transvalvular gradient, aortic valve replacement can be safely performed with outcomes similar to patients with high valvular gradients.

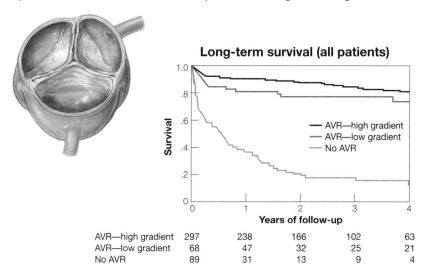

Long-term survival (all patients)

AVR—high gradient	297	238	166	102	63
AVR—low gradient	68	47	32	25	21
No AVR	89	31	13	9	4

Similarly, in the presence of chronic aortic regurgitation and severe LV dysfunction, aortic valve replacement can be performed with low risk. Since 1990, hospital mortality was 0% for patients with normal or reduced left ventricular function.

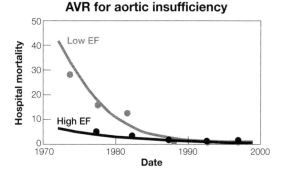

AVR for aortic insufficiency

A New Cleveland Clinic Heart Center

Construction is under way for a new Heart Center facility at the Cleveland Clinic Foundation. The Heart Center will provide the latest in technological advancements and offer state-of-the-art operating rooms and cardiology labs. These innovations will be placed in an optimum environment for patients and their families. The main pavilion of the Heart Center will house outpatient diagnostic facilities, 115 examination rooms, and offices for 129 physicians. A technology building will house the latest medical advancements available in 16 cardiothoracic operating rooms, 12 cardiac catheterization labs, 8 electrophysiology labs, a coronary care unit, a heart failure unit, and 2 surgical intensive care units. A new hospital tower will provide 288 private rooms for our patients, with a focus on amenities that promote our "healing hospitality" concept for patient care. In addition, a fully equipped conference center will enable doctors from around the world to meet, confer, and share knowledge. When complete, the Cleveland Clinic Heart Center will provide over 1 million square feet of space. The Heart Center is scheduled to open in 2008.

Appendix B

The Care Delivery Value Chain

Value-based competition requires a transformation of health care delivery. The integrated practice unit model implies a very different conception of care delivery from the prevailing approach. Care is organized around medical conditions, and is medically integrated across specialties, treatments, and services, and over time. Dedicated teams utilize facilities designed for maximum value in care delivery for the medical condition being addressed. Care over the full care cycle is tightly coordinated, and patient information is extensively and seamlessly shared. Results (outcomes and costs) are measured, analyzed, and reported. All the entities involved in the integrated practice unit accept joint responsibility and accountability for performance.

To help make the ideas of value-based competition concrete and operational, we introduced the care delivery value chain (CDVC) in chapter 5. The CDVC offers a systematic framework to delineate and analyze the process of care delivery in a medical condition. It is constructed for a medical condition, not for an individual procedure or intervention. The focus of the CDVC is on the activities involved in patient care, with non–care delivery activities (e.g., contracting, billing) treated as supporting activities (and not included in the figures).

The CDVC is both a descriptive and a normative tool: it helps a provider understand how it configures care delivery today, how its role in the CDVC relates to other entities, how its CDVC compares to other providers and to medical knowledge, and how it can modify its structure and processes to improve patient value. Chapter 5 (see the box "Transforming the Care Delivery Value Chain") sets forth a series of analytical questions to guide the investigation of a CDVC from a patient value perspective.

We have found that the notion of a value chain is sufficiently unfamiliar to indicate that health care practitioners and other readers can benefit from more detailed discussion of how to construct and map the CDVC.

Also, the concept comes to life when readers can see a number of concrete examples. This appendix further describes the CDVC framework and how to map a care delivery value chain for a particular medical condition. It then discusses three examples covering different types of medical conditions: chronic kidney disease (stages 1 to 4), stroke in a major vessel, and breast cancer. These examples include a chronic disease (chronic kidney disease), emergency care (stroke), and care involving both surgery and other major procedures (breast cancer). In these examples, the CDVC presented is meant to capture the essential activities but is far from exhaustive. We also include a brief overview of each medical condition, as well as commentary on some of the important issues for the configuration and management of care delivery that arise in each medical condition.

These examples are far from comprehensive. However, they help bring the CDVC framework to life and provide guidance in applying it. Over time, our hope is that the range and depth of available CDVC examples will grow to include many medical conditions, along with knowledge about how they are best defined, configured, organized, and managed.

Delineating Types of Care Delivery Activities

Care delivery consists of a myriad of different types of activities, such as consultation with the patient, prescribing medication, ordering and interpreting tests, performing surgery, conducting physical therapy, monitoring disease progression, and countless others. Care delivery activities can be linked, which means that the way one activity is performed affects the results of others. For example, the approach to rehabilitation can affect the results of surgery, and the type of surgery chosen may affect or be affected by appropriate adjuvant therapies.

The particular set of activities involved in care for each medical condition will differ, and the activities may be modified to some extent for individual patients.[1] The delineation of activities can take place at varying levels of detail. A particular surgical procedure, for example, can be broken down into the numerous constituent activities. It is easy to become overwhelmed by sheer complexity.

If we step back, however, care delivery in any medical condition consists of some characteristic types of activities, which are shown in the headings in figure 5-5. Distinguishing each type of activity can be revealing in its own right, as we will discuss. As a group, these types of activities constitute the cycle of care. The types tend to occur in a sequence, although there are feedback loops. While it is common in health care to examine processes and guidelines at a very detailed and granular level around specific services or procedures, what is often missing is a perspective on the cycle of care as a whole. Delineating the care delivery value chain allows a holistic view of the process and enables a broader approach to value improvement.

Every CDVC starts with *monitoring/preventing*. (Figure 5-5 illustrates some specific examples of each type of activity, but those shown are by no means exhaustive.) Monitoring/preventing activities include tracking a patient's circumstances, assessing risk, and taking steps to prevent or reduce the seriousness of illness or injury. These activities can have a major impact on value through early detection and limiting the need for treatment. This part of the care delivery value chain is often overlooked, undervalued, or minimized. In general, physicians are not compensated for keeping patients healthy, but for the things they do to treat illness.

Diagnosing is a well-accepted part of the care cycle. As we have discussed, diagnosing is not one activity but an entire set of activities, including testing, medical history, evaluation involving multiple specialists, and constructing a plan for treatment. Diagnostic activities are distinct from treatment, and diagnosis may well benefit from a broader array of skills. The quality and accuracy of diagnosis has a major impact on the value of care delivered. Organizing diagnosis into a dedicated unit within an integrated practice unit can be beneficial given the differing nature of the activities involved. Much of the information underlying diagnoses can be electronically shared, which facilitates consultations across providers and second opinions.

Preparing is a category of activities that can be overlooked or not given systematic attention. Careful preparation before intervention or other subsequent care can improve results and efficiency downstream. As in other fields, good setup in health care can be important to good execution.

Intervening refers to the set of activities involved in reversing or mitigating a condition, such as drug therapy, surgery, chemotherapy, or other procedures. We use *intervening* rather than the term *treating* to highlight the fact that interventions themselves are only part of overall treatment. There can be several types of interventions available in treating a medical condition, which can be used separately or in combination.

Recovery/rehabilitating is part of care for every medical condition, but, like preparing, it is often not addressed with adequate attention or resources. Especially once a patient leaves a unit or is discharged from the hospital, the continued responsibility for the patient's ongoing recovery is often unclear and not proactively managed. Patients, as some physicians have told us, are sometimes "discharged into Neverland," which undermines outcomes and can lead to additional costs. Managing recovery well, conversely, often improves results and reduces rehospitalizations, as was illustrated by the example of home monitoring by Sentara described in chapter 5.

Monitoring/managing is the last part of the care cycle, although it can require feedback loops to earlier stages when a disease progresses or complications arise. This set of activities can also significantly improve the longer-term results of care, and reduce the need for additional care. Good monitoring/managing reduces the probability of feedback loops in which the patient requires further diagnosis, preparation, intervention, and recovery. The importance to patient value of long-term monitoring/management is becoming more and more accepted, though this set of activities is often seen as completely outside of the normal care cycle. Specialist organizations have grown up to offer disease management services because many mainstream providers do not see this role as part of their business.

Accessing refers to the steps involved in gaining access to the patient, including patient visits, movement within the care setting, and other means. Access in some form is required for all other activities. Accessing and moving patients is important to value because it involves time, cost, patient handling, delays, and postponements for both providers and patients. New forms of patient access are emerging, such as remote monitoring and Internet consultations.

Measuring refers to the measurement of a patient's medical circumstances. Measurement is necessary across the care delivery chain—that is, in screening, diagnosis, conducting procedures, tracking recovery, and monitoring for recurrence of problems. Numerous measures of the patient's condition are collected, often repeatedly. Measurement involves a cross-cutting, cumulative, and potentially expensive set of activities that requires systematic management as well as the ability to aggregate and share data across individual entities and the care cycle. Today, measurement is often handled piecemeal and could benefit from unified processes and infrastructure.

Finally, *informing* refers to notifying, educating, and coaching the patient. Informing is needed throughout the entire care cycle and can have a major influence on patient results. Numerous studies document the improvement in value when patients are informed and involved, and when they participate in managing their disease or condition. In breast cancer treatment, for example, patients who understand what to expect both comply better with instructions and report higher satisfaction. Informing is not always seen as a distinct set of activities, however, and may take place on a hit-or-miss basis. Systematic attention to how and when to inform patients, how to inform them cost-effectively, and what staff should play informing roles is key for value improvement.

Mapping the Care Delivery Value Chain for a Practice Unit

The CDVC provides the basic framework for structuring integrated practice units, coordinating the care cycle, designing facilities, configuring the process of care, developing practice standards, defining and collecting the right information, and accumulating costs.

Mapping the CDVC for a medical condition starts with identifying the set of activities in each stage of care. In diagnosing, for example, the discrete activities involved in creating the diagnosis and developing the treatment plan should be delineated, along with the types of measures that need to be gathered and the types of information that need to be conveyed to the patient. The point here is not to mandate what activities should be performed and how, but to understand what is actually done. Documenting the process of care delivery is a precondition for measuring value and making improvements.

In mapping the CDVC, the labels and examples in figure 5-5 serve only as a starting point. In each integrated practice unit, the specific activities will be different. Constructing a CDVC often requires judgments in defining and categorizing particular activities, as well as deciding the level of detail at which the analysis should be conducted. Care delivery activities can be identified at varying levels of granularity. In-patient rehabilitation, for example, can be displayed as one activity or broken down into numerous discrete activities, especially in rehabilitation from complex medical conditions such as strokes or orthopedic injuries.

The general principle is to begin by delineating the CDVC at a level of detail that allows the overall care cycle to be understood, includes all the important groups of activities, and encompasses the different organizational units and separate entities involved in care. Such an analysis allows a broad examination of the full care cycle together with the important linkages and handoffs. The CDVC can then be further refined to greater levels of detail as the analysis proceeds.

Constructing a CDVC requires other judgments as well. Perhaps the most basic is the question of boundaries: what is the appropriate medical condition or conditions around which to organize care, and what are the beginning and end of the care cycle? A medical condition should include the set of related illnesses or injuries that are best treated in an integrated care delivery process. The care cycle begins early enough to allow value-enhancing monitoring and prevention, and ends late enough to capture the value of long-term disease management. The boundaries of the CDVC, in turn, should determine the appropriate organizational structure, reporting relationships, and unit for which costs and revenues are aggregated.

If seemingly similar medical conditions require very different sets of care delivery activities, they should probably be seen as separate medical conditions and organized as separate integrated practice units. Conversely, if traditionally distinct practices require repeated coordination and integrated facilities in order to deliver excellent results, then consideration should be given to treating them as components of a broader practice unit. For example, a diabetic care practice unit may include integrated care for co-occurring vision, renal, heart, vascular, and other conditions within the specialized team, even though the same provider may have a separate practice unit for nondiabetic cardiac care. Practice unit boundaries need not, and should not, be mutually exclusive from the point of view of specialties and medical problems.

To illustrate how to map the CDVC, we consider three representative examples.

Management of Chronic Kidney Disease (Stages 1 to 4)

A representative care delivery value chain for one medical condition, chronic kidney disease (CKD), is shown in figure B-1 (note that we have omitted support activities in this and the other examples for reasons of clarity and space). This example is not meant to be exhaustive, but to illustrate the CDVC applied to a particular case.

Chronic kidney disease is a condition affecting an estimated 20 million Americans. It is defined as abnormal kidney function that has not degraded to the point of end stage renal disease (ESRD), which requires renal replacement therapy (dialysis) or kidney transplantation. CKD is often associated with other medical conditions, such as hypertension, cardiovascular disease, urologic disorders, and diabetes. CKD can often be successfully managed for long periods of time, and its progression can be slowed, especially if the condition is addressed early.

Constructing a CDVC for chronic kidney disease, as in any medical condition, requires choices about boundaries. One boundary question is whether CKD care should be a separate chain or whether the chain should encompass the multiple chronic conditions that can co-occur (e.g., diabetes, heart ailments). Here, we treat CKD as a distinct medical condition because, for many patients, a separate, focused chain will deliver the best value, including coordination with care for other conditions across chains. However, for some patient groups, such as diabetics, it may be beneficial to include CKD care as part of a broader practice unit because of the need for ongoing, complex-to-manage linkages in the care delivery process for such patients. Such choices are exactly the questions that the CDVC framework aims to raise and help address.

The other boundary question related to CKD is the extent of the care cycle. In kidney disease, physicians have traditionally thought in terms of five stages, with end stage renal disease (ESRD) as stage 5. Based on our work with nephrologists in multiple regions, we have chosen here to define CKD (the first four stages) as a distinct medical condition in terms

FIGURE B-1

The care delivery value chain for chronic kidney disease

	Monitoring/ preventing	Diagnosing	Preparing	Intervening	Recovering/ rehabilitating	Monitoring/ managing
Knowledge management						
Informing	• Lifestyle counseling • Diet counseling	• Explanation of the diagnosis and implications	• Lifestyle counseling • Diet counseling • Education on procedures	• Medication counseling and compliance follow-up • Lifestyle and diet counseling	• Medication counseling and compliance follow-up • Lifestyle and diet counseling	• Medication compliance follow-up • Lifestyle and diet counseling • Renal replacement therapy (RRT) options counseling
Measuring	• Serum creatinine • Glomerular filtration rate (GFR) • Proteinuria	• Special urine tests • Renal ultrasound • Serological testing • Renal artery angio • Kidney biopsy • Nuclear med. scans	• Procedure-specific pretesting	• Procedure-specific measurements	• Kidney function tests	• Kidney function tests • Bone metabolism • Anemia
Accessing	• Office visits • Lab visits	• Office visits • Lab visits	• Various	• Office visits • Hospital visits	• Office/lab visits • Telephone/internet interaction	• Office/lab visits • Telephone/internet interaction
	Monitoring/ preventing • Monitoring renal function (at least annually) • Monitoring and addressing risk factors (e.g., blood pressure) • Early nephrologist referral for abdominal kidney function	**Diagnosing** • Medical and family history • Directed advanced testing • Consultation with other specialists • Data integration • Formal diagnosis • Formulate a treatment plan	**Preparing** • Procedure-specific preparation (e.g., diet, medication) • Tight blood pressure control • Tight diabetes control	**Intervening** Pharmaceutical • Kidney function (ACE inhibitors, ARBs) Procedures • Renal artery angioplasty Urological (if needed) Endocrinological (if needed) • Vascular access graft at stage 4	**Recovering/ rehabilitating** • Fine-tuning of the drug regimen • Determining supporting nutritional modifications	**Monitoring/ managing** • Managing renal function • Managing kidney side effects of other treatments (e.g., cardiac catheterization) • Managing the effects of associated diseases (e.g., diabetes, hypertension, uremia) • Referral for RRT

Provider margin

Patient value (Health results per unit of cost)

Feedback loops

Legend:
☐ Nephrology practice
☐ Other provider entities

of organizing care from a value perspective. We treat ESRD as two differ-ent though linked medical conditions, dialysis and kidney transplanta-tion, even though the same nephrologist may care for the patient during all three.

CKD and ESRD involve very different sets of activities, with different facilities and skills: limiting the progression of renal failure is an entirely different challenge from effective renal replacement, and dialysis man-agement and kidney transplantation also require very different care deliv-ery value chains governed by very different drivers of patient value. The care delivery value chains for CKD and ESRD are mutually exclusive—any given patient is either involved in one chain or the other at a point in time. Many patients with CKD may not progress to ESRD.

There are important links among the three chains that need to be man-aged. First, there needs to be a transfer of patient information in moving from CKD to dialysis to transplantation. Second, a patient in advanced CKD will benefit from timely installation of a vascular access graft (prefer-ably an arteriovenous fistula) before dialysis is required.[2] Third, a feed-back loop to CKD will be needed if a transplantation patient develops CKD with the new kidney, which is not uncommon.

Our judgment, based on expert input we have drawn on in preparing this example, is that more insight and more benefit in terms of improving patient value is gained by characterizing these conditions as three linked chains rather than a single chain. However, note that the CDVC frame-work is aimed at motivating and providing a framework for carrying on just this kind of discussion. Different providers can and will make differ-ent choices about how to organize and structure care delivery based on their patient populations, capabilities, and insights. What is most impor-tant is that every provider make a conscious and thoughtful choice about the best way to define the medical conditions and practice units in which it will participate, and to organize accordingly. Instead, too many providers simply follow conventions based on history and medical specialties.

Figure B-1 provides an overview of the full CKD care cycle, without attempting to capture all the relevant details. As with every care cycle, care for chronic kidney disease begins with prevention, especially for pa-tients at high risk. Such prevention activities should be part of excellent primary care. Primary care is also usually the place where an abnormality in kidney function is detected, and where the process of addressing chronic kidney disease begins.

Figure B-1 illustrates the various entities involved in the CKD cycle of care. In addition to the primary care physician, outpatient care managed by a nephrologist normally constitutes much of the care cycle. Clinical laboratories have an important and sustained role, while surgery and other procedures may be needed for some patients. Other specialists, such as urologists and endocrinologists, may have a role. The number of different entities involved in CKD care raises significant challenges in terms of data sharing and integration, as well as challenges in the coordination of decisions and treatments.

The care delivery value chain for CKD can be highly *iterative*. As patient circumstances evolve (e.g., kidney function degrades or other conditions arise), new measurement and diagnosis become necessary and new treatment plans may be needed. As the condition progresses, new entities may become involved in diagnosis or in delivering additional interventions. If a patient develops new medical conditions, or existing related conditions such as hypertension become severe, adjustments are needed.

The CDVC for chronic kidney disease also needs to be structured to deal with the fact that CKD patients are subject to complications and side effects from other seemingly unrelated treatments, such as the use of contrast agents in cardiac catheterization. Anticipating such side effects, factoring them into care decisions, and managing their consequences is an important aspect of the CKD care cycle. How to assemble the appropriate information, anticipate complications, and organize care to coordinate such decision making are important challenges.

This example illustrates an important principle underlying the integrated practice unit model. While there will inevitably be variations among patients, the aim is to recognize and address these variations within an integrated structure designed for expertise in the patient's primary condition, rather than an ad hoc structure involving uncoordinated specialists.

Stroke Care: Major Blood Vessel

Stroke is a relatively common medical emergency, involving about 700,000 cases per year in the United States. Strokes occur for a variety of reasons, with prominent risk factors including high blood pressure, tobacco use, diabetes, artery disease or heart disease, sickle cell disease, high blood cholesterol, obesity, excessive alcohol or drug use, family history, and prior strokes or heart attacks.[3]

About 20 percent of all strokes involve a large clot in a major blood vessel in the brain. Such strokes have the potential to halt blood flow to major sections of the brain, which kills brain tissue and results in severe patient consequences. Without successful and timely therapy for such strokes, the prognosis is bleak: death or severe disability. In the United States, stroke leads to about 163,000 deaths per year and is the leading cause of long-term disability. Stroke-related medical costs in 2005 were estimated at about $56.8 billion, of which $16.3 billion were attributable to acute care, $18.7 billion to long-term care, and $21.8 billion to lost income.[4]

Large clots in major vessels are quite resistant to systemic drug-based clot-dissolving therapies. For many such clots, the only means to clear them is mechanical intervention via a catheter in the brain, or drugs delivered via a catheter directly to the clot.

Stroke care, especially for major vessels, is highly time sensitive. Unless the treatment is delivered quickly (within a few hours for major vessel clots), the affected area of the brain is lost. Getting the patient to the right hospital quickly, securing timely imaging, and intervening promptly are essential to achieving good outcomes.

The CDVC for a major stroke is shown in figure B-2. Ideally, there should be a prevention element in the chain, which is especially important when prior strokes have occurred. Preventive activities can potentially take place as part of primary care, or as part of CDVCs for medical conditions that represent important stroke risk factors.

Once a stroke involving a major vessel has occurred, stroke care can involve a number of different entities: an ambulance company, an acute hospital, a rehabilitation hospital, and a long-term care facility (nursing home). Within the acute hospital, numerous organizational units often play a role: the emergency room, the imaging unit, the angioplasty suite, neurological intensive care, a hospital ward, and the rehabilitation unit, among others. Multiple types of medical skills must be brought together, as partially illustrated in the figure.

To successfully address a stroke involving a major vessel, the hospital must have sophisticated, twenty-four-hour, on-call imaging capability, including a computed tomographic (CT) scanner capable of CT angiography (CTA) as well as a magnetic resonance imaging (MRI) scanner. While the national standard of care for stroke requires a CT scanner, most hospitals lack round-the-clock access to MRI capability, and only a few hospitals have an MRI machine in the emergency room. MRI scans are essential in making a definitive diagnosis of the location and consequences of a stroke, and in determining the best treatment option for major stroke cases.

Since care must be delivered as soon after the stroke as possible, timely ambulance transport or another means of getting the patient to an appropriately equipped hospital quickly is important. Also, the ease and timeliness of patient transport inside the hospital, including the time required to place patients on imaging machines and move them between different treatment locations within the hospital, can have a major influence on the time to treatment and on patient results.

The care delivery value chain for strokes involving a major blood vessel

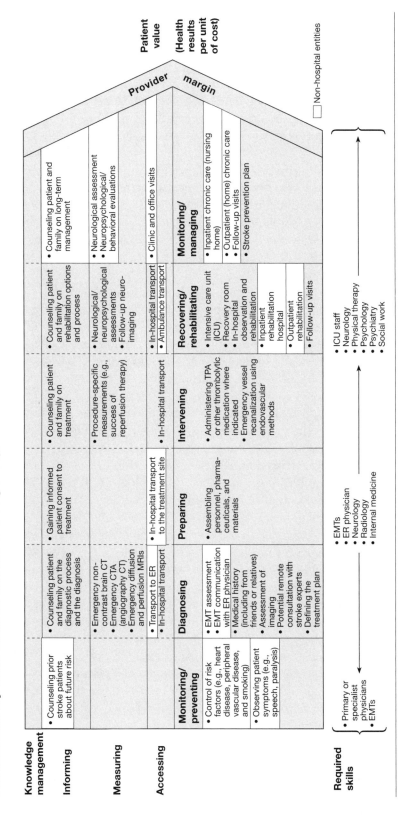

Breast Cancer Care

Each year, about 200,000 new cases of breast cancer are diagnosed in the United States and about 50,000 women die of the disease. A family history of breast cancer is a major risk factor, as are obesity and high-fat diets.

Patients with breast cancer may also have other conditions, such as postmenopausal hormonal imbalance or a history of Hodgkin's disease. From a patient value perspective, breast cancer care can be treated as a distinct medical condition with its own CDVCs. Separate care delivery chains should be responsible for postmenopausal hormonal management and Hodgkin's disease care, although there are linkages. Since prolonged use of some combinations of hormones raises the risk of breast cancer, as can radiation treatment for Hodgkin's disease, the presence of these conditions should affect the frequency of breast cancer screening.

A representative CDVC for breast cancer care is shown in figure B-3. As in all CDVCs, the breast cancer care cycle begins with monitoring and prevention. Early detection of breast cancer enables more effective treatment, so self-exams to detect lumps should begin in a woman's teens. Age, family history, and the results of genetic screening influence the frequency with which routine mammography should occur. Current practice involves annual screening via mammography at age forty, or ten years prior to the youngest age at which a family member contracted the disease. Risk counseling, reminders about self-checks, and the organization of mammograms normally take place within the practice of a primary care physician (PCP) or obstetrician/gynecologist (OB/GYN). The consistency of these activities across providers is uneven and a major issue affecting patient value.

In current practice, a positive mammogram or self-detection usually results in a referral to either a breast specialist or general surgeon for biopsy and other diagnostic procedures such as MRI or ultrasound (new imaging technologies now being tested may enable further diagnostic tests to be performed in the office of a PCP or OB/GYN). The diagnostic tests determine the size and location of the mass, whether it is malignant, and, if so, whether it is invasive or noninvasive. Genetic evaluation can also help to determine the type of cancer. In addition, metastatic tests (chest x-rays, bone scans, and CT scans) may be performed to determine whether the cancer has spread. New blood tests are becoming available that measure markers to help determine which patients should have metastatic tests.

After diagnosis, there are numerous choices to be made by the physician and the patient in terms of treatment. Extensive education and decision support for the patient is needed in this process because there are

The care delivery value chain for breast cancer

Knowledge management

Informing
- Education and reminders about regular exams
- Lifestyle and diet counseling

- Counseling patient and family on the diagnostic process and the diagnosis

- Explaining and supporting patient choices of treatment

- Counseling patient and family on treatment and prognosis

- Counseling patient and family on rehabilitation options and process

- Counseling patient and family on long-term risk management

Measuring
- Self-exams
- Mammograms

- Mammograms
- Ultrasound
- MRI
- Biopsy
- BRACA 1, 2 …

- Procedure-specific measurements

- Range of movement
- Side effects measurement

- Recurring mammograms (every 6 months for the first 3 years)

Accessing
- Office visits
- Mammography lab visits

- Office visits
- Lab visits
- High-risk clinic visits

- Office visits
- Hospital visits

- Hospital stay
- Visits to outpatient or radiation chemo-therapy units

- Office visits
- Rehabilitation facility visits

- Office visits
- Lab visits
- Mammographic labs and imaging center visits

Monitoring/preventing
- Medical history
- Monitoring for lumps
- Control of risk factors (obesity, high-fat diet)
- Clinical exams
- Genetic screening

Diagnosing
- Medical history
- Determining the specific nature of the disease
- Genetic evaluation
- Choosing a treatment plan

Preparing
- Medical counseling
- Surgery prep (anesthetic risk assessment, EKG)
- Patient and family psychological counseling
- Plastic or oncoplastic surgery evaluation

Intervening
- Surgery (breast preservation or mastectomy, onco-plastic alternative)
- Adjuvant therapies (hormonal medica-tion, radiation, and/or chemotherapy)

Recovering/rehabilitating
- In-hospital and outpatient wound healing
- Psychological counseling
- Treatment of side effects (skin damage, neurotoxic, cardiac, nausea, lymphedema, and chronic fatigue)
- Physical healing

Monitoring/managing
- Periodic mammography
- Other imaging
- Follow-up clinical exams for the next 2 years
- Treatment for any continued side effects

Provider margin

Patient value (Health results per unit of cost)

☐ Breast cancer specialist
☐ Other provider entities

interdependencies between surgical options and potential adjuvant therapies. Lumpectomy, mastectomy (several possible types), and oncoplastic surgery (which includes breast reconstruction) with either lumpectomy or mastectomy are options. The choice depends on the disease stage and patient preferences. The choice of type of surgery, as well as the patient's age and stage of cancer, affect decisions about adjuvant therapies (hormonal therapy, radiation, or chemotherapy, or a combination of these). For example, some women choose mastectomy over breast-preserving surgery (lumpectomy) because lumpectomy requires subsequent radiation and thus regular travel to a radiation facility for six weeks. Radiation also introduces risks of long-term side effects. Thus, the surgical options cannot be considered in isolation, even though adjuvant therapies will be delivered by different physicians at different times. Family education is also important prior to surgery because of the relatively high divorce rate for women after breast cancer surgery.

There is generally no reimbursement for patient education and counseling in the current system. However, the overall health and well-being of the patient is enhanced by including these services explicitly in the care cycle. Moreover, empirical evidence demonstrates that informed, involved breast cancer patients not only have better compliance but are also more likely to perceive their treatment as successful.

Preparation for surgery involves medical counseling as well as such activities as a presurgical electrocardiogram and anesthetic risk assessment. Plastic or oncoplastic surgery evaluation also needs to occur at this point. Surgery is performed in a hospital or surgery center. Reconstructive surgery can be done later, but in most cases occurs at the time of malignant tissue removal. Hormonal medication (e.g., tamoxifen) is prescribed at the time of the postoperative recovery. Recovery from surgery includes wound healing, psychological counseling, and physical therapy, each of which is associated with both in-hospital and outpatient activities.

Adjuvant therapy follows surgery. Lumpectomy (and sometimes mastectomy) is followed by radiation, which today requires that the patient go to the radiation facility regularly (often daily) for six weeks. New techniques are allowing radiation to be completed in five days, making travel or commuting far easier. Patients who have radiation must be monitored for years for skin damage. The use of chemotherapy depends on the patient's age and stage of cancer. Patients who have chemotherapy must be monitored for chronic fatigue, nausea, cardiac effects, and neurotoxic effects.

Surgery and other treatments do not cure breast cancer, but hopefully turn it into a chronic rather than an acute disease. Regular mammography, other imaging, and clinical exams continue throughout the patient's life. If surgery was performed by a general surgeon, long-term follow-up often reverts to the OB/GYN or PCP. If surgery was performed by a breast specialist, the surgeon may continue the long-term monitoring and hormonal medication. Thus, the general surgeons are more likely to see care as a surgical intervention, whereas breast cancer specialists are more naturally inclined toward a care-cycle perspective.

As we have described, a variety of types of skills and specialists can be involved in breast cancer care. While care of breast cancer is often managed by a combination of OB/GYNs and general surgeons, condition-specific specialists are increasingly important as understanding of the disease improves. Accurate reading of mammograms depends on volume of experience, so high-volume centers with experienced radiologists offer superior results. Pathologists who specialize in breasts are becoming more common, with more experience and specialized expertise in understanding the type or subtype of malignancy. Specialized breast surgeons tend to have physician practices that include more services for long-term follow-up, patient advocacy, or social work services, as well as physician assistants who can perform monitoring and consultation activities for patients with no signs of recurrence. While breast surgeons' practices are narrower in terms of the medical conditions served, then, they are broader in terms of the CDVC and the care cycle.

The breast cancer CDVC draws attention to the array of physicians involved in care across the cycle. As one physician aptly explained, a significant part of his job is to ensure there are no "holes in the floor" for the patient to fall through. For example, early signs of secondary lymphedema, a swelling that may occur in the arms of breast cancer patients due to removal of lymph nodes, may be missed if the patient reports these symptoms to someone caring for a different aspect of the disease. Better results are achieved with early physical therapy, but this opportunity is sometimes missed until lymphedema is more extreme. Another "hole" in the care cycle occurs when imaging or clinical exams are skipped. A full-care-cycle view, with clear assignment of responsibility at each stage, will lead to better systems to ensure appropriate long-term monitoring.

Notes

Chapter 1

1. In some nations, such as the United Kingdom, costs are increasing based on deliberate choices to boost spending because of perceived deficiencies in the system.

2. U.S. Census Bureau (2001, 2002); DeNavas-Walt, Proctor, and Mills (2005). In 1987, there were 31 million uninsured Americans. The percentage of uninsured Americans rose from 12.9 percent in 1987 to 15.7 percent in 2004. The rise was continuous except for a brief decline in 1999–2000.

3. Starfield (2000b).

4. Commonwealth Fund/Harvard/Harris Interactive (2001); Blendon et al. (2003).

5. Ibid.

6. OECD data cited in Friedman (2001) and World Health Organization (2004).

7. These results may be significantly affected by poor access to primary care; see Starfield (2000b). Rates of deaths from medical errors appear to be lower in the United States (see chapter 3). A study by Schoen et al. (2005) indicates that a greater percentage of American patients report problems and errors in outpatient care than patients in Australia, Canada, France, Germany, and New Zealand. Again, the lack of universal primary care and the fragmented system of care in the United States contribute to the extreme frustration of Americans with their health care system. Yet, on several of the study's measures of serious health consequences, such as rehospitalization from complications during recovery or significant health consequences from reported medication errors, the U.S. patients reported better results than any country but Germany.

8. Druss et al. (2002).

9. Committee on Quality of Health Care in America, Institute of Medicine (2001). Appendix A of this report reviewed more than seventy peer-reviewed medical articles documenting quality problems of these three types.

10. McGlynn et al. (2003). The authors examined the thirty conditions in depth, reviewing established national guidelines, the medical literature, and proposed indicators of quality to establish the process of care that should be followed. The authors found little difference in the proportion of recommended care received across preventive care (54.9 percent), acute care (53.5 percent), and chronic care (56.1 percent). The study did find large differences in the percentage

of recommended care that was actually delivered when classified by medical condition, ranging from 10.5 percent of the recommended care for alcohol dependency to 78.7 percent for senile cataracts. See also Fonarow et al. (2003) and Wennberg and Cooper (1999).

11. Woolf et al. (2004); Bertoni et al. (2005).

12. Kohn, Corrigan, and Donaldson (2000); Committee on Quality of Health Care in America, Institute of Medicine (2001); Chassin et al. (1998); Advisory Commission on Consumer Protection and Quality in the Health Care Industry (1998).

13. HealthGrades (2004).

14. Starfield (2000b); Weingart et al. (2000).

15. Weingart et al. (2000).

16. See the discussion and notes in chapter 8.

17. Chandra, Shanantu, and Seabury (2005) found that 40 percent of malpractice payments involved malpractice in diagnosis. Phillips et al. (2004) found that one third of unambiguous negligence claims in medical malpractice suits involving primary care were due to diagnosis error. The validity of the claim was based on a peer review by a panel of uninvolved physicians.

18. See, for example, Bates et al. (1997); Kohn, Corrigan, and Donaldson (2000); and Committee on Quality of Health Care in America, Institute of Medicine (2001).

19. Zhan and Miller (2003).

20. Weingart et al. (2000).

21. Wennberg and Cooper (1999); Martin et al. (2002).

22. Ibid.

23. Fisher et al. (2003a, 2003b); Wennberg and Cooper (1999).

24. Baicker and Chandra (2004).

25. See the box "How Good Outcome Information Arose" in chapter 4 for a fuller discussion.

26. Kane et al. (2004); Bohmer et al. (2005). See also the section in chapter 5 entitled "Choose the Range and Types of Services Provided."

27. Coye et al. (2003).

28. Balas and Boren (2000).

29. See also Committee on Quality of Health Care in America, Institute of Medicine (2001), which reviews a number of papers showing slow adoption of established guidelines, as well as Gawande (2004), which gives a sense of how innovation and adoption occur. Many other studies document slow adoption of established guidelines and proven practices, such as Davis et al. (1995), Grimshaw and Russell (1993), Wells (2000), Davis and Taylor-Vaisey (1997), Mosca et al. (2005), Denton et al. (2003), LaBresh et al. (2004), Galvin (2005), and Pathman et al. (1996).

30. AHA/ASHMR Survey (2002); U.S. Department of Health and Human Services, Office of the Assistant Secretary for Planning and Evaluation (2002).

31. Physicians are quick to point out that if the administrative burden were decreased, they could reduce prices or provide more free care to those who need it.

32. PricewaterhouseCoopers and the American Hospital Association (2001).

33. Woolhandler and Himmelstein (1997); Woolhandler, Himmelstein, and Wolfe (2004); and Woolhandler, Campbell, and Himmelstein (2004).

34. Woolhandler and Himmelstein (1997)

35. Connolly (2005).

36. Mayne (2004).

37. Mercer Human Resource Consulting (2004a).

38. Hewitt Associates (2003a, 2003b). Hewitt Associates found that CEO and COO concern about health care costs was so universal that the question was removed from its 2005 survey. (Communication with Joanne Laffrey, Hewitt Associates, March 29, 2005.)

39. Mercer Human Resources Consulting (2004a).

Chapter 2

1. Economists refer to competition that creates or expands value as non–zero sum, or *positive sum*. Competition that creates no value, but only determines how value is divided, is called *zero sum*. Often, zero-sum competition degenerates to negative-sum competition because the competitive process increases costs without offsetting gains. For a discussion of the roots of the zero-sum idea in game theory, see Aumann (1987).

2. See, for example, Relman (2005).

3. Centers for Medicare and Medicaid, Office of the Actuary, National Health Statistics Group, "National Health Expenditures."

4. Fee reductions on specific conditions to attract a stream of patients with those conditions can create a win-win situation in which the provider gains expertise and efficiency that enables success at lower prices.

5. A group of AHA member hospitals wrote a letter in December 2003 to the Secretary of Health and Human Services asking for clarification and change in the thick "regulatory morass" that seemed to require hospitals to bill full prices to the uninsured and pursue "aggressive efforts to collect from all patients." The Secretary responded, saying that hospitals may charge discounted prices to uninsured patients. See T. G. Thompson (2004).

6. Medical bills are the second leading cause of personal bankruptcy.

7. Federal Trade Commission and U.S. Department of Justice (2004); Dranove (2000).

8. Some notable exceptions are discussed in chapter 5.

9. Kaiser Family Foundation (2004), section 5, "Trends in the Structure of the Health Care Marketplace."

10. Martinez (2002).

11. Sizable markets, such as Asheville and Greensboro, North Carolina, have gone from two hospital systems to one. See Jaklevic (2000).

12. Capps and Dranove (2004). Other data also reveals that hospital price increases are highest for those institutions with the most bargaining power, such as children's hospitals with a monopoly in their region. See, for example, Jaklevic (2000).

13. Federal Trade Commission and U.S. Department of Justice (2004) reviews the literature and testimony on mergers.

14. Providers object to the suggestion that they become "focused factories" that standardize care for a narrowly focused set of services (Herzlinger, 1997, 1999a). This objection is valid for many areas of care, but concern regarding narrow specialization is not a good reason for trying to provide all services for all patients without achieving excellence.

15. Coordinated care across providers, when it is needed, will also get far easier when medical records are truly integrated rather than held by each separate provider and not made easily available to other providers. The current medical records system creates an artificial rationale for broad-line providers.

16. We discuss stroke care further in chapters 4 and 5.

17. Some providers argue that any narrowing of services will result in a dispro-portionately high loss of patients because referring doctors expect every patient to be treated at the hospital to which they refer, and the diagnosis is often not clear at the time of referral.

18. For example, in organ transplants, where risk-adjusted outcome data is pub-licly available, even when the referring doctors are aware that the data shows better outcomes for a non-local provider, they often assume the patient can only get reim-bursement for coverage at the closest provider, so they refer to that provider group.

19. Some observers argue that managed care plans are offering what healthy subscribers want when they enroll. However, subscribers should become much more focused on the services available from the health plan *at the time of illness or injury*.

20. Families know about their chronic conditions, but health plans have not generally competed to serve subscribers with chronic illnesses, since they are ex-pensive to serve compared to healthy subscribers.

21. See the discussion and notes in chapter 1, especially Committee on Quality of Health Care in America, Institute of Medicine (2001), which reviews more than seventy articles published in peer-reviewed journals that document health care quality problems; Wennberg and Cooper (1999); Baicker and Chandra (2004); Fisher et al. (2003a, 2003b); and McGlynn et al. (2003).

22. Advocates of "managed care" (in the best sense of the phrase) envision a system in which physicians are supported with information and up-to-date guide-lines by a well-administered system that coaches rather than handcuffs them to enable better judgment. We talk later about the challenges of achieving this in practice, and the powerful alternative of achieving these goals with patient-centered, value-based competition on results.

23. This is an example of supply-induced demand, in which hospital beds and physicians' schedules are filled to capacity.

24. Immediate readmission would not count as a separate admission. However, if a second surgery is needed, or if the patient does not recover fully or develops complications such as surgical adhesions, for example, the subsequent care will be paid for again.

25. See Kessler and McClellan (2002) for a study of the costs and productivity losses from defensive medicine. Studying elderly patients with cardiac illness, the authors estimate a savings in hospital costs of $4.76 for each $1 reduction in litiga-tion costs for the insurer (intuitively, this result says that more litigation results in doctors practicing more defensive medicine). This study found no improved health associated with higher spending.

26. U.S. Department of Health and Human Services, Office of the Assistant Sec-retary for Planning and Evaluation (2002).

27. Although out-of-network care is not inherently more expensive, hospitals charge list prices to out-of-network patients that may be two to four times as high as negotiated in-network prices. The difference between the amount the payer will reimburse and the artificially high list prices essentially makes out-of-network care prohibitively expensive for many patients.

28. Communication with Dr. Leroy Hood, Institute for Systems Biology, Octo-ber 8, 2004.

29. The quality of health care has multiple dimensions, and different patients will value them differently in their choices. Researchers working on relevant mea-

sures look at dimensions such as risk-adjusted outcomes, satisfaction, length of disease-free intervals, mortality, length of stay, repeat surgeries, and infection rates.

30. Wennberg and Cooper (1999) examine U.S. Medicare data. See their chapter 5, "Practice Variations and the Quality of Surgical Care for Common Conditions," 139–174. See also Baicker and Chandra (2004).

31. Wennberg and Cooper (1999).

32. Ironically, as providers have become more alike in services offered, they remain dissimilar in the processes used and results delivered, reducing value for the patients who receive substandard care.

33. The full-service model has also slowed the development of coordinated care across separate facilities and procedures for patient transport.

34. E. S. Fisher et al. (2004).

35. See the earlier discussion and notes in the section "Competition to Increase Bargaining Power."

36. Data on hospital spending show similar trends. The hospital spending rate was 3.2 percent in 1997, 3.1 percent in 1998, and 5.1 percent in 1999 (U.S. Department of Labor, Bureau of Labor Statistics, n.d.). Reflecting these premium growth trends, employer spending on health benefits also saw declining growth rates from 1990 to 1996, but the rate of increase has climbed each year since then. For more data on employer health care spending trends, see Mercer Human Resources Consulting (2005).

37. Essentially, this restarted the medical arms race of the 1980s in a new form, as we discuss in chapter 3.

38. Professional ethics and professional pride are now the primary motivations for improving quality and efficiency. The incentives in the system should not work against them. We discuss this further in the section "The Wrong Incentives for Providers."

39. Gawande (2004) discusses how most doctors believe they are well above average, although roughly half must be below average. He also provides a vivid example of how learning occurs when results are compared. The story of improvements in care in cystic fibrosis is a strong testament to the power of information and the value of the work being done by Don Berwick at the Institute for Healthcare Improvement.

40. Hibbard, Stockard, and Tusler (2003).

41. Thus, an old problem reappears in the new system. Even in the days of fee for service, competition among providers was suppressed by referrals based on personal connections and limited information. See chapter 3.

42. For instance, the government requires reporting of objective information about airline performance.

43. In the *U.S. News and World Report* ranking, "[i]n Ophthalmology, Pediatrics, Psychiatry, Rehabilitation, and Rheumatology [the remaining five specialties], hospitals were ranked only by their reputation among board-certified specialists. This is because mortality data for pediatric facilities are unavailable and are irrelevant or unreliable in the other specialties. Ranked hospitals were cited by at least 3 percent of responding physicians" (Comarow, 2004).

The technical criteria require a hospital to provide at least nine of twenty technology-intensive patient services: angioplasty, cardiac catheterization lab, cardiac intensive care beds, computed tomography scanner, diagnostic radioisotope facility, diagnostic mammography services, extracorporeal shock wave lithotripter, magnetic resonance imaging, medical/surgical intensive care, neonatal intensive care, oncology services, open heart surgery, pediatric intensive care beds, positron emission tomography scanner, reproductive health, single photon emission computed tomography, transplant services, ultrasound, and x-ray radiation therapy (O'Muircheartaigh and Murphy, 2004). This standard discourages specialization, while stimulating hospital demand for expensive technology for expensive technology's sake.

44. Kane, Needleman, and Rudell (2004); Bohmer et al. (2005); Pisano, Bohmer, and Edmondson (2001).

45. We describe how this information developed in chapter 4.

46. Pennsylvania Health Care Cost Containment Council 2002 data; see Winslow (1990).

47. Winslow (1990). The Pennsylvania Health Care Cost Containment Council 1988 data were also previously available on the council's Web site at http://www.PHC4.org.

48. Schneider and Epstein (1996).

49. Becher and Chassin (2001).

50. Mehrotra, Bodenheimer, and Dudley (2003) discuss fifteen employer coalition initiatives to measure health care quality in eleven communities throughout the United States. See also the Committee for Economic Development (2002).

51. These examples are discussed further in chapter 4. See also Burton (1999); Bodenheimer and Sullivan (1998); Farley et al. (2003); and Rosenthal, Quinn, and Harper (1997).

52. Preferred Global Health (2001).

53. Dr Foster (2005).

54. See also the discussion on information in chapter 4.

55. O'Connor, Llewellyn-Thomas, and Flood (2004); Wennberg and Cooper (1999).

56. Wennberg and Cooper (1999), 226–229.

57. Bodenheimer et al. (2002) found that better-informed patients have better outcomes and lower costs. Patients who adopted a self-management education process showed better outcomes for asthma, arthritis, and diabetes. Fewer hospitalizations generated savings of $750 per patient.

58. O'Connor, Llewellyn-Thomas, and Flood (2004); Bodenheimer et al. (2002); Wennberg and Cooper (1999).

59. Ibid.

60. Today, patients who dare to haggle with doctors can obtain discounts from list prices. Because these discounts can be significant but the process is contentious, companies have emerged that negotiate discounted prices for individual patients. With transparent prices, however, doctors and patients would not need to haggle about price and could focus instead on the medical needs at hand. For a discussion on haggling, see Costell (2002a, 2002b).

61. Newhouse and the Insurance Experiment Group (1996) found that uninformed patients with lower copayments sought more medical care, but the patients' only choice was more care or less. Since there was no process of informing patients about outcomes, their choice did not necessarily translate into better outcomes. O'Connor, Llewellyn-Thomas, and Flood (2004) also found that less-informed patients chose more expensive, more invasive care, which is consistent with uninformed patients confusing more treatment with better health. The idea that people seek better health is far more logical than the idea that people always want more medical care, which implies they desire pain, risk, and inconvenience.

62. O'Connor, Llewellyn-Thomas, and Flood (2004).

63. This literature is discussed in chapters 6 and 7.

64. Kleinke (1998).

65. More generally, health plans fail to advise patients about or direct patients to surgeons with lower rates of repeat surgeries.

66. For example, when a bill seems to be in error, the health plan simply refuses payment rather than try to sort it out. When payment is refused, the hospital or physician group bills the patient or grieving family, who must pay the bill or contest the error on their own.

67. If most patients questioned and contested bills, it would become far less expensive for providers and health plans to improve billing practices and get it right the first time than to deal with the patients' queries. However, most patients do not pursue this option, due possibly to lack of awareness and the challenges of dealing with large bureaucracies.

68. Patients may also be billed as though they were going out of network when they receive care from an in-network doctor without the required referrals.

69. Out-of-network or "list" price may be as much as four times higher than negotiated prices.

70. The patient is charged list price, but the payer reimburses 70 percent of what it would owe if it had a contract with the out-of-the-network provider. Because bargained-down contract prices are often 50 percent of list price (or less), paying 70 percent of that portion of the bill only reimburses 35 percent of it. The patient must pay the remaining 65 percent because the patient cannot bargain with the hospital to get the in-network price. (The percentage paid by the patient may be more or less than 65 percent depending on the size of the health plan's negotiated in-network discounts.)

71. HCIA (1997) shows that the median U.S. HMO faces 22 percent disenrollment every year.

72. McGlynn et al. (2003).

73. While this chart data does not specifically measure readmission, the data discussed in chapter 1 reveal large numbers of errors and low standards of care in the past decade when admission numbers turned upward.

74. Wennberg, Freeman, and Culp (1987).

75. Wennberg (2005); Fisher et al. (2003a, 2003b); Baicker and Chandra (2004). There is usually no evidence to suggest how often a patient should be seen. A doctor with more time tends to see patients more frequently.

76. Wennberg (2005) calls this type of overtreatment bias "subliminal" in the sense that it does not seem to stem from conscious decisions to overtreat.

77. Committee on Quality of Health Care in America, Institute of Medicine (2001).

78. Dean et al. (2001)

79. Communication with Brent James, February 16, 2005, and July 15, 2005.

80. Many employers are self-insured but hire health plans to administer their benefits. Even these employers tended to go along with approaches that appeared to contain costs in the short term.

Chapter 3

1. Gordon (1992).

2. Gabel (1999).

3. Since 1946, more than $4.6 billion in Hill-Burton grant funds, plus $1.5 billion in loans, have been directed to 6,800 health care facilities in over 4,000 communities (U.S. Department of Health and Human Services, Health Resources

and Services Administration, n.d.). However, some of the new facilities, especially in rural areas, lacked physicians to staff them.

4. Nichols et al. (2004).

5. For a discussion of the many skewed incentives in U.S. health care in the 1980s and early 1990s, see Teisberg, Porter, and Brown (1994b).

6. Section 1877 of the Social Security Act, enacted in 1989, prohibited physician referrals of Medicare patients for clinical laboratory services in facilities where the physicians had financial interests. The legislation has since been expanded in 1992 and 1993 to apply to Medicaid and Medicare beneficiaries and, in the 2003 Medicare Modernization Act, to specifically target specialty hospitals. See Centers for Medicare and Medicaid Services (2005a).

7. A major ischemic stroke requires complex intervention to save the area of the brain around the site of the blockage, and managing a more complex recovery. A minor stroke requires only observation of the patient and diagnosis of the stroke's cause to determine appropriate preventive treatment to reduce the risk of a future large stroke.

8. Enthoven (1993, 2003, 2004).

9. See chapter 1, figure 1-17.

10. Robinson and Luft (1987) first described the arms race competition in health care.

11. These facilities, however, were rarely designed around patient value in addressing particular medical conditions, as we discuss in chapter 5.

12. See, for example, Pauly (2004) and Relman (2005).

13. See U.S. General Accounting Office (2003b) and Casalino, Devers, and Brewster (2003).

14. The percentage of persons under age sixty-five who are uninsured passed 15 percent in 1991 and has risen since then to over 17.7 percent in 2003 (Hoffman, Carbaugh, and Cook, 2004; Committee on the Consequences of Uninsurance, Board on Health Care Services, Institute of Medicine of the National Academies, 2004).

15. Hunter (2004).

16. Applied Research and Analysis Directorate, Health Policy Research Program (2003). See also note 17.

17. World Health Organization (2002a); Applied Research and Analysis Directorate, Health Policy Research Program (2003); Wilson et al. (1999). Due to the lack of universal primary care coverage and care cycle fragmentation, U.S. patients express more frustration about their care and perceive more mistakes than citizens of five other countries, even though they report fewer rehospitalizations and fewer significant health consequences from outpatient medication errors (Schoen et al., 2005). The frustration of U.S. patients signals a serious problem in the United States. However, there are significant quality problems in other nations as well.

18. Eckbo (2005).

19. The Institute of Medicine estimated 44,000 to 88,000 deaths from medical errors in 1999; the U.S. population was 279 million. HealthGrades estimated 195,000 deaths from medical errors in 2002. The U.S. population in 2002 was 288 million.

20. For a discussion of HIPAA implementation of notification of privacy policies, see Upham and Gue (n.d.).

21. Herzlinger (1997).

22. Herzlinger (2004a) offers an authoritative compilation of contributions on consumer-driven health care. Many of the suggestions made in this edited volume

can be beneficial in a broader context in which competition is redefined in the ways we describe here.

23. Herzlinger (1997) proposes focused factories that are specialized around particular areas of treatment. In her writing, Herzlinger uses the example of Jiffy Lube, which provides oil changes but leaves other parts of the car to others. This model is applicable to relatively few areas of care.

24. Nichols et al. (2004) documents extensive interviews conducted over a decade of research in twelve communities that show that an increasing number of individuals believe that market-based solutions, which are strongly identified with consumer-driven health care, have failed. The authors do reveal the state of thinking about U.S. health care; however, their analysis assumes throughout that competition in health care means either competition among health plans or competition among hospitals and networks.

25. Kohn, Corrigan, and Donaldson (2000).

26. Each of these results was discussed in chapter 1. The citations to the relevant studies are included there.

27. Midwest Business Group on Health in collaboration with Juran Institute, Inc., and the Severyn Group, Inc. (2003). Fisher et al. (2003a, 2003b) estimate 30 percent waste in Medicare spending, and Milstein (2004) estimates 40 percent waste in the system.

28. For a discussion of studies of the effect of fatigue on rates of medical error, see Landrigan et al. (2004).

29. In its own words, "The National Quality Forum is a private, not-for-profit membership organization created to develop and implement a national strategy for healthcare quality measurement and reporting. The mission of the NQF is to improve American healthcare through endorsement of consensus-based national standards for measurement and public reporting of healthcare performance data that provide meaningful information about whether care is safe, timely, beneficial, patient-centered, equitable and efficient." The NQF was formed in 1998 in response to the President's Advisory Commission on Consumer Protection and Quality in the Health Care Industry. See http://www.qualityforum.org/.

For information on the Institute for Healthcare Improvement, see its Web site, http://www.ihi.org/ihi/about, and its progress report (available on the site). For information about the National Committee for Quality Assurance, see its Web site, http://www.ncqa.org/about/about.htm.

30. See Birkmeyer et al. (2000); Committee for Economic Development (2002); Sarudi (2001); Boeing Company (2001); Lovern (2001); Midwest Business Group on Health (2001); and R. Pollack (2002). See also Leapfrog's Web site, http://www.leapfroggroup.org/home.

31. Berwick et al. (2003).

32. Leapfrog's compendium of pay-for-performance initiatives can be found at http://ir.leapfroggroup.org/compendium/compendiumresult.cfm.

33. Snyder and Anderson (2005).

34. Gawande (2004).

35. Another national guideline, that tPA must be administered within three hours to be effective, is also problematic. Some patients can benefit from later administration.

36. Wennberg (2005) discusses the problem of not rewarding doctors for helping to educate and inform patients. He points this out as a weakness in current pay-for-performance proposals.

37. The Medicare for All proposal is the Expanded and Improved Medicare for All U.S. National Health Insurance Act, HR 676.

38. See, for example, Nichols et al. (2004) and Enthoven (2004).

39. A single payer's purchasing process is likely to resemble government procurement in areas such as defense, where bureaucracy reigns, suppliers have become highly concentrated, and weapons are extremely costly and subject to large overruns.

40. Revenue Act of 1978.

41. Medical savings accounts (MSAs) were simultaneously proposed by several individuals, but are most strongly associated with John Goodman and Richard Rahn, who laid out such a plan in 1984 (Goodman and Rahn, 1984). Also in 1984, Singapore created its Medisave program, in which all employees contributed 6 percent of their income to accounts that could be used for nonreimbursed medical costs. A medical savings plan was introduced in South Africa in 1993 by a private insurer, and MSAs are now widespread there.

42. Health Insurance Portability and Accountability Act of 1996.

43. This history is developed from the following sources: Saleem (2003); National Center for Policy Analysis (2004); Tanner (1992); Office of Personnel Management (n.d.).

44. Health plans may still choose to pay for preventive care (such as vaccinations and early detection of treatable diseases) or cover other treatments that clearly reduce overall costs irrespective of HSA limits. This should not be necessary if HSA accounts are adequately funded. Indeed, studies so far show that patients with HSAs do not forgo preventive care. However, the point remains that it is important to ensure that patients are not forgoing prescriptions or other effective care because of out-of-pocket costs.

45. Aetna (2004) discusses Aetna's results from studying the behavior of nearly 14,000 subscribers of its Aetna HealthFund plan.

46. Similar to the results from Aetna, the National Center for Policy Analysis (2004) describes the experiences of two companies offering HSAs. Assurant Health reported that 43 percent of HSA applicants did not have prior health plan coverage and 70 percent of purchasers were over forty years old. E-HealthInsurance reported that 32 percent of HSA applicants did not have health plan coverage in the preceding six-month period. E-HealthInsurance also reported that half of the applicants earned less than $35,000.

47. For example, see Newhouse and the Insurance Experiment Group (1996).

48. Lieber (2004). Lockheed Martin, Medtronic, and Wells Fargo also offer an employee option of MSAs.

49. Committee for Economic Development (2002).

50. Ibid.

51. Value-based competition will require all participants in the system, including pharmaceutical companies, to compete to create value. The incentive to create new, more effective, and less expensive drugs will be strong. As we discuss in chapter 7, consumer advertising to encourage drug usage should decrease as data on results is improved.

Chapter 4

1. Cutler et al. (1999) analyzes cardiac medicine. Separately, Cutler and McClellan (2001) find that technological advances are worth far more than costs in four of the five conditions they analyzed, and equal to cost in the fifth.

2. Morris (1999).

3. Nordhaus (1999) examines the benefits of spending on health care in the United States and finds the value of increased longevity to be almost as large as the value of all other goods and services consumed by Americans. This suggests that failing to consider the value of health care, and trying simply to reduce its costs, can lead to very misguided priorities. In a separate study with different methods, Murphy and Topel (1999) calculate the economic value of increases in life expectancy as the single largest source of gains in living standards. Neither study includes the benefits of reductions in sickness or improvements in quality of life from better health, which would add even more to the value (Luce et al., 2004).

4. Some studies suggest that drug spending is rising primarily due to increased use of effective drugs, rather than price increases. See, for example, Dubois et al. (2000) and Kleinke (2000). Lichtenberg (2001) analyzes the relationship between new-drug use and medical expenditures and finds that use of newer drugs reduces mortality and morbidity and substantially reduces total medical expenditure, including large reductions in inpatient expenditures. However, there are also examples of drugs that do not clearly increase value, including examples of new drugs that are not more effective and examples of increased drug spending due to increased prices.

5. Studies have found that requiring patients to pay for drugs sometimes results in higher overall costs because the resulting failure to use the drugs raises other costs by more than the drug costs. The results are strongest in mental health but are not limited to that area. In such cases, health plans and patients will benefit if the health plan has the flexibility to cover drugs fully and thus encourage an effective and less-expensive therapy. See Soumerai et al. (1994); Kleinke (2001); and Lichtenberg (1996, 2001).

6. Price controls appear to have stifled innovation in many other industries and countries. For example, the French pharmaceutical industry once ranked second in producing innovative drugs. After years of price controls, France is now ranked ninth. Similar suppression of drug innovation can be observed in other price-controlled systems, including Italy, Spain, and Canada.

7. The ALLHAT Officers and Coordinators for the ALLHAT Collaborative Research Group (2002). We thank Dr. Robert Flaherty from Montana State University for bringing this example to our attention.

8. Lichtenberg (2000) looks at the drivers of the longevity increases analyzed by Nordhaus (1999) and Murphy and Topel (1999). He finds that medical innovation in the form of new drugs and medical expenditures contributes to increased longevity, and suggests that increased development of new drugs may be a more cost-effective way of increasing life expectancy than increased medical expenditures.

9. This reality is illustrated vividly by the differences in results for treating cystic fibrosis patients described in Gawande (2004).

10. Note that more experienced and effective providers will often enjoy higher margins due to their expertise and efficiency. As we discuss, rewarding good providers with more patients, and allowing substandard providers to attract fewer patients, would be a much more important motivator for excellent providers than small changes in prices or bonuses.

11. Administration of aspirin to patients with heart attack symptoms is one of the process measures widely used, including by Medicare. See Centers for Medicare and Medicaid Services (2004a).

12. Fisher (2005).

13. Wennberg (2005) points out that the incentive to overtreat is often subliminal. Physicians do not consciously decide to overtreat patients just to earn more

money, but rather they believe that fully using medical capacity—their time and available hospital facilities—is the right thing to do. We are sympathetic to this view. Given the uncertainty they face and the lack of evidence they have or use, physicians are inclined to do more for patients when they can. But that may not improve results or value. One implication of his observation is that requiring doctors to do less may seem unethical to them unless they can see evidence that doing less improves outcomes for the patient. So, again, focusing on results is crucial.

14. Transplant outcome data, for example, is verified by checking whether the patient had a subsequent transplant by a different provider and whether Social Security records indicate that the patient has died.

15. Herzlinger (1997) advocates the movement to "focused factories" and the standardization of health care delivery, which relates to the question of market or business definition. We believe that the notion of focused factories is too narrow a view of how providers should structure care delivery. See chapter 5.

16. Milstein points to the need for measures of "longitudinal efficiency" (Milstein, 2004; Fisher et al., 2004). He observes that some providers may have lower costs for treating an entire episode of acute care, or for a year of treatment for a chronic condition, even if parts of the delivered care have a higher unit price and concludes that longitudinal efficiency is more important than the unit price. Analysis of care cycles and the care delivery value chain (chapter 5 and appendix B) reveal factors that underlie longitudinal efficiency and can enable the development of the measures of longitudinal efficiency that Milstein identifies as nonexistent.

17. The journal *Disease Management* was launched in 1998. For a discussion of disease management literature, see chapters 6 and 7.

18. Coresh et al. (2003).

19. Bolton (2003).

20. Ofsthun et al. (2003). Some studies conclude that early intervention in chronic kidney disease more than doubles the chances of survival six months after onset. A timely referral of patients with early stages of chronic kidney disease requires a collaboration among primary care physicians, who screen patients and begin patient education, a disease management program to provide for further education, and surgical preparation for dialysis if the disease progresses.

21. The preferred vascular access for dialysis is an arteriovenous fistula, which significantly lowers the rate of complications with dialysis (Centers for Medicare and Medicaid Services, 2004d) but requires surgery to install the fistula before dialysis begins. In the United States, only 31 percent of patients have a fistula installed, compared to 81 percent in Europe and 93 percent in Japan (Rayner et al., 2004).

22. Stack (2003). Stack also concluded that mortality risks were 20 percent lower for patients who saw a nephrologist at least twice in the year before dialysis therapy initiation.

23. Villagra and Ahmed (2004); Gold and Kongstvedt (2003).

24. The concept of the productivity frontier defines the relationship between quality and cost. The frontier itself charts the relationship between quality and cost if a producer utilizes all available best practices in terms of methods, technologies, equipment, skills, and so on. This frontier constantly shifts outward as new best practices are developed. If a producer is not operating on this frontier, moving toward it by adopting best practices can improve quality with no cost sacrifice, lower cost with no quality sacrifice, or improve quality and cost at the same time (see figure 4-2). In health care, given the absence of value-based competition

at the condition level, numerous providers are operating well off the productivity frontier. For further discussion, see Porter (1996).

25. The abundant evidence of poor-quality care and care below accepted medical standards in the United States is discussed in chapter 1.

26. See, for example, Fisher et al. (2003a, 2003b).

27. Kohn, Corrigan, and Donaldson (2000).

28. Midwest Business Group on Health in collaboration with Juran Institute, Inc., and The Severyn Group, Inc. (2003). The estimate is based on literature review and Juran Institute experience with hospital clients. Dartmouth research (Fisher et al., 2003a, 2003b) estimates 30 percent waste in Medicare spending. Milstein (2004) estimates 40 percent waste in the system.

29. Wennberg and Cooper (1999). This study of Medicare practices throughout the United States also found that increased per capita spending did not eliminate the underserving of patients, particularly for preventive care (see page 200). More recent studies confirm these results, finding that more specialist care did not mean that the basic care had been provided, just that more money had been spent.

30. Trevelyan (2002).

31. Longman (2005).

32. Ibid.

33. See the many articles and presentations by Brent C. James on quality improvement in health care. These and other examples are discussed in chapter 5.

34. Morris (1999).

35. Kizer (2003) discusses the "strong and persistent" literature finding that better outcomes are associated with experience and volume. See, for example, Showstack et al. (1987), Marwick (1992), Birkmeyer et al. (2002), and Begg et al. (2002) for studies considering the relationship of hospital volume and results. Other studies, such as Birkmeyer et al. (2003), show that the hospital and volume relationship is driven by the volumes and outcomes of specific surgeons. Still other studies show the benefit of a practiced team. See, for example, Young et al. (1997). Huckman and Pisano (2005) show that the team matters by demonstrating that the surgeon's volume at a specific hospital matters more than his or her overall volume. Bohmer et al. (2005) looks at learning curves on two dimensions, showing that at community hospitals costs are driven down faster for procedures in which they have higher volume, and that at tertiary care hospitals, learning is faster on how to treat more complex cases, of which they treat more. The different dimensions of learning reflect the different areas of higher volumes of experience.

36. See Murray and Teasdale (2005) and Gandjour, Bannenberg, and Lauterbach (2003).

37. Even the most skeptical researchers note the threshold effect. See for example, Sowden et al. (1997). In addition, the more recent literature is stronger than the earlier literature in showing the correlation of experience and outcomes, in part because it uses better risk adjustment and in part because of the more sophisticated understanding of learning, rather than volume, as the key driver of improvement.

38. Kerlikowske et al. (1998).

39. Smith-Bindman et al. (2005).

40. Outsourcing to specialists is possible for some biologic samples, such as in amniocentesis, where samples can be shipped at ambient temperatures.

41. In carotid endarterectomies (surgical procedures that remove plaque from the carotid artery to reduce the risk of stroke associated with stenosis, a narrowing

of blood vessels), for example, mortality rates are lower for patients at hospitals where the procedure is performed at least seventy times per year than at hospitals where it is performed fewer than forty times per year (1.7 percent vs. 2.5 percent). Hospitals that perform a high volume of carotid endarterectomies and also participate in clinical trials, signifying the systematic study of new methods of treatment, have even lower mortality rates (1.5 percent). See Wennberg et al. (1998).

42. Choudhry, Fletcher, and Soumerai (2005) reviewed sixty-two studies and found an inverse relationship between quality of care and the physician's age, underscoring the importance of competence, results, and learning, not age or numbers of years in practice.

43. M. D. Anderson continues to provide second opinions for other types of cancer.

44. We are grateful to Dr. Gil Gonzalez for bringing this example to our attention.

45. See chapters 6 and 7.

46. Coye et al. (2003) discuss the adoption and diffusion of innovations in medicine even if only a portion of patients is involved.

47. Fakhry et al. (2004); Watts et al. (1999, 2004); Centers for Disease Control (2005).

48. Hesdorffer, Ghajar, and Iacono (2002). Also, CarePath (2005a) reports that in 66 percent of cases, fewer than 75 percent of the guidelines are implemented.

49. CarePath (2005b).

50. See also Huckman and Pisano (2005) and Siegrist and Kane (2003).

51. Progress on patient choice must be assigned high priority so that information and choice reinforce each other. With information, people want choice. When choice is available, individuals seek information. The Preferred Global Health example, discussed later in this chapter and in chapter 6, illustrates that enough information can be found today to identify the world-class providers. And if patients are bold enough to ask, many physicians will discuss their experience and past outcomes.

52. In many areas of medicine, the standardization of a "focused factory" (Herzlinger, 1999a) would be inappropriate.

53. Fuhrmans (2005c).

54. See Iezzoni (2003) and Knaus (2002).

55. See National Cancer Institute (2004).

56. See U.S. Cystic Fibrosis Foundation (2004).

57. Gawande (2004).

58. Ibid.

59. Starting in 1998, the registry has evolved from capturing basic patient data to enabling center-by-center performance comparisons. See Schechter and Margolis (2005). Until recently, the Cystic Fibrosis Foundation registry contained aggregated data by patient by year (e.g., how many visits per year the patient had) rather than encounter-level information on the patient-physician interaction. In 2003, inspired in part by the Genentech-funded Epidemiologic Study of Cystic Fibrosis, the Foundation added a Web application enabling the participating centers to enter real-time information about each patient visit into the registry (communication with Dr. Bruce Marshall, Director of Clinical Affairs, on October 12, 2005; communication with Dr. Jeff Wagener on October 13, 2005).

60. Communication with Dr. Bruce Marshall, Director of Clinical Affairs at Cystic Fibrosis Foundation, September 2, 2005. The Cystic Fibrosis Foundation estimates that 95 percent of the 22,000 patients treated at accredited centers are in the reg-

istry, and that an additional 400 to 500 patients (mostly lightly affected adults) are not in the registry because they are treated by community pulmonologists outside the accredited centers.

61. See American Association of Kidney Patients (1999) and the United States Renal Data System Web site (http://www.usrds.org).

62. USRDS is funded by the National Institute of Diabetes and Digestive and Kidney Diseases (part of NIH) and the Centers for Medicare and Medicaid Services.

63. USRDS also collects data from the United Network of Organ Sharing on the outcomes of ESRD patients receiving a kidney transplant.

64. Communication with Cynthia Lambert, Medical Quality Manager for ESRD Network of New England, September 1, 2005. Since the data is based on Medicare reimbursement code UB 92, acute dialysis facilities in hospitals are also excluded from the database.

65. Filtration rates (or "treatment adequacy"), like other medical results, depends on the patient's risk factors as well as on the care processes. In this case, comorbidities (such as whether the patient is diabetic) and the type of vascular access contribute significantly to outcomes.

66. Communication with Cynthia Lambert, Medical Quality Manager for ESRD Network of New England, September 1, 2005.

67. Nissenson and Rettig (1999).

68. See, for example, Fisher et al. (2003a, 2003b).

69. Knaus (2002) has a brief history of the development of APACHE.

70. Knaus et al. (1986).

71. Cerner (2002, 2004).

72. Knaus (2005).

73. Afessa et al. (2005).

74. APACHE risk-adjusted outcome measures were also used in the Cleveland Health Quality Choice experiment discussed in this chapter.

75. Joint Commission on Accreditation of Healthcare Organizations (2005).

76. Knaus (2005) makes this point in an editorial accompanying the Mayo Clinic study, Afessa et al. (2005).

77. More than a decade later, Congress mandated that the Veterans Administration report risk-adjusted surgical outcomes and compare them to national average results.

78. Grover (2005).

79. Technically, the New York Department of Health requested rather than required the data. However, given that the department set payment rates until 1996 and has regulatory powers to approve or revoke Certificates of Need for cardiac programs, no hospital refused the request (Becher and Chassin, 2001).

80. Chassin (2002). See also figures 2-6 and 2-7 and the accompanying discussion in chapter 2.

81. California's CABG mortality reporting started in 1997 as a voluntary reporting effort led jointly by the Pacific Business Group on Health and the California Office of Statewide Health Planning and Development. Initially, 77 of the 121 CABG-performing hospitals in the state reported their data. The passage of California Senate Bill 680 in 2001 replaced the voluntary program with the mandatory California CABG Outcomes Reporting Program (CCORP), which began data collection in January 2003. See California CABG Mortality Reporting Program (2005).

82. New Jersey followed the New York measurement procedures exactly and has seen its risk-adjusted mortality drop from 4.02 percent in 1994 to 2.56 percent

in 1999 (communication with Dr. Mark Chassin, January 31, 2005; New Jersey Department of Health and Senior Services, 2001).

83. Cumulatively, STS has spent more than $12 million on the effort, financed mostly by physician fees for becoming part of the database (communication with Mike Hogan, Director of Government Relations for the Society of Thoracic Surgeons, September 23, 2005). Each physician practice or hospital is also required to hire a full- or part-time data manager who is responsible for data entry and data integrity (Society of Thoracic Surgeons, 2003).

84. See, for example, Ferguson et al. (2002a) and Grover et al. (2001).

85. As the expected mortality for the sicker, older, and more overweight patient cohort rose by 35 percent, the observed risk-adjusted mortality dropped by 30 percent during the period that results data has been collected, shared, and analyzed (Rich, 2005).

86. Fifty-eight peer-reviewed studies have been published so far using the data.

87. New techniques are not just discussed, but demonstrated on animal organs.

88. Orringer (2001). See also Ferguson et al. (2000).

89. Fifteen of these measures come directly from the STS database, including outcome measures such as the need for surgical re-exploration and risk-adjusted mortality (both in-hospital and thirty-day postoperative mortality). See Society of Thoracic Surgeons (2004).

90. Rich (2005.)

91. Orringer (2001).

92. Patients whose transplant fails sometimes do not communicate with the provider. The families of patients who die sometimes do not inform providers. Thus, transplant center data may tend to overrepresent survivorship. For example, 60 percent of kidney transplant losses are unknown to the institution that performed the transplant. The UNOS process verifies and collects comprehensive data.

93. Scientific Registry of Transplant Recipients (2005).

94. Joint Commission on Accreditation of Healthcare Organizations (2005).

95. See discussion in Knaus (2002).

96. See, for example, O'Connor, Llewellyn-Thomas, and Flood (2004); Wennberg and Cooper (1999); and Bodenheimer et al. (2002).

97. Burton (1999); Farley et al. (2003).

98. Neuhauser and Harper (2002).

99. Rosenthal, Quinn, and Harper (1997).

100. Given the imperfections in outcome measures, it is understandable that employers did not immediately respond to the reports. On the other hand, the data were collected for almost a decade. Some companies have reported that when medical inflation eased in the late 1990s, they became less focused on health plans and less aggressive about quality issues. The result was a major lost opportunity.

101. Hannan et al. (1994); Dziuban et al. (1994); Peterson et al. (1998).

102. Peterson et al. (1998). Also see figure 2-7 and its accompanying text.

103. Chassin (2002).

104. Gawande (2004).

105. In Pennsylvania, a study by Schneider and Epstein (1996) of why outcome measures seemed not to affect choices revealed that the referring doctors were unaware of the published outcome data, so their referrals of patients to providers with worse risk-adjusted outcomes and higher costs were not intentional. The cases of United Resource Networks and Preferred Global Health, discussed in chap-

ter 6 and later in this chapter, both demonstrate patient responsiveness to outcome data where expert advisors are involved. O'Connor, Llewellyn-Thomas, and Flood (2004) demonstrates that patients with decision support services use data to make logical, often cost-saving decisions consistent with both medical evidence and their own values. See also Bodenheimer et al. (2002), and Wennberg and Cooper (1999).

106. See Elswick (2001), Appleby (2002), and Herzlinger (2004a). Freudenheim (2000) quotes Brian Marcotte, vice president of benefits for Honeywell, on this point.

107. The Committee on Quality of Health Care in America (2001) recommended a $1 billion innovation fund for the next three to five years to spur advances.

108. See for example, Pauly (2004) and Relman (2005). Also, D. Wennberg et al. (1997) and Fisher and Wennberg (2003) show that more supply of capital equipment, such as cardiac catheterization labs, increases demand for its use.

109. Medtap International (2004).

110. Rettig (1994).

111. Lubitz and Riley (1993). In contrast, non-Medicare costs, specifically the costs of long-term care, are shown in three studies to be higher for people who die older: during the last ninety days of life (Temkin-Greener et al., 1992), the last year of life (Scitovsky, 1984), and the last two years of life (Spillman and Lubitz, 2000).

112. Perls, Alpert, and Fretts (1997).

113. Kramer (1995).

114. Hoffman and Rice (1996). Note that the definition of chronic conditions can be broad, which the authors make clear.

115. Murphy and Topel (1999) find that medical innovation in the form of new drugs and medical expenditures contributes to increased longevity and suggests that increased development of new drugs may be a more cost-effective way of increasing life expectancy than increased medical expenditure. Cutler and McClellan (2001), Cutler, McClellan, and Newhouse (1998), Cutler et al. (1999), Cosgrove (2000), and Lasker Charitable Trust/Funding First (1999), among others, articulate this point of view.

116. Researchers at Harvard's Center for Risk Analysis have developed a database of more than 700 cost-utility ratios for pharmaceutical therapies, surgical procedures, and diagnostic procedures. See Neumann (2000) and Neumann et al. (2000).

117. Pardes et al. (1999).

118. Knaus (2005).

119. Grove (2005).

120. Apache Medical Systems (2000).

121. The Acute Respiratory Distress Syndrome Network (2000).

122. Pronovost et al. (2004).

Chapter 5

1. Indeed, this problem is not uncommon in other types of professional service organizations.

2. Addressing medical conditions over the full cycle of care is consistent with the concept of clinical microsystems, which posits that the key question is whether the health care system is providing care that meets patients' needs for high-quality and high-value care, and that this question must be asked at the level of microsystems (care for patients with a given condition) rather than at the level of the specialty (e.g., cardiac services or oncology) or the level of the hospital system. See http://www.clinicalmicrosystem.org and Batalden and Splaine (2002).

3. U.S. Cystic Fibrosis Foundation Registry (1998).

4. This dedication has also resulted in the commercialization of such inventions as the chest-thumping vest, used by some 45,000 patients suffering from cystic fibrosis and other lung diseases worldwide. See Gawande (2004).

5. Fairview has achieved more carried-to-term pregnancies and live births for women with cystic fibrosis than any other provider in the country.

6. Fairview-University Children's Hospital (2005).

7. Financial viability for a provider organization does not come from maximizing revenue at any cost, but from generating revenues that yield a positive margin. The task is not to maximize the number of revenue-producing services to cover fixed overhead, but to match the overhead to the services that the organization can deliver effectively and efficiently. The task is not to fill excess capacity with more service lines, but to adjust capacity to the needs of the service lines in which a provider excels.

8. For example, Florida passed a law in 2004 that "prohibits any hospital that restricts its medical and surgical services primarily to cardiac, orthopedic, surgical or oncology practices" regardless of ownership (Romano, 2004a). On the federal level, the 2003 Medicare drug law included a moratorium on new specialty hospitals through June 8, 2005.

9. Kane, Needleman, and Rudell (2004, 2005). These studies have been misinterpreted to conclude that community hospitals are a better value for all care. However, the studies only considered secondary care, of which 40 percent was in obstetrics and gynecology.

10. Bohmer et al. (2005).

11. Ironically, the Stark law is an unnecessary complication to such value-enhancing integration of care. See chapter 8.

12. See, for example, Enthoven and Tollen (2005). This paper mistakenly equates vertical integration of the health plan and provider network with full-cycle care. The two are logically separate. Full-cycle care does not require an integrated health plan. Conversely, poor integration of care across the cycle can and does frequently occur in vertically integrated systems.

13. Dartmouth researchers and practitioners have taken significant steps in addressing improvement in value for patients by focusing on the level at which patients experience care for a condition ("clinical microsystems"), rather than on the hospital (or "macrosystem") level. We share with the clinical microsystems perspective a focus on patient-centric care, on improving value at the level at which care is delivered and value is created, and on the need for integration in the cycle of care for a condition as the patient experiences it. See Batalden and Splaine (2002) and http://www.clinicalmicrosystem.org. Clinical microsystems, however, are more loosely and sometimes more broadly defined than an integrated practice unit. For example, Dartmouth's Clinical Microsystem Web site (http://www.clinicalmicrosystem.org) explains that microsystems "can be naturally occurring clinical providers and their support staff who do not work in close proximity but who share a subpopulation of patients and who are, more or less, aware or unaware of themselves as a small system. They, in effect, provide a 'care team' or 'care group' without walls and shape clinical policy (in a more or less planned or unplanned manner). For example: urologists practicing in a group, side by side and independently." Presumably, an improved microsystem would look like a practice unit integrated over the cycle of care. Just as every provider has care delivery value chains (discussed later in this chapter), even if they have not analyzed them, so

every provider participates in microsystems, with varying degrees of awareness and effectiveness in delivering value for patients.

14. See chapter 4. In cardiac surgery, for example, the American College of Surgeons has recommended that each team perform at least 150 operations per year. See "Guidelines for Minimal Standards in Cardiac Surgery" (1984) and DeWeese, Urschel, and Waldhausen (1991).

15. Note that *multidisciplinary* does not mean full service. Instead, it refers to a more effective way to provide care for each medical condition.

16. Chetney (2003).

17. Not only do prevailing organization structures co-mingle diagnosis and treatment, but reimbursement levels favoring treatment also reinforce this structure. Today there is low reimbursement for many types of diagnosis, follow-up effort, and prevention. Instead, there is a clear bias toward procedures and treatment. There has also been little effort to devise measures for the cost-effectiveness of diagnosis or prevention. Both diagnosis and prevention can raise health care value substantially, and separating and measuring these functions is important.

18. Communication with Brent James, September 8, 2004.

19. Intermountain Health Care 2003 annual report.

20. Without results data, providers can perform unneeded surgery that does not help, and patients can be misled into thinking that everything (including surgery) should be attempted to reduce their pain and improve functionality. Some critics see spine surgery as expensive but unnecessary care because the patient can experience no significant improvement in functionality or pain reduction after the operation. Data measuring improvement for the Boston Spine Group's patients is important in demonstrating the value of such surgery in the first place, while also demonstrating the excellence of the group's own results.

21. Becker (2003).

22. Corporate practice of medicine laws, which make it difficult for corporations to employ physicians, are an example of ill-advised regulations that stand in the way of value creation. We discuss these laws in chapter 8.

23. Herzlinger, for example, proposed the idea of "focused factories" for health care delivery, using examples such as McDonald's and Jiffy Lube. The idea is that there should be multiple, homogenous units for addressing each condition that would embody best practices.

24. Milstein (2004) and Fisher et al. (2004) also have made the point that measurement needs to address the "longitudinal efficiency" over the full cycle of acute care (or over a specified time period for chronic care). See also note 16 in chapter 4.

25. Intermountain Health Care (2005), Havenstein (2005).

26. Communication with Dr. David Burton, August 2, 2005.

27. Gawande (2004).

28. For an authoritative treatment of risk adjustment, see Iezzoni (2003).

29. For detailed materials, see http://wiqualitycollaborative.org.

30. See the Quality Reports section of the Dartmouth-Hitchcock Medical Center Web site (http://dhmc.org).

31. Weissman et al. (2005).

32. Some counter this suggestion with concerns about how doctors will be able to learn how to practice if substantial experience in a field is required to begin serving patients. We do not believe that doctors should learn at the expense of unsuspecting and uninformed patients. Instead, doctors should learn by working at an institution with an experienced, excellent team. The experience gained can

provide the basis for opening new services. Or, new services can be supported by, or affiliated with, leading providers in a practice area, as we will discuss.

33. Higher margins result from superior efficiency, the ability to charge higher prices, or both. Because better outcomes are often achieved with efficient processes and fewer mistakes, excellent providers may not choose to charge higher prices. They will benefit from the flow of patients and the resulting virtuous circle (see figure 5-2).

34. This is the nature of positive-sum competition. Patients and health plans benefit from value gains, while providers will also benefit in terms of reputation, patient flow, and efficiency.

35. Urbina (2006) describes the skewed incentives in care for diabetes.

36. In organ transplants, for example, the best providers tend to offer the most favorable discounts. See chapter 6.

37. Communication with Dr. Delos Cosgrove, October 24, 2005.

38. Beckley (2003).

39. Communication with Robert Reznik, President, Prizm Development, Inc.

40. For a description of the concept of the value chain, see Porter (1985, 1996, 2001).

41. Note that the display of activities in health care is somewhat different than in a typical business.

42. Communication with Dr. John Mendelsohn, December 12, 2005.

43. Estimates of time spent on clinical care range from 19 percent for residents (Green, 1995) to 51 percent for physicians in academic medical centers (Cohen et al., 2000), 55 percent (Gottschalk and Flocke, 2005) to 61 percent (Gilchrist et al., 2005) for family physicians (American Academy of Family Physicians, 2005a), and 77 percent for mental health providers in VA hospitals (Sullivan et al., 2003).

44. Some highly specialized facilities, such as angiography suites, will appropriately be shared even by high-volume, excellent providers given the small number of procedures in a single medical condition.

45. National Business Group on Health (2004).

46. Examples include the Veterans Administration hospitals, Beth Israel, Brigham and Women's, Intermountain Health Care, the Cleveland Clinic, and the University of Pittsburgh Medical Center. See also Massachusetts Technology Collaborative (2003) and New England Healthcare Institute (2004).

47. The architecture of the Internet greatly enhances the ability to introduce IT modules incrementally. See Porter (2001).

48. This section draws on extensive discussions with Donald Berwick and Maureen Bisognano of the Institute for Healthcare Improvement. The Institute has published a wide array of studies on practice improvement. See the bibliography.

49. Uhlig et al. (2002).

50. American Medical Association (2005); McCue (2005); Institute for Healthcare Improvement (2004).

51. Communication with Brent James, July 15, 2005. The most expensive provider had costs that were two and one half times IHC's costs.

52. James (n.d.), "An Introduction to Clinical Quality Improvement."

53. We are grateful to Dr. Andrew Fishleder for this example.

54. Gawande (2002).

55. We are grateful to Dr. Jo Shapiro for bringing this example to our attention.

56. In Sweden, as we discuss in chapter 8, the publication and discussion of outcome measures spurs efforts to improve even when patients have limited choices of providers. Professional pride and responsibility are strong.

57. Gawande (2002).

58. http://www.ortholearnctr.org.

59. New England Baptist Bone and Joint Institute (2005).

60. We are grateful to Dr. Jo Shapiro for bringing this example to our attention.

61. American Academy of Family Physicians (2005b).

62. Surprisingly, the effect of physician organization on administrative costs in health care has largely escaped scrutiny, with most of the criticism heaped on health plans.

63. Adverse selection is also sometimes referred to as a "lemons problem." The idea is that less able physicians might choose a staff model because their income is more secure. For the average provider institution, careful tracking of results is the best protection from adverse selection.

64. The SF-36 Questionnaire includes thirty-six questions that measure the burden of disease.

Chapter 6

1. Consumer-directed health care (see Herzlinger, 2004a, for example, pp. 12, 195, and 799) focuses on the choice of a health plan as the key choice. While we believe that competition among health plans can add value, the more decisive choice is the choice of provider at the medical condition level.

2. Newhouse (1996) is a compelling study of how uninformed patients make medical choices. The study results, that insured patients want more health care, contrast sharply with the results of studies of informed patients. With information and access to decision support, patients can distinguish between more health *care* and more health, so they make evidence-based choices, often for less care. See, for example, O'Connor, Llewellyn-Thomas, and Flood (2004), Bodenheimer et al. (2002), and Wennberg and Cooper (1999).

3. Martinez (2004).

4. Fuhrmans (2004); Fitzgerald (2004).

5. Health plans need to enable members to get excellent care, rather than level the field and just direct members to the lowest-cost provider. This does not deny the importance of process improvement, which will be a high priority for providers when outcomes are transparent and excellence is rewarded. For a significant example of process improvement, see the discussion about the Institute for Healthcare Improvement's 100,000 lives campaign in chapter 5.

6. Rosenthal et al. (2004) has tables summarizing pay-for-quality strategies by a number of health plans and employer coalitions.

7. The most commonly quoted figure for providers' administrative expenses is Woolhandler and Himmelstein's 1997 estimate that administrative costs constitute 26 percent of hospital expenditures.

8. Villagra and Ahmed (2004).

9. Gold and Kongstvedt (2003).

10. National Committee for Quality Assurance (2004).

11. Harvard Pilgrim (2004).

12. In consumer-driven health care, consumers choose among health plans that compete to distinguish themselves (Herzlinger, 2002, 2004a). Consumer-driven health care will be enabled by competition at the right level. It will continue to be slow to take hold until health care competition is redefined to be value based and results oriented. Choice among health plans is not sufficient.

13. There will be coordination, and in some cases special subgroups, established for sets of co-occurring conditions.

14. Fisher et al. (2003a, 2003b) and Wennberg and Cooper (1999) demonstrate the importance of understanding medical outcomes at the end of life, when better treatment and more treatment may be at odds. Their research has found higher patient and family satisfaction with medical treatment at the end of life when it was less invasive and involved fewer procedures and less hospitalization. Such insight would be overlooked if outcomes were interpreted to mean only length of life.

15. United Resource Networks, for example, uses the codes to figure out which transplant centers take the most difficult cases, to avoid overrating centers that get the easiest patients. Outcomes, experience, and experience with difficult cases are all factored into their analysis.

16. See the discussion later in this chapter in the section titled "Shift the Nature of Information Sharing with Providers."

17. United Resource Networks home page: http://www.urnweb.com.

18. National Cancer Institute (2005a) shows survival rates. National Cancer Institute (2005b) has data on participation in clinical trials.

19. Communication with Jeffrey Kang, July 21, 2005.

20. Communication with Jeffrey Kang, August 1, 2005.

21. See the discussion in chapter 4.

22. Preferred Global Health is described in chapters 2 and 4.

23. Committee on Quality of Health Care in America (2001).

24. Goetzel et al. (2005) reviews forty-four studies specifically addressing the return on investment in disease management and finds that even considering only the direct medical cost savings, ROI is usually positive.

25. Villagra and Ahmed (2004).

26. Wellpoint, Inc. (2002).

27. This includes the "core conditions" of diabetes, coronary artery disease, congestive heart failure, chronic obstructive pulmonary disease, asthma, and end stage renal disease, as well as the "impact conditions" of osteoarthritis, acid-related stomach disorders, low back pain, osteoporosis, fibromyalgia, atrial fibrillation/anticoagulant therapy, chronic hepatitis and cirrhosis, incontinence, irritable bowel syndrome, pressure ulcers, and inflammatory bowel disease.

28. Gold and Kongstvedt (2003); Gold and Johnson (2004).

29. Gold and Kongstvedt (2003). Critics point out that patients with a new diagnosis are "best behaved" in the first year after learning of their disease. However, this does not negate the finding that those in a disease management program had better outcomes and lower costs than those with a newly diagnosed disease and no disease management program.

30. Gold and Johnson (2004).

31. Hoffman et al. (1996); Hoffman and Rice (1996). This cost estimate is for direct health care costs only; it does not include the indirect costs of lost productivity for the person with a chronic condition or that person's caregivers.

32. Hoffman et al. (1996); Hoffman and Rice (1996).

33. Martinez (2004); Aetna (2005).

34. See the section "Actively Support Provider and Treatment Choice with Information and Unbiased Counseling" earlier in this chapter.

35. Gawande (2005).

36. Best Doctors (2005).

37. HEDIS stands for Health Plan Employer Data and Information Set. The measures include consumer satisfaction, access to care, and plan physicians' compliance with treatment guidelines.

38. Dalzell (1999).

39. Communications with Brent James, February 16, 2005, and July 15, 2005.

40. A part of the issue with health plan portability was addressed in the Consolidated Omnibus Budget Reconciliation Act (COBRA) of 1986. Individuals leaving employment have the right to temporarily (for eighteen months) continue their group health coverage with the same health plan. Normally, the coverage continues at the same (negotiated) rate, but the individual assumes responsibility for the employer's contribution to plan cost. After eighteen months, the price changes to a non-negotiated rate that can be much higher.

41. Firms that heavily involved capitation reinsured many patients in response to financial difficulty (Martinez, 2004).

42. Connecting for Health (2004a, 2004b).

43. Health plans and their "business associates" are covered under HIPAA regulation, which requires compliance with rules and the potential for HHS audits. Service providers such as providers of individual patient records may choose to avoid a direct business association with health plans and offer their services directly to consumers. Health plans (or employers) could offer reduced health plan payments or lower deductibles to members (or employees) who contracted for patient records services.

44. Herzlinger (2002) draws this parallel, as have others.

45. Ferrara (1995); Massaro and Wong, (1995); Goldman, Buchanan, and Keeler (2000); Yip and Hsiao (1997). Cost reductions are also consistent with Joe Newhouse's and RAND's findings that copayments create incentives for using less care.

46. Aetna (2004).

47. Although increased payment responsibility leads to self-rationing, better-informed patients have been shown to choose less invasive and therefore less expensive care. See Wennberg (2005) and the discussion and end notes in chapter 4.

48. See, for example, O'Connor et al. (2004), Wennberg and Cooper (1999), and Bodenheimer et al. (2002).

Chapter 7

1. Notably Herzlinger (1999a, 2004a).

2. Angell (2004).

3. Baker et al. (2003).

4. Researchers at Harvard's Center for Risk Analysis have developed a database of more than 700 cost-utility ratios for pharmaceutical therapies, surgical procedures, and diagnostic procedures. Some drugs provide immediate cost savings and actually save more (in averted hospital care, for example) than they cost to administer. Long-term anticoagulant therapy for lung cancer patients with acute deep venous thrombosis is an example. Many other drugs are cost-effective in that although they do not immediately save money, they have health benefits far exceeding their costs. See Neumann (2000), Neumann and Olchanski (2003), and Neumann et al. (2000). Also see Dubois et al. (2000) and Kleinke (2000), both of which find many uses of drugs that increase spending on drugs and increase value. Of course, some expensive drugs do not increase value.

5. Newhouse (1992) argues that increased technology use can increase welfare, but the analysis and discussion stay at an aggregate level, at which the benefits of specific new technologies cannot be measured. Cutler and McClellan (2001) examine the value of new technology for five conditions (heart attacks, low-birth-weight infants, depression, cataracts, and breast cancer) and find the medical benefits worth the cost of care in four of the five.

6. For example, Bellinger et al. (1995), Bellinger et al. (2003), and Newburger et al. (2003).

7. Herzlinger (2002), for example, advocates putting consumers in charge of their choice of health plan and improving information and incentives so that better choices will occur. Herzlinger (2004a) extends this argument to emphasize the role that employers could play in creating change in consumer behavior. Consumer involvement, however, is not sufficient to create the needed changes in U.S. health care to drive rapid quality and efficiency improvement. Major changes in the nature and level of health care competition will be necessary. When value-based competition is enabled and pursued, consumer-driven health care will be possible.

8. Accepting personal responsibility does not mean opting out of health care coverage, as we will discuss later in this chapter. Rather, all consumers need to embrace the importance of universal coverage to ensure fairness, reduce cross subsidies, minimize inefficiencies, and contain overall health care costs.

9. See the discussion in chapter 2. Physicians cite cooperation and compliance (in filling and taking prescriptions, doing exercises or physical therapy, and following diet guidelines, for example) as significant factors in reducing costs and enabling effective care. Patient responsibility is not only a matter of making choices but also of enabling treatment to succeed.

10. For example, Bodenheimer et al. (2002) found better-informed patients had better outcomes for asthma, arthritis, and diabetes. Fewer hospitalizations generated savings of $750 per patient.

11. Connecting for Health (2004a, 2004b).

12. First Market Research (2005), Krasner (2005).

13. Blue Cross Blue Shield plans in a number of states, in addition to other leading health plans, have initiated this practice, in which doctors are paid for e-mail correspondence, and patients make a copayment. This trend is also discussed in chapters 6 and 8.

14. Coye and Detmer (1998).

15. Some observers have portrayed competition as consumers jumping from provider to provider based on price. This sort of competition is not what value-based competition on results is all about.

16. Ferrara (1995); Massaro and Wong (1995); Goldman, Buchanan, and Keeler (2000); Yip and Hsiao (1997).

17. Aetna Web site (http://www.aetna.com/index.htm).

18. HSAs may also have a self-rationing effect for low-income patients who lack out-of-pocket resources. The safe harbor provisions for insurance coverage below the deductible may need to include preventive care for low-income patients.

19. See Towers Perrin (2005) and Towers Perrin HR Services (2005). Mercer Human Resource Consulting (2003) also shows a 15 percent cost increase in the total health benefit cost per employee in 2002 and a 10.1 percent increase in 2003. The study predicted the 2004 increase to be 13 percent, but the actual figure was 7.5 percent. While lower than expected, this still outpaces inflation. See figure 1-17.

20. Connolly (2005). Ford reported in 2003 that health care added $1,000 to the cost of every car it makes in the United States (Mayne, 2004).

21. Mercer Human Resource Consulting (2004a).

22. Mercer Human Resource Consulting (2004b).

23. Hewitt Associates (2004a). The following year, Hewitt researchers perceived that concerns over health care costs were so universal that Hewitt did not even repeat the question.

24. See Birkmeyer et al. (2000); Mehrotra, Bodenheimer, and Dudley (2003); Committee for Economic Development (2002); Boeing Company (2001); Ceniceros (2001c); Freudenheim (2000); Midwest Business Group on Health (2001); and Sarudi (2001).

25. The initial Leapfrog evidence-based hospital referral parameters included five adult conditions: coronary artery bypass surgery, percutaneous coronary interventions, pancreatic resection, abdominal aortic aneurysm repair, and esophageal resection (Birkmeyer, Finlayson, and Birkmeyer, 2001). The parameters were later expanded to include three high-risk neonatal conditions: expected birth weight less than 1,500 grams, gestational age less than 32 weeks, or prenatal diagnosis of major congenital anomaly (Leapfrog Group, 2004).

26. Agency for Healthcare Research and Quality (2005).

27. Birkmeyer et al. (2004).

28. Berwick et al. (2003).

29. Mercer Human Resource Consulting (2004b).

30. The literature on the value of disease management is large and growing exponentially. The Committee on Quality of Health Care in America (2001) cites an indexed bibliography of 400 peer-reviewed studies on the topic. It concludes that disease management clearly improves health outcomes. Goetzel et al. (2005) reviews forty-four studies specifically addressing the return on investment in disease management and finds that even considering only the direct medical cost savings, ROI is usually positive. For a discussion of two health plans' case studies that document significant returns to disease management, see the discussion in chapter 6.

31. Some observers point out that most (60 percent) chronic disease occurs for older Americans, giving employers less incentive to reduce the costs that Medicare will ultimately bear. We suspect that the short-term mind-set is even more powerful. As employers begin to think in terms of health value instead of just costs, the benefits of disease management will be better understood.

32. Communication with Denise Stump, Scotts Miracle-Gro, November 21, 2005.

33. Ibid.

34. According to the 2005 National Business Group on Health/Watson Wyatt (2005) trends survey, "Managing Health Care Costs in a New Era," the number of employers with such programs nearly doubled in 2004, to 68 percent.

35. The survey (National Business Group on Health/Watson Wyatt, 2005) tapped 555 employers with at least 1,000 workers, with information gathered in late 2004 and January 2005. It is not a representative sample of all employers, but reflects the experience of the nation's largest companies.

36. O'Connell (2004); Whole Health Management (2005).

37. High-deductible health plans together with a health savings account are often called *consumer-directed health plans*.

38. Health Care Policy Roundtable (2004); Freudenheim (2005a).

Chapter 8

1. Worse still, a Department of Health and Human Services requirement that hospitals bill those without insurance at list price, and make attempts to collect on these bills, led to many situations in which the uninsured actually subsidized the insured, and where medical bills drove lower-income individuals into bankruptcy. These issues are discussed in chapter 2. In response to awareness of these inequities, the Secretary of Health and Human Services published a letter to the president of

the American Hospital Association on February 19, 2004, stating that "hospitals can provide discounts to uninsured and underinsured patients who cannot afford their hospital bills." See T. G. Thompson (2004).

2. As we discussed in earlier chapters, ours is not a proposal for fragmenting care—quite the opposite. Much of today's care is physician centric or institution centric, rather than designed to best deliver value to patients. The result is duplication of services and fragmentation of care delivery over the full cycle of care.

3. Medicare plus Medicaid and Medicaid State Children's Health Insurance Program (SCHIP) expansion now accounts for 45.6 percent of expenditures, with Medicare representing 17 percent of expenditures. The federal government estimates that Medicare will account for about 20 percent of health care expenditures in 2015, with Medicare plus Medicaid and SCHIP expansion accounting for 49 percent that year (Heffler et al., 2005).

4. In a world of cost shifting, Medicare's discounting pressures have benefited other health plans in pulling prices down. If Medicare pursues value creation, other health plans are likely to follow as well. The question is whether these experiments will become the norm, which remains far from certain given past experience.

5. The Institute of Medicine is currently working to create a list that could be the basis of explicit policy about what is covered. The state of Oregon attempted to face the choice of covered services head-on in the 1990s, revealing the complexity of the task. See Department of Human Services, Health Services, Office of Medical Assistance Programs (2004) and Fox and Leichter (1993).

6. Wennberg, Fisher, and Skinner (2002); Wennberg et al. (2004b).

7. We will pay particular attention in this chapter to the role of insurance and coverage in reinforcing value-based competition or undermining it.

8. Romney (2004); Dembner (2005).

9. The Hill-Burton Act (1946) required hospitals to provide free care to those who needed it. Historically, however, hospitals were largely segregated. African Americans were turned away from white-only hospitals. The legacy of hospital discrimination is one of the reasons for racial differences in health care delivery and health outcomes.

10. Starfield (1998, 2000a, 2000b) shows that the major benefits of universal insurance accrue only when it facilitates primary care. Also, international studies comparing quality find the provision of primary care to be the most favorable factor in the U.K. system, which otherwise has significant problems with waiting, rationing, and preventable medical errors (Hussey et al., 2004).

11. Peterson et al. (1994) indicates that insurance coverage is certainly not the full explanation for racial disparities in health care. In a retrospective discharge analysis from the Veterans' Health Administration, this study found that African Americans admitted with myocardial infarction were less likely to receive catheterization or revitalization procedures than whites, even after correction for complications and the condition of the patient. Woolf et al. (2004) analyze excess mortality among African Americans and demonstrate the urgency of achieving equivalent care for improving aggregate U.S. health care outcomes.

12. The Commonwealth Fund Health Care Opinion Leaders Survey found that more than half of respondents supported this approach, but health care providers did not (Commonwealth Fund, February 2005, November–December 2004).

13. In addition to direct costs of free care, there are large indirect costs, such as the cost of poorer health for people without primary care or any sort of disease management counseling, the costs of collection agencies and court expenses for bill collection, and administrative costs.

14. Even if mandatory universal coverage is not achieved immediately, there are compelling arguments to address the issue of primary care for the uninsured. Both equity (given the racial and income-based disparities in health care in the United States) and efficiency (given the benefits of universal primary care) suggest the need to move in this direction. Newhouse and the Insurance Experiment Group (1996) suggests that rather than subsidizing all primary care for the poor, screening for conditions such as high blood pressure could be done for free, enabling the better provision of free care that is of high value.

15. Agency for Healthcare Research and Quality (2000).

16. The risk pool section of HealthInsurance.org's Web site (http://healthinsurance .org/riskpoolinfo.html) has information on states with insurance plans for people who have been denied insurance due to health history.

17. Critics argue that if the highest-risk members are randomly assigned, gaming and selection will move to the next riskiest tier of members. But gaming and selection are costly. With lower-risk members, incentives to encourage disenrollment become less strong. Also, the definition of the threshold for high risk can be adjusted to limit gaming.

18. Newhouse and the Insurance Experiment Group (1996) found that patients respond to higher copayments by seeking less care. This is not surprising given the lack of information the patients faced, as well as referrals that were not evidence based. The underlying assumption, that all U.S. care was good, was a common misperception at that time. Patients were informed about the costs they would bear, but not about the quality of outcomes by different providers or the benefits of various prevention, treatment, and disease management approaches. The study found that the forgone (or excess) care chosen did not correlate with health outcomes. That is a logical result of patients' (and often doctors') lack of information. The only real choice was self-rationing of care. Patients had information on costs and no reliable information on difference in outcomes, so trade-offs in health value were not apparent and patients simply sought less care when it cost them more.

19. The Commonwealth Fund's February 2005 survey of health care opinion leaders found that 84 percent supported this approach for expanding coverage options for individuals and small businesses.

20. Greenberger (2005a).

21. Westmoreland (2001).

22. Romney (2004); Dembner (2005).

23. Where re-underwriting is illegal, insurers can still discontinue a whole plan and then effectively reinsure everyone in the plan. There would be less incentive for this if risk pools ensured that all health plans covered their share of the most expensive members.

24. The quality and length of life are sometimes expressed as disability-adjusted life years.

25. Wennberg (2005); Fisher et al. (2003a, 2003b).

26. Mandatory insurance without a minimum coverage standard will result in exclusions of certain medical conditions, which effectively makes some covered individuals uninsured.

27. Information collected once can be used by any number of parties at virtually no incremental cost. In economists' terms, information is a public good, and government has an important role in ensuring that public goods are available.

28. The Department of Health and Human Services contains two sister research agencies: the National Institutes of Health (NIH) is responsible for biomedical

research, and the Agency for Healthcare Research and Quality (AHRQ) is responsible for health services research.

29. AHRQ's stated goals are to work with both the public and private sectors to identify the most effective ways to organize, manage, finance, and deliver high-quality care, reduce medical errors, and improve patient safety. AHRQ has a very small budget relative to the National Institutes of Health (NIH), which is responsible for biomedical research. This reflects the general lack of understanding that still persists about the crucial role of results information in enabling competition and improving value in health care delivery (see the discussion in chapter 4). NIH spending will have a much higher return when health care competition shifts to value-based competition on results.

30. These reports include facility characteristics, utilization data, and costs (both in total and for Medicare patients). Data is reported by DRG and by provider. CMS publishes these cost reports, which can be purchased for about $100.

31. President's Advisory Commission on Consumer Protection and Quality in the Health Care Industry (1998).

32. "Steps should be taken to ensure that comparative information on health care quality is valid, reliable, comprehensible, and widely available in the public domain" (President's Advisory Commission on Consumer Protection and Quality in the Health Care Industry, 1998).

33. Even if such data is made public in a difficult-to-interpret form, information companies and health plans will benefit from it and create more accessible forms of the information.

34. Knaus (2002).

35. American Academy of Family Physicians (2005a).

36. Caplan et al. (1990).

37. Hallinan (2005).

38. Pierce (1995).

39. We are grateful to Dr. Robert H. Bode at New England Baptist Hospital for bringing this example to our attention.

40. See chapter 4 for a discussion of the studies on experience, learning, and results.

41. Clear measures will help consumers distinguish between highly experienced practitioners who are set in their ways and those who have learned and improved based on experience.

42. In chapters 2 and 6 we discuss the use of complex, opaque billing as a means of cost shifting among hospitals, health plans, and patients.

43. Counter to past practices of requiring the low-income uninsured to pay the full list prices, the Minnesota attorney general has reached an agreement with Minnesota hospitals giving price breaks (below list) to people with incomes below $125,000 at about half of the state's hospitals (Office of Minnesota Attorney General, 2005).

44. Hospitals, which are not in the business of bill collection, complied by turning over unpaid accounts to collection agencies, which collected aggressively. For a discussion of hospital billing practices for uninsured or low-income patients and their relation to Department of Health and Human Services requirements and other legal requirements, see Watson (2004), Pryor and Seifert (2003), Lagnado (2003), and T. G. Thompson (2004).

45. Centers for Medicare and Medicaid Services (2004b); T. G. Thompson (2004).

46. Out-of-network copayments, for example, usually include 30 percent of the in-network reimbursement rate plus 100 percent of the difference between the in-network price and the provider's list price, which is typically about double the in-network price. The patient's responsibility, then, amounts to a total of about 65 percent of the list price. Moreover, if a complication occurs in the course of out-of-network care, insurance often will not cover any of the costs related to the complication. As a result, the cost and risk of out-of-network care are prohibitive for many patients, even if the out-of-network provider is far superior. As we discuss in the section on limiting price discrimination, ending in-network contracting altogether is a better approach.

47. Individual patients will not negotiate prices in almost all cases. Instead, a health plan or service will negotiate on behalf of many patients and will have significant bargaining power.

48. Roughly 2,000 heart transplants per year are performed in the United States.

49. The Commission on Systemic Interoperability published recommendations in October 2005 that included changing the Stark laws to enable information sharing and interoperable systems.

50. Such efforts are also a predictable response to a flawed pricing system in which low reimbursement rates for some services are subsidized by other, more profitable services that specialty hospitals target. Medicare reimbursement rates drive many of these cross subsidies. General hospitals worry that specialty hospitals will serve only patients with the DRGs that are profitable, and, within those DRGs, serve only patients with less complex problems that cost less to treat. Without the cross subsidies in DRG payments, the concern about specialty hospitals would be significantly reduced.

51. U.S. General Accounting Office (2003a).

52. Medicare Payment Advisory Commission (2004), 213–214.

53. Romano (2004b).

54. Eventually, physicians should also have to regularly demonstrate competence. This could involve results data, as well as demonstrating competence using simulations or simulators, as airline pilots are required to do.

55. There have also been studies that found that mergers raise prices the most when they occur in highly concentrated markets, but increase prices less in less concentrated markets. A 2004 joint report by the Federal Trade Commission and U.S. Department of Justice (FTC/DOJ) includes a lengthy discussion of the debates about the reasons for and results of mergers. The report also cites David Dranove's statement: "I have asked many providers why they wanted to merge. Although publicly they all invoked the synergies mantra, virtually everyone states privately that the main reason for merging was to avoid competition and/or obtain market power" (Dranove, 2000, p. 122).

56. FTC/DOJ (2004).

57. FTC/DOJ (2004).

58. FTC/DOJ (2004) contains an extensive discussion of group purchasing organizations (GPOs); see its chapter 4, 34–46.

59. FTC/DOJ (2004), chapter 4, 37.

60. Concerns raised in the FTC/DOJ hearings on GPOs also include side payments to gain exclusive contracts, GPO management compensation based on supplier fee income rather than on hospital savings, supplier payments to obtain market share, and new entrants with value-enhancing products being blocked from access to hospital sales.

61. We are grateful to David Crowder, MD, of Foundation Coal Company for bringing this point to our attention. See Crowder (2004).

62. Some attribute excess demand for medical care entirely to the lack of payment responsibility of patients. However, physician-induced demand also contributes, due to both defensive medicine and to practice standards that are not evidence based. Physician-induced demand is higher for patients who bear no personal responsibility for the bills and in situations in which information is not easily available to inform value-driven decisions by patients and physicians.

63. We thank Dr. Jeff Kang for articulating the need for a change in medical perspective from defensive medicine to offensive development of a high-quality risk-adjusted results record.

64. In 2005, President Bush proposed malpractice reform modeled on California law that would cap at $250,000 the amount a provider could be required to pay a patient for pain and suffering (beyond the cost of medical services). The proposal also included restrictions so that old cases cannot be brought to court years after the medical treatment occurred, and that enable judgments to be paid over time rather than in a lump sum.

65. Kaiser Family Foundation (2005). See also note 3 in this chapter.

66. Wennberg (2005) discusses the phenomenon of supply-sensitive care. He attributes it to the generally held assumption that medical facilities should be fully utilized, finding that more care is given for a disease when there are more doctors specializing in that type of care or more hospital beds for a given population, or both. Much supply-sensitive care is for chronic diseases, for which there are very few evidence-based guidelines. Studies of the amount of care and the amount of spending indicate that more hospitalizations, doctor visits, ICU stays, and spending do not improve outcomes or satisfaction. For example, see Fisher et al. (2003a, 2003b).

67. See the discussion in chapter 3. The RBRVS reduced the bias toward procedures, but did not eliminate it. Moreover, since most physicians are independent agents, not employees of the hospital, the physicians' incentives to perform procedures are not undone by the hospitals' incentives to reduce costs within a DRG.

68. Outcomes are poorer in that there is increased morbidity, such as swelling due to the lack of lymph nodes.

69. Originally Medicare used ten process checks.

70. See, for example, Gawande (2004). As the average medical outcome improves over time, the best providers tend to stay ahead of the pack, improving their results even more rapidly.

71. McGlynn et al. (2003) showed that on average Americans get 55 percent of the care that is medically indicated and also that the delivery of consultative and educational services is often neglected. Without measures to document that skipping these time-consuming steps reduces quality, they are easy to neglect.

72. Wennberg (2005) found that twenty-six hospitals had roughly the same occupancy rate and that excess bed capacity created more hospitalizations. It would be far preferable to reallocate excess beds to areas of care with proven excellence rather than allow excess capacity to lead to overuse in many substandard services.

73. Migliori (2005) showed that in the experience of United Resource Networks, patients balance four categories of considerations in making medical choices in organ transplants: results, speed (waiting time), cost, and comfort.

74. Health Care Financing Administration (1998); Myerson (1994).

75. Centers for Medicare and Medicaid Services (2005b).

76. Medicare could improve its calculation of reimbursement rates. Prices for new methods of care should be set based on value versus alternate methods. This will encourage value improvement and innovation much more than reimbursement based on cost. Medicare can devise gain-sharing models to cover new, value-enhancing care delivery approaches (see chapter 6). Geographic adjustments in reimbursement need to be modified or restructured to facilitate value-enhancing competition across geography. Price adjustments for teaching hospitals need to be phased out and replaced with direct compensation for teaching that does not distort competition in care delivery services. Finally, adjustments in prices for hospitals treating more low-income (but non-Medicare) patients is not a logical approach to dealing with free care. Compensation should be based on the services actually delivered.

77. National Governors Association Center for Best Practices (2003).

78. Ibid.

79. Ibid.

80. Kirschner, Marincola, and Teisberg (1994); Silverstein, Garrison, and Heinig (1995).

81. World Health Organization (2004). There are statistical issues that may penalize the United States. Some countries define stillbirth as any baby who lives less than twenty-four hours. Others, including the United States, count any child born alive as a live birth and include those who die within twenty-four hours in the infant mortality statistics. But U.S. statistics still do not compare well even to industrialized countries that count live births immediately.

82. See, for example, Starfield (2000b) and Woolf et al. (2004). Hussey et al. (2004) also finds universal access to primary care to be a strength of the United Kingdom. But even with universal coverage, there are problems; Blendon et al. (2003) finds shortfalls in primary care in all five industrialized nations surveyed.

83. One could argue that lack of data and the myth that expensive care is good care has brought patients to the United States. It is widely agreed, however, that the best of U.S. medical care is truly excellent, and wealthy international patients travel to these preeminent providers for good reason.

84. Kohn, Corrigan, and Donaldson (2000); HealthGrades (2004). The U.S. population in 1999 was 279 million and in 2002 was 288 million.

85. World Health Organization (2002a).

86. Schoen et al. (2005).

87. Eckbo (2005). See also Michel (2004).

88. World Health Organization (2002a); Wilson et al. (1999).

89. Applied Research and Analysis Directorate (2003). See also Michel (2004).

90. While it might at first seem obvious that a more consistent global price would be a better solution, the issue is complicated by poverty, the health care needs of developing countries, and the bargaining power of monopoly national health services.

91. Ministry of Health, Singapore (http://www.moh.gov.sg/corp/index.do).

92. World Health Organization (2000).

93. Interview with Göran Henriks, the Chief of Learning and Innovation for the Jönköping *lan* council.

94. Public hospitals in France do more research than private providers, so the difference is not all due to efficiency. See Arnold (2004) and Sandier, Paris, and Polton (2004).

95. Chia (2002).

96. National Center for Policy Analysis (2000).

97. Leading U.S. hospitals treated about 60,000 international patients in 1997, and medical travel is growing.

98. "Get Well Away" (2004), p. 76.

Appendix B

1. Activities are related to the concept of processes that is prevalent in total quality management literature. The concept of activities, their types, and the linkages among them is more general and more illuminating for examining the overall strategy and organization of a service line.

2. Without a fistula, access to veins for dialysis can become the limiting factor in how long a patient can receive dialysis. Ensuring that the fistula is installed in time is important because the site needs to heal before dialysis.

3. American Heart Association (2005).

4. American Heart Association (2005) reports estimated direct and indirect costs of strokes. We attribute all $14.9 billion of direct hospital expenditures and $1.5 billion of the $2.9 billion direct physicians and other professionals expenditures to acute care and count $13.2 billion of nursing home care, $2.9 billion in home health care, $1.2 billion in drugs and other medical durables, and the remaining $1.4 billion of the physician expenditures as long-term care.

Bibliography

Ackerman, T. "Center Will Stop Giving 2nd Opinions on Cancer." *Houston Chronicle,* August 11, 2004.

Acute Respiratory Distress Syndrome Network. "Ventilation with Lower Tidal Volumes as Compared with Traditional Tidal Volumes for Acute Lung Injury and the Acute Respiratory Distress Syndrome." *New England Journal of Medicine* 342 (2000): 1301–1308.

Advisory Commission on Consumer Protection and Quality in the Health Care Industry. *Quality First: Better Health Care for All Americans.* 1998. http://www .hcqualitycommission.gov/final/.

Aetna. "Aetna Research Shows Positive Impact of Consumerism on Health Care Decisions." Press release. February 16, 2004. http://www.aetna.com/news/2004/ pr_20040216a.htm.

———. "Reproductive Health Fact Sheet." 2005. http://www.aetna.com/presscenter/ kit/women_health/reproductive_health_factSheet.html.

Afessa, B., M. T. Keegan, R. D. Hubmayr, J. M. Naessens, O. Gajic, K. H. Long, and S. G. Peters. "Evaluating the Performance of an Institution Using an Intensive Care Unit Benchmark." *Mayo Clinic Proceedings* 80 (2005):174–180. http://www .mayoclinicproceedings.com/inside.asp?a=1&ref=8002a2.

Agency for Healthcare Research and Quality. Healthcare Cost and Utilization Project Fact Book No. 5. "Preventable Hospitalizations: Window into Primary and Preventive Care, 2000." http://www.ahrq.gov/data/hcup/factbk5/factbk5a.htm.

———. "30 Safe Practices for Better Health Care." Fact Sheet. AHRQ Publication no. 04-P025. March 2005. http://www.ahrq.gov/qual/30safe.pdf.

AHA/ASHRM Survey of Hospital Experience with Professional Liability Insurance. Statement of the American Hospital Association before the Federal Trade Commission Health Care Competition Law and Policy Workshop, September 9–10, 2002. http://www.hospitalconnect.com/ahapolicyforum/trendwatch/content/ tw020618medliap1.pdf.

Albert, T. "Dressed for Success: Re-covering Patients." *American Medical News,* August 27, 2001. http://www.ama-assn.org/amednews/2001/08/27/prsa0827.htm.

The ALLHAT Officers and Coordinators for the ALLHAT Collaborative Research Group. "Major Outcomes in High-Risk Hypertensive Patients Randomized to Angiotensin-Converting Enzyme Inhibitor or Calcium Channel Blocker vs Diuretic: The Antihypertensive and Lipid-Lowering Treatment to Prevent Heart

Attack Trial (ALLHAT)." *Journal of the American Medical Association* 288, no. 23 (2002): 2981–2997.

Altman, S. H., and D. Shactman. "Should We Worry About Hospitals' High Administrative Costs?" *New England Journal of Medicine* 336, no. 11 (1997): 798–799.

American Academy of Family Physicians. "AAFP Clinical Recommendations." 2005a. http://www.aafp.org/x132.xml.

_____. "Fundamentals of Management." 2005b. http://www.aafp.org/fom.xml.

American Association of Kidney Patients. "Washington Report: The Medicare End-Stage Renal Disease (ESRD) Program." Special issue, *aakpRENALIFE* 15, no. 2 (1999). http://www.aakp.org/AAKP/RenalifeArt/1990s/washingtonspecial99.htm.

American Heart Association. *Heart Disease and Stroke Statistics—2005 Update.* Dallas: American Heart Association, 2005. http://www.americanheart.org/downloadable/heart/1105390918119HDSStats2005Update.pdf.

American Hospital Association. "Medical Liability Insurance: Looming Crisis?" *TrendWatch* 4, no. 3 (2002): 1–4.

_____. *AHA Annual Survey Database: Fiscal Year 2001.* Chicago: Health Forum, 2003. Survey available at http://www.ahaonlinestore.com.

_____. *Trends Affecting Hospitals and Health Systems: TrendWatch Chartbook 2003.* Washington, DC: American Hospital Association, 2004.

_____. *AHA Annual Survey Database: Fiscal Year 2003.* Chicago: Health Forum, 2005.

American Hospital Association Board of Trustees. "Statement of Principles and Guidelines." *Hospital Billing and Collection Practices*, December 17, 2003.

American Medical Association. *Current Procedural Terminology.* 4th ed. Chicago: American Medical Association, 2004.

_____. "Helping Make Hospitals Safer: Patient Safety Campaign Gets It Right." Editorial. *American Medical News*, January 14, 2005.

Andersen, R. N., and B. L. Smith. "Deaths: Leading Causes for 2002." *National Vital Statistics Reports* 53, no. 17. Hyattsville, MD: National Center for Health Statistics, 2005.

Anell, A., and M. Willis. "International Comparison of Health Care Systems Using Resource Profiles." *Bulletin of the World Health Organization* 78, no. 6 (2000): 770–778.

Angell, M. "The Doctor as Double Agent." *Kennedy Institute of Ethics Journal* 3, no. 3 (1993): 279–286.

_____. *The Truth About the Drug Companies: How They Deceive Us and What to Do About It.* New York: Random House, 2004.

Aoki, N. "Biotech Speaks Up: Feeling Vulnerable, Industry Seeks a Voice in Latest Debate over Prescription Drug Prices." *The Boston Globe*, October 3, 2000. http://www.biohope.org/media/article.cfm?articleid=210&state=MA.

Apache Medical Systems. "Of Mice and Men—APACHE Simulator Helps Reduce Clinical Trial Costs, Speed FDA Approval; Computer Model Simulates Human Drug Testing." Press release. August 31, 2000. http://www.apache-msi.com/news/simulator.shtml.

Appleby, J. "Frustrated Doctors Rebel Against Insurers." *USA Today*, July 20, 2000.

_____. "Firms Offer Medical Data Services." *USA Today*, January 22, 2002.

Applied Research and Analysis Directorate, Health Policy Research Program. "Request for Proposals for Synthesis Research RFP 014. Governance Choices and Health Care Quality: A Focus on Patient Safety." 2003. http://www.hc-sc.gc.ca/iacb-dgiac/arad-draa/english/rmdd/rfp/rfp014.html.

Arnold, M. "France Prescribes Bitter Medicine for Ailing Health System Tipped into Crisis by the Summer Heatwave." *Financial Times,* January 20, 2004.

Asch, S. M., E. A. McGlynn, M. M. Hogan, R. A. Hayward, P. Shekelle, L. Rubenstein, J. Keesey, J. Adams, and E. A. Kerr. "Comparison of Quality of Care for Patients in the Veterans Health Administration and Patients in a National Sample." *Annals of Internal Medicine* 141, no. 12 (2004): 938–945.

Associated Press. "Facts and Figures on the Finances of Doctors and Hospitals." *Associated Press Newswires,* January 22, 2001a.

_____. "U.S. Health Care System Said Lacking." *The New York Times,* March 2, 2001b.

Aston, G. "OIG: Medicare HMOs' Administrative Spending Excessive." *AMNews,* February 21, 2000.

Aumann, R. J. "Game Theory." In *The New Palgrave: A Dictionary of Economics,* edited by John Eatwell, Murray Milgate, and Peter Newman. London: Macmillan; New York: Stockton Press; Tokyo: Maruzen, 1987.

Baicker, K., and A. Chandra. "Medicare Spending, the Physician Workforce, and Beneficiaries' Quality of Care." *Health Affairs* Web exclusive (April 7, 2004): W4-184; W4-197. http://content.healthaffairs.org/cgi/reprint/hlthaff.w4.184v1.

Baker, G. B. "Integrating Technology and Disease Management—The Challenges." *Healthplan* 43, no. 5 (2002): 60–62, 64–66.

Baker, L., H. Birnbaum, J. Geppert, D. Mishol, and E. Moyneur. "The Relationship Between Technology Availability and Health Care Spending." *Health Affairs* Web exclusive (July–December, 2003): W3-537–W3-551.

Balas, E. A., and S. A. Boren. "Managing Clinical Knowledge for Health Care Improvement." In *Yearbook of Medical Informatics 2005: Ubiquitous Health Care Systems,* edited by R. Haux and C. Kulikowski, 65–70. Stuttgart, Germany: Schattauer Verlagsgesellschaft, 2005.

Balas, E. A., S. Weingarten, C. T. Garb, D. Blumenthal, S. A. Boren, and G. D. Brown. "Improving Preventive Care by Prompting Physicians." *Archives of Internal Medicine* 160, no. 3 (2000): 301–308.

Bansal, D., V. Gaddam, Y. W. Aude, J. Bissett, I. Fahdi, L. Garza, J. Joseph, B. Molavi, B. V. Pai, A. Sinha, E.S. Smith 3rd, and J. L. Mehta. "Trends in the Care of Patients with Acute Myocardial Infarction at a University-Affiliated Veterans Affairs Medical Center." *Journal of Cardiovascular Pharmacology and Therapeutics* 10, no. 1 (2005): 39–44.

Basting, T. "The Field of Disease Management at a Crossroads: An Interview with David B. Nash, M.D., M.B.A." *Disease Management* 4, no. 2 (2001): 35–38.

Batalden, P., and M. Splaine. "What Will It Take to Lead the Continual Improvement and Innovation of Health Care in the Twenty-First Century?" *Quality Management in Health Care* 11, no. 1 (2002): 45–54.

Bates, D. W., et al. "The Cost of Adverse Drug Events in Hospitalized Patients." *Journal of the American Medical Association* 277, no. 4 (1997): 307–311.

Becher, E. C., and M. R. Chassin. "Improving the Quality of Health Care: Who Will Lead?" *Health Affairs* 20, no. 5 (2001): 164–179.

Becker, C. "Spine-Tingling Prospects." *Modern Healthcare,* November 10, 2003.

_____. "Preparing for the Worst: GPOs Fear Fallout from Senate Hearings." *Modern Healthcare,* August 30, 2004, 8–9.

Beckley, E. T. "Visicu to the Rescue." *Modern Physician,* March 2003.

Beever, C., H. Burns, and M. Karbe. "U.S. Health Care's Technology Cost Crisis." *Strategy+Business,* March 31, 2004. http://www.strategy-business.com/press/enewsarticle/enews033104.

Begg, C. B., et al. "Variations in Morbidity After Radical Prostatectomy." *New England Journal of Medicine* 346, no. 15 (2002): 1138–1144.

Bellandi, D. "Spinoffs, Big Deals Dominate in '99." *Modern Healthcare,* January 10, 2000.

_____. "The Deals Are Off." *Modern Healthcare,* January 8, 2001.

Bellinger, D. C., R. A. Jonas, L. A. Rappaport, D. Wypij, G. Wernovsky, K. C. Kuban, P. D. Barnes, G. L. Holmes, P. R. Hickey, R. D. Strand, et al. "Developmental and Neurologic Status of Children After Heart Surgery with Hypothermic Circulatory Arrest or Low-Flow Cardiopulmonary Bypass." *New England Journal of Medicine* 332, no. 9 (1995): 549–555.

Bellinger, D. C., D. Wypij, A. J. duPlessis, L. A. Rappaport, R. A. Jonas, G. Wernovksy, and J. W. Newburger. "Neurodevelopmental Status at Eight Years in Children with D-Transposition of the Great Arteries: The Boston Circulatory Arrest Trial." *Journal of Thoracic and Cardiovascular Surgery* 126 (2003): 1385–1396.

Benko, L. B., and D. Bellandi. "The Rough and Tumble of It: Hospitals Flexing Their Muscles in Contract Disputes with Insurers." *Modern Healthcare,* March 19, 2001.

Bennett, J., and H. H. Hovey. "Companies Feel Pinch of Rising Health Costs." *The Wall Street Journal,* online edition, July 17, 2002.

Berk, M. L., and A. C. Monheit. "The Concentration of Health Expenditures: An Update." *Health Affairs* 11, no. 4 (1992): 145–149.

_____. "The Concentration of Health Care Expenditures, Revisited." *Health Affairs* 20, no. 2 (2001): 9–18.

Berk, M. L., A. C. Monheit, and Michael M. Hagan. "How the U.S. Spent Its Health Care Dollar: 1929–1980." *Health Affairs* 7, no. 4 (1998): 46–60.

Berndt, E. R., S. N. Finkelstein, P. E. Greenberg, R. H. Howland, A. Keith, A. J. Rush, J. Russell, and M. B. Keller. "Workplace Performance Effects from Chronic Depression and Its Treatment." *Journal of Health Economics* 17 (1998): 511–535.

Berndt, E. R., R. G. Frank, and T. G. McGuire. "Alternative Insurance Arrangements and the Treatment of Depression: What Are the Facts?" *American Journal of Managed Care* 3, no. 2 (1997): 243–250.

Bernson, M. E. "On Medical Education Reform at Harvard and Beyond: A Perspective with Jo Shapiro, MD, Harvard Medical School." *Next Generation,* November 2004. http://www.nextgenmd.org/vol1-2/shapirov1i2.html.

Bertoni, A. G., K. L. Goonan, D. E. Bonds, M. C. Whitt, D. C. Goff Jr., and F. L. Brancati. "Racial and Ethnic Disparities in Cardiac Catheterization for Acute Myocardial Infarction in the United States, 1995–2001." *Journal of the National Medical Association* 97, no. 3 (2005): 1–7.

Berwick, D. M. "Continuous Improvement as an Ideal in Health Care." *New England Journal of Medicine* 320, no. 1 (1989): 53–56.

_____. "Eleven Worthy Aims for Clinical Leadership of Health System Reform." *Journal of the American Medical Association* 272, no. 10 (1994): 797–802.

_____. "A Primer on Leading the Improvement of Systems." *British Medical Journal* 312 (1996a): 619–622.

_____. "Quality Comes Home." *Annals of Internal Medicine* 125, no. 10 (1996b): 839–843.

_____. *Escape Fire: Designs for the Future of Health Care.* San Francisco: Jossey Bass, 2004.

Berwick, D. M., N. A. DeParle, D. M. Eddy, P. M. Ellwood, A. C. Enthoven, G. C. Halvorson, K. W. Kizer, E. A. McGlynn, U. E. Reinhardt, R. D. Reischauer, W. L.

Roper, J. W. Rowe, L. D. Schaeffer, J. E. Wennberg, and G. R. Wilensky. "Paying for Performance: Medicare Should Lead." *Health Affairs* 22, no. 6 (2003): 8–10.

Berwick, D. M., A. B. Godfrey, and J. Roessner. *Curing Health Care: New Strategies for Quality Improvement.* San Francisco: John Wiley and Sons, 1990.

Berwick, D. M., B. C. James, and M. Coye. "The Connections Between Quality Measurement and Improvement." *Medical Care* 41, no. 1 (2003): I30–139.

Berwick, D. M., and T. W. Nolan. "Physicians as Leaders in Improving Health Care: A New Series in *Annals of Internal Medicine.*" *Annals of Internal Medicine* 128, no. 4 (1998): 289–292.

Best Doctors. "Best Doctors v. Disease Management." *Insights,* April 2005. http://www .bestdoctors.com/bd/insightsqtrly.pdf.

Birkmeyer, J. D. "High-Risk Surgery—Follow the Crowd." *Journal of the American Medical Association* 283 (2000): 1191–1193.

Birkmeyer, J. D., et al. *The Potential Benefits of Universal Adoption.* Leapfrog Patient Safety Standards. Dartmouth Medical School, November 2000.

———. *The Leapfrog Group's Patient Safety Practices, 2003: The Potential Benefits of Universal Adoption.* February 2004. http://www.leapfroggroup.org/media/file/ Leapfrog-Birkmeyer.pdf.

Birkmeyer, J. D., E. V. Finlayson, and C. M. Birkmeyer. "Volume Standards for High-Risk Surgical Procedures: Potential Benefits of the Leapfrog Initiative." *Surgery* 130, no. 3 (2001): 415–422.

Birkmeyer, J. D., A. E. Siewers, E. V. Finlayson, T. A. Stukel, F. L. Lucas, I. Batista, H. G. Welch, and D. E. Wennberg. "Hospital Volume and Surgical Mortality in the United States." *New England Journal of Medicine* 346, no. 15 (2002): 1128–1137.

Birkmeyer, J. D., J. S. Skinner, and D. E. Wennberg. "Will Volume-Based Referral Strategies Reduce Costs or Just Save Lives?" *Health Affairs* 21, no. 5 (2002): 234–241.

Birkmeyer, J. D., T. A. Stukel, A. E. Siewers, P. P. Goodney, D. E. Wennberg, and F. L. Lucas. "Surgeon Volume and Operative Mortality in the United States." *New England Journal of Medicine* 349, no. 22 (2003): 2117–2127.

Birkmeyer, N. J., J. N. Weinstein, A. N. Tosteson, T. D. Tosteson, J. S. Skinner, J. D. Lurie, R. Deyo, and J. E. Wennberg. "Design of the Spine Patient Outcomes Research Trial (SPORT)." *Spine* 27, no. 12 (2002): 1361–1372.

Blendon, R. J., C. Schoen, C. DesRoches, R. Osborn, and K. Zapert. "Common Concerns Amid Diverse Systems: Health Care Experiences in Five Countries." *Health Affairs* 22, no. 3 (2003): 106–121.

Blumenthal, D. "Decisions, Decisions: Why the Quality of Medical Decisions Matters." *Health Affairs* Web exclusive (October 7, 2004). http://content.healthaffairs .org/cgi/reprint/hlthaff.var.124v1.

Blumenthal, D., C. Vogeli, L. Alexander, and M. Pittman. "A Five-Nation Hospital Survey: Commonalities, Differences, and Discontinuities." The Commonwealth Fund. May 2004. http://www.cmwf.org/usr_doc/blumenthal_5nathospsurvey_734.pdf.

Boccuzzi, S. J. "Proceedings of a Symposium: Economics and Cost-Effectiveness in Evaluating the Value of Cardiovascular Therapies." *American Heart Journal* 137, no. 5 (1999): S62–S66.

Bodenheimer, T., K. Lorig, H. Holman, and K. Grumbach. "Patient Self-Management of Chronic Disease in Primary Care." *Journal of the American Medical Association* 288, no. 19 (2002): 2469–2475.

Bodenheimer, T., and K. Sullivan. "How Large Employers Are Shaping the Health Care Marketplace—Second of Two Parts." *New England Journal of Medicine* 338, no. 15 (1998): 1084–1088.

Boeing Company. "Boeing Initiates Local Community Health Care Collaboration to Improve Patient Safety." News release. July 12, 2001.

Bogdanich, W. "Two Powerful Groups Hold Sway over Buying at Many Hospitals." *The New York Times*, March 4, 2002.

Bohmer, R. M. J., A. C. Edmondson, and L. R. Feldman. "Intermountain Health Care." Case 9-603-066. Boston: Harvard Business School, 2002.

Bohmer, R. M. J., I. M. Nembhard, and R. Galvin. "Bridges to Excellence: Bringing Quality Health Care to Life." Case 604-030. Boston: Harvard Business School, 2004.

Bohmer, R. M. J., A. B. Winslow, A. C. Edmondson, and G. P. Pisano. "Team Learning Trade-offs: When Improving One Critical Dimension of Performance Inhibits Another." Working paper 05-047, Harvard Business School, Boston, 2005.

Bolton, W. K. "Renal Physicians Association Clinical Practice Guideline: Appropriate Patient Preparation for Renal Replacement Therapy: Guideline Number 3." *Journal of the American Society of Nephrologists* 14, no. 5 (2003): 1406–1410.

Bolton, W. K., and W. F. Owen Jr. "Preparing the Patient for Renal Replacement Therapy. Teamwork Optimizes Outcomes." *Postgraduate Medicine* 111, no. 6 (2002): 97–98, 101–104, 107–108. http://www.postgradmed.com/issues/2002/06_02/bolton.htm.

Boodman, S. "'Seeds' Show Effect on Early Prostate Cancer." *The Washington Post,* September 15, 1998.

Born, P., and C. J. Simon. "Patients and Profits: The Relationship Between HMO Financial Performance and Quality of Care." *Health Affairs* 20, no. 2 (2001): 167–174.

Borus, J. F. "Recognizing and Managing Residents' Problems and Problem Residents." *Academy of Radiology* 4 (1997): 527–533.

Boyles, W. R. "Consumer-Driven Health Plans. How Much of a Change?" *Healthplan* 44, no. 4 (2003): 32–34.

Brennan, T. A. "Luxury Primary Care—Market Innovation or Threat to Access?" *New England Journal of Medicine* 345, no. 15 (2002): 1165–1168.

Brown, G. B., and E. O. Teisberg. "A Script—Innovation Is the Key." *EIU Healthcare International*, 1st Quarter (1997): 79–88.

Brown-Beasley, M. W. "Telemonitoring Exploits Use of Existing Low-Cost Technology." *Telemedicine* 3, no. 1 (1995): 8.

Brummel-Smith, K. V., C. Boult, L. Boult, and J. T. Pacala. "Geriatrics in Managed Care: Systems of Care for Older Populations of the Future." Department of Family Practice and Community Health, University of Minnesota Medical School, 1996.

Bulkeley, W. M. "Mayo, IBM Join to Mine Medical Data." *The Wall Street Journal*, August 4, 2004.

Burda, D. "Raining on Competition. Florida's Specialty Hospital Ban Is a Bad Idea for Patients." *Modern Healthcare*, July 12, 2004.

Burns, L. R., J. Cacciamani, J. Clement, and W. Aquino. "The Fall of the House of AHERF: The Allegheny Bankruptcy." *Health Affairs* 19, no. 1 (2000): 7–41.

Burton, T. M. "Operation That Rated Hospitals Was Success, but the Patient Died." *The Wall Street Journal*, August 23, 1999.

_____. "Fatal Blockages: Stroke Victims Are Often Taken To Wrong Hospital." Wall Street Journal, May 9, 2005.

Butler, L. "Momentum Builds for Adding Drug Coverage to Medicare." *American Medical News,* February 14, 2000.

Butler, S. M. "A New Policy Framework for Health Care Markets." *Health Affairs* 23, no. 2 (2004): 22–24.

California CABG Mortality Reporting Program. *The California Report on Coronary Artery Bypass Graft Surgery, Hospital Data 2000–2002*. February 2005. http://www.oshpd .cahwnet.gov/HQAD/Outcomes/Studies/cabg/2000-2002Report/CCMRP0002.pdf.

Calmes, J. "Bill of Rights for Patients Poses Dilemma for Democratic Party." *The Wall Street Journal,* August 29, 2000.

Calmes, J., and L. McGinley. "Budget Office Sees Slower Growth in Health Programs." *The Wall Street Journal,* January 17, 1997.

Campion, F. X., and M. S. Rosenblatt. "Quality Assurance and Medical Outcomes in the Era of Cost Containment." *Surgical Clinics of North America* 76, no. 1 (1996): 139–159.

Capello, D. "The Better Doctor, an Interview with Atul Gawande." *New Yorker Online*, December 6, 2004 (posted November 29, 2004).

Caper, P. "Database Strategies for the Management of Clinical Decision Making." In *New Perspectives in Health Care Economics*. London: Mediq Ltd., 1991.

Caplan, R. A., K. L. Posner, R. J. Ward, and F. W. Cheney. "Adverse Respiratory Events in Anesthesia: A Closed Claims Analysis." *Anesthesiology* 72, no. 5 (1990): 828–833.

Capps, C., and D. Dranove. "Hospital Consolidation and Negotiated PPO Prices." *Health Affairs* 23, no. 2 (2004): 175–181.

Carbonin, P., R. Bernabei, G. Zuccala, and G. Gambassi. "Health Care of Older Persons, a Country Profile: Italy." *Journal of the American Geriatrics Society* 45, no. 12 (1997): 1519–1522.

CarePath, Inc. "Commonwealth of Virginia: Medicare Cost Reduction, Improved Patient Outcome." CarePath, Inc. Internal document. February 2005a.

———. Web site. 2005b. http://www.carepathbm.com/.

Carpenter, D. P. "The Political Economy of FDA Drug Review: Processing, Politics, and Lessons for Policy." *Health Affairs* 23, no. 1 (2004): 52–63.

Casalino, L. P., K. J. Devers, and L. R. Brewster. "Focused Factories? Physician-Owned Specialty Facilities." *Health Affairs* 22, no. 6 (2003): 56–67.

Ceniceros, R. "Provider Clout Leads to Higher Health Plan Costs." *Business Insurance,* April 2, 2001a, 11.

———. "Buyers' Clout Carries Cost." *Business Insurance,* August 27, 2001b, 1, 21.

———. "Pacific Business Group on Health Endorses Consumer-Driven Plan." *Business Insurance,* November 12, 2001c, 3.

Center for Justice and Democracy. "Bush and HMOs: Myth vs. Reality." March 23, 2001. http://www.centerjd.org/press/release/01-03-23b.htm.

Centers for Disease Control. "Facts about Traumatic Brain Injury." Factsheet. March 2005. http://www.cdc.gov/Migrated_Content/Fact_Sheet/Freeform_Fact_Sheet_ (General)/Facts_About_TBI.pdf.

Centers for Medicare and Medicaid Services. "CMS Statistics: Medicare State Enrollment." http://www.cms.hhs.gov/statistics/enrollment/.

———. Office of the Actuary, National Health Statistics Group. National Health Expenditures Aggregate and Per Capita Amounts, Percent Distribution, and Average Annual Percent Growth, by Source of Funds: Selected Calendar Years 1960–2004. http://www.cms.hhs.gov/NationalHealthExpendData/downloads/tables .pdf.

———. "CMS Announces Guidelines for Reporting Hospital Quality Data." Press release. January 28, 2004a. http://www.cms.hhs.gov/media/press/release.asp? Counter=955.

———. "Questions on Charges for the Uninsured." February 17, 2004b. http:// www.cms.hhs.gov/FAQ_Uninsured.pdf.

_____. "CMS Launches 'Fistula First' Initiative to Improve Care and Quality of Life for Hemodialysis Patients." April 14, 2004c. http://www.cms.hhs.gov/media/press/release.asp?Counter=1007.

_____. *2004 Annual Report, End Stage Renal Disease Clinical Performance Measures Project.* Baltimore: Department of Health and Human Services, Centers for Medicare and Medicaid Services, Office of Clinical Standards and Quality, December 2004d. http://www.cms.hhs.gov/esrd/2004_AR_final.pdf.

_____. "Physicians' Referrals to Health Care Entities with Which They Have Financial Relationships." 2005a. http://www.cms.hhs.gov/medlearn/refphys.asp.

_____. "Medicare 'Pay For Performance (P4p)' Initiatives." Factsheet. January 31, 2005b. http://www.cms.hhs.gov/media/press/release.asp?Counter=1343.

Cerner. "St. Mary's Medical Center: APACHE Highlights Ways to Improve Care of the Sickest Patients." Case study. 2002. http://www.cerner.com/public/filedownload.asp?LibraryID=9907.

_____. "Cerner Apache III for ICU: The Unified Approach to Outcomes Measurement." Brochure. 2003. http://www.cerner.com/public/filedownload.asp?LibraryID=15385.

_____. "Sarasota Memorial Hospital: Data Analysis Drives ICU Improvements." Case study. 2004. http://www.cerner.com/public/filedownload.asp?LibraryID=9906.

_____. Millenium Apache Web site. 2005. http://www.cerner.com/public/MillenniumSolution.asp?id=3562.

Chandra, A., S. Nundy, and S. A. Seabury. "The Growth of Physician Medical Malpractice Payments: Evidence from the National Practitioner Data Bank." *Health Affairs* Web exclusive (May 31, 2005). http://content.healthaffairs.org/cgi/reprint/hlthaff.w5.240v1.

Chapman, R. H., and P. J. Neumann. "Web Site Offers Comprehensive List of Cost-Utility Ratios in Health and Medicine." *Harvard Center for Risk Analysis* 8, no. 8 (November 2000).

Charbonneau, A., A. K. Rosen, R. R. Owen, A. Spiro 3rd, A. S. Ash, D. R. Miller, L. Kazis, B. Kader, F. Cunningham, and D. R Berlowitz. "Monitoring Depression Care: In Search of an Accurate Quality Indicator." *Medical Care* 42, no. 6 (June 2004): 522–531.

Chassin, M. R. "Achieving and Sustaining Improved Quality: Lessons from New York State and Cardiac Surgery." *Health Affairs* 21, no. 4 (2002): 40–51.

Chassin, M. R., R. W. Galvin, and the National Roundtable on Health Care Quality. "The Urgent Need to Improve Health Care Quality." *Journal of the American Medical Association* 280, no. 11 (1998): 1000–1005.

Cheng, T. M. "Taiwan's New National Health Insurance Program: Genesis and Experience So Far." *Health Affairs* 22, no. 3 (2003): 61–76.

Chennisi, D., and G. LeGrow. "The Next-Generation Health Plan: Product Innovation." *Healthplan* 44, no. 4 (2003): 63–64.

Chernew, M. E., R. A. Hirth, and D. M. Cutler. "Increased Spending on Health Care: How Much Can the United States Afford?" *Health Affairs* 22, no. 4 (2003): 15–25.

Chetney, R. "The Cardiac Connection Program: Home Care That Doesn't Miss a Beat." *Home Healthcare Nurse* 21, no. 10 (2003): 680–686.

Chia, N. C. "Health for All: Financing and Delivery Issues." In *Singapore Economy in the 21st Century*, edited by Koh Ai Tee et al. Singapore: McGraw Hill, 2002.

Choudhry, N. K., R. H. Fletcher, and S. B. Soumerai. "Systematic Review: The Relationship Between Clinical Experience and Quality of Health Care." *Annals of Internal Medicine* 142, no. 4 (2005): 260–273.

Clancy, C. M., and K. Cronin. "Evidence-Based Decision Making: Global Evidence, Local Decisions." *Health Affairs* 24, no. 1 (2005): 151–162.

Clarfield, M. A., A. Paltiel, Y. Gindin, B. Morginstin, and T. Dwolatzky. "Country Profile: Israel." *Journal of the American Geriatrics Society* 48, no. 8 (2000): 980–984.

Cockburn, I. M. "The Changing Structure of the Pharmaceutical Industry." *Health Affairs* 23, no. 1 (2004): 10–22.

Cockburn, I. M., H. L. Bailit, E. R. Berndt, and S. N. Finkelstein. "Loss of Work Productivity Due to Illness and Medical Treatment." *Journal of Occupational and Environmental Medicine* 41, no. 11 (1999): 948–953.

Cohen, M. D., D. R. Hawes, G. D. Hutchins, W. D. McPhee, M. B. LaMasters, and R. P. Fallon. "Activity-Based Cost Analysis: A Method of Analyzing the Financial and Operating Performance of Academic Radiology Departments." *Radiology* 215 (2000): 708–716.

Comarow, A. "Finding the Right Hospital for You." *U.S. News & World Report* 127, no. 3 (1999): 72–73.

_____. "Best Hospitals 2004, Methodology Behind the Rankings" *U.S. News.com.* September 6, 2004. http://www.usnews.com/usnews/health/hosptl/methodology .htm.

Commission on Systemic Interoperability. *Ending the Document Game: Connecting and Transforming Your Healthcare Through Information Technology.* Washington, DC: Government Printing Office, 2005. http://endingthedocumentgame.gov/ PDFs/entireReport.pdf.

Committee on the Consequences of Uninsurance, Board on Health Care Services, Institute of Medicine of the National Academies. *Insuring America's Health: Principles and Recommendations.* Washington, DC: National Academies Press, 2004.

Committee for Economic Development, Research and Policy Committee. *A New Vision for Health Care: A Leadership Role for Business.* New York: Committee for Economic Development, 2002. http://www.ced.org/docs/report/report_healthcare.pdf.

Committee on Quality of Health Care in America, Institute of Medicine. *Crossing the Quality Chasm: A New Health System for the 21st Century.* Washington, DC: National Academies Press, 2001.

Commonwealth Fund. *First Report and Recommendations of the Commonwealth Fund's International Working Group on Quality Indicators: A Report to Health Ministers of Australia, Canada, New Zealand, the United Kingdom, and the United States.* June 2004. http://www.cmwf.org/usr_doc/ministers_complete2004report_ 752.pdf.

_____. Health Care Opinion Leaders Survey. November–December 2004. http:// www.cmwf.org/usr_doc/Opinion_leaders_topline.pdf.

_____. Health Care Opinion Leaders Survey. February 2005. http://www.cmwf .org/usr_doc/HCOL_survey2_tables.pdf

_____. Health Care Opinion Leaders Survey. April 2005. http://www.cmwf.org/ surveys/surveys_show.htm?doc_id=275633.

Commonwealth Fund/Harvard/Harris Interactive. "2001 Commonwealth Fund International Health Policy Survey." 2001. http://www.cmwf.org/surveys/surveys_ show.htm?doc_id=228169.

Connecting for Health, Markle Foundation. *Achieving Electronic Connectivity in Health Care: A Preliminary Road Map from the Nation's Public and Private-Sector Healthcare Leaders.* Markle Foundation and The Robert Wood Johnson Foundation. July 2004a. http://www.connectingforhealth.org/resources/cfh_aech_ roadmap_072004.pdf.

_____. *Connecting Americans to Their Healthcare: Final Report.* Markle Foundation and The Robert Wood Johnson Foundation. July 2004b. http://www.connecting forhealth.org/resources/wg_eis_final_report_0704.pdf.

Connolly, C. "U.S. Firms Losing Health Care Battle, GM Chairman Says." *The Washington Post,* February 11, 2005.

Consumer-Purchaser Disclosure Project. *The State Experience in Health Quality Data Collection.* Washington, DC: National Partnership for Women & Families, May 2004. http://healthcaredisclosure.org/resources/files/DataCollection.pdf.

Consumer's Medical Resource. http://www.consumersmedical.com.

Conto, A., and P. Gnemi. "Advanced Strategies in Designing New Chemicals: Further Problems or a New Challenge for the Chemical Industry?" *Chemical Market Reporter,* October 30, 2000.

Cooke, R. *Dr. Folkman's War: Angiogenesis and the Struggle to Defeat Cancer.* New York: Random House, 2001.

Coresh, J., B. C. Astor, T. Greene, G. Eknoyan, and A. S. Levey. "Prevalence of Chronic Kidney Disease and Decreased Kidney Function in the Adult US Population: Third National Health and Nutrition Examination Survey." *American Journal of Kidney Disease* 41, no. 1 (2003): 1–12.

Cosgrove, D. M. "The Innovation Imperative." Presidential address, 80th annual meeting of the American Association for Thoracic Surgery, Toronto, Ontario, May 1, 2000.

_____. "The Value of Health Care: Changing the Debate." Presented at the City Club Forum, Cleveland, Ohio, January 21, 2005.

Costell, D. "Can We Talk Price?" *The Wall Street Journal,* February 8, 2002a.

_____. "How to Haggle." *The Wall Street Journal,* February 8, 2002b.

Council on Ethical and Judicial Affairs, American Medical Association. "Ethical Issues in Managed Care." *Journal of the American Medical Association* 273, no. 4 (1995): 330–335.

Cowart, R. G. "Surges in Mergers Make Cost-Cutting a Necessity." *Managed Healthcare,* February 1, 2000.

Coye, M. J., W. M. Aubry, and W. Yu for the Health Technology Center. "The 'Tipping Point' and Health Care Innovations: Advancing the Adoption of Beneficial Technologies." Presented at Accelerating Quality Improvement in Health Care Strategies to Speed the Diffusion of Evidence-Based Innovations, Washington, DC, January 27–28, 2003.

Coye, M. J., and D. E. Detmer. "Quality at a Crossroads." *Millbank Quarterly Journal of Public Health and Health Care Policy* 76, no. 4 (1998). http://www.milbank.org/quarterly/764featcoye.html.

Crabtree, P. "Orange County, Calif., Medical Groups Drop HMOs." *The Orange County Register,* December 15, 1998.

Crowder, D. F. "Health Care Strategies for Foundation Coal Company." Unpublished paper, 8th draft, October 12, 2004.

Cuellar, A. E., and P. J. Gertler. "Strategic Integration of Hospitals and Physicians." Working paper, Haas School of Business, University of California–Berkeley, May 1, 2002. http://faculty.haas.berkeley.edu/gertler/working_papers/hospital_vi_5_10_02.pdf.

Cunningham, P. J. "Targeting Communities with High Rates of Uninsured Children." *Health Affairs* Web exclusive (July 25, 2001). http://content.healthaffairs.org/cgi/content/abstract/hlthaff.w1.20v1.

Cutler, D. M. "Cutting Costs and Improving Health: Making Reform Work." *Health Affairs* 14, no. 1 (1995): 161–172.

_____. "Declining Disability Among the Elderly." *Health Affairs* 20, no. 6 (2001): 11–27.

_____. *Your Money or Your Life: Strong Medicine for America's Health Care System.* Cary, NC: Oxford University Press, 2004.

Cutler, D. M., and E. R. Berndt, eds. *Medical Care Output and Productivity.* NBER Studies in Income and Wealth 63. Cambridge, MA: National Bureau of Economic Research, 2001.

Cutler, D. M., and A. Garber, eds. *Frontiers in Health Policy Research.* Vol. 6. Cambridge, MA: MIT Press, 2003.

Cutler, D. M., and M. McClellan. "Is Technological Change in Medicine Worth It?" *Health Affairs* 20, no. 5 (2001): 11–29.

Cutler, D. M., M. McClellan, and J. P. Newhouse. "The Costs and Benefits of Intensive Treatment for Cardiovascular Disease." NBER working paper W6514, National Bureau of Economic Research, Cambridge, MA, April 1998, 1–34. http://www.nber.org/papers/w6514.

Cutler, D. M., M. McClellan, J. P. Newhouse, and D. Remler. "Pricing Heart Attack Treatments." NBER working paper W7089, National Bureau of Economic Research, Cambridge, MA, 1999.

Cutler, D. M., and L. Sheiner, "The Geography of Medicare." *American Economic Review,* May 1999, 228–233.

"The Cutting Edge of Virtual Reality." *The Economist,* March 22, 2001, 44–46. http://www.ynl.t.u-tokyo.ac.jp/~nakamura/Economist_com.htm.

Dahl, D. "Hospitals, HMOs Pursue Consolidation to Cut Costs." *Boston Business Journal,* July 8, 1994.

Dalzell, M. D. "Physician, HEDIS (Health Employer Data and Information Set) Thyself." *Managed Care* 8, no. 3 (1999): 54, 57.

Danzon, P. M., and M. V. Pauly. "Insurance and New Technology: From Hospital to Drugstore." *Health Affairs* 20, no. 5 (September–October 2001): 86–100.

Darlin, D. "No-Brainer Health Care Is Passé." *The New York Times,* October 29, 2005.

Davis, D. A., and A. Taylor-Vaisey. "Translating Guidelines into Practice: A Systematic Review of Theoretic Concepts, Practical Experience and Research Evidence in the Adoption of Clinical Practice Guidelines." *Canadian Medical Association Journal* 157, no. 4 (1997): 408–416.

Davis, D. A., M. A. Thomson, A. D. Oxman, and R. B. Haynes. "Changing Physician Performance: A Systematic Review of the Effect of Continuing Medical Education Strategies." *Journal of the American Medical Association* 274, no. 9 (1995): 700–705.

Davis, K. "Will Consumer-Directed Health Care Improve System Performance?" Issue Brief, The Commonwealth Fund, August 2004.

Dean, N. C., M. P. Silver, K. A. Bateman, B. James, C. J. Hadlock, D. Hale. "Decreased Mortality After Implementation of a Treatment Guideline for Community-Acquired Pneumonia." *American Journal of Medicine* 110, no. 6 (2001): 451–457.

Dembner, A. "Romney Seeks 'First-Class' Health Plan for Poor." *The Boston Globe,* February 18, 2005. http://www.boston.com/news/local/massachusetts/articles/2005/02/18/romney_seeks_first_class_health_plan_for_poor/.

DeNavas-Walt, C., B. D. Proctor, and R. J. Mills. *Income, Poverty, and Health Insurance Coverage in the United States: 2004.* U.S. Census Bureau, Current Population Reports no. P60-229. Washington, DC: Government Printing Office, 2005. http://www.census.gov/prod/2005pubs/p60-229.pdf.

Denton, T. A., G. C. Fonarow, K. A. LaBresh, and A. Trento. "Secondary Prevention After Coronary Bypass: The American Heart Association 'Get with the Guidelines' Program." *Annals of Thoracic Surgery* 75, no. 3 (2003): 758–760.

Department of Human Services, Health Services, Office of Medical Assistance Programs. *The Oregon Health Plan: An Historical Overview.* February 2004. http://www.oregon.gov/DHS/healthplan/data_pubs/ohpoverview0204.pdf.

Devers, K. J., L. R. Brewster, and P. B. Ginsburg. "Specialty Hospitals: Focused Factories or Cream Skimmers?" Issue Brief no. 62, Center for Studying Health System Change, April 2003, 1–4.

Dewar, H. "Healthcare Unites Senate GOP." *Washingtonpost.com.* July 18, 1999. http://www.washingtonpost.com/wp-srv/politics/special/healthcare/stories/senate071899.htm.

DeWeese, J. A., H. C. Urschel Jr., and J. A. Waldhausen. "Guidelines for Minimal Standards in Cardiac Surgery: American College of Surgeons." *Bulletin of the American College of Surgeons* 76, no. 8 (1991): 27–29.

Dimick, J. B., J. D. Birkmeyer, and G. R. Upchurch Jr. "Measuring Surgical Quality: What's the Role of Provider Volume?" *World Journal of Surgery,* September 8, 2005.

Doolan, D. F., D. W. Bates, and B. C. James. "The Use of Computers for Clinical Care: A Case Series of Advanced U.S. Sites." *Journal of American Medical Informatics Association* 10, no. 1 (2003): 94–107.

Dooren, J. "Health Coverage in U.S. Rises for Children, But Slips in Total." *The Wall Street Journal,* July 1, 2004.

Dranove, D. *The Economic Evolution of American Health Care: From Marcus Welby to Managed Care.* Princeton, NJ: Princeton University Press, 2000.

Dreyfuss, R. "Which Doctors?" *The New Republic,* June 22, 1998, 22–25.

Dr Foster. "Research, Analysis and Communication." 2005. http://www.drfoster.co.uk/hp/index.asp.

Druss, B. G., S. C. Marcus, M. Olfson, and H. A. Pincus. "The Most Expensive Medical Conditions in America." *Health Affairs* 21, no. 4 (2002): 105–111.

Dubois, R. W., A. J. Chawla, C. A. Neslusan, M. W. Smith, and S. Wade. "Explaining Drug Spending Trends: Does Perception Match Reality?" *Health Affairs* 19, no. 2 (2000): 231–239.

Dudley, R. A., K. L. Johansen, R. Brand, D. J. Rennie, and A. Milstein. "Selective Referral to High-Volume Hospitals: Estimating Potentially Avoidable Deaths." *Journal of the American Medical Association* 283, no. 9 (2000): 1159–1166.

Dunn, K. "Innovation Is Driven by the Possibility of Profit." *The Washington Post,* October 1, 2000.

Dziuban, S. W., et al. "How a New York Cardiac Surgery Program Uses Outcomes Data." *Annals of Thoracic Surgery* 58, no. 6 (1994): 1871–1876.

Eagle, K. A., A. J. Garson, G. A. Beller, and C. Sennett. "Closing the Gap Between Science and Practice: The Need for Professional Leadership." *Health Affairs* 22, no. 2 (2003): 196–201.

Easterbrook, G. "Old News." *The New Republic,* October 30, 2000.

Eckbo, P. "Building a Global Independent Patient Services Organisation to Improve Critical Illness Care: Addressing the Incentives, Cost and Quality Issues in Healthcare." Presentation to the World Health Congress, April 7, 2005.

Eddy, D. M. "Evidence-Based Medicine: A Unified Approach." *Health Affairs* 24, no. 1 (2005): 9–17.

Eddy, D. M., and J. Billings. "The Quality of Medical Evidence: Implications for Quality of Care." *Health Affairs* 7, no. 1 (1988): 19–32.

Edlin, M. "Disease Management Proves Itself at Geisinger." *Healthplan* 44, no. 4 (2003a): 55–58.

———. "Success in Rural Telemedicine." *Healthplan* 44, no. 4 (2003b): 60–62.

Edmondson, A. C., R. Bohmer, and G. P. Pisano. "Disrupted Routines: Team Learning and New Technology Adaptation." *Administrative Science Quarterly* 46 (2001a): 685–716.

———. "Speeding Up Team Learning." *Harvard Business Review*, October 2001b, 5–11.

Edmondson, A., G. P. Pisano, R. Bohmer, and A. Winslow. "Learning How and Learning What: Effects of Tacit and Codified Knowledge on Performance Improvement Following Technology Adoption." *Decision Sciences* 34, no. 2 (2003): 197–223.

Edwards, M., and J. Hamilton. "10 Deals That Changed Biotechnology." *Signals*, November 17, 1998. http://www.signalsmag.com.

Eisenberg, D. "Curing Managed Care." *Time*, June 12, 2000.

Eisenberg, R. "Reexamining Drug Regulation from the Perspective of Innovation Policy." University of Michigan faculty workshop, November 15, 2002.

Ellrodt, G. R., M. Robertson, Y. Hong, and K. LaBresh for the American Heart Association. "Get with the Guidelines: Coronary Artery Disease Program Narrows the Gender Associated Treatment Gap." Poster presented at the American Heart Association's Scientific Sessions. Orlando, FL. November 9, 2003. http://content.healthaffairs.org/cgi/reprint/hlthaff.w5.74v1.

Elswick, J. "Honeywell Cites Success with Medical Decision Support Tool." *Employee Benefit News*, October 1, 2001.

Enthoven, A. C. "How Employers Boost Health Costs." *The Wall Street Journal*, January 24, 1992.

———. "The History and Principles of Managed Competition." *Health Affairs* 12 (1993): 24–48.

———. "Employment-Based Health Insurance Is Failing: Now What?" *Health Affairs* Web exclusive (May 28, 2003): W3-237–W3-249.

———. "Market Forces and Efficient Health Care Systems." *Health Affairs* 23, no. 2 (2004): 25–27.

Enthoven, A. C., and L. A. Tollen. "Competition in Health Care: It Takes Systems to Pursue Quality and Efficiency." *Health Affairs* Web exclusive (September 7, 2005). http://content.healthaffairs.org/cgi/reprint/hlthaff.w5.420v1.

Escarce, J. J., K. Kapur, G. F. Joyce, and K. A. Van Vorst. "Medical Care Expenditures Under Gatekeeper and Point-of-Service Arrangements." *Health Services Research* 36, no. 6 (2001): 1037–1057.

Fairview-University Children's Hospital. "Cystic Fibrosis Center Outcomes Data." 2005. http://www.fairviewchildrens.org/outcomes/mcfc-intro.htm.

Fakhry, S. M., A. L. Trask, M. A. Waller, and D. D. Watts; IRTC Neurotrauma Task Force. "Management of Brain-Injured Patients by an Evidence-Based Medicine Protocol Improves Outcomes and Decreases Hospital Charges." *Journal of Trauma* 56, no. 3 (2004): 492–499; discussion 499–500.

Fallon Community Health Plan. "Disease Management Takes Center Stage at National Conference." Press release. April 15, 2003. http://www.fchp.org/news/press/PressRelease.aspx?cid=411.

FamiliesUSA. "The 106th Congress: How Federal Managed Care Legislation Affects You." http://www.familiesusa.org/site/PageServer?pagename=media_updates_compare2.

Farley, D. O., M. C. Haims, D. J. Keyser, S. S. Olmsted, S. V. Curry, and M. Sorbero. *Regional Health Quality Improvement Coalitions: Lessons Across the Life Cycle.* Santa Monica, CA: RAND Corporation, 2003. http://www.rand.org/publications/ TR/TR102/.

Farria, D., and S. A. Feig. "An Introduction to Economic Issues in Breast Imaging." *Radiologic Clinics of North America* 38, no. 4 (2000): 825–842.

Federal Trade Commission, Health Care Services and Products Division, Bureau of Competition. *FTC Antitrust Actions in Health Care Services and Products.* Washington, DC: Federal Trade Commission, 2003. http://www.ftc.gov/bc/ hcupdate030401.pdf.

Federal Trade Commission and U.S. Department of Justice. *Improving Health Care: A Dose of Competition.* July 2004. http://www.usdoj.gov/atr/public/health_ care/204694.pdf.

Fendrick, A. M. "The Role of Economic Evaluation in the Diagnosis and Treatment of *Helicobacter pylori* Infection." *Gastroenterology Clinics* 29, no. 4 (2000): 837–851.

Fendrick, A. M., J. T. McCort, M. E. Chrenew, R. A. Hirth, C. Patel, and B. S. Bloom. "Immediate Eradication of *Helicobacter pylori* in Patients with Previously Documented Peptic Ulcer Disease: Clinical and Economic Effects." *American Journal of Gastroenterology* 92, no. 11 (1997): 2017–2024.

Ferguson, T. B., Jr., L. P. Coombs, and E. D. Peterson. "Internal Thoracic Artery Grafting in the Elderly Patient Undergoing Coronary Artery Bypass Grafting: Room for Process Improvement?" *Journal of Thoracic and Cardiovascular Surgery* 123 (2002a): 869–880.

———. "Preoperative Beta-Blocker Use and Mortality and Morbidity Following CABG Surgery in North America." *Journal of the American Medical Association* 287, no. 17 (2002b): 2221–2227.

Ferguson, T. B., Jr., S. W. Dziuban Jr., F. H. Edwards, M. C. Eiken, A. Laurie, W. Shroyer, P. C. Pairolero, R. P. Anderson, and F. L. Grover. "The STS National Database: Current Changes and Challenges for the New Millennium." *Annals of Thoracic Surgery* 69 (2000): 680–691.

Ferguson, T. B., Jr., B. G. Hammill, E. D. Peterson, and E. R. DeLong. "A Decade of Change—Risk Profiles and Outcomes for Isolated Coronary Artery Bypass Grafting Procedures, 1990–1999: A Report from the STS National Database Committee and the Duke Clinical Research Institute." *Annals of Thoracic Surgery* 73 (2002):480–490.

Ferguson, T. B., Jr., E. D. Peterson, L. P. Coombs, M. C. Eiken, M. L. Carey, F. L. Grover, and E. R. DeLong. "Use of Continuous Quality Improvement to Increase Use of Process Measures in Patients Undergoing Coronary Artery Bypass Graft Surgery: A Randomized Controlled Trial." *Journal of the American Medical Association* 90, no. 1 (2003): 49–56.

Fernandopulle, R., T. Ferris, A. Epstein, B. McNeil, J. Newhouse, G. Pisano, and D. Blumenthal. "A Research Agenda for Bridging the Quality Chasm." *Health Affairs* 22, no. 2 (2003): 178–190.

Ferrara, P. "More Than a Theory: Medical Savings Accounts at Work." Cato Policy Analysis. The Cato Institute, Washington, DC, March 14, 1995. http://www.cato .org/pubs/pas/pa-220es.html.

Ferris, T. G., Y. Chang, D. Blumenthal, and S. D. Pearson. "Leaving Gatekeeping Behind—Effects of Opening Access to Specialists for Adults in a Health Maintenance Organization." *New England Journal of Medicine* 345, no. 18 (2001): 1312–1317.

Finkelstein, S. N., E. R. Berndt, P. E. Greenberg, R. A. Parsley, J. M. Russell, and M. B. Keller. "Improvement in Subjective Work Performance After Treatment of Chronic Depression: Some Preliminary Results." *Psychopharmacology Bulletin* 32, no. 1 (1996): 33–40.

First Market Research. "The Massachusetts Public and Primary Care Physicians React to a New Quality/Cost Information System." Marketing research study conducted for Harvard Pilgrim HealthCare. October 2005.

Fisher, E. "More Care Is Not Better Care." *Expert Voices*, Issue 7, January 2005. http://www.nihcm.org/ExpertV7.pdf.

Fisher, E. S., and H. G. Welch. "Avoiding the Unintended Consequences of Growth in Medical Care: How Might More Be Worse?" *Journal of the American Medical Association* 281, no. 5 (1999): 446–453.

Fisher, E. S., D. E. Wennberg, and T. A. Stukel. "Hospital Readmission Rates for Cohorts of Medicare Beneficiaries in Boston and New Haven." *New England Journal of Medicine* 331, no. 15 (1994): 989–994.

Fisher, E. S., D. E. Wennberg, T. A. Stukel, and D. J. Gottlieb. "Variations in the Longitudinal Efficiency of Academic Medical Centers." *Health Affairs* Web exclusive (October 7, 2004). http://content.healthaffairs.org/cgi/reprint/hlthaff.var.19v1.

Fisher, E. S., D. E. Wennberg, T. A. Stukel, D. J. Gottlieb, F. L. Lucas, and É. L. Pinder. "The Implications of Regional Variations in Medicare Spending. Part 1: The Content, Quality, and Accessibility of Care." *Annals of Internal Medicine* 138, no. 4 (2003a): 273–287.

⸻. "The Implications of Regional Variations in Medicare Spending. Part 2: Health Outcomes and Satisfaction with Care." *Annals of Internal Medicine* 138, no. 4 (2003b): 288–298.

Fisher, E. S., and J. E. Wennberg. "Health Care Quality, Geographic Variations, and the Challenge of Supply-Sensitive Care." *Perspectives in Biology and Medicine* 46, no. 1 (2003): 69–79.

Fitzgerald, C. L. "Highmark Reins in Diagnostic Imaging." *Physicians News Digest*, October 2004.

Fonarow, G. C., C. W. Yancy, S. F. Chang, and ADHERE Scientific Advisory Board and Investigators. "Variation in Heart Failure Quality of Care Indicators Among U.S. Hospitals: Analysis of 230 Hospitals in ADHERE." *Journal of Cardiac Failure* 9, no. 5, supplement (2003): S82.

Fox, D. M., and H. M. Leichter. "State Model: Oregon. The Ups and Downs of Oregon's Rationing Plan." *Health Affairs* 12, no. 2 (1993): 66–70.

Freudenheim, M. "Advice Is the Newest Prescription in Health Costs." *The New York Times*, April 9, 2000.

⸻. "Many Hospitals Resist Computerized Patient Care." *The New York Times*, April 6, 2004.

⸻. "60 Companies Plan to Sponsor Health Coverage for Uninsured." *The New York Times*, January 27, 2005a.

⸻. "Digital Rx: Take Two Aspirins and E-Mail Me in the Morning." *The New York Times*, March 2, 2005b.

Friedman, M. "How to Cure Health Care." *Public Interest* 142 (Winter 2001): 3.

Fronstin, P. "Sources of Health Insurance and Characteristics of the Uninsured: Analysis of the March 1999 Current Population Survey." *EBRI Issue Brief* 217 (2000): 1–26.

⸻. "Defined Contribution Health Benefits." *EBRI Issue Brief* 231 (2001): 1–30.

Fuchs, V. R. "What's Ahead for Health Insurance in the United States?" *New England Journal of Medicine* 346, no. 23 (2002): 1822–1824.

Fuchs, V. R., and H. C. Sox Jr. "Physicians' Views of the Relative Importance of Thirty Medical Innovations." *Health Affairs* 20, no. 5 (2001): 30–42.

Fuhrmans, V. "Attacking Rise in Health Costs, Big Company Meets Resistance." *The Wall Street Journal*, July 13, 2004.

_____. "Radical Surgery." *The Wall Street Journal*, February 11, 2005a.

_____. "Early-Warning Tool for Unsafe Drugs." *The Wall Street Journal*, April 28, 2005b.

_____. "Insurer Reveals What Doctors Really Charge." *The Wall Street Journal*, August 18, 2005c.

Gaba, D. M., and S. K. Howard. "Fatigue Among Clinicians and the Safety of Patients." *New England Journal of Medicine* 347, no. 16 (2002): 1249–1255.

Gabel, J. R. "Job-Based Health Insurance, 1977–1998: The Accidental System Under Scrutiny." *Health Affairs* 18, no. 6 (1999): 62–74.

Gabel, J., A. LoSasso, and T. Rice. "Consumer-Driven Health Plans: Are They More Than Talk Now?" *Health Affairs* Web exclusive (December 8, 2003): W395–W407. http://content.healthaffairs.org/cgi/content/full/hlthaff.w2.395v1/DC1.

Galen Institute. "Aetna HealthFund: A Consumer Directed Health Plan Study." February 11, 2004. http://www.galen.org/fileuploads/Aetna.pdf.

Galvin, R. "Purchasing Health Care: An Opportunity for a Public-Private Partnership." *Health Affairs* 22, no. 2 (2003): 191–195.

_____. "'A Deficiency of Will and Ambition': A Conversation with Donald Berwick." *Health Affairs* Web exclusive (January 12, 2005). http://content.healthaffairs.org/cgi/content/full/hlthaff.w5.1/DC1?eaf.

Gandjour, A., A. Bannenberg, and K. W. Lauterbach. "Threshold Volumes Associated with Higher Survival in Health Care: A Systematic Review." *Medical Care* 41 (2003): 1129–1141.

Garber, A. M. "Evidence-Based Coverage Policy." *Health Affairs* 20, no. 5 (2001): 62–82.

Gardner, J. "Provider Relief Gaining." *Modern Healthcare*, September 4, 2000.

Garson, A., Jr. "The Duke Cost-Effectiveness Programs." Presented at The Academic Health Center in the 21st Century, Duke Private Sector Conference, 1995. http://conferences.mc.duke.edu/privatesector/dpsc1995/ahc.htm.

_____. "The U.S. Health Care System 2010: Problems, Principles, and Potential Solutions." *Circulation* 101, no. 16 (2000): 2015–2016.

Garvey, J. M. "Beyond 'Compliance' to Participation and More." *Health Industry Today*, May 1998.

Gatsonis, C. A., A. M. Epstein, J. P. Newhouse, S. L. Normand, and B. J. McNeil. "Variations in the Utilization of Coronary Angiography for Elderly Patients with an Acute Myocardial Infarction: An Analysis Using Hierarchical Logistic Regression." *Medical Care* 33, no. 6 (1995): 625–642.

Gawande, A. *Complications: A Young Surgeon's Notes on an Imperfect Science.* New York: Picador, 2002.

_____. "The Bell Curve: What Happens When Patients Find Out How Good Their Doctors Really Are?" *New Yorker Online*, December 6, 2004 (posted on November 29, 2004). http://www.newyorker.com/fact/content/?041206fa_fact.

_____. "Piecework: Medicine's Money Problem." *New Yorker Online*, April 4, 2005 (posted on March 28, 2005).

"Get Well Away; Medical Tourism to India." *The Economist* (London), October 9, 2004, 76.

Gilchrist, V., G. McCord, S. L. Schrop, B. D. King, K. F. McCormick, A. M. Oprandi, B. A. Selius, M. Cowher, R. Maheshwary, F. Patel, A. Shah, B. Tsai, and M. Zaharna. "Physician Activities During Time Out of the Examination Room."*Annals of Family Medicine* 3 (2005): 494–499.

Gilmartin, R. V. "America's Revolution in Health Care: Increasing Competition and Choice; Improving People's Health." Presented at the Executives' Club of Chicago, February 27, 1997. *Executive Speeches* (August–September 1997).

Gingrich, N. "Transforming Health and Health Care to a 21st Century System." Draft, December 12, 2002.

Ginsburg, P. B. "The Role of Society in Making Distributive Judgments." *Health Affairs* 14, no. 3 (1995): 283.

_____. "Health Spending: Questioning the Assumptions." *Health Affairs* 18, no. 1 (1999): 272–274, 276–277.

_____. "Controlling Health Care Costs." *New England Journal of Medicine* 351, no. 16 (2004): 1591–1593.

Ginsburg, P. B., L. B. LeRoy, and G. T. Hammons. "Medicare Physician Payment Reform." *Health Affairs* 9, no. 1 (1990): 178–188.

Ginsburg, P. B., and K. E. Thorpe. "Can All-Payer Rate Setting and the Competitive Strategy Coexist?" *Health Affairs* 11, no. 2 (1992): 73–86.

Glassberg, H. "Hospitals in 'Most Wired' Ranking Make Progress on Electronic Records." *The Wall Street Journal Online*, July 19, 2004.

Gleason, S., K. L. Furie, M. H. Lev, J. O'Donnell, P. M. McMahon, M. T. Beinfeld, E. Halpern, M. Mullins, G. Harris, W. J. Koroshetz, and G. S. Gazelle. "Potential Influence of Acute CT on Inpatient Costs in Patients with Ischemic Stroke." *Academic Radiology* 8, no. 10 (2001): 955–964.

Glied, S., and S. E. Little. "The Uninsured and the Benefits of Medical Progress." *Health Affairs* 22, no. 4 (2003): 210–219.

Godfrey, A. B., D. M. Berwick, and J. Roessner. "Ten Lessons Learned—How Quality Management Really Works in Health Care." *Quality Progress* 4 (April 1992): 23–27.

Godfrey, M., and C. Kerrigan. "Specialty Practice Improvement and Redesign L3." Presented at the sixth annual International Summit on Redesigning the Clinical Office Practice, Washington, DC, March 31, 2005.

Goetzel, R. Z., R. J. Ozminkowski, V. G. Villagra, and J. Duffy. "Return on Investment in Disease Management: A Review." *Health Care Financing Review* 26, no. 4 (Summer 2005): 1–19.

Gold, W. R., and A. Johnson. "Disease Management." Presented at the NASCHIP Conference, Minneapolis, MN, October 2004. http://www.naschip.org/Evaluating%20Disease%20Management%20-%20Gold-Johnson%20Presentation%20-%20NASCHIP%202004.pdf.

Gold, W. R., and P. Kongstvedt. "How Broadening DM's Focus Helped Shrink One Plan's Costs." *Managed Care*, November 2003.

Goldberg, I. "How to Ensure That Medicine Incorporates the Best of Science." *Ophthalmology Clinics of North America* 13, no. 1 (2000): 7–14.

Goldie, S. J. "Preventing Cervical and Anal Cancer in HIV-Positive Women and Men: Using Disease-Specific Models to Develop Clinical Guidelines." *Harvard Center for Risk Analysis* 8, no. 2 (February 2000).

Goldman, D., J. Buchanan, and E. Keeler. "Simulating the Impact of Medical Savings Accounts on Small Business." *Health Services Research* 35, no. 1, part 1 (2000): 53–75.

Goldsmith, J., D. Blumenthal, and W. Rishel. "Federal Health Information Policy: A Case of Arrested Development." *Health Affairs* 22, no. 4 (2003): 44–55.

Goldstein, A. "Rebel Candidacy Roils Ailing AMA." *The Washington Post,* June 15, 1998.

Goodman, J., and R. Rahn. "Salvaging Medicare with an IRA." *The Wall Street Journal,* March 20, 1984.

Goodman, W. G., et al. "Coronary-Artery Calcification in Young Adults with End-Stage Renal Disease Who Are Undergoing Dialysis." *New England Journal of Medicine* 342, no. 20 (2000): 1478–1483.

Goozner, M. "The Price Isn't Right." *American Prospect,* September 11, 2000, 25–29.

Gordon, J. S. "How America's Health Care Fell Ill." *American Heritage* 43, no. 3 (1992): 49–65.

Gottschalk, A., and S. A. Flocke. "Time Spent in Face-to-Face Patient Care and Work Outside the Examination Room." *Annals of Family Medicine* 3 (2005): 488–493.

Graham, J. D. "An Investor's Look at Life-Saving Opportunities." *Harvard Center for Risk Analysis* 7, no. 1 (February 1999).

Grandjean, E. M., P. H. Berthet, R. Ruffmann, and P. Leuenberger. "Cost-Effectiveness Analysis of Oral N-Acetylcysteine as a Preventive Treatment in Chronic Bronchitis." *Pharmacological Research* 42, no. 1 (2000): 39–50.

Grazier, K. L., and G'Sell Associates. *Group Medical Insurance Large Claims Database Collection and Analysis.* SOA Monograph M-HB97-1. Illinois: Society of Actuaries, 1997.

Green, M. J. "What (If Anything) Is Wrong with Residency Overwork?" *Annals of Internal Medicine* 123, no. 7 (1995): 512–517.

Greenberg, P. E., T. Sisitsky, R. C. Kessler, S. N. Finkelstein, E. R. Berndt, J. R. Davidson, J. C. Ballenger, and A. J. Fyer. "The Economic Burden of Anxiety Disorders in the 1990s." *Journal of Clinical Psychiatry* 60, no. 7 (1999): 427–435.

Greenberg, P. E., L. E. Stiglin, S. N. Finkelstein, and E.R. Berndt. "Depression: A Neglected Major Illness." *Journal of Clinical Psychiatry* 54, no. 11 (1993): 419–424.

Greenberger, S. S. "Romney Eyes Penalties for Those Lacking Insurance." *The Boston Globe,* June 22, 2005a. http://www.boston.com/news/local/massachusetts/articles/2005/06/22/romney_eyes_penalties_for_those_lacking_insurance/?page=1.

———. "Health Plan Pressures Massachusetts Firms." *The Boston Globe,* October 30, 2005b. http://www.boston.com/business/articles/2005/10/30/health_plan_pressures_mass_firms/

Greene, J. "Boosting Adult Immunizations." *Healthplan* 44, no. 4 (2003): 50–53.

Griffen, F. D. "Statement of American College of Surgeons to House Energy and Commerce Subcommittee on Health in Regards to Patient Safety and Quality Initiatives." June 9, 2005. http://www.facs.org/ahp/testimony/patientsafety.html.

Grimshaw, J. M., and I. T. Russell. "Effect of Clinical Guidelines on Medical Practice: A Systematic Review of Rigorous Evaluations." *Lancet* 342, no. 8883 (1993): 1317–1322.

Groopman, J. *Second Opinions.* New York: Viking, 2000.

Grove, A. S. "Efficiency in the Health Care Industries: A View from the Outside." *Journal of the American Medical Association* 294, no. 4 (2005): 490–492.

Grover, F. L. "Capitalizing on Existing STS and DCRI Resources." Presentation to the Institute of Medicine Subcommittee on Pay for Performance, Washington, DC, September 1, 2005.

Grover, F. L., A. L. Shroyer, K. Hammermeister, F. H. Edwards, T. B. Ferguson Jr., S. W. Dziuban Jr., J. C. Cleveland Jr., R. E. Clark, and G. McDonald. "A Decade's

Experience with Quality Improvement in Cardiac Surgery Using the Veterans Affairs and Society of Thoracic Surgeons National Databases." *Annals of Surgery* 234, no. 4 (2001): 464–472.

"Guidelines for Minimal Standards in Cardiac Surgery." *Bulletin of the American College of Surgeons* 69, no. 1 (1984): 67–69.

Gurwitz, J. H., et al. "Incidence and Preventability of Adverse Drug Events Among Older Persons in the Ambulatory Setting." *Journal of the American Medical Association* 289, no. 9 (2003): 1107–1116.

Hackensack University Medical Center. "About Us." http://www.humc.com/html/about.html.

_____. "Hackensack University Medical Center and Nicole Miller Present Fashion Rx for Haute Hospital Wear." http://www.humc.com/gown/index.html.

Hallam, K. "Cutting Costs but Not Quality of Care." *Modern Healthcare,* February 21, 2000.

Hallinan, J. T. "Heal Thyself: Once Seen as Risky, One Group of Doctors Changes Its Ways." *The Wall Street Journal,* June 21, 2005.

Halm, E. A., C. Lee, and M. R. Chassin. "How Is Volume Related to Quality in Health Care? A Systematic Review of the Research Literature." In *Interpreting the Volume-Outcome Relationship in the Context of Health Care Quality,* edited by Maria Hewitt, 27–102. Washington, DC: National Academies Press, 2000.

_____. "Is Volume Related to Outcome in Health Care? A Systematic Review and Methodologic Critique of the Literature." *Annals of Internal Medicine* 137, no. 6 (2002): 511–520.

Hamed, A., A. Lee, X. S. Ren, D. R. Miller, F. Cunningham, H. Zhang, and L. E. Kazis. "Use of Antidepressant Medications: Are There Differences in Psychiatric Visits Among Patient Treatments in the Veterans Administration?" *Medical Care* 42, no. 6 (2004): 551–559.

Hamilton, D. P., and R. Winslow. "Do Statins Help Prevent Cancer? Few Tests Slated." *The Wall Street Journal,* May 20, 2005.

Hammitt, J. K. "Valuing Health: Quality-Adjusted Life Years or Willingness to Pay." *Risk in Perspective* 11, no. 1 (2003).

Hamory, B., K. McKinley, and G. Nelson. "Using Metrics to Promote Excellence: From the Frontline to the Front Office and Beyond." Presented at Fall Microsystem Invitational, Fairlee, VT, October 6, 2005.

Hannan, E. L., et al. "Improving the Outcomes of Coronary Artery Bypass Mortality in New York State." *Journal of the American Medical Association* 271, no. 10 (1994): 761–766.

Harvard Pilgrim. "Harvard Pilgrim Health Care Named #1 Health Plan in America." Press release. September 23, 2004.

Havenstein, H. "GE, health care firm partner to develop medical IT systems." *Computerworld,* July 11, 2005. http://www.computerworld.com/softwaretopics/software/appdev/story/0,10801,103102,00.html.

Hawker, G. A., J. G. Wright, P. C. Coyte, J. I. Williams, B. Harvey, R. Glazier, A. Wilkins, and E. M. Badley. "Determining the Need for Hip and Knee Arthroplasty: The Role of Clinical Severity and Patients' Preferences." *Medical Care* 39, no. 3 (2001): 206–216.

Hayward, R. S., M. C. Wilson, S. R. Tunis, E. B. Bass, and G. Guyatt. "Users' Guides to the Medical Literature: VIII. How to Use Clinical Practice Guidelines: A. Are the Recommendations Valid?" *Journal of the American Medical Association* 274, no. 4 (1995): 570–574.

HCIA. *Guide to the Managed Care Industry*. Baltimore: HCIA, 1997.

Health Care Financing Administration. "Medicare Participating Heart Bypass Center Demonstration." Extramural research report. September 1998.

Healthcare Infection Control Practices Advisory Committee. "Guidance on Public Reporting of Healthcare-Associated Infections." February 28, 2005. http://www.cdc.gov/ncidod/hip/PublicReportingGuide.pdf.

Health Care Policy Roundtable. "Four Million Uninsured Workers to be Given Access to Affordable Health Care by Coalition of Fortune 500 Companies." Press release. May 10, 2004. http://www.hcpr.org/press/2004/pr_051004.asp.

HealthGrades. *Patient Safety in American Hospitals*. July 2004. http://www.healthgrades.com/media/english/pdf/HG_Patient_Safety_Study_Final.pdf.

Heffler, S., S. Smith, S. Keehan, C. Borger, M. K. Clemens, and C. Truffer. "Trends: U.S. Health Spending Projections for 2004–2014." *Health Affairs* Web exclusive (February 23, 2005). http://content.healthaffairs.org/cgi/reprint/hlthaff.w5.74v1.

Heffner, J. E. "Miracles and Magic Bullets: Translating Science into Better Care." *Critical Care Medicine* 28, no. 10 (2000): 3572–3573.

Heindenreich, P., and M. McClellan. "Trends in Heart Attack Treatments and Outcomes, 1975–1995." In *Medical Care Output and Productivity*, edited by David M. Cutler and Ernst R. Berndt. Chicago: University of Chicago Press, 2001.

Helms, R. B. "The Tax Treatment of Health Insurance: Early History and Evidence, 1940–1970." In *Empowering Health Care Consumers Through Tax Reform*, edited by Grace-Marie Arnett. Ann Arbor: University of Michigan Press, 1999.

Herzlinger, R. E. "Why Data Systems in Nonprofit Organizations Fail." *Harvard Business Review*, January–February 1977, 81–86.

———. "Can We Control Health Care Costs?" *Harvard Business Review*, March–April 1978, 102–110.

———. "How Companies Tackle Health Care Costs: Part II." *Harvard Business Review*, September–October 1985, 108–120.

———. "The Failed Revolution in Health Care—The Role of Management." *Harvard Business Review*, March–April 1989, 95–103.

———. "Healthy Competition." *The Atlantic*, August 1991, 69–81.

———. "Market-Driven Health Care." *Harvard Business Review*, September–October 1997, 200–204.

———. *Market-Driven Health Care: Who Wins, Who Loses in the Transformation of America's Largest Service Industry*. Boulder, CO: Perseus Book Group, 1999a.

———. *Protection of the Health Care Consumer*. Washington, DC: Progressive Policy Institute, 1999b. http://www.ppionline.org/ppi_ci.cfm?contentid=1344&knlgAreaID=111&subsecid=138.

———. "The 'Truth' About Managed Care." *Journal of Health Politics, Policy and Law* 24, no. 5 (1999c).

———. "Let's Put Consumers in Charge of Health Care." *Harvard Business Review*, July 2002, 4–11.

———. "Prix-Fixe Rip-Off." *The Wall Street Journal*, June 13, 2003.

———, ed. *Consumer-Driven Health Care*. San Francisco: John Wiley & Sons, 2004a.

———. "An IT Trojan Horse . . . Feds Should Stay Out of 'Evidence-Based' Medicine." *Modern Healthcare*, September 6, 2004b.

———. "Uncle Sam Is No Doctor." *USA Today*, March 28, 2005.

Herzlinger, R. E., and D. Calkins. "How Companies Tackle Health Care: Part III." *Harvard Business Review*, January–February 1986, 70–80.

Herzlinger, R. E., and W. S. Krasker. "Who Profits from Nonprofits?" *Harvard Business Review,* January–February 1987, 93–106.

Herzlinger, R. E., and R. Parsa-Parsi. "Consumer-Driven Health Care: Lessons from Switzerland." *Journal of the American Medical Association* 292, no. 10 (2004): 1213–1220.

Herzlinger, R. E., and J. Schwartz. "How Companies Tackle Health Care Costs: Part I." *Harvard Business Review,* July–August 1985, 69–72.

Hesdorffer, D. C., J. Ghajar, and L. Iacono. "Predictors of Compliance with the Evidence-Based Guidelines for Traumatic Brain Injury Care: A Survey of United States Trauma Centers." *Journal of Trauma* 52, no. 6 (2002): 1202–1209.

Hewitt Associates. "Employers Concerned About the Impact of Rising Health Care Costs and Are Evaluating Alternatives." News release. January 14, 2003a. http://was4.hewitt.com/hewitt/resource/newsroom/pressrel/2003/01-14-03.htm.

———. "Hewitt Study Shows Employers Critically Concerned with Health Care Costs and Looking for Creative Solutions." News release. December 2, 2003b. http://was4.hewitt.com/hewitt/resource/newsroom/pressrel/2003/12-02-03.htm.

———. *Health Care Expectations: Future Strategy and Directions.* Lincolnshire, IL: Hewitt Associates, 2004a. http://was4.hewitt.com/hewitt/resource/rptspubs/subrptspubs/hcexpectations_2004.pdf.

———. "Health Care Costs Show Signs of Moderating, but Still Outpace Inflation." News release. October 11, 2004b.

———. "Hewitt Study Shows Employers Seeking to Attack Root Causes of Health Care Cost Inflation." News release. January 10, 2005.

Hibbard, J. H., J. Stockard, and M. Tusler. "Does Publicizing Hospital Performance Stimulate Quality Improvement Efforts?" *Health Affairs* 22, no. 2 (2003): 84–94.

Hillner, B. E., T. J. Smith, and C. E. Desch. "Hospital and Physician Volume or Specialization and Outcomes in Cancer Treatment: Importance in Quality of Cancer Care." *Journal of Clinical Oncology* 18, no. 11 (2000): 2327–2340.

Himmelstein, D. U., S. Woolhandler, and S. M. Wolfe. "Administrative Waste in the U.S. Health Care System in 2003: The Cost to the Nation, the States, and the District of Columbia, with State-specific Estimates of Potential Savings." *International Journal of Health Services: Planning, Administration, Evaluation* 34, no. 1 (2004): 79–86.

Hirsch, J. "Patent Fight Delays Cheaper Drug Cancer." *The Los Angeles Times,* September 6, 2000.

Hixson, J. S. "Six Questions Everyone Should Ask About Health System Reform: An Application of Basic Economics." *Galen Institute Health Policy Report,* March 2002, 1–25.

Hoffman, C., A. Carbaugh, and A. Cook. *Health Insurance Coverage in America: 2003 Data Update.* Washington, DC: Kaiser Commission on Medicaid and the Uninsured, 2004.

Hoffman, C., and D. P. Rice. *Chronic Care in America: A 21st Century Challenge.* Princeton, NJ: The Robert Wood Johnson Foundation, 1996.

Hoffman, C., D. P. Rice, and H. Y. Sung. "Persons with Chronic Conditions: Their Prevalence and Costs." *Journal of the American Medical Association* 276, no. 18 (1996): 1473–1479.

Hsiao, W. C. "Medical Savings Accounts: Lessons from Singapore." *Health Affairs* 14, no. 2 (1995): 260–266.

Hu, J. C., K. F. Gold, C. L. Pashos, S. S. Mehta, and M. S. Litwin. "Role of Surgeon Volume in Radical Prostatectomy Outcomes." *Journal of Clinical Oncology* 21, no. 3 (2003): 401–405.

Huckman, R. S., and G. P. Pisano. "The Effect of Organizational Context on Individual Performance: Evidence from Cardiac Surgery." Working paper 03-083, Harvard Business School, Boston, 2003.

———. "Adopting New Technologies: Turf Battles in Coronary Revascularization." *New England Journal of Medicine* 352, no. 9 (2005): 857–859.

Hun, J. C., et al. "Role of Surgeon Volume in Radical Prostatectomy Outcomes." *Journal of Clinical Oncology* 21, no. 3 (2003): 401–405.

Hunter, J. "The History of ThedaCare." ThedaCare internal document. June 30, 2004.

Hussey, P. S., G. F. Anderson, R. Osborn, C. Feek, V. McLaughlin, J. Millar, and A. Epstein. "How Does the Quality of Care Compare in Five Countries?" *Health Affairs* 23, no. 3 (2004): 89–99.

Iezzoni, L. I., ed. *Risk Adjustment for Measuring Healthcare Outcomes.* 3rd ed. Chicago: Health Administration Press, 2003.

Iglehart, J. K. "A Bias Toward Action: A Conversation with Leonard Schaeffer." *Health Affairs* Web exclusive (2003). http://content.healthaffairs.org/cgi/reprint/hlthaff.w1.30v1.pdf.

Ingebretsen, M. "Electronic Medical Records Could Save $78 Billion a Year." *The Wall Street Journal*, January 21, 2005.

Institute for Healthcare Improvement. "100K Lives Campaign." 2004. http://www.ihi.org/IHI/Programs/Campaign.htm.

Institute of Medicine. *Fostering Rapid Advances in Health Care: Learning from System Demonstrations.* Washington, DC: National Academies Press, 2002.

Intermountain Health Care. "GE Healthcare and IHC Establish New Research Center to Develop Electronic Health Record Technologies." News release. July 6, 2005. http://www.ihc.com/xp/ihc/aboutihc/news/article26.xml.

Irving Levin Associates, Inc. "Mergers and Acquisitions Database." January 23, 2004. http://www.levinassociates.com/m&adatabase/introduction.htm.

Jacob, J. A. "CIGNA De-capitates, Returns to Fee-for-Service Payments." *American Medical News,* April 10, 2000a. http://www.ama-assn.org/amednews/2000/04/10/mksc0410.htm.

———. "Fee for Service Rebounding as Insurers Rethink Capitation." *American Medical News,* May 22–29, 2000b. http://www.ama-assn.org/amednews/2000/05/22/bil10522.htm.

Jaklevic, M. C. "What Hospitals 'See' They Get." *Modern Health Care* 30, no. 10 (2000): 60–62.

James, B. C. "Curing vs. Caring." Introduction to Clinical Quality Improvement Course. http://www.ihc.com/xp/ihc/documents/institute/caring.ppt.

———. "Deployment: Clinical Integration." Introduction to Clinical Quality Improvement Course. http://www.ihc.com/xp/ihc/documents/institute/clinical_intg.ppt.

———. "An Introduction to Clinical Quality Improvement." Introduction to Clinical Quality Improvement Course. http://www.ihc.com/xp/ihc/documents/institute/intro.ppt.

———. "Quality Controls Cost." Introduction to Clinical Quality Improvement Course. http://www.ihc.com/xp/ihc/documents/institute/qual-cost.ppt.

———. "Understanding Variation." Introduction to Clinical Quality Improvement Course. http://www.ihc.com/xp/ihc/documents/institute/variation.ppt.

_____. "Making It Easy to Do It Right [Editorial]." *New England Journal of Medicine* 345, no. 13 (2001a): 991–993.

_____. "Making Quality Pay—Shared Benefit Payment Methods." Presentation to the American Health Quality Association, Scottsdale, AZ, June 1, 2001b. http://www.ihc.com/xp/ihc/documents/institute/ahqa61.ppt.

_____. "The Scientific Basis of Quality Improvement." Presented at the fourth International Conference on the Scientific Basis of Health Services, Sydney, Australia, September 22, 2001c. http://www.ihc.com/xp/ihc/documents/institute/nsw922.ppt.

_____. "Quality Improvement Opportunities in Health Care—Making It Easy to Do It Right." *Journal of Managed Care Pharmacy* 8, no. 5 (2002a): 394–399.

_____. "Physicians and Quality Improvement in Hospitals: How Do You Involve Physicians in TQM?" *Quality and Participation* 25, no. 2 (2002b): 56–63.

_____. "Information System Concepts for Quality Measurement." *Medical Care* 41, no. 1 (2003): I71–I79.

Jeffords, J., and E. Kennedy. "What Should Constitute a Patients' Bill of Rights?" *Roll Call,* March 26, 2001.

Jencks, S. F., et al. "Quality of Medical Care Delivered to Medicare Beneficiaries." *Journal of American Medical Association* 284, no. 13 (2000): 1670–1676.

Joint Commission on Accreditation of Healthcare Organizations. "Important Notice Re: ICU Measure Set." July 1, 2005. http://www.jcaho.org/pms/core+measures/icunotificationtomeasurementsystems.pdf.

Kaiser Family Foundation. *Trends and Indicators in the Changing Health Care Marketplace: 2004 Update.* Menlo Park, CA: Kaiser Family Foundation, 2004. http://www.kff.org/insurance/7031/loader.cfm?url=/commonspot/security/getfile.cfm&PageID=36095.

_____. *Medicare Chart Book 2005.* http://www.kff.org/medicare/7284.cfm.

Kaiser Family Foundation and Health Research and Educational Trust. "Employer Health Benefits 2003 Annual Survey." 2003. http://www.kff.org/insurance/ehbs2003-abstract.cfm.

_____. "Employer Health Benefits 2004 Annual Survey." 2004. http://www.kff.org/insurance/7148/index.cfm.

Kane, N. M., J. Needleman, and L. Rudell. "Comparing the Clinical Quality and Cost in Academic Health Centers and in Community Hospitals." Research Brief no. 2, Pioneer Institute for Public Policy Research, Boston, November 2004.

_____. "Comparing the Clinical Quality and Cost in Academic Health Centers and in Community Hospitals." Policy Dialogue no. 56, Pioneer Institute for Public Policy Research, Boston, January 2005.

Katz, J. T., and L. W. Tishler. "Promoting Humanism in Your Medical Interns." Presented at the 2005 APDIM Spring meeting. http://www.im.org/AAIM/Meetings/Docs/APDIM/Wksp106-HumanismForResidents.pdf.

Kaufman, M. "Report Says Drugmakers Innovate Less, Modify More." *Washingtonpost.com,* May 29, 2002.

Keen, J., D. Light, and N. Mays. *Public-Private Relations in Health Care.* London: King's Fund, 2001.

Kerlikowske, K., D. Grady, J. Barclay, S. D. Frankel, S. H. Ominsky, E. A. Sickles, and V. Ernster. "Variability and Accuracy in Mammographic Interpretation Using the American College of Radiology Breast Imaging Reporting and Data System." *Journal of the National Cancer Institute* 90, no. 23 (1998): 1801–1809.

Kerr, E. A., R. B. Gerzoff, S. L. Krein, J. V. Selby, J. D. Piette, J. D. Curb, W. H. Herman, D. G. Marrero, K. M. Narayan, M. M. Safford, T. Thompson, and C. M. Mangione. "Diabetes Care Quality in the Veterans Affairs Health Care System and Commercial Managed Care: The TRIAD Study." *Annals of Internal Medicine* 141, no. 4 (2004): 272–281.

Kertesz, L. "What Is Fueling the Increase in Health Care Costs?" *Healthplan* 43, no. 3 (2002): 38–42.

Kessler, D., and M. McClellan. "The Effects of Hospital Ownership on Medical Productivity." NBER working paper 8537, National Bureau of Economic Research, Cambridge, MA, October 2001.

_____. "How Liability Law Affects Medical Productivity." *Journal of Health Economics* 21 (2002): 931–955.

Kirschner, M. W., E. Marincola, and E. O. Teisberg. "The Role of Biomedical Research in Health Care Reform." *Science* 266, no. 5182, new series (1994): 49–51.

Kizer, K. W. "The Volume-Outcome Conundrum." *New England Journal of Medicine* 349, no. 22 (2003): 2159–2161.

Kleinke, J. D. *Bleeding Edge: The Business of Health Care in the New Century.* Gaithersburg, MD: Aspen Publishers, 1998.

_____. "Just What the HMO Ordered: The Paradox of Increasing Drug Costs." *Health Affairs* 19, no. 2 (2000): 78–91.

_____. "The Price of Progress: Prescription Drugs in the Health Care Market." *Health Affairs* 20, no. 5 (2001): 43–60.

_____. "Access Versus Excess: Value-Based Cost Sharing for Prescription Drugs." *Health Affairs* 23, no. 1 (2004): 34–47.

Knaus, W. A. "APACHE 1978–2001: The Development of a Quality Assurance System Based on Prognosis: Milestones and Personal Reflections." *Archives of Surgery* 137, no. 1 (2002): 37–41.

_____. "Improving Intensive Care Performance: Complex Paths to Simple Truths." *Mayo Clinic Proceedings* 80 (2005):164–165. http://www.mayoclinic proceedings.com/inside.asp?AID=838&UID.

Knaus, W. A., E. A. Draper, D. P. Wagner, J. E. Zimmerman. "An Evaluation of Outcome from Intensive Care in Major Medical Centers." *Annals of Internal Medicine* 104, no. 3 (1986): 410–418.

Knox, R. A. "Boston Hospital Pulls Out of Medicare HMO Business." *The Boston Globe,* August 27, 1999.

Koberstein, W. "Market Chaos, Marketing Order: Agency Roundtable 2000." *Pharmaceutical Executive,* September 1, 2000, 46–72.

Kohn, L. T., J. M. Corrigan, and M. S. Donaldson, eds. Committee on Quality of Health Care in America, Institute of Medicine. *To Err Is Human.* Washington, DC: National Academy Press, 2000.

Kolata, G. "A Conversation with Victor Fuchs: An Economist's View of Health Care Reform." *The New York Times,* May 2, 2000a.

_____. "For Those Who Can Afford It, Old-Style Medicine Returns." *The New York Times,* March 17, 2000b.

Kowalczyk, L. "Blue Cross OK's Fee Hikes for Physicians." *The Boston Globe,* May 28, 2000.

_____. "Hospitals Raising Rates for HMOs Hikes Cast Doubt on Cost Control of Managed Care." *The Boston Globe,* March 18, 2001.

Kramer, A. M. "Health Care for Elderly Persons—Myths and Realities." *New England Journal of Medicine* 332, no. 15 (1995): 1027–1029.

Krasner, J. "Doctors, Patients Want Data on Cost, Quality, Study Finds." *The Boston Globe*, October 18, 2005.

Kruzikas, D. T., H. J. Jiang, D. Reus, M. L. Barrett, R. M. Coffey, and R. Andrews. *Preventable Hospitalizations: Window into Primary and Preventive Care, 2000.* HCUP Fact Book No. 5; AHRQ Publication no. 04-0056. Rockville, MD: Agency for Healthcare Research and Quality, 2004.http://www.ahrq.gov/data/hcup/factbk5/.

Kuttner, R. "Managed Care and Medical Education." *New England Journal of Medicine* 341, no. 14 (1999): 1092–1096.

LaBresh, K. A., A. G. Ellrodt, R. Gliklich, J. Liljestrand, and R. Peto. "Get with the Guidelines for Cardiovascular Secondary Prevention: Pilot Results." *Archives of Internal Medicine* 164, no. 2 (2004): 203–209.

Lagnado, L. "Call It Yale v. Yale—Law-School Clinic Is Taking Affiliated Hospital to Court over Debt-Collection Tactics." *The Wall Street Journal*, November 14, 2003.

Lagnado, L., and J. Lublin. "Hospital Chief Is Picked to Revive Distressed Area." *The Wall Street Journal,* September 6, 2000.

Lamb, R. M., D. M. Studdert, R. M. J. Bohmer, D. M. Berwick, and T. A. Brennan. "Hospital Disclosure Practices: Results of a National Survey." *Health Affairs* 22, no. 2 (2003): 73–83.

Lambrew, J. M., and A. Garson Jr. "Small but Significant Steps to Help the Uninsured." The Commonwealth Fund. January 2003. http://www.cmwf.org/programs/insurance/lambrew_smallsignificant_bn_585.asp.

Landrigan, C. P., J. M. Rothschild, J. W. Cronin, R. Kaushal, E. Burdick, J. T. Katz, C. M. Lilly, P. H. Stone, S. W. Lockley, D. W. Bates, and C. A. Czeisler. "Effect of Reducing Interns' Work Hours on Serious Medical Errors in Intensive Care Units." *New England Journal of Medicine* 351, no. 18 (2004): 1838–1848.

Landro, L. "Doctor 'Scorecards' Are Proposed in a Health-Care Quality Drive." *The Wall Street Journal*, March 25, 2004.

_____. "The Informed Patient: Health-Care Quality Programs Under Fire." *The Wall Street Journal,* July 6, 2005.

Lasker Charitable Trust/Funding First. "Exceptional Returns: The Economic Value of America's Investment in Medical Research." Presented at the Conference on the Economic Value of America's Investment in Medical Research, December 1999.

Leapfrog Group. "Evidence-Based Hospital Referral." Factsheet. April 7, 2004. http://www.leapfroggroup.org/media/file/Leapfrog-Evidence-based_Hospital_Referral_Fact_Sheet.pdf.

Leatherman, S., et al. "The Business Case for Quality: Case Studies and an Analysis." *Health Affairs* 22, no. 2 (2003): 17–30.

Lester, H., and J. Q. Tritter. "Medical Error: A Discussion of the Medical Construction of Error and Suggestions for Reforms of Medical Education to Decrease Error." *Medical Education* 35 (2001): 855–861.

Lettau, M., and T. Buchmueller. "Comparing Benefit Costs for Full and Part-Time Workers." *Monthly Labor Review* 122, no. 3 (1999): 30–35.

Levin-Epstein, M. "Managed Care Again Seen on Capitol Hill as Ripe for Reform." *Managed Care,* March 2001. http://www.managedcaremag.com/archives/0103/0103.washington.html.

Levy, F. H. "Excess Hospitalization Costs Attributable to Medical Injuries." *American Academy of Pediatrics Grand Rounds*, no. 11 (January 2004): 7–8.

Lewis, D. E. "Health Professionals Unionize to Take on HMOs." *New York Times Syndicate*, March 27, 2001.

Lichtenberg, F. R. "Do (More and Better) Drugs Keep People out of Hospitals?" *American Economic Review* 86, no. 2 (1996): 384–388.

_____. "Sources of U.S. Longevity Increase, 1960–1997." CESifo working paper 405, CESifo, Munich, Germany, December 2000.

_____. "The Benefits and Costs of Newer Drugs: Evidence from the 1996 Medical Expenditure Panel Survey." NBER working paper 8147, National Bureau of Economic Research, Cambridge, MA, March 2001.

_____. "Pharmaceutical Innovation, Mortality Reduction, and Economic Growth." In *Measuring the Gains from Medical Research: An Economic Approach*, edited by K. M. Murphy and R. H. Topel. Chicago: University of Chicago Press, 2003.

Lieber, R. "New Way to Curb Medical Costs: Make Employees Feel the Sting." *The Wall Street Journal*, June 23, 2004.

Lim, M. K. "Quest for Quality Care and Patient Safety: The Case of Singapore." *Quality and Safety in Health Care* 13, no. 1 (2004): 71–75.

Longman, P. "The Best Care Anywhere." *Washington Monthly*, January/February, 2005, 39–48.

Loop, F. D., B. W. Lytle, D. M. Cosgrove, R. W. Stewart, M. Goormastic, G. W. Williams, L. A. R. Golding, C. C. Gill, P. C. Taylor, W. C. Sheldon, and W. L. Proudfit. "Influence of the Internal-Mammary-Artery Graft on 10-Year Survival and Other Cardiac Events." *New England Journal of Medicine* 314, no. 1 (1986): 1–6.

Lorig, K. R., P. Ritter, A. L. Stewart, D. S. Sobel, B. W. Brown Jr., A. Bandura, V. M. Gonzalez, D. D. Laurent, and H. R. Holman. "Chronic Disease Self-Management Program: 2-Year Health Status and Health Care Utilization Outcomes." *Medical Care* 39, no. 11 (2001): 1217–1223.

Lovern, E. "Minding Hospitals' Business." *Modern Health Care* 31, no. 22 (2001): 30–33.

Lubitz, J. D., and G. F. Riley. "Trends in Medicare Payments in the Last Year of Life." *New England Journal of Medicine* 328, no. 15 (1993): 1092–1096.

Lucci, A., and M. O. Sherman. "Assessment of the Current Medicare Reimbursement System for Breast Cancer." *Breast Diseases: A Year Book Quarterly* 16, no. 2 (2005).

Luce, B. R., F. Sloan, J. Mauskopf, and C. Paramore. "Estimating the Value of Investment: Medicare and Overall U.S. Health Care Services." Presented at the 2004 Annual Research Meeting, San Diego, CA, June 6, 2004. http://www.academy health.org/2004/ppt/luce.ppt.

Luft, H. S., J. P. Bunker, and A. C. Enthoven. "Should Operations Be Regionalized? The Empirical Relation Between Surgical Volume and Mortality." *New England Journal of Medicine* 301, no. 25 (1979): 1364–1369.

Lukacs, S. L., E. K. France, A. E. Baron, and L. A. Crane. "Effectiveness of an Asthma Management Program for Pediatric Members of a Large Health Maintenance Organization." *Archives of Pediatric Adolescent Medicine* 156, no. 9 (2002): 872–876.

Lytle, B. W., E. H. Blackstone, F. D. Loop, P. L. Houghtaling, J. H. Arnold, R. Akhrass, P. M. McCarthy, and D. M. Cosgrove. "Two Internal Thoracic Artery Grafts Are Better Than One." *Journal of Thoracic and Cardiovascular Surgery* 117, no. 5 (1999): 855–872.

Lytle, B. W., E. H. Blackstone, J. F. Sabik, P. Houghtaling, F. D. Loop, and D. M. Cosgrove. "The Effect of Bilateral Internal Thoracic Artery Grafting on Survival During 20 Postoperative Years." *Annals of Thoracic Surgery* 78, no. 6 (2004): 2005–2014.

MacStravic, S. "Rethinking the Question 'Does Disease Management Work?'" *HealthLeaders News*, October 31, 2005.

Magnusson, P. "Your Doctor May Be in Again; Even Clinton Is Embracing Medical Savings Accounts." *BusinessWeek*, December 30, 1996, 49.

Mahoney, M. E. "Innovative Mind-set: Revitalize or Dismantle When There's Something More Suitable." *Hospitals & Health Networks*, August 5, 1994.

"Major Trends Affecting the Health Care Industry." In *Plunkett's Health Care Industry Almanac 1999–2000*, 7–20. Houston, TX: Plunkett Research, 1999.

Marshall, M. N., P. G. Shekelle, R. H. Brook, and S. Leatherman. *Dying to Know: Public Release of Information About Quality of Health Care*. Santa Monica, CA: The Nuffield Trust and RAND Corporation, 2000.

Martin, A., L. Whittle, K. Levit, G. Won, and L. Hinman. "Health Care Spending During 1991–1998: A Fifty-State Review." *Health Affairs* 21, no. 4 (2002): 112–126.

Martinez, B. "How Insurance Payments Can Work Against Less-Invasive Biopsies." *The Wall Street Journal*, March 28, 2001.

———. "Strong Medicine: With New Muscle, Hospitals Squeeze Insurers on Rates— After Era of Dominant HMOs, Providers Turn the Tables by Consolidating Locally—HCA's $8,465 Chest-Pain Bill." *The Wall Street Journal*, April 12, 2002.

———. "Road to Recovery—Behind Aetna's Turnaround: Small Steps to Pare Costs of Care." *The Wall Street Journal*, August 13, 2004.

Marwick, C. "Using High-Quality Providers to Cope with Today's Rising Health Care Costs." *Journal of the American Medical Association* 268, no. 16 (1992): 2142–2145.

Massachusetts Technology Collaborative in partnership with New England Health Institute. *Advanced Technologies to Lower Health Care Costs and Improve Quality*. Westborough, MA: Massachusetts Technology Park Corporation, 2003. http://www.massinsight.com/docs/AdvancedTechnologies_MTC_NEHI.pdf.

Massaro, T. A., and Y-N. Wong. "Positive Experience with Medical Savings Accounts in Singapore." *Health Affairs* 14, no. 2 (1995): 267–272.

Matthews, M. "Drug Prices: A Solution—Adopt Policies to Encourage Competition, Not Corporate Restraint." *Barron's*, September 16, 2000a.

———. "Prices, Profits and Prescriptions: The Pharmatech Industry in the New Economy." Policy Report no. 157, Institute for Policy Innovation, Lewisville, TX, November 28, 2000b.

Maxwell, J., F. Briscoe, S. Davidson, L. Eisen, M. Robbins, P. Temin, and C. Young. "Managed Competition in Practice: 'Value Purchasing' by Fourteen Employers." *Health Affairs* 17, no. 3 (1998): 216–226.

Mayne, E. "Ford: Health Costs Could Drive Investment Overseas." *The Detroit News*, July 20, 2004.

Mays, G. P., G. Claxton, and B. C. Strunk. "Tiered-Provider Networks: Patients Face Cost-Choice Trade-offs." Issue Brief no. 71, Center for Studying Health System Change, November 2003. http://www.hschange.com/CONTENT/627/?topic=topic03.

McArdle, F. B., P. Neuman, M. Kitchman, K. Kirland, and D. Yamamoto. "Large Firms' Retiree Health Benefits Before Medicare Reform: 2003 Survey Results." *Health Affairs* Web exclusive (January 14, 2004). http://content.healthaffairs.org/cgi/content/abstract/hlthaff.w4.7.

McCue, M. T. "Immunizations Ensure Long-Term Health for All." *Managed Healthcare*, July 1999.

_____. "I'm Losing My Patience." *Managed Healthcare Executive*, February 2005.

McGlynn, E. A., S. Asch, J. Adams, J. Keesey, J. Hicks, A. DeCristofaro, and E. A. Kerr. "The Quality of Health Care Delivered to Adults in the United States." *New England Journal of Medicine* 348, no. 26 (2003): 2635–2645.

McKinnell, H. "Health Care in the 21st Century." Panel discussion on the topic "Who Will Pay for 21st Century Health Care?" World Economic Forum, Davos, Switzerland, February 2, 1998.

_____. *A Call to Action: Taking Back Healthcare for Future Generations*. New York: McGraw-Hill Professional, 2005.

M. D. Anderson Cancer Center. "Breast Center Dedicated to Patients who Intend to Be Treated Here." *FYI*, September 27, 2004.

Medicare Payment Advisory Commission. Public Meeting, November 17, 2004. Transcript. http://www.medpac.gov/public_meetings/transcripts/1104_allcombined_transc.pdf.

MEDTAP International, Inc. *The Value of Investment in Health Care: Better Care, Better Lives*. Bethesda, MD: MEDTAP International, 2004. http://www.medtap.com/Products/HP_FullReport.pdf.

Mehrotra, A., T. Bodenheimer, and R. Adams Dudley. "Employers' Efforts to Measure and Improve Hospital Quality: Determinants of Success." *Health Affairs* 22, no. 2 (2003): 60–71.

Meier, B. "A Region's Hospital Supplies: Costly Ties." *The New York Times*, October 8, 2002. http://www.mrmi.org/GPO_Issue/NYHA_PremierNYT100802.pdf.

Mello, M. M., and T. A. Brennan. "The Controversy over High-Dose Chemotherapy with Autologous Bone Marrow Transplant for Breast Cancer." *Health Affairs* 20, no. 5 (2001): 101–117.

Mello, M. M., D. M. Studdert, and T. A Brennan. "The Leapfrog Standards: Ready to Jump from Marketplace to Courtroom?" *Health Affairs* 22, no. 2 (2003): 45–59.

Meltsner, S. "For-Profit or Not: Where's the Best Care?" *Medical Economics,* July 1998.

Mercer Human Resource Consulting. News release. December 8, 2003. http://www.mercerhr.com/pressrelease/details.jhtml/dynamic/idcontent/1121535.

_____. *National Survey of Employer-Sponsored Health Plans 2003*. New York: Mercer Human Resource Consulting, 2004a.

_____. "Health Benefit Costs Rises 7.5% in 2004, Lowest Increase in Five Years." News release. November 22, 2004b.

_____. *National Survey of Employer-Sponsored Health Plans 2004*. New York: Mercer Human Resource Consulting, 2005.

Michel, P. "Quality Improvement and Accreditation in French Hospitals: Progress and Questions." *Gastroenterology Clinical Biology* 28, no. 12 (2004): 1229–1230.

Midwest Business Group on Health. "Leapfrog Group Update." *The Bulletin,* December 2001, 3.

Midwest Business Group on Health in collaboration with Juran Institute, Inc., and The Severyn Group, Inc. *Reducing the Costs of Poor-Quality Health Care Through Responsible Purchasing Leadership*. 2nd printing. Chicago: MBGH, 2003.

Migliori, R. J. "Creating Competition Within Health Care: Leveraging a Centers of Excellence Model." Presented at the World Health Congress, Washington, DC, January 30, 2005.

Milstein, A. Testimony to the U.S. Senate Health, Education, Labor and Pension Committee. January 28, 2004. http://healthcaredisclosure.org/docs/files/Testimony012804.pdf.

Mokyr, J. "Induced Technical Innovation and Medical History: An Evolutionary Approach." *Journal of Evolutionary Economics* 8 (1998): 119–137.

Montgomery Research, Inc. *Health Care Technology: Innovating Clinical Care Through Technology.* Vol. 1. San Francisco: Montgomery Research, 2003.

Moore-Ede, M. *The Twenty-Four Hour Society: Understanding Human Limits in a World That Never Stops.* Reading, MA: Addison-Wesley, 1993.

Morris, C. R. "The Health-Care Economy Is Nothing to Fear." *Atlantic Monthly,* December 1999, 86–96.

Morrisey, M. A. "Competition in Hospital and Health Insurance Markets: A Review and Research Agenda." *Health Services Research* 36, no. 1, part II (2001).

Morrison, I *Health Care in the New Millennium: Vision, Values, and Leadership.* San Francisco: Jossey-Bass, 2000.

Mosca, L., A. H. Linfante, E. J. Benjamin, K. Berra, S. N. Hayes, B. W. Walsh, R. P. Fabunmi, J. Kwan, T. Mills, and S. L. Simpson. "National Study of Physician Awareness and Adherence to Cardiovascular Disease Prevention Guidelines." *Circulation* 111, no. 4 (2005): 499–510.

Moses, H. "The Market Has Failed Health Care. Long Live the Market!" The Boston Consulting Group, 2001.

Moses, H., and J. B. Martin. "Academic Relationships with Industry." *Journal of the American Medical Association* 285, no. 7 (2001): 933–935.

Mukamel, D .B., and A. I. Mushlin. "Quality Care Information Makes a Difference: An Analysis of Market Share and Price Changes After Publication of the New York Cardiac Surgery Mortality Reports." *Medical Care* 36, no. 7 (1998): 945–954.

Mulligan, D., M. Shapiro, and D. Walrod. "Managing Risk in Healthcare." *The McKinsey Quarterly* no. 3 (1996): 95–105.

Murphy, K. M., and R. H. Topel. "The Economic Value of Medical Research." Presented at the Conference on the Economic Value of America's Investment in Medical Research, December 1999.

———, eds. *Measuring the Gains from Medical Research: An Economic Approach.* Chicago: University of Chicago Press, 2003.

Murray, G., and G. Teasdale. *The Relationship Between Volume and Health Outcomes: Report of Volume/Outcome Sub-Group to Advisory Group to National Framework for Service Change NHS Scotland.* February 2005. http://www.show.scot.nhs.uk/ sehd/nationalframework/Documents/VolumeOutcomeReportWebsite.pdf.

Myerson, A. R. "It's a Business. No, It's a Religion." *The New York Times,* February 13, 1994.

Nash, D. B., D. Shulkin, F. Comite, R. Loeppke, B. Van Cleave, R. Kane, J. Christianson, and D. Pousma. "Measurement of the Impact of Winona Health Online." *Disease Management* 4, no. 1 (2001): 15–18.

National Business Group on Health. "National Business Group on Health Releases Charitable Corporate Donation Guidelines—Emphasis on Information Technology Investments Will Yield Most Benefits." Press release. October 27, 2004. http://www.wbgh.com/pressrelease.cfm?printPage=1&id=38.

National Business Group on Health/Watson Wyatt. *Managing Health Care Costs in a New Era: 10th Annual National Business Group on Health/Watson Wyatt Survey Report 2005.* Watson Wyatt Worldwide, 2005. http://www.watsonwyatt.com/ research/resrender.asp?id=w-821&page=1.

National Cancer Institute. "Annual Report to the Nation Finds Cancer Incidence and Death Rates on the Decline: Survival Rates Show Significant Improvement."

Press release. June 3, 2004. http://www.cancer.gov/newscenter/pressreleases/
ReportNation2004release.

_____. "Cancer Progress Report—2003 Update: Survival." April 29, 2005a.
http://progressreport.cancer.gov/doc.asp?pid=1&did=21&chid=13&coid=32&
mid=vpco#cancer.

_____. "Cancer Progress Report—2003 Update: Treatment." March 30, 2005b.
http://progressreport.cancer.gov/doc.asp?pid=1&did=21&mid=vcol&chid=12.

National Center for Health Statistics. *Health, United States, 2004 with Chartbook on
Trends in the Health of Americans.* Hyattsville, MD: National Center for Health
Statistics, 2004. http://www.cdc.gov/nchs/data/hus/hus04.pdf.

National Center for Policy Analysis. "Medical Savings Accounts in South Africa."
June 2000. http://www.ncpa.org/studies/s234/s234.html.

_____. "A Brief History of Health Savings Accounts." August 11, 2004. http://www
.ncpa.org/prs/tst/20040811_hsa_history.htm.

National Committee for Quality Assurance. *State of Health Care Quality: 2004.*
Washington, DC: National Committee for Quality Assurance. http://www.ncqa
.org/communications/SOMC/SOHC2004.pdf.

National Governors Association Center for Best Practices. "Disease Management:
The New Tool for Cost Containment and Quality Care." Issue brief. February
2003. http://www.nga.org/cda/files/031403DISEASEMGMT.pdf.

National Institute for Health Care Management Research and Education Foundation. *Changing Patterns of Pharmaceutical Innovation.* Washington, DC: NIHCM
Foundation, 2002. http://www.nihcm.org/innovations.pdf.

National Quality Forum. *National Voluntary Consensus Standards for Hospital Care:
An Initial Performance Measure Set.* Washington, DC: The National Quality
Forum, 2003.

National Vaccine Advisory Committee. "Lessons Learned from a Review of the
Development of Selected Vaccines." *Pediatrics* 104, no. 4. (1999): 942–950.

Neuhauser, D., and D. L. Harper. "Too Good to Last: Did Cleveland Health Quality
Choice Leave a Legacy and Lessons to Be Learned?" *Quality and Safety in Health
Care* 11, no. 2 (2002): 202–203.

Neumann, P. J. "Are Pharmaceuticals Cost-Effective? Lessons for the Medicare
Drug Benefit Debate." *Risk in Perspective* 8, no. 5 (May 2000). http://www
.hcra.harvard.edu/risk.html.

Neumann, P., and N. Olchanski. "A Web-Based Registry of Cost-Utility Analyses."
Risk in Perspective 11, no. 3 (September 2003). http://www.ispor.org/news/
articles/Feb04/registry.asp.

Neumann, P. J., E. A. Sandberg, C. M. Bell, P. W. Stone, and R. H. Chapman. "Are
Pharmaceuticals Cost-Effective? A Review of the Evidence." *Health Affairs* 19,
no. 2 (2000): 92–109.

New England Baptist Bone and Joint Institute. "Bioskills Learning Center." Brochure.
2005.

New England Healthcare Institute. *Remote Physiological Monitoring, Innovation in the
Management of Heart Failure.* NEHI Innovation Series. Cambridge, MA: NEHI,
2004. http://www.nehi.net/CMS/admin/cms/_uploads/docs/HF Report.pdf.

Newburger, J. W., D. Wypij, D. C. Bellinger, L. A. Rappaport, A. J. duPlessis, D.
Almirall, D. L. Wessel, R. A. Jonas, and G. Wernovsky. "Length of Stay After
Infant Heart Surgery Is Related to Cognitive Outcome at Age 8 Years." *Journal
of Pediatrics* 143 (2003): 67–73.

Newhouse, J. P. "Medical Care Costs: How Much Welfare Loss?" *Journal of Economic Perspectives* 6, no. 3 (1992): 3–21.

Newhouse, J. P., and the Insurance Experiment Group. *Free for All? Lessons from the RAND Health Insurance Experiment.* Cambridge, MA: Harvard University Press, 1996.

Newhouse, J. P., and P. C. Weiler. "Reforming Medical Malpractice and Insurance." *Regulation: The Cato Review of Business & Government*, no. 14 (Fall 1991): 4.

New Jersey Department of Health and Senior Services. *Cardiac Surgery in New Jersey: Technical Report.* 2001. http://www.state.nj.us/health/hcsa/cabgs01/cabg_technical01.pdf.

New York State Department of Health. *Coronary Artery Bypass Surgery in New York State: 1989–1991.* Albany, NY: New York State Department of Health, 1992.

_____. *Coronary Artery Bypass Surgery in New York State: 1990–1992.* Albany, NY: New York State Department of Health, 1993.

_____. *Coronary Artery Bypass Surgery in New York State: 1993–1994.* Albany, NY: New York State Department of Health, 1995.

_____. *Coronary Artery Bypass Surgery in New York State: 1993–1995.* Albany, NY: New York State Department of Health, 1997.

_____. *Coronary Artery Bypass Surgery in New York State: 1995–1997.* Albany, NY: New York State Department of Health, 2000.

Nichols, L. M., P. B. Ginsburg, R. A. Berenson, J. Christianson, and R. E. Hurley. "Are Market Forces Strong Enough to Deliver Efficient Health Care Systems? Confidence Is Waning." *Health Affairs* 23, no. 2 (2004): 8–21.

Nissenson, A. R., and R. A. Rettig. "Medicare's End-Stage Renal Disease Program: Current Status and Future Prospects." *Health Affairs* 18, no. 1 (1999): 161–179.

Nodhturft, V., et al. "Chronic Disease Self-Management." *Nursing Clinics of North America* 35, no. 2 (2000): 507–518.

Nordhaus, W. D. *The Health of Nations: The Contribution of Improved Health to Living Standards.* New York: Lasker Foundation, 1999. http://www.laskerfoundation.org/reports/pdf/healthofnations.pdf.

_____. "The Health of Nations: The Contribution of Improved Health to Living Standards." In *Measuring the Gains from Medical Research*, edited by K. M. Murphy and Robert Topel, 9–41. Chicago: University of Chicago Press, 2003.

Null, G., C. Dean, M. Feldman, and D. Rasio. "Death by Medicine." Nutrition Institute of America. October 2003. http://www.niausa.org/research/DeathByMedicine/DeathByMedicine1.htm.

O'Connell, B. "Clinics Treat Workers, Trim Companies' Costs." *The Chicago Tribune*, December 13, 2004.

O'Connor, A. M., H. A. Llewellyn-Thomas, and A. B. Flood. "Modifying Unwarranted Variations in Health Care: Shared Decision Making Using Patient Decision Aids." *Health Affairs* Web exclusive (October 7, 2004). http://content.healthaffairs.org/cgi/content/full/hlthaff.var.63/DC2.

O'Connor, G. T., H. B. Quinton, N. D. Traven, L. D. Ramunno, T. A. Dodds, T. A. Marciniak, and J. E. Wennberg. "Geographic Variation in the Treatment of Acute Myocardial Infarction: the Cooperative Cardiovascular Project." *Journal of the American Medical Association* 281, no. 7 (1999): 627–633.

Office of Minnesota Attorney General. "Agreement Between Attorney General and Minnesota Hospitals Will Provide Fair Pricing to Uninsured Patients, Establish

Code of Conduct for Debt Collection Practices." Press release. May 5, 2005. http://www.ag.state.mn.us/consumer/PR/PR_050505HospitalFairPricing.htm.

Office of Personnel Management. "High Deductible Health Plans (HDHP) with Health Savings Accounts (HSA)." http://www.opm.gov/hsa/chart.asp.

Ofsthun, N., J. Labrecque, E. Lacson, M. Keen, and J. M. Lazarus. "The Effects of Higher Hemoglobin Levels on Mortality and Hospitalization in Hemodialysis Patients." *Kidney International* 63, no. 5 (2003): 1908–1914.

Omoigui, N. A., D. P. Miller, K. J. Brown, K. Annan, D. Cosgrove 3rd, B. Lytle, F. Loop, and E. J. Topol. "Outmigration for Coronary Bypass Surgery in an Era of Public Dissemination of Clinical Outcomes." *Circulation* 93, no. 1 (1996): 27–33.

O'Muircheartaigh, C., A. Burke, and W. Murphy. *The 2004 Index of Hospital Quality.* Chicago: National Opinion Research Center at the University of Chicago, 2004. http://www.norc.org/new/methrep_2004F.pdf.

O'Reilly, B. "Why Doctors Aren't Curing Ulcers." *Fortune,* June 9, 1997, 100–112.

Ornstein, C. "Threats from Doctors, Hospitals to Quit Aetna's Network Spread Nationwide." *The Dallas Morning News,* June 1, 1999.

Orringer, M. B. "STS Database Activities and You: 'What's in It for Me?'" *Annals of Thoracic Surgery* 72, no. 1 (2001): 1–2.

Pardes, H., K. G. Manton, E. S. Lander, H. D. Tolley, A. D. Ullian, and H. Palmer. "Effects of Medical Research on Health Care and the Economy." *Science* 283 (1999): 36–37.

Parker-Pope, T. "Budget Beauty: Doctors Offer Cheaper Cosmetic Procedures." *The Wall Street Journal*, December 3, 2002.

Passell, P., for Funding First. *Exceptional Returns: The Economic Value of America's Investment in Medical Research.* New York: Mary Lasker Foundation, 2000.

Pathman, D. E., T. R. Konrad, G. L. Freed, V. A. Freeman, and G. G. Koch. "The Awareness-to-Adherence Model of the Steps to Clinical Guideline Compliance. The Case of Pediatric Vaccine Recommendations." *Medical Care* 34, no. 9 (1996): 873–889.

Pauly, M. V. "What If Technology Never Stops Improving? Medicare's Future Under Continuous Cost Increases." *Specialty Law Digest Health Care Law* 308 (December 2004): 9–26.

Pear, R. "Insurers Object to New Provision in Medicare Law." *The New York Times*, August 22, 2004.

Perlin, J. B., R. M. Kolodner, and R. H. Roswell. "The Veterans Health Administration: Quality, Value, Accountability, and Information as Transforming Strategies for Patient-Centered Care." *American Journal of Managed Care* 10, no. 11, pt. 2 (2004): 828–836.

Perls, T. T., L. Alpert, and R. C. Fretts. "Middle-Aged Mothers Live Longer." *Nature* 389 (1997): 133.

Perrin, D. *HSA Road Rules for Consumers, Employers, Insurers, Banks, Credit Unions and Administrators.* 1st ed. Washington, DC: HSA Insider Corporation, 2004. http://www.hsainsider.com/HSA%20Road%20Rules%20Dec%207th.pdf.

Perry, C. "Bush to Push Sweeping Health Reform." *Physicians News Digest.* January 2003. http://www.physiciansnews.com/cover/103.html.

Petersen, A. "Nursing Homes Face Insurance Crunch." *The Wall Street Journal*, June 3, 2004.

Peterson, E. D., et al. "Racial Variation in Cardiac Procedure Use and Survival Following Acute Myocardial Infarction in the Department of Veterans Affairs." *Journal of the American Medical Association* 271, no. 15 (1994): 1175–1180.

Peterson, E. D., et al. "The Effects of New York's Bypass Surgery Provider Profiling on Access to Care and Patient Outcomes in the Elderly." *Journal of the American College of Cardiology* 32, no. 4 (1998): 993–999.

Peterson, E. D., L. P. Coombs, E. R. DeLong, C. K. Haan, and T. B. Ferguson. "Procedural Volume as a Marker of Quality for CABG Surgery." *Journal of the American Medical Association* 291, no. 2 (2004): 195–201.

Pham, A. "New Blue Cross Plan in Peril: Partners Won't Participate." *The Boston Globe,* September 9, 1999.

Phillips, R. L., Jr., L. A. Bartholomew, S. M. Dovey, G. E. Fryer Jr., T. J. Miyoshi, and L. A. Green. "Learning from Malpractice Claims About Negligent, Adverse Events in Primary Care in the United States." *Quality and Safety in Health Care* 13, no. 2 (2004): 121–126.

Pierce, E. C., Jr. "Anesthesia Safety and Mortality Studies in the 1950s through 1970s." Anesthesia Patient Safety Foundation History Overview. The 34th Rovenstine Lecture. Presented at the annual meeting of the American Society of Anesthesiologists, Atlanta, GA, October 1995. http://www.apsf.org/about/rovenstine/part3.mspx.

Pisano, G. P. "Knowledge, Integration, and the Locus of Learning: An Empirical Analysis of Process Development." *Strategic Management Journal* 15 (1994): 85–100.

Pisano, G. P., R. Bohmer, and A. C. Edmondson. "Organizational Differences in Rates of Learning: Evidence from the Adoption of Minimally Invasive Cardiac Surgery." *Management Science* 47, no. 6 (2001): 752.

Pittsburgh Regional Healthcare Initiative. http://www.prhi.org/.

Polastro, E. T., and S. Tulcinsky. "Outsourcing Pharmaceutical Contract Research and Manufacturing: What Does the Future Hold?" *Chemical Market Reporter,* October 30, 2000.

Pollack, A. "Protecting a Favorable Image." *The New York Times,* November 4, 2000.

Pollack, R. "One Leap Forward, Two Leaps Back." *Trustee,* January 2002, 29–32.

Powell, J. "First Seniority Loses 40 More Doctors." *The Boston Herald,* August 11, 1999.

———. "Groups Seek Medigap Help." *The Boston Herald,* August 28, 1999.

Porter, M. E. *Competitive Advantage: Creating and Sustaining Superior Performance.* New York: Free Press, 1985.

———. "What Is Strategy?" *Harvard Business Review,* November–December 1996.

———. *On Competition.* Boston: Harvard Business School Press, 1998.

———. "Strategy and the Internet." *Harvard Business Review,* March 2001.

Porter, M. E., and E. O. Teisberg. "Fixing Competition in U.S. Health Care." HBR Research Report, June 2004a.

Porter, M. E., and E. O. Teisberg. "Redefining Competition in Health Care." *Harvard Business Review,* June 2004b.

Preferred Global Health. "The Independent Patient Organization." Company literature. April 2001.

President's Advisory Commission on Consumer Protection and Quality in the Health Care Industry. *Quality First: Better Health Care for All Americans.* 1998. http://www.hcqualitycommission.gov/final/.

PricewaterhouseCoopers and the American Hospital Association. *Patients or Paperwork? The Regulatory Burden Facing America's Hospitals.* 2001. http://pwchealth.com/cgi-local/hcregister.cgi?link=pdf/ahapaperwork.pdf.

Pronk, N., et al. "Relationship Between Modifiable Health Risks and Short-Term Health Care Charges." *Journal of the American Medical Association* 282, no. 23 (1995): 2235–2239.

Pronovost, P. J., et al. "Evaluation of the Culture of Safety: Survey of Clinicians and Managers in an Academic Medical Center." *Quality and Safety in Health Care* 12, no 6. (2003): 405–410.

Pronovost, P. J., M. L. Rinke, K. Emery, C. Dennison, C. Blackledge, and S. M. Bernholtz. "Interventions to Reduce Mortality Among Patients Treated in Intensive Care Units." *Journal of Critical Care* 19 (2004): 158–164.

Prosser, E. S. "The Road to Drug Delivery." *Chemical and Industry,* October 2, 2000, 632.

Pryor, C., and R. Seifert. "Unintended Consequences: How Federal Regulations and Hospital Policies Can Leave Patients in Debt." The Commonwealth Fund. June 2003. http://www.cmwf.org/programs/insurance/pryor_unintendedconsequences_653.pdf.

Rakowski, H. "Planning Strategically: Preparing for the New Millennium." *American Heart Journal* 137, no. 5 (1999).

Ray, G. T., et al. "The Cost of Health Conditions in a Health Maintenance Organization." *Medical Care Research and Review* 57, no. 1 (2000): 92–109.

Raymond, J., and A. B. Gesalman. "Why Drugs Cost So Much." *Newsweek,* September 25, 2000.

Rayner, H. C., A. Besarab, W. W. Brown, A. Disney, A. Saito, and R. L. Pisoni. "Vascular Access Results from the Dialysis Outcomes and Practice Patterns Study (DOPPS): Performance Against Kidney Disease Outcomes Quality Initiative (K/DOQI) Clinical Practice Guidelines." *American Journal of Kidney Disease* 44, no. 5, suppl. 3 (2004): 22–26.

Reinhardt, U. E. "Does the Aging of the Population Really Drive the Demand for Health Care?" *Health Affairs* 22, no. 6 (2003): 27–39.

Reinhardt, U. E., and T. M. Cheng. "Costs of Health Care Administration in the United States and Canada." *New England Journal of Medicine* 349, no. 25 (2003): 2461–2464.

Reinhardt, U. E., P. S. Hussey, and G. F. Anderson. "U.S. Health Care Spending in an International Context." *Health Affairs* 23, no. 3 (2004): 10–25.

Relman, A. S. "The Health of Nations: Medicine and the Free Market." *New Republic,* March 7, 2005.

Renal Physicians Association. *RPA Advanced CKD Patient Management Toolkit.* Rockville, MD: Renal Physicians Association, July 2004. http://www.renalmd.org/toolkit/form_toolkit.cfm.

Rettig, R. A. "Medical Innovation Duels Cost Containment." *Health Affairs* 13, no. 3 (1994): 7–27.

Reynolds, R. A., J. A. Rizzo, and M. L. Gonzalez. "The Cost of Medical Professional Liability." *Journal of the American Medical Association* 257, no. 20 (1987): 2776–2781.

Rice, D. P., T. A. Hodgson, and A. N. Kopstein. "The Economic Costs of Illness: A Replication and Update." *Health Care Financing Review* 7, no. 1 (1985): 61–80.

Rich, J. "Measuring Physician Quality and Efficiency of Care for Medicare Beneficiaries." Testimony to House Committee on Ways and Means. Health Subcommittee, March 15th, 2005.

Richmond, R. "Doctors See Healthy Returns in Digital Records." *The Wall Street Journal,* December 7, 2004.

Robbins, J. "Should Pharmaceutical Prices Be Regulated?" *Hospitals & Health Networks,* October 1, 2000.

Roberts, J. "Who Pays the Bill and Who Makes the Profit in Treating Chronic Disease?" *Western Journal of Medicine* 172, no. 2 (2000): 76–77.

Roberts, M., W. Hsiao, P. Berman, and M. Reich. *Getting Health Reform Right: A Guide to Improving Performance and Equity.* Oxford, England: Oxford University Press, 2004.

The Robert Wood Johnson Foundation. *Annual Report.* Princeton, NJ: The Robert Wood Johnson Foundation, 1994.

Robinson, J. C. "From Managed Care to Consumer Health Insurance: The Fall and Rise of Aetna." *Health Affairs* 23, no. 2 (2004): 43–55.

Robinson, J. C., and H. S. Luft. "Competition and the Cost of Hospital Care, 1972 to 1982." *Journal of the American Medical Association* 257, no. 23 (1987): 3241–3245.

Romano, M. "Stay out of Florida." *Modern Healthcare,* July 5, 2004a.

_____. "This Year's Model." *Modern Healthcare,* August 2, 2004b.

_____. "Indefinite Delay." *Modern Healthcare,* August 30, 2004c.

Romano, P. S., J. J. Geppert, S. Davies, M. R. Miller, A. Elixhauser, and K. M. McDonald. "A National Profile of Patient Safety in U.S. Hospitals." *Health Affairs* 22, no. 2 (2003): 154–166.

Romney, M. "My Plan for Massachusetts Health Insurance Reform." *The Boston Globe,* November 21, 2004. http://www.boston.com/news/globe/editorial_opinion/oped/articles/2004/11/21/my_plan_for_massachusetts_health_insurance_reform/.

Rosenberg, L. E. "Exceptional Economic Returns on Investments in Medical Research." *Medical Journal of Australia* 177, no. 7 (2002): 368–371.

Rosenthal, Elizabeth. "The HMO Catch: When Healthier Isn't Cheaper." *The New York Times,* March 16, 1997.

Rosenthal, G. E., L. Quinn, and D. L. Harper. "Declines in Hospital Mortality Associated with a Regional Initiative to Measure Hospital Performance." *American Journal of Medical Quality* 12, no. 2 (1997): 103–112.

Rosenthal, M. B., R. Fernandopulle, H. R. Song, and B. Landon. "Paying for Quality: Providers' Incentives for Quality Improvement." *Health Affairs* 23, no. 2 (2004): 127–141.

Rubin, R. J., K. A. Dietrich, and A. D. Hawk. "Clinical and Economic Impact of Implementing a Comprehensive Diabetes Management Program in Managed Care." *Journal of Clinical Endocrinology and Metabolism* 83, no. 8 (1998): 2635–2642.

Saleem, H. T. "Health Spending Accounts." U.S. Department of Labor, Bureau of Labor Statistics. December 19, 2003. http://www.bls.gov/opub/cwc/cm20031022ar01p1.htm.

Sales, M. M., F. E. Cunningham, P. A. Glassman, M. A. Valentino, and C. B. Good. "Pharmacy Benefits Management in the Veterans Health Administration: 1995 to 2003." *American Journal of Managed Care* 11, no. 2 (2005): 104–112.

Salkever, A. "A Paperless Health-Care System?" *Business Week Online,* July 7, 2004. http://www.businessweek.com/technology/content/jul2004/tc2004077_8164_tc_171.htm.

Sandier, S., V. Paris, and D. Polton. *Health Care Systems in Transition: France.* Copenhagen, Denmark: WHO Regional Office for Europe on behalf of the European Observatory on Health Systems and Policies, 2004. http://www.euro.who.int/document/e83126.pdf.

Santiago, J. M. "The Costs of Treating Depression." *Journal of Clinical Psychiatry* 54, no. 11 (1993): 425–426.

Sarudi, D. "The Leapfrog Effect." *Hospitals & Health Networks* 75, no. 5 (2001): 32–36.

Schechter, M. S., and P. Margolis. "Improving Subspecialty Healthcare: Lessons from Cystic Fibrosis." *Journal of Pediatrics* 147, no. 3 (2005): 295–301.

Schneider, E. C., and A. M. Epstein. "Influence of Cardiac-Surgery Performance Reports on Referral Practices and Access to Care. A Survey of Cardiovascular Specialists." *New England Journal of Medicine* 335, no. 4 (1996): 251–256.

———. "Use of Public Performance Reports: A Survey of Patients Undergoing Cardiac Surgery." *Journal of the American Medical Association* 279, no. 20 (1998): 1638–1642.

Schneller, E. S. "The Value of Group Purchasing in the Health Care Supply Chain." School of Health Administration and Policy, Arizona State University, 2000.

Schodek, D., and M. Steinberg. "Patient Transport Module: PTM Feasibility Study." Harvard University Graduate School of Design, Cambridge, MA, 2003.

Schoen, C., R. Osborn, P. T. Huynh, M. Doty, K. Davis, K. Zapert, and J. Peugh. "Primary Care and Health System Performance: Adults' Experiences in Five Countries: Differing Performance Levels Among Countries Highlight the Potential for Improvement and Cross-National Learning." *Health Affairs* Web exclusive (October 28, 2004). http://content.healthaffairs.org/cgi/reprint/hlthaff.w4 .487v1.

Schoen, C., R. Osborn, P. T. Huynh, M. Doty, K. Zapert, J. Peugh, and K. Davis. "Taking the Pulse of Health Care Systems: Experiences of Patients with Health Problems in Six Countries." *Health Affairs* Web exclusive (November 3, 2005). http://content.healthaffairs.org/cgi/reprint/hlthaff.w5.509v3.

Scientific Registry of Transplant Recipients. "Center and OPO-Specific Reports, July 2005." http://www.ustransplant.org/csr_0507/csrDefault.aspx.

Scitovsky, A. A. "The High Cost of Dying: What Do the Data Show?" *Milbank Quarterly* 62, no. 4 (1984): 591–608.

Selecky, C. "Evaluating Coordination of Care in Medicaid: Improving Quality and Clinical Outcomes." Statement as President-elect of the DMAA before the House Committee on Energy and Commerce Health Subcommittee, October 15, 2003.

Selker, H. P. "Systems for Comparing Actual and Predicted Mortality Rates: Characteristics to Promote Cooperation in Improving Hospital Care." *Annals of Internal Medicine* 118, no. 10 (1993): 820–822.

Selker, H. P., J. L. Griffith, and R. B. D'Agostino. "A Time-Insensitive Predictive Instrument for Acute Myocardial Infarction Mortality: A Multicenter Study." *Medical Care* 29, no. 12 (1991): 1196–1211.

Sexton, J. B., E. J. Thomas, and R. L. Helmreich. "Error, Stress, and Teamwork in Medicine and Aviation: Cross Sectional Surveys." *British Medical Journal* 320, no. 3237 (2000): 745–749.

Shaller, D., S. Sofaer, S. D. Findlay, J. H. Hibbard, and S. Delbanco. "Consumers and Quality-Driven Health Care: A Call to Action." *Health Affairs* 22, no. 2 (2003): 95–101.

Shapiro, I., M. Shapiro, and D. Wilcox. "Measuring the Value of Cataract Surgery." Paper presented at the NBER-CRIW conference on health care prices, Bethesda, MD, June 1998.

———. "Measuring the Value of Cataract Surgery." In *Medical Care Output and Productivity*, edited by David M. Cutler and Ernst R. Berndt. Chicago: University of Chicago Press, 2001.

Showstack, J. A., K. E. Rosenfeld, D. W. Granick, H. S. Luft, R. W. Schaffarzick, and J. Fowles. "Association of Volume with Outcome of Coronary Artery Bypass Graft Surgery." *Journal of the American Medical Association* 257, no. 6 (1987): 785–789.

Sidorov, J., R. Shull, J. Tomcavage, S. Girolami, N. Lawton, and R. Harris. "Does Diabetes Disease Management Save Money and Improve Outcomes? A Report of Simultaneous Short-Term Savings and Quality Improvement Associated with a Health Maintenance Organization-Sponsored Disease Management Program Among Patients Fulfilling Health Employer Data and Information Set Criteria." *Diabetes Care* 25, no. 4 (2002): 684–689.

Siegrist, R. B., Jr., and N. M. Kane. "Exploring the Relationship Between Inpatient Hospital Costs and Quality of Care." *American Journal of Managed Care* 9, special no. 1 (June 2003): SP43–49.

Silverman, E. M., J. S. Skinner, and E. S. Fisher. "The Association Between For-Profit Hospital Ownership and Increased Medicare Spending." *New England Journal of Medicine* 341, no. 6 (1999): 420–426.

Silverstein, S. C., H. H. Garrison, and S. J. Heinig. "A Few Basic Economic Facts About Research in the Medical and Related Life Sciences." *Federation of American Scientists for Experimental Biology Journal* 9, no. 10 (1995): 833–840.

Simmons, H. E. "Lessons from the Failed Healthcare Debate." *Healthcare Forum* 41, no. 1 (1998): 46–50.

_____. "Why Health Care Quality Must Be Improved and Why Health System Reform Must Occur." Presentation to the American Federation of Teachers and the National Education Association, Washington, DC, March 31, 2001.

Simon, G. E., et al. "Depression and Work Productivity: The Comparative Costs of Treatment Versus Nontreatment." *Journal of Occupational and Environmental Medicine* 43, no. 1 (2001): 2–9.

Sirio, C. A., K. T. Segel, D. J. Keyser, E. I. Harrison, J. C. Lloyd, R. J. Weber, C. A. Muto, D. G. Webster, V. Pisowicz, and K. W. Feinstein. "Pittsburgh Regional Healthcare Initiative: A Systems Approach for Achieving Perfect Patient Care." *Health Affairs* 22, no. 5 (2003): 157–165.

Skinner, J., and J. E. Wennberg. "Exceptionalism or Extravagance? What's Different About Health Care in South Florida?" *Health Affairs* Web exclusive (August 13, 2003). http://content.healthaffairs.org/cgi/content/abstract/hlthaff.w3.372v1.

Smith-Bindman, R., P. Chu, D. L. Miglioretti, C. Quale, R. D. Rosenberg, G. Cutter, B. Geller, P. Bacchetti, E. A. Sickles, and K. Kerlikowske. "Physician Predictors of Mammographic Accuracy." *Journal of the National Cancer Institute* 97, no. 5 (2005): 358–367.

Smits, H., B. Zarowitz, V. K. Sahney, and L. Savitz. "The Business Case for Pharmaceutical Management: A Case Study of Henry Ford Health System." The Commonwealth Fund. April 2003. http://www.cmwf.org/usr_doc/smits_bcs_pharmaceuticalmanagement_613.pdf.

Snoots, W. M. "Information Technology and the Medical Profession: A Curse or an Opportunity?" *Baylor University Medical Center Proceedings* 15, no. 2 (2002): 138–142.

Snyder, C., and G. Anderson. "Do Quality Improvement Organizations Improve the Quality of Hospital Care for Medicare Beneficiaries?" *Journal of the American Medical Association* 293, no. 23 (2005): 2900–2907.

Society of Thoracic Surgeons. *National Adult Cardiac Surgery Database and Outcomes Program Participation Manual.* Chicago: Society of Thoracic Surgeons, 2003. http://www.ctsnet.org/file/DatabaseManual2003.pdf.

_____. "STS National Database Measures Used in National Consensus Standards Intended to Improve Cardiac Surgery Outcomes." Press release. December 10, 2004. http://www.sts.org/sections/communications/pressreleases/Press%20Releases/article.html.

Souba, W. W., and D. W. Wilmore. "Judging Surgical Research: How Should We Evaluate Performance and Measure Value?" Departments of Surgery, the Massachusetts General Hospital and the Brigham and Women's Hospital, Harvard Medical School, Boston, 2000.

Soumerai, S., et al. "Effects of a Limit on Medicaid Drug-Reimbursement Benefits on the Use of Psychotropic Agents and Acute Mental Health Services by Patients with Schizophrenia." *New England Journal of Medicine* 331, no. 10 (1994): 650–655.

Sowden, A. J., R. Grilli, and N. Rice. *The Relationship Between Hospital Volume and Quality of Health Outcomes.* CRD Report 8, pt. 1. York: Centre for Reviews and Dissemination, 1997.

Spear, S. J., and M. Schmidhofer. "Ambiguity and Workarounds as Contributors to Medical Error." *Annals of Internal Medicine* 142, no. 8 (2005): 627–630.

Spillman, B. C., and J. Lubitz. "The Effect of Longevity on Spending for Acute and Long-Term Care." *New England Journal of Medicine* 342, no. 19 (2000): 1409–1415.

Stack, A. G. "Impact of Timing of Nephrology Referral and Pre-ESRD Care on Mortality Risk Among New ESRD Patients in the United States." *American Journal of Kidney Disease* 41, no. 2 (2003): 310–318.

Stackhouse, J. "The Eureka Formula." *The Globe and Mail,* October 18, 2000. http://www.theglobeandmail.com/series/America/1018.html.

Starfield, B. *Primary Care: Balancing Health Needs, Services, and Technology.* New York: Oxford University Press, 1998.

_____. "Evaluating the State Children's Health Insurance Program: Critical Considerations." *Annual Review of Public Health,* no. 21 (2000a): 569–585.

_____. "Is US Health Really the Best in the World?" *Journal of the American Medical Association* 284, no. 4 (2000b): 483–485.

Steinberg, C. "Overview of the U.S. Health Care System." American Hospital Association. 2003. http://www.hospitalconnect.com/aha/resource_center/statistics/statistics.html.

Steinberg, E. P., and B. R. Luce. "Evidence Based? Caveat Emptor!" *Health Affairs* 24, no. 1 (2005): 80–92.

Steinhauer, J. "Rebellion in White: Doctors Pulling Out of HMO Systems." *The New York Times,* January 10, 1999.

Steinman, T. I., J. Dickmeyer, W. D. Mattern, A. R. Nissenson, and T. F. Parker. "Disease Management for ESRD: The Time Has Come." *Dialysis and Transplantation* 29, no. 10 (2000): 602.

Stewart, A., J. K. Schmier, and B. R. Luce. "Economics and Cost-Effectiveness in Evaluating the Value of Cardiovascular Therapies. A Survey of Standards and Guidelines for Cost-Effectiveness Analysis in Health Care." *American Heart Journal* 137 (1999): S53–S61.

Stewart, W. F., J. A. Ricci, E. Chee, and D. Morganstein. "Lost Productive Work Time Costs from Health Conditions in the United States: Results from the American Productivity Audit." *Journal of Occupational and Environmental Medicine* 45, no. 12 (2003): 1234–1246.

Stipp, D. "Gene Chip Breakthrough." *Fortune,* March 31, 1997, 58–76.

_____. "Why Pfizer." *Fortune,* May 11, 1998.

Stone, V. E., G. R. Seage 3rd, T. Hertz, and A. M. Epstein. "The Relation Between Hospital Experience and Mortality for Patients with AIDS." *Journal of the American Medical Association* 268, no. 19 (1992): 2655–2661.

Street A., R. Carr-Hill, and J. Posnett. "Is Hospital Performance Related to Expenditure on Management?" *Journal of Health Services and Residential Policy* 4 (1999): 16–23.

Strunk, B. C., P. B. Ginsburg, and J. R. Gabel. "Tracking Health Care Costs. Hospital Care Surpasses Drugs as the Key Cost Driver." *Health Affairs* Web exclusive (September 26, 2001). http://content.healthaffairs.org/cgi/content/full/hlthaff .w1.39v1/DC1.

Sullivan, G., K. J. Jinnett, S. Mukherjee, and K. L. Henderson. "How Mental Health Providers Spend Their Time: A Survey of 10 Veterans Health Administration Mental Health Services." *Journal of Mental Health Policy and Economics* 6, no. 2 (2003): 89–97.

Sullivan, S. D., and K. B. Weiss. "Health Economics of Asthma and Rhinitis II. Assessing the Value of Interventions." *Journal of Allergy and Clinical Immunology* 107, no. 2 (2001): 203–210.

Switzer, G. E., E. A. Halm, C. H. Chang, B. S. Mittman, M. B. Walsh, and M. J. Fine. "Physician Awareness and Self-Reported Use of Local and National Guidelines for Community-Acquired Pneumonia." *Journal of General Internal Medicine* 18, no. 10 (2003): 816.

Symes, D. R. "Physician Data Entry Is the Solution." *Health Management Technology* 20, no. 4 (1999): 34, 36–37.

Tanner, M. "Health Care Reform: The Good, the Bad, and the Ugly." Cato Policy Analysis no. 184. The Cato Institute, Washington, DC, November 24, 1992. http://www.cato.org/pubs/pas/pa184.html.

Taurel, S. "We'd Be Worse Off Without 'Greedy' Drug-Makers." *The Houston Chronicle,* October 30, 2000.

Taylor, M. "Merger Exemption Protest." *Modern Healthcare,* September 4, 2000a.

_____. "Two Provider-Owned HMOs Probed." *Modern Healthcare,* April 10, 2000b.

_____. "Medicare Reform Provision Could Cost Employers, Clarification May Ease Collections from Primary Payers." *Business Insurance,* January 12, 2004a.

_____. "Surveying the Competition." *Modern Healthcare,* July 26, 2004b.

Teisberg, E. O., M. E. Porter, and G. B. Brown. "Innovation, Information, and Competition: a Lasting Cure for American Health Care." White paper (unpublished), February 1994a.

_____. "Innovation: Medicine's Best Cost-Cutter." *The New York Times,* February 27, 1994b.

_____. "Making Competition in Health Care Work." *Harvard Business Review,* July–August 1994c, 131–141.

_____. "Finding a Lasting Cure for U.S. Health Care." *Harvard Business Review,* September–October 1994d, 45–52.

_____. "The Debate on Health Care Reform Continues." *Harvard Business Review,* November–December 1994e.

Temkin-Greener, H., M. R. Meiners, E. A. Petty, and J. S. Szydlowski. "The Use and Cost of Health Services Prior to Death: A Comparison of the Medicare-Only and the Medicare-Medicaid Elderly Populations." *Milbank Quarterly* 70, no. 4 (1992): 679–701.

Theis, S. "Clinic Gives Japan Docs Inside View." *Plain Dealer,* February 2, 2000.

Thomas, R. "Brains on Drugs in Washington." *Smartmoney.com,* September 27, 2000.

Thompson, K. M. "Kid at Risk." *Harvard Center for Risk Analysis* 8, no. 4 (2000).

Thompson, L. "Disease Management Programs: Improving Health While Reducing Costs?" Center on an Aging Society Issue Brief no. 4, Robert Wood Johnson Foundation, Princeton, NJ, January 2004.

Thompson, T. G., Secretary of Health and Human Services. Letter to R. J. Davidson, President, American Hospital Association. February 19, 2004. http://www.hhs.gov/news/press/2004pres/20040219.html.

Towers Perrin. *Towers Perrin 2006 Health Care Cost Survey.* Stamford, CT: Towers Perrin, 2005.

Towers Perrin HR Services. "Employers Face 8% Increase in Health Care Costs in 2006." Press release. September 28, 2005. http://www.towersperrin.com/hrservices/webcache/towers/United_States/press_releases/2005_09_28/2005_09_28.htm.

Trevelyan, E. W. "The Performance Management System of the Veterans Health Administration (A)." Unpublished case, Boston, Harvard School of Public Health, 2002.

Uhlig, P. N. "Understanding the New World of Health Care." *Annals of Thoracic Surgery* 64, no. 5 (1997): 1451–1445.

Uhlig, P. N., J. Brown, A. K. Nason, A. Camelio, and E. Kendall. "John M. Eisenberg Patient Safety Awards. System Innovation: Concord Hospital." *Joint Commission Journal on Quality Improvement* 28, no. 12 (2002): 666–672.

United Health Foundation. *America's Health: State Health Rankings, 2004 Edition. A Call to Action for People and Their Communities.* Minnetonka, MN: United Health Foundation, 2004. http://www.unitedhealthfoundation.org/mediakit/shrmediakit/State Health 2004.pdf.

Upham, R., and D. Gue. "Communicating to Patients About HIPAA Privacy: Have We Achieved Compliance or Complacency?" HIPAAdvisory. http://www.hipaadvisory.com/action/compliance/communicating.htm.

Urbina, I. "Bad Blood: In the Treatment of Diabetes, Success Often Does Not Pay." *The New York Times,* January 11, 2006.

U.S. Census Bureau. "Current Population Survey, 2001." U.S. Bureau of Labor Statistics. http://www.bls.gov/cps/home.htm.

_____. "Current Population Survey, 2002." U.S. Bureau of Labor Statistics. http://www.bls.gov/cps/home.htm.

U.S. Cystic Fibrosis Foundation. "Facts About CF." May 2004. http://www.cff.org/UploadedFiles/publications/files/FactsAboutCFonLH%200504.pdf.

U.S. Cystic Fibrosis Foundation Registry. "Survival Curve." 1998. http://www.fairviewchildrens.org/outcomes/mcfc6.htm.

U.S. Department of Health and Human Services, Health Resources and Services Administration. "The Hill-Burton Free Care Program." http://www.hrsa.gov/osp/dfcr/about/aboutdiv.htm.

U.S. Department of Health and Human Services, Office of the Assistant Secretary for Planning and Evaluation. *Confronting the New Health Care Crisis: Improving Health Care Quality and Lowering Costs by Fixing Our Medical Liability System.* Washington, DC: Department of Health and Human Services, 2002. http://aspe.hhs.gov/daltcp/reports/litrefm.htm.

U.S. Department of Labor, Bureau of Labor Statistics. http://www.bls.gov.

U.S. General Accounting Office. *Medicaid Managed Care: States' Safeguards for Children with Special Needs Vary Significantly.* GAO/HEHS-00-169. Washington, DC:

U.S. General Accounting Office; Health, Education, and Human Services Division, 2000a. http://www.gao.gov/cgi-bin/getrpt?GAO/HEHS-00-169.

_____. *Medicare+Choice: Payments Exceed Cost of Fee-for-Service Benefits, Adding Billions to Spending.* GAO/HEHS-00-161. Washington, DC: U.S. General Accounting Office; Health, Education, and Human Services Division, 2000b. http://www.gao.gov/cgi-bin/getrpt?GAO/HEHS-00-161.

_____. "Specialty Hospitals: Information on National Market Share, Physician Ownership, and Patients Served." GAO-03-683R. April 18, 2003a. http://www.gao.gov/new.items/d03683r.pdf.

_____. "Specialty Hospitals: Geographic Location, Services Provided, and Financial Performance." GAO-04-167. October 2003b. http://www.gao.gov/new.items/d04167.pdf.

U.S. Senate. Testimony of Richard A. Norling, chairman and CEO, Premier Incorporated, before the Subcommittee on Antitrust, Competition, and Business and Consumer Rights, Committee on the Judiciary, April 20, 2002. http://www.premierinc.com/all/newsroom/news-public/resource-center/norling-written-testimony.doc.

Van Den Bulcke, D., H. Zhang, and X. Li. "Interaction Between the Business Environment and the Corporate Strategic Positioning of Firms in the Pharmaceutical Industry: A Study of the Entry and Expansion Path of MNEs into China." *Management International Review,* October 2000, 353–377.

Villagra, V. G., and T. Ahmed. "Effectiveness of a Disease Management Program for Patients with Diabetes." *Health Affairs* 23, no. 4 (2004): 255–266.

Villarosa, L. "Studies Tie Success of Some Operations to Number a Hospital Does." *The New York Times,* April 11, 2002.

Vitelli, T. *The Story of Intermountain Health Care.* Salt Lake City, UT: Intermountain Health Care, 1995.

Wagner, E. H., B. T. Austin, C. Davis, M. Hindmarsh, J. Schaefer, and A. Bonomi. "Improving Chronic Illness Care: Translating Evidence Into Action." *Health Affairs* 20, no. 6 (2001): 64–78.

Wagner, E. H., P. Barrett, M. J. Barry, W. Barlow, and F. J. Fowler Jr. "The Effect of a Shared Decision Making Program on Rates of Surgery for Benign Prostatic Hyperplasia. Pilot Results." *Medical Care* 33, no. 8 (1995): 765–770.

Walsh, M. W. "Hospital Network's Switch Is Blow to Novation." *The New York Times,* November 23, 2002.

Walshe, K., and S. M. Shortell. "When Things Go Wrong: How Health Care Organizations Deal with Major Failures." *Health Affairs* 23, no. 3 (2004): 103–111.

Watson, S. D. "Sticker Shock—Hospital Billing and Class Action Litigation." *Lahey Clinic Medical Ethics Journal* (Fall 2004): 4, 12.

Watts, D. D., D. Hanfling, M. A. Waller, C. Gilmore, S. M. Fakhry, and A. L. Trask. "An Evaluation of the Use of Guidelines in Prehospital Management of Brain Injury." *Prehospital Emergency Care* 8, no. 3 (2004): 254–261.

Watts, D. D., M. Roche, R. Tricarico, F, Poole, J. J. Brown Jr., G. B. Colson, A. L. Trask, and S. M. Fakhry. "The Utility of Traditional Prehospital Interventions in Maintaining Thermostasis." *Prehospital Emergency Care* 3, no. 2 (1999): 115–122.

Weber, J. "Should the FDA Lower the Threshold?" *Business Week,* August 11, 1997.

Weingart, S. N., R. M. Wilson, R. W. Gibberd, and B. Harrison. "Epidemiology and Medical Error." *British Medical Journal* 320 (2000): 774–777.

Weissman, J. S., C. L. Annas, A. M. Epstein, E. C. Schneider, B. Clarridge, L. Kirle, C. Gatsonis, S. Feibelmann, and N. Ridley. "Error Reporting and Disclosure

Systems: Views from Hospital Leaders." *Journal of American Medical Association* 293, no. 11 (2005): 1359–1366.

Weller, C. D. *Patient Choice Organizations. The Next Generation After Capitation and Managed Care.* Aspen Special Report. Gaithersburg, Maryland: Aspen Publishers, 1997.

———. "Decapitating Healthcare." *Modern Healthcare,* August 31, 1998.

———. "Science Innovation Groups and Cluster Theory: The Next Generation After Managed Care." Draft. June 29, 2000.

Wellpoint, Inc. *Wellpoint by Design.* Annual report 2002. http://media.corporate-ir .net/media_files/irol/82/82476/reports/wellpoint2002AR.pdf.

Wells, K. B., C. Sherbourne, M. Schoenbaum, N. Duan, L. Meredith, J. Unutzer, J. Miranda, M. F. Carney, and L. V. Rubenstein. "Impact of Disseminating Quality Improvement Programs for Depression in Managed Primary Care: A Randomized Controlled Trial." *Journal of American Medical Association* 283, no. 2 (2000): 212–220.

Wennberg, D., J. Dickens Jr., D. Soule, M. Kellett Jr., D. Malenka, J. Robb, T. Ryan Jr., W. Bradley, P. Vaitkus, M. Hearne, G. O'Connor, and R. Hillman. "The Relationship Between the Supply of Cardiac Catheterization Laboratories, Cardiologists and the Use of Invasive Cardiac Procedures in Northern New England." *Journal of Health Services Research and Policy* 2, no. 2 (1997): 75–80.

Wennberg, D. E., and J. E. Wennberg. "Addressing Variations: Is There Hope for the Future?" *Health Affairs* Web exclusive (December 10, 2003). http://content .healthaffairs.org/cgi/reprint/hlthaff.w3.614v1.

Wennberg, J. E. "Variation in Use of Medicare Services Among Regions and Selected Academic Medical Centers: Is More Better?" Duncan W. Clark Lecture, presented at the New York Academy of Medicine, New York, January 24, 2005. http://www.dartmouthatlas.org/lectures/NYAM_Lecture_FINAL.pdf.

———. "The More Things Change. . . : The Federal Government's Role in the Evaluative Sciences." *Health Affairs* Web exclusive (June 25, 2003). http://content .healthaffairs.org/cgi/reprint/hlthaff.w3.308v1.

Wennberg, J. E., and M. M. Cooper, eds. *The Dartmouth Atlas of Health Care in the United States.* The Trustees of Dartmouth College. Chicago: AHA Press, 1999. http://www.dartmouthatlas.com/atlaslinks/99atlas.php.

Wennberg, J. E., E. S. Fisher, and J. S. Skinner. "Geography and the Debate over Medicare Reform." *Health Affairs* Web exclusive (February 13, 2002). http:// content.healthaffairs.org/cgi/reprint/hlthaff.w2.96v1.

Wennberg, J. E., E. S. Fisher, T. A. Stukel, J. S. Skinner, S. M. Sharp, and K. K. Bronner. "Use of Hospitals, Physician Visits, and Hospice Care During Last Six Months of Life Among Cohorts Loyal to Highly Respected Hospitals in the United States." *British Medical Journal* 328 (2004a): 607–611.

Wennberg, J. E., E. S. Fisher, T. A. Stukel, and S. M. Sharp. "Use of Medicare Claims Data to Monitor Provider-Specific Performance Among Patients with Severe Chronic Illness." *Health Affairs* Web exclusive (October 7, 2004b). http://content .healthaffairs.org/cgi/reprint/hlthaff.var.5v1.

Wennberg, J. E., J. L. Freeman, and W. J. Culp. "Are Hospital Services Rationed in New Haven or Over-utilised in Boston?" *Lancet* 23, no. 1 (1987): 1185–1189.

Wennberg, J. E., and A. Gittelsohn. "Variations in Medical Care Among Small Areas." *Scientific American* 246, no. 1 (1982): 120–134.

Wennberg, J. E., F. L. Lucas, J. D. Birkmeyer, C. E. Bredenberg, and E. S. Fisher. "Variation in Carotid Endarterectomy Mortality in the Medicare Population:

Trial Hospitals, Volume and Patient Characteristics." *Journal of the American Medical Association* 279, no. 16 (1998): 1278–1281.

Wessel, D., and W. Bogdanich. "Closed Market: Laws of Economics Often Don't Apply in Health-Care Field." *The Wall Street Journal,* January 22, 1992.

Westmoreland, T. M., Director of Health Care Financing Administration, Department of Health and Human Services. Letter to State Medicaid directors, "Outstationing—Pregnant Women and Children Applying for Medicaid at Locations Other Than Welfare Offices." January 18, 2001. http://www.cms.hhs.gov/states/letters/smd01181.pdf.

White House. "Key Components of the President's Health Care Reform Agenda." News release. February 11, 2002.

Whole Health Management. "Case Study: Discovery Communications." 2005. http://www.wholehealthnet.com/files/PDF/WH_casestudy_discoverychannel.pdf.

Wilson, J. "New Technology Designed to Save Time, Improve Health Care." *The Dover Post*, January 7, 2004.

Wilson, M. C., et al. "Users' Guides to the Medical Literature: VIII. How to Use Clinical Practice Guidelines: B. What Are the Recommendations and Will They Help You in Caring for Your Patients?" *Journal of the American Medical Association* 274, no. 20 (1995): 1630–1632.

Wilson, R. M., B. T. Harrison, R. W. Gibberd, and J. D. Hamilton. "An Analysis of the Causes of Adverse Events from the Quality in Australian Health Care Study." *Medical Journal of Australia* 170, no. 9 (1999): 411–415.

Winkelman, J. W., J. L. Aitken, and D. R. Wybenga. "Cost Savings in a Hospital Clinical Laboratory with a Pay-for-Performance Incentive Program for Supervisors." *Archives of Pathology and Laboratory Medicine* 115 (1991): 38–41.

Winslow, R. "Data Spur Debate on Hospital Quality." *The Wall Street Journal*, May 24, 1990.

Winslow, R., and L. McGinley. "Back on the Front Burner: Health Care Is Once Again High on the Legislative Agenda, and Once Again, Consensus Won't Be Easy." *The Wall Street Journal*, February 21, 2001. http://www.aahpechochamber.tv/buzz/clippings/2001/01_02_21_backburner.cfm.

Woolf, S. H., R. E. Johnson, G. E. Fryer Jr., G. Rust, and D. Satcher. "The Health Impact of Resolving Racial Disparities: An Analysis of US Mortality Data." *American Journal of Public Health* 94, no. 12 (2004): 2078–2081.

Woolhandler, S., and D. U. Himmelstein. "The Deteriorating Administrative Efficiency of the U.S. Health Care System." *New England Journal of Medicine* 324, no. 18 (1991): 1253–1258.

_____."Costs of Care and Administration at For-Profit and Other Hospitals in the United States." *New England Journal of Medicine* 336, no. 11 (1997): 769–774.

World Health Organization. *Obesity: Preventing and Managing the Global Epidemic.* Geneva, Switzerland: World Health Organization, 1977.

_____. *The World Health Report 2000. Health Systems: Improving Performance.* Geneva, Switzerland: World Health Organization, 2000. http://www.who.int/entity/whr/2000/en/whr00_en.pdf.

_____. "Quality of Care: Patient Safety. Report by the Secretariat." A55/13. Fifty-fifth World Health Assembly, March 23, 2002a. http://www.who.int/gb/ebwha/pdf_files/WHASS/ea5513.pdf.

_____. *The World Health Report 2002. Reducing Risks, Promoting Healthy Life.* Geneva, Switzerland: World Health Organization, 2002b. www.who.int/entity/whr/2002/en/whr02_en.pdf.

_____. *The World Health Report 2004. Changing History.* Geneva, Switzerland: World Health Organization, 2004. http://www.who.int/entity/whr/2004/en/report04_en.pdf.

_____. *World Health Report 2005, Make Every Mother and Child Count.* 2005. http://www.who.int/whr/2005/whr2005_en.pdf.

Woolhandler, S., T. Campbell, and D. U. Himmelstein. "Health Care Administration in the United States and Canada: Micromanagement, Macro Costs." *International Journal of Health Services* 34, no. 1 (2004): 65–78.

Wright, J. D., and M. C. Weinstein. "Gains in Life Expectancy from Medical Interventions—Standardizing Data on Outcomes." *New England Journal of Medicine* 339, no. 6 (1998): 380–386.

Wyke, A. "Can Patients Drive the Future of Health Care?" *Harvard Business Review,* July–August 1997, 145–146.

Yip, W. C., and W. C. Hsiao. "Medical Saving Accounts: Lessons from China." *Health Affairs* 15, no. 6 (1997): 244–251.

Young, G. J., M. P. Charns, J. Daley, M. G. Forbes, W. Henderson, and S. F. Khuri. "Best Practices for Managing Surgical Services: The Role of Coordination." *Health Care Management Review* 22, no. 4 (1997): 72–81.

Zeidel, M. L., and B. C. James. "Improving the Quality of Health Care in America: What Medical Schools, Leading Medical Journals, and Federal Funding Agencies Can Do." *American Journal of Medicine* 112, no. 2 (2002): 165–167.

Zhan, C., and M. R. Miller. "Excess Length of Stay, Charges and Mortality Attributable to Medical Injuries During Hospitalization." *Journal of the American Medical Association* 290, no. 14 (2003): 1868–1874.

Zwanziger, J., G. A. Melnick, and A. Bamezai. "Costs and Price Competition in California Hospitals, 1980–1990." *Health Affairs* 13, no. 4 (1994): 118–126.

Index

About the Authors

MICHAEL E. PORTER is the Bishop William Lawrence University Professor, based at Harvard Business School. A leading authority on competitive strategy and the competitiveness of countries, regions, and cities, Professor Porter's ideas and personal leadership have influenced countless governments, companies, and scholars across the globe. His ideas on strategy are taught in virtually every business school in the world, and his thinking on competitiveness has become an integral part of modern economic development theory and practice. Professor Porter's work on health care dates back more than a decade.

An aerospace engineering graduate of Princeton, Professor Porter earned both an M.B.A. from the Harvard Business School, where he was a George F. Baker Scholar, and a Ph.D. in business economics from Harvard University. He has received numerous awards and honors, including the Adam Smith Award of the National Association of Business Economists, national honors in a number of countries, and the highest award of the Academy of Management for scholarly contributions to management.

ELIZABETH OLMSTED TEISBERG is an associate professor at the University of Virginia's Darden Graduate School of Business, where she received the Frederick S. Morton Leadership Award. Her expertise is in strategy, innovation, and risk analysis. She was previously an associate professor at the Harvard Business School.

In addition to researching health care for over a decade, Professor Teisberg has analyzed strategy in medical device and biotech companies, real options, research and development decisions, medical innovation, and strategic response to uncertainty. She has authored numerous cases and articles in professional publications, and coauthored *The Portable MBA*, which has been published in five languages.

Professor Teisberg's M.S. and Ph.D. are from the Stanford University School of Engineering. She also holds a master of engineering from the University of Virginia and an A.B., summa cum laude, from Washington University in St. Louis. She is a member of Phi Beta Kappa.